W9-CUP-074

DRINKtionary®

**Cocktails ○ Shooters ○ Manhattans ○ Martinis
Margaritas ○ Frozen Drinks ○ Hot Drinks**

A Series

by Elmo Strutter™

*Over 6000 recipes! From the classics to the trendiest,
its all here in this easy-to-use dictionary-style reference.*

Published in the United States of America by
Drinktionary® LLC
Louisville, Kentucky
www.drinktionary.com
www.bartendersbook.com
contactus@drinktionary.com

In conjunction with
Four Colour Imports, Ltd.
2410 Frankfort Avenue
Louisville, Kentucky 40206
www.fourcolour.com

Printed in China

Cover and Image designs by Robert Garrison, Lexington, Kentucky

Research and Authoring by Elmo Strutter™, Pete (Rison) Hosbach

Editing by Pete (Rison) Hosbach, Laura Hosbach, Linda Book

Layout and design by TreeMouse Design
liltreemouse@aol.com

0 9 8 7 6 5 4 3 2

To my best friend and wife, Laura.

About the Author

Elmo Strutter™ - the drink doctor. He grew up on Cape Cod, Massachusetts and lived in Boston and New York City. A graduate of Boston College, he now lives in Louisville, Kentucky.

It took Elmo Strutter™ 13 years to discover and compile the 6000 recipes in Drinktionary®. He began by tending bar in Manhattan and Cape Cod in the 90's. As he collected thousands of recipes from his customers and through research, he recorded them everywhere he could – on napkins, notebook paper and inside the covers of other recipe books.

Originally creating his name, Elmo Strutter™, as a funny, anonymous and memorable pseudonym for his bartending identity, he has evolved into the author and the drink doctor.

After Drinktionary® was published, people from all walks of life began asking Elmo Strutter™ for his advice on drink recipes for upcoming events. All in good fun, people eventually came to him for recommendations for personal situations like a break up with a girlfriend, a hard day at work or a celebration. One day someone called Elmo Strutter™ the drink doctor. It stuck, and the laughs continue.

Elmo Strutter™ created Drinktionary® to share his knowledge with everyone who enjoys a good drink and likes to have a good time. If you meet him, ask the drink doctor what recipe from Drinktionary® that he prescribes for you!

- This book contains adult language and content and is intended for readers of legal, alcohol drinking ages. Please serve and consume alcoholic recipes responsibly, know when to say when, and do not drink and drive!

- Signature cocktail creations are noted with *** following the recipe name.

- Trademark rights to the names of the liquors, mixers, foods and names found in this book are owned by their respective owners.

- Please be watching our website and the book stores as Drinktionary® is a series by Elmo Strutter™ with updates and more books.

- If you know of a cocktail recipe that is not listed in this book, or if you have a creation of your own, then please email us.

  Contact Drinktionary®: contactus@drinktionary.com

  Order additional books: order@drinktionary.com

  Visit the website: www.drinktionary.com
  www.bartendingbook.com

- As the author of this book, I want everyone to enjoy it and to have as much fun as possible. With that in mind, I would like each of you to please drink and serve alcoholic cocktails responsibly, and do not drink and drive. Thank you.

– Elmo Strutter™

Introduction

Drinktionary® is a collection of cocktail recipes that are arranged to resemble a dictionary. Containing more than 6000 recipes, it is the most complete and modern compilation of mixed drink recipes available with more than 5000 cocktail recipes and 1200 shooter recipes as well as sections listing manhattans, martinis, margaritas, frozen and hot drink concoctions.

Arranged in alphabetical order, recipes are located quickly—like they would be in a dictionary. Recipe quantities are translated and listed in parts for easy adaptation to each establishment's rules for liquor amounts and glass sizes. Drinktionary® is a universal guide that can be used in any setting—from a five star restaurant in New York City to a local bar in Rome to a private party with your friends.

The Layout of Drinktionary®

Drinktionary® is divided into seven sections. Each is separated by a tabbed page for easy location, and all of the recipes are listed alphabetically. The first section has over 380 pages of cocktail recipes—ranging from the classics to the trendiest. The second section contains almost 90 pages of shooters. Tabbed sections for manhattans, martinis, margaritas, frozen and hot drinks follow, so you can easily locate popular cocktail styles and their ingredients.

Reading the Recipes

The recipes in Drinktionary® contain the drink name, the required liquors, the mixers (if needed), any specific instructions and the suggested glassware. Liquors are described as generically as possible without altering the recipe (or the fun in the name), so be sure to ask your customers if they prefer specific brands of liquors.

Understanding Parts

It is important to understand parts. Bars, restaurants, clubs and individual bartenders have different measurements for a "shot" of liquor. A shot of liquor is the total quantity, or volume, of liquor to be poured into a specific cocktail. It may vary from ¾ of an ounce to 2 ½ ounces for each cocktail—depending on the rules of the establishment. Therefore, the quantity of total liquor for each cocktail recipe in this book has been listed by parts. A part is an amount. The total number of parts equals the total volume of liquor per drink. Parts will vary by recipe. Some will have only one part while others will have many.

Even though most of your cocktail recipes call for liquors and mixers, the most important measurements are parts of liquor in each drink. The best way to understand the parts of the liquor is to imagine a shot glass or jigger for measurement as illustrated in the examples below. Its volume is equal to your establishment's rules for total liquor quantity to be poured into a cocktail. If you are making a recipe with only one required liquor, then the amount of that liquor poured into the cocktail should fill the entire imagined shot glass. If you are mixing a cocktail that requires two liquors of equal amounts (or parts), then you would pour the same amount of each liquor into your imaginary shot glass to fill it. You would do the same if the cocktail required three or more liquors of equal parts as well. The parts together equal the total shot quantity each particular bar allows. Let's see some examples and focus only on the liquor.

Example #1:

ANTIFREEZE-
1 part Green Crème de Menthe, 1 part Vodka

The recipe for "ANTIFREEZE" exemplifies a cocktail with equal parts of two liquors. Figure 1 shows how these parts would look in your imaginary shot glass.

Figure 1: ANTIFREEZE

• • • • • • • •

Example #2:

TOXIC WASTE -
1 part Blue Curaçao, 1 part Melon Liqueur, 1 part Vodka

The recipe for "TOXIC WASTE" exemplifies a cocktail requiring two or more liquors of the same amount. Each is listed as 1 part. This indicates that the liquors are poured in equal parts. Figure 2 shows how these parts would look in your imaginary shot glass.

Figure 2: TOXIC WASTE

Example #3:

ROASTED TOASTED ALMOND (1)-
2 parts Coffee Liqueur, 1 part Amaretto, 1 part Vodka

The recipe for "ROASTED TOASTED ALMOND" exemplifies a cocktail requiring three different liquors with one of them requiring twice as much as the others. Figure 3 shows how these parts would look in your imaginary shot glass.

Figure 3: ROASTED TOASTED ALMOND (1)

• • • • • • • •

Example #4:

APRICOT PIE-
2 parts Apricot Brandy, 2 parts Light Rum, 1 part Sweet Vermouth

The recipe for "APRICOT PIE" exemplifies a cocktail requiring three different liquors that total five parts—2 parts apricot brandy, 2 parts light rum and 1 part sweet vermouth. Figure 4 shows how these parts would look in your imaginary shot glass.

Figure 4: APRICOT PIE

Terminology

Neat or Up: Served in a glass without ice.

On the Rocks: Served in a glass with ice.

Strain: You will strain the contents of a recipe when you want to chill them and mix them before pouring them into a glass with no ice. This is most common when preparing in a cocktail glass. To strain you should mix all of the ingredients of a recipe (unless otherwise noted) into a shaker or mixing glass with ice. Then use a metal strainer or another glass to allow the liquid contents to be poured into your service glass without allowing the ice to pass through.

Muddle: Crushing and mixing dry ingredients with liquid ones at the bottom of the glass.

Float: Usually a last step, pouring the liquor or mixer to be a final layer on top of the mixed cocktail in its glass is floating.

Lace: Lacing is when you use your thumb on the top of the bottle or pouring spout or when you allow the liquor to pour down the stem of the bar spoon to allow the ingredient to collect and float in the middle of the cocktail in the specified glass.

Top: When directed to top, you should add the ingredient after mixing and pouring the others into the glass.

Fill: When the recipe directs you to fill, this is the last step to the mixing. Pour or mix the ingredients into the required glass and then fill the last part on top of the mixture.

Layer: Layering is exactly what it implies—pouring one ingredient on top of the other without allowing them to mix in the glass. For example:

FOURTH (4ᵀᴴ) OF JULY TOOTER-
1 part Grenadine, 1 part Vodka, 1 part Blue Curaçao
(Layer in order in Cocktail Glass—no ice)

The recipe for "FOURTH (4ᵀᴴ) OF JULY TOOTER" exemplifies a cocktail requiring the non-alcoholic mixer in layering process. The grenadine is listed with the liquors as the first ingredient to be layered. Figure 5 shows how these parts would look as they are layered in a cocktail glass.

Figure 5: 4ᵀᴴ OF JULY TOOTER

Combining the Mixers with the Liquor Parts

Topped and laced ingredients are added as the last step after the cocktail is mixed in the glass. Layered cocktails following the layering procedure described above.

- Mixing in cocktail and shot glasses! Unless specific instructions are given for a cocktail, most drinks are mixed following these general rules. Pour the liquors and the mixers into a shaker with ice, shake or stir and strain into the glass. Generally, no ice is added to cocktail glasses. The mixtures are chilled and strained into them and are served up.

- If you are serving the drink in a highball, collins, rocks or sour glass, then these are the guidelines to follow. If there are no carbonated mixers, then fill the glass with ice. Pour the liquor and mixers into the glass at the same time. This is fast, and it allows for a more blended, better tasting mix of the ingredients. You may also conclude these steps by placing a small shaker over the top of the glass, turning them upside down so that the bottom of the drink glass is facing up and shaking. This not only better mixes the ingredients, but also adds a little show. If a drink calls for carbonated mixers, then simply pour the liquor and mixers at the same time into the iced glass. Do not shake.

- Mixing margaritas! Although Drinktionary® will provide the most common glassware and recipe, you must first determine a few things before mixing a margarita—frozen, up, or on the rocks? Salt or no salt? Margaritas can be enjoyed in any combination and will vary by person. To make a margarita with salt (either frozen or on the rocks) you should take a lime wedge and use it to moisten the rim of the glass. Then dip the glass into cocktail salt and proceed to mix the recipe. To make a frozen margarita, follow the procedures outlined below for making frozen drinks. To make a margarita up or on the rocks, mix it as you would if you were making a drink in a cocktail glass (but with or without ice) as described above.

- Making frozen drinks can be an art. The most difficult part is determining the perfect amount of ice to add to the blender. If you work at a restaurant or bar, then you may be fortunate enough to have a blending machine that automatically dispenses the right amount of crushed ice, but if you don't then practice will make perfect. You will first need to determine how much crushed ice you will need to fill your specific sized daiquiri glass. Then you will want to determine how much room the ingredients from the recipe will take in the glass and decrease your amount of ice. The best way to determine this is to simply practice with your blender with ice and water before making the cocktails. In order for the cocktail to taste correctly you will want the ingredients of your blender to be the perfect amount to pour into the glass or glasses you are filling. Extra takes away from the taste, and less makes a smaller drink.

Once you determine the amount of ice, then making the concoction is a breeze. Simply add your ice and all of the ingredients into the blender and blend. For recipes that require ice cream you may want to use less ice than for those that just contain juices. Remember to add any carbonated mixers like sodas, beer or champagne after you blend the other ingredients to avoid carbonation overflow.

Glassware

As liquor quantities differ from bar to bar, so does glassware. Drinktionary® recommends the most common glassware to allow for easy adaptation to your own establishment's inventory, but it can be easily substituted.

Glassware common for mixed cocktails with liquor and mixers are the highball, collins and sour glasses. Drinktionary® recommends highball glasses for the majority of mixed cocktail recipes, but any glass can be substituted. Common substitutions include parfait and pousse café glasses that are generally the same size but have small stems by the base.

These three would be the most commonly used.

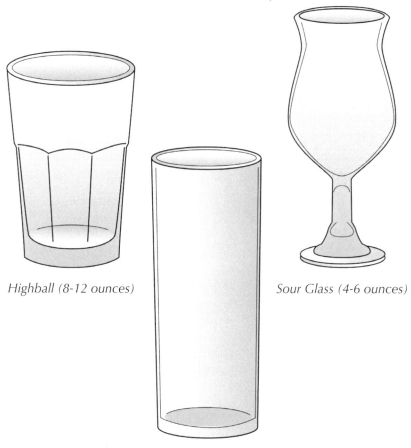

Highball (8-12 ounces)

Sour Glass (4-6 ounces)

Collins (10-14 ounces)

Drinks served "up" with no ice are prepared in a cocktail glass. These are sometimes called martini glasses. Pony and cordial glasses can be used as well, but the cocktail glass is the most popular.

Smaller cocktails, that are common both with mixers and without, use an old-fashioned or rocks glass.

Cocktail (3-6 ounces)

Rocks Glass (3-6 ounces)

Certain types of drinks use specific types of glasses that are not part of the common bar. Examples are the sherry glass, smaller snifters and different size wine and beer glasses. Below are the most common additional glassware used in Drinktionary®'s recipes.

*The shot glass
(for measuring or
serving shooters)
(1 ½ - 2 ounces)*

*The beer mug
(12 ounces)*

The daiquiri glass for frozen drinks (10-14 ounces)

The snifter

The Irish Coffee Cup for hot drinks (8-10 ounces)

The wine glass

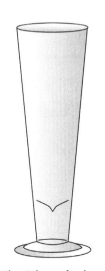

The Pilsner for beer (fancier than the pint glass) (12-14 ounces)

The champagne flute

Liquors

The basic liquors to have on hand for a small bar are:

Amaretto • Blended Whiskey • Bourbon Whiskey • Brandy • Brown Crème de Caçao • Canadian Whiskey • Coffee Liqueur • Dark Rum • Dry Vermouth • Gin • Green Crème de Menthe • Irish Cream Liqueur • Irish Whiskey • Light Rum • Scotch Whiskey • Sour Mash Whiskey • Sweet Vermouth • Tequila • Triple Sec • Vodka • White Crème de Caçao • White Crème de Menthe

Some additional liquors for the more creative cocktails:

151-proof Rum • Anisette • Banana Liqueur • Beer • Bénédictine • Blue Curaçao • Butterscotch Schnapps • Campari • Champagne • Cinnamon Schnapps • Coconut Rum • Cognac Crème de Cassis • Drambuie® • Galliano® • Goldschläger® • Grand Marnier® • Green Chartreuse • Hazelnut Liqueur • Irish Mist® • Jägermeister® • Licorice Liqueur • Melon Liqueur • Peach Schnapps • Peppermint Schnapps • Raspberry Liqueur • Red Dubonnet® • Red Wine • Sambuca • Sherry • Sloe Gin • Southern Comfort® • Spiced Rum • Tia Maria® • White Dubonnet® • White Wine • Yellow Chartreuse • Various fruit schnapps and brandy

• • • • • • • •

Mixers

Common mixers behind the bar are:

Bitters • Club Soda • Coconut Milk or Piña Colada Mix • Cola • Cranberry Juice • Grapefruit Juice • Grenadine • Horseradish • Hot Sauce • Light Cream or Milk • Lime Juice • Orange Juice • Orgeat Syrup (Almond) • Pepper • Pineapple Juice • Salt • Strawberry Margarita Mix • Simple Syrup • Sour Mix • Sugar • Tonic Water • Worcestershire Sauce

Garnishes

The cocktail recipes are listed with the garnishes assumed unless otherwise indicated. Remember that cocktail garnishes are intended to complement the mixer in the drink. Dark drinks in a cocktail glass usually use a cherry garnish. Cherries are also used for manhattans, sours and tropical drinks. Light drinks in a cocktail glass generally use a lemon twist. Twists and olives are used for martinis. Highball drinks use garnishes that resemble the liquor or mixer flavor of the cocktail. Limes are mostly used for drinks with tonic water, cola and cranberry juice, and lemons are commonly used in club soda mixers. Oranges are used to complement orange or citrus flavored liquor, and they are good for sour and tropical cocktails. Pineapples are frequently used in tropical drinks.

Common garnishes are:

Celery • Cherries • Chocolate Sprinkles • Cinnamon • Cocktail Onions • Fresh Mint • Lemon Slices • Lime Slices • Olives • Orange Slices • Pineapple Wedges • Strawberries • Whipped Cream

Adapting or Changing a Recipe from One Type to Another

Drinktionary® recommends the most common form of each recipe, but feel free to experiment with different variations of each drink. If it's supposed to be served in a cocktail glass and you want to make it a frozen cocktail, then follow the directions for frozen drinks. When making smaller drinks to larger drinks (like a shooter to a cocktail), add more of the mixers to fill the new glass size. Decrease the amount of mixers when changing larger drinks to smaller drinks (like a highball to a shooter). You shouldn't have to change the parts of the alcohol as that amount should stay constant. If you want to add flavor to a recipe, then add another part of a flavored schnapps or brandy.

• • • • • • • •

Bar Set Up – Tools of the Trade

Along with the Drinktionary®, liquor, beer, wine, mixers, garnishes and glassware the bar should have the following tools:

Bar spoon (for mixing, lacing, stirring and muddling) • Blender (for making frozen drinks) • Bottle Opener • Can Opener • Knife (for cutting fruit, etc.) • Ice Bucket and Tongs • Rag • Shaker or Mixing Glass (for pouring recipes into glasses without the ice) • Shot Glass or Jigger (for measuring) • Strainer

Bartenders' Responsibilities

As a bartender you have two main areas of responsibility—to your customers and to your establishment.

To your customers and friends you should know when they have had enough to drink. You should be able to mix the cocktail that is requested, and it should be mixed so that it tastes good. If the cocktail is overwhelmed by a heavy alcohol taste, then it is made incorrectly. Unless of course, it is straight liquor with no mixers. As the bartender, you must be in control of the bar to ensure order and safety while allowing the patrons to be relaxed and comfortable. You need to subtly command your control while remaining friendly and trustworthy. With this balance both you and your customers will have fun, and the bar will stay busy.

To the bar you need to provide efficient, accurate and fast accumulation of sales. Adhere to accurate liquor pours as specified by the total liquor count per cocktail desired by your employer. Be conscious of prompt and friendly service to your patrons, and keep your bar clean, organized and stocked.

Be a Better Bartender

Have the necessary tools and supplies with you behind the bar that will make you a better bartender. Along with the usual tools consider several objects that you can keep in your pocket like two pens (one for you and one to lend to customers), a lighter (to light someone's cigarette), two books of matches (to give to customers) and a pack of gum. Throughout a shift bartenders are often asked for these items. Too often they have to search for these items or they do not have them. Also, keep a pack of cigarettes and a current daily newspaper behind the bar. You may not want them, but a customer might.

Customer service is very important and requires a love for your job and patience, especially when you are tired and busy. Keep your patrons happy. Always greet them with a smile, and if you are busy and can not wait on them immediately, then acknowledge them with eye contact so they know that you are on your way to them. Make an effort to know the names of your regular customers. Greet them by name, and remember their favorite cocktails. Enable your customers to feel as if this is "their" bar and that you are "their" bartender. Always keep your bar clean and dry, clear empty glasses and plates frequently, refill bar snacks and empty ashtrays often. Try placing clean, damp and neatly folded rags at various spots around the bar, so you do not have to reach or look for a rag when you need one. If your bar has a buy-back policy (giving a free drink to regular customers or giving every fifth or so drink on the house), then utilize this tool to reward good customers and to increase your tips. Buy-backs should be used sparingly and should be reserved for patrons that are good for the bar and good to the bartender. Remember, patience and a smile are needed and are often forgotten. The bartender is there for the customers—to serve, to listen, to advise and sometimes to allow privacy.

Showmanship is another important aspect of being a better bartender. Familiarize yourself with your glassware so that when you strain the contents from the shaker you pour the perfect amount into the glass. This will differ on the glass and on the number of drinks being poured. Pouring a martini will require a different amount than pouring five of the same kind of shooters. When you make a perfect pour, there is no waste and you look professional. When mixing a classy drink like a manhattan or a rob roy, take extra care in preparing it. Chill the glass, put some show into it and pour the perfect amount into the glass. Upgrade glassware for fancy cocktails, upscale customers or special occasions. Use a snifter instead of a rocks glass or a wine glass instead of a highball, for example.

Flip through the pages of this book, and have fun discovering new shooters and cocktails. I hope you will have fun with this manual and that it will increase your fun, sales, service and tips.

Cocktails

ABSINTHE SPECIAL-
   Anisette
   Water, Powdered Sugar, splash Orange Bitters
   (Mix into Cocktail Glass—no ice)

ABSOLUTE REDHEAD-
   Absolut® Peppar Vodka
   Lime Juice, splash Cranberry Juice *(Mix into Small Rocks Glass—ice)*

ACACIA-
   4 parts Gin, 1 part Bénédictine, splash Cherry Brandy
   Lime Juice *(Mix into Cocktail Glass—no ice)*

ACAPULCO (1)-
   2 parts Light Rum, 1 part Triple Sec
   Sour Mix *(Mix into Small Rocks Glass—ice)*

ACAPULCO (2)-
   Tequila
   Grapefruit Juice, Pineapple Juice *(Mix into Highball Glass—ice)*

ACAPULCO BLUE-
   2 parts Tequila, 1 part Blue Curaçao
   Sugar, Club Soda *(Mix into Highball Glass—ice)*

ACAPULCO CLAM DIGGER-
   Tequila
   Tomato Juice, Clam Juice, Horseradish, Hot Sauce, Worcestershire Sauce,
      splash Lime Juice
   (Mix into Highball Glass—ice)

ACAPULCO JOY-
   1 part Coffee Liqueur, 1 part Peach Schnapps
   Vanilla Ice Cream, Banana, top Whipped Cream
   (Blend with ice in Daiquiri Glass)

ACAPULCOCO-
   2 parts Coffee Liqueur, 2 parts Tequila, 1 part Coconut Rum, 1 part Dark Rum
   (Mix into Cocktail Glass—no ice)

ACAPULCOCO ZOMBIE (1)-
   1 part Dark Rum, 1 part Tequila, 1 part Vodka,
      splash White Crème de Menthe (lace)
   Orange Juice, Pineapple Juice *(Mix into Highball Glass—ice)*

ACCORDION-
   3 parts Brandy, 1 part Dry Vermouth, 1 part Sweet Vermouth, splash Triple Sec
   (Mix into Cocktail Glass—no ice)

ACHAMPANDO-
   Dry Vermouth
   Sour Mix, Club Soda (top)
   (Mix into Highball Glass—ice)

ADAM-
>Dark Rum
>Lime Juice, splash Grenadine *(Mix into Cocktail Glass—no ice)*

ADAM AND EVE (1)-
>1 part Brandy, 1 part Forbidden Fruit Liqueur, 1 part Gin
>splash Sour Mix *(Mix into Cocktail Glass—no ice)*

ADAM AND EVE (2)-
>Apple Schnapps, Cranberry Schnapps
>Club Soda, splash Lemon-Lime Soda *(Mix into Highball Glass—ice)*

ADDINGTON-
>1 part Dry Vermouth, 1 part Sweet Vermouth
>Club Soda *(Mix into Highball Glass—ice)*

ADIOS MOTHER-
>1 part Blue Curaçao, 1 part Gin, 1 part Spiced Rum, 1 part Vodka
>Sour Mix *(Mix into Highball Glass—ice)*

ADIOS MOTHER F**KER-
>1 part Blue Curaçao, 1 part Gin, 1 part Light Rum, 1 part Tequila,
>   1 part Triple Sec, 1 part Vodka
>Orange Juice, Pineapple Juice
>*(Mix into Highball Glass—ice. Serve with drinking straw, drink all at once.)*

ADMIRAL (1)-
>1 part Bourbon Whiskey, 1 part Dry Vermouth
>Lime Juice *(Mix into Cocktail Glass—no ice)*

ADMIRAL (2)-
>4 parts Gin, 1 part Cherry Brandy
>Lime Juice *(Mix into Cocktail Glass—no ice)*

ADMIRAL BENBOW-
>2 parts Gin, 1 part Dry Vermouth
>Lime Juice *(Mix into Cocktail Glass—no ice)*

ADMIRAL GROWNEY-
>4 parts Gin, 1 part Dry Vermouth
>Lime Juice *(Mix into Cocktail Glass—no ice)*

ADMIRAL VERNON-
>3 parts Light Rum, 1 part Grand Marnier®, splash Amaretto
>Lime Juice *(Mix into Cocktail Glass—no ice)*

ADMIRAL X-RAY COCKTAIL-***
>4 parts Spiced Rum, 1 part Amaretto, 1 part Melon Liqueur
>Cranberry Juice, Orange Juice, Pineapple Juice, splash Grenadine
>*(Mix into Highball Glass—ice)*

ADMIRALTY-
>2 parts Gin, 1 part Apricot Brandy, 1 part Dry Vermouth
>splash Lime Juice *(Mix into Cocktail Glass—no ice)*

A

ADONIS-
2 parts Dry Sherry, 1 part Sweet Vermouth
splash Orange Bitters *(Mix into Cocktail Glass—no ice)*

ADRIENNE'S DREAM-
4 parts Brandy, 1 part Peppermint Schnapps, 1 part White Crème de Caçao
Sour Mix, Club Soda (top) *(Mix into Highball Glass—ice)*

ADULT LONG ISLAND ICED TEA-
1 part Gin, 1 part Light Rum, 1 part Triple Sec, 1 part Vodka
(Mix into Cocktail Glass—no ice)

ADULT HOT CHOCOLATE-
Peppermint Schnapps
Hot Chocolate, top Whipped Cream *(Mix into Irish Coffee Cup—no ice)*

ADULT ROOT BEER FLOAT-
1 part Coffee Liqueur, 1 part Galliano®
Vanilla Ice Cream, fill Cola *(Blend in with ice Daiquiri Glass)*

AFFAIR-
Strawberry Schnapps
Cranberry Juice, Orange Juice, splash Club Soda
(Mix into Highball Glass—ice)

AFFINITY-
1 part Dry Vermouth, 1 part Scotch Whiskey, 1 part Sweet Vermouth
Orange Bitters *(Mix into Cocktail Glass—no ice)*

AFFIRMATIVE ACTION-
2 parts Vodka, 1 part Cognac
Orange Juice *(Mix into Highball Glass—ice)*

AFTER DINNER-
1 part Apricot Brandy, 1 part Triple Sec
Lime Juice *(Mix into Cocktail Glass—no ice)*

AFTER FIVE (1)-
1 part Irish Cream Liqueur, 1 part Peppermint Schnapps
(Mix into Small Rocks Glass—ice)

AFTER FIVE (2)-
1 part Coffee Liqueur, 1 part Irish Cream Liqueur, 1 part Peppermint Schnapps
(Layer in Order in Cocktail Glass—no ice)

AFTER EIGHT-
1 part Coffee Liqueur, 1 part Irish Cream Liqueur, 1 part White Crème de
Menthe *(Layer in Order in Cocktail Glass—no ice)*

AFTER EIGHT MARTINI-
2 parts Irish Cream Liqueur, 2 parts Vodka, 1 part Green Crème de Menthe
(Layer in Order in Cocktail Glass—no ice)

AFTER NINE-
1 part Coffee Liqueur, 1 part Irish Cream Liqueur, 1 part Peach Schnapps
(Layer in Order in Cocktail Glass—no ice)

AFTER SEX-
2 parts Vodka, 1 part Banana Liqueur
Orange Juice *(Mix into Highball Glass—ice)*

AFTER SUPPER-
1 part Apricot Brandy, 1 part Triple Sec
Sour Mix *(Mix into Cocktail Glass—no ice)*

AFTERSHOCK-
1 part Cherry Brandy, 1 part Coconut Rum, 1 part Drambuie®
Lemonade *(Mix into Highball Glass—ice)*

AGENT 99-
1 part Grand Marnier®, 1 part Blue Curaçao, 1 part Sambuca
(Layer in Order in Cocktail Glass—no ice)

AGENT ORANGE (1)-
1 part Apple Schnapps, 1 part Gin, 1 part Light Rum, 1 part Melon Liqueur,
   1 part Southern Comfort®, 1 part Vodka, 1 part Yukon Jack® Canadian
   Whiskey
splash Grenadine, fill Orange Juice *(Mix into Highball Glass—ice)*

AGENT ORANGE (2)-
1 part Jack Daniel's® Tennessee Sour Mash Whiskey, 1 part Southern Comfort®
Orange Juice *(Mix into Highball Glass—ice)*

AGENT PROVOCATEUR-
2 parts Light Rum, 1 part Coconut Rum, 1 part Melon Liqueur, 1 part Triple Sec
Sour Mix
(Mix into Highball Glass—ice)

AGINCOURT-
2 parts Dry Vermouth, 2 parts Sweet Vermouth, 1 part Amaretto
Lime Juice *(Mix into Cocktail Glass—no ice)*

AGGRAVATION-
1 part Coffee Liqueur, 1 part Scotch Whiskey
(Mix into Cocktail Glass—no ice)

AIR GUNNER-
Vodka, splash Blue Curaçao
Sour Mix *(Mix into Highball Glass—ice)*

AIRHEAD-
Peach Schnapps
Cranberry Juice *(Mix into Highball Glass—ice)*

ALABAMA-
1 part Brandy, 1 part Triple Sec
Sour Mix *(Mix into Cocktail Glass—no ice)*

ALABAMA FIZZ-
Gin
Sour Mix, splash Club Soda
(Mix into Highball Glass—ice)

ALABAMA K. O.-
1 part Banana Liqueur, 1 part Sloe Gin, 1 part Southern Comfort® (float)
Orange Juice *(Mix into Highball Glass—ice)*

ALABAMA MARTINI-
4 parts Vodka, 1 part Blended Whiskey, 1 part Galliano®
Orange Juice *(Mix into Cocktail Glass—no ice)*

ALABAMA SLAMMA-
2 parts Coffee Liqueur, 2 parts Cognac, 1 part Amaretto,
    1 part Blackberry Brandy, 1 part Dry Vermouth
Lime Juice *(Mix into Highball Glass—ice)*

ALABAMA SLAMMER (1)-
2 parts Amaretto, 2 parts Southern Comfort®, 1 part Sloe Gin
Orange Juice *(Mix into Highball Glass—ice)*

ALABAMA SLAMMER (2)-
1 part Amaretto, 1 part Southern Comfort®, 1 part Sloe Gin
Orange Juice, Pineapple Juice *(Mix into Highball Glass—ice)*

ALABAMA SLAMMER (3)-
1 part Galliano®, 1 part Southern Comfort®, 1 part Sloe Gin, 1 part Triple Sec
Orange Juice *(Mix into Highball Glass—ice)*

ALABAZAM-
Cognac, splash Triple Sec
Sour Mix, splash Orange Bitters *(Mix into Small Rocks Glass—ice)*

ALAMO SPLASH-
Tequila
Orange Juice, Pineapple Juice, splash Lemon-Lime Soda
(Mix into Highball Glass—ice)

ALASKA-
2 parts Gin, 1 part Yellow Chartreuse
Orange Bitters *(Mix into Cocktail Glass—no ice)*

ALBEMARLE FIZZ-
Gin, splash Raspberry Liqueur
Sour Mix, splash Club Soda *(Mix into Highball Glass—ice)*

ALBERTO MARTINI-
Citrus Vodka
Cranberry Juice *(Mix into Cocktail Glass—no ice)*

ALBERTO TOMBA-
3 parts Gin, 1 part Plum Brandy
Orange Juice, Lime Juice *(Mix into Cocktail Glass—no ice)*

ALEXANDER-
1 part Gin (or Brandy), 1 part White Crème de Caçao
Light Cream or Milk, sprinkle Nutmeg
(Mix into Cocktail Glass—no ice)

ALEXANDER NEVSKY-
1 part Apricot Brandy, 1 part Vodka
Orange Juice, splash Lime Juice *(Mix into Highball Glass—ice)*

ALEXANDER'S BROTHER-
1 part Gin, 1 part White Crème de Caçao
Light Cream or Milk *(Mix into Cocktail Glass—no ice)*

ALEXANDER'S SISTER (1)-
1 part Gin, 1 part Green Crème de Menthe
Light Cream or Milk, sprinkle Nutmeg *(Mix into Cocktail Glass—no ice)*

ALEXANDER'S SISTER (2)-
2 parts Cognac, 1 part White Crème de Menthe
Light Cream or Milk *(Mix into Cocktail Glass—no ice)*

ALEXANDRA-
4 parts Amaretto, 1 part Crème de Almond, 1 part White Crème de Caçao
Light Cream or Milk *(Mix into Cocktail Glass—no ice)*

ALFIE-
Citrus Vodka, splash Triple Sec
Pineapple Juice *(Mix into Cocktail Glass—no ice)*

ALFONSO SPECIAL-
2 parts Grand Marnier®, 1 part Dry Vermouth, 1 part Gin,
    splash Sweet Vermouth
splash Bitters *(Mix into Cocktail Glass—no ice)*

ALFREDO-
1 part Campari, 1 part Gin *(Mix into Small Rocks Glass—ice)*

ALGAE-
1 part Blue Curaçao, 1 part Melon Liqueur, 1 part Raspberry Schnapps,
    1 part Vodka
Sour Mix, fill Lemon-Lime Soda *(Mix into Highball Glass—ice)*

ALGONQUIN-
2 parts Blended Whiskey, 1 part Dry Vermouth
Pineapple Juice *(Mix into Cocktail Glass—no ice)*

ALHAMBRA-
3 parts Brandy, 1 part Drambuie®, 1 part Fino Sherry
(Mix into Small Rocks Glass—ice)

ALHAMBRA ROYALE-
Brandy
Hot Chocolate, top Whipped Cream *(Mix into Irish Coffee Cup—no ice)*

ALICE-
2 parts Scotch Whiskey, 1 part Kümmel®, 1 part Sweet Vermouth
(Mix into Cocktail Glass—no ice)

ALICE IN WONDERLAND-
1 part Grand Marnier®, 1 part Tequila, 1 part Tia Maria®
(Mix into Small Rocks Glass—ice)

ALICE MINE-
2 parts Grand Marnier®, 1 part Dry Vermouth, 1 part Gin,
   splash Sweet Vermouth
splash Bitters *(Mix into Cocktail Glass—no ice)*

ALIEN SECRETION-
1 part Coconut Rum, 1 part Melon Liqueur
Sour Mix *(Mix into Highball Glass—ice)*

ALIEN URINE SAMPLE-
1 part Banana Liqueur, 1 part Coconut Rum, 1 part Melon Liqueur,
   1 part Peach Schnapps, splash Blue Curaçao
Sour Mix, top Club Soda *(Mix into Highball Glass—ice)*

ALL-AMERICAN DAIQUIRI, THE-
*(Three layers: Blue, Red, White: Blended with ice & layered in order
in Daiquiri Glass)*
1. 1 part Light Rum or Vodka
   Sour Mix, Blueberry Daiquiri Mix, blend with ice
2. 1 part Light Rum or Vodka
   Sour Mix, Strawberry Daiquiri Mix, blend with ice
3. Whipped Cream

ALL-AMERICAN FIZZ-
2 parts Gin, 1 part Cognac
Lime Juice, Grenadine, fill Club Soda *(Mix into Highball Glass—ice)*

ALLEGHENY (1)-
2 parts Bourbon Whiskey, 2 parts Dry Vermouth, 1 part Blackberry Brandy
Sour Mix *(Mix into Cocktail Glass—no ice)*

ALLEGHENY (2)-
1 part Blackberry Brandy, 1 part Bourbon Whiskey, 1 part Dry Vermouth
Lime Juice, splash Bitters *(Mix into Cocktail Glass—no ice)*

ALLELUIA-
Tequila, splash Blue Curaçao, splash Maraschino Liqueur
Sour Mix, fill Tonic Water
(Mix into Highball Glass—ice)

ALLEN-
1 part Gin, 1 part Maraschino Liqueur
Sour Mix *(Mix into Cocktail Glass—no ice)*

ALLIANCE-
1 part Dry Vermouth, 1 part Gin, splash Aquavit®
(Mix into Small Rocks Glass—ice)

ALLIED REQUIREMENTS-
2 parts Dry Vermouth, 1 part Gin, splash Licorice Liqueur
splash Bitters *(Mix into Cocktail Glass—no ice)*

ALLIES-
1 part Dry Vermouth, 1 part Gin, splash Kümmel®
(Mix into Cocktail Glass—no ice)

ALLIGATOR-
1 part Melon Liqueur, 1 part Triple Sec, 1 part Vodka
Orange Juice, Sour Mix, top Lemon-lime Soda *(Mix into Highball Glass—ice)*

ALMERIA-
1 part Coffee Liqueur, 1 part Light Rum
splash Light Cream or Milk *(Mix into Cocktail Glass—no ice)*

ALMOND COCKTAIL-
2 parts Gin, 1 part Dry Vermouth, splash Amaretto
(Mix into Small Rocks Glass—ice)

ALMOND CHOCOLATA-
Amaretto
Hot Chocolate, top Whipped Cream *(Mix into Irish Coffee Cup—no ice)*

ALMOND COFFEE-
Amaretto
Coffee, top Whipped Cream *(Mix into Irish Coffee Cup—no ice)*

ALMOND DELIGHT-
2 parts Amaretto, 1 part Brown Crème de Caçao
Light Cream or Milk *(Mix into Highball Glass—ice)*

ALMOND FROST-
2 parts Amaretto, 1 part Cognac, 1 part Coconut Liqueur
Orange Juice, Light Cream or Milk *(Blend with ice in Daiquiri Glass)*

ALMOND JOY-
1 part Amaretto, 1 part Brown Crème de Caçao, 1 part Coconut Liqueur
Light Cream or Milk *(Mix into Highball Glass—ice)*

ALMOND JOY MARTINI-
1 part Hazelnut Liqueur, 1 part Vodka, 1 part White Crème de Caçao
splash Coconut Milk *(Mix into Cocktail Glass—no ice)*

ALMOST AMANDA-
Gin
Grapefruit Juice, Sour Mix *(Mix into Cocktail Glass—no ice)*

ALOHA-
2 parts Vodka, 1 part Apricot Brandy
Pineapple Juice *(Mix into Cocktail Glass—no ice)*

ALOHA BUBBLY-
Dry White Wine
Pineapple Juice, Sugar, Club Soda *(Mix into Highball Glass—ice)*

ALTERED STATE-
1 part Pear Schnapps, 1 part Irish Cream Liqueur, 1 part Coffee Liqueur
(Layer in Order in Cocktail Glass with no ice)

ALTERNATE-
1 part Crème de Cassis, 1 part Melon Liqueur
Pineapple Juice
(Mix into Highball Glass—ice)

ALZHEIMERS-
1 part Canadian Whiskey, 1 part Citrus Vodka
Cola *(Mix into Highball Glass—ice)*

AMAGANSETT-
3 parts Gin, 1 part Anisette, 1 part Dry Vermouth,
    splash White Crème de Menthe
(Mix into Cocktail Glass—no ice)

AMALFI-
3 parts Bourbon Whiskey, 1 part Galliano®, splash Amaretto
Lime Juice, fill Club Soda *(Mix into Highball Glass—ice)*

AMARETTO CAFE-
Amaretto
Coffee, top Whipped Cream *(Mix into Irish Coffee Cup—no ice)*

AMARETTO MIST-
Amaretto
(Mix into Small Rocks Glass—crushed ice)

AMARETTO ROSE-
Amaretto
Lime Juice, Club Soda *(Mix into Highball Glass—ice)*

AMARETTO SOUR-
Amaretto
Sour Mix *(Mix into Sour Glass—ice)*

AMARETTO STONE SOUR-
Amaretto
Orange Juice, Sour Mix *(Mix into Sour Glass—ice)*

AMARETTO STINGER-
2 parts Amaretto, 1 part White Crème de Menthe
(Mix into Cocktail Glass—no ice)

AMARETTO SUPREME-
4 parts Cognac, 1 part Amaretto
Light Cream or Milk *(Mix into Cocktail Glass—no ice)*

AMARETTO TEA-
Amaretto
Hot Tea, top Whipped Cream *(Mix into Irish Coffee Cup—no ice)*

AMBASSADOR WEST-
2 parts Brandy, 1 part Gin, splash Dry Vermouth
Olive Garnish *(Mix into Cocktail Glass—no ice)*

AMBER AMOUR-
Amaretto
Sour Mix, Club Soda *(Mix into Highball Glass—ice)*

AMBER DAIQUIRI-
4 parts Dark Rum, 1 part Triple Sec
Lime Juice *(Blend with ice in Daiquiri Glass)*

AMBROSIA (1)-
4 parts Apple Schnapps, 4 parts Brandy, 1 part Triple Sec,
fill Chilled Champagne
Lime Juice *(Mix into Champagne Flute—no ice)*

AMBROSIA (2)-
2 parts Coconut Rum, 1 part Dark Rum, 1 part Triple Sec
Orange Juice, Light Cream or Milk *(Blend with ice in Daiquiri Glass)*

AMBULANCE CHASER-
Cognac, splash Port
splash Worcestershire Sauce, Pepper *(Mix into Cocktail Glass—no ice)*

AMERICAN APPLE PIE-
Cinnamon Schnapps
Apple Juice *(Mix into Highball Glass—ice)*

AMERICAN BEAUTY (1)-
1 part Brandy, 1 part Dry Vermouth, 1 part Port (lace),
splash White Crème de Menthe
Orange Juice, Grenadine *(Mix into Cocktail Glass—no ice)*

AMERICAN BEAUTY (2)-
3 parts Cognac, 1 part Dry Vermouth, 1 part Port (lace),
splash White Crème De Menthe
Orange Juice, splash Grenadine *(Mix into Cocktail Glass—no ice)*

AMERICAN DREAM (1)-
Red Wine, splash Bourbon Whiskey, splash Sweet Vermouth
fill Cola *(Mix into Highball Glass—ice)*

AMERICAN DREAM (2)-
1 part Amaretto, 1 part Brown Crème de Caçao, 1 part Coffee Liqueur,
1 part Hazelnut Liqueur
(Mix into Cocktail Glass—no ice)

AMERICAN FIZZ-
1 part Brandy, 1 part Gin
Lime Juice, splash Grenadine *(Mix into Highball Glass—ice)*

AMERICAN FLAG (1)-
1 part Grenadine, 1 part White Crème de Caçao, 1 part Blue Curaçao
(Layer in Order in Cocktail Glass—no ice)

AMERICAN FLAG (2)-
1 part Blue Curaçao, 1 part Peppermint Schnapps, 1 part Crème de Noyaux
(Layer in Order in Cocktail Glass—no ice)

AMERICAN FLYER-
Light Rum, fill Champagne
Sour Mix *(Mix into Champagne Flute—no ice)*

AMERICAN GLORY-
Champagne
Lemonade, Orange Juice
(Mix into Highball Glass or Champagne Flute with ice)

AMERICAN GROG-
Light Rum
Hot Water, Sour Mix *(Mix into Irish Coffee Cup—no ice)*

AMERICAN ROSE-
Brandy, splash Licorice Liqueur
splash Grenadine *(Mix into Cocktail Glass—no ice)*

AMERICANA-
Champagne, splash Jack Daniel's® Tennessee Sour Mash Whiskey
Sugar, Bitters *(Mix into Champagne Flute—no ice)*

AMERICANO-
1 part Campari, 1 part Sweet Vermouth
Club Soda *(Mix into Highball Glass—ice)*

AMETHYST-
2 parts Dry Vermouth, 2 parts Vodka, 1 part Blue Curaçao
splash Lime Juice, splash Grenadine *(Mix into Cocktail Glass—no ice)*

AMORE-
2 parts Amaretto, 1 part Coffee Liqueur
Light Cream or Milk, Vanilla Ice Cream *(Blend with ice in Daiquiri Glass)*

AMORE-ADE-
2 parts Amaretto, 1 part Triple Sec
Club Soda *(Mix into Highball Glass—ice)*

AMOROUS DUO-
4 parts Raspberry Liqueur, 1 part Amaretto
Vanilla Ice Cream *(Blend with ice in Daiquiri Glass)*

AMSTERDAM-
3 parts Gin, 1 part Triple Sec
Orange Juice *(Mix into Small Rocks Glass—ice)*

ANAL PROBE-
2 parts Light Rum, 1 part Coffee Liqueur
Cola *(Mix into Highball Glass—ice)*

ANATOLE COFFEE-
1 part Coffee Liqueur, 1 part Cognac, 1 part Hazelnut Liqueur
Cold Coffee, top Whipped Cream *(Blend with ice in Daiquiri Glass)*

ANCHORS AWEIGH (1)-
Bourbon Whiskey, splash Maraschino Liqueur, splash Peach Schnapps,
    splash Triple Sec
Light Cream or Milk *(Mix into Highball Glass—ice)*

ANCHORS AWEIGH (2)-
2 parts Vodka, 1 part Blackberry Brandy, 1 part Blue Curaçao
(Mix into Cocktail Glass—no ice)

ANDALUSIA-
3 parts Dry Sherry, 1 part Brandy, 1 part Light Rum
(Mix into Cocktail Glass—no ice)

ANDALUSIAN SMILE-
3 parts Dry Sherry, 1 part Cognac, 1 part Light Rum
splash Bitters *(Mix into Small Rocks Glass—ice)*

ANEJO BANGER-
4 parts Tequila, 1 part Galliano® (float)
Orange Juice *(Blend with ice in Daiquiri Glass)*

ANEJO PACIFICO-
Tequila
Passion Fruit Juice, Sour Mix *(Mix into Cocktail Glass—no ice)*

ANESTHETIC-
3 parts Gin, 1 part Cognac, 1 part Dry Vermouth
Sugar, splash Orange Bitters *(Mix into Small Rocks Glass—ice)*

ANGEL FACE-
2 parts Gin, 1 part Apple Brandy, 1 part Apricot Brandy
(Mix into Cocktail Glass—no ice)

ANGEL MARTINI-
3 parts Vodka, 1 part Hazelnut Liqueur *(Mix into Cocktail Glass—no ice)*

ANGEL'S DELIGHT-
1 part Grenadine, 1 part Triple Sec, 1 part Sloe Gin, 1 part Light Cream or Milk
(Layer in Order in Cocktail Glass—no ice)

ANGEL'S KISS-
1 part White Crème de Caçao, 1 part Sloe Gin, 1 part Brandy
1 part Light Cream or Milk *(Layer in Order in Cocktail Glass—no ice)*

ANGEL'S TIP-
1 part Coffee Liqueur, 1 part Irish Cream Liqueur
(Layer in Order in Cocktail Glass—no ice)

ANGEL'S TIT-
Brown Crème de Caçao
Light Cream or Milk, Cherry Garnish *(Mix into Cocktail Glass—no ice)*

ANGEL'S TREAT-
2 parts Dark Rum, 1 part Amaretto
Chocolate Milk, top Whipped Cream, top Chocolate sprinkles
(Mix into Cocktail Glass—no ice)

ANGEL'S WING-
1 part Brandy, 1 part White Crème de Caçao, 1 part Light Cream or Milk
(Layer in Order in Cocktail Glass—no ice)

ANGLER'S COCKTAIL-
Gin
Orange Bitters, Bitters, splash Grenadine *(Mix into Small Rocks Glass—ice)*

ANGRY BULL-
Light Rum
Beef Bouillon, splash Worcestershire Sauce, splash Hot Sauce
(Mix into Cocktail Glass—no ice)

ANITA'S SATISFACTION-
Gin
splash Grenadine, splash Bitters, splash Orange Bitters
(Mix into Cocktail Glass—no ice)

ANKLE BREAKER-
2 parts 151-proof Rum, 1 part Cherry Brandy
Sour Mix *(Mix into Highball Glass—ice)*

ANISETTE COFFEE-
1 part Anisette, 1 part Gin
Coffee, top Whipped Cream *(Mix into Irish Coffee Cup—no ice)*

ANNA'S BANANA-
Vodka
Lime Juice, Bananas, Honey *(Blend with ice in Daiquiri Glass)*

ANNA'S WISH-
2 parts Dark Rum, 1 part Triple Sec
Pineapple Juice *(Mix into Highball Glass—ice)*

ANNAPOLIS FIZZ-
Gin, splash Raspberry Liqueur
Sour Mix, splash Club Soda *(Mix into Highball Glass—ice)*

ANNIVERSARY COCKTAIL-
1 part Brandy, 1 part Gin
splash Orange Bitters *(Mix into Cocktail Glass—no ice)*

ANTE-
2 parts Apple Brandy, 2 parts Red Dubonnet®, 1 part Triple Sec
(Mix into Cocktail Glass—no ice)

ANTHONY'S SPUR-
3 parts Gin, 1 part Dry Vermouth, 1 part Sweet Vermouth
Orange Juice *(Mix into Cocktail Glass—no ice)*

ANTIBES-
3 parts Gin, 1 part Bénédictine
Grapefruit Juice *(Mix into Highball Glass—ice)*

ANTOINE SPECIAL-
1 part Red Dubonnet®, 1 part Dry Vermouth (float)
(Mix into Wine Glass—no ice)

ANTOINE'S LULLABY-
Dark Rum, splash Orange Curaçao, splash Port
Lime Juice *(Mix into Cocktail Glass—no ice)*

ANY PORT IN A STORM-
3 parts Ruby Port, 1 part Cognac, splash Maraschino Liqueur
Lime Juice, fill Club Soda *(Mix into Highball Glass—ice)*

APACHE-
1 part Coffee Liqueur, 1 part Irish Cream Liqueur, 1 part Melon Liqueur
(Layer in order in Cocktail Glass—no ice)

APERITIVO-
1 part Gin, 1 part Sambuca
splash Orange Bitters *(Mix into Cocktail Glass—no ice)*

APOCALYPSE-
2 parts Peppermint Schnapps, 1 part Bourbon Whiskey, 1 part Coffee Liqueur,
1 part Vodka *(Mix into Cocktail Glass—no ice)*

APOLLO 1-
3 parts Apple Brandy, 1 part Gin, 1 part Triple Sec
(Mix into Small Rocks Glass—ice)

APOLLO 4-
3 parts Apple Brandy, 1 part Gin, 1 part Triple Sec, 1 part Vanilla Liqueur
(Mix into Small Rocks Glass—ice)

APOLLO COOLER-
Metaxa, splash Licorice Liqueur
splash Lime Juice, fill Club Soda *(Mix into Highball Glass—ice)*

APPETIZER-
Blended Whiskey, splash Triple Sec
splash Bitters *(Mix into Cocktail Glass—no ice)*

APPIAN WAY-
3 parts Gin, 1 part Amaretto, 1 part Strega
Orange Slice Garnish *(Mix into Cocktail Glass—no ice)*

APPLE BLOSSOM-
Apple Brandy
Apple Juice, splash Sour Mix
(Mix into Highball Glass with ice or blend with ice in Daiquiri Glass)

APPLE BLOW FIZZ-
Apple Brandy
Sour Mix, splash Club Soda *(Mix into Highball Glass—ice)*

APPLE BRANDY-
Apple Brandy
Sour Mix, Grenadine *(Mix into Cocktail Glass—no ice)*

APPLE BRANDY HIGHBALL-
Apple Brandy
Ginger Ale or Club Soda *(Mix into Highball Glass—ice)*

APPLE BRANDY RICKEY-
Apple Brandy
Lime Juice, Club Soda *(Mix into Highball Glass—ice)*

APPLE BRANDY SOUR-
Apple Brandy
Sour Mix *(Mix into Sour Glass—ice)*

APPLE BUCK-
Apple Brandy, splash Ginger Brandy
Lime Juice, fill Ginger Ale *(Mix into Highball Glass—ice)*

APPLE CALABASH-
1 part Apple Brandy, 1 part Coconut Rum, 1 part Cranberry Brandy,
    1 part Spiced Rum
Pineapple Juice, Light Cream or Milk *(Blend with ice in Daiquiri Glass)*

APPLE CAR-
1 part Apple Schnapps, 1 part Triple Sec
Sour Mix *(Mix into Cocktail Glass—no ice)*

APPLE CART-
1 part Apple Brandy, 1 part Triple Sec
Lime Juice *(Mix into Cocktail Glass—no ice)*

APPLE CHILL-
Apple Schnapps
Pineapple Juice, splash Lime Juice
(Mix into Highball Glass—ice)

APPLE CRISP-
1 part Butterscotch Schnapps, 1 part Sour Apple Schnapps, 1 part Vodka
(Mix into Cocktail Glass—no ice)

APPLE COBBLER-
1 part Apple Schnapps, 1 part Goldschläger®, 1 part Irish Cream Liqueur
(Mix into Cocktail Glass—no ice)

APPLE COLADA-
Apple Schnapps
Coconut Milk, splash Light Cream or Milk *(Blend with ice in Daiquiri Glass)*

APPLE EDEN-
Vodka
Apple Juice *(Mix into Highball Glass—ice)*

APPLE GRANNY CRISP-
2 parts Apple Schnapps, 1 part Brandy, 1 part Irish Cream Liqueur
Vanilla Ice Cream, Graham Cracker Crumbs, top Whipped Cream
(Blend with ice in Daiquiri Glass)

APPLE KNOCKER-
Apple Brandy, splash Sweet Vermouth
Orange Juice, splash Sour Mix *(Mix into Highball Glass—ice)*

APPLE MANHATTAN-
2 parts Bourbon Whiskey, 1 part Apple Brandy
(Mix into Cocktail Glass—no ice)

APPLE PIE (1)-
1 part Apple Schnapps, 1 part Vodka
Pineapple Juice, sprinkle Cinnamon
(Mix into Highball Glass—ice)

APPLE PIE (2)-
1 part Light Rum, 1 part Sweet Vermouth, splash Apple Schnapps
Sour Mix, Grenadine
(Mix into Cocktail Glass—no ice)

APPLE PIE (3)-
2 parts Light Rum, 1 part Apple Brandy, 1 part Sweet Vermouth,
splash Apricot Brandy
Lime Juice, splash Grenadine *(Mix into Cocktail Glass—no ice)*

APPLE PIE (4)-
2 parts Dark Rum, 1 part Sweet Vermouth, splash Apple Brandy
Lime Juice, splash Grenadine
(Mix into Cocktail Glass—no ice)

APPLE PIE A LA MODE-
2 parts Coconut Rum, 2 parts Spiced Rum, 1 part Apple Brandy
Light Cream or Milk *(Mix into Highball Glass—ice)*

APPLE RIVER INNER TUBE-
1 part Brandy, 1 part Brown Crème de Caçao
Vanilla Ice Cream, Spiced Apple Ring Garnish
(Blend with ice in Daiquiri Glass)

APPLE RUM-DUM-
1 part Apple Brandy, 1 part Light Rum, splash Amaretto
splash Lime Juice, fill Club Soda
(Mix into Highball Glass—ice)

APPLE RUM RICKEY-
1 part Apple Schnapps, 1 part Light Rum
Lime Juice, Club Soda
(Mix into Highball Glass—ice)

APPLE ROUGE-
1 part Apple Brandy, 1 part Red Dubonnet®
(Mix into Cocktail Glass—no ice)

APPLE SIDECAR-
3 parts Apple Brandy, 1 part Triple Sec
Lime Juice *(Mix into Cocktail Glass—no ice)*

APPLE SMILE-
Apple Brandy
Sour Mix, splash Grenadine *(Mix into Cocktail Glass—no ice)*

APPLE SWIZZLE-
2 parts Apple Brandy, 1 part Light Rum
Water, Sour Mix, splash Bitters *(Mix into Highball Glass—ice)*

APPLE TART-
1 part Amaretto, 1 part Apple Brandy
Orange Juice *(Mix into Highball Glass—ice)*

APPLED RUM COOLER-
3 parts Light Rum, 1 part Apple Brandy
Lime Juice, Club Soda *(Mix into Highball Glass—ice)*

APPLETINI-
1 part Apple Brandy, 1 part Vodka, 1 part Triple Sec
(Mix into Cocktail Glass—no ice)

APRES SKI-
1 part Coffee Liqueur, 1 part Peppermint Schnapps,
   1 part White Crème de Caçao
(Mix into Cocktail Glass—no ice)

APRICOCIOUS-
Apricot Brandy
Orange Juice, Pineapple Juice *(Mix into Highball Glass—ice)*

APRICOT ANISETTE COLLINS-
2 parts Gin, 1 part Anisette, 1 part Apricot Brandy
Sour Mix, splash Club Soda *(Mix into Highball Glass—ice)*

APRICOT BLUSH-
1 part Apricot Brandy, 1 part Vodka
(Mix into Small Rocks Glass—ice)

APRICOT BRANDY RICKEY-
Apricot Brandy
Lime Juice, Club Soda *(Mix into Highball Glass—ice)*

APRICOT COCKTAIL-
Apricot Brandy, splash Gin
Sour Mix, Orange Juice *(Mix into Cocktail Glass—no ice)*

APRICOT COOLER-
Apricot Brandy
Sugar, Ginger Ale or Club Soda
(Mix into Highball Glass—ice)

APRICOT CREAM SPRITZ-
Apricot Brandy, (fill Sparkling Wine after blend)
Light Cream Milk *(Blend with ice in Wine Glass)*

APRICOT FIZZ-
Apricot Brandy
Sour Mix, splash Club Soda *(Mix into Highball Glass—ice)*

APRICOT JERK-
2 parts Apricot Brandy, 1 part Coconut Rum, 1 part Dark Rum
Light Cream or Milk
(Mix into Highball Glass with ice or blend with ice in Daiquiri Glass)

APRICOT LADY-
1 part Apricot Brandy, 1 part Light Rum, splash Triple Sec
Lime Juice *(Mix into Small Rocks Glass—ice)*

APRICOT ORANGE FIZZ-
1 part Apricot Brandy, 1 part Light Rum
Orange Juice, Lime Juice, Club Soda
(Mix into Highball Glass—ice)

APRICOT PIE-
2 parts Apricot Brandy, 2 parts Light Rum, 1 part Sweet Vermouth
splash Lime Juice, splash Grenadine
(Mix into Cocktail Glass—no ice)

APRICOT QUEEN-
2 parts Light Rum, 1 part Apricot Brandy, 1 part Triple Sec
Lime Juice *(Mix into Cocktail Glass—no ice)*

APRICOT SOUR-
Apricot Brandy
Sour Mix *(Mix into Sour Glass—ice)*

APRICOT STONE SOUR-
Apricot Brandy
Orange Juice, Sour Mix *(Mix into Sour Glass—ice)*

APRICOT SWEETIE-
1 part Apricot Brandy, 1 part Dark Rum, 1 part Gin
Lime Juice, Grenadine *(Blend with ice in Daiquiri Glass)*

APRIHOT-
Apricot Brandy
Hot Water *(Mix into Irish Coffee Cup—no ice)*

APRIL FOOL-
Apple Schnapps
Cranberry Juice, Vanilla Ice Cream *(Blend with ice in Daiquiri Glass)*

AQUA MARINA-
Champagne, splash Green Crème de Menthe, splash Vodka
splash Lime Juice *(Mix into Champagne Flute—no ice)*

AQUAMAN-
1 part Aquavit, 1 part Gin, splash Dry Vermouth
(Mix into Cocktail Glass—no ice)

AQUARIAN SPECIAL-
1 part Forbidden Fruit Liqueur, 1 part Gin, 1 part Triple Sec
(Mix into Cocktail Glass—no ice)

AQUARIUS-
3 parts Blended Whiskey, 1 part Cherry Brandy
Cranberry Juice *(Mix into Small Rocks Glass—ice)*

AQUEDUCT-
2 parts Vodka, 1 part Apricot Brandy, 1 part Triple Sec
Lime Juice *(Mix into Cocktail Glass—no ice)*

ARAGO-
1 part Banana Liqueur, 1 part Cognac
top Whipped Cream *(Mix into Cocktail Glass—no ice)*

ARAWAK CUP-
Dark Rum, splash Amaretto
Pineapple Juice, Passion Fruit Juice, Lime Juice
(Mix into Cocktail Glass—no ice)

ARCHBISHOP-
2 parts Gin, 1 part Green Ginger Wine, splash Bénédictine
(Mix into Small Rocks Glass—ice)

ARCTIC JOY-
1 part Peppermint Schnapps, 1 part White Crème de Caçao
Light Cream or Milk
(Mix into Highball Glass—ice)

ARDMORE-
2 parts Scotch Whiskey, 1 part Cherry Brandy, 1 part Sweet Vermouth
Orange Juice *(Mix into Cocktail Glass—no ice)*

ARGYLL-
2 parts Apple Brandy, 2 parts Scotch Whiskey, 1 part Gin
Honey *(Mix into Cocktail Glass—no ice)*

ARISE MY LOVE-
Chilled Champagne, splash Green Crème de Menthe
(Mix into Champagne Flute—no ice)

AROUND THE WORLD-
1 part Gin, 1 part Green Crème de Menthe
Pineapple Juice *(Mix into Highball Glass—ice)*

ARROWHEAD-
2 parts Dark Rum, 1 part Banana Liqueur, 1 part Southern Comfort®
Lemonade, splash Lime Juice
(Mix into Highball Glass—ice)

ARTHUR TOMPKINS-
4 parts Gin, 1 part Grand Marnier®
Lime Juice *(Mix into Highball Glass—ice)*

ARTILLERY-
2 parts Gin, 1 part Sweet Vermouth
Bitters *(Mix into Cocktail Glass—no ice)*

ARTIST'S SPECIAL-
1 part Blended Whiskey, 1 part Sherry
Sour Mix *(Mix into Cocktail Glass—no ice)*

ARUBA-
4 parts Gin, 1 part Triple Sec
Sour Mix *(Mix into Highball Glass—ice)*

ASIAN MARTINI-
Vodka, splash Ginger Schnapps
Orange Twist *(Mix into Cocktail Glass—no ice)*

ASS KICKER-
1 part 100-proof Vodka, 1 part Goldschläger®, 1 part Peppermint Schnapps,
    1 part Tequila, 1 part Triple Sec, 1 part Vodka
Orange Juice, Pineapple Juice
(Mix into Highball Glass—ice)

ASSASSIN-
1 part Jack Daniel's® Tennessee Sour Mash Whiskey,
    1 part Peppermint Schnapps, 1 part Tequila
Cola *(Mix into Highball Glass—ice)*

ASSASSINO-
2 parts Blended Whiskey, 1 part Dry Vermouth, splash Sambuca
Pineapple Juice, Club Soda *(Mix into Highball Glass—ice)*

ASSOCIATION SPECIAL-
2 parts Gin, 1 part Sweet Vermouth
splash Bitters *(Mix into Cocktail Glass—no ice)*

ASTORIA-
2 parts Gin, 1 part Dry Vermouth
splash Orange Bitters *(Mix into Cocktail Glass—no ice)*

ASTRONAUT-
1 part Jamaican Rum, 1 part Vodka
Lime Juice, Passion Fruit Juice *(Mix into Highball Glass—ice)*

ASSISTED SUICIDE-
2 parts 100-proof Vodka, 1 part Jägermeister®
Jolt® Cola *(Mix into Highball Glass—ice)*

ATLANTIC BREEZE-
2 parts Light Rum, 1 part Apricot Brandy, 1 part Galliano® (lace)
Pineapple Juice, splash Lime Juice, splash Grenadine
(Mix into Highball Glass—ice)

ATOMIC ORANGE MARTINI-
1 part Melon Liqueur, 1 part Vodka
Orange Juice *(Mix into Cocktail Glass—no ice)*

ATTA BOY-
2 parts Gin, 1 part Dry Vermouth
Grenadine *(Mix into Cocktail Glass—no ice)*

ATTENTION-
1 part Anisette, 1 part Crème de Noyaux, 1 part Gin
splash Orange Bitters *(Mix into Cocktail Glass—no ice)*

ATTITUDE-
1 part Peach Schnapps, 1 part Vodka *(Mix into Small Rocks Glass—ice)*

AUBADE-
Light Rum
Lime Juice, Grenadine, fill Tonic Water *(Mix into Highball Glass—ice)*

AUNT AGATHA-
Light Rum
Orange Juice, splash Bitters *(Mix into Highball Glass—ice)*

AUNT JEMIMA-
1 part Brandy, 1 part White Crème de Caçao, 1 part Bénédictine
(Layer in Order in Cocktail Glass—no ice)

AUNT MARY-
Light Rum
Tomato Juice, splash Worcestershire Sauce, splash Hot Sauce, Salt, Pepper
(Mix into Highball Glass—ice)

AURORA-
1 part Amaretto, 1 part Coconut Liqueur, 1 part Triple Sec
Pineapple Juice *(Mix into Highball Glass—ice)*

AUSTRALIAN VIRGIN-
2 parts White Wine, 1 part Dark Rum
Pineapple Juice, splash Grenadine
(Mix into Highball Glass—ice)

AVALANCHE (1)-
1 part Coffee Liqueur, 1 part White Crème de Caçao, 1 part Southern Comfort®
(Layer in Order in Cocktail Glass—no ice)

AVALANCHE (2)-
1 part Gin, 1 part White Crème de Caçao
Light Cream or Milk *(Mix into Cocktail Glass—no ice)*

AVIATION-
Gin, splash Apricot Brandy, splash Cherry Brandy
Lime Juice *(Mix into Cocktail Glass—no ice)*

AVRIL-
4 parts Canadian Whiskey, 1 part Cranberry Schnapps
(Mix into Cocktail Glass—no ice)

AWOL-
2 parts Scotch Whiskey, 1 part Amaretto, 1 part Triple Sec
Lime Juice *(Mix into Small Rocks Glass—ice)*

AXE MURDERER-
1 part Amaretto, 1 part Gin, 1 part Light Rum, 1 part Peach Schnapps,
1 part Southern Comfort®, 1 part Tequila, 1 part Triple Sec
Pineapple Juice, Grenadine, splash Lemon-Lime Soda
(Mix into Highball Glass—ice)

AZTEC SURFBOARD-
3 parts Tequila, 1 part Brandy, splash Amaretto, splash Blue Curaçao
Grapefruit Juice, Orange Juice
(Mix into Highball Glass—ice)

AZTECA (1)-
1 part Coffee Liqueur, 1 part Light Rum, 1 part White Crème de Caçao,
splash Triple Sec
(Mix into Cocktail Glass—no ice)

AZTECA (2)-
1 part Coffee Liqueur, 1 part Tequila, 1 part White Crème de Caçao,
splash Triple Sec
(Mix into Cocktail Glass—no ice)

AZULUNA-
2 parts Light Rum, 1 part Blue Curaçao
Pineapple Juice, Coconut Milk
(Blend with ice in Daiquiri Glass)

– NOTES –

B-1-
1 part Amaretto, 1 part Coffee Liqueur, 1 part Irish Cream Liqueur, 1 part Vodka
(Mix into Cocktail Glass—no ice)

B-2-
1 part Coffee Liqueur, 1 part Hazelnut Liqueur, 1 part Irish Cream Liqueur,
1 part Vodka
Light Cream or Milk *(Mix into Highball Glass—ice)*

B-28-
1 part Irish Cream Liqueur, 1 part Coffee Liqueur, 1 part Amaretto,
1 part Butterscotch Schnapps
(Layer in Order in Cocktail Glass—no ice)

B-51-
1 part Irish Cream Liqueur, 1 part Coffee Liqueur, 1 part Light Rum
(Layer in Order in Cocktail Glass—no ice)

B-52-
1 part Coffee Liqueur, 1 part Irish Cream Liqueur, 1 part Grand Marnier®
(Layer in Order in Cocktail Glass—no ice)

B-52 BOMBER-
Coffee Liqueur, Light Crème de Caçao, Vodka
Light Cream or Milk *(Mix into Highball Glass—ice)*

B-52 with a BOMBAY® DOOR-
1 part Coffee Liqueur, 1 part Irish Cream Liqueur, 1 part Grand Marnier®,
1 part Bombay® Gin
(Layer in Order in Cocktail Glass—no ice)

B-53-
1 part Coffee Liqueur, 1 part Sambuca, 1 part Grand Marnier®
(Layer in Order in Cocktail Glass—no ice)

B-54-
1 part Coffee Liqueur, 1 part Irish Cream Liqueur, 1 part Grand Marnier®,
1 part Tequila
(Layer in Order in Cocktail Glass—no ice)

B-57-
1 part Coffee Liqueur, 1 part Triple Sec, 1 part Sambuca
(Layer in Order in Glass with no ice)

B & B-
1 part Bénédictine, 1 part Brandy (float)
(Mix into Cocktail Glass—no ice)

B. B. C. (1)-
Blackberry Brandy
Cola *(Mix into Highball Glass—ice)*

B. B. C. (2)-
1 part Bénédictine, 1 part Baileys® Irish Cream Liqueur, 1 part Cointreau
(Layer in Order in Cocktail Glass—no ice)

B. B. C. (3)-
1 part Irish Cream Liqueur, 1 part Banana Liqueur
Piña Colada Mix *(Mix into Highball Glass—ice)*

B. B. G.-
1 part Bénédictine, 1 part Baileys® Irish Cream Liqueur, 1 part Grand Marnier®
(Layer in Order in Cocktail Glass—no ice)

B. M. A.-
1 part Amaretto, 1 part Brandy
Hot Chocolate, Coffee *(Mix into Irish Coffee Cup—no ice)*

B. M. SLIDER-
1 part Coffee Liqueur, 1 part Southern Comfort®
Light Cream or Milk *(Mix into Cocktail Glass—no ice)*

B. V. D.-
1 part Dry Vermouth, 1 part Gin, 1 part Light Rum
(Mix into Cocktail Glass—no ice)

BABBIE'S SPECIAL-
Apricot Brandy, splash Gin
Light Cream or Milk *(Mix into Cocktail Glass—no ice)*

BABE RUTH-
1 part Hazelnut Liqueur, 1 part Vodka
(Layer in Order in Cocktail Glass—no ice)

BABY ASPIRIN-
3 parts Coconut Rum, 1 part Triple Sec
Orange Juice, Pineapple Juice, splash Grenadine
(Mix into Highball Glass—ice)

BABY BLUE MARTINI-
1 part Blue Curaçao, 1 part Vodka
Sour Mix *(Mix into Cocktail Glass—no ice)*

BABY'S BOTTOM-
3 parts Blended Whiskey, 1 part White Crème de Caçao,
    1 part White Crème de Menthe
(Mix into Cocktail Glass—no ice)

BACCHUS-
2 parts Brandy, 1 part Apricot Brandy
Lime Juice *(Mix into Small Rocks Glass—ice)*

BACHELOR'S BAIT-
Gin
splash Orange Bitters, splash Grenadine
(Mix into Cocktail Glass—no ice)

BACK BAY BALM-
Gin
Cranberry Juice, splash Lime Juice, splash Orange Bitters, top Club Soda
(Mix into Highball Glass—ice)

BACK SEATER-
1 part Apple Brandy, 1 part Brandy, 1 part Triple Sec
splash Lime Juice *(Mix into Cocktail Glass—no ice)*

BACK STREET BANGER-
1 part Jack Daniel's® Tennessee Sour Mash Whiskey, 1 part Irish Cream Liqueur
(Mix into Small Rocks Glass—ice)

BACKBURNER-
2 parts Peppermint Schnapps, 1 part Coffee Liqueur, 1 part Light Rum
(Mix into Cocktail Glass—no ice)

BACON & TOMATO SANDWICH-
1 part Dark Rum, 1 part Gin, 1 part Light Rum
Lemonade *(Mix into Highball Glass—ice)*

BAD ATTITUDE-
1 part Amaretto, 1 part Gin, 1 part Light Rum, 1 part Tequila, 1 part Triple Sec,
1 part Vodka
Cranberry Juice, Orange Juice, Pineapple Juice, splash Grenadine
(Mix into Highball Glass—ice)

BAD HABIT-
1 part Peach Schnapps, 1 part Vodka *(Mix into Small Rocks Glass—ice)*

BAD STING-
1 part Grenadine, 1 part Sambuca, 1 part Grand Marnier®, 1 part Tequila
(Layer in Order in Cocktail Glass—no ice)

BAHAMA BREEZE-
1 part Banana Liqueur, 1 part Melon Liqueur
Coconut Milk, Pineapple Juice, Orange Juice
(Blend with ice in Daiquiri Glass)

BAHAMA MAMA (1)-
2 parts Coconut Rum, 2 parts Dark Rum, 1 part 151-proof Rum,
1 part Coffee Liqueur
Sour Mix, Pineapple Juice *(Mix into Highball Glass—ice)*

BAHAMA MAMA (2)-
1 part Dark Rum, 1 part Gold Rum, 1 part Light Rum
Orange Juice, Pineapple Juice, Sour Mix, splash Grenadine
(Mix into Highball Glass—ice)

BAHAMA MAMA (3)-
2 parts Spiced Rum, 1 part Coconut Rum, 1 part Dark Rum
Orange Juice, splash Grenadine *(Mix into Highball Glass—ice)*

BAHIA COOLER-
2 parts Coconut Rum, 1 part Dark Rum, 1 part Light Rum
Pineapple Juice *(Mix into Highball Glass—ice)*

BAILEYROUSKIE-
1 part Coffee Liqueur, 1 part Irish Cream Liqueur, 1 part Vodka
Light Cream or Milk
(Mix into Cocktail Glass—no ice)

BAIRN-
2 parts Scotch Whiskey, 1 part Triple Sec
splash Orange Bitters *(Mix into Small Rocks Glass—ice)*

BAJA BANANA-BOAT MARGARITA-
2 parts Tequila, 1 part Banana Liqueur
Sour Mix, Bananas (optional)
(Mix into Cocktail Glass with no ice or blend with ice in Daiquiri Glass)

BALANCHINE'S BELLE-
3 parts Red Dubonnet®, 1 part Dry Vermouth *(Mix into Cocktail Glass—no ice)*

BALD HEAD-
Gin, splash Anisette, splash Dry Vermouth *(Mix into Cocktail Glass—no ice)*

BALD PUSSY-
1 part Blueberry Schnapps, 1 part Melon Liqueur, 1 part Triple Sec,
    1 part Vodka
Lime Juice, Lemon-Lime Soda *(Mix into Highball Glass—ice)*

BALD-HEADED WOMAN-
151-proof Rum
Grapefruit Juice *(Mix into Highball Glass—ice)*

BALI HAI-
1 part Gin, 1 part Light Rum, splash Amaretto, Champagne (top)
Sour Mix *(Mix into Highball Glass—ice)*

BALL-PEEN HAMMER-
3 parts Vodka, 1 part Rye Whiskey
splash Lime Juice *(Mix into Cocktail Glass—no ice)*

BALLET RUSSE-
2 parts Vodka, 1 part Crème de Cassis
Sour Mix *(Mix into Small Rocks Glass—ice)*

BALLISTIC MISSILE-
1 part Amaretto, 1 part Grand Marnier®
Pineapple Juice *(Mix into Highball Glass—ice)*

BALLSBRIDGE BRACER-
2 parts Irish Whiskey, 1 part Irish Mist®
Orange Juice *(Mix into Highball Glass—ice)*

BALLYLICKEY BELT-
Irish Whiskey
Honey, fill Club Soda *(Mix into Highball Glass—ice)*

BALMORAL-
3 parts Scotch Whiskey, 1 part Dry Vermouth, 1 part Sweet Vermouth
splash Bitters *(Mix into Cocktail Glass—no ice)*

BALTIMORE BRACER-
1 part Anisette, 1 part Brandy
splash Light Cream or Milk (optional) *(Mix into Cocktail Glass—no ice)*

BALTIMORE EGGNOG-
1 part Brandy, 1 part Jamaican Rum, 1 part Madeira Wine
Sugar, Light Cream or Milk *(Mix into Highball Glass—ice)*

BAMBOO-
2 parts Dry Sherry, 1 part Dry Vermouth
splash Orange Bitters *(Mix into Cocktail Glass—no ice)*

BANANA B. JONES-
Banana Liqueur
Coconut Milk, Vanilla Ice Cream, Bananas, top Whipped Cream
(Blend with ice in Daiquiri Glass)

BANANA BALM-
2 parts Vodka, 1 part Banana Liqueur
splash Lime Juice, fill Club Soda *(Mix into Highball Glass—ice)*

BANANA BANSHEE-
1 part Banana Liqueur, 1 part White Crème de Caçao
Light Cream or Milk *(Mix into Highball Glass—ice)*

BANANA BERRY BLENDER-
2 parts Raspberry Liqueur, 1 part Banana Liqueur
Vanilla Ice Cream *(Blend with ice in Daiquiri Glass)*

BANANA BIRD-
Bourbon Whiskey, splash Banana Liqueur, splash Triple Sec
Light Cream or Milk *(Mix into Cocktail Glass—no ice)*

BANANA BLISS-
1 part Banana Liqueur, 1 part Light Rum
Light Cream or Milk, Orange Juice, splash Grenadine, splash Bitters
(Mix into Highball Glass—ice)

BANANA BOAT (1)-
1 part Banana Liqueur, 1 part Coconut Rum
Pineapple Juice *(Mix into Highball Glass—ice)*

BANANA BOAT (2)-
1 part Banana Liqueur, 1 part Tequila
Lime Juice *(Mix into Highball Glass—ice)*

BANANA BOOMER-
1 part Banana Liqueur, 1 part Light Rum
Orange Juice, Pineapple Juice *(Mix into Highball Glass—ice)*

BANANA CHI CHI-
1 part Banana Liqueur, 1 part Vodka
Coconut Milk, Pineapple Juice, Banana
(Blend with ice in Daiquiri Glass)

BANANA COLADA-
1 part Light Rum, 1 part Dark Rum
Pineapple Juice, Coconut Milk, Bananas
(Blend with ice in Daiquiri Glass)

BANANA COW-
1 part Banana Liqueur, 1 part Light Rum
Light Cream or Milk, splash Grenadine *(Mix into Cocktail Glass—no ice)*

BANANA CREAM PIE-
1 part Banana Liqueur, 1 part Vodka, 1 part White Crème de Caçao
Light Cream or Milk *(Mix into Highball Glass—ice)*

BANANA DAIQUIRI-
3 parts Light Rum, 1 part Triple Sec
Sour Mix, Bananas, Honey *(Blend with ice in Daiquiri Glass)*

BANANA DI AMORE-
1 part Amaretto, 1 part Banana Liqueur
Orange Juice, Sour Mix *(Blend with ice in Daiquiri Glass)*

BANANA FOSTER-
3 parts Spiced Rum, 1 part Banana Liqueur
Vanilla Ice Cream, 1 Banana *(Blend with ice in Daiquiri Glass)*

BANANA ITALIANO-
1 part Banana Liqueur, 1 part Galliano®
Light Cream or Milk
(Mix into Highball Glass with ice or blend with ice in Daiquiri Glass)

BANANA MAMA-
1 part Banana Liqueur, 1 part Coconut Rum, 1 part Dark Rum,
    1 part Light Rum
Pineapple Juice, Strawberry Daiquiri Mix *(Blend with ice in Daiquiri Glass)*

BANANA MAMBA-
Banana Liqueur
Orange Juice, Pineapple Juice, splash Lime Juice
(Mix into Highball Glass—ice)

BANANA MILK SHAKE-
2 parts Light Rum, 1 part Banana Liqueur
Light Cream or Milk, splash Grenadine
(Mix into Highball Glass with ice or blend with ice in Daiquiri Glass)

BANANA MOO-
Banana Liqueur
Light Cream or Milk *(Mix into Highball Glass—ice)*

BANANA NUT BREAD (1)-
2 parts Banana Liqueur, 2 parts Hazelnut Liqueur, 1 part Dry Sherry
Vanilla Ice Cream *(Blend with ice in Daiquiri Glass)*

BANANA NUT BREAD (2)-
2 parts Banana Liqueur, 2 parts Hazelnut Liqueur, 1 part Dry Sherry,
    1 part Vanilla Liqueur
Light Cream or Milk *(Mix into Highball Glass—ice)*

BANANA POPSICLE-
Banana Liqueur
Coconut Milk, Orange Sherbet *(Blend with ice in Daiquiri Glass)*

BANANA PUDDING-
1 part Coffee Liqueur, 2 parts Banana Liqueur, 1 part Irish Cream Liqueur
(Layer in Order in Cocktail Glass—no ice)

BANANA PUNCH-
3 parts Vodka, 1 part Apricot Brandy, 1 part Banana Liqueur
Lime Juice, Club Soda *(Mix into Highball Glass—ice)*

BANANA RUM CREAM-
3 parts Dark Rum, 1 part Banana Liqueur
Light Cream or Milk *(Mix into Highball Glass—ice)*

BANANA SLIP-
1 part Banana Liqueur, 1 part Irish Cream Liqueur
(Layer in Order in Cocktail Glass—no ice)

BANANA SLUSHEE-
1 part Banana Liqueur, 1 part Dark Rum
Orange Juice, Sugar *(Blend with ice in Daiquiri Glass)*

BANANA SOMBRERO-
1 part Banana Liqueur, 1 part Coffee Liqueur
Light Cream or Milk *(Mix into Highball Glass—ice)*

BANANA SPLIT (1)-
4 parts Banana Liqueur, 1 part Crème de Noyaux,
    1 part White Crème de Caçao
splash Light Cream or Milk, splash Grenadine
(Blend with ice in Daiquiri Glass)

BANANA SPLIT (2)-
1 part Swiss Chocolate Almond Liqueur, 1 part Strawberry Schnapps,
    1 part Banana Liqueur *(Layer in Order in Cocktail Glass—no ice)*

BANANA SPLIT (3)-
1 part Brown Crème de Caçao, 1 part Amaretto, 1 part Strawberry Schnapps,
    1 part Banana Liqueur *(Layer in Order in Cocktail Glass—no ice)*

BANANA TREE-
2 parts Banana Liqueur, 1 part Galliano®, 1 part White Crème de Caçao
Vanilla Ice Cream, Bananas *(Blend with ice in Daiquiri Glass)*

BANANARAMA-
2 parts Banana Liqueur, 1 part Triple Sec
Light Cream or Milk, splash Bitters
(Mix into Highball Glass—ice)

BANANAS BARBADOS-
2 parts Spiced Rum, 1 part Banana Liqueur
Hot Chocolate, top Whipped Cream
(Mix into Irish Coffee Cup—no ice)

BANCHORY-
1 part Scotch Whiskey, 1 part Sherry
splash Orange Juice, splash Sour Mix *(Mix into Cocktail Glass—no ice)*

BANDANA-
   2 parts Blended Whiskey, 1 part Banana Liqueur
   splash Lime Juice, splash Orange Juice
   (Mix into Cocktail Glass—no ice)

BANDITO-
   Banana Liqueur
   Light Cream or Milk *(Mix into Highball Glass—ice)*

BANFF-
   3 parts Canadian Whiskey, 1 part Cherry Brandy, 1 part Grand Marnier®
   splash Bitters *(Mix into Cocktail Glass—no ice)*

BANK HOLIDAY-
   1 part Bourbon Whiskey, 1 part Brandy, 1 part Galliano®,
      1 part White Crème de Caçao
   Light Cream or Milk *(Mix into Cocktail Glass—no ice)*

BANJINO-
   3 parts Gin, 1 part Banana Liqueur
   Orange Juice *(Mix into Cocktail Glass—no ice)*

BANNISTER-
   1 part Apple Schnapps, 1 part Gin, splash Licorice Liqueur
   splash Grenadine *(Mix into Cocktail Glass—no ice)*

BANSHEE-
   2 parts Banana Liqueur, 1 part White Crème de Caçao
   Light Cream or Milk *(Mix into Cocktail Glass—no ice)*

BAR BANDIT-
   2 parts Tequila, 1 part Dry Vermouth, 1 part Raspberry Liqueur,
      1 part Sweet Vermouth
   Grenadine, fill Club Soda
   (Mix into Highball Glass—ice)

BARBADOS PUNCH-
   Spiced Rum, splash Triple Sec
   Pineapple Juice, Lime Juice *(Mix into Highball Glass—ice)*

BARBARA-
   2 parts Vodka, 1 part White Crème de Caçao
   Light Cream or Milk *(Mix into Highball Glass—ice)*

BARBARELA-
   2 parts Triple Sec, 1 part Sambuca *(Mix into Small Rocks Glass—ice)*

BARBARIAN-
   Tequila
   Pineapple Juice, splash Grenadine, splash Lime Juice
   (Mix into Highball Glass—ice)

BARBARY COAST-
   1 part Gin, 1 part Rum, 1 part Scotch Whiskey, 1 part White Crème de Caçao
   Light Cream or Milk *(Mix into Cocktail Glass—no ice)*

BARBIZON-
3 parts Blended Whiskey, 1 part Bénédictine, splash Triple Sec
Lime Juice *(Mix into Cocktail Glass—no ice)*

BAREFOOT & PREGNANT-
2 parts Brandy, 1 part Dry Vermouth, splash White Crème de Menthe
splash Grenadine *(Mix into Cocktail Glass—no ice)*

BARKING DOG-
1 part Dry Vermouth, 1 part Gin, 1 part Sweet Vermouth
splash Bitters *(Mix into Cocktail Glass—no ice)*

BARN BURNER-
Vodka
Tomato Juice, splash Hot Sauce *(Mix into Cocktail Glass—no ice)*

BARN DOOR-
Vodka
Pineapple Juice, splash Cranberry Juice (lace) *(Mix into Highball Glass—ice)*

BARNSTORMER-
3 parts Canadian Whiskey, 1 part Peppermint Schnapps, splash Brown Crème
    de Caçao, splash White Crème de Caçao
Lime Juice *(Mix into Small Rocks Glass—ice)*

BARNEY BARNATO-
1 part Brandy, 1 part Red Dubonnet®, splash Triple Sec
splash Bitters *(Mix into Cocktail Glass—no ice)*

BARNUM-
2 parts Gin, 1 part Apricot Brandy
splash Lime Juice, splash Bitters *(Mix into Cocktail Glass—no ice)*

BARON-
3 parts Gin, 1 part Dry Vermouth, 1 part Sweet Vermouth, 1 part Triple Sec
(Mix into Cocktail Glass—no ice)

BARRACUDA-
2 parts Gold Rum, 1 part Galliano®, fill Champagne
Pineapple Juice, Sour Mix *(Mix into Champagne Flute—no ice)*

BARRACUDA BITE-
Light Rum
Sour Mix, fill Club Soda *(Mix into Highball Glass—ice)*

BARRIER BREAKER-
3 parts Dark Rum, 1 part Triple Sec, splash Blue Curaçao
Coffee, top Whipped Cream *(Mix into Irish Coffee Cup—no ice)*

BARRIER REEF-
2 parts Gin, 1 part Triple Sec, splash Blue Curaçao, splash Grand Marnier®
Vanilla Ice Cream *(Blend with ice in Daiquiri Glass)*

BARROW BLUES-
2 parts Blue Curaçao, 1 part Coconut Rum, 1 part Light Rum
Pineapple Juice *(Mix into Highball Glass—ice)*

BARTENDER'S SPECIAL-
Gin
Lime Juice, Passion Fruit Juice, splash Bitters *(Mix into Cocktail Glass—no ice)*

BARTMAN-
1 part Apple Brandy, 1 part Light Rum
Orange Juice, Lime Juice, splash Grenadine *(Mix into Highball Glass—ice)*

BARTON SPECIAL-
2 parts Apple Schnapps, 1 part Gin, 1 part Scotch Whiskey
(Mix into Small Rocks Glass—ice)

BASIC BILL-
3 parts Light Rum, 1 part Grand Marnier®, 1 part Red Dubonnet®
splash Bitters *(Mix into Cocktail Glass—no ice)*

BASIN STREET-
2 parts Bourbon Whiskey, 1 part Triple Sec
Sour Mix *(Mix into Cocktail Glass—no ice)*

BASTARDIZED SCREWDRIVER-
Light or Dark Rum
Orange Juice *(Mix into Highball Glass—ice)*

BAT BITE-
Dark Rum
Cranberry Juice *(Mix into Highball Glass—ice)*

BATTERED, BRUISED & BLEEDING-
1 part Grenadine, 1 part Melon Liqueur, 1 part Blue Curaçao
(Layer in Order in Cocktail Glass—no ice)

BAVARIAN COFFEE-
1 part Coffee Liqueur, 1 part Peppermint Schnapps
Coffee, sprinkle Chocolate *(Mix into Irish Coffee Cup—no ice)*

BAY BOMBER-
1 part Bombay® Gin, 1 part Light Rum, 1 part Tequila, 1 part Triple Sec,
   1 part Vodka, 1 part 151-proof Rum (lace)
Cranberry Juice, Orange Juice, Pineapple Juice, Sour Mix
(Blend with ice in Daiquiri Glass)

BAY BREEZE-
Vodka
Cranberry Juice, Pineapple Juice *(Mix into Highball Glass—ice)*

BAY CITY BOMBER-
1 part Gin, 1 part Rum, 1 part Tequila, 1 part Vodka,
   splash 151-proof Rum (top)
Orange Juice, Pineapple Juice, Cranberry Juice, Sour Mix
(Blend with ice in Daiquiri Glass)

BAY HORSE-
3 parts Blended Whiskey, 1 part Brown Crème de Caçao,
   1 part Licorice Liqueur
Light Cream or Milk, sprinkle Nutmeg *(Mix into Small Rocks Glass—ice)*

BAYARD FIZZ-
Gin, splash Cherry Liqueur, splash Raspberry Liqueur
Sour Mix, splash Club Soda *(Mix into Highball Glass—ice)*

BAZOOKA-
2 parts Southern Comfort®, 1 part Banana Liqueur
splash Grenadine, top Whipped Cream *(Mix into Cocktail Glass—no ice)*

BAZOOKA JOE-
1 part Blue Curaçao, 1 part Banana Liqueur, 1 part Irish Cream Liqueur
(Layer in Order in Glass with no ice)

BEACH BABY-
1 part Coconut Rum, 1 part Irish Cream Liqueur
Light Cream or Milk *(Mix into Cocktail Glass—no ice)*

BEACH BERRY-
Raspberry Liqueur
Orange Juice, splash Lime Juice, splash Grenadine
(Mix into Highball Glass—ice)

BEACH BUM'S COOLER-
4 parts Irish Cream Liqueur, 1 part Banana Liqueur, 1 part Light Rum
Coconut Milk, Vanilla Ice Cream, Milk, Banana
(Blend with ice in Daiquiri Glass)

BEACH CRUISER-
Spiced Rum
Cranberry Juice, Pineapple Juice *(Mix into Highball Glass—ice)*

BEACH PARTY-
Light Rum
Orange Juice, Pineapple Juice, splash Grenadine
(Blend with ice in Daiquiri Glass)

BEACHCOMBER-
3 parts Light Rum, 1 part Triple Sec
Sour Mix, Grenadine, Sugar Rim
(Mix into Cocktail Glass—no ice)

BEADLER TO THE FRONT-
2 parts Dark Rum, 1 part Banana Liqueur, 1 part Licorice Liqueur
splash Bitters *(Mix into Cocktail Glass—no ice)*

BEADLESTONE-
1 part Dry Vermouth, 1 part Scotch Whiskey
(Mix into Cocktail Glass—no ice)

BEALS COCKTAIL-
3 parts Scotch Whiskey, 1 part Dry Vermouth, 1 part Sweet Vermouth
(Mix into Cocktail Glass—no ice)

BEAM ME UP SCOTTY (1)-
1 part Banana Liqueur, 1 part Coffee Liqueur, 1 part Irish Cream Liqueur
(Mix into Cocktail Glass—no ice)

B

BEAM ME UP SCOTTY (2)-
1 part Banana Liqueur, 1 part Coffee Liqueur, 1 part Irish Cream Liqueur
Light Cream or Milk *(Mix into Highball Glass—ice)*

BEANSY'S BATTLEGROUND-
2 parts Sweet Vermouth, 1 part Brandy, splash Licorice Liqueur
splash Bitters *(Mix into Cocktail Glass—no ice)*

BEARDED CLAM-
1 part Amaretto, 1 part Canadian Whiskey
Cranberry Juice *(Mix into Highball Glass—ice)*

BEAUTY ON THE BEACH-
1 part Grand Marnier®, 1 part Light Rum, 1 part Southern Comfort®
splash Lime Juice, splash Orange Bitters
(Mix into Cocktail Glass—no ice)

BEAUTY SPOT (1)-
2 parts Gin, 1 part Dry Vermouth, 1 part Sweet Vermouth
Orange Juice, Grenadine (on bottom) *(Mix into Cocktail Glass—no ice)*

BEAUTY SPOT (2)-
Gin, splash White Crème de Caçao
splash Grenadine (top) *(Mix into Cocktail Glass—no ice)*

BEDROOM FARCE-
2 parts Dark Rum, 1 part Bourbon Whiskey, splash Galliano®
Hot Chocolate, top Whipped Cream
(Mix into Irish Coffee Cup—no ice)

BEE STINGER-
3 parts Blackberry Brandy, 1 part White Crème de Menthe
(Mix into Cocktail Glass—no ice)

BEE'S KISS-
Light Rum
Light Cream or Milk, Honey
(Mix into Highball Glass—ice)

BEE'S KNEES-
Gin
Lime Juice, Honey *(Mix into Small Rocks Glass—ice)*

BEE-STUNG LIPS-
Light Rum
Light Cream or Milk, Honey *(Mix into Cocktail Glass—no ice)*

BEER BUSTER-
100-proof Vodka, fill Beer
Hot Sauce *(Mix into Highball Glass—ice)*

BEETLEJUICE-
2 parts Brown Crème de Caçao, 2 parts White Crème de Caçao, 1 part Coffee
Liqueur, 1 part Peppermint Schnapps
Light Cream or Milk *(Mix into Cocktail Glass—no ice)*

BELFAST CAR BOMB-
12 oz. Stout Beer, 1 part Scotch Whiskey, 1 part Irish Cream Liqueur
(Drop Scotch Whiskey in Shot Glass into Mug of Beer and float Irish Cream Liqueur)

BELLADONNA-
1 part Dark Rum, 1 part Light Rum
Cranberry Juice, Orange Juice, Pineapple Juice *(Mix into Highball Glass—ice)*

BELLE MELON-
3 parts Melon Liqueur, 1 part Vodka
Light Cream or Milk *(Mix into Cocktail Glass—no ice)*

BELLE OF ELLIS ISLAND-
4 parts Dry Vermouth, 1 part Brandy, splash Triple Sec
Sugar, splash Orange Bitters *(Mix into Cocktail Glass—no ice)*

BELLINI-
Chilled Champagne
Peach Juice, splash Sour Mix, splash Grenadine
(Mix into Champagne Flute—no ice)

BELMONT-
Gin, splash Raspberry Liqueur
Light Cream or Milk *(Mix into Cocktail Glass—no ice)*

BELMONT STAKES-
2 parts Vodka, 1 part Light Rum, 1 part Strawberry Schnapps
splash Lime Juice, splash Grenadine *(Mix into Cocktail Glass—no ice)*

BEND ME OVER-
1 part Amaretto, 1 part Vodka
Orange Juice, splash Sour Mix *(Mix into Highball Glass—ice)*

BENGAL-
3 parts Brandy, 1 part Maraschino Liqueur, 1 part Triple Sec
Pineapple Juice, splash Bitters *(Mix into Cocktail Glass—no ice)*

BENNETT-
Gin
Lime Juice, Orange Bitters, Sugar *(Mix into Cocktail Glass—no ice)*

BENT NAIL-
3 parts Canadian Whiskey, 1 part Drambuie®, splash Cherry Brandy
(Mix into Small Rocks Glass—ice)

BENTLEY-
2 parts Apple Brandy, 1 part Red Dubonnet® *(Mix into Cocktail Glass—no ice)*

BERLIN MARTINI-
Vodka, splash Black Sambuca, splash Peach Schnapps
(Mix into Cocktail Glass—no ice)

BERMUDA BOUQUET-
4 parts Gin, 2 parts Apricot Brandy, 1 part Triple Sec
Orange Juice, Sour Mix, splash Grenadine *(Mix into Highball Glass—ice)*

BERMUDA HIGHBALL-
1 part Brandy, 1 part Dry Vermouth, 1 part Gin
Ginger Ale or Club Soda *(Mix into Highball Glass—ice)*

BERMUDA ROSE-
3 parts Gin, 1 part Apricot Brandy
Grenadine *(Mix into Cocktail Glass—no ice)*

BERMUDA TRIANGLE-
2 parts Peach Schnapps, 1 part Spiced Rum
Orange Juice *(Mix into Small Rocks Glass—ice)*

BERNARDO-
Gin, splash Triple Sec
Lime Juice, splash Bitters *(Mix into Cocktail Glass—no ice)*

BERNARD'S BEVIE-
3 parts Gin, 1 part Dry Vermouth, 1 part Sweet Vermouth, splash Bénédictine
(Mix into Cocktail Glass—no ice)

BERRIES & CREAM-
2 parts Berry Schnapps, 1 part Spiced Rum, splash Raspberry Liqueur,
   splash Strawberry Schnapps
Light Cream or Milk *(Mix into Highball Glass—ice)*

BERRISSIMO-
1 part Blackberry Brandy, 1 part Strawberry Schnapps
Orange Juice, Pineapple Juice, Club Soda (top) *(Mix into Highball Glass—ice)*

BERRY FIZZ-
4 parts Gin, 1 part Maraschino Liqueur, splash Raspberry Liqueur
Lime Juice, fill Club Soda *(Mix into Highball Glass—ice)*

BERRY WALL-
1 part Gin, 1 part Sweet Vermouth, splash Triple Sec
(Mix into Cocktail Glass—no ice)

BERTA'S SPECIAL-
Tequila
Lime Juice, Honey, Orange Bitters, Club Soda *(Mix into Highball Glass—ice)*

BETSY ROSS-
1 part Brandy, 1 part Port, splash Triple Sec *(Mix into Cocktail Glass—no ice)*

BETTER THAN ANYTHING-
1 part Brandy, 1 part Cherry Brandy, splash Triple Sec
splash Lime Juice, splash Grenadine *(Mix into Cocktail Glass—no ice)*

BETTER THAN SEX-
1 part Coffee Liqueur, 1 part Grand Marnier®, 1 part Haagen Dazs® Cream
   Liqueur, 1 part Hazelnut Liqueur
Light Cream or Milk *(Mix into Highball Glass—ice)*

BETWEEN THE SHEETS (1)-
1 part Brandy, 1 part Light Rum, 1 part Triple Sec
Sour Mix *(Mix into Cocktail Glass—no ice)*

BETWEEN THE SHEETS (2)-
1 part Blue Curaçao, 1 part Brandy, 1 part Light Rum
Sour Mix *(Mix into Highball Glass—ice)*

BEVERLY HILLS-
2 parts Triple Sec, 1 part Coffee Liqueur, 1 part Cognac
(Mix into Cocktail Glass—no ice)

BIANCO-
3 parts Bourbon Whiskey, 1 part Dry Vermouth
splash Bitters *(Mix into Cocktail Glass—no ice)*

BIBLE BELT-
2 parts Bourbon Whiskey, 1 part Triple Sec
Sour Mix, Sugared Rim *(Mix into Highball Glass—ice)*

BIFFY-
2 parts Gin, 1 part Citrus Rum
Lime Juice *(Mix into Highball Glass—ice)*

BIG APPLE-
4 parts Apple Brandy, 1 part Amaretto
Apple Juice *(Mix into Highball Glass—ice)*

BIG BAMBOO-
2 parts 151-proof Rum, 2 parts Light Rum, 1 part Triple Sec
Orange Juice, Pineapple Juice, Sour Mix *(Mix into Highball Glass—ice)*

BIG BAND CHARLIE-
3 parts Dark Rum, 1 part Melon Liqueur, 1 part Triple Sec
Lime Juice *(Mix into Highball Glass—ice)*

BIG BLUE SKY-
1 part Blue Curaçao, 1 part Coconut Liqueur, 1 part Light Rum
Pineapple Juice *(Mix into Highball Glass—ice)*

BIG BOY-
2 parts Brandy, 1 part Citrus Vodka, 1 part Triple Sec
(Mix into Cocktail Glass—no ice)

BIG CHILL-
1 part Coffee Liqueur, 1 part Green Crème de Menthe
top Chocolate Sprinkles *(Mix into Cocktail Glass—no ice)*

BIG CHILL, THE-
1 part Coconut Rum, 1 part Dark Rum
Cranberry Juice, Orange Juice, Pineapple Juice
(Blend with ice in Daiquiri Glass)

BIG DIPPER-
1 part Apricot Brandy, 1 part White Crème de Caçao
Light Cream or Milk, splash Grenadine *(Mix into Cocktail Glass—no ice)*

BIG KAHUNA (1)-
3 parts Gin, 1 part Blue Curaçao, splash Sweet Vermouth
Pineapple Juice *(Mix into Highball Glass—ice)*

BIG KAHUNA (2)-
3 parts Gin, 1 part Triple Sec, splash Sweet Vermouth
Pineapple Juice *(Mix into Cocktail Glass—no ice)*

BIG RED-
2 parts Dry Vermouth, 2 parts Sweet Vermouth, 1 part Sloe Gin
splash Orange Bitters *(Mix into Small Rocks Glass—ice)*

BIG RED HOOTER-
1 part Amaretto, 1 part Tequila
Pineapple Juice, Grenadine *(Mix into Highball Glass—ice)*

BIG ROLLER-
1 part Amaretto, 1 part Banana Liqueur, 1 part Coffee Liqueur
(Mix into Cocktail Glass—no ice)

BIG TITTY DRINK-
Coconut Rum
Pineapple Juice *(Mix into Highball Glass—ice)*

BIG YELLOW BANANA-
2 parts Vodka, 1 part Banana Liqueur
Lime Juice, fill Club Soda *(Mix into Highball Glass—ice)*

BIGWOOD GIRLS-
2 parts Light Rum, 1 part Brandy, 1 part Triple Sec
Lime Juice *(Mix into Cocktail Glass—no ice)*

BIJOU COCKTAIL-
1 part Gin, 1 part Green Chartreuse, 1 part Sweet Vermouth
splash Orange Bitters *(Mix into Cocktail Glass—no ice)*

BIKINI-
2 parts Vodka, 1 part Light Rum
Sour Mix, Light Cream or Milk, Sugar *(Mix into Cocktail Glass—no ice)*

BIKINI LINE-
1 part Raspberry Liqueur, 1 part Tia Maria®, 1 part Vodka
(Mix into Cocktail Glass—no ice)

BIKINI WAX-
2 parts Vodka, 1 part Light Rum
Light Cream or Milk, splash Sour Mix *(Mix into Cocktail Glass—no ice)*

BILL LEAVES TOWN-
Blended Whiskey, splash Sweet Vermouth
splash Grenadine *(Mix into Cocktail Glass—no ice)*

BILLY TAYLOR-
Gin
Sour Mix, Club Soda *(Mix into Highball Glass—ice)*

BIRD-OF-PARADISE FIZZ-
Gin
Sour Mix, Club Soda, splash Grenadine *(Mix into Highball Glass—ice)*

BIRTH CONTROL-
1 part Gin, 1 part Rye Whiskey *(Mix into Small Rocks Glass—ice)*

BISCAYNE COCKTAIL-
2 parts Gin, 1 part Forbidden Fruit Liqueur, 1 part Light Rum
Lime Juice *(Mix into Cocktail Glass—no ice)*

BISHOP-
Burgundy Wine
Sour Mix, Orange Juice, Sugar *(Mix into Wine Glass—no ice)*

BISCUIT NECK-
1 part Amaretto, 1 part Bourbon Whiskey, 1 part Hazelnut Liqueur,
1 part Irish Cream Liqueur *(Mix into Cocktail Glass—no ice)*

BITCH SLAP-
1 part 100-proof Vodka, 1 part Gin, 1 part Light Rum, 1 part Vodka
fill Lemonade, splash Lemon-Lime Soda *(Mix into Highball Glass—ice)*

BITCH ON WHEELS-
4 parts Gin, 1 part Dry Vermouth, 1 part White Crème de Menthe,
splash Sambuca *(Mix into Cocktail Glass—no ice)*

BITE OF THE IGUANA-
2 parts Tequila, 1 part Triple Sec, 1 part Vodka
Orange Juice, Sour Mix, splash Lemon-Lime Soda
(Mix into Highball Glass—ice)

BITTER BIKINI-
3 parts Campari, 2 parts Dry Vermouth, 1 part Triple Sec
(Mix into Small Rocks Glass—ice)

BITTERSWEET-
1 part Dry Vermouth, 1 part Sweet Vermouth
splash Bitters, splash Orange Bitters *(Mix into Cocktail Glass—no ice)*

BLACK & BLUE-
1 part Black Raspberry Liqueur, 1 part Blue Curaçao, 1 part Tequila
(Mix into Small Rocks Glass—ice)

BLACK & GOLD-
1 part Black Sambuca, 1 part Goldschläger® *(Mix into Small Rocks Glass—ice)*

BLACK & TAN-
6 oz. Ale, 6 oz. Stout *(Layer in Order in Beer Mug)*

BLACK BABY-
Coffee Liqueur
Light Cream or Milk, Cola *(Mix into Highball Glass—ice)*

BLACK BALTIMORE-
2 parts Brandy, 1 part Black Sambuca *(Mix into Cocktail Glass—no ice)*

BLACK BITCH-
1 part Black Sambuca, 1 part Irish Cream Liqueur, 2 parts 151-proof Rum
(Layer in Order in Cocktail Glass—no ice)

BLACK CAT-
Black Cherry Liqueur
Cranberry Juice, Cola *(Mix into Highball Glass—ice)*

BLACK CHERRY-
1 part Coffee Liqueur, 1 part Irish Cream Liqueur, 1 part Raspberry Liqueur,
   1 part Vodka
Light Cream or Milk, splash Cola, Cherry Garnish
(Mix into Highball Glass—ice)

BLACK CHERRY MARGARITA-
2 parts Black Cherry Liqueur, 1 part Tequila
Orange Juice, Sour Mix
(Mix into Cocktail Glass with no ice or blend with ice in Daiquiri Glass)

BLACK DAIQUIRI-
3 parts Dark Rum, 1 part Triple Sec
Sour Mix, Honey *(Blend with ice in Daiquiri Glass)*

BLACK DEATH-
1 part Bourbon Whiskey, 1 part Dry Vermouth, splash Blackberry Brandy
Lime Juice *(Mix into Small Rocks Glass—ice)*

BLACK DEVIL (1)-
1 part Dark Rum, 1 part Green Crème de Menthe
(Layer in Order in Cocktail Glass—no ice)

BLACK DEVIL (2)-
4 parts Dark Rum, 1 part Dry Vermouth *(Mix into Cocktail Glass—no ice)*

BLACK DOG-
Bourbon Whiskey, splash Dry Vermouth, splash Blackberry Brandy
(Mix into Small Rocks Glass—ice)

BLACK DRAGON-
1 part Mint Liqueur, 1 part Coffee Liqueur, 1 part Scotch Whiskey
(Layer in Order in Cocktail Glass—no ice)

BLACK DUBLINSKI-
1 part Coffee Liqueur, 1 part Irish Cream Liqueur, 1 part Vodka,
   splash Dry Sherry *(Mix into Cocktail Glass—no ice)*

BLACK EYE-
1 part Blackberry Brandy, 1 part Vodka *(Mix into Small Rocks Glass—ice)*

BLACK EYED SUSAN-
4 parts Grand Marnier®, 1 part Brandy, 1 part White Crème de Menthe
(Mix into Cocktail Glass—no ice)

BLACK FOREST (1)-
1 part Vodka, 1 part Raspberry Liqueur (lace)
Sour Mix *(Mix into Highball Glass—ice)*

BLACK FOREST (2)-
1 part Chocolate Liqueur, 1 part Raspberry Liqueur
Cappuccino *(Mix into Irish Coffee Cup—no ice)*

BLACK GOLD-
1 part Jägermeister®, 1 part Goldschläger®
(Mix into Small Rocks Glass—ice)

BLACK HAWK-
2 parts Blended Whiskey, 1 part Sloe Gin
(Mix into Cocktail Glass—no ice)

BLACK HONEY-
2 parts Coffee Liqueur, 1 part Drambuie®
Coffee, top Whipped Cream *(Mix into Irish Coffee Cup—no ice)*

BLACK JACK-
2 parts Cherry Brandy, 1 part Brandy
Coffee, top Whipped Cream *(Mix into Irish Coffee Cup—no ice)*

BLACK ICE-
3 parts Vodka, 1 part Blackberry Brandy *(Mix into Cocktail Glass—no ice)*

BLACK KENTUCKY-
1 part Black Sambuca, 2 parts Bourbon Whiskey
(Layer in Order in Cocktail Glass—no ice)

BLACK LADY-
4 parts Grand Marnier®, 1 part Coffee Liqueur, splash Brandy
(Mix into Cocktail Glass—no ice)

BLACK LICORICE-
1 part Coffee Liqueur, 1 part Sambuca *(Mix into Small Rocks Glass—ice)*

BLACK MAGIC (1)-
2 parts Vodka, 1 part Coffee Liqueur
splash Sour Mix *(Mix into Small Rocks Glass—ice)*

BLACK MAGIC (2)-
1 part Black Sambuca, 1 part Vodka *(Mix into Small Rocks Glass—ice)*

BLACK MANHATTAN-
Irish Whiskey, splash Sweet Vermouth *(Mix into Cocktail Glass—no ice)*

BLACK MARBLE-
Russian Vodka
Olive and Orange Slice Garnish *(Mix into Small Rocks Glass—ice)*

BLACK MARIA-
1 part Coffee Brandy, 1 part Light Rum
Coffee, Sugar, top Whipped Cream *(Mix into Irish Coffee Cup—no ice)*

BLACK MARTINI-
Vodka, splash Raspberry Liqueur
Lemon Twist Garnish *(Mix into Cocktail Glass—no ice)*

BLACK MONDAY-
2 parts Dark Rum, 1 part Black Sambuca, splash Cherry Brandy
Lime Juice *(Mix into Cocktail Glass—no ice)*

BLACK ORCHID-
1 part Blue Curaçao, 1 part Light Rum
Cranberry Juice, Grenadine, splash Lemon-Lime Soda
(Mix into Highball Glass—ice)

BLACK PAGODA-
3 parts Brandy, 1 part Dry Vermouth, 1 part Sweet Vermouth, splash Triple Sec
(Mix into Cocktail Glass—no ice)

BLACK ROSE-
Light Rum
Coffee, Sugar, top Whipped Cream
(Mix into Irish Coffee Cup—no ice)

BLACK RUSSIAN-
2 parts Vodka, 1 part Coffee Liqueur
(Mix into Cocktail Glass—no ice)

BLACK SHEEP-
Blackberry Brandy
Lime Juice *(Mix into Cocktail Glass—no ice)*

BLACK STRIPE-
Dark Rum
Hot Water, Molasses, Honey *(Mix into Irish Coffee Cup—no ice)*

BLACK THORN (1)-
2 parts Sloe Gin, 1 part Sweet Vermouth *(Mix into Cocktail Glass—no ice)*

BLACK THORN (2)-
Irish Whiskey, splash Anisette, splash Dry Vermouth
(Mix into Cocktail Glass—no ice)

BLACK TIE-
1 part Drambuie®, 1 part Scotch Whiskey, 1 part Amaretto
(Layer in Order in Glass with no ice)

BLACK VELVET-
1 part Stout Beer, 1 part Champagne
(Layer in Order in Champagne Flute)

BLACK VELVETEEN-
3 parts Stout Beer, 1 part Hard Cider *(Beer Mug)*

BLACK WATCH-
2 parts Scotch Whiskey, 1 part Coffee Liqueur
splash Soda *(Mix into Cocktail Glass—no ice)*

BLACK WIDOW-
1 part Dark Rum, 1 part Southern Comfort®
Sour Mix *(Mix into Highball Glass—ice)*

BLACK WITCH-
Gold Rum, splash Apricot Brandy, splash Dark Rum
Pineapple Juice *(Mix into Highball Glass—ice)*

BLACKBERRIES & CREAM-
1 part Banana Liqueur, 1 part Blackberry Brandy, 1 part Coconut Liqueur
Pineapple Juice, splash Light Cream or Milk
(Mix into Highball Glass with ice or blend with ice in Daiquiri Glass)

BLACKBERRY SIP-
1 part Blackberry Brandy, 1 part Vodka
Sour Mix *(Mix into Cocktail Glass—no ice)*

BLACKBERRY SLAMMER-
2 parts Brandy, 2 parts Coffee Liqueur, 1 part Amaretto, 1 part Blackberry
 Brandy, 1 part Dry Vermouth
Lime Juice *(Mix into Highball Glass—ice)*

BLACKPOOL TOWER-
2 parts Irish Cream Liqueur, 1 part Apricot Brandy, splash Gin
(Mix into Cocktail Glass—no ice)

BLANCHE-
2 parts Anisette, 2 parts Triple Sec, 1 part White Curaçao
(Mix into Cocktail Glass—no ice)

BLARNEY STONE-
Irish Whiskey, splash Anisette, splash Cherry Liqueur, splash Triple Sec
splash Bitters *(Mix into Cocktail Glass—no ice)*

BLASTER (1)-
1 part Triple Sec, 1 part Coffee Liqueur, 1 part Irish Cream Liqueur
(Layer in Order in Glass with no ice)

BLASTER (2)-
Jägermeister®, fill Red Bull® *(Mix into Highball Glass—ice)*

BLENDED COMFORT-
2 parts Bourbon Whiskey, 1 part Southern Comfort®, splash Dry Vermouth
Sour Mix *(Mix into Highball Glass—ice)*

BLIGHTER BOB-
2 parts Light Rum, 1 part Crème de Cassis, 1 part Dark Rum
Orange Juice, splash Bitters, fill Ginger Ale *(Mix into Highball Glass—ice)*

BLIMEY-
Scotch Whiskey
Sour Mix *(Mix into Cocktail Glass—no ice)*

BLINDER-
Scotch Whiskey
Grapefruit Juice, splash Grenadine *(Mix into Highball Glass—ice)*

BLINKER-
Blended Whiskey
Grapefruit Juice, splash Grenadine *(Mix into Highball Glass—ice)*

BLIZZARD-
Blended Whiskey
Cranberry Juice, splash Sour Mix *(Blend with ice in Daiquiri Glass)*

BLIZZARD, THE-
1 part Brandy, 1 part Coffee Liqueur, 1 part Irish Cream Liqueur,
1 part Light Rum
Light Cream or Milk, Vanilla Ice Cream
(Blend with ice in Daiquiri Glass)

BLOCK & FALL-
2 parts Brandy, 2 parts Triple Sec, 1 part Apple Brandy, 1 part Licorice Liqueur
(Mix into Cocktail Glass—no ice)

BLONDE JENNY-
3 parts Dry Vermouth, 1 part Gin
Orange Juice, splash Orange Bitters *(Mix into Cocktail Glass—no ice)*

BLONDE MARTINI-
Vodka, splash Lillet
Orange Twist Garnish *(Mix into Cocktail Glass—no ice)*

BLOOD & SAND (1)-
1 part Cherry Brandy, 1 part Scotch Whiskey, 1 part Sweet Vermouth
Orange Juice *(Mix into Cocktail Glass—no ice)*

BLOOD & SAND (2)-
1 part Dry Vermouth, 1 part Gin, 1 part Strawberry Schnapps, 1 part Sweet
Vermouth *(Mix into Cocktail Glass—no ice)*

BLOOD CLOT-
Southern Comfort®
fill Lemon-Lime Soda, splash Grenadine (lace)
(Do Not Mix, Serve with Drinking Straw, Drink all at once.)
(Mix into Highball Glass—ice)

BLOODHOUND-
2 parts Gin, 1 part Dry Vermouth, 1 part Sweet Vermouth
(Mix into Cocktail Glass—no ice)

BLOODY BRAIN-
1 part Blended Whiskey, 1 part Irish Cream Liqueur
Grenadine (float) *(Mix into Cocktail Glass—no ice)*

BLOODY BREW-
2 parts Beer, 1 part Vodka
Tomato Juice, Salt *(Mix into Highball Glass—ice)*

BLOODY BULL-
Vodka
fill ½ Tomato Juice and ½ Beef Bouillon, splash Worcestershire Sauce,
Salt, Pepper
(Mix into Highball Glass—ice)

BLOODY CAESAR-
Vodka
Littleneck Quahog Clam (on bottom of glass), Tomato Juice, splash
Worcestershire Sauce, splash Hot Sauce, Horseradish, Celery Salt,
Lime Wedge
(Mix into Cocktail Glass—no ice)

BLOODY MARIA-
Tequila
Tomato Juice, splash Sour Mix, splash Hot Sauce, dash Celery Salt, dash
    Ground Pepper *(Mix into Highball Glass—ice)*

BLOODY MARY-
Vodka
Tomato Juice, Worcestershire Sauce, Sour Mix, Horseradish, splash Lime Juice,
    dash Whole Black Pepper, dash Salt and Pepper, dash Celery Salt
(Mix into Highball Glass—ice)

BLOOMSBURY BLAST-
1 part Gin, 1 part Sherry, splash Cherry Brandy, splash Dry Vermouth,
    splash Sweet Vermouth, splash Triple Sec, splash White Crème de Caçao
Lime Juice *(Mix into Cocktail Glass—no ice)*

BLOW JOB (1)-
1 part Coffee Liqueur, 1 part Irish Cream Liqueur, 1 part Vodka
top Whipped Cream *(Mix into Champagne Flute—no ice)*

BLOW JOB (2)-
1 part Banana Liqueur, 1 part Coffee Liqueur, 1 part Irish Cream Liqueur
top Whipped Cream
(Mix into Champagne Flute—no ice)

BLOW JOB (3)-
Irish Cream Liqueur
top Whipped Cream *(Mix into Champagne Flute—no ice)*

BLOW JOB (4)-
Amaretto
top Whipped Cream *(Mix into Champagne Flute—no ice)*

BLUE ANGEL-
2 parts Brandy, 1 part Blue Curaçao, 1 part Vanilla Liqueur
Light Cream or Milk *(Mix into Cocktail Glass—no ice)*

BLUE BALLS-
1 part Blue Curaçao, 1 part Coconut Rum, 1 part Peach Schnapps
Sour Mix, top Lemon-Lime Soda *(Mix into Highball Glass—ice)*

BLUE BAYOU (1)-
2 parts Spiced Rum, 1 part Blue Curaçao
Light Cream or Milk, Vanilla Ice Cream
(Blend with ice in Daiquiri Glass)

BLUE BAYOU (2)-
1 part Blue Curaçao, 1 part Vodka
Grapefruit Juice, Pineapple Juice *(Mix into Highball Glass—ice)*

BLUE BEARD-
1 part Blueberry Brandy, 1 part Vodka *(Mix into Cocktail Glass—no ice)*

BLUE BIRD-
3 parts Gin, 1 part Triple Sec
splash Bitters *(Mix into Cocktail Glass—no ice)*

BLUE BLAZER-
Blended Whiskey
Hot Water, Sugar *(Mix into Irish Coffee Cup—no ice)*

BLUE CANARY-
Gin, splash Blue Curaçao
Grapefruit Juice *(Mix into Cocktail Glass with crushed ice)*

BLUE CARNATION-
1 part Blue Curaçao, 1 part White Crème de Caçao
Light Cream or Milk *(Mix into Highball Glass—ice)*

BLUE CHIMNEY SMOKE-
Tequila, splash Blue Curaçao (float)
Orange Juice *(Mix into Highball Glass—ice)*

BLUE CLOUD-
2 parts Amaretto, 1 part Blue Curaçao
Vanilla Ice Cream, top Whipped Cream *(Blend with ice in Daiquiri Glass)*

BLUE COOL-
2 parts Peppermint Schnapps, 1 part Blue Curaçao
Lemon-Lime Soda *(Mix into Highball Glass—ice)*

BLUE DAIQUIRI-
3 parts Light Rum, 1 part Blue Curaçao
Sour Mix, Honey *(Blend with ice in Daiquiri Glass)*

BLUE DENIM-
1 part Bourbon Whiskey, 1 part Dry Vermouth, splash Blue Curaçao
splash Bitters *(Mix into Small Rocks Glass—ice)*

BLUE DEVIL-
4 parts Gin, 1 part Blue Curaçao, 1 part Cherry Liqueur
Sour Mix *(Mix into Cocktail Glass—no ice)*

BLUE GLORY-
Peppermint Schnapps, splash Blue Curaçao
Lemon-Lime Soda *(Mix into Highball Glass—ice)*

BLUE GRASS-
Bourbon Whiskey, splash Maraschino Liqueur
Lime Juice, Pineapple Juice *(Mix into Highball Glass—ice)*

BLUE HAWAII-
1 part Blue Curaçao, 1 part Light Rum, 1 part White Crème de Caçao
Pineapple Juice, splash Light Cream or Milk *(Mix into Highball Glass—ice)*

BLUE HAWAIIAN-
1 part Blue Curaçao, 1 part Coconut Rum
Pineapple Juice *(Mix into Highball Glass—ice)*

BLUE KAMIKAZE-
1 part Blue Curaçao, 1 part Vodka
Lime Juice *(Mix into Highball Glass—ice)*

BLUE LADY-
Blue Curaçao
Lime Juice, Lemon-Lime Soda *(Mix into Highball Glass—ice)*

BLUE LAGOON (1)-
1 part Blue Curaçao, 1 part Vodka
Lemonade *(Mix into Highball Glass—ice)*

BLUE LAGOON (2)-
Blue Curaçao
Lemon-Lime Soda *(Mix into Highball Glass—ice)*

BLUE LEMONADE-
1 part Blue Curaçao, 1 part Vodka
Lemonade *(Mix into Highball Glass—ice)*

BLUE MARGARITA-
3 parts Tequila, 1 part Blue Curaçao
Sour Mix
(Mix into Cocktail Glass with no ice or blend with ice in Daiquiri Glass)

BLUE MARLIN-
2 parts Light Rum, 1 part Blue Curaçao
Lime Juice *(Mix into Small Rocks Glass—ice)*

BLUE MEANIE-
2 parts Tequila, 1 part Blue Curaçao
Sour Mix *(Mix into Highball Glass—ice)*

BLUE MONDAY (1)-
2 parts Vodka, 1 part Triple Sec, splash Blue Curaçao
(Mix into Cocktail Glass—no ice)

BLUE MONDAY (2)-
3 parts Canadian Whiskey, 1 part Blueberry Brandy, splash Brandy
(Mix into Cocktail Glass—no ice)

BLUE MONDAY (3)-
3 parts Vodka, 1 part Blue Curaçao
(Mix into Small Rocks Glass—ice)

BLUE MOON-
2 parts Gin, 1 part Blue Curaçao *(Mix into Cocktail Glass—no ice)*

BLUE MOUNTAIN-
3 parts Light Rum, 1 part Tia Maria®, 1 part Vodka
Orange Juice, splash Lime Juice *(Mix into Highball Glass—ice)*

BLUE PASSION-
1 part Blue Curaçao, 1 part Spiced Rum
Sour Mix *(Mix into Highball Glass—ice)*

BLUE SHARK-
2 parts Tequila, 2 parts Vodka, 1 part Blue Curaçao
(Mix into Cocktail Glass—no ice)

BLUE STAR-
2 parts Gin, 1 part Blue Curaçao, 1 part Lillet
Orange Juice *(Mix into Small Rocks Glass—ice)*

BLUE SUEDE SHOES-
1 part Blue Curaçao, 1 part Vodka
Club Soda *(Mix into Highball Glass—ice)*

BLUE TAIL FOX-
1 part Blue Curaçao, 1 part Brown Crème de Caçao
Light Cream or Milk *(Mix into Highball Glass—ice)*

BLUE TANGO-
2 parts Vodka, 1 part Blue Curaçao, 1 part Dry Vermouth
Lime Juice *(Mix into Cocktail Glass—no ice)*

BLUE TRAIN-
1 part Blue Curaçao, 1 part Gin
Lime Juice *(Mix into Highball Glass—ice)*

BLUE VALIUM-
1 part Gin, 1 part Light Rum, 1 part Tequila, 1 part Triple Sec, 1 part Vodka,
1 part Blue Curaçao
Sour Mix, Cola *(Mix into Highball Glass—ice)*

BLUE VELVET-
1 part Melon Liqueur, 1 part Raspberry Liqueur (drizzle Whipped Cream with
splash Blue Curaçao)
Vanilla Ice Cream, top Whipped Cream
(Blend with ice in Daiquiri Glass)

BLUE WHALE-
1 part Blue Curaçao, 1 part Vodka or Light Rum
Sour Mix *(Mix into Highball Glass—ice)*

BLUE WATCH-
2 parts Spiced Rum, 1 part Blue Curaçao
Ginger Ale *(Mix into Highball Glass—ice)*

BLUE WAVE-
1 part Blue Curaçao, 1 part Light Rum
Lime Juice, Pineapple Juice *(Mix into Highball Glass—ice)*

BLUEBERRY FREEZE-
1 part Blueberry Schnapps, 1 part Vodka
Coconut Milk, Pineapple Juice, Vanilla Ice Cream
(Blend with ice in Daiquiri Glass)

BLUEBERRY MARTINI-
Gin, splash Blue Curaçao, splash Raspberry Liqueur
(Mix into Cocktail Glass—no ice)

BLUEBERRY RUMBA-
2 parts Light Rum, 1 part Blueberry Schnapps, 1 part Blue Curaçao, 1 part
Dark Rum, 1 part Triple Sec
Lemonade, Pineapple Juice *(Mix into Highball Glass—ice)*

BLURRICANE-
1 part Blue Curaçao, 1 part Peppermint Schnapps, 1 part Goldschläger®,
1 part Jägermeister®, 1 part Bourbon Whiskey, 1 part Licorice Liqueur
(Layer in Order in Cocktail Glass—no ice)

BLUSHIN' RUSSIAN-
1 part Coffee Liqueur, 1 part Vodka
Vanilla Ice Cream, Strawberries *(Blend with ice in Daiquiri Glass)*

BLUSHING BARMAID-
1 part Amaretto, 1 part Campari
Lime Juice, fill Club Soda *(Mix into Highball Glass—ice)*

BOARDWALK BREEZER-
3 parts Dark Rum, 1 part Banana Liqueur
Pineapple Juice, splash Lime Juice, splash Grenadine
(Mix into Highball Glass—ice)

BOB DANBY-
2 parts Red Dubonnet®, 1 part Brandy *(Mix into Cocktail Glass—no ice)*

BOBBY BURNS-
1 part Scotch Whiskey, 1 part Sweet Vermouth, splash Bénédictine
(Mix into Cocktail Glass—no ice)

BOCCE BALL-
1 part Amaretto, 1 part Vodka
Orange Juice, Club Soda *(Mix into Highball Glass—ice)*

BODEGA BOLT-
1 part Gin, 1 part Sherry
Club Soda *(Mix into Highball Glass—ice)*

BOILERMAKER-
12 oz. Beer, 1 part Whiskey *(Drop Whiskey in Shot Glass into Beer Mug)*

BOLERO-
2 parts Light Rum, 1 part Apple Brandy, splash Sweet Vermouth
(Mix into Cocktail Glass—no ice)

BOLO-
Light Rum
Orange Juice, Sour Mix *(Mix into Highball Glass—ice)*

BOLSHOI PUNCH-
Vodka, splash Crème de Cassis, splash Light Rum
Sour Mix *(Mix into Small Rocks Glass—ice)*

BOMB, THE-
1 part Banana Liqueur, 1 part Peach Schnapps, 1 part Sour Apple Schnapps
Pineapple Juice, Lemon-Lime Soda
(Mix into Highball Glass—ice)

BOMBAY COCKTAIL-
2 parts Brandy, 1 part Dry Vermouth, 1 part Sweet Vermouth, splash Anisette,
splash Triple Sec *(Mix into Cocktail Glass—no ice)*

B

BON APPETIT-
1 part Gin, 1 part Red Dubonnet®
Orange Juice, splash Bitters *(Mix into Highball Glass—ice)*

BON TON-
2 parts Gold Rum, 2 parts Southern Comfort®, 1 part Grand Marnier®
Lime Juice, splash Orange Bitters *(Mix into Cocktail Glass—no ice)*

BONAIRE BOOTY-
2 parts Brown Crème de Caçao, 1 part Amaretto, 1 part Light Rum
Light Cream or Milk *(Mix into Cocktail Glass—no ice)*

BONAVENTURE-
3 parts Canadian Whiskey, 1 part Cherry Brandy
Lime Juice, Orange Juice *(Mix into Highball Glass—ice)*

BONGO COLA-
2 parts Gold Rum, 1 part Coffee Liqueur, splash Cherry Brandy
Pineapple Juice, splash Lime Juice, fill Cola *(Mix into Highball Glass—ice)*

BONNIE PRINCE-
4 parts Gin, 1 part Drambuie®, 1 part Wine *(Mix into Cocktail Glass—no ice)*

BONSAI PIPELINE-
2 parts Tropical Fruit Schnapps, 1 part Vodka *(Mix into Small Rocks Glass—ice)*

BOOM BANG-
3 parts Gin, 1 part Sherry, splash Scotch Whiskey (float)
(Mix into Cocktail Glass—no ice)

BOOMER-
2 parts Tequila, 1 part Apricot Brandy
Orange Juice, Sour Mix *(Mix into Highball Glass—ice)*

BOOMERANG-
2 parts Gin, 1 part Dry Vermouth, splash Maraschino Liqueur
splash Bitters *(Mix into Cocktail Glass—no ice)*

BOOSTER-
Brandy, splash Triple Sec *(Mix into Cocktail Glass—no ice)*

BOOT HILL-
4 parts Blended Whiskey, 1 part Apple Schnapps
Sour Mix *(Mix into Cocktail Glass—no ice)*

BOOT SCOOTER-
1 part Cinnamon Schnapps, 1 part Coffee Liqueur
(Mix into Small Rocks Glass—ice)

BOOTLEGGER-
1 part Jack Daniel's® Tennessee Sour Mash Whiskey , 1 part Southern Comfort®,
1 part Tequila *(Mix into Small Rocks Glass—ice)*

BORA BORA-
1 part Raspberry Liqueur, 1 part Tropical Fruit Schnapps
Pineapple Juice *(Mix into Highball Glass—ice)*

BORDER CROSSING-
Tequila
Cola, Lime Juice *(Mix into Highball Glass—ice)*

BORDEVER-
Bourbon Whiskey
Ginger Ale *(Mix into Cocktail Glass—no ice)*

BORINQUEN-
Light Rum, splash 151-proof Rum
Lime Juice, Orange Juice, Passion Fruit Juice
(Mix into Small Rocks Glass—ice)

BORROWED TIME-
3 parts Canadian Whiskey, 1 part Port
splash Grenadine *(Mix into Cocktail Glass—no ice)*

BOSOM CARESSER-
2 parts Brandy, 2 parts Madeira Wine, 1 part Triple Sec
(Mix into Cocktail Glass—no ice)

BOSS, THE-
3 parts Bourbon Whiskey, 1 part Amaretto *(Mix into Small Rocks Glass—ice)*

BOSSA NOVA-
2 parts Dark Rum, 1 part Apricot Brandy, 1 part Galliano®
Pineapple Juice, splash Lime Juice *(Mix into Highball Glass—ice)*

BOSTON COCKTAIL-
1 part Apricot Brandy, 1 part Gin
Sour Mix, Grenadine *(Mix into Cocktail Glass—no ice)*

BOSTON COOLER-
Light Rum
Sour Mix, Ginger Ale or Club Soda *(Mix into Highball Glass—ice)*

BOSTON GOLD-
2 parts Vodka, 1 part Banana Liqueur
Orange Juice *(Mix into Highball Glass—ice)*

BOSTON SIDECAR-
1 part Brandy, 1 part Light Rum, 1 part Triple Sec
Lime Juice *(Mix into Cocktail Glass—no ice)*

BOSTON SOUR-
Blended Whiskey
Sour Mix *(Mix into Highball Glass—ice)*

BOSTON WALLBANGER-
1 part Vodka, 1 part Galliano® (lace)
Orange Juice, splash Light Cream or Milk
(Mix into Highball Glass—ice)

BOSWELLIAN BOOSTER-
2 parts Dry Vermouth, 1 part Brandy
Sour Mix, splash Orange Bitters *(Mix into Small Rocks Glass—ice)*

BOTTOM LINE, THE-
Vodka
Lime Juice, fill Tonic Water *(Mix into Highball Glass—ice)*

BOURBON A LA CRÈME-
2 parts Bourbon Whiskey, 1 part Brown Crème de Caçao
Vanilla Beans *(Mix into Cocktail Glass—no ice)*

BOURBON COBBLER-
Bourbon Whiskey
Lime Juice, Grapefruit Juice, Almond Extract *(Mix into Small Rocks Glass—ice)*

BOURBON COLLINS-
Bourbon Whiskey
Sour Mix, splash Club Soda *(Mix into Highball Glass—ice)*

BOURBON HIGHBALL-
Bourbon Whiskey
Ginger Ale or Club Soda *(Mix into Highball Glass—ice)*

BOURBON SATIN-
1 part Bourbon Whiskey, 1 part White Crème de Caçao
Light Cream or Milk *(Mix into Cocktail Glass—no ice)*

BOURBON SIDECAR-
2 parts Bourbon Whiskey, 1 part Triple Sec
Lime Juice *(Mix into Highball Glass—ice)*

BOURBON SLOE GIN FIZZ-
2 parts Bourbon Whiskey, 1 part Sloe Gin
Sour Mix, splash Club Soda *(Mix into Highball Glass—ice)*

BOURBON STREET-
1 part Amaretto, 1 part Bourbon Whiskey *(Mix into Cocktail Glass—no ice)*

BOWTON NELL-
3 parts Light Rum, 1 part Brandy, 1 part Gin
Orange Juice, Lime Juice, splash Grenadine, top Club Soda
(Mix into Highball Glass—ice)

BOXCAR-
1 part Gin, 1 part Triple Sec
Lime Juice, splash Grenadine *(Mix into Highball Glass—ice)*

BOYD OF THE LOCH-
1 part Dry Vermouth, 1 part Scotch Whiskey *(Mix into Cocktail Glass—no ice)*

BRAIN BLENDER-
2 parts Southern Comfort®, 1 part Banana Liqueur, 1 part Light Rum,
    1 part Peach Schnapps, splash Bénédictine
Grenadine, Orange Juice *(Mix into Highball Glass—ice)*

BRAIN CANDY-
2 parts Green Crème de Menthe, 1 part Vodka
Mountain Dew® *(Mix into Cocktail Glass—no ice)*

BRAIN ERASER-
2 parts Vodka, 1 part Amaretto, 1 part Coffee Liqueur
fill Club Soda (Do Not Mix, Serve with Drinking Straw, Drink all at once.)
(Mix into Highball Glass—ice)

BRAIN STORM-
Blended Whiskey, splash Bénédictine, splash Dry Vermouth
(Mix into Cocktail Glass—no ice)

BRAIN'S BELIEF-
3 parts Light Rum, 1 part Brown Crème de Caçao
Sour Mix, Cold Tea *(Mix into Highball Glass—ice)*

BRANDIED MADEIRA-
2 parts Brandy, 2 parts Madeira Wine, 1 part Dry Vermouth
(Mix into Small Rocks Glass—ice)

BRANDIED PEACHES & CREAM-
1 part Peach Brandy, 1 part Peach Schnapps
Coconut Milk, Vanilla Ice Cream
(Blend with ice in Daiquiri Glass)

BRANDIED PORT-
1 part Brandy, 1 part Port, splash Maraschino Liqueur
Sour Mix *(Mix into Small Rocks Glass—ice)*

BRANDY ALEXANDER-
1 part Brandy, 1 part Brown Crème de Caçao
Light Cream or Milk *(Mix into Cocktail Glass—no ice)*

BRANDY BERRY FIX-
Brandy, splash Strawberry Schnapps
Water, Sour Mix *(Mix into Highball Glass—ice)*

BRANDY BLAZER-
Brandy
Sugar Cube, Orange Peel (ignite, optional) {extinguish flame before drinking}
(Mix into Irish Coffee Cup—no ice)

BRANDY BLIZZARD-
3 parts Brandy, 1 part White Crème de Menthe
Lime Juice, fill Ginger Ale
(Mix into Highball Glass—ice)

BRANDY BUCK-
4 parts Brandy, 1 part White Crème de Caçao
Lime Juice, fill Club Soda *(Mix into Highball Glass—ice)*

BRANDY CASSIS-
Brandy, splash Crème de Cassis
Sour Mix *(Mix into Cocktail Glass—no ice)*

BRANDY CHAMPERELLE-
1 part Brandy, 1 part Triple Sec, 1 part Yellow Chartreuse, 1 part Anisette
(Layer in Order in Cocktail Glass—no ice)

BRANDY COBBLER-
Brandy
Club Soda, Sugar *(Mix into Highball Glass—ice)*

BRANDY COCKTAIL-
Brandy
Sugar, Bitters *(Mix into Cocktail Glass—no ice)*

BRANDY COLLINS-
Brandy
Sour Mix, splash Club Soda *(Mix into Highball Glass—ice)*

BRANDY CRUSTA-
4 parts Brandy, 1 part Triple Sec, splash Maraschino Liqueur
Sour Mix, splash Bitters *(Mix into Cocktail Glass—no ice)*

BRANDY DAISY-
Brandy
Sour Mix, splash Grenadine *(Mix into Highball Glass—ice)*

BRANDY EGGNOG-
Brandy
Sugar, sprinkle Nutmeg *(Mix into Highball Glass—ice)*

BRANDY FANCY-
Brandy, splash Maraschino Liqueur
splash Bitters, splash Orange Bitters *(Mix into Cocktail Glass—no ice)*

BRANDY FIX-
Brandy
Water, Sour Mix *(Mix into Highball Glass—ice)*

BRANDY FIZZ-
Brandy
Sour Mix, splash Club Soda *(Mix into Highball Glass—ice)*

BRANDY FLIP-
Brandy
Light Cream or Milk, Sugar *(Mix into Highball Glass—ice)*

BRANDY GUMP-
Brandy
Lime Juice, splash Grenadine *(Mix into Cocktail Glass—no ice)*

BRANDY HIGHBALL-
Brandy
Ginger Ale or Club Soda *(Mix into Highball Glass—ice)*

BRANDY HUMMER-
1 part Brandy, 1 part Coffee Liqueur
Vanilla Ice Cream *(Blend with ice in Daiquiri Glass)*

BRANDY JULEP-
Brandy
Sugar, Mint Leaves *(Mix into Highball Glass—ice)*

BRANDY MELBA-
4 parts Brandy, 1 part Peach Schnapps, 1 part Raspberry Liqueur
Lime Juice, splash Orange Bitters *(Mix into Cocktail Glass—no ice)*

BRANDY MILK PUNCH-
Brandy
Light Cream or Milk, Sugar *(Mix into Highball Glass—ice)*

BRANDY OLD-FASHIONED-
Brandy
Sugar, splash Water, splash Bitters *(Mix into Small Rocks Glass—ice)*

BRANDY PUFF-
Brandy
Light Cream or Milk, fill Club Soda *(Mix into Highball Glass—ice)*

BRANDY RIM-
1 part Banana Liqueur, 1 part Blackberry Liqueur, 1 part Light Rum
Orange Juice, Grenadine *(Mix into Highball Glass—ice)*

BRANDY SANGAREE-
1 part Brandy, 1 part Port (float)
Club Soda, Sugar, sprinkle Nutmeg *(Mix into Highball Glass—ice)*

BRANDY SLING-
Brandy
Water, Sour Mix *(Mix into Small Rocks Glass—ice)*

BRANDY SMASH-
Brandy
Club Soda, Sugar (muddle), Mint Leaves *(Mix into Small Rocks Glass—ice)*

BRANDY SOUR-
Brandy
Sour Mix *(Mix into Sour Glass—ice)*

BRANDY SPECIAL-
Brandy, splash Triple Sec
Sugar, splash Bitters *(Mix into Cocktail Glass—no ice)*

BRANDY SQUIRT-
Brandy
Club Soda, Sugar, Grenadine *(Mix into Highball Glass—ice)*

BRANDY SWIZZLE-
Brandy
Water, Sour Mix, Bitters *(Mix into Highball Glass—ice)*

BRANDY TODDY-
Brandy
Water, Sugar *(Mix into Small Rocks Glass—one ice cube)*

BRANDY VERMOUTH-
4 parts Brandy, 1 part Sweet Vermouth
Bitters *(Mix into Cocktail Glass—no ice)*

BRANDY ZOOM-
Brandy
Hot Water, Light Cream or Milk, Honey *(Mix into Irish Coffee Cup—no ice)*

BRANTINI-
2 parts Brandy, 1 part Gin, splash Dry Vermouth
(Mix into Small Rocks Glass—ice)

BRASS FIDDLE, THE-
2 parts Peach Schnapps, 1 part Sour Mash Whiskey
Pineapple Juice, Orange Juice, splash Grenadine
(Blend with ice in Daiquiri Glass)

BRASS MONKEY-
1 part Light Rum, 1 part Vodka
Orange Juice *(Mix into Highball Glass—ice)*

BRASSY BLONDE-
Blended Whiskey, splash Strawberry Schnapps
Grapefruit Juice, top Club Soda *(Mix into Highball Glass—ice)*

BRAVE BULL-
2 parts Tequila, 1 part Coffee Liqueur *(Mix into Small Rocks Glass—ice)*

BRAZEN HUSSY-
1 part Triple Sec, 1 part Vodka
Lime Juice *(Mix into Cocktail Glass—no ice)*

BRAZIL-
1 part Dry Sherry, 1 part Dry Vermouth, splash Anisette
Bitters *(Mix into Cocktail Glass—no ice)*

BRAZILIAN COFFEE-
Bahai® Coffee Liqueur
Coffee, top Whipped Cream *(Mix into Irish Coffee Cup—no ice)*

BRAZILIAN MONK-
1 part Brown Crème de Caçao, 1 part Coffee Liqueur, 1 part Hazelnut Liqueur,
   splash Dry Sherry
Vanilla Ice Cream *(Blend with ice in Daiquiri Glass)*

BREAKFAST-
Gin
splash Grenadine *(Mix into Small Rocks Glass—ice)*

BREAKFAST EGGNOG-
4 parts Apricot Brandy, 1 part Triple Sec
Light Cream or Milk, sprinkle Nutmeg *(Mix into Highball Glass—ice)*

BREEZE PUNCH-
Dark Rum
Passion Fruit Juice, Sour Mix *(Mix into Highball Glass—ice)*

BRESNAN-
1 part Dry Vermouth, 1 part Sweet Vermouth, splash Crème de Cassis
Lime Juice *(Mix into Cocktail Glass—no ice)*

BRIAN'S BELIEF-
3 parts Light Rum, 1 part Brown Crème de Caçao
Cold Tea, Sour Mix *(Mix into Highball Glass—ice)*

BRIDESMAID COOLER-
Gin
Sour Mix, splash Bitters, fill Ginger Ale *(Mix into Highball Glass—ice)*

BRIGADOON-
1 part Dry Vermouth, 1 part Scotch Whiskey
Grapefruit Juice *(Mix into Highball Glass—ice)*

BRIGHTON PUNCH-
1 part Bénédictine, 1 part Bourbon Whiskey, 1 part Brandy
Orange Juice, Sour Mix, Club Soda *(Mix into Highball Glass—ice)*

BRITISH COMFORT-
3 parts Southern Comfort®, 1 part Gin
Orange Juice, splash Lime Juice *(Mix into Highball Glass—ice)*

BRITTANY-
Gin, splash Amer Picon
Orange Juice, Sour Mix *(Mix into Cocktail Glass—no ice)*

BROADWAY MARTINI-
Gin, splash White Crème de Menthe *(Mix into Cocktail Glass—no ice)*

BROADWAY SMILE-
1 part Triple Sec, 1 part Citrus Rum, 1 part Crème de Cassis
(Layer in Order in Cocktail Glass—no ice)

BROKEN DOWN GOLF CART-
1 part Melon Liqueur, 1 part Amaretto, 1 part Cranberry Juice
(Layer in Order in Cocktail Glass—no ice)

BROKEN SPUR-
2 parts Port, 1 part Sweet Vermouth, splash Triple Sec
(Mix into Cocktail Glass—no ice)

BROKER'S THOUGHT-
1 part Bourbon Whiskey, 1 part Light Rum
Sour Mix, Light Cream or Milk *(Mix into Highball Glass—ice)*

BRONX CHEER-
Apricot Brandy
Raspberry Soda *(Mix into Highball Glass—ice)*

BRONX COCKTAIL-
1 part Dry Vermouth, 1 part Gin, 1 part Sweet Vermouth
splash Orange Juice *(Mix into Cocktail Glass—no ice)*

BRONX MARTINI-
Vodka
splash Bitters, Orange Twist Garnish
(Mix into Cocktail Glass—no ice)

BRONX RIVER-
   3 parts Gin, 1 part Sweet Vermouth
   Sour Mix *(Mix into Cocktail Glass—no ice)*

BRONX SILVER-
   2 parts Gin, 1 part Dry Vermouth
   Orange Juice *(Mix into Highball Glass—ice)*

BRONX TERRACE-
   1 part Dry Vermouth, 1 part Gin
   Lime Juice *(Mix into Cocktail Glass—no ice)*

BROOKLYN (1)-
   3 parts Blended Whiskey, 1 part Dry Vermouth, splash Maraschino Liqueur
   splash Bitters *(Mix into Cocktail Glass—no ice)*

BROOKLYN (2)-
   3 parts Gin, 1 part Sweet Vermouth
   Orange Juice, sprinkle Nutmeg *(Mix into Cocktail Glass—no ice)*

BROWN BEAR-
   2 parts Cognac, 1 part Coffee Liqueur *(Mix into Small Rocks Glass—ice)*

BROWN BOMBER-
   1 part Peanut Liqueur, 1 part White Crème de Caçao
   Light Cream or Milk *(Mix into Highball Glass—ice)*

BROWN COCKTAIL-
   2 parts Dark Rum, 2 parts Gin, 1 part Dry Vermouth
   (Mix into Cocktail Glass—no ice)

BROWN COW-
   1 part Brown Crème de Caçao, 1 part Vodka
   Light Cream or Milk *(Mix into Cocktail Glass—no ice)*

BROWN DERBY-
   Dark Rum
   Lime Juice, Maple Syrup *(Mix into Small Rocks Glass—ice)*

BROWN EYE OPENER-
   1 part Amaretto, 1 part Butterscotch Schnapps, 1 part Coffee Liqueur,
      1 part 100-proof Vodka, 1 part Irish Cream Liqueur
   (Mix into Cocktail Glass—no ice)

BRUISED HEART-
   1 part Peach Schnapps, 1 part Raspberry Liqueur, 1 part Vodka
   Cranberry Juice *(Mix into Highball Glass—ice)*

BRUTE-
   1 part Amaretto, 1 part Brown Crème de Caçao
   Vanilla Ice Cream *(Blend with ice in Daiquiri Glass)*

BUBBLEGUM (1)-
   1 part Banana Liqueur, 1 part Melon Liqueur, 1 part Vodka
   Orange Juice, Grenadine *(Mix into Highball Glass—ice)*

BUBBLEGUM (2)-
1 part Amaretto, 1 part Banana Liqueur, 1 part Yukon Jack® Canadian Liqueur
Orange Juice, Light Cream or Milk, Grenadine
(Mix into Highball Glass—ice)

BUBBLEGUM (3)-
1 part Banana Liqueur, 1 part Peach Schnapps, 1 part Vodka
Orange Juice *(Mix into Highball Glass—ice)*

BUBBLEGUM (4)-
1 part Banana Liqueur, 1 part Peach Schnapps, 1 part Southern Comfort®,
1 part Vodka *(Mix into Small Rocks Glass—ice)*

BUBBLEGUM (5)-
1 part Banana Liqueur, 1 part Southern Comfort®
Light Cream or Milk, splash Grenadine (lace)
(Mix into Highball Glass—ice)

BUBBLY MINT-
Champagne, splash White Crème de Menthe
(Mix into Champagne Flute—no ice)

BUBY-
Gin
Lime Juice, splash Grenadine *(Mix into Cocktail Glass—no ice)*

BUCCANEER-
1 part Coffee Liqueur, 1 part Dark Rum, 1 part Light Rum
Pineapple Juice, Light Cream or Milk
(Mix into Highball Glass with ice or blend with ice in Daiquiri Glass)

BUCK JONES-
2 parts Light Rum, 1 part Sweet Sherry
Lime Juice, Ginger Ale or Club Soda
(Mix into Highball Glass—ice)

BUCK, THE-
2 parts Brandy, 1 part White Crème de Menthe
Lime Juice, fill Ginger Ale *(Mix into Highball Glass—ice)*

BUCKING IRISH-
Irish Whiskey
Ginger Ale *(Mix into Highball Glass—ice)*

BUCKS FIZZ-
Gin
Orange Juice, Sugar *(Mix into Highball Glass—ice)*

BUDDY'S FAVORITE-
Bourbon Whiskey
Water *(Mix into Highball Glass—no ice)*

BULL & BEAR-
2 parts Bourbon Whiskey, 1 part Triple Sec
Lime Juice, splash Grenadine *(Mix into Cocktail Glass—no ice)*

BULL FIGHT-
Aquavit
Beef Bouillon, splash Worcestershire Sauce, splash Lime Juice
(Mix into Highball Glass—ice)

BULL FROG (1)-
Vodka, splash Triple Sec
Lemonade *(Mix into Highball Glass—ice)*

BULL FROG (2)-
Vodka
Sour Mix, Lime Juice
(Mix into Highball Glass—ice)

BULL SH*T-
1 part Light Rum, 1 part Peach Schnapps or 1 part Pear Schnapps
(Mix into Small Rocks Glass—ice)

BULL SHOT-
Vodka
Beef Bouillon, splash Worcestershire Sauce, dash Salt and Pepper
(Mix into Small Rocks Glass—ice)

BULL'S EYE-
Brandy
Cider, Ginger Ale or Club Soda
(Mix into Highball Glass—ice)

BULL'S MILK-
2 parts Brandy, 1 part Light Rum
Light Cream or Milk, Sugar, sprinkle Nutmeg
(Mix into Highball Glass—ice)

BULLDOG-
2 parts Cherry Brandy, 1 part Gin
Lime Juice *(Mix into Cocktail Glass—no ice)*

BULLDOG CAFE-
1 part Brandy, 1 part Gin, 1 part Rye Whiskey, 1 part Sweet Vermouth,
splash Triple Sec *(Mix into Cocktail Glass—no ice)*

BULLDOG HIGHBALL-
Gin
Orange Juice, Club Soda *(Mix into Highball Glass—ice)*

BUMBLEBEE (1)-
1 part Citrus Rum, 1 part Vodka *(Mix into Cocktail Glass—no ice)*

BUMBLEBEE (2)-
Gin
Honey, splash Lime Juice *(Mix into Cocktail Glass—no ice)*

BUMBLEBEE (3)-
3 parts Blackberry Brandy, 1 part White Crème de Menthe
(Mix into Cocktail Glass—no ice)

BUMBLEBEE (4)-
1 part Coffee Liqueur, 1 part Irish Cream Liqueur, 1 part Sambuca
(Mix into Cocktail Glass—no ice)

BUMBO-
Dark Rum
Lime Juice, splash Grenadine, sprinkle Nutmeg
(Mix into Cocktail Glass—no ice)

BUN WARMER-
1 part Apricot Brandy, 1 part Southern Comfort®
Hot Cider, Cinnamon Stick
(Mix into Irish Coffee Cup—no ice)

BUNKY PUNCH-
1 part Melon Liqueur, 1 part Peach Schnapps, 1 part Vodka
Grape Juice, Orange Juice, Cranberry Juice
(Blend with ice in Daiquiri Glass)

BUNNY BONANZA-
2 parts Tequila, 1 part Apple Brandy, splash Triple Sec
Sour Mix *(Mix into Highball Glass—ice)*

BUNNY HUG-
1 part Anisette, 1 part Blended Whiskey, 1 part Gin
(Mix into Cocktail Glass—no ice)

BURBERRY-
Gin, splash Maraschino Liqueur
Sugar, splash Orange Bitters *(Mix into Cocktail Glass—no ice)*

BURFENTAILOR-
2 parts Sweet Vermouth, 1 part Brandy, 1 part Gin, splash Licorice Liqueur
Lime Juice, splash Grenadine
(Mix into Small Rocks Glass—ice)

BURGUNDY BISHOP-
1 part Light Rum, fill Red Wine
Sour Mix *(Mix into Wine Glass—no ice)*

BURNING SUN-
Strawberry Schnapps
Pineapple Juice *(Mix into Highball Glass—ice)*

BURN'S NIGHT SPECIAL-
1 part Scotch Whiskey, 1 part Sweet Vermouth, splash Bénédictine
(Mix into Cocktail Glass—no ice)

BURNT ALMOND-
Amaretto
Light Cream or Milk *(Mix into Small Rocks Glass—ice)*

BURNT EMBERS-
3 parts Light Rum, 1 part Apricot Brandy
Pineapple Juice *(Mix into Highball Glass—ice)*

BURNT MARTINI-
2 parts Gin, 1 part Blended Whiskey *(Mix into Cocktail Glass—no ice)*

BURY ME DEEP-
3 parts Gin, 1 part Raspberry Liqueur, 1 part Scotch Whiskey
Orange Juice, Lemonade *(Mix into Highball Glass—ice)*

BUSHRANGER-
2 parts Light Rum, 1 part Red Dubonnet®
Bitters *(Mix into Cocktail Glass—no ice)*

BUSHWHACKER-
1 part Amaretto, 1 part Coffee Liqueur, 1 part Irish Cream Liqueur,
 1 part Light Rum
Light Cream or Milk
(Mix into Small Rocks Glass—ice)

BUTTAFUOCO-
4 parts Tequila, 1 part Cherry Brandy, 1 part Galliano®
Lime Juice, fill Club Soda
(Mix into Highball Glass—ice)

BUTTER COLADA-
3 parts Butterscotch Schnapps, 1 part Light Rum
Coconut Milk, splash Light Cream or Milk
(Blend with ice in Daiquiri Glass)

BUTTER PECAN (1)-
2 parts Hazelnut Liqueur, 1 part Butterscotch Schnapps, 1 part Vanilla Liqueur
Light Cream or Milk *(Mix into Highball Glass—ice)*

BUTTER PECAN (2)-
Hazelnut Liqueur
Vanilla Ice Cream, Butter Pecan Ice Cream
(Blend with ice in Daiquiri Glass)

BUTTERBALL (1)-
1 part Irish Cream Liqueur, 1 part Butterscotch Schnapps
(Layer in Order in Cocktail Glass—no ice)

BUTTERBALL (2)-
1 part Butterscotch Schnapps, 1 part Irish Cream Liqueur
Light Cream or Milk *(Mix into Highball Glass—ice)*

BUTTERNUT COFFEE-
1 part Amaretto, 1 part Butterscotch Schnapps
Coffee, top Whipped Cream *(Mix into Irish Coffee Cup—no ice)*

BUTTERSCOTCH COLLINS-
3 parts Scotch Whiskey, 1 part Drambuie®
Sour Mix, splash Club Soda *(Mix into Highball Glass—ice)*

BUTTERY FINGER-
1 part Butterscotch Schnapps, 1 part Coffee Liqueur, 1 part Irish Cream
 Liqueur, 1 part Vodka *(Mix into Cocktail Glass—no ice)*

BUTTERY NIPPLE-
1 part Butterscotch Schnapps, 1 part Irish Cream Liqueur, 1 part Vodka
(Mix into Cocktail Glass—no ice)

BUTTERY NIPPLE WITH AN ATTITUDE-
1 part Butterscotch Schnapps, 1 part Irish Cream Liqueur, splash Peppermint
Schnapps *(Mix into Cocktail Glass—no ice)*

BUTTOCK CLENCHER-
1 part Gin, 1 part Tequila, splash Melon Liqueur
Lemonade, Pineapple Juice *(Mix into Highball Glass—ice)*

BUTTON HOOK-
1 part Anisette, 1 part Apricot Brandy, 1 part Brandy, 1 part White Crème de
Menthe *(Mix into Cocktail Glass—no ice)*

BUTTONED LIP-
1 part Coconut Rum, 1 part Spiced Rum
Diet Cola, splash Orange Juice *(Mix into Highball Glass—ice)*

BUZZ LIGHTYEAR-
1 part Melon Liqueur, 1 part Vodka
Orange Juice *(Mix into Highball Glass—ice)*

BUZZARD'S BREATH-
1 part Amaretto, 1 part Coffee Liqueur, 1 part Peppermint Schnapps
(Mix into Small Rocks Glass—ice)

– NOTES –

Black Opal - Vodka, Gin, rum, triple sec,
blackberry liquor, Blue Curacao liquor,
Seven-up, sweet + sour

C. C. KAZI-
Tequila
Cranberry Juice, Lime Juice *(Mix into Highball Glass—ice)*

C-SPOT-
Peach Schnapps
Cranberry Juice *(Mix into Highball Glass—ice)*

CABARET-
Gin, splash Bénédictine, splash Dry Vermouth
Bitters *(Mix into Cocktail Glass—no ice)*

CABER TOSS-
1 part Gin, 1 part Scotch Whiskey, splash Licorice Liqueur
(Mix into Cocktail Glass—no ice)

CABLECAR-
2 parts Gin, 1 part Triple Sec
Lime Juice *(Mix into Small Rocks Glass—ice)*

CABLEGRAM-
Blended Whiskey
Sour Mix, Ginger Ale *(Mix into Highball Glass—ice)*

CACTUS BANGER-
3 parts Tequila, 1 part Galliano® (float)
Orange Juice *(Mix into Highball Glass—ice)*

CACTUS BERRY-
1 part Tequila, 1 part Triple Sec, 1 part Red Wine
Sour Mix, splash Lime Juice, splash Lemon-Lime Soda
(Mix into Cocktail Glass—no ice)

CACTUS BITE-
Tequila, splash Drambuie®, splash Triple Sec
Sour Mix, splash Bitters
(Mix into Cocktail Glass—no ice)

CACTUS BOWL-
2 parts Light Rum, 1 part Amaretto, 1 part Spiced Rum
Pineapple Juice, splash Lime Juice
(Blend with ice in Daiquiri Glass)

CACTUS COLADA-
2 parts Tequila, 1 part Melon Liqueur
Coconut Milk, Pineapple Juice *(Blend with ice in Daiquiri Glass)*

CACTUS FEVER-
Margarita Schnapps
Lime Wedge, Salted Rim *(Mix into Cocktail Glass—no ice)*

CACTUS MARGARITA-
Tequila
Pineapple Juice, Sour Mix
(Mix into Cocktail Glass with no ice or blend with ice in Daiquiri Glass)

CACTUS SPIKE-
1 part Margarita Schnapps, 1 part Sloe Gin
Orange Juice, Sour Mix *(Mix into Cocktail Glass—no ice)*

CADIZ-
2 parts Blackberry Brandy, 2 parts Dry Sherry, 1 part Triple Sec
Light Cream or Milk *(Mix into Small Rocks Glass—ice)*

CAFE AMARETTO-
Amaretto
Coffee, top Whipped Cream *(Mix into Irish Coffee Cup—no ice)*

CAFE AMOUR-
2 parts Cognac, 1 part Amaretto
Coffee, top Whipped Cream *(Mix into Irish Coffee Cup—no ice)*

CAFE AUX COGNAC-
Cognac
Coffee, Sugar, top Whipped Cream *(Mix into Irish Coffee Cup—no ice)*

CAFE BARBADOS-
2 parts Dark Rum, 1 part Tia Maria®
Coffee, top Whipped Cream *(Mix into Irish Coffee Cup—no ice)*

CAFE BONAPARTE-
Brandy
Cappuccino, top Whipped Cream *(Mix into Irish Coffee Cup—no ice)*

CAFE CABANA-
Coffee Liqueur
Club Soda *(Mix into Highball Glass—ice)*

CAFE CARIBBEAN-
1 part Amaretto, 1 part Light Rum
Coffee, Sugar, top Whipped Cream *(Mix into Irish Coffee Cup—no ice)*

CAFE DE PARIS-
Gin, splash Anisette
Light Cream or Milk *(Mix into Cocktail Glass—no ice)*

CAFE DIABLO-
2 parts Cognac, 1 part Triple Sec (ignite, optional) {extinguish
    flame before drinking}
Coffee, top Whipped Cream *(Mix into Irish Coffee Cup—no ice)*

CAFE DI AMARETTO-
Amaretto
Coffee, top Whipped Cream *(Mix into Irish Coffee Cup—no ice)*

CAFE DON JUAN-
1 part Coffee Liqueur, 1 part Dark Rum
Coffee, Sugared Rim *(Mix into Irish Coffee Cup—no ice)*

CAFE FOSTER-
2 parts Dark Rum, 1 part Banana Liqueur
Coffee, top Whipped Cream *(Mix into Irish Coffee Cup—no ice)*

CAFE FRENCH-
2 parts Amaretto, 2 parts Triple Sec, 1 part Irish Cream Liqueur
Coffee, top Whipped Cream *(Mix into Irish Coffee Cup—no ice)*

CAFE GRANDE-
1 part Brown Crème de Caçao, 1 part Grand Marnier®, 1 part Tia Maria®
Coffee, Cherry Garnish *(Mix into Irish Coffee Cup—no ice)*

CAFE HENRY THE THIRD-
1 part Brandy, 1 part Coffee Liqueur, 1 part Galliano®, 1 part Grand Mariner
Coffee, Cinnamon Rim, top Whipped Cream
(Mix into Irish Coffee Cup—no ice)

CAFE L'ORANGE -
2 parts Grand Marnier®, 1 part Cognac, 1 part Triple Sec
Coffee, top Whipped Cream *(Mix into Irish Coffee Cup—no ice)*

CAFE MARNIER-
Grand Marnier®
Coffee, top Whipped Cream *(Mix into Irish Coffee Cup—no ice)*

CAFE MICHELLE-
2 parts Amaretto, 2 parts Coffee Liqueur, 1 part Irish Cream Liqueur
Coffee, top Whipped Cream *(Mix into Irish Coffee Cup—no ice)*

CAFE NELSON-
1 part Hazelnut Liqueur, 1 part Irish Cream Liqueur
Coffee, top Whipped Cream, sprinkle Nuts *(Mix into Irish Coffee Cup—no ice)*

CAFE PREGO-
3 parts Amaretto, 1 part Brandy
Coffee, top Whipped Cream *(Mix into Irish Coffee Cup—no ice)*

CAFE ROMANO-
1 part Coffee Liqueur, 1 part Sambuca
Light Cream or Milk *(Mix into Cocktail Glass—no ice)*

CAFE ROYALE-
Brandy or Cognac
Coffee, Sugar Cube (soak Sugar Cube in Brandy, ignite, drop in Coffee,
  optional) {extinguish flame before drinking}
(Mix into Irish Coffee Cup—no ice)

CAFE SAN JUAN-
Dark Rum
Cold Coffee, Sugar *(Mix into Highball Glass—ice)*

CAFE SEIYOKEN-
1 part Light Rum, 1 part Melon Liqueur, 1 part Sake
Coffee, splash Lime Juice, top Whipped Cream
(Mix into Irish Coffee Cup—no ice)

CAFE THEATRE-
1 part Irish Cream Liqueur, 1 part White Crème de Caçao, splash Brown
  Crème de Caçao, splash Hazelnut Liqueur
Coffee, top Whipped Cream *(Mix into Irish Coffee Cup—no ice)*

CAFE TOLEDO-
1 part Coffee Liqueur, 1 part Irish Cream Liqueur
Coffee, Chocolate Syrup, top Whipped Cream
(Mix into Irish Coffee Cup—no ice)

CAFE ZURICH-
1 part Amaretto, 1 part Anisette, 1 part Cognac
Coffee, Honey, top Whipped Cream *(Mix into Irish Coffee Cup—no ice)*

CAIPIRINHA-
Golden Rum
Sugar, Lime Wedges *(Mix into Small Rocks Glass—ice)*

CAITHNESS COMFORT-
Scotch Whiskey, splash Triple Sec
Light Cream or Milk, Honey *(Mix into Highball Glass—ice)*

CAITLIN'S CURE-
Gin
splash Grenadine, splash Bitters, splash Orange Bitters
(Mix into Cocktail Glass—no ice)

CAJUN MARTINI (1)-
Vodka, splash Dry Vermouth
Jalapeno Pepper Garnish *(Mix into Cocktail Glass—no ice)*

CAJUN MARTINI (2)-
Pepper Vodka, splash Dry Vermouth *(Mix into Cocktail Glass—no ice)*

CAJUN MARY-
Pepper Vodka
Tomato Juice, Worcestershire Sauce, Sour Mix, Horseradish, splash Lime Juice,
    dash Whole Black Pepper, dash Salt and Pepper, dash Celery Salt
(Mix into Highball Glass—ice)

CALEDONIA-
1 part Brandy, 1 part Brown Crème de Caçao
Light Cream or Milk, sprinkle Cinnamon
(Mix into Small Rocks Glass—ice)

CALEIGH-
3 parts Scotch Whiskey, 1 part Blue Curaçao, 1 part White Crème de Caçao
(Mix into Cocktail Glass—no ice)

CALICO JACK-
1 part Bourbon Whiskey, 1 part Dark Rum
Sour Mix *(Mix into Cocktail Glass—no ice)*

CALIFORNIA COFFEE-
1 part California Brandy, 1 part California Sherry
Coffee, splash Orange Juice, splash Lime Juice, top Whipped Cream
(Mix into Irish Coffee Cup—no ice)

CALIFORNIA COOLER-
Vodka
Orange Juice, Club Soda *(Mix into Highball Glass—ice)*

CALIFORNIA DREAM-
2 parts Tequila, 1 part Sweet Vermouth, splash Dry Vermouth
(Mix into Cocktail Glass—no ice)

CALIFORNIA DRIVER-
Vodka
Grapefruit Juice, Orange Juice *(Mix into Highball Glass—ice)*

CALIFORNIA ICED TEA-
1 part Light Rum, 1 part Gin, 1 part Tequila, 1 part Triple Sec
Orange Juice, Pineapple Juice, Sour Mix *(Mix into Highball Glass—ice)*

CALIFORNIA LEMONADE (1)-
Blended Whiskey
Sour Mix, Club Soda *(Mix into Highball Glass—ice)*

CALIFORNIA LEMONADE (2)-
1 part Brandy, 1 part Gin, 1 part Vodka
Orange Juice, Sour Mix, splash Grenadine *(Mix into Highball Glass—ice)*

CALIFORNIA ROOT BEER (1)-
2 parts Vodka, 1 part Galliano®
Cola *(Mix into Highball Glass—ice)*

CALIFORNIA ROOT BEER (2)-
1 part Coffee Liqueur, 1 part Galliano®
Club Soda, splash Cola *(Mix into Highball Glass—ice)*

CALIFORNIA ROOT BEER (3)-
1 part Coffee Liqueur, 1 part Galliano®, splash Beer (top)
Cola *(Mix into Highball Glass—ice)*

CALIFORNIA SKY-
1 part Blue Curaçao 1 part Coconut Rum, 1 part 151-proof Rum (lace)
Pineapple Juice, ignite, (optional) {extinguish flame before drinking}
(Mix into Highball Glass—ice)

CALIFORNIA SURFER-
1 part Coconut Rum, 1 part Jägermeister®
Pineapple Juice *(Mix into Highball Glass—ice)*

CALIFORNIAN-
Vodka
Grapefruit Juice, Orange Juice *(Mix into Highball Glass—ice)*

CALM VOYAGE-
1 part Light Rum, 1 part Strega
Lime Juice, splash Passion Fruit Juice *(Blend with ice in Champagne Flute)*

CALVADOS-
2 parts Apple Brandy, 1 part Triple Sec
Orange Juice, splash Orange Bitters *(Mix into Cocktail Glass—no ice)*

CALYPSO COFFEE-
1 part Jamaican Rum, 1 part Tia Maria®
Coffee, top Whipped Cream *(Mix into Irish Coffee Cup—no ice)*

CALYPSO COFFEE (USA)-
1 part Brown Crème de Caçao, 1 part Light Rum, splash Amaretto (top)
Coffee *(Mix into Irish Coffee Cup—no ice)*

CALYPSO COOLER-
1 part Dark Rum, 1 part Peach Schnapps, 1 part Spiced Rum
Orange Juice, splash Lime Juice, splash Grenadine, Club Soda (top)
(Mix into Highball Glass—ice)

CAMEL DRIVER-
1 part Sambuca, 1 part Irish Cream Liqueur
(Layer in Order in Glass with no ice)

CAMEL'S COFFEE-
2 parts Coffee Liqueur, 1 part Cognac, 1 part Light Rum, 1 part Strega
Cold Coffee *(Mix into Highball Glass—ice)*

CAMERON'S KICK-
1 part Irish Whiskey, 1 part Scotch Whiskey
Sour Mix, Orange Bitters
(Mix into Cocktail Glass—no ice)

CAMP GRENADA-
Campari
Grapefruit Juice, Pineapple Juice, splash Grenadine, fill Lemon-Lime Soda
(Mix into Highball Glass—ice)

CAMPOBELLO-
1 part Campari, 1 part Gin, 1 part Sweet Vermouth
(Mix into Cocktail Glass—no ice)

CAMSHAFT-
2 parts Vodka, 1 part Campari
Orange Juice, Passion Fruit Juice, Lemonade
(Mix into Highball Glass—ice)

CANADA COCKTAIL-
3 parts Canadian Whiskey, 1 part Triple Sec
Sugar, splash Bitters *(Mix into Cocktail Glass—no ice)*

CANADIAN APPLE-
4 parts Canadian Whiskey, 1·part Apple Brandy
Sour Mix *(Mix into Highball Glass—ice)*

CANADIAN BLACKBERRY FIZZ-
2 parts Canadian Whiskey, 1 part Blackberry Brandy
Sour Mix, splash Club Soda *(Mix into Highball Glass—ice)*

CANADIAN BREEZE-
Canadian Whiskey, splash Maraschino Liqueur
Pineapple Juice, Lime Juice *(Mix into Small Rocks Glass—ice)*

CANADIAN CHERRY-
3 parts Canadian Whiskey, 1 part Cherry Brandy
Sour Mix, Orange Juice
(Mix into Small Rocks Glass—ice)

CANADIAN COCKTAIL-
4 parts Canadian Whiskey, 1 part Triple Sec
Sugar, Bitters *(Mix into Cocktail Glass—no ice)*

CANADIAN COFFEE-
Canadian Whiskey
Coffee, top Whipped Cream *(Mix into Irish Coffee Cup—no ice)*

CANADIAN CREAM-
Canadian Rye Whiskey
Light Cream or Milk, Honey *(Mix into Cocktail Glass—no ice)*

CANADIAN DAISY-
Canadian Whiskey, splash Brandy, splash Raspberry Liqueur
Sour Mix, splash Grenadine *(Mix into Highball Glass—ice)*

CANADIAN MOOSE-
1 part Coffee Liqueur, 1 part Irish Cream Liqueur, 1 part Canadian Whiskey
(Layer in Order in Cocktail Glass—no ice)

CANADIAN OLD-FASHIONED-
Canadian Whiskey
Sugar, splash Water, splash Bitters *(Mix into Small Rocks Glass—ice)*

CANADIAN PINEAPPLE-
Canadian Whiskey, splash Maraschino Liqueur
Sour Mix *(Mix into Small Rocks Glass—ice)*

CANADIAN SALAD-
2 parts Canadian Whiskey, 1 part Brandy, 1 part Irish Mist®,
    1 part Scotch Whiskey
Orange Juice, Sour Mix
(Mix into Highball Glass—ice)

CANADIAN TEA-
Canadian Whiskey
Hot Tea *(Mix into Irish Coffee Cup—no ice)*

CANADO SALUDO-
Light Rum
Orange Juice, Pineapple Juice, Sour Mix, Grenadine, Bitters
(Mix into Small Rocks Glass—ice)

CANAL STREET DAISY-
Blended Whiskey
Orange Juice, Sour Mix, Club Soda *(Mix into Highball Glass—ice)*

CANDLE IN THE WINDOW-
Light Rum, splash Bourbon Whiskey, splash Brown Crème de Caçao,
    splash Cherry Brandy
Coffee, splash Light Cream or Milk, top Whipped Cream
(Mix into Irish Coffee Cup—no ice)

CANDY-
1 part Brandy, 1 part Galliano®, splash Maraschino Liqueur
Orange Sherbet *(Blend with ice in Daiquiri Glass)*

CANDY APPLE (1)-
1 part Apple Schnapps, 1 part Cinnamon Schnapps
Apple Juice *(Mix into Cocktail Glass—no ice)*

CANDY APPLE (2)-
1 part Apple Schnapps, 1 part Peach Schnapps
Cranberry Juice *(Mix into Highball Glass—ice)*

CANDY ASS-
1 part Irish Cream Liqueur, 1 part Raspberry Liqueur, 1 part White
Crème de Caçao *(Mix into Cocktail Glass—no ice)*

CANDY BAR (1)-
1 part Hazelnut Liqueur, 1 part Vodka *(Mix into Small Rocks Glass—ice)*

CANDY BAR (2)-
1 part Brown Crème de Caçao, 1 part Coffee Liqueur, 1 part Hazelnut Liqueur
Light Cream or Milk *(Mix into Highball Glass—ice)*

CANDY CANE-
1 part Green Crème de Menthe, 1 part Peppermint Schnapps
(Layer in Order in Cocktail Glass—no ice)

CANDY PANTS-
3 parts Blended Whiskey, 1 part Cherry Brandy
Sour Mix, splash Grenadine *(Mix into Cocktail Glass—no ice)*

CANDY STORE-
1 part Amaretto, 1 part Crème de Noyaux, 1 part Raspberry Liqueur
Cookies n' Cream Ice Cream, top Whipped Cream
(Blend with ice in Daiquiri Glass)

CANYON QUAKE-
1 part Amaretto, 1 part Brandy, 1 part Irish Cream Liqueur
Light Cream or Milk *(Blend with ice in Daiquiri Glass)*

CAPE COD COOLER-
2 parts Sloe Gin, 1 part Gin, splash Amaretto
Cranberry Juice, splash Lime Juice *(Mix into Highball Glass—ice)*

CAPE CODDER-
Vodka
Cranberry Juice *(Mix into Highball Glass—ice)*

CAPE COLADA-
1 part Peach Schnapps, 1 part Vodka
Coconut Milk, Cranberry Juice, Sour Mix *(Blend with ice in Daiquiri Glass)*

CAPE GRAPE-
Vodka
Grapefruit Juice, splash Cranberry Juice *(Mix into Highball Glass—ice)*

CAPE OF GOOD WILL-
3 parts Light Rum, 1 part Apricot Brandy
Orange Juice, Lime Juice, splash Orange Bitters
(Mix into Cocktail Glass—no ice)

CAPE TOWN-
1 part Blended Whiskey, 1 part Dry Vermouth, splash Triple Sec
splash Bitters *(Mix into Cocktail Glass—no ice)*

CAPITAL PUNISHMENT-
1 part Amaretto, 1 part Jack Daniel's® Tennessee Sour Mash Whiskey
(Mix into Small Rocks Glass—ice)

CAPPUCCINO COCKTAIL-
1 part Coffee Liqueur, 1 part Vodka
Light Cream or Milk *(Mix into Cocktail Glass—no ice)*

CAPPUCCINO MOCHA-
1 part Brown Crème de Caçao, 1 part Coffee Liqueur
Cappuccino, top Whipped Cream *(Mix into Irish Coffee Cup—no ice)*

CAPPUCCINO SAUSALITO-
1 part Amaretto, 1 part Coffee Liqueur
Coffee, Hot Chocolate, top Whipped Cream
(Mix into Irish Coffee Cup—no ice)

CAPRI-
1 part Banana Liqueur, 1 part White Crème de Caçao
Light Cream or Milk *(Mix into Small Rocks Glass—ice)*

CAPRICCIO-
2 parts Amaretto, 1 part Brandy, 1 part Coffee Liqueur
Coffee, top Whipped Cream *(Mix into Irish Coffee Cup—no ice)*

CAPTAIN COOK-
3 parts Gin, 1 part Maraschino Liqueur
Orange Juice *(Mix into Cocktail Glass—no ice)*

CAPTAIN DEW-
Captain Morgan® Original Spiced Rum
Mountain Dew® *(Mix into Highball Glass—ice)*

CAPTAIN KIDD-
1 part Brandy, 1 part Dark Rum, 1 part Brown Crème de Caçao
(Mix into Cocktail Glass—no ice)

CAPTAIN'S TABLE-
Gin, splash Maraschino Liqueur
Orange Juice, splash Grenadine, fill Ginger Ale *(Mix into Highball Glass—ice)*

CAR CRASH-
1 part Amaretto, 1 part Peach Schnapps, 1 part Southern Comfort®
Orange Juice, Sour Mix, splash Grenadine *(Mix into Highball Glass—ice)*

CARA MIA-
2 parts Gin, 1 part Dry Vermouth, 1 part Sherry, splash Triple Sec
(Mix into Cocktail Glass—no ice)

CARA SPOSA-
1 part Coffee Liqueur, 1 part Triple Sec
Light Cream or Milk *(Mix into Cocktail Glass—no ice)*

CARACAS-
Scotch Whiskey, splash Amaretto, splash Triple Sec
Sour Mix *(Mix into Cocktail Glass—no ice)*

CARAMEL APPLE-
1 part Butterscotch Schnapps, 1 part Sour Apple Schnapps
(Mix into Cocktail Glass—no ice)

CARAMEL APPLE MARTINI-
2 parts Vodka, 1 part Butterscotch Schnapps, 1 part Sour Apple Schnapps
(Mix into Cocktail Glass—no ice)

CARAMEL NUT-
1 part Butterscotch Schnapps or Caramel Liqueur, 1 part White
  Crème de Caçao
Vanilla Ice Cream, Chopped Nuts Garnish *(Blend with ice in Daiquiri Glass)*

CARDINAL-
3 parts Light Rum, 1 part Maraschino Liqueur, splash Triple Sec
splash Grenadine *(Mix into Cocktail Glass—no ice)*

CARIB BREEZER-
1 part Banana Liqueur, 1 part Melon Liqueur, 1 part Vodka
Pineapple Juice *(Blend with ice in Daiquiri Glass)*

CARIBBEAN BEACH PARTY-
1 part Banana Liqueur, 1 part Dark Rum
Coconut Milk, Pineapple Juice, Cranberry Juice, Grenadine
(Mix into Highball Glass with ice or blend with ice in Daiquiri Glass)

CARIBBEAN BERRY-
2 parts Spiced Rum, 1 part Coconut Rum, 1 part Melon Liqueur,
  1 part Peach Schnapps
Cranberry Juice *(Mix into Highball Glass—ice)*

CARIBBEAN BREEZE (1)-
4 parts Dark Rum, 1 part Banana Liqueur
Pineapple Juice, splash Lime Juice, splash Grenadine, splash Orange Bitters
(Mix into Highball Glass—ice)

CARIBBEAN BREEZE (2)-
1 part Banana Liqueur, 1 park Dark Rum
Coconut Milk, Pineapple Juice, Sour Mix, Grenadine
(Mix into Highball Glass with ice or blend with ice in Daiquiri Glass)

CARIBBEAN CHAMPAGNE-
Champagne, splash Banana Liqueur, splash Light Rum
(Mix into Champagne Flute—no ice)

CARIBBEAN CHAT-
Spiced Rum, splash White Crème de Caçao
Orange Juice, Club Soda *(Mix into Highball Glass—ice)*

CARIBBEAN COCKTAIL-
2 parts Dark Spiced Rum, 1 part Apricot Brandy
Cranberry Juice *(Mix into Highball Glass—ice)*

CARIBBEAN COFFEE-
Dark Rum
Coffee, splash Light Cream or Milk, Sugar, top Whipped Cream
(Mix into Irish Coffee Cup—no ice)

CARIBBEAN COOLER-
1 part Apricot Brandy, 1 part Coconut Rum, 1 part Dark Rum
Light Cream or Milk
(Mix into Highball Glass with ice or blend with ice in Daiquiri Glass)

CARIBBEAN CRUISE-
2 parts Vodka, 1 part Coconut Rum, 1 part Light Rum
Pineapple Juice, splash Grenadine *(Mix into Highball Glass—ice)*

CARIBBEAN GRASSHOPPER-
1 part Coconut Liqueur, 1 part Green Crème de Menthe, 1 part White
    Crème de Caçao
Light Cream or Milk *(Mix into Highball Glass—ice)*

CARIBBEAN ICE CREAM-
1 part Coffee Liqueur, 1 part Dark Rum
Vanilla Ice Cream, splash Light Cream or Milk
(Blend with ice in Daiquiri Glass)

CARIBBEAN KISS-
3 parts Dark Rum, 1 part Amaretto, 1 part Coffee Liqueur (Coffee Liqueur Rim)
Light Cream or Milk, sprinkle Cinnamon, Brown sugar (Rim)
(Mix into Highball Glass—ice)

CARIBBEAN MADRAS-
Dark Rum
Cranberry Juice, Orange Juice *(Mix into Highball Glass—ice)*

CARIBBEAN MARGARITA-
1 part Banana Liqueur, 1 part Tequila
Coconut Milk, Sour Mix, Pineapple Juice, Grenadine
(Mix into Highball Glass with ice or blend with ice in Daiquiri Glass)

CARIBBEAN MARTINI-
2 parts Vodka, 1 part Coconut Rum
Splash Pineapple Juice *(Mix into Cocktail Glass—no ice)*

CARIBBEAN PUNCH-
1 part Banana Liqueur, 1 part Dark Rum
Coconut Milk, Pineapple Juice, Orange Juice *(Mix into Highball Glass—ice)*

CARIBBEAN ROMANCE-
1 part Amaretto, 1 part Light Rum
Orange Juice, Pineapple Juice, Grenadine (float)
(Mix into Highball Glass—ice)

CARIBBEAN SCREWDRIVER-
1 part Banana Liqueur, 1 part Coconut Rum, 1 part Peach Schnapps
Orange Juice, Pineapple Juice, Light Cream or Milk
(Mix into Highball Glass—ice)

CARIBBEAN SMUGGLER-
2 parts Dark Rum, 1 part Triple Sec
Orange Juice, Sour Mix, fill Lemon-Lime Soda
(Mix into Highball Glass—ice)

CARIBBEAN SUNSET-
Red Wine, splash Triple Sec
splash Orange Bitters, fill Club Soda *(Mix into Wine Glass—no ice)*

CARIBE-
Spiced Rum
Pineapple Juice, splash Lime Juice *(Mix into Cocktail Glass—no ice)*

CAROL COCKTAIL
2 parts Brandy, 1 part Sweet Vermouth *(Mix into Cocktail Glass—no ice)*

CAROLI-
4 parts Gin, 1 part Apricot Brandy
splash Orange Bitters *(Mix into Cocktail Glass—no ice)*

CAROLINA-
Tequila
Light Cream or Milk, splash Grenadine, splash Vanilla Extract, Cherry Garnish
(Mix into Cocktail Glass—no ice)

CARROT CAKE-
1 part Butterscotch Schnapps, 1 part Goldschläger®, 1 part Irish Cream Liqueur
(Mix into Cocktail Glass—no ice)

CARUSO-
2 parts Gin, 1 part Dry Vermouth, 1 part Green Crème de Menthe
(Mix into Cocktail Glass—no ice)

CASABLANCA-
Light Rum, splash Maraschino Liqueur, splash Triple Sec
Lime Juice *(Mix into Cocktail Glass—no ice)*

CASCO BAY LEMONADE-
Citrus Vodka
Sour Mix, splash Cranberry Juice, splash Lemon-Lime Soda
(Mix into Highball Glass—ice)

CASINO COCKTAIL-
Gin, splash Maraschino Liqueur
Sour Mix, Orange Bitters
(Mix into Cocktail Glass—no ice)

CASINO COFFEE-
1 part Amaretto, 1 part Brandy, 1 part Brown Crème de Caçao
Coffee, top Whipped Cream, top Chocolate Sprinkles
(Mix into Irish Coffee Cup—no ice)

CASSIS A LA CRÈME-
Crème de Cassis, splash Hazelnut Liqueur
Light Cream or Milk *(Mix into Cocktail Glass—no ice)*

CASTLE DIP-
1 part Apple Brandy, 1 part White Crème de Menthe, splash Licorice Liqueur
(Mix into Cocktail Glass—no ice)

CAT & FIDDLE-
3 parts Canadian Whiskey, 1 part Triple Sec, splash Licorice Liqueur,
splash White Dubonnet® *(Mix into Cocktail Glass—no ice)*

CAT'S EYE-
Dry Vermouth, splash Yellow Chartreuse
splash Orange Bitters *(Mix into Cocktail Glass—no ice)*

CATALINA-
1 part Vodka, 1 part White Port, splash Campari
splash Grenadine *(Mix into Cocktail Glass—no ice)*

CATALINA MARGARITA-
3 parts Tequila, 1 part Blue Curaçao, 1 part Peach Schnapps
Sour Mix *(Mix into Cocktail Glass—no ice)*

CATHERINE OF SHERIDAN SQUARE-
3 parts Dark Rum, 1 part Tia Mia®
Cold Coffee, splash Light Cream or Milk
(Mix into Irish Coffee Cup—ice)

CAVANAUGH'S SPECIAL-
1 part Amaretto, 1 part Coffee Liqueur (layer on top), 1 part White
Crème de Caçao
Vanilla Ice Cream, top Whipped Cream *(Blend with ice in Daiquiri Glass)*

CEASEFIRE-
1 part Cherry Brandy, 1 part Dry Vermouth, 1 part Scotch Whiskey
Lemonade *(Mix into Highball Glass—ice)*

CELTIC BULL-
Irish Whiskey
Beef Bouillon, Tomato Juice, splash Worcestershire Sauce
(Mix into Highball Glass—ice)

CELTIC MIX-
1 part Irish Whiskey, 1 part Scotch Whiskey
splash Lime Juice, splash Bitters *(Mix into Cocktail Glass—no ice)*

CENTENARIO-
3 parts Light Rum, 1 part Coffee Liqueur, 1 part Triple Sec
Lime Juice, Grenadine *(Mix into Highball Glass—ice)*

CENTRAL PARK-
2 parts Apple Brandy, 2 parts Apricot Brandy, 1 part Cherry Brandy, 1 part Gin,
splash Maraschino Liqueur
Orange Juice, splash Grenadine (float)
(Mix into Cocktail Glass—no ice)

CENTRAL PARK WEST-
3 parts Gin, 1 part Cherry Brandy
Lime Juice *(Mix into Cocktail Glass—no ice)*

CHALULA CREAM-
3 parts Jamaican Rum, 1 part Cherry Liqueur
Lime Juice, Light Cream or Milk *(Mix into Cocktail Glass—no ice)*

CHAMPAGNE CHARISMA-
2 parts Champagne, 1 part Vodka, splash Peach Schnapps
Cranberry Juice, Raspberry Sherbet *(Blend with ice in Daiquiri Glass)*

CHAMPAGNE COCKTAIL-
Champagne
Sugar, Bitters *(Mix into Champagne Flute—no ice)*

CHAMPAGNE CORNUCOPIA SWIRL-
1 part Champagne, 1 part Peach Schnapps, 1 part Vodka
Rainbow Sherbet (Pour over Cranberry Juice after blend)
(Blend with ice in Daiquiri Glass)

CHAMPAGNE JULEP-
Champagne
Sugar, Fresh Mint *(Mix into Champagne Flute—no ice)*

CHAMPAGNE ROYAL-
Champagne, splash Raspberry Liqueur *(Mix into Cocktail Glass—no ice)*

CHAMPS ELYSEES-
2 parts Brandy, Yellow Chartreuse
Sour Mix, Bitters *(Mix into Cocktail Glass—no ice)*

CHANGUIRONGO-
Tequila
Ginger Ale *(Mix into Highball Glass—ice)*

CHANNEL 64-
1 part Banana Liqueur, 1 part Irish Cream Liqueur, 1 part Eggnog Liqueur
(Layer in Order in Cocktail Glass—no ice)

CHANTICLEER-
Gin, splash Raspberry Liqueur
Lime Juice *(Mix into Small Rocks Glass—ice)*

CHAOS CALMER-
3 parts Gin, 1 part Triple Sec
Orange Juice, splash Lime Juice, splash Grenadine
(Mix into Highball Glass—ice)

CHAPALA-
Tequila, splash Triple Sec
Orange Juice, Lime Juice, Grenadine *(Mix into Small Rocks Glass—ice)*

CHAPEL HILL-
3 parts Bourbon Whiskey, 1 part Triple Sec
Lime Juice *(Mix into Cocktail Glass—no ice)*

CHARGER-
3 parts Dark Rum, 1 part Cherry Brandy
Sour Mix *(Mix into Cocktail Glass—no ice)*

CHARLES COCKTAIL-
1 part Brandy, 1 part Sweet Vermouth
Bitters *(Mix into Cocktail Glass—no ice)*

CHARLES' NIGHTCAP-
1 part Brandy, 1 part Pear Brandy *(Mix into Cocktail Glass—no ice)*

CHARLESTON-
1 part Cherry Brandy, 1 part Dry Vermouth, 1 part Gin, 1 part Maraschino
   Liqueur, 1 part Sweet Vermouth, 1 part Triple Sec
(Mix into Cocktail Glass—no ice)

CHARLIE CHAPLIN-
1 part Apricot Brandy, 1 part Sloe Gin
Lime Juice *(Mix into Small Rocks Glass—ice)*

CHARMER-
Scotch Whiskey, splash Blue Curaçao, splash Dry Vermouth
splash Orange Bitters *(Mix into Cocktail Glass—no ice)*

CHARRO-
Tequila
Coffee, splash Light Cream or Milk, top Whipped Cream
(Mix into Irish Coffee Cup—no ice)

CHARTBUSTER-
1 part Coconut Liqueur, 1 part Strawberry Schnapps
Pineapple Juice *(Mix into Highball Glass—ice)*

CHATHAM COCKTAIL-
4 parts Gin, 1 part Ginger Brandy
Sour Mix *(Mix into Cocktail Glass—no ice)*

CHEAP MAN'S PIÑA COLADA-
Coconut Rum
Pineapple Juice, splash Light Cream or Milk
(Blend with ice in Daiquiri Glass)

CHEAP SUNGLASSES-
2 parts Melon Liqueur, 1 part Peach Schnapps
Orange Juice, Pineapple Juice, Sour Mix, splash Lemon-Lime Soda
(Mix into Highball Glass—ice)

CHEESE SANDWICH-
3 parts Melon Liqueur, 1 part Triple Sec, splash Dark Rum
Lemonade, splash Lime Juice *(Mix into Highball Glass—ice)*

CHELSEA-
2 parts Dry Vermouth, 1 part Bourbon Whiskey, 1 part Blackberry Brandy,
   1 part Triple Sec
splash Lime Juice *(Mix into Cocktail Glass—no ice)*

CHELSEA HOTEL-
3 parts Gin, 1 part Triple Sec
splash Lime Juice *(Mix into Cocktail Glass—no ice)*

CHELSEA SIDECAR-
1 part Gin, 1 part Triple Sec
Lime Juice *(Mix into Cocktail Glass—no ice)*

CHERIE-
2 parts Light Rum, 1 part Cherry Brandy, 1 part Triple Sec
Lime Juice *(Mix into Cocktail Glass—no ice)*

CHERRIED CREAM RUM-
3 parts Light Rum, 1 part Cherry Brandy
Light Cream or Milk *(Mix into Cocktail Glass—no ice)*

CHERRIES FROM HEAVEN-
Cherry Brandy
splash Lime Juice, splash Bitters, fill Tonic Water
(Mix into Highball Glass—ice)

CHERRY BLOSSOM (1)-
3 parts Brandy, 1 part Cherry Brandy, 1 part Triple Sec
Lime Juice
(Mix into Cocktail Glass—no ice)

CHERRY BLOSSOM (2)-
2 parts Cherry Brandy, 1 part Dark Rum
Cranberry Juice, splash Lime Juice, splash Grenadine
(Mix into Cocktail Glass—no ice)

CHERRY BOMB (1)-
1 part Cherry Brandy, 1 part Light Rum
Sour Mix *(Mix into Cocktail Glass—no ice)*

CHERRY BOMB (2)-
1 part Coconut Rum, 1 part Tequila, 1 part Vodka
Pineapple Juice, splash Light Cream or Milk, splash Grenadine
(Mix into Highball Glass—ice)

CHERRY CHOCOLATE FREEZE-
1 part Brown Crème de Caçao, 1 part Cherry Brandy
Chocolate Ice Cream *(Blend with ice in Daiquiri Glass)*

CHERRY COBBLER-
4 parts Gin, 1 part Cherry Brandy, 1 part Crème de Cassis
Sour Mix *(Mix into Highball Glass—ice)*

CHERRY COCKTAIL-
1 part Danish Cherry Wine, 1 part Vodka
Lime Juice *(Mix into Wine Glass—no ice)*

CHERRY COLA (1)-
Cherry Brandy
Cola *(Mix into Highball Glass—ice)*

CHERRY COLA (2)-
2 parts Dark Rum, 1 part Cherry Brandy
Cola *(Mix into Highball Glass—ice)*

CHERRY COOLER-
 Cherry Vodka or Cherry Brandy
 Cola *(Mix into Highball Glass—ice)*

CHERRY DAIQUIRI-
 3 parts Light Rum, 1 part Cherry Brandy
 Sour Mix *(Blend with ice in Daiquiri Glass)*

CHERRY FIZZ-
 Cherry Brandy
 Sour Mix, splash Club Soda *(Mix into Highball Glass—ice)*

CHERRY FLIP-
 Cherry Brandy
 Light Cream or Milk, Sugar, sprinkle Nutmeg *(Mix into Highball Glass—ice)*

CHERRY HOUND-
 Black Cherry Schnapps
 Grapefruit Juice *(Mix into Highball Glass—ice)*

CHERRY KISS-
 1 part Irish Cream Liqueur, 1 part Raspberry Liqueur
 (Layer in Order in Cocktail Glass—no ice)

CHERRY MARGARITA-
 2 parts Cherry Brandy, 2 parts Tequila, 1 part Triple Sec
 Sour Mix
 (Mix into Cocktail Glass with no ice or blend with ice in Daiquiri Glass)

CHERRY PIE-
 3 parts Vodka, 1 part Cherry Brandy, 1 part Brandy
 (Mix into Cocktail Glass—no ice)

CHERRY REPAIR KIT-
 1 part Amaretto, 1 part White Crème de Caçao, splash Maraschino Liqueur
 Light Cream or Milk, splash Grenadine
 (Mix into Highball Glass with ice or blend with ice in Daiquiri Glass)

CHERRY RUM-
 Light Rum, splash Cherry Brandy
 Light Cream or Milk *(Mix into Cocktail Glass—no ice)*

CHERRY SLING-
 Cherry Brandy
 Water, Sour Mix *(Mix into Highball Glass—ice)*

CHERRY SOUR-
 1 part Blended Whiskey, 1 part Cherry Brandy
 Sour Mix *(Mix into Sour Glass— ice)*

CHERRY TREE CLIMBER-
 2 parts Cherry Brandy, 2 parts White Crème de Caçao,
  1 part Peppermint Schnapps
 Vanilla Ice Cream
 (Blend with ice in Daiquiri Glass)

CHERRY VANILLA-
2 parts Maraschino Liqueur, 1 part Cherry Liqueur, 1 part White
   Crème de Caçao
Light Cream or Milk, Vanilla Ice Cream, Maraschino Cherries
(Blend with ice in Daiquiri Glass)

CHESHIRE CAT-
1 part Peach Schnapps, 1 part Spiced Rum
Orange Juice *(Mix into Highball Glass—ice)*

CHI-CHI (1)-
Vodka
Coconut Milk, Pineapple Juice
(Blend with ice in Daiquiri Glass)

CHI CHI (2)-
3 parts Light Rum, 1 part Blackberry Brandy
Pineapple Juice *(Mix into Highball Glass—ice)*

CHICAGO COCKTAIL-
Brandy, splash Triple Sec
Bitters *(Mix into Small Rocks Glass—ice)*

CHICAGO FIZZ-
1 part Light Rum, 1 part Port
Sour Mix, splash Club Soda *(Mix into Highball Glass—ice)*

CHILLY CHOCOLATE MINT-
1 part Coconut Rum, 1 part Dark Rum, 1 part Peppermint Schnapps
Light Cream or Milk, Chocolate Syrup
(Blend with ice in Daiquiri Glass)

CHILLY IRISHMAN-
2 parts Irish Whiskey, 1 part Coffee Liqueur, 1 part Irish Cream Liqueur
Cold Espresso, Vanilla Ice Cream, Sugar
(Blend with ice in Daiquiri Glass)

CHIMNEY FIRE
Amaretto
Hot Cider, sprinkle Cinnamon *(Mix into Irish Coffee Cup—no ice)*

CHINESE COCKTAIL-
1 part Jamaican Rum, 1 part Maraschino Liqueur, 1 part Triple Sec
Bitters, Grenadine *(Mix into Cocktail Glass—no ice)*

CHINESE TORTURE-
1 part Canton Liqueur, 1 part 151-proof Rum *(Mix into Cocktail Glass—no ice)*

CHIP SHOT-
Light Rum
Cranberry Juice, Pineapple Juice *(Mix into Highball Glass—ice)*

CHIQUITA-
1 part Banana Liqueur, 1 part Triple Sec
splash Light Cream or Milk *(Mix into Cocktail Glass—no ice)*

CHITA RIVER-
1 part Beer, 1 part Tequila
Lime Juice *(Mix into Cocktail Glass—no ice)*

CHOCO-BANANA SMASH-
Irish Cream Liqueur
Light Cream or Milk, Vanilla Extract, Vanilla Ice Cream, top Chocolate
Sprinkles *(Blend with ice in Daiquiri Glass)*

CHOCOLADA-
3 parts Light Rum, 1 part Coffee Liqueur, 1 part Dark Rum
Chocolate Syrup, Coconut Milk *(Blend with ice in Daiquiri Glass)*

CHOCOLATE ALMOND-
Amaretto, splash Coconut Liqueur
Light Cream or Milk, Chocolate Syrup *(Mix into Highball Glass—ice)*

CHOCOLATE ALMOND CREAM-
1 part Amaretto, 1 part White Crème de Caçao
Vanilla Ice Cream *(Blend with ice in Daiquiri Glass)*

CHOCOLATE BANANA-
1 part Banana Liqueur, 1 part Brown Crème de Caçao, 1 part Dark Rum
Hot Chocolate, top Whipped Cream *(Mix into Irish Coffee Cup—no ice)*

CHOCOLATE BANANA BANSHEE-
1 part Banana Liqueur, 1 part Coffee Liqueur, 1 part White Crème de Caçao
Light Cream or Milk *(Mix into Highball Glass—ice)*

CHOCOLATE BLACK RUSSIAN-
2 parts Vodka, 1 part Coffee Liqueur
Chocolate Ice Cream *(Blend with ice in Daiquiri Glass)*

CHOCOLATE BRANDY HUMMER-
1 part Brandy, 1 part Coffee Liqueur
Chocolate Ice Cream *(Blend with ice in Daiquiri Glass)*

CHOCOLATE COCKTAIL-
1 part Port, 1 part Yellow Chartreuse
Sugar *(Mix into Cocktail Glass—no ice)*

CHOCOLATE COFFEE-
2 parts Cognac, 1 part Brown Crème de Caçao
Coffee, splash Light Cream or Milk, top Whipped Cream
(Mix into Irish Coffee Cup—no ice)

CHOCOLATE COFFEE KISS-
1 part Coffee Liqueur, 1 part Irish Cream Liqueur, splash Brown Crème de
Caçao, splash Grand Marnier®
Coffee, Chocolate Syrup, top Whipped Cream
(Mix into Irish Coffee Cup—no ice)

CHOCOLATE CORVETTE (1)-
3 parts Dark Rum, 1 part Brown Crème de Caçao
Hot Chocolate, splash Light Cream or Milk, top Whipped Cream
(Mix into Irish Coffee Cup—no ice)

CHOCOLATE CORVETTE (2)-
2 parts Dark Rum, 1 part Brown Crème de Caçao, 1 part Coffee Liqueur
splash Light Cream or Milk *(Mix into Cocktail Glass—no ice)*

CHOCOLATE COVERED BANANA-
Coconut Rum
Chocolate Syrup, Bananas, Vanilla Ice Cream, top Whipped Cream
(Blend with ice in Daiquiri Glass)

CHOCOLATE COVERED CHERRY-
1 part Amaretto, 1 part Coffee Liqueur, 1 part White Crème de Caçao
splash Grenadine (lace) *(Mix into Cocktail Glass—no ice)*

CHOCOLATE COVERED STRAWBERRY-
1 part Strawberry Schnapps, 1 part White Crème de Caçao
Light Cream or Milk *(Mix into Highball Glass—ice)*

CHOCOLATE DAISY-
1 part Brandy, 1 part Port
Sour Mix, Grenadine *(Mix into Highball Glass—ice)*

CHOCOLATE FILP-
1 part Brandy, 1 part Sloe Gin
Light Cream or Milk, Sugar, sprinkle Nutmeg
(Mix into Highball Glass—ice)

CHOCOLATE KISS (1)-
2 parts Cognac, 1 part Raspberry Liqueur
Hot Chocolate, top Whipped Cream
(Mix into Irish Coffee Cup—no ice)

CHOCOLATE KISS (2)-
1 part Brown Crème de Caçao, 1 part Cognac, 1 part Raspberry Liqueur
(Mix into Cocktail Glass—no ice)

CHOCOLATE MARTINI-
Vodka, splash White Crème de Caçao *(Mix into Cocktail Glass—no ice)*

CHOCOLATE MILK SHAKE-
2 parts Brown Crème de Caçao, 1 part Coffee Liqueur,
1 part Irish Cream Liqueur
Light Cream or Milk *(Mix into Highball Glass—ice)*

CHOCOLATE MINT (1)-
2 parts Gin, 1 part Green Crème de Menthe, 1 part Peppermint Schnapps
Hot Chocolate, top Whipped Cream
(Mix into Irish Coffee Cup—no ice)

CHOCOLATE MINT (2)-
1 part Coffee Liqueur, 1 part Green Crème de Menthe, 1 part Peppermint
Schnapps *(Mix into Cocktail Glass—no ice)*

CHOCOLATE MINT KISS (1)-
2 parts Brown Crème de Caçao, 1 part White Crème de Menthe
Chocolate Syrup *(Mix into Cocktail Glass—no ice)*

CHOCOLATE MINT KISS (2)-
1 part Brown Crème de Caçao, 1 part Coffee Liqueur, 1 part White Crème de Menthe *(Mix into Cocktail Glass—no ice)*

CHOCOLATE MINT RUM-
2 parts Dark Rum, 1 part Brown Crème de Caçao, 1 part 151-proof Rum, splash White Crème de Menthe
splash Light Cream or Milk *(Mix into Cocktail Glass—no ice)*

CHOCOLATE MONKEY-
2 parts Banana Liqueur, 1 part Light Rum
Chocolate Ice Cream, Bananas *(Blend with ice in Daiquiri Glass)*

CHOCOLATE PARADISE-
Peppermint Schnapps
Chocolate Milk *(Mix into Highball Glass—ice)*

CHOCOLATE RUM-
2 parts Light Rum, 1 part White Crème de Caçao, 1 part White Crème de Menthe, splash 151-proof Rum
Light Cream or Milk *(Mix into Small Rocks Glass—ice)*

CHOCOLATE SAILOR-
2 parts Brown Crème de Caçao, 1 part Gin
Cola *(Mix into Highball Glass—ice)*

CHOCOLATE SIN (1)-
Peppermint Schnapps
Hot Chocolate, top Whipped Cream *(Mix into Irish Coffee Cup—no ice)*

CHOCOLATE SIN (2)
1 part White Crème de Caçao, 1 part Peppermint Schnapps
(Mix into Cocktail Glass—no ice)

CHOCOLATE SOLDIER (1)-
2 parts Gin, 1 part Red Dubonnet®
Lime Juice *(Mix into Cocktail Glass—no ice)*

CHOCOLATE SOLDIER (2)-
2 parts Brown Crème de Caçao, 1 part Cognac, 1 part Dry Vermouth, splash Triple Sec *(Mix into Cocktail Glass—no ice)*

CHOCOLATE SNOW BEAR-
1 part Amaretto, 1 part Brown Crème de Caçao
Chocolate Syrup, French Vanilla Ice Cream, Vanilla Extract, top Whipped Cream *(Blend with ice in Daiquiri Glass)*

CHOCOLATE SUNDAE-
1 part Irish Cream Liqueur, 1 part White Crème de Cacao, 1 part Coffee Liqueur, top Whipped Cream
(Layer in Order in Cocktail Glass—no ice)

CHOCOLATE TOASTED ALMOND (1)-
1 part Amaretto, 1 part Coffee Liqueur
Light Cream or Milk, Chocolate Syrup *(Mix into Highball Glass—ice)*

CHOCOLATE TOASTED ALMOND (2)-
1 part Amaretto, 1 part Brown Crème de Caçao, 1 part Coffee Liqueur
Light Cream or Milk *(Mix into Highball Glass—ice)*

CHOCOLATE VICE (1)-
3 parts Dark Rum, 1 part Bourbon Whiskey, 1 part Brown Crème de Caçao
Hot Chocolate, top Whipped Cream
(Mix into Irish Coffee Cup—no ice)

CHOCOLATE VICE (2)-
2 parts Dark Rum, 1 part Bourbon Whiskey, 1 part Brown Crème de Caçao,
    1 part Coffee Liqueur *(Mix into Cocktail Glass—no ice)*

CHOCOLATE XS-
1 part Brown Crème de Caçao, 1 part Dark Rum, 1 part Irish Cream Liqueur
Chocolate Milk, Chocolate Ice Cream, top Chocolate sprinkles
(Blend with ice in Daiquiri Glass)

CHOCOLATIER-
1 part Light Rum, 1 part White Crème de Caçao
Chocolate Ice Cream, top Whipped Cream
(Blend with ice in Daiquiri Glass)

CHOCOLATIER CAKE-
1 part Brown Crème de Caçao, 1 part Brandy
Light Cream or Milk *(Layer in Order in Cocktail Glass—no ice)*

CHOKER-
Scotch Whiskey, splash Licorice Liqueur
splash Bitters *(Mix into Cocktail Glass—no ice)*

CHOP NUT-
2 parts Light Rum, 1 part Coconut Rum, 1 part White Crème de Caçao,
    splash Hazelnut Liqueur
Orange Juice *(Mix into Small Rocks Glass—ice)*

CHRISTIAN'S COCKTAIL-
1 part Medium Sherry, 1 part Scotch Whiskey
Orange Juice, Sour Mix *(Mix into Cocktail Glass—no ice)*

CHRISTMAS TREE-
1 part Green Crème de Menthe, 1 part Grenadine, 1 part Irish Cream Liqueur
(Layer in Order in Cocktail Glass—no ice)

CHRYSANTHEMUM-
1 part Bénédictine, 1 part Dry Vermouth, splash Licorice Liqueur
(Mix into Cocktail Glass—no ice)

CHUCK RASPBERRY-
3 parts Raspberry Liqueur, 1 part Amaretto
Pineapple Juice, splash Grenadine *(Mix into Highball Glass—ice)*

CHUNNEL-
2 parts Grand Marnier®, 1 part Gin, 1 part Sweet Vermouth
splash Bitters *(Mix into Cocktail Glass—no ice)*

CIAO BABY-
Dark Rum
Strawberry Daiquiri Mix, Sour Mix, splash Grenadine
(Blend with ice in Daiquiri Glass)

CINCINNATI-
6 oz. Beer
fill Club Soda *(Beer Mug)*

CINNACCINO-
2 parts Spiced Rum, 1 part Cinnamon Schnapps
Cappuccino *(Mix into Irish Coffee Cup—no ice)*

CINNAMON ROLL-
Cinnamon Schnapps, splash Apple Schnapps
(Mix into Cocktail Glass—no ice)

CINNAMON TOAST-
Spiced Rum
Hot Apple Cider, Sugar and Cinnamon Rim
(Mix into Irish Coffee Cup—no ice)

CIQUITA-
1 part Banana Liqueur, 1 part Vodka
Light Cream or Milk *(Mix into Highball Glass—ice)*

CITRON BOMB-
1 part Citrus Vodka, 1 part Grand Marnier®
Orange Juice, Lemons *(Mix into Highball Glass—ice)*

CITRON NEON-
3 parts Citrus Vodka, 2 parts Melon Liqueur, 1 part Blue Curaçao
Sour Mix *(Mix into Highball Glass—ice)*

CITRONELLA COOLER-
Citrus Vodka
Lemonade, Cranberry Juice, splash Lime Juice *(Mix into Highball Glass—ice)*

CITRUS BANANA FLIP-
Dark Rum
Club Soda, Orange Juice, Light Cream or Milk, Lime Juice, Brown Sugar,
    Bananas *(Blend with ice in Daiquiri Glass)*

CITRUS CACTUS-
Tequila, splash Anisette
Sour Mix, splash Grenadine *(Mix into Cocktail Glass—no ice)*

CITRUS COOLER-
2 parts Dark Rum, 1 part Triple Sec
Orange Juice, Sour Mix, top Lemon-Lime Soda
(Mix into Highball Glass—ice)

CITY SLICKER-
2 parts Brandy, 1 part Triple Sec, splash Licorice Liqueur
(Mix into Cocktail Glass—no ice)

CIVIL WAR-
1 part Jack Daniel's® Tennessee Sour Mash Whiskey, 1 part Yukon Jack®
Canadian Liqueur
Cranberry Juice *(Mix into Highball Glass—ice)*

CLAM DIGGER-
Vodka
Clam Juice, Tomato Juice, splash Hot Sauce, splash Worcestershire Sauce, Salt,
Pepper *(Mix into Highball Glass—ice)*

CLAM DIGGER'S BLANKET-***
Irish Cream Liqueur
Hot Chocolate, top Whipped Cream *(Mix into Irish Coffee Cup—no ice)*

CLAMATO-
Vodka
Clam Juice, Tomato Juice *(Mix into Small Rocks Glass—ice)*

CLARET COBBLER-
Claret
Club Soda, Sugar *(Mix into Wine Glass—no ice)*

CLARET LEMONADE-
Claret or Red Wine
Sour Mix, Water *(Mix into Highball Glass—no ice)*

CLARIDGE COCKTAIL-
1 part Dry Vermouth, 1 part Gin, splash Apricot Brandy, splash Triple Sec
(Mix into Cocktail Glass—no ice)

CLASSIC COCKTAIL-
3 parts Brandy, 1 part Maraschino Liqueur, 1 part Triple Sec
Lime Juice *(Mix into Small Rocks Glass—ice)*

CLIMAX (1)-
1 part Amaretto, 1 part Banana Liqueur, 1 part Triple Sec, 1 part Vodka,
1 part White Crème de Caçao
Light Cream or Milk
(Mix into Highball Glass—ice)

CLIMAX (2)-
1 part Coffee Liqueur, 1 part Southern Comfort®
top Whipped Cream *(Mix into Small Rocks Glass—ice)*

CLOAK & DAGGER-
Jamaican Rum
Cola, splash Orange Bitters *(Mix into Highball Glass—ice)*

CLOISTER-
4 parts Gin, 1 part Yellow Chartreuse
Grapefruit Juice, Sour Mix *(Mix into Cocktail Glass—no ice)*

CLOUD 9-
1 part Amaretto, 1 part Black Raspberry Liqueur, 1 part Irish Cream Liqueur
Vanilla Ice Cream, half Peanut Butter Cup Garnish
(Blend with ice in Daiquiri Glass)

CLOUDY SKY-
Sloe Gin
Lime Juice, fill Ginger Ale *(Mix into Highball Glass—ice)*

CLOVE COCKTAIL-
2 parts Sweet Vermouth, 1 part Muscatel, 1 part Sloe Gin
(Mix into Cocktail Glass—no ice)

CLOVER CLUB COCKTAIL-
Gin
Lime Juice, Grenadine *(Mix into Cocktail Glass—no ice)*

CLOVER LEAF-
Gin
Lime Juice, Grenadine *(Mix into Cocktail Glass—no ice)*

CLUB COCKTAIL-
2 parts Gin, 1 part Sweet Vermouth *(Mix into Cocktail Glass—no ice)*

CLUB MED-
2 parts Vodka, 1 part Raspberry Liqueur
Pineapple Juice, Lime Juice *(Mix into Highball Glass—ice)*

COBANA-
1 part Banana Liqueur, 1 part Coffee Liqueur, 1 part Strawberry Schnapps
(Mix into Cocktail Glass—no ice)

COBANA COFFEE-
1 part Banana Liqueur, 1 part Strawberry Schnapps
Coffee, Sugar, top Whipped Cream *(Mix into Irish Coffee Cup—no ice)*

COBBLER (GENERIC)-
(Any Liqueur)
Club Soda, Sugar *(Mix into Highball Glass—ice)*

COBBLER, THE-
Sherry, splash Triple Sec
Sugar, splash Grenadine *(Mix into Cocktail Glass—no ice)*

COCAINE (1)-
1 part Raspberry Liqueur, 1 part Southern Comfort®, 1 part Vodka
Cranberry Juice, Orange Juice *(Mix into Highball Glass—ice)*

COCAINE (2)-
1 part Raspberry Liqueur, 1 part Vodka
Grapefruit Juice *(Mix into Highball Glass—ice)*

COCAINE LADY-
1 part Coffee Liqueur, 1 part Irish Cream Liqueur, 1 part Light Rum,
    1 part Vodka
Light Cream or Milk, Cola (float) *(Mix into Highball Glass—ice)*

COCK & BULL SHOT-
Vodka
Beef Bouillon, Chicken Bouillon, Lime Juice, splash Hot Sauce, splash
    Worcestershire Sauce, Salt, Pepper *(Mix into Highball Glass—ice)*

COCK-A-BENDY-
2 parts Scotch Whiskey, 1 part Sweet Vermouth, splash Campari
(Mix into Small Rocks Glass—ice)

COCO CHANEL-
1 part Coffee Liqueur, 1 part Gin
Light Cream or Milk *(Mix into Cocktail Glass—no ice)*

COCO JAVA-
1 part Coconut Liqueur, 1 part Coffee Liqueur
Hot Chocolate, top Whipped Cream
(Mix into Irish Coffee Cup—no ice)

COCO LOCO (1)-
2 parts Tequila, 1 part Gin, 1 part Light Rum
Pineapple Juice, Sour Mix *(Mix into Highball Glass—ice)*

COCO LOCO (2)-
1 part Coconut Rum, 1 part Dark Rum
Coconut Milk, Papaya Juice, Pineapple Juice, Orange Juice, Grenadine
(Blend with ice in Daiquiri Glass)

COCOBANANA-
2 parts Banana Liqueur, 2 parts Light Rum, 1 part Amaretto,
    1 part Coconut Rum
Pineapple Juice, Coconut Milk, Bananas, Vanilla Ice Cream
(Blend with ice in Daiquiri Glass)

COCOMACOQUE-
1 part Light Rum, 1 part Red Wine
Pineapple Juice, Orange Juice, Lime Juice *(Mix into Highball Glass—ice)*

COCONUT BROWNIE-
2 parts Spiced Rum, 1 part Coconut Rum
Hot Chocolate, top Whipped Cream *(Mix into Irish Coffee Cup—no ice)*

COCONUT CLIMBER-
2 parts Coconut Rum, 1 part Mango Liqueur, 1 part Spiced Rum
Light Cream or Milk, Orange Juice, splash Grenadine
(Mix into Highball Glass—ice)

COCONUT COLA-
Coconut Rum
Cola *(Mix into Highball Glass—ice)*

COCONUT DAIQUIRI-
1 part Coconut Rum, 1 part Dark Rum
Sour Mix, Coconut Milk *(Blend with ice in Daiquiri Glass)*

COCONUT GIN-
1 part Coconut Liqueur, 1 part Gin
Lime Juice *(Mix into Small Rocks Glass—ice)*

COCONUT MONKEY-
1 part Apricot Brandy, 1 part Coconut Rum
Pineapple Juice *(Mix into Highball Glass—ice)*

COCONUT TEQUILA-
1 part Coconut Liqueur, 1 part Tequila
Lime Juice *(Mix into Small Rocks Glass—ice)*

COFFEE ALEXANDER-
1 part Brown Crème de Caçao, 1 part Coffee Liqueur
Light Cream or Milk *(Mix into Cocktail Glass—no ice)*

COFFEE BERRY (1)-
1 part Coffee Liqueur, 1 part Hazelnut Liqueur, 1 part Raspberry Liqueur
Light Cream or Milk *(Mix into Highball Glass—ice)*

COFFEE BERRY (2)-
1 part Hazelnut Liqueur, 1 part Raspberry Liqueur
Coffee, top Whipped Cream *(Mix into Irish Coffee Cup—no ice)*

COFFEE BRANDY HUMMER-
1 part Brandy, 1 part Coffee Liqueur
Coffee, Ice Cream *(Blend with ice in Daiquiri Glass)*

COFFEE BREAK-
1 part Brandy, 1 part Coffee Liqueur
Coffee, top Whipped Cream, Cherry Garnish
(Mix into Irish Coffee Cup—no ice)

COFFEE CHASER-
1 part Coffee Liqueur, 1 part Grand Marnier®
Coffee, top Whipped Cream *(Mix into Irish Coffee Cup—no ice)*

COFFEE COCKTAIL-
1 part Brandy, 1 part Port
Sugar, sprinkle Nutmeg *(Mix into Small Rocks Glass—ice)*

COFFEE COOLER-
1 part Coffee Liqueur, 1 part Vodka
Cold Coffee, Light Cream or Milk, Sugar, Coffee Ice Cream
(Blend with ice in Daiquiri Glass)

COFFEE EGGNOG-
2 parts Blended Whiskey, 1 part Coffee Liqueur
Light Cream or Milk, Instant Coffee, Sugar
(Blend with ice in Daiquiri Glass)

COFFEE FANTASY-
Irish Cream Liqueur
Cold Coffee, Light Cream or Milk *(Mix into Highball Glass—ice)*

COFFEE FLING-
Drambuie®
Coffee, Sugar, top Whipped Cream
(Mix into Irish Coffee Cup—no ice)

COFFEE FLIP-
1 part Brandy, 1 part Port
Light Cream or Milk, Sugar, sprinkle Nutmeg
(Mix into Highball Glass—ice)

COFFEE FLOAT-
2 parts Blended Whiskey, 1 part Crème de Noyaux
Coffee, Vanilla Ice Cream *(Mix into Irish Coffee Cup—no ice)*

COFFEE GRASSHOPPER-
1 part Coffee Liqueur, 1 part White Crème de Menthe
Light Cream or Milk
(Mix into Small Rocks Glass—ice)

COFFEE HUMMER-
1 part Coffee Liqueur, 1 part Light Rum
Vanilla Ice Cream *(Blend with ice in Daiquiri Glass)*

COFFEE KEOKEE-
1 part Brandy, 1 part Coffee Liqueur
Coffee, top Whipped Cream *(Mix into Irish Coffee Cup—no ice)*

COFFEE NUT-
1 part Amaretto, 1 part Hazelnut Liqueur
Coffee, top Whipped Cream *(Mix into Irish Coffee Cup—no ice)*

COFFEE NUT SUNDAE-
1 part Amaretto, 1 part Hazelnut Liqueur
Coffee Ice Cream, top Whipped Cream *(Blend with ice in Daiquiri Glass)*

COFFEE OLD-FASHIONED-
Bourbon Whiskey
Club Soda, Water, Sugar, Bitters, Instant Coffee Grinds, muddle
(Mix into Small Rocks Glass—ice)

COFFEE ROYALE-
Brandy
Coffee, splash Light Cream or Milk, Sugar, top Whipped Cream
(Mix into Irish Coffee Cup—no ice)

COFFEE SOUR-
Coffee Liqueur
Sour Mix *(Mix into Sour Glass—ice)*

COFFEE STICK-
3 parts Coffee Liqueur, 1 part Sambuca
Light Cream or Milk *(Mix into Cocktail Glass—no ice)*

COGNAC COUPLING-
3 parts Cognac, 2 parts Port, 1 part Anisette
Lime Juice *(Mix into Small Rocks Glass—ice)*

COGNAC HIGHBALL-
Cognac
Ginger Ale or Club Soda *(Mix into Highball Glass—ice)*

COLADASCOPE-
2 parts Light Rum, 1 part Triple Sec
Pineapple Juice, Lime Juice, Coconut Milk
(Mix into Highball Glass with ice or blend with ice in Daiquiri Glass)

COLD DECK (1)-
2 parts Brandy, 1 part Sweet Vermouth, splash White Crème de Menthe
(Mix into Cocktail Glass—no ice)

COLD DECK (2)-
2 parts Brandy, 1 part Peppermint Schnapps, 1 part Sweet Vermouth
(Mix into Cocktail Glass—no ice)

COLD KISS-
3 parts Blended Whiskey, 1 part Peppermint Schnapps, splash White Crème de
Caçao *(Mix into Cocktail Glass—no ice)*

COLD PORRIDGE-
Scotch Whiskey
Light Cream or Milk, Honey *(Mix into Small Rocks Glass—ice)*

COLDCOCKED-
Southern Comfort®
Piña Colada Mix, Cola, top Whipped Cream *(Blend with ice in Daiquiri Glass)*

COLLINS (GENERIC)-
(Any Liqueur)
Sour Mix, splash Club Soda *(Mix into Highball Glass—ice)*

COLONIAL COCKTAIL-
Gin, splash Maraschino Liqueur
Grapefruit Juice, Olive Garnish *(Mix into Cocktail Glass—no ice)*

COLONY CLUB-
Gin, splash Licorice Liqueur
splash Orange Bitters *(Mix into Cocktail Glass—no ice)*

COLORADO BULLDOG-
1 part Coffee Liqueur, 1 part Vodka
Light Cream or Milk, fill Cola *(Mix into Highball Glass—ice)*

COLUMBIA-
2 parts Light Rum, 1 part Raspberry Liqueur
Lime Juice *(Mix into Cocktail Glass—no ice)*

COLUMBUS COCKTAIL-
3 parts Dark Rum, 1 part Apricot Brandy
Lime Juice *(Mix into Small Rocks Glass—ice)*

COMBO-
Dry Vermouth, splash Brandy, splash Triple Sec
Bitters, Sugar *(Mix into Small Rocks Glass—ice)*

COMFORTABLE BROTHER-
1 part Hazelnut Liqueur, 1 part Southern Comfort®
(Mix into Small Rocks Glass—ice)

COMFORTABLE FIRE-
Southern Comfort®
Hot Apple Cider, Cinnamon Stick *(Mix into Irish Coffee Cup—no ice)*

COMFORTABLE FUZZY SCREW-
1 part Peach Schnapps, 1 part Southern Comfort®, 1 part Vodka
Orange Juice *(Mix into Highball Glass—ice)*

COMFORTABLE FUZZY SCREW AGAINST THE WALL-
1 part Southern Comfort®, 1 part Peach Schnapps, 1 part Vodka,
  splash Galliano®
Orange Juice *(Mix into Highball Glass—ice)*

COMFORTABLE MOCHA-
Southern Comfort®
Hot Chocolate, Coffee, top Whipped Cream
(Mix into Irish Coffee Cup—no ice)

COMFORTABLE PIRATE-
3 parts Captain Morgan® Original Spiced Rum, 1 part Southern Comfort®
Pineapple Juice *(Mix into Highball Glass—ice)*

COMFORTABLE SCREW-
1 part Southern Comfort®, 1 part Vodka
Orange Juice *(Mix into Highball Glass—ice)*

COMFORTABLE SCREW AGAINST THE WALL-
1 part Southern Comfort®, 1 part Vodka, splash Galliano®
Orange Juice *(Mix into Highball Glass—ice)*

COMFORTING COFFEE-
1 part Bourbon Whiskey, 1 part Southern Comfort®, splash Brown
  Crème de Caçao
Coffee, splash Light Cream or Milk, top Whipped Cream
(Mix into Irish Coffee Cup—no ice)

COMMANDO-
2 parts Bourbon Whiskey, 1 part Triple Sec, splash Licorice Liqueur
Lime Juice *(Mix into Highball Glass—ice)*

COMMODORE-
Blended Whiskey
Sour Mix, Orange Bitters *(Mix into Cocktail Glass—no ice)*

COMMONWEALTH COCKTAIL-
4 parts Canadian Whiskey, 1 part Grand Marnier®
Lime Juice, Orange Twist Garnish *(Mix into Cocktail Glass—no ice)*

COMMUNICATOR-
3 parts Dark Rum, 1 part Galliano®, splash Brown Crème de Caçao
(Mix into Small Rocks Glass—ice)

COMPADRE-
3 parts Tequila, 1 part Cherry Liqueur
splash Grenadine, splash Orange Bitters *(Mix into Cocktail Glass—no ice)*

CONCHITA-
Tequila
Grapefruit Juice, splash Lime Juice *(Mix into Small Rocks Glass—ice)*

CONCORDE-
Cognac, fill Champagne
Apple Juice *(Mix into Champagne Flute—no ice)*

CONEY ISLAND BABY-
2 parts Peppermint Schnapps, 1 part Brown Crème de Caçao
Club Soda *(Mix into Highball Glass—ice)*

CONFIRMED BACHELOR-
Gin
Lime Juice, splash Grenadine
(Mix into Cocktail Glass—no ice)

CONNECTICUT BULLDOG-
4 parts Gin, 1 part Light Rum
Sour Mix *(Mix into Cocktail Glass—no ice)*

CONNOISSEUR'S TREAT-
3 parts Cognac, 1 part Dark Rum
Sour Mix *(Mix into Small Rocks Glass—ice)*

CONTINENTAL-
4 parts Light Rum, 1 part Green Crème de Menthe
Sour Mix *(Mix into Cocktail Glass—no ice)*

COOL-AID (1)-
1 part Amaretto, 1 part Melon Liqueur
Apple Juice *(Mix into Highball Glass—ice)*

COOL-AID (2)-
1 part Amaretto, 1 part Melon Liqueur, 1 part Southern Comfort®
Cranberry Juice *(Mix into Highball Glass—ice)*

COOL BREEZE-
Vodka
Cranberry Juice, Pineapple Juice, splash Ginger Ale
(Mix into Highball Glass—ice)

COOL BLUE MARTINI-
Gin or Vodka, splash Blue Curaçao, splash Dry Vermouth
splash Lime Juice *(Mix into Cocktail Glass—no ice)*

COOL CARLOS-
2 parts Triple Sec (float), 1 part Dark Rum
Cranberry Juice, Pineapple Juice, splash Sour Mix
(Mix into Highball Glass—ice)

COOL COLONEL-
2 parts Bourbon Whiskey, 1 part Southern Comfort®
Iced Tea, Sour Mix, top Club Soda
(Mix into Highball Glass—ice)

COOL JAZZ-
1 part Banana Liqueur, fill Dry White Wine
Lime Juice, Banana Slice Garnish *(Mix into Wine Glass—ice)*

COOL KISS-
Amaretto
Vanilla Ice Cream, Strawberry Margarita Mix *(Blend with ice in Daiquiri Glass)*

COOL OPERATOR-
2 parts Melon Liqueur, 1 part Light Rum, 1 part Vodka
Grapefruit Juice, Orange Juice, splash Lime Juice
(Blend with ice in Daiquiri Glass)

COOLER (GENERIC)-
(Any Liqueur)
Club Soda, Sugar, fill Ginger Ale *(Mix into Highball Glass—ice)*

COOLER BY THE LAKE-
White Wine, splash Peach Schnapps
Cranberry Juice, splash Sour Mix, fill Club Soda *(Mix into Wine Glass—ice)*

COON DOG-
1 part Blackberry Liqueur, 1 part Jack Daniel's® Tennessee Sour Mash Whiskey
(Mix into Small Rocks Glass—ice)

COOPERSTOWN-
2 parts Gin, 1 part Dry Vermouth, 1 part Sweet Vermouth
Mint Leaf Garnish *(Mix into Cocktail Glass—no ice)*

COPACABANA BANANA-
1 part Gold Rum, 1 part Vodka, splash Amaretto, splash Banana Liqueur
Lime Juice *(Mix into Cocktail Glass—no ice)*

COPENHAGEN DREAM-
3 parts Gin, 1 part Aquavit
Sour Mix, splash Light Cream or Milk *(Mix into Highball Glass—ice)*

COPPER PENNY-
2 parts Amaretto, 1 part White Crème de Caçao
Light Cream or Milk *(Mix into Highball Glass—ice)*

COPPERHEAD-
Vodka
Ginger Ale *(Mix into Highball Glass—ice)*

CORAL GOLD-
2 parts Gold Rum, 2 parts Triple Sec, 1 part Peppermint Schnapps
(Mix into Cocktail Glass—no ice)

CORAL REEF-
2 parts Coconut Rum, 1 part Vodka
Strawberry Margarita Mix *(Blend with ice in Daiquiri Glass)*

CORCOVADO-
2 parts Tequila, 1 part Drambuie®, splash Blue Curaçao
Lemonade *(Mix into Highball Glass—ice)*

CORDIAL DAISY-
Cherry Brandy, splash Triple Sec
Sour Mix, splash Club Soda *(Mix into Highball Glass—ice)*

CORDLESS SCREWDRIVER-
Vodka
Sugar-covered Orange Garnish *(Mix into Cocktail Glass—no ice)*

CORDOVA-
2 parts Gin, 1 part Sweet Vermouth, splash Licorice Liqueur
splash Light Cream or Milk *(Mix into Cocktail Glass—no ice)*

CORKSCREW-
3 parts Light Rum, 1 part Dry Vermouth, 1 part Peach Brandy
(Mix into Cocktail Glass—no ice)

CORNELL-
Gin, splash Cherry Liqueur
Lime Juice *(Mix into Cocktail Glass—no ice)*

CORONADO-
Gin, splash Cherry Brandy, splash Triple Sec
Pineapple Juice *(Mix into Small Rocks Glass—ice)*

CORONATION (1)-
1 part Gin, fill Champagne
Sugar, Ice *(Mix into Champagne Flute—no ice)*

CORONATION (2)-
1 part Dry Vermouth, 1 part Sherry, splash Maraschino Liqueur
splash Orange Bitters *(Mix into Cocktail Glass—no ice)*

CORONATION (3)-
2 parts Brandy, 1 part Triple Sec, splash Peach Schnapps, splash White Crème
de Menthe *(Mix into Cocktail Glass—no ice)*

CORPSE REVIVER (1)-
1 part Citrus Rum, 1 part Gin, 1 part Triple Sec, splash Licorice Liqueur
Lime Juice *(Mix into Cocktail Glass—no ice)*

CORPSE REVIVER (2)-
2 parts Apple Brandy, 1 part Brandy, splash Sweet Vermouth
(Mix into Cocktail Glass—no ice)

CORVETTE-
1 part Sloe Gin, 1 part Southern Comfort®, splash Campari
Lemonade *(Mix into Highball Glass—ice)*

COSMOPOLITAN (COSMOPOLITAN MARTINI)-
2 parts Vodka, 1 part Triple Sec
Cranberry Juice, Lime Juice *(Mix into Cocktail Glass—no ice)*

COSMOS-
Vodka
Lime Juice *(Mix into Cocktail Glass—no ice)*

COSSACK-
1 part Cognac, 1 part Vodka
Sour Mix *(Mix into Cocktail Glass—no ice)*

COSTA DEL SOL-
2 parts Gin, 1 part Apricot Brandy, 1 part Grand Marnier®
(Mix into Small Rocks Glass—ice)

COUNT CURREY-
1 part Gin, fill Champagne
Sugar *(Mix into Champagne Flute—no ice)*

COUNT STROGANOFF-
3 parts Vodka, 1 part Triple Sec, 1 part White Crème de Caçao
(Mix into Small Rocks Glass—ice)

COUNTRY & WESTERN-
1 part Coconut Rum, 1 part Dark Rum
Orange Juice, Pineapple Juice *(Mix into Highball Glass—ice)*

COUNTRY CREAM-
2 parts Coffee Liqueur, 2 parts Pear Brandy, 1 part Campari,
1 part Raspberry Liqueur
Vanilla Ice Cream *(Blend with ice in Daiquiri Glass)*

COWBOY-
Blended Whiskey or Rye Whiskey
Light Cream or Milk *(Mix into Cocktail Glass—no ice)*

COWBOY COCKSUCKER-
1 part Butterscotch Schnapps, 1 part Irish Cream Liqueur, splash Goldschläger®
(Mix into Cocktail Glass—no ice)

COWGIRL-
Bourbon Whiskey
Light Cream or Milk, Honey *(Mix into Cocktail Glass—no ice)*

COWGIRL'S PRAYER-
Tequila
Lemonade, Lime Juice *(Mix into Highball Glass—ice)*

CRANBERRY BOGG-
Cranberry Brandy
Ginger Ale *(Mix into Highball Glass—ice)*

CRANBERRY COOLER-
Amaretto
Orange Juice, Cranberry Juice *(Mix into Highball Glass—ice)*

CRANBERRY KISS-
2 parts Spiced Rum, 1 part Peppermint Schnapps
Cranberry Juice, Sour Mix *(Mix into Highball Glass—ice)*

CRANIUM MELTDOWN-
1 part 151-proof Rum, 1 part Coconut Rum, 1 part Raspberry Liqueur
Pineapple Juice *(Mix into Highball Glass—ice)*

CRATER FACE-
1 part Bourbon Whiskey, 1 part Madeira Wine, splash Banana Liqueur
splash Grenadine *(Mix into Small Rocks Glass—ice)*

CRAZY BEN-
    Bénédictine
    Splash Sour Mix, fill Club Soda *(Mix into Highball Glass—ice)*

CRAZY CURTIS -***
    Dewar's® Scotch Whiskey, splash Cognac (top)
    (Mix into Small Rocks Glass—ice)

CRAZY ITALIAN-
    1 part Amaretto, 1 part Irish Cream Liqueur *(Mix into Cocktail Glass—no ice)*

CRAZY NUN-
    1 part Anisette, 1 part Tequila *(Mix into Small Rocks Glass—ice)*

CREAM FIZZ-
    Gin
    Sour Mix, Light Cream or Milk, splash Club Soda
    (Mix into Highball Glass—ice)

CREAM PUFF-
    Light Rum
    Light Cream or Milk, Sugar, Club Soda *(Mix into Highball Glass—ice)*

CREAM SODA-
    Amaretto
    Club Soda *(Mix into Highball Glass—ice)*

CREAMSICLE (1)-
    Vanilla Liqueur
    Orange Juice, splash Light Cream or Milk *(Mix into Highball Glass—ice)*

CREAMSICLE (2)-
    Amaretto
    Orange Juice, splash Light Cream or Milk *(Mix into Highball Glass—ice)*

CREAMSICLE (3)-
    1 part Triple Sec, 1 part White Crème de Caçao
    Light Cream or Milk *(Mix into Highball Glass—ice)*

CREAMY BUSH-
    1 part Bushmill's® Irish Whiskey, 1 part Irish Cream Liqueur
    (Mix into Cocktail Glass—no ice)

CREAMY GIN SOUR-
    1 part Gin, 1 part Triple Sec
    Sour Mix, Light Cream or Milk, Club Soda (top)
    (Blend with ice in Daiquiri Glass)

CREAMY MIMI-
    1 part Sweet Vermouth, 1 part Vodka, splash Triple Sec, splash White Crème de
        Caçao *(Mix into Small Rocks Glass—ice)*

CREAMY ORANGE-
    1 part Brandy, 1 part Cream Sherry
    Orange Juice, splash Light Cream or Milk *(Mix into Cocktail Glass—no ice)*

CREAMY SCREWDRIVER-
  Vodka
  Orange Juice, Sugar *(Blend with ice in Daiquiri Glass)*

CRÈME DE CAFE-
  2 parts Coffee Liqueur, 1 part Anisette, 1 part Light Rum
  Light Cream or Milk *(Mix into Small Rocks Glass—ice)*

CRÈME DE GIN-
  3 parts Gin, 1 part White Crème de Menthe
  Orange Juice, Lime Juice *(Mix into Cocktail Glass—no ice)*

CRÈME DE MENTHE FRAPPE-
  Green Crème de Menthe
  (Mix into Cocktail Glass—crushed ice)

CRÈMESICKLE (1)-
  1 part Galliano®, 1 part White Crème de Caçao
  Orange Juice, splash Light Cream or Milk *(Mix into Highball Glass—ice)*

CRÈMESICKLE (2)-
  1 part Galliano®, 1 part Triple Sec
  Orange Juice, splash Light Cream or Milk *(Mix into Highball Glass—ice)*

CREOLE-
  Light Rum
  Lime Juice, Hot Sauce, Beef Bouillon, Salt, Pepper, Green Cherry, Red Cherry
    Garnish *(Mix into Cocktail Glass—no ice)*

CREOLE LADY-
  1 part Bourbon Whiskey, 1 part Madeira Wine
  splash Grenadine, Green Cherry, Red Cherry Garnish
  (Mix into Cocktail Glass—no ice)

CRICKET-
  1 part Green Crème de Menthe, 1 part White Crème de Caçao, splash Brandy
  Light Cream or Milk *(Mix into Highball Glass—ice)*

CRIME OF PASSION-
  Dark Rum, splash Raspberry Liqueur
  Passion Fruit Juice, Vanilla Ice Cream, fill Cream Soda
  (Blend with ice in Daiquiri Glass)

CRIMSON COCKTAIL-
  2 parts Gin, 1 part Port (float)
  Lime Juice, Grenadine *(Mix into Cocktail Glass—no ice)*

CRIMSON SUNSET-
  Gin, splash Tawny Port (float)
  Lime Juice, splash Grenadine *(Mix into Cocktail Glass—no ice)*

CRIMSON TIDE-
  1 part 151 part-proof Rum, 1 part Coconut Rum, 1 part Raspberry Liqueur,
    1 part Southern Comfort®, 1 part Tropical Fruit Schnapps, 1 part Vodka
  Cranberry Juice, Lemon-Lime Soda *(Mix into Highball Glass—ice)*

CRISP APPLE-
2 parts Apple Brandy, 1 part Amaretto, 1 part Tequila, splash Triple Sec
Lime Juice *(Mix into Small Rocks Glass—ice)*

CROCODILE COOLER-
2 parts Citrus Vodka, 2 parts Melon Liqueur, 1 part Triple Sec
Sour Mix, fill Lemon-Lime Soda *(Mix into Highball Glass—ice)*

CROOKED SISTER-
1 part Gin, 1 part Triple Sec, 1 part White Crème de Caçao
(Mix into Small Rocks Glass—ice)

CROW-
Blended Whiskey
Lime Juice, splash Grenadine *(Mix into Cocktail Glass—no ice)*

CROW'S NEST-
1 part Gin, 1 part Sweet Sherry *(Mix into Small Rocks Glass—ice)*

CROWN-
Scotch Whiskey
splash Lime Juice, splash Grenadine *(Mix into Cocktail Glass—no ice)*

CRUISE CONTROL-
1 part Apricot Brandy, 1 part Light Rum, 1 part Triple Sec
splash Lime Juice, Club Soda *(Mix into Highball Glass—ice)*

CRYPTO NUGGET-
2 parts Apple Schnapps, 1 part Blue Curaçao, 1 part Vodka
Lime Juice *(Mix into Cocktail Glass—no ice)*

CRYSTAL SLIPPER-
Blue Curaçao
Orange Bitters *(Mix into Cocktail Glass—no ice)*

CUBA LIBRE-
Light Rum
Cola, splash Lime Juice, Lime Wedge Garnish *(Mix into Highball Glass—ice)*

CUBA LIBRE ESPANA-
1 part Dark Rum, 1 part Light Rum, 1 part Sweet Sherry
Lime Juice, fill Cola *(Mix into Highball Glass—ice)*

CUBAN CHERRY-
2 parts Light Rum, 1 part Bourbon Whiskey, 1 part Brown Crème de Caçao,
    1 part Cherry Brandy
Light Cream or Milk *(Mix into Highball Glass—ice)*

CUBAN COCKTAIL (1)-
Light Rum
Sour Mix *(Mix into Cocktail Glass—no ice)*

CUBAN COCKTAIL (2)-
2 parts Brandy, 1 part Apricot Brandy
Lime Juice *(Mix into Cocktail Glass—no ice)*

CUBAN MANHATTAN-
1 part Dry Vermouth, 1 part Light Rum, 1 part Sweet Vermouth
splash Bitters
(Mix into Cocktail Glass—no ice)

CUBAN MISSILE-
2 parts Brandy, 1 part Apricot Brandy
Lime Juice *(Mix into Cocktail Glass—no ice)*

CUBAN SPECIAL-
Light Rum, splash Triple Sec
Pineapple Juice, Lime Juice *(Mix into Cocktail Glass—no ice)*

CUBANO-
Light Rum
Sour Mix *(Mix into Cocktail Glass—no ice)*

CULROSS-
4 parts Light Rum, 1 part Apricot Brandy, 1 part Lillet
Lime Juice *(Mix into Cocktail Glass—no ice)*

CUPID-
Sherry
splash Sour Mix, sprinkle Cayenne Pepper
(Mix into Cocktail Glass—no ice)

CUPID'S COCOA-
1 part Amaretto, 1 part Coffee Liqueur
Coffee, top Whipped Cream *(Mix into Irish Coffee Cup—no ice)*

CUPID'S KISS-
2 parts Crème de Noyaux, 1 part White Crème de Caçao
Light Cream or Milk, Strawberry Garnish
(Mix into Highball Glass—ice)

CYCLONE ATTACK-
Blue Curaçao
Lime Juice *(Layer in Order in Glass with no ice)*

CYRANO-
1 part Irish Cream Liqueur, 1 part Grand Marnier®, splash Raspberry Liqueur
(Layer in Order in Cocktail Glass—no ice)

CZAR-
1 part Grand Marnier®, 1 part Vodka, fill White Wine
splash Lime Juice, splash Orange Bitters
(Mix into Wine Glass—ice)

CZARINA-
1 part Apricot Brandy, 1 part Dry Vermouth, 1 part Vodka
splash Bitters *(Mix into Cocktail Glass—no ice)*

– NOTES –

DC-3-
1 part Brown Crème De Cacao, 1 part Sambuca, 1 part Irish Cream Liqueur
(Layer in Order in Cocktail Glass—no ice)

DC-9-
1 part Coffee Liqueur, 1 part Sambuca, 1 part Light Rum
(Layer in Order in Glass with no ice)

D-DAY-
1 part 151-proof Rum, 1 part Banana Liqueur, 1 part Citrus Vodka,
  1 part Raspberry Liqueur
Orange Juice *(Mix into Highball Glass—ice)*

DAGGER-
1 part Tequila, 1 part White Crème de Cacao, 1 part Peach Schnapps
(Layer in Order in Cocktail Glass—no ice)

DAILY BRUIN-
2 parts Gin, 1 part Apple Brandy, 1 part Sweet Vermouth
Lime Juice, splash Grenadine *(Mix into Cocktail Glass—no ice)*

DAILY DOUBLE-
1 part Amaretto, 1 part Southern Comfort®
Cranberry Juice, Orange Juice, Pineapple Juice
(Mix into Small Rocks Glass—ice)

DAILY DOUBLE C-
1 part Dry Vermouth, 1 part Light Rum
2 Cherries Garnish *(Mix into Small Rocks Glass—ice)*

DAILY MAIL-
Scotch Whiskey, splash Amaretto, splash Blue Curaçao
Sour Mix *(Mix into Highball Glass—ice)*

DAIQUIRI-
Light Rum, splash Triple Sec (optional)
Sour Mix
(Mix into Cocktail Glass with no ice or blend with ice in Daiquiri Glass)

DAISY-
Tequila
Lime Juice, splash Grenadine, splash Club Soda
(Mix into Small Rocks Glass—ice)

DAISY (GENERIC)-
(Any Liqueur)
Sour Mix, splash Grenadine *(Mix into Beer Mug—ice)*

DAISY DUELLER-
Sour Mash Whiskey, splash Triple Sec
splash Sour Mix, Club Soda *(Mix into Highball Glass—ice)*

DAMBUSTER-
3 parts Rum, 1 part Coffee Liqueur
splash Ginger Ale, fill Light Cream or Milk *(Mix into Highball Glass—ice)*

DAMN-THE-WEATHER-
Gin, splash Sweet Vermouth, splash Triple Sec
splash Orange Juice *(Mix into Cocktail Glass—no ice)*

DAMN-YOUR-EYES-
3 parts Light Rum, 1 part White Dubonnet®, splash Dry Vermouth
(Mix into Cocktail Glass—no ice)

DAMNED IF YOU DO-
3 parts Blended Whiskey, 1 part Cinnamon Schnapps
(Mix into Small Rocks Glass—ice)

DANCE WITH A DREAM-
4 parts Brandy, 1 part Triple Sec, splash Anisette
(Mix into Cocktail Glass—no ice)

DANCIN' BONES-
4 parts Dry Vermouth, 1 part Maraschino Liqueur, 1 part Sweet Vermouth
splash Orange Bitters *(Mix into Cocktail Glass—no ice)*

DANDY-
1 part Canadian Whiskey, 1 part Red Dubonnet®, splash Triple Sec
splash Bitters *(Mix into Cocktail Glass—no ice)*

DANGEROUS LIASONS-
1 part Tia Maria®, 1 part Triple Sec
splash Sour Mix *(Mix into Cocktail Glass—no ice)*

DANIEL BOONE-
3 parts Bourbon Whiskey, 1 part Triple Sec
Grapefruit Juice *(Mix into Highball Glass—ice)*

DANISH COFFEE-
Haagen-Dazs® Cream Liqueur
Coffee, top Whipped Cream *(Mix into Irish Coffee Cup—no ice)*

DANISH GIN FIZZ-
4 parts Gin, 1 part Cherry Brandy
Sour Mix, splash Club Soda *(Mix into Highball Glass—ice)*

DANISH MARY-
Aquavit
Bloody Mary Mix *(Mix into Highball Glass—ice)*

DANNY'S DOWNFALL-
1 part Blended Whiskey, 1 part Gin, 1 part Sweet Vermouth
(Mix into Cocktail Glass—no ice)

DARB-
1 part Apricot Brandy, 1 part Dry Vermouth, 1 part Gin
Sour Mix *(Mix into Cocktail Glass—no ice)*

DARBY-
Gin
Grapefruit Juice, Sour Mix *(Mix into Cocktail Glass—no ice)*

DARK & LOVELY (1)-
1 part Coffee Liqueur, 1 part Hazelnut Liqueur, 1 part Irish Cream Liqueur
(Mix into Cocktail Glass—no ice)

DARK & LOVELY (2)-
1 part Coffee Liqueur, 1 part Hazelnut Liqueur, 1 part Irish Cream Liqueur
Light Cream or Milk *(Mix into Highball Glass—ice)*

DARK EYES-
3 parts Vodka, 1 part Blackberry Brandy
Lime Juice *(Mix into Cocktail Glass—no ice)*

DARK LAGOON-
1 part Blue Curaçao, fill Pineapple Wine
splash Grenadine *(Mix into Wine Glass—ice)*

DARK NIGHTMARE-
4 parts Coffee Liqueur, 1 part Goldschläger®
Light Cream or Milk *(Mix into Highball Glass—ice)*

DARTH VADER-
2 parts Jägermeister®, 1 part Gin, 1 part Light Rum, 1 part Tequila,
1 part Triple Sec, 1 part Vodka
Sour Mix *(Mix into Highball Glass—ice)*

DARTMOUTH GREEN-
3 parts Gin, 1 part Green Crème de Menthe, splash Kümmel
Lime Juice *(Mix into Cocktail Glass—no ice)*

DAVID BAREFACE-
3 parts Light Rum, 1 part White Crème de Caçao
Light Cream or Milk
(Mix into Cocktail Glass—no ice)

DAVIS-
1 part Dry Vermouth, 1 part Jamaican Rum, splash Raspberry Liqueur
Lime Juice *(Mix into Cocktail Glass—no ice)*

DAVIS BRANDY-
2 parts Brandy, 1 part Dry Vermouth
splash Grenadine, splash Bitters *(Mix into Cocktail Glass—no ice)*

DAYTONA DAYDREAM-
Spiced Rum
Pink Grapefruit Juice, Chocolate Milk, splash Grenadine
(Mix into Highball Glass—ice)

DE RIGUEUR-
Blended Whiskey
Grapefruit Juice, Honey *(Mix into Cocktail Glass—no ice)*

DeROSIER-
2 parts Light Rum, 1 part Bourbon Whiskey, 1 part Brown Crème de Caçao,
splash Cherry Brandy
(Mix into Cocktail Glass—no ice)

DEANNE-
2 parts Vodka, 1 part Sweet Vermouth, 1 part Triple Sec
(Mix into Cocktail Glass—no ice)

DEATH BY CHOCOLATE-
2 parts Irish Cream Liqueur, 1 part Brown Crème de Caçao, 1 part Vodka
Chocolate Ice Cream *(Blend with ice in Daiquiri Glass)*

DEATH BY SEX-
1 part Amaretto, 1 part Peach Schnapps, 1 part Sloe Gin, 1 part Southern
    Comfort®, 1 part Triple Sec, 1 part Vodka
Cranberry Juice, Orange Juice *(Mix into Highball Glass—ice)*

DEATH IN THE AFTERNOON-
1 part Licorice Liqueur, fill Champagne
(Mix into Champagne Flute—no ice)

DEAUVILL-
1 part Apple Brandy, 1 part Brandy, 1 part Triple Sec
Sour Mix *(Mix into Cocktail Glass—no ice)*

DEBUTANTE'S DREAM-
1 part Bourbon Whiskey, 1 part Brandy
Orange Juice, splash Lime Juice *(Mix into Cocktail Glass—no ice)*

DECADENCE-
1 part Coffee Liqueur, 1 part Hazelnut Liqueur, 1 part Irish Cream Liqueur
(Layer in Order in Cocktail Glass—no ice)

DECEIVER-
2 parts Tequila, 1 part Galliano® *(Mix into Small Rocks Glass—ice)*

DEEP DARK SECRET-
3 parts Dark Rum, 1 part Coffee Liqueur, 1 part Light Rum
Light Cream or Milk *(Mix into Cocktail Glass—no ice)*

DEEP SEA-
1 part Dry Vermouth, 1 part Gin, splash Anisette
Orange Bitters *(Mix into Cocktail Glass—no ice)*

DEEP SEA DIVER-
3 parts Dark Rum, 1 part Light Rum, 1 part Triple Sec, 1 part 151-proof Rum
Sour Mix *(Mix into Highball Glass—ice)*

DEEP THROAT (1)-
1 part Coffee Liqueur, 1 part Vodka
top Whipped Cream *(Mix into Champagne Flute—no ice)*

DEEP THROAT (2)-
1 part Coffee Liqueur, 1 part Grand Marnier®
top Whipped Cream *(Mix into Champagne Flute—no ice)*

DEJA VU-
1 part Coconut Liqueur, 1 part Triple Sec, splash Amaretto
Orange Juice *(Mix into Highball Glass—ice)*

DELILAH-
2 parts Gin, 1 part Triple Sec
Lime Juice *(Mix into Small Rocks Glass—ice)*

DELMONICO (1)-
2 parts Gin, 1 part Brandy, 1 part Dry Vermouth, 1 part Sweet Vermouth
(Mix into Cocktail Glass—no ice)

DELMONICO (2)-
2 parts Gin, 1 part Dry Vermouth
Orange Bitters *(Mix into Cocktail Glass—no ice)*

DELTA-
4 parts Blended Whiskey, 1 part Southern Comfort®
Sour Mix *(Mix into Highball Glass—ice)*

DEMPSEY-
1 part Apple Brandy, 1 part Gin, splash Anisette
Grenadine *(Mix into Cocktail Glass—no ice)*

DEPTH BOMB-
1 part Apple Brandy, 1 part Brandy
splash Sour Mix, splash Grenadine *(Mix into Small Rocks Glass—ice)*

DEPTH CHARGE-
12 oz. Beer, 1 part Schnapps or Whiskey
(drop Schnapps or Whiskey in Shot Glass into Mug of Beer)

DERBY DAIQUIRI-
Light Rum
Orange Juice, splash Sour Mix *(Blend with ice in Daiquiri Glass)*

DERBY FIZZ-
Bourbon Whiskey, splash Triple Sec
Sour Mix, splash Club Soda *(Mix into Highball Glass—ice)*

DERBY SPECIAL-
3 parts Light Rum, 1 part Triple Sec
Orange Juice, Sour Mix *(Blend with ice in Daiquiri Glass)*

DESERT GLOW-
1 part Peach Schnapps, 1 part Tequila
Orange Juice *(Mix into Highball Glass—ice)*

DESERT SHIELD-
3 parts Vodka, 1 part Cranberry Liqueur
Cranberry Juice *(Mix into Highball Glass—ice)*

DESERT SUNRISE (1)-
1 part Blue Curaçao, 1 part Margarita Schnapps
Orange Juice, Sour Mix *(Mix into Highball Glass—ice)*

DESERT SUNRISE (2)-
Vodka
Orange Juice, Pineapple Juice, Grenadine (lace), (stir with straw for "sunrise")
(Mix into Highball Glass—ice)

DESERT THRILLER MARGARITA-
Margarita Schnapps
Lime, Salted Rim
(Mix into Cocktail Glass with no ice or blend with ice in Daiquiri Glass)

DETROIT DAISY-
Dark Rum
Lime Juice, splash Grenadine *(Mix into Highball Glass—ice)*

DEVIL'S ADVOCATE-
3 parts Gin, 1 part Apple Brandy
Lime Juice, splash Grenadine *(Mix into Cocktail Glass—no ice)*

DEVIL'S COCKTAIL-
1 part Dry Vermouth, 1 part Port
Sour Mix *(Mix into Cocktail Glass—no ice)*

DEVIL'S DELIGHT (1)-
1 part Brandy, 1 part Grand Marnier®, 1 part Triple Sec, 1 part Vodka
Sour Mix, splash Lime Juice *(Mix into Highball Glass—ice)*

DEVIL'S DELIGHT (2)-
1 part Blue Curaçao, 1 part Brandy, 1 part Grand Marnier®, 1 part Vodka
Sour Mix, splash Lime Juice *(Mix into Highball Glass—ice)*

DEVIL'S TAIL-
2 parts Light Rum, 1 part Vodka, splash Apricot Brandy
Lime Juice, Grenadine *(Blend with ice in Daiquiri Glass)*

DI AMORE DREAM-
2 parts Amaretto, 1 part White Crème de Caçao
Orange Juice, Vanilla Ice Cream *(Blend with ice in Daiquiri Glass)*

DIABLO-
2 parts White Port, 1 parts Dry Vermouth
Lime Juice *(Mix into Cocktail Glass—no ice)*

DIABOLINI-
2 parts Gin, 2 parts Light Rum, 1 part Triple Sec
Lime Juice *(Mix into Cocktail Glass—no ice)*

DIAMOND FIZZ-
1 part Gin, fill Champagne
Sour Mix *(Mix into Champagne Flute—2 ice cubes)*

DIAMOND HEAD-
3 parts Gin, 1 part Triple Sec, splash Sweet Vermouth
Pineapple Juice *(Mix into Cocktail Glass—no ice)*

DIANA-
1 part White Crème de Menthe, 1 part Brandy (float)
(Mix into Cocktail Glass—no ice)

DIANNE-ON-THE-TOWER-
4 parts Light Rum, 1 part Bourbon Whiskey, splash Brown Crème de Caçao,
splash Cherry Brandy *(Mix into Cocktail Glass—no ice)*

DICKIE WARD-
Scotch Whiskey
Ginger Ale, splash Bitters *(Mix into Highball Glass—ice)*

DIESEL-
1 part Lager, splash Blue Currant, 1 part Hard Cider
(Layer in Order in Beer Mug)

DINAH-
Blended Whiskey
Sour Mix, Mint Leaf Garnish *(Mix into Cocktail Glass—no ice)*

DINGLE DRAM-
3 parts Irish Whiskey, 1 part Irish Mist®, splash White Crème de Caçao (float)
Cold Coffee, Club Soda, top Whipped Cream *(Mix into Highball Glass—ice)*

DINGO-
1 part Amaretto, 1 part Light Rum, 1 part Southern Comfort®
Sour Mix, Orange Juice, splash Grenadine *(Mix into Highball Glass—ice)*

DINNER CLUB BABES-***
1 part Amaretto, 1 part Southern Comfort®
Cranberry Juice, Orange Juice *(Mix into Highball Glass—ice)*

DIPLOMAT-
3 parts Dry Vermouth, 1 part Sweet Vermouth, splash Maraschino Liqueur
Bitters, Lemon Slice, Cherry Garnish *(Mix into Cocktail Glass—no ice)*

DIRTY BANANA-
2 parts Coffee Liqueur, 1 part Light Rum
Light Cream or Milk, Bananas, Sugar *(Blend with ice in Daiquiri Glass)*

DIRTY DIAPER-
1 part Amaretto, 1 part Melon Liqueur, 1 part Raspberry Liqueur,
     1 part Southern Comfort®, 1 part Vodka
Orange Juice *(Mix into Highball Glass—ice)*

DIRTY DICK'S DOWNFALL-
4 parts Gin, 1 part Campari, 1 part Dry Gin *(Mix into Cocktail Glass—no ice)*

DIRTY GIRL SCOUT-
1 part Coffee Liqueur, 1 part Irish Cream Liqueur, splash Green Crème de
     Menthe *(Mix into Small Rocks Glass—ice)*

DIRTY GIRL SCOUT COOKIE (1)-
2 parts Irish Cream Liqueur, 1 part Green Crème de Menthe
(Mix into Cocktail Glass—no ice)

DIRTY GIRL SCOUT COOKIE (2)-
2 parts Irish Cream Liqueur, 1 part Green Crème de Menthe
Light Cream or Milk *(Mix into Highball Glass—ice)*

DIRTY HARRY-
1 part Grand Marnier®, 1 part Tia Maria®
(Mix into Cocktail Glass—no ice)

DIRTY MARTINI-
Gin, Splash Dry Vermouth
Splash Olive Juice, Olive garnish *(Mix into Cocktail Glass—no ice)*

DIRTY MOTHER-
2 parts Brandy, 1 part Coffee Liqueur
(Mix into Cocktail Glass—no ice)

DIRTY SEX ON THE BEACH-
2 parts Peach Schnapps, 1 part Melon Liqueur, 1 part Raspberry Liqueur
Pineapple Juice *(Mix into Highball Glass—ice)*

DIRTY SOCK-
Scotch Whiskey
Pineapple Juice *(Mix into Highball Glass—ice)*

DIRTY VIRGIN-
3 parts Gin, 1 part Brown Crème de Caçao
(Mix into Small Rocks Glass—ice)

DIRTY WHITE MOTHER (1)-
3 parts Brandy, 1 part Coffee Liqueur
Light Cream or Milk (float) *(Mix into Small Rocks Glass—ice)*

DIRTY WHITE MOTHER (2)-
1 part Coffee Liqueur, 1 part Tequila
Light Cream or Milk (float) *(Mix into Small Rocks Glass—ice)*

DISAPPOINTED LADY-
1 part Brandy, 1 part Crème de Noyaux, 1 part Tia Maria®
Orange Juice, splash Grenadine *(Mix into Highball Glass—ice)*

DISCOVERY BAY-
3 parts Brandy, 1 part Triple Sec
Lemon Sherbet, fill Ginger Ale *(Mix into Highball Glass—ice)*

DIXIE COCKTAIL-
2 parts Gin, 1 part Dry Vermouth, splash Anisette
Orange Juice *(Mix into Cocktail Glass—no ice)*

DIXIE DEW-
3 parts Bourbon Whiskey, 1 part Triple Sec, 1 part White Crème de Menthe
(Mix into Cocktail Glass—no ice)

DIXIE JULEP-
Bourbon Whiskey
Sugar, Mint leaves *(Mix into Highball Glass—ice)*

DIXIE STRINGER-
Bourbon Whiskey, splash Southern Comfort®, splash White Crème de Menthe
(Mix into Cocktail Glass—no ice)

DIXIE WHISKEY-
Bourbon Whiskey, splash Triple Sec, splash White Crème de Menthe
Bitters, Sugar *(Mix into Cocktail Glass—no ice)*

DIZZY BUDDHA-
  1 part Amaretto, 1 part Banana Liqueur, 1 part Coconut Rum, 1 part Coffee
    Liqueur, 1 part Dark Rum, 1 part Melon Liqueur, 1 part Southern
    Comfort®, 1 part Vodka
  Orange Juice, Pineapple Juice, Grenadine *(Mix into Highball Glass—ice)*

DO BE CAREFUL-
  1 part Gin, 1 part Triple Sec
  splash Grenadine, splash Lime Juice *(Mix into Cocktail Glass—no ice)*

DOCTOR-
  Citrus Rum
  Lime Juice *(Mix into Small Rocks Glass—ice)*

DOCTOR BIRD-
  Light Rum
  Light Cream or Milk, Honey, splash Grenadine
  (Mix into Cocktail Glass—no ice)

DOCTOR COCKTAIL-
  2 parts Citrus Rum, 1 part Spiced Rum
  Lime Juice *(Mix into Cocktail Glass—no ice)*

DOCTOR COOK-
  Gin, splash Maraschino Liqueur
  splash Sour Mix *(Mix into Cocktail Glass—no ice)*

DOCTOR DAWSON-
  Tequila
  Sour Mix, splash Bitters, fill Club Soda *(Mix into Highball Glass—ice)*

DOCTOR FUNK-
  Jamaican Rum, splash Anisette
  Sour Mix, splash Grenadine, fill Club Soda *(Mix into Highball Glass—ice)*

DOCTOR PEPPER (1)-
  1 part Amaretto, 1 part Spiced Rum
  Cola *(Mix into Highball Glass—ice)*

DOCTOR PEPPER (2)-
  1 part Amaretto, 1 part 151-proof Rum, fill Beer *(Beer Mug)*

DOCTOR PIPPER-
  3 parts Amaretto, 1 part 151-proof Rum, fill Beer
  (drop Shot of Liqueur into Beer Mug)

DOCTOR'S ORDERS-
  1 part Brandy, 1 part Forbidden Fruit Liqueur, 1 part Gin
  Lime Juice *(Mix into Cocktail Glass—no ice)*

DODGE SPECIAL-
  1 part Gin, 1 part Triple Sec
  Grape Juice *(Mix into Highball Glass—ice)*

DOG PISS-
  1 part Southern Comfort®, 1 part Vodka, fill Beer *(Beer Mug)*

DOG SLED-
Canadian Whiskey
Orange Juice, splash Lime Juice, splash Grenadine
(Mix into Highball Glass—ice)

DOG'S NOSE-
1 part Gin, fill Ale *(Beer Mug)*

DOLLAR BILL-
1 part Light Rum, 1 part Melon Liqueur
splash Lime Juice
(Mix into Cocktail Glass—no ice)

DOLLY O'DARE-
2 parts Dry Vermouth, 2 parts Gin, 1 part Apricot Brandy
(Mix into Cocktail Glass—no ice)

DOMINICAN COCO LOCO-
3 parts Coconut Rum, 1 part Amaretto
Pineapple Juice, splash Light Cream or Milk, splash Grenadine
(Mix into Highball Glass—ice)

DON JUAN-
1 part Dark Rum, 1 part Tequila
Pineapple Juice, Grapefruit Juice *(Mix into Cocktail Glass—no ice)*

DONNA'S DELIGHT-
2 parts Apricot Brandy, 2 parts Brandy, 1 part Amaretto
(Mix into Cocktail Glass—no ice)

DOONESBURY DASH-
3 parts Gin, 3 parts Medium Sherry, 1 part Dry Vermouth, 1 part Sweet
Vermouth, splash Cherry Brandy, splash Triple Sec, splash White
Crème de Caçao
Lime Juice *(Mix into Highball Glass—ice)*

DORADO-
Tequila
Lime Juice, Honey *(Mix into Highball Glass—ice)*

DORALTO-
Tequila
Sour Mix, splash Bitters, fill Tonic Water
(Mix into Highball Glass—ice)

DORCHESTER NIGHT CAP-
1 part Brandy, 1 part Galliano®, splash White Crème de Menthe
(Mix into Cocktail Glass—no ice)

DOUBLE MINT-
Spearmint Schnapps, splash Green Crème de Menthe
Coffee, top Whipped Cream *(Mix into Irish Coffee Cup—no ice)*

DOUBLE STANDARD SOUR-
1 part Blended Whiskey, 1 part Gin
Sour Mix, Grenadine *(Mix into Sour Glass— ice)*

DOUBLE TROUBLE-
2 parts Brandy, 1 part Dry Vermouth
splash Grenadine, splash Bitters *(Mix into Cocktail Glass—no ice)*

DOUBLOON-
1 part Jamaican Rum, 1 part Light Rum, 1 part 151-proof Rum, splash Anisette, splash Triple Sec
Grapefruit Juice, Orange Juice *(Mix into Highball Glass—ice)*

DOUGLAS FAIRBANKS-
2 parts Gin, 1 part Apricot Brandy
Sour Mix *(Mix into Cocktail Glass—no ice)*

DOUGLAS TOWN-
2 parts Coffee Liqueur, 1 part Tequila
Lime Juice *(Mix into Cocktail Glass—no ice)*

DOWN COMFORTER-
3 parts Southern Comfort®, 1 part Gin
Orange Juice, Lime Juice *(Mix into Cocktail Glass—no ice)*

DOWN THE HATCH-
Blended Whiskey, splash Blackberry Brandy
splash Orange Bitters *(Mix into Cocktail Glass—no ice)*

DOWN UNDER-
Vodka, splash Brandy, splash Crème de Cassis, splash Triple Sec
(Mix into Cocktail Glass—no ice)

DOWNSIDER-
3 parts Tequila, 1 part Banana Liqueur, 1 part Galliano®
Light Cream or Milk, splash Lime Juice, splash Grenadine, splash Bitters
(Mix into Cocktail Glass—no ice)

DOYLES' DELIBERATION-
2 parts Vodka, 1 part Melon Liqueur *(Mix into Cocktail Glass—no ice)*

DRAGON FIRE-
1 part Green Crème de Menthe, 1 part Pepper Vodka
(Mix into Cocktail Glass—no ice)

DRAGONFLY-
Gin
Ginger Ale *(Mix into Highball Glass—ice)*

DRAGON SLAYER-
2 parts Blueberry Schnapps, 1 part Blue Curaçao, 1 part Coconut Rum, 1 part Vodka
Orange Juice, Pineapple Juice, splash Grenadine, fill Lemon-Lime Soda
(Mix into Highball Glass—ice)

DRAGON'S BREATH-
2 parts Beer, 2 parts Gin, 2 parts 100-proof Vodka, 2 parts Vodka, 1 part Dark Rum, 1 part Peppermint Schnapps
fill Cola *(Mix into Highball Glass—ice)*

DRAINPIPE-
1 part Blue (or Green) Curaçao, 1 part Irish Cream Liqueur
fill Cola *(Mix into Highball Glass with no ice)*

DRAWBRIDGE-
White Wine, splash Blue Curaçao
top Club Soda *(Mix into Wine Glass—ice)*

DREAM COCKTAIL-
2 parts Brandy, 1 part Triple Sec, splash Anisette
(Mix into Cocktail Glass—no ice)

DREAM SHAKE-
1 part Irish Cream Liqueur, 1 part Tia Maria®
(Mix into Cocktail Glass—no ice)

DREAMSICLE-
Amaretto
Vanilla Ice Cream, splash Orange Juice, splash Light Cream or Milk
(Blend with ice in Daiquiri Glass)

DREAMY MONKEY-
2 parts Vodka, 1 part Banana Liqueur, 1 part Brown Crème de Caçao
Light Cream or Milk, Banana, Vanilla Ice Cream
(Blend with ice in Daiquiri Glass)

DRINK OF THE GODS-
2 parts Vodka, 1 part Blueberry Schnapps
Pineapple Juice
(Mix into Highball Glass—ice)

DRINKING MAN'S FRUIT CUP, THE-
2 parts Gold Rum, 1 part Jamaican Rum
Cranberry Juice, Orange Juice, fill Lemon-Lime Soda
(Mix into Highball Glass—ice)

DRIVE AWAY-
1 part Amaretto, 1 part Dark Rum
Grapefruit Juice, Orange Juice *(Mix into Highball Glass—ice)*

DROOG'S DATE-
Light Rum, splash Cherry Brandy, splash Triple Sec
Lime Juice *(Mix into Cocktail Glass—no ice)*

DRY HOLE-
2 parts Light Rum, 1 part Apricot Brandy, 1 part Triple Sec
Lime Juice, fill Club Soda *(Mix into Highball Glass—ice)*

DU BARRY-
2 parts Gin, 1 part Dry Vermouth, splash Anisette
splash Bitters, Orange Slice *(Mix into Cocktail Glass—no ice)*

DUBLIN SOUR-
3 parts Irish Whiskey, 1 part Triple Sec, splash Raspberry Liqueur (float)
Lime Juice *(Mix into Cocktail Glass—no ice)*

DUBONNET COCKTAIL-
2 parts Red Dubonnet®, 1 part Gin
splash Orange Bitters *(Mix into Cocktail Glass—no ice)*

DUBONNET FIZZ-
Red Dubonnet®, splash Cherry Brandy
Orange Juice, Sour Mix, Club Soda *(Mix into Highball Glass—ice)*

DUBONNET HIGHBALL-
Red Dubonnet®
Ginger Ale or Club Soda *(Mix into Highball Glass with 2 ice cubes)*

DUBONNET MANHATTAN-
1 part Blended Whiskey, 1 part Red Dubonnet®
Cherry Garnish *(Mix into Cocktail Glass—no ice)*

DUBONNET NEGRONI-
2 parts Gin, 1 part Campari, 1 part Red Dubonnet®
(Mix into Cocktail Glass—no ice)

DUCHESS-
3 parts Anisette, 1 part Dry Vermouth, 1 part Sweet Vermouth
(Mix into Cocktail Glass—no ice)

DUCK FART (1)-
1 part Coffee Liqueur, 1 part Irish Cream Liqueur, 1 part Canadian Rye
Whiskey *(Layer in Order in Cocktail Glass—no ice)*

DUCK FART (2)-
1 part Coffee Liqueur, 1 part Brown Crème de Caçao, 1 part Irish Cream
Liqueur *(Layer in Order in Cocktail Glass—no ice)*

DUCK PIN-
1 part Raspberry Liqueur, 1 part Southern Comfort®
Pineapple Juice *(Mix into Highball Glass—ice)*

DUKE-
Triple Sec, splash Maraschino Liqueur, fill Champagne
Orange Juice, Sour Mix *(Mix into Champagne Flute—no ice)*

DUKE OF MARLBOROUGH-
Sweet Vermouth, splash Raspberry Liqueur
Lime Juice *(Mix into Cocktail Glass—no ice)*

DUKE'S A CHAMP-
2 parts Vodka, 1 part Blackberry Brandy
(Mix into Cocktail Glass—no ice)

DUNDEE-
Gin, splash Drambuie®, splash Scotch Whiskey
splash Lime Juice *(Mix into Small Rocks Glass—ice)*

DUNLOP-
2 parts Light Rum, 1 part Sherry
splash Bitters *(Mix into Small Rocks Glass—ice)*

DUPLEX-
   1 part Dry Vermouth, 1 part Sweet Vermouth
   Orange Bitters *(Mix into Cocktail Glass—no ice)*

DUSTY BILL-
   3 parts Canadian Whiskey, 1 part Apple Brandy, splash Brandy
   Sour Mix *(Mix into Highball Glass—ice)*

DUSTY DOG-
   Vodka, splash Crème de Cassis
   splash Lime Juice, splash Bitters, fill Ginger Ale *(Mix into Highball Glass—ice)*

DUTCH COFFEE-
   Chocolate Liqueur
   Coffee, top Whipped Cream *(Mix into Irish Coffee Cup—no ice)*

DUTCH TREAT-
   3 parts Gin, 1 part Aquavit
   Sour Mix, splash Light Cream or Milk *(Mix into Highball Glass—ice)*

DUTCH VELVET-
   1 part Banana Liqueur, 1 part Chocolate Mint Liqueur
   Light Cream or Milk *(Mix into Cocktail Glass—no ice)*

DUVAL-
   2 parts Triple Sec, 1 part Sambuca *(Mix into Cocktail Glass—no ice)*

DYNASTY-
   1 part Amaretto, 1 part Southern Comfort® *(Mix into Cocktail Glass—no ice)*

– NOTES –

_____

_____

_____

_____

_____

_____

_____

_____

_____

_____

_____

_____

E. T.-
1 part Irish Cream Liqueur, 1 part Melon Liqueur, 1 part Vodka
(Mix into Cocktail Glass—no ice)

EAGER BEAVER-
2 parts Coffee Liqueur, 2 parts Light Rum, 1 part Triple Sec
(Mix into Cocktail Glass—no ice)

EAGLE-
2 parts Gin, 1 part Crème de Yvette
Sour Mix *(Mix into Cocktail Glass—no ice)*

EARL OF SARDINIA-
3 parts Campari, 1 part Crème de Cassis
Grapefruit Juice, splash Pineapple Juice, splash Grenadine
(Mix into Highball Glass—ice)

EARTHQUAKE (1)-
1 part Anisette, 1 part Blended Whiskey, 1 part Gin
(Mix into Cocktail Glass—no ice)

EARTHQUAKE (2)-
2 parts Bourbon Whiskey, 2 parts Gin, 1 part Anisette
(Mix into Cocktail Glass—no ice)

EARTHQUAKE COOLER-
1 part Triple Sec, 1 part Vodka, 1 part Champagne (lace)
splash Lime Juice, splash Orange Bitters *(Mix into Cocktail Glass—no ice)*

EAST INDIA (1)-
Brandy, splash Jamaican Rum, splash Triple Sec
Pineapple Juice, Bitters *(Mix into Cocktail Glass—no ice)*

EAST INDIA (2)-
1 part Dry Sherry, 1 part Dry Vermouth
Orange Bitters *(Mix into Cocktail Glass—no ice)*

EAST SIDE-
2 parts Amaretto, 2 parts Light Rum, 1 part Coconut Rum
Light Cream or Milk *(Mix into Highball Glass—ice)*

EASTER EGG-
1 part Raspberry Liqueur, 1 part Tia Maria®, 1 part Light Cream or Milk
(Layer in Order in Cocktail Glass—no ice)

EASTERN MANHATTAN-
Japanese Whiskey, Splash Anisette, Splash Sweet Vermouth
(Mix into Cocktail Glass—no ice)

EASY SAZERAC-
Bourbon Whiskey, splash Anisette
splash Water, splash Bitters, Sugar, muddle *(Mix into Small Rocks Glass—ice)*

EAT HOT DEATH-
151-proof Rum
Lime Juice *(Mix into Small Rocks Glass—ice)*

ECLIPSE (1)-
2 parts Sloe Gin, 1 part Gin
splash Lime Juice, Grenadine (on Bottom) *(Mix into Cocktail Glass—no ice)*

ECLIPSE (2)-
Amaretto, splash Brown Crème de Caçao
Orange Juice, Chocolate Ice Cream *(Blend with ice in Daiquiri Glass)*

ECLIPSE (3)-
Old Bushmill's® Black Bush Irish Whiskey
Club Soda *(Mix into Highball Glass—ice)*

EDITH DAY-
Gin
Grapefruit Juice, Sugar *(Mix into Highball Glass—ice)*

EH BOMB-
1 part Tequila, 1 part White Crème de Menthe, 1 part Licorice Liqueur, 1 part
Irish Cream Liqueur *(Layer in Order in Cocktail Glass—no ice)*

EIFFEL TOWER-
2 parts Brandy, 2 parts Vodka, 1 part Anisette, 1 part Triple Sec
(Mix into Cocktail Glass—no ice)

EL CID-
Tequila, splash Amaretto
Lime Juice, splash Grenadine, fill Tonic Water *(Mix into Highball Glass—ice)*

EL DIABLO-
Tequila, splash Crème de Cassis
splash Lime Juice, fill Ginger Ale *(Mix into Highball Glass—ice)*

EL MORO-
2 parts Gin, 1 part Dry Vermouth
Orange Juice, splash Orange Bitters, Sugar *(Mix into Cocktail Glass—no ice)*

EL PRESIDENTE (1)-
Light Rum
Lime Juice, Pineapple Juice, Grenadine *(Mix into Cocktail Glass—no ice)*

EL PRESIDENTE (2)-
2 parts Light Rum, 1 part Dry Vermouth
splash Bitters *(Mix into Cocktail Glass—no ice)*

EL REVOLTO-
1 part Peppermint Schnapps, 1 part Irish Cream Liqueur, 1 part Triple Sec
(Layer in Order in Cocktail Glass—no ice)

EL SALVADOR-
2 parts Light Rum, 1 part Hazelnut Liqueur,
splash Lime Juice, splash Grenadine *(Mix into Cocktail Glass—no ice)*

EL TORO SANGRIENTO (BLOODY BULL)-
Vodka
fill ½ Tomato Juice, ½ Beef Bouillon, splash Worcestershire Sauce, Salt, Pepper
(Mix into Highball Glass—ice)

ELECTRIC BANANA-
2 parts Banana Liqueur, 1 part Coconut Liqueur, 1 part Melon Liqueur
Light Cream or Milk, Orange Juice, Pineapple Juice
(Mix into Highball Glass—ice)

ELECTRIC ICED TEA-
1 part Blue Curaçao, 1 part Gin, 1 part Light Rum, 1 part Tequila, 1 part Vodka
Sour Mix, fill Lemon-Lime Soda
(Mix into Highball Glass with ice or blend with ice in Daiquiri Glass)

ELECTRIC JAM-
3 parts Vodka, 1 part Blue Curaçao
Sour Mix, fill Lemon-Lime Soda *(Mix into Highball Glass—ice)*

ELECTRIC LEMONADE (1)-
1 part Gin, 1 part Light Rum, 1 part Tequila, 1 part Vodka, splash Triple Sec
Sour Mix, top Lemon-Lime Soda *(Mix into Highball Glass—ice)*

ELECTRIC LEMONADE (2)-
1 part Blue Curaçao, 1 part Gin, 1 part Light Rum, 1 part Tequila, 1 part Vodka
Sour Mix, top Lemon-Lime Soda *(Mix into Highball Glass—ice)*

ELECTRIC SCREWDRIVER-
2 parts Amaretto, 1 part Southern Comfort®
Orange Juice *(Mix into Highball Glass—ice)*

ELECTRIC SURFBOARD-
Blue Curaçao
Pineapple Juice, splash Grenadine, splash Lemon-Lime Soda (top)
(Mix into Highball Glass—ice)

ELECTRIC WATERMELON-
1 part Light Rum, 1 part Melon Liqueur, 1 part Triple Sec, 1 part Vodka
Orange Juice, Lemon-Lime Soda, splash Grenadine (lace)
(Mix into Highball Glass—ice)

ELEPHANT LIPS-
3 parts Dark Rum, 1 part Banana Liqueur
Lime Juice *(Mix into Cocktail Glass—no ice)*

ELK'S OWN-
2 parts Blended Whiskey, 1 part Port
Sour Mix, Pineapple Garnish *(Mix into Cocktail Glass—no ice)*

EMERALD BAY-
1 part Vodka, 1 part Green Crème de Menthe (float)
Pineapple Juice, Sour Mix, Pineapple Garnish *(Mix into Highball Glass—ice)*

EMERALD COOLER-
2 parts Gin, 1 part Green Crème de Menthe
splash Lime Juice, fill Club Soda *(Mix into Highball Glass—ice)*

EMERALD FOREST-
Gin, splash Green Crème de Menthe, splash White Crème de Menthe
(Mix into Cocktail Glass—no ice)

EMERALD ISLE (1)-
　　Gin, splash Green Crème de Menthe
　　Bitters *(Mix into Cocktail Glass—no ice)*

EMERALD ISLE (2)-
　　1 part Green Crème de Menthe, 1 part Irish Whiskey
　　Vanilla Ice Cream, top Club Soda *(Blend with ice in Daiquiri Glass)*

EMERSON-
　　2 parts Gin, 1 part Sweet Vermouth, splash Maraschino Liqueur
　　Lime Juice *(Mix into Cocktail Glass—no ice)*

EMPIRE-
　　2 parts Gin, 1 part Apple Brandy, 1 part Apricot Brandy
　　(Mix into Cocktail Glass—no ice)

END OF MY ROPE-
　　Hazelnut Liqueur, splash Banana Liqueur
　　Pineapple Juice, splash Bitters *(Mix into Cocktail Glass—no ice)*

ENEBRIATOR-
　　1 part Amaretto, 1 part Gin, 1 part Triple Sec, 1 part Vodka
　　Pineapple Juice *(Mix into Highball Glass—ice)*

ENGLISH COFFEE-
　　1 part Coffee Liqueur, 1 part Gin, splash Triple Sec
　　Coffee, top Whipped Cream *(Mix into Irish Coffee Cup—no ice)*

ENGLISH HIGHBALL-
　　1 part Brandy, 1 part Gin, 1 part Sweet Vermouth
　　Ginger Ale or Club Soda *(Mix into Highball Glass—ice)*

ENGLISH ROSE-
　　2 parts Gin, 1 part Apricot Brandy, 1 part Dry Vermouth
　　Grenadine, Lime Juice, Sugared Rim, Cherry Garnish
　　(Mix into Cocktail Glass—no ice)

ENTWISTLE'S ERROR-
　　Dark Rum
　　splash Lime Juice, fill Tonic Water *(Mix into Highball Glass—ice)*

ERIC THE RED-
　　3 parts Scotch Whiskey, 1 part Cherry Brandy, splash Dry Vermouth
　　(Mix into Small Rocks Glass—ice)

ERMINE TAIL-
　　Sambuca
　　Light Cream or Milk (float), sprinkle Instant Espresso Coffee Grinds (top)
　　(Mix into Highball Glass—ice)

ERUPTION-
　　Canadian Whiskey, splash Crème de Cassis *(Mix into Cocktail Glass—no ice)*

ESCOFFIER-
　　2 parts Apple Brandy, 1 part Triple Sec, 1 part Red Dubonnet®
　　splash Bitters *(Mix into Cocktail Glass—no ice)*

E

ESKIMO KISS-
1 part Amaretto, 1 part Cherry Brandy, 1 part Swiss Chocolate Almond Liqueur
top Whipped Cream *(Mix into Cocktail Glass—no ice)*

ESMERALDA-
Tequila
Lime Juice, Honey, splash Bitters (optional) *(Mix into Cocktail Glass—no ice)*

ESPANA-
2 parts Dark Rum, 1 part Apple Brandy, splash Sweet Vermouth
splash Orange Bitters *(Mix into Cocktail Glass—no ice)*

ESQUIMAUX CRÈME-
2 parts Canadian Whiskey, 1 part Grand Marnier®
Light Cream or Milk, splash Lime Juice, sprinkle Nutmeg, sprinkle Cinnamon
(Mix into Highball Glass—ice)

ETHEL DUFFY-
1 part Apricot Brandy, 1 part Triple Sec, 1 part White Crème de Menthe
(Mix into Cocktail Glass—no ice)

EUROPEAN COCKTAIL-
2 parts Gin, 1 part Cream Sherry, 1 part Dry Vermouth, 1 part Red Dubonnet®,
    splash Grand Marnier®
(Mix into Cocktail Glass—no ice)

EVANS-
Rye Whiskey, splash Apricot Brandy, splash Triple Sec
(Mix into Cocktail Glass—no ice)

EVANS RESCUES THE DAMSEL OF GARSTANG TOWER-
2 parts Dry Vermouth, 2 parts Gin, 2 parts Sweet Vermouth,
    1 part Strawberry Schnapps
splash Orange Bitters
(Mix into Cocktail Glass—no ice)

EVE-
Pink Sparkling Wine, splash Cognac, splash Licorice Liqueur, splash Triple Sec
Sugar *(Mix into Wine Glass—ice)*

EVE'S APPLE DAIQUIRI-
Spiced Rum, splash Apple Brandy
Orange Juice, Sour Mix *(Blend with ice in Daiquiri Glass)*

EVERGLADES SPECIAL-
1 part Light Rum, 1 part White Crème de Caçao, splash Coffee Liqueur
Light Cream or Milk *(Mix into Highball Glass—ice)*

EVERYBODY'S IRISH-
Irish Whiskey, splash Green Chartreuse, splash Green Crème de Menthe
(Mix into Cocktail Glass—no ice)

EVERYTHING BUT-
1 part Blended Whiskey, 1 part Gin, splash Apricot Brandy
Orange Juice, Sour Mix *(Mix into Highball Glass—ice)*

EXECUTIVE SUNRISE-
Tequila, splash Crème de Cassis (lace)
Orange Juice (Freshly squeezed, optional) *(Mix into Highball Glass—ice)*

EXTACY-
2 parts Melon Liqueur, 1 part 151-proof Rum, 1 part Citrus Vodka,
1 part Blue Curaçao (lace)
Pineapple Juice *(Mix into Highball Glass—ice)*

EXTERMINATOR-
Vodka, splash Sherry *(Mix into Cocktail Glass—no ice)*

EYE DROP-
1 part Licorice Liqueur, 1 part Peppermint Schnapps, 1 part Vodka
(Mix into Small Rocks Glass—ice)

EYE OPENER (1)-
Light Rum, splash Anisette, splash Triple Sec, splash White Crème de Caçao
Sugar *(Mix into Cocktail Glass—no ice)*

EYE OPENER (2)-
1 part Dark Rum, 1 part Jamaican Rum, splash Triple Sec
Orange Juice, Grapefruit Juice *(Mix into Highball Glass—ice)*

– NOTES –

_____

_____

_____

_____

_____

_____

_____

_____

_____

_____

_____

_____

_____

_____

.50 CALIBER-
1 part Gin, 1 part Bourbon Whiskey, 1 part Sour Mash Whiskey, 1 part Vodka
Lemon-Lime Soda *(Mix into Highball Glass—ice)*

44D-
1 part Coffee Liqueur, 1 part Peach Schnapps, 1 part Vodka
splash Grenadine *(Mix into Cocktail Glass—no ice)*

401-
1 part Coffee Liqueur, 1 part Banana Liqueur, 1 part Irish Cream Liqueur, 1 part
Yukon Jack® Canadian Liqueur *(Layer in Order in Cocktail Glass—no ice)*

'57 CHEVY-
1 part Grand Marnier®, 1 part Southern Comfort®, 1 part Vodka
Pineapple Juice *(Mix into Highball Glass—ice)*

'57 CHEVY (WITH A WHITE LICENSE PLATE)-
1 part White Crème de Caçao, 1 part Vodka *(Mix into Small Rocks Glass—ice)*

'57 T-BIRD-
1 part Amaretto, 1 part Grand Marnier®, 1 part Southern Comfort®
Pineapple Juice *(Mix into Cocktail Glass—no ice)*

501 BLUE-
1 part Blueberry Schnapps, 1 part Blue Curaçao, 1 part Vodka
Sour Mix, splash Lemon-Lime Soda *(Mix into Highball Glass—ice)*

F-16-
1 part Coffee Liqueur, 1 part Hazelnut Liqueur, 1 part Irish Cream Liqueur
(Layer in Order in Cocktail Glass—no ice)

F-52-
1 part Coffee Liqueur, 1 part Irish Cream Liqueur, 1 part Hazelnut Liqueur
(Layer in Order in Cocktail Glass—no ice)

F. B. I. FIZZ-
1 part Bourbon Whiskey, 1 part Cherry Brandy, 1 part Spiced Rum
fill Club Soda *(Mix into Highball Glass—ice)*

F. U.-
Hazelnut Liqueur
Lemon-Lime Soda *(Mix into Highball Glass—ice)*

FACE OFF-
1 part Grenadine, 1 part Green Crème de Menthe, 1 part Blue Curaçao,
1 part Sambuca *(Layer in Order in Cocktail Glass—no ice)*

FAIR & WARMER-
2 parts Light Rum, 1 part Sweet Vermouth, splash Triple Sec
(Mix into Cocktail Glass—no ice)

FAIRBANKS-
1 part Apricot Brandy, 1 part Dry Vermouth, 1 part Gin
splash Lime Juice, splash Grenadine
(Mix into Cocktail Glass—no ice)

FAIRY BELLE-
    2 parts Gin, 1 part Apricot Brandy
    splash Grenadine *(Mix into Cocktail Glass—no ice)*

FALLEN ANGEL-
    Gin, splash White Crème de Menthe
    Lime Juice, Bitters, Cherry Garnish *(Mix into Cocktail Glass—no ice)*

FALLING STAR-
    Spiced Rum
    Orange Juice, splash Lime Juice, fill Tonic Water *(Mix into Highball Glass—ice)*

FANCY BRANDY-
    Brandy, splash Triple Sec
    Bitters, Sugar *(Mix into Cocktail Glass—no ice)*

FANCY FREE-
    Rye Whiskey, splash Maraschino Liqueur
    Sour Mix, splash Bitters, splash Orange Bitters
    (Mix into Cocktail Glass—no ice)

FANCY GIN-
    Gin, splash Triple Sec
    Bitters, Sugar *(Mix into Cocktail Glass—no ice)*

FANCY WHISKEY-
    Blended Whiskey, splash Triple Sec
    Bitters, Sugar *(Mix into Cocktail Glass—no ice)*

FANS-
    2 parts Scotch Whiskey, 1 part Triple Sec
    Grapefruit Juice *(Mix into Highball Glass—ice)*

FANTASIO-
    1 part Brandy, 1 part Dry Vermouth, splash Maraschino Liqueur,
        splash White Crème de Menthe *(Mix into Cocktail Glass—no ice)*

FARE THEE WELL-
    3 parts Gin, 1 part Dry Vermouth, splash Sweet Vermouth, splash Triple Sec
    (Mix into Cocktail Glass—no ice)

FARMER GILES-
    Gin, splash Dry Vermouth, splash Sweet Vermouth
    splash Bitters *(Mix into Cocktail Glass—no ice)*

FARMER'S COCKTAIL-
    2 parts Gin, 1 part Dry Vermouth, 1 part Sweet Vermouth
    Bitters *(Mix into Cocktail Glass—no ice)*

FARMER'S MILK-
    Scotch Whiskey
    Light Cream or Milk, Sugar, sprinkle Nutmeg *(Mix into Highball Glass—ice)*

FARTHINGALE-
    1 part Dry Vermouth, 1 part Gin, 1 part Sweet Vermouth
    splash Bitters *(Mix into Cocktail Glass—no ice)*

FAST LAP-
4 parts Gin, 1 part Licorice Liqueur
Orange Juice, splash Grenadine *(Mix into Small Rocks Glass—ice)*

FAT CAT-
2 parts Irish Cream Liqueur, 1 part Amaretto, 1 part Banana Liqueur
(Mix into Cocktail Glass—no ice)

FAT FACE-
3 parts Gin, 1 part Apricot Brandy
splash Grenadine *(Mix into Cocktail Glass—no ice)*

FATHER SHERMAN-
3 parts Brandy, 1 part Apricot Brandy
Orange Juice *(Mix into Cocktail Glass—no ice)*

FATHER'S MILK-
Bourbon Whiskey
Light Cream or Milk, Sugar *(Mix into Highball Glass—ice)*

FAVORITE COCKTAIL-
1 part Apricot Brandy, 1 part Dry Vermouth, 1 part Gin
Lime Juice *(Mix into Cocktail Glass—no ice)*

FELONY FRAPPE-***
2 parts Blueberry Schnapps, 1 part Light Rum
Strawberry Daiquiri Mix, splash Sour Mix, top Whipped Cream
(Blend with ice in Daiquiri Glass)

FEROCIOUS FLIP-
1 part Brandy, fill Ruby Port
splash Light Cream or Milk, Sugar, sprinkle Nutmeg
(Mix into Wine Glass—no ice)

FERN GULLY-
1 part Coconut Rum, 1 part Dark Rum, splash Crème de Noyaux
Orange Juice, splash Lime Juice *(Mix into Highball Glass—ice)*

FERRARI-
2 parts Dry Vermouth, 1 part Amaretto *(Mix into Small Rocks Glass—ice)*

FERRIS WHEEL-
1 part Brandy, 1 part Sambuca *(Mix into Cocktail Glass—no ice)*

FESTIVAL-
1 part Apricot Brandy, 1 part White Crème de Caçao
Light Cream or Milk, splash Grenadine *(Mix into Highball Glass—ice)*

FIESTA-
1 part Apple Brandy, 1 part Dry Vermouth, 1 part Light Rum
splash Lime Juice, splash Grenadine *(Mix into Cocktail Glass—no ice)*

FIFTH (5th) AVENUE-
1 part Brown Crème de Caçao, 1 part Apricot Brandy
1 part Light Cream or Milk *(Layer in Order in Cocktail Glass—no ice)*

FIFTY-FIFTY-
1 part Dry Vermouth, 1 part Gin *(Mix into Cocktail Glass—no ice)*

FIG LEAF-
1 part Light Rum, 1 part Sweet Vermouth
Lime Juice, splash Bitters *(Mix into Cocktail Glass—no ice)*

FIJI FIZZ-
3 parts Dark Rum, 1 part Bourbon Whiskey, splash Cherry Brandy
Cola, splash Orange Bitters *(Mix into Highball Glass—ice)*

FILBY-
2 parts Gin, 1 part Amaretto, 1 part Campari, 1 part Dry Vermouth
(Mix into Cocktail Glass—no ice)

FINE & DANDY-
3 parts Gin, 1 part Triple Sec
Lime Juice, Bitters, Cherry Garnish *(Mix into Cocktail Glass—no ice)*

FINO MARTINI-
Gin, splash Fino Sherry *(Mix into Cocktail Glass—no ice)*

FIRE & ICE-
Pepper Vodka, splash Dry Vermouth *(Mix into Cocktail Glass—no ice)*

FIRE BALL (1)-
Cinnamon Schnapps, splash Cherry Brandy *(Mix into Cocktail Glass—no ice)*

FIRE BALL (2)-
1 part Coffee Liqueur, 1 part Licorice Liqueur
(Layer in Order in Cocktail Glass—no ice)

FIRE BALL (3)-
1 part Brandy, 1 part Sambuca
(Layer in Order in Cocktail Glass—no ice)

FIRE BOMB-
1 part Sour Mash Whiskey, 1 part Tequila, 1 part Vodka
splash Hot Sauce *(Mix into Small Rocks Glass—ice)*

FIRE BREATHING DRAGON-
1 part Campari, 1 part Tequila, 1 part 151-proof Rum
(Mix into Small Rocks Glass—ice)

FIRE ENGINE-
Jägermeister®
Club Soda, splash Grenadine *(Mix into Highball Glass—ice)*

FIRE ENGINE WITH AN ALARM-
1 part Jägermeister®, 1 part Vodka
Club Soda, splash Grenadine *(Mix into Highball Glass—ice)*

FIRE FLY-
Vodka
Grapefruit Juice, splash Grenadine (lace) *(Mix into Highball Glass—ice)*

FIRE IN HEAVEN-
151-proof Rum
splash Hot Sauce *(Mix into Small Rocks Glass—ice)*

FIRE ISLAND SUNRISE-
1 part Light Rum, 1 part Vodka
Orange Juice, Lemonade, splash Cranberry Juice
(Mix into Highball Glass—ice)

FIRECRACKER (1)-
1 part Cherry Brandy, 1 part Cinnamon Schnapps
splash Hot Sauce *(Mix into Small Rocks Glass—ice)*

FIRECRACKER (2)-
1 part Raspberry Liqueur, 1 part Vodka
Sour Mix *(Mix into Highball Glass—ice)*

FIRECRACKER (3)-
1 part Raspberry Liqueur, 1 part Tequila
Sour Mix *(Mix into Highball Glass—ice)*

FIRECRACKER (4)-
1 part Blended Whiskey, 1 part Raspberry Liqueur
Sour Mix *(Mix into Highball Glass—ice)*

FIREMAN'S SOUR-
Light Rum
Sour Mix, Grenadine, splash Club Soda *(Mix into Sour Glass— ice)*

FIRESTORM-
1 part Cinnamon Schnapps, 1 part Peppermint Schnapps,
    1 part 151-proof Rum
(Mix into Small Rocks Glass—ice)

FIRST LOVE-
2 parts Champagne, 1 part Gin, splash Cherry Liqueur
Sugar *(Mix into Cocktail Glass—no ice)*

FIRST NIGHTER-
Gin, splash Cherry Liqueur, splash White Dubonnet®, fill Sparkling Wine
(Mix into Highball Glass—ice)

FIVE BEFORE FLYING-
1 part Banana Liqueur, 1 part Bourbon Whiskey, 1 part Southern Comfort®,
    splash Brandy, splash White Crème de Caçao
Coffee, splash Light Cream or Milk, top Whipped Cream
(Mix in Irish Coffee Cup—no ice)

FIX (GENERIC)-
(Any Liqueur)
Water, Sour Mix *(Mix into Highball Glass—ice)*

FJORD-
2 parts Brandy, 1 part Aquavit
Orange Juice, Lime Juice, splash Grenadine
(Mix into Cocktail Glass—no ice)

FLAG-
splash Crème de Yvette, 1 part Apricot Brandy with splash Triple Sec (mixed), 1 part Red Wine *(Layer in Order in Cocktail Glass—no ice)*

FLAME THROWER-
1 part Brown Crème de Caçao, 1 part Bénédictine *(Layer in Order in Cocktail Glass—no ice)*

FLAMING ARMADILLO-
1 part Tequila, 1 part Amaretto, 1 part 151-proof Rum (ignite, optional) {extinguish flame before drinking} *(Layer in Order in Cocktail Glass—no ice)*

FLAMING ASSHOLE-
1 part Blueberry Brandy, 1 part 151 proof-proof Rum, 1 part Tequila *(Cocktail Glass with no ice)*

FLAMING BLUE F**K-
1 part Sambuca, 1 part Blue Curaçao (ignite, optional) (drink through straw) {extinguish flame before drinking} *(Layer in Order in Cocktail Glass—no ice)*

FLAMING COCAINE-
1 part Cinnamon Schnapps, 1 part Vodka Cranberry Juice *(Mix into Highball Glass—ice)*

FLAMING DIAMOND-
1 part Strawberry Schnapps, 1 part Peppermint Schnapps, 1 part Grand Marnier® *(Layer in Order in Cocktail Glass—no ice)*

FLAMING DOCTOR PEPPER-
1 part Amaretto, 1 part Light Rum *(Layer in Order in Shot Glass)*, 12 oz. Beer (ignite, optional) {extinguish flame before drinking} *(drop Shot Glass into Mug of Beer)*

FLAMING ORGASM-
1 part 151 part-proof Rum, 12 oz. Lager *(Drop Rum in Shot Glass into Mug of Beer)*

FLAMING ORGY-
1 part Grenadine, 1 part Green Crème de Menthe, 1 part Brandy, 1 part Tequila *(Layer in Order in Cocktail Glass—no ice)*

FLAMINGO-
3 parts Gin, 1 part Apricot Brandy Lime Juice, Grenadine *(Mix into Cocktail Glass—no ice)*

FLEET STREET-
3 parts Gin, 1 part Sweet Vermouth, splash Dry Vermouth, splash Triple Sec splash Lime Juice *(Mix into Cocktail Glass—no ice)*

FLIM FLAM-
2 parts Light Rum, 1 part Triple Sec Orange Juice, Lime Juice *(Mix into Cocktail Glass—no ice)*

FLINTLOCK-
3 parts Bourbon Whiskey, 1 part Apple Brandy, splash Peppermint Schnapps
splash Lime Juice, splash Grenadine *(Mix into Cocktail Glass—no ice)*

FLINTSTONE-
3 parts Bourbon Whiskey, 1 part Apple Brandy, 1 part Peppermint Schnapps
splash Lime Juice, splash Grenadine *(Mix into Cocktail Glass—no ice)*

FLIP (GENERIC)-
(Any Liqueur)
Light Cream or Milk, Sugar *(Mix into Highball Glass—ice)*

FLIPPER-
2 parts Gin, 1 part Amaretto, splash Campari, splash Dry Vermouth
(Mix into Cocktail Glass—no ice)

FLIRTING WITH THE SANDPIPER-
3 parts Light Rum, 1 part Cherry Brandy
Orange Juice, splash Orange Bitters *(Mix into Highball Glass—ice)*

FLORADORA COOLER-
Gin
Club Soda, Sour Mix, Grenadine *(Mix into Highball Glass—ice)*

FLORIDA-
Gin, splash Cherry Brandy, splash Triple Sec
Orange Juice, Lime Juice *(Mix into Cocktail Glass—no ice)*

FLORIDA BANANA-
2 parts Vodka, 1 part Banana Liqueur, 1 part Coconut Liqueur
Orange Juice, Banana Garnish
(Mix into Highball Glass with ice or blend with ice in Daiquiri Glass)

FLORIDA DAIQUIRI-
4 parts Dark Rum, 1 part Cherry Brandy
Grapefruit Juice, Sour Mix *(Blend with ice in Daiquiri Glass)*

FLORIDA FREEZE-
1 part Coconut Rum, 1 part Dark Rum
Pineapple Juice, Orange Juice *(Blend with ice in Daiquiri Glass)*

FLORIDA GATOR-
3 parts Gold Rum, 1 part Maraschino Liqueur, 1 part Triple Sec
Orange Juice *(Mix into Cocktail Glass—no ice)*

FLORIDA PUNCH-
4 parts Dark Rum, 1 part Cognac
Grapefruit Juice, Orange Juice *(Mix into Highball Glass—ice)*

FLORIDA STONE SOUR-
1 part Amaretto, 1 part Hazelnut Liqueur
Orange Juice, Sour Mix *(Mix into Highball Glass—ice)*

FLYING DUTCHMAN-
Gin, splash Triple Sec *(Mix into Small Rocks Glass—ice)*

FLYING F**K-
1 part Sambuca, 1 part Sour Mash Whiskey
(Layer in Order in Cocktail Glass—no ice)

FLYING GRASSHOPPER-
1 part Green Crème de Menthe, 1 part Vodka, 1 part White Crème de Menthe
(Mix into Cocktail Glass—no ice)

FLYING HORSE-
2 parts Vodka, 1 part Cherry Brandy
Light Cream or Milk
(Mix into Highball Glass—ice)

FLYING KANGAROO-
1 part Coconut Rum, 1 part Vodka, splash Galliano®
Orange Juice, Pineapple Juice, splash Light Cream or Milk
(Mix into Highball Glass—ice)

FLYING MONKEY-
1 part Coffee Liqueur, 1 part Banana Liqueur, 1 part Irish Cream Liqueur
(Layer in Order in Cocktail Glass—no ice)

FLYING SAUCER-
2 parts Light Rum, 1 part Citrus Rum, 1 part Dry Vermouth
splash Grenadine *(Mix into Cocktail Glass—no ice)*

FLYING SCOTCHMAN-
1 part Scotch Whiskey, 1 part Sweet Vermouth
Bitters, Sugar *(Mix into Cocktail Glass—no ice)*

FOCAL POINT-
1 part Light Rum, 1 part Melon Liqueur
splash Lime Juice, splash Grenadine (lace) *(Mix into Cocktail Glass—no ice)*

FOG CITY BLUES-
3 parts Blue Curaçao, 1 part White Crème de Caçao
Light Cream or Milk *(Mix into Cocktail Glass—no ice)*

FOG CUTTER (1)-
3 parts Light Rum, 1 part Brandy, 1 part Gin, 1 part Sweet Sherry (lace)
Orange Juice, Lime Juice, splash Orgeat (Almond) Syrup (optional)
(Mix into Highball Glass—ice)

FOG CUTTER (2)-
1 part Brandy, 1 part Gin, 1 part Light Rum
Pineapple Juice, Sour Mix
(Mix into Highball Glass—ice)

FOG HORN (1)-
Gin
Lime Juice, Ginger Ale *(Mix into Highball Glass—ice)*

FOG HORN (2)-
2 parts Brandy, 1 part Blue Curaçao
sprinkle Nutmeg *(Mix into Cocktail Glass—no ice)*

FOG HORN (3)-
2 parts Brandy, 1 part Triple Sec
sprinkle Nutmeg *(Mix into Cocktail Glass—no ice)*

FOGGY AFTERNOON-
2 parts Vodka, 1 part Apricot Brandy, 1 part Triple Sec, splash Banana Liqueur
splash Lime Juice, Cherry Garnish *(Mix into Cocktail Glass—no ice)*

FOGGY DAY-
1 part Gin, 1 part Licorice Liqueur *(Mix into Small Rocks Glass—ice)*

FONDLING FOOL-
3 parts Brandy, 2 parts Madeira Wine, 1 part Triple Sec
(Mix into Cocktail Glass—no ice)

FONTAINEBLEAU SPECIAL-
2 parts Anisette, 2 parts Brandy, 1 part Dry Vermouth
(Mix into Cocktail Glass—no ice)

FOOL'S GOLD-
1 part Galliano®, 1 part Vodka *(Mix into Small Rocks Glass—ice)*

FORBIDDEN JUNGLE-
3 parts Coconut Rum, 1 part Peach Schnapps
Pineapple Juice, splash Lime Juice, splash Grenadine
(Mix into Highball Glass—ice)

FOREIGN AFFAIR-
2 parts Cognac, 1 part Anisette
(Mix into Cocktail Glass—no ice)

FORESTER-
1 part Bourbon Whiskey, 1 part Maraschino Liqueur
Lime Juice *(Mix into Small Rocks Glass—ice)*

FORNICATION-
1 part Irish Cream Liqueur, 1 part Tia Maria®
(Layer in Order in Cocktail Glass—no ice)

FORT LAUDERDALE-
3 parts Light Rum, 1 part Sweet Vermouth
Orange Juice, Lime Juice *(Mix into Small Rocks Glass—ice)*

FORTY-FORTH (44TH) STREET-
1 part Brandy, 1 part Dark Rum
Sour Mix *(Mix into Cocktail Glass—no ice)*

FOUR LEAF CLOVER-
1 part Green Crème de Menthe, 1 part Irish Whiskey
Light Cream or Milk *(Mix into Highball Glass—ice)*

FOUR WHEELER-
Dark Rum
Orange Juice, Pineapple Juice, Coconut Milk
(Blend with ice in Daiquiri Glass)

FOURTH DEGREE-
1 part Dry Vermouth, 1 part Gin, 1 part Sweet Vermouth,
    splash Licorice Liqueur *(Mix into Cocktail Glass—no ice)*

FOURTH (4TH) OF JULY (1)-
1 part Grenadine, 2 parts Blue Curaçao, 2 parts Light Rum
(Layer in Order in Cocktail Glass—no ice)

FOURTH (4TH) OF JULY (2)-
1 part Grenadine, 2 parts Vodka, 2 parts Blue Curaçao
(Layer in Order in Cocktail Glass—no ice)

FOURTH (4TH) OF JULY TOOTER-
1 part Grenadine, 1 part Vodka, 1 part Blue Curaçao
(Layer in Order in Cocktail Glass—no ice)

FOX & HOUNDS-
3 parts Bourbon Whiskey, 1 part Licorice Liqueur
Sour Mix *(Mix into Cocktail Glass—no ice)*

FOX HOUND-
Brandy, splash Kümmel
Cranberry Juice, splash Lime Juice *(Mix into Highball Glass—ice)*

FOX RIVER-
Rye Whiskey, splash Brown Crème de Caçao
Bitters *(Mix into Cocktail Glass—no ice)*

FOX TAIL-
Sambuca
Light Cream or Milk (float), sprinkle Instant Coffee Grinds
(Mix into Cocktail Glass—no ice)

FOX TROT (1)-
Dark Rum, splash Triple Sec
Sour Mix *(Mix into Cocktail Glass—no ice)*

FOX TROT (2)-
Light Rum, splash Triple Sec
Lime Juice *(Mix into Small Rocks Glass—ice)*

FOXY LADY-
2 parts Amaretto, 1 part Brown Crème de Caçao
Light Cream or Milk *(Mix into Highball Glass—ice)*

FRAISE FIZZ-
2 parts Gin, 1 part Strawberry Schnapps
Sour Mix, splash Club Soda *(Mix into Highball Glass—ice)*

FRANKENJACK-
2 parts Gin, 1 part Apricot Brandy, 1 part Dry Vermouth, splash Triple Sec
(Mix into Cocktail Glass—no ice)

FRAPPE-
(Any Liqueur)
(Blend with ice in Daiquiri Glass)

FRAZZLED STRAWBERRY-
Strawberry Schnapps
Ginger Ale *(Mix into Highball Glass—ice)*

FRED'S SPECIAL-
Rye Whiskey
Lime Juice, fill Cola *(Mix into Highball Glass—ice)*

FREDDY FUDPUCKER-
Tequila, splash Galliano® (float)
Orange Juice *(Mix into Highball Glass—ice)*

FREE SILVER-
3 parts Gin, 1 part Dark Rum
Sour Mix, splash Light Cream or Milk, Club Soda
(Mix into Highball Glass—ice)

FREEBASE-
1 part Coffee Liqueur, 1 part Light Rum, 1 part Dark Rum, 1 part 151-proof
   Rum (float) *(Mix into Cocktail Glass—no ice)*

FREIGHT TRAIN-
1 part Sour Mash Whiskey, 1 part Tequila *(Mix into Small Rocks Glass—ice)*

FRENCH "75"-
1 part Gin, fill Champagne
Sour Mix *(Mix in Champagne Flute—no ice)*

FRENCH "125"-
1 part Brandy, fill Champagne
Sour Mix *(Mix in Champagne Flute—no ice)*

FRENCH COFFEE-
Grand Marnier®
Coffee, top Whipped Cream
(Mix in Irish Coffee Cup—no ice)

FRENCH COLADA-
2 parts Light Rum, 1 part Cognac, splash Crème de Cassis
Pineapple Juice, Coconut Milk
(Mix into Highball Glass with ice or blend with ice in Daiquiri Glass)

FRENCH CONNECTION (1)-
1 part Cognac, 1 part Grand Marnier® *(Mix into Cocktail Glass—no ice)*

FRENCH CONNECTION (2)-
2 parts Cognac, 1 part Amaretto *(Mix into Small Rocks Glass—ice)*

FRENCH CONNECTION (3)-
2 parts Brandy, 1 part Amaretto *(Mix into Small Rocks Glass—ice)*

FRENCH CURVE-
White Wine, splash Maraschino Liqueur, splash Licorice Liqueur
Lemon Garnish, Orange Garnish
(Mix into Wine Glass—ice)

FRENCH DAIQUIRI-
  Light Rum, splash Crème de Cassis
  Sour Mix *(Blend with ice in Daiquiri Glass)*

FRENCH DREAM-
  3 parts Irish Cream Liqueur, 1 part Raspberry Liqueur
  (Mix into Cocktail Glass—no ice)

FRENCH FANTASY-
  1 part Black Raspberry Liqueur, 1 part Grand Marnier®
  Orange Juice, Cranberry Juice *(Mix into Highball Glass—ice)*

FRENCH GREEN DRAGON-
  1 part Cognac, 1 part Green Chartreuse *(Mix into Small Rocks Glass—ice)*

FRENCH KISS (1)-
  1 part Dry Vermouth, 1 part Sweet Vermouth *(Mix into Cocktail Glass—no ice)*

FRENCH KISS (2)-
  2 parts Bourbon Liqueur, 1 part Apricot Brandy
  splash Lime Juice, splash Grenadine *(Mix into Cocktail Glass—no ice)*

FRENCH MARTINI-
  1 part Black Raspberry Liqueur, 1 part Vodka *(Mix into Cocktail Glass—no ice)*

FRENCH REVOLUTION-
  4 parts Brandy, 1 part Raspberry Liqueur, fill Champagne
  (Mix in Champagne Flute—no ice)

FRENCH ROSE-
  1 part Cherry Liqueur, 1 part Gin *(Mix into Cocktail Glass—no ice)*

FRENCH SUMMER, THE-
  Raspberry Liqueur
  Club Soda *(Mix into Highball Glass—ice)*

FRENCH TICKLER-
  1 part Goldschläger®, 1 part Grand Marnier® *(Mix into Cocktail Glass—no ice)*

FRENCH TOAST-
  1 part Butterscotch Schnapps, 1 part Cinnamon Schnapps, 1 part Irish Cream
    Liqueur *(Mix into Cocktail Glass—no ice)*

FRIAR TUCK-
  Hazelnut Liqueur, splash Brandy
  Lime Juice, splash Grenadine *(Mix into Cocktail Glass—no ice)*

FRIAR'S COFFEE-
  Bénédictine
  Coffee, Sugar, top Whipped Cream *(Mix in Irish Coffee Cup—no ice)*

FRIDAY-
  Light Rum
  Orange Juice or Mango Juice, splash Lime Juice
  (Mix into Highball Glass with ice or blend with ice in Daiquiri Glass)

FRIGHTLEBERRY MURZENQUEST-
2 parts Vodka, 1 part Galliano®, 1 part Triple Sec, splash Maraschino Liqueur
Lime Juice, splash Bitters
(Mix into Cocktail Glass—no ice)

FRIGID HAIRY VIRGIN-
2 parts Light Rum, 1 part Triple Sec
Pineapple Juice
(Mix into Highball Glass with ice or blend with ice in Daiquiri Glass)

FRISCO-
3 parts Blended Whiskey, 1 part Bénédictine
Lime Juice *(Mix into Cocktail Glass—no ice)*

FRISCO SOUR-
4 parts Blended Whiskey, 1 part Bénédictine
Sour Mix *(Mix into Sour Glass— ice)*

FRISKY WITCH-
1 part Sambuca, 1 part Vodka
Black Licorice Stick Garnish
(Mix into Small Rocks Glass—ice)

FROBISHER-
1 part Gin, fill Champagne
splash Bitters *(Mix in Champagne Flute—no ice)*

FROG LICK-
1 part Vodka, 1 part Yukon Jack® Canadian Liqueur
Lime Juice *(Mix into Small Rocks Glass—ice)*

FROOT LOOP-
2 parts Apple Brandy, 1 part Cherry Brandy, 1 part Vodka
Orange Juice *(Mix into Highball Glass—ice)*

FROST HEAVES-
1 part Jägermeister®, 1 part Yukon Jack® Perma Frost Schnapps
(Mix into Small Rocks Glass—ice)

FROSTBITE-
4 parts Tequila, 1 part White Crème de Caçao, splash Blue Curaçao
Light Cream or Milk
(Mix into Highball Glass with ice or blend with ice in Daiquiri Glass)

FROSTY NOGGIN-
3 parts Light Rum, 1 part White Crème de Menthe
Eggnog, Vanilla Ice Cream, top Whipped Cream
(Blend with ice in Daiquiri Glass)

FROUPE-
1 part Brandy, 1 part Sweet Vermouth, splash Bénédictine
(Mix into Cocktail Glass—no ice)

FROZEN APPLE-
Apple Schnapps
Sour Mix *(Blend with ice in Daiquiri Glass)*

FROZEN BERKELEY-
3 parts Light Rum, 1 part Brandy
Passion Fruit Juice, Lime Juice *(Blend with ice in Daiquiri Glass)*

FROZEN BIKINI-
2 parts Vodka, 1 part Peach Schnapps, fill Champagne
Orange Juice, Peach Juice, splash Sour Mix *(Blend with ice in Daiquiri Glass)*

FROZEN BRANDY & RUM-
1 part Brandy, 1 part Light Rum
Sour Mix *(Blend with ice in Daiquiri Glass)*

FROZEN CITRON NEON-
3 parts Citrus Vodka, 2 parts Melon Liqueur, 1 part Blue Curaçao
Sour Mix *(Blend with ice in Daiquiri Glass)*

FROZEN CRAN RAZZ-
2 parts Tequila, 1 part DeKuyper® Razzmatazz Black Raspberry Liqueur
Cranberry Juice, splash Sour Mix *(Blend with ice in Daiquiri Glass)*

FROZEN DAIQUIRI-
Light Rum, splash Triple Sec (optional)
Sour Mix *(Blend with ice in Daiquiri Glass)*

FROZEN FUZZY-
2 parts Peach Schnapps, 1 part Triple Sec
Lime Juice, Grenadine, splash Lemon-Lime Soda
(Blend with ice in Daiquiri Glass)

FROZEN MARGARITA-
3 parts Tequila, 1 part Triple Sec
Sour Mix *(Blend with ice in Daiquiri Glass)*

FROZEN MATADOR-
Tequila
Pineapple Juice, splash Lime Juice *(Blend with ice in Daiquiri Glass)*

FROZEN MINT DAIQUIRI-
Light Rum
Sour Mix, Mint Leaves *(Blend with ice in Daiquiri Glass)*

FROZEN PINEAPPLE DAIQUIRI-
Light Rum
Pineapple Slices, Sour Mix *(Blend with ice in Daiquiri Glass)*

FROZEN SNOWBALL-
2 parts Gin, 1 part Sambuca, 1 part White Crème de Menthe
Light Cream or Milk *(Blend with ice in Daiquiri Glass)*

FRU-FRU-
1 part Banana Liqueur, 1 part Peach Schnapps
Pineapple Juice, Lime Juice *(Mix into Highball Glass—ice)*

FRUIT DAIQUIRI-
2 parts Light Rum, 1 part White Crème de Caçao, 1 part (Fruit Liqueurs)
Fruit, splash Sour Mix *(Blend with ice in Daiquiri Glass)*

FRUIT LOOP (1)-
1 part Amaretto, 1 part Blue Curaçao
Grenadine, Light Cream or Milk
(Mix into Highball Glass—ice)

FRUIT LOOP (2)-
Citrus Rum
Cranberry Juice, Pineapple Juice *(Mix into Highball Glass—ice)*

FRUIT MARGARITA-
2 parts Tequila, 1 part Triple Sec, 1 part (Fruit Liqueurs)
Sour Mix *(Mix into Cocktail Glass—no ice)*

FRUIT MARGARITA (FROZEN)-
2 parts Tequila, 1 part Triple Sec, 1 part (Fruit Liqueurs)
Fruit, splash Sour Mix *(Blend with ice in Daiquiri Glass)*

FRUIT OF THE LOOM-
1 part Apple Schnapps, 1 part Peach Schnapps
Cranberry Juice *(Mix into Highball Glass—ice)*

FRUIT RUM FRAPPE-
2 parts Light Rum, 1 part Banana Liqueur, 1 part Crème de Cassis
Orange Juice *(Blend with ice in Daiquiri Glass)*

FRUITY SMASH-
1 part Banana Liqueur, 1 part Cherry Brandy
Vanilla Ice Cream *(Blend with ice in Daiquiri Glass)*

FRUITY ZIMA-
Zima®, splash Raspberry Liqueur *(Mix into Highball Glass—ice)*

FUNKY MONKEY-
1 part Coffee Liqueur, 1 part Irish Cream Liqueur, 1 part Peach Schnapps
(Mix into Cocktail Glass—no ice)

FURLONG TOO LATE, A-
1 part Light Rum, fill Ginger Beer *(Beer Mug)*

FUSION COSMO-
3 parts Vodka, 1 part Triple Sec
Cranberry Juice, splash Lime Juice
(Mix into Cocktail Glass—no ice)

FUZZY ASTRONAUT-
1 part Peach Schnapps, 1 part Vodka
Tang® Mix *(Mix into Highball Glass—ice)*

FUZZY BALLS-
1 part Melon Liqueur, 1 part Peach Schnapps, 1 part Vodka
Cranberry Juice, Grapefruit Juice *(Mix into Highball Glass—ice)*

FUZZY BROTHER-
3 parts Brandy, 1 part Peach Schnapps
Orange Juice *(Mix into Highball Glass—ice)*

FUZZY CHARLIE (1)-
2 parts Coconut Rum, 2 parts Spiced Rum, 1 part Peach Schnapps
Orange Juice *(Mix into Highball Glass—ice)*

FUZZY CHARLIE (2)-
3 parts Dark Rum, 1 part Banana Liqueur, 1 part Coconut Rum
Pineapple Juice, top Ginger Ale
(Mix into Highball Glass—ice)

FUZZY DICK-
1 part Coffee Liqueur, 1 part Grand Marnier®
Coffee, top Whipped Cream
(Mix in Irish Coffee Cup—no ice)

FUZZY FRUIT-
Peach Schnapps
Grapefruit Juice *(Mix into Highball Glass—ice)*

FUZZY IRISHMAN-
1 part Raspberry Liqueur, 1 part Butterscotch Schnapps, 1 part Irish Cream
Liqueur *(Layer in Order in Cocktail Glass—no ice)*

FUZZY MEXICAN
1 part Peach Schnapps, 1 part Tequila
Orange Juice
(Mix into Highball Glass—ice)

FUZZY MONKEY-
1 part Banana Liqueur, 1 part Peach Schnapps, 1 part Vodka
Orange Juice *(Mix into Highball Glass—ice)*

FUZZY MOTHER-
1 part Tequila, 1 part 151-proof Rum (lace) (ignite, optional) {extinguish flame
before drinking}
(Mix into Cocktail Glass—no ice)

FUZZY NAVEL-
Peach Schnapps
Orange Juice *(Mix into Highball Glass—ice)*

FUZZY NUT-
4 parts Peach Schnapps, 1 part Amaretto
Hot Chocolate, top Whipped Cream *(Mix in Irish Coffee Cup—no ice)*

FUZZY PISSBOMB-
Peach Schnapps
Mountain Dew® *(Mix into Highball Glass—ice)*

FUZZY SCREW-
1 part Peach Schnapps, 1 part Vodka
Orange Juice *(Mix into Highball Glass—ice)*

FUZZY SCREW AGAINST THE WALL-
1 part Peach Schnapps, 1 part Vodka, splash Galliano® (top)
Orange Juice *(Mix into Highball Glass—ice)*

FUZZY WUZZY-
1 part Peach Schnapps, 1 part Vodka
Orange Juice *(Mix into Highball Glass—ice)*

FUZZY ZIMA-
Peach Schnapps, fill Zima® *(Mix into Highball Glass—ice)*

– NOTES –

G4-
1 part Amaretto, 1 part Irish Cream Liqueur
(Layer in order in Cocktail Glass—no ice)

G. & C.-
1 part Cognac, 1 part Galliano® *(Mix into Cocktail Glass—no ice)*

G-BOY-
1 part Grand Marnier®, 1 part Hazelnut Liqueur, 1 part Irish Cream Liqueur
(Mix into Cocktail Glass—no ice)

G-SPOT-
1 part Southern Comfort®, 1 part Peach Schnapps
Orange Juice *(Mix into Highball Glass—ice)*

G-STRING-
Vodka, splash Brown Crème de Caçao
splash Light Cream or Milk *(Mix into Cocktail Glass—no ice)*

G. T. O.-
1 part Amaretto, 1 part Gin, 1 part Light Rum, 1 part Southern Comfort®,
1 part Vodka
Orange Juice, splash Grenadine *(Mix into Highball Glass—ice)*

GABLES COLLINS-
1 part Crème de Noyaux, 1 part Vodka
Club Soda, splash Lime Juice, splash Pineapple Juice
(Mix into Highball Glass—ice)

GADZOOKS-
1 part Apricot Brandy, 1 part Dry Vermouth, 1 part Gin, splash Cherry Brandy
splash Lime Juice *(Mix into Cocktail Glass—no ice)*

GAELIC COFFEE-
2 parts Brown Crème de Caçao, 1 part Irish Cream Liqueur,
1 part Irish Whiskey
Coffee, splash Light Cream or Milk, top Whipped Cream
(Mix into Irish Coffee Cup—no ice)

GALACTIC ALE-
3 parts Blue Curaçao, 3 parts Vodka, 1 part Black Raspberry Liqueur
Lime Juice *(Mix into Cocktail Glass—no ice)*

GALATOIRES GLORY-
2 parts Southern Comfort®, 1 part Brandy
Lime Juice, splash Grenadine *(Mix into Cocktail Glass—no ice)*

GALE AT SEA-
3 parts Vodka, 1 part Blue Curaçao, 1 part Dry Vermouth, 1 part Galliano®
(Mix into Cocktail Glass—no ice)

GALE FORCE-
2 parts Gin, 1 part Gold Rum, splash 151-proof Rum
Orange Juice, splash Lime Juice
(Mix into Highball Glass—ice)

GALLIANO HOT SHOT-
Galliano®
Coffee, top Whipped Cream *(Mix into Irish Coffee Cup—no ice)*

GALWAY BAY-
1 part Coffee Liqueur, 1 part Irish Cream Liqueur, 1 part Peppermint Schnapps
Light Cream or Milk
(Mix into Highball Glass with ice or blend with ice in Daiquiri Glass)

GALWAY GREY-
2 parts Vodka, 1 part Triple Sec, 1 part White Crème de Caçao
Light Cream or Milk, Lime Juice *(Mix into Highball Glass—ice)*

GARETH GLOWWORM-
3 parts Light Rum, 1 part White Crème de Caçao, splash Cherry Brandy (lace)
Light Cream or Milk *(Mix into Cocktail Glass—no ice)*

GASPER-
1 part Apricot Brandy, 1 part Gin *(Mix into Cocktail Glass—no ice)*

GATES OF HELL-
Tequila, splash Cherry Brandy (lace)
Lime Juice *(Mix into Small Rocks Glass—ice)*

GAUGUIN-
Light Rum
Passion Fruit Juice, Lime Juice *(Mix into Small Rocks Glass—ice)*

GAULT'S GUMPTION-
3 parts Canadian Whiskey, 1 part Peach Schnapps, splash Sweet Vermouth
(Mix into Cocktail Glass—no ice)

GAZETTE-
2 parts Brandy, 1 part Sweet Vermouth
Sour Mix *(Mix into Cocktail Glass—no ice)*

GEISHA-
2 parts Bourbon Whiskey, 1 part Sake
Sour Mix *(Mix into Highball Glass—ice)*

GENE SPLICE-
1 part Raspberry Liqueur, 1 part Tequila, 1 part Vodka
Lime Juice, Pineapple Juice *(Mix into Highball Glass—ice)*

GENERAL HARRISON'S EGGNOG-
Red Wine
Sugar, sprinkle Nutmeg *(Mix into Wine Glass—no ice)*

GENEVA CONVENTION-
4 parts Vodka, 1 part 100-proof Vodka, 1 part Goldschläger®
(Mix into Cocktail Glass—no ice)

GENEVA SUMMIT-
1 part Southern Comfort®, 1 part Vodka, splash Peppermint Schnapps
Orange Juice, Lime Juice, splash Lemon-Lime Soda (top)
(Mix into Highball Glass—ice)

GENOA-
2 parts Vodka, 1 part Campari
Orange Juice *(Mix into Highball Glass—ice)*

GENT OF THE JURY-
4 parts Gin, 1 part Cherry Brandy
Pineapple Juice, splash Lime Juice, splash Grenadine
(Mix into Highball Glass—ice)

GENTLE BEN-
1 part Gin, 1 part Tequila, 1 part Vodka
Orange Juice *(Mix into Highball Glass—ice)*

GENTLE BULL-
2 parts Tequila, 1 part Coffee Liqueur
Light Cream or Milk *(Mix into Highball Glass—ice)*

GENTLEMAN'S CLUB-
1 part Brandy, 1 part Gin, 1 part Sweet Vermouth
Club Soda *(Mix into Highball Glass—ice)*

GENTLEMAN'S COCKTAIL-
2 parts Bourbon Whiskey, 1 part Brandy, 1 part White Crème de Menthe
Club Soda *(Mix into Highball Glass—ice)*

GENTLEMAN'S TODDY-
1 part Jamaican Rum, 1 part Puerto Rican Rum
Hot Water, Sour Mix *(Mix into Irish Coffee Cup—no ice)*

GEORGIA MINT JULEP-
1 part Brandy, 1 part Peach Brandy
Sugar, Mint Leaves, muddle *(Mix into Highball Glass—ice)*

GEORGIA PEACH (1)-
3 parts Vodka, 1 part Peach Schnapps
Lemonade, splash Grenadine *(Mix into Highball Glass—ice)*

GEORGIA PEACH (2)-
2 parts Vodka, 1 part Peach Brandy
Peach Juice, splash Lime Juice *(Mix into Highball Glass—ice)*

GEORGIA PEACH FIZZ-
3 parts Brandy, 1 part Peach Brandy, splash Banana Liqueur
Sour Mix, splash Club Soda
(Mix into Highball Glass—ice)

GEORGIAN SUNRISE-
3 parts Tequila, 1 part Peach Schnapps, 1 part Strawberry Schnapps
Sour Mix *(Mix into Highball Glass—ice)*

GERALDINE-
3 parts Canadian Whiskey, 1 part Red Dubonnet®, 1 part Yellow Chartreuse, splash Dry Vermouth
splash Bitters
(Mix into Cocktail Glass—no ice)

GERRY FORD-
2 parts Brandy, 1 part Aquavit
Orange Juice, Lime Juice, splash Grenadine *(Mix into Cocktail Glass—no ice)*

GET LAID-
2 parts Vodka, 1 part Raspberry Liqueur
Pineapple Juice, splash Cranberry Juice *(Mix into Highball Glass—ice)*

GHETTO BLASTER-
1 part Coffee Liqueur, 1 part Metaxa, 1 part Tequila, 1 part Rye Whiskey
(Layer in Order in Cocktail Glass—no ice)

GHOSTBUSTER-
1 part Coffee Liqueur, 1 part Irish Cream Liqueur, 1 part Vodka
(Mix into Small Rocks Glass—ice)

GIBSON-
Gin or Vodka, splash Vermouth
Onion Garnish *(Mix into Cocktail Glass—no ice)*

GILLIGAN'S ISLAND-
3 parts Light Rum, 1 part Maraschino Liqueur
Grapefruit Juice, Lime Juice *(Mix into Cocktail Glass—no ice)*

GILROY-
Cherry Brandy, splash Dry Vermouth
Lime Juice, splash Orange Bitters *(Mix into Cocktail Glass—no ice)*

GIMLET-
Gin or Vodka
splash Lime Juice *(Mix into Cocktail Glass—no ice)*

GIMLEY-
Gin or Vodka
splash Sour Mix *(Mix into Cocktail Glass—no ice)*

GIN & BERRIES-
4 parts Gin, 1 part Strawberry Liqueur
splash Sour Mix, Strawberry Daiquiri Mix, top Club Soda
(Blend with ice in Daiquiri Glass)

GIN & IT-
2 parts Gin, 1 part Sweet Vermouth *(Mix into Cocktail Glass—no ice)*

GIN & SIN-
Gin
Lime Juice, Orange Juice, Grenadine *(Mix into Cocktail Glass—no ice)*

GIN & TONIC-
Gin
Tonic Water *(Mix into Highball Glass—ice)*

GIN ALEXANDER-
1 part Brown Crème de Caçao, 1 part Gin
Light Cream or Milk, sprinkle Nutmeg or Cinnamon
(Mix into Cocktail Glass—no ice)

GIN ALOHA-
1 part Gin, 1 part Triple Sec
Pineapple Juice, Orange Bitters
(Mix into Cocktail Glass—no ice)

GIN BUCK-
Gin
Lime Juice, Ginger Ale *(Mix into Small Rocks Glass—ice)*

GIN CASSIS-
3 parts Gin, 1 part Crème de Cassis
Lime Juice *(Mix into Highball Glass—ice)*

GIN COBBLER-
Gin
Club Soda, Sugar *(Mix into Highball Glass—ice)*

GIN COCKTAIL-
Gin
splash Bitters *(Mix into Cocktail Glass—no ice)*

GIN COOLER-
Gin
Club Soda, Sugar, fill Ginger Ale
(Mix into Highball Glass—ice)

GIN DAIQUIRI-
3 parts Gin, 1 part Light Rum
Sour Mix
(Mix into Cocktail Glass with no ice or blend with ice in Daiquiri Glass)

GIN DAISY-
Gin
Sour Mix, splash Grenadine *(Mix into Highball Glass—ice)*

GIN FIX-
Gin
Water, Sour Mix *(Mix into Highball Glass—ice)*

GIN FIZZ-
Gin
Sour Mix, splash Club Soda *(Mix into Highball Glass—ice)*

GIN HIGHBALL-
Gin
Club Soda or Ginger Ale *(Mix into Highball Glass—ice)*

GIN MILK PUNCH-
Gin
Light Cream or Milk, Sugar, sprinkle Nutmeg
(Mix into Highball Glass—ice)

GIN RICKEY-
Gin
Club Soda, splash Lime Juice *(Mix into Highball Glass—ice)*

GIN SANGAREE-
Gin, splash Port
Club Soda, Sugar, splash Water, sprinkle Nutmeg
(Mix into Highball Glass—ice)

GIN SIDECAR-
2 parts Gin, 1 part Triple Sec
Lime Juice *(Mix into Small Rocks Glass—ice)*

GIN SLING-
Gin
Water, Sour Mix *(Mix into Highball Glass—ice)*

GIN SMASH-
Gin
Club Soda, Sugar, Mint Leaves *(Mix into Small Rocks Glass—ice)*

GIN SOUR-
Gin
Sour Mix *(Mix into Sour Glass—ice)*

GIN SQUIRT-
Gin
Club Soda, Sugar, Grenadine *(Mix into Highball Glass—ice)*

GIN STINGER-
4 parts Gin, 1 part White Crème de Menthe *(Mix into Cocktail Glass—no ice)*

GIN SWIZZLE
Gin
Water, Sour Mix, Bitters *(Mix into Highball Glass—ice)*

GIN THING-
Gin
Lime Juice, Ginger Ale *(Mix into Highball Glass—ice)*

GIN TODDY-
Gin
Water, Sugar *(Mix into Small Rocks Glass—ice)*

GIN TODDY (HOT)-
Gin
Hot Water, Sugar, sprinkle Nutmeg *(Mix into Irish Coffee Cup—no ice)*

GINGER BEER-
12 oz. Dark Beer, top Ginger Brandy *(Beer Mug)*

GINGER BREEZE-
Light Rum, splash Cherry Brandy
Orange Juice, top Ginger Ale
(Mix into Highball Glass—ice)

GINGER COLADA-
2 parts Dark Rum, 1 part Coconut Rum, 1 part Ginger Brandy
Pineapple Juice *(Blend with ice in Daiquiri Glass)*

GINGER JOLT-
2 parts Blended Whiskey, 1 part Ginger Wine
fill Club Soda *(Mix into Highball Glass—ice)*

GINGER SNAP (1)-
3 parts Spiced Rum, 1 part Ginger Brandy
Eggnog, Ginger Snap Cookie
(Blend with ice in Daiquiri Glass)

GINGER SNAP (2)-
3 parts Vodka, 1 part Ginger Wine
fill Club Soda *(Mix into Highball Glass—ice)*

GINGERBREAD-
1 part Butterscotch Schnapps, 1 part Cinnamon Schnapps,
    1 part Irish Cream Liqueur
Light Cream or Milk *(Mix into Highball Glass—ice)*

GINGERBREAD MAN-
1 part Coffee Liqueur, 1 part Irish Cream Liqueur, 1 part Goldschläger®
(Layer in Order in Cocktail Glass with no ice)

GINZA MARY-
2 parts Vodka, 1 part Sake
Tomato Juice, splash Lime Juice, splash Soy Sauce, splash Hot Sauce, Pepper
(Mix into Highball Glass—ice)

GIRL MOM WARNED YOU ABOUT, THE-
1 part Grenadine, 1 part Triple Sec, 1 part Light Rum, 1 part Melon Liqueur,
    1 part Blue Curaçao
(Layer in Order in Cocktail Glass with no ice)

GIRL SCOUT COOKIE (1)-
2 parts Coffee Liqueur, 1 part Green Crème de Menthe
Light Cream or Milk *(Mix into Highball Glass—ice)*

GIRL SCOUT COOKIE (2)-
2 parts Coffee Liqueur, 1 part Peppermint Schnapps
Light Cream or Milk *(Mix into Highball Glass—ice)*

GIRL SCOUT COOKIE (3)-
1 part Brown Crème de Caçao, 1 part Green Crème de Menthe
Light Cream or Milk *(Mix into Highball Glass—ice)*

GIRL SCOUT COOKIE (4)-
1 part Coffee Liqueur, 1 part Irish Cream Liqueur, 1 part Peppermint Schnapps
(Mix into Cocktail Glass—no ice)

GLACIER MINT-
3 parts Vodka, 1 part Citrus Vodka, 1 part Green Crème de Menthe
(Mix into Cocktail Glass—no ice)

GLAD EYES-
3 parts Licorice Liqueur, 1 part Peppermint Schnapps
(Mix into Cocktail Glass—no ice)

GLADIATOR-
1 part Amaretto, 1 part Southern Comfort®
Orange Juice, top Lemon-Lime Soda *(Mix into Highball Glass—ice)*

GLADIATOR STINGER-
1 part Brandy, 1 part Peppermint Schnapps, 1 part Sambuca
(Mix into Cocktail Glass—no ice)

GLADYS DELIGHT-
Dry Vermouth, splash Sweet Vermouth
Ginger Ale, splash Grenadine *(Mix into Highball Glass—ice)*

GLASGOW-
Scotch Whiskey, splash Crème de Noyaux, splash Dry Vermouth
Lime Juice *(Mix into Small Rocks Glass—ice)*

GLASNOST-
4 parts Vodka, 1 part Peppermint Schnapps *(Mix into Cocktail Glass—no ice)*

GLASS TOWER-
2 parts Light Rum, 2 parts Peach Schnapps, 2 parts Triple Sec, 2 parts Vodka,
    1 part Sambuca
Lemon-Lime Soda *(Mix into Highball Glass—ice)*

GLITTER & TRASH-
Gin, splash Vodka
Lemon-Lime Soda *(Mix into Highball Glass—ice)*

GLOOM CHASER-
1 part Grand Marnier®, 1 part Triple Sec
Lime Juice, splash Grenadine *(Mix into Cocktail Glass—no ice)*

GLOOM LIFTER-
2 parts Blended Whiskey, 1 part Brandy, splash Raspberry Liqueur
Sour Mix *(Mix into Highball Glass—ice)*

GO FOR BROKE-
1 part Dry Vermouth, 1 part Gin, splash Triple Sec
splash Bitters *(Mix into Cocktail Glass—no ice)*

GO-GO JUICE-
1 part Blue Curaçao, 1 part Gin, 1 part Light Rum, 1 part Vodka, 1 part Tequila
Orange Juice, Sour Mix, top Lemon-Lime Soda *(Mix into Highball Glass—ice)*

GO GIRL!-
1 part Raspberry Liqueur, 1 part Vodka
splash Sour Mix, splash Club Soda *(Mix into Cocktail Glass—no ice)*

GODCHILD-
1 part Amaretto, 1 part Vodka
Light Cream or Milk *(Mix into Highball Glass—ice)*

GODFATHER-
2 parts Bourbon or Scotch Whiskey, 1 part Amaretto
(Mix into Small Rocks Glass—ice)

GODMOTHER (1)-
2 parts Vodka, 1 part Amaretto *(Mix into Small Rocks Glass—ice)*

GODMOTHER (2)-
2 parts Vodka, 1 part Coffee Liqueur *(Mix into Small Rocks Glass—ice)*

GOLD MARGARITA (1)-
3 parts Tequila, 1 part Grand Marnier®
Sour Mix *(Mix into Cocktail Glass—no ice)*

GOLD MARGARITA (2)-
3 parts Gold Tequila, 1 part Triple Sec
Lime Juice *(Mix into Cocktail Glass—no ice)*

GOLDEN APPLE CIDER-
Goldschläger®
Hot Apple Cider *(Mix into Irish Coffee Cup—no ice)*

GOLDEN BOY-
3 parts Bourbon Whiskey, 1 part Light Rum
Orange Juice, splash Sour Mix, Grenadine (lace)
(Mix into Cocktail Glass—no ice)

GOLDEN BRONX-
Gin, splash Dry Vermouth, splash Sweet Vermouth
splash Orange Juice *(Mix into Cocktail Glass—no ice)*

GOLDEN CADILLAC-
2 parts Galliano®, 1 part White Crème de Caçao
Light Cream or Milk *(Mix into Highball Glass—ice)*

GOLDEN CHAIN-
1 part Brandy, 1 part Triple Sec, splash Yellow Chartreuse
Lime Juice *(Mix into Cocktail Glass—no ice)*

GOLDEN DAWN (1)-
2 parts Apple Brandy, 1 part Apricot Brandy, 1 part Gin
Orange Juice, Grenadine *(Mix into Small Rocks Glass—ice)*

GOLDEN DAWN (2)-
Gin, splash Apricot Brandy
Orange Juice *(Mix into Cocktail Glass—no ice)*

GOLDEN DAZE-
3 parts Gin, 1 part Peach Brandy
Orange Juice *(Mix into Cocktail Glass—no ice)*

GOLDEN DRAGON-
2 parts Brandy, 1 part Yellow Chartreuse
(Mix into Cocktail Glass—no ice)

GOLDEN DREAM (1)-
2 parts Galliano®, 1 part White Crème de Caçao, splash Triple Sec
Orange Juice, Light Cream or Milk
(Mix into Highball Glass—ice)

GOLDEN DREAM (2)-
4 parts Galliano®, 1 part Triple Sec
splash Orange Juice, splash Light Cream or Milk
(Mix into Cocktail Glass—no ice)

GOLDEN FIZZ-
Gin
Sour Mix, splash Club Soda *(Mix into Highball Glass—ice)*

GOLDEN FRAPPE-
Port
Orange Juice, Sour Mix *(Mix into Highball Glass—ice)*

GOLDEN FRIENDSHIP-
1 part Amaretto, 1 part Light Rum, 1 part Sweet Vermouth
Ginger Ale *(Mix into Highball Glass—ice)*

GOLDEN FROG-
1 part Galliano®, 1 part Strega, 1 part Vodka
Lime Juice *(Mix into Cocktail Glass—no ice)*

GOLDEN GATE-
1 part Gin, 1 part Light Rum, 1 part White Crème de Caçao,
    splash 151-proof Rum
Lime Juice *(Mix into Highball Glass—ice)*

GOLDEN GLOW (1)-
2 parts Bourbon Whiskey, 1 part Dark Rum
Orange Juice, Sour Mix, splash Grenadine (float)
(Mix into Cocktail Glass—no ice)

GOLDEN GLOW (2)-
1 part Blackberry Brandy, 1 part Galliano®, 1 part Green Crème de Menthe
(Mix into Small Rocks Glass—ice)

GOLDEN HORNET-
4 parts Gin, 1 part Sherry, 1 part Scotch Whiskey (float)
(Mix into Cocktail Glass—no ice)

GOLDEN OLDIE-
2 parts Dark Rum, 1 part Banana Liqueur
Pineapple Juice *(Mix into Highball Glass—ice)*

GOLDEN PANTHER-
1 part Blended Whiskey, 1 part Brandy, 1 part Gin, splash Dry Vermouth
Orange Juice
(Mix into Highball Glass—ice)

GOLDEN ROOSTER-
4 parts Gin, 1 part Apricot Brandy, 1 part Dry Vermouth, 1 part Triple Sec
(Mix into Cocktail Glass—no ice)

GOLDEN SCREW-
Vodka
Orange Juice, splash Bitters *(Mix into Cocktail Glass—no ice)*

GOLDEN SLIPPER-
2 parts Apricot Brandy, 1 part Yellow Chartreuse
(Mix into Cocktail Glass—no ice)

GOLF COCKTAIL-
2 parts Gin, 1 part Dry Vermouth
splash Bitters *(Mix into Cocktail Glass—no ice)*

GONE TOMORROW-
Gin
splash Lime Juice (lace), Cherry Stem Garnish
(Mix into Small Rocks Glass—ice)

GOOBER-
1 part Black Raspberry Liqueur, 1 part Melon Liqueur, 1 part Triple Sec,
1 part Vodka
Orange Juice, Pineapple Juice, Grenadine
(Mix into Highball Glass—ice)

GOOD & PLENTY (1)-
1 part Anisette, 1 part Blackberry Brandy
(Mix into Cocktail Glass—no ice)

GOOD & PLENTY (2)-
1 part Anisette, 1 part Licorice Liqueur
(Mix into Cocktail Glass—no ice)

GOOD & PLENTY (3)-
1 part Coffee Liqueur, 1 part Vodka, splash Anisette
Vanilla Ice Cream *(Blend with ice in Daiquiri Glass)*

GOOD BYE-
1 part Brandy, 1 part Sloe Gin
Lime Juice *(Mix into Cocktail Glass—no ice)*

GOOD COFFEE-
100-proof Vodka
Double Espresso *(Mix into Irish Coffee Cup—no ice)*

GOOD GOLLY-
3 parts Dark Rum, 1 part Galliano®, splash Brown Crème de Caçao
Coffee, Light Cream or Milk (float) *(Mix into Irish Coffee Cup—no ice)*

GOOD NIGHT SWEETHEART-
1 part Apricot Brandy, 1 part Brandy, 1 part Port
Sour Mix, sprinkle Cinnamon *(Mix into Highball Glass—ice)*

GOOMBAY SMASH-
1 part Coconut Rum, 1 part Dark Rum, splash Triple Sec
Pineapple Juice, Sour Mix, Orange Juice, Grenadine
(Mix into Highball Glass with ice or blend with ice in Daiquiri Glass)

GORGEOUS-
1 part Grand Marnier®, 1 part Amaretto
(Mix into Layer in Order in Cocktail Glass with no ice)

GORILLA MILK-
2 parts Light Rum, 1 part Banana Liqueur, 1 part Coffee Liqueur, 1 part Irish
    Cream Liqueur
Light Cream or Milk, Banana Garnish *(Mix into Highball Glass—ice)*

GORILLA PUNCH-
2 parts Vodka, 1 part Blue Curaçao
Orange Juice, Pineapple Juice *(Mix into Highball Glass—ice)*

GORILLA SNOT-
1 part Port, 1 part Irish Cream Liqueur
(Layer in Order in Cocktail Glass—no ice)

GORKY PARK-
Vodka
Sour Mix, splash Grenadine, splash Bitters *(Mix into Cocktail Glass—no ice)*

GRACELAND-
2 parts Dry Vermouth, 2 parts Sweet Vermouth, 1 part Scotch Whiskey
splash Bitters *(Mix into Cocktail Glass—no ice)*

GRADEAL SPECIAL-
2 parts Light Rum, 1 part Apricot Brandy, 1 part Gin
Sugar *(Mix into Cocktail Glass—no ice)*

GRAND AM-
1 part Amaretto, 1 part Grand Marnier® *(Mix into Cocktail Glass—no ice)*

GRAND APPLE-
2 parts Apple Brandy, 1 part Cognac, 1 part Grand Marnier®
(Mix into Small Rocks Glass—ice)

GRAND FINALE-
2 parts Amaretto, 1 part Coconut Liqueur, 1 part Hazelnut Liqueur
Light Cream or Milk *(Mix into Highball Glass—ice)*

GRAND GOLD-
3 parts Gold Tequila, 1 part Grand Marnier®
Sour Mix, splash Orange Juice *(Mix into Cocktail Glass—no ice)*

GRAND HOTEL-
1 part Gin, 1 part Grand Marnier®, splash Dry Vermouth
splash Lime Juice *(Mix into Cocktail Glass—no ice)*

GRAND MASTER-
4 parts Scotch Whiskey, 1 part Peppermint Schnapps
Club Soda *(Mix into Highball Glass—ice)*

GRAND MATADOR-
3 parts Tequila, 1 part Grand Marnier®, 1 part Vanilla Liqueur
(Mix into Small Rocks Glass—ice)

GRAND MOMENT-
2 parts Gin, 1 part Grand Marnier®
Lime Juice *(Mix into Cocktail Glass—no ice)*

GRAND OCCASION-
3 parts Light Rum, 1 part Grand Marnier®, 1 part White Crème de Caçao
Lime Juice *(Mix into Cocktail Glass—no ice)*

GRAND PASSION-
Gin
Passion Fruit Juice, splash Bitters *(Mix into Cocktail Glass—no ice)*

GRAND ROYAL FIZZ-
Gin, splash Maraschino Liqueur
Orange Juice, Sour Mix, Light Cream or Milk, splash Club Soda
(Mix into Highball Glass—ice)

GRAND SLAM-
2 parts Citrus Rum, 1 part Dry Vermouth, 1 part Sweet Vermouth
(Mix into Cocktail Glass—no ice)

GRANVILLE-
Gin, splash Apple Brandy, splash Grand Marnier®
splash Lime Juice *(Mix into Cocktail Glass—no ice)*

GRAPE CRUSH (1)-
1 part Raspberry Liqueur, 1 part Vodka
Cranberry Juice, splash Sour Mix
(Mix into Highball Glass—ice)

GRAPE CRUSH (2)-
1 part Raspberry Liqueur, 1 part Vodka
Sour Mix, splash Lemon-Lime Soda
(Mix into Highball Glass—ice)

GRAPE SHOT-
3 parts Tequila, 1 part Triple Sec
Grape Juice *(Mix into Cocktail Glass—no ice)*

GRAPE SLUSH-
1 part Light Rum, 1 part Tequila, 1 part Vodka
Grape Soda *(Mix into Highball Glass—ice)*

GRAPE VODKA FROTH-
Vodka
Grape Juice, Lime Juice *(Mix into Small Rocks Glass—ice)*

GRAPEFRUIT COCKTAIL-
Gin, splash Maraschino Liqueur
Grapefruit Juice *(Mix into Cocktail Glass—no ice)*

GRAPEFRUIT HIGHBALL-
Light Rum
Grapefruit Juice *(Mix into Highball Glass—ice)*

GRAPEFRUIT NOG-
Brandy
Grapefruit Juice, Lime Juice, Honey
(Blend with ice in Daiquiri Glass)

GRAPEVINE-
Gin
Grape Juice, splash Lime Juice, splash Grenadine
(Mix into Highball Glass—ice)

GRASS IS GREENER-
2 parts Light Rum, 1 part Green Crème de Menthe
Lime Juice *(Mix into Highball Glass—ice)*

GRASS SKIRT-
1 part Gin, 1 part Triple Sec
Pineapple Juice, splash Grenadine *(Mix into Highball Glass—ice)*

GRASSHOPPER-
1 part Green Crème de Menthe, 1 part White Crème de Caçao
Light Cream or Milk *(Mix into Cocktail Glass—no ice)*

GRATEFUL DEAD-
1 part Gin, 1 part Light Rum, 1 part Raspberry Liqueur, 1 part Triple Sec,
   1 part Vodka
Sour Mix *(Mix into Cocktail Glass—no ice)*

GRAVEL GERTIE-
Vodka
Tomato Juice, Clam Juice, splash Worcestershire Sauce, splash Lime Juice,
   splash Hot Sauce, Salt, Pepper, Horseradish
(Mix into Highball Glass—ice)

GRAVEYARD-
1 part Bourbon Whiskey, 1 part Scotch Whiskey, 1 part Gin, 1 part Light Rum,
   1 part Tequila, 1 part Triple Sec, 1 part Vodka, fill ½ Beer & ½ Stout
(Beer Mug)

GREAT BALLS OF FIRE-
1 part Goldschläger®, 1 part Cinnamon Schnapps, 1 part Cherry Brandy
(Layer in Order in Cocktail Glass—no ice)

GREAT DANE-
2 parts Aquavit, 1 part Cherry Brandy
Cranberry Juice, splash Orange Bitters *(Mix into Cocktail Glass—no ice)*

GREAT HEAD-
3 parts Canadian Whiskey, 1 part Apple Brandy
(Mix into Cocktail Glass—no ice)

GREAT SECRET-
4 parts Gin, 1 part Lillet
splash Bitters *(Mix into Cocktail Glass—no ice)*

GREEK BUCK-
Brandy, splash Licorice Liqueur (float)
Lime Juice, fill Ginger Ale *(Mix into Highball Glass—ice)*

GREEK COFFEE-
Metaxa
Coffee, top Whipped Cream *(Mix into Irish Coffee Cup—no ice)*

GREEK REVOLUTION-
1 part Grenadine, 1 part Licorice Liqueur, 1 part Galliano®
(Layer in Order in Cocktail Glass—no ice)

GREEN APPLE-
Southern Comfort®, splash Melon Liqueur
Sour Mix *(Mix into Highball Glass—ice)*

GREEN BACK-
1 part Gin, 1 part Green Crème de Menthe
Sour Mix *(Mix into Cocktail Glass—no ice)*

GREEN CHARTREUSE NECTAR-
2 parts Apricot Schnapps, 1 part Green Chartreuse
(Mix into Cocktail Glass—no ice)

GREEN CHILI-
1 part Peach Schnapps, 1 part Melon Liqueur
splash Hot Sauce *(Mix into Cocktail Glass—no ice)*

GREEN DEMON-
1 part Light Rum, 1 part Melon Liqueur, 1 part Vodka
Lemonade *(Mix into Highball Glass—ice)*

GREEN DEVIL-
1 part Gin, 1 part Green Crème de Menthe
Lime Juice, Mint Leaves *(Mix into Small Rocks Glass—ice)*

GREEN DINOSAUR-
1 part Gin, 1 part Light Rum, 1 part Melon Liqueur, 1 part Tequila,
    1 part Triple Sec, 1 part Vodka
Sour Mix, splash Lemon-Lime Soda *(Mix into Highball Glass—ice)*

GREEN DRAGON (1)-
3 parts Gin, 1 part Green Crème de Menthe, 1 part Kümmel
Lime Juice, Orange Bitters *(Mix into Cocktail Glass—no ice)*

GREEN DRAGON (2)-
2 parts Russian Vodka, 1 part Green Chartreuse
(Mix into Cocktail Glass—no ice)

GREEN DRAGON (3)-
3 parts Gin, 1 part Green Crème de Menthe, 1 part Jägermeister®
splash Lime Juice, splash Bitters *(Mix into Cocktail Glass—no ice)*

GREEN EYED MONSTER-
4 parts Irish Whiskey, 2 parts Green Crème de Menthe, 1 part Sweet Vermouth
splash Bitters *(Mix into Cocktail Glass—no ice)*

GREEN EYES-
1 part Blue Curaçao, 1 part Vodka, splash Triple Sec (float)
Orange Juice, Green Cherry Garnish *(Mix into Highball Glass—ice)*

GREEN FANTASY-
1 part Dry Vermouth, 1 part Melon Liqueur, 1 part Vodka
(Mix into Cocktail Glass—no ice)

G

GREEN FIRE-
Gin, splash Green Crème de Menthe, splash Kümmel
(Mix into Cocktail Glass—no ice)

GREEN FIZZ-
Gin, splash Green Crème de Menthe
Sour Mix, splash Club Soda
(Mix into Highball Glass—ice)

GREEN FLY-
3 parts Vodka, 1 part Green Crème de Menthe, 1 part White Crème de Menthe
(Mix into Cocktail Glass—no ice)

GREEN FROG, THE-
4 parts Dark Rum, 1 part Blue Curaçao, splash White Crème de Menthe
Orange Juice
(Mix into Highball Glass with ice or blend with ice in Daiquiri Glass)

GREEN GABLES-
2 parts Sweet Vermouth, 1 part Gin, splash Green Chartreuse
(Mix into Cocktail Glass—no ice)

GREEN GENIE-
Green Chartreuse, Tequila *(Mix into Cocktail Glass—no ice)*

GREEN GOBLIN-
½ pint Hard Cider, ½ pint Lager, Blue Curaçao *(Layer in Order in Beer Mug)*

GREEN GODDESS-
1 part Melon Liqueur, 1 part Scotch Whiskey, splash Dry Vermouth
Lemon-Lime Soda *(Mix into Highball Glass—ice)*

GREEN HORNET (1)-
Lime Vodka
Lemon-Lime Soda *(Mix into Highball Glass—ice)*

GREEN HORNET (2)-
3 parts Brandy, 1 part Green Crème de Menthe
(Mix into Small Rocks Glass—ice)

GREEN ISLAND-
Vodka, splash Green Crème de Menthe
Pineapple Juice, Sour Mix *(Mix into Highball Glass—ice)*

GREEN LAGOON-
1 part Gin, 1 part Green Crème de Menthe
Pineapple Juice *(Mix into Highball Glass—ice)*

GREEN LANTERN (1)-
Melon Liqueur
Orange Juice, Lemon-Lime Soda *(Mix into Highball Glass—ice)*

GREEN LANTERN (2)-
2 parts Hpnotiq®, 1 part Vodka
fill Red Bull® *(Mix into Highball Glass—ice)*

GREEN LIZARD-
2 parts Green Chartreuse, 1 part 151-proof Rum
(Mix into Small Rocks Glass — ice)

GREEN MIRAGE-
2 parts Vodka, 1 part Galliano®, splash Blue Curaçao, splash Dry Vermouth
(Mix into Cocktail Glass — no ice)

GREEN MIST-
1 part Scotch Whiskey, 1 part Green Crème de Menthe
Lime Juice *(Mix into Cocktail Glass — no ice)*

GREEN OPAL-
2 parts Anisette, 1 part Gin *(Mix into Cocktail Glass — no ice)*

GREEN ORCHID-
2 parts Green Crème de Menthe, 1 part Licorice Liqueur
fill Club Soda *(Mix into Highball Glass — ice)*

GREEN ROOM-
1 part Brandy, 1 part Dry Vermouth, splash Triple Sec
(Mix into Cocktail Glass — no ice)

GREEN RUSSIAN-
1 part Melon Liqueur, 1 part Vodka
Light Cream or Milk *(Mix into Highball Glass — ice)*

GREEN SCORPION-
1 part Jack Daniel's® Tennessee Sour Mash Whiskey, 1 part Vodka,
splash Blue Curaçao
fill Lemon-Lime Soda *(Mix into Highball Glass — ice)*

GREEN SNEAKER-
2 parts Vodka, 1 part Melon Liqueur, 1 part Triple Sec
Orange Juice *(Mix into Highball Glass — ice)*

GREEN SPIDER-
3 parts Vodka, 1 part Green Crème de Menthe
(Mix into Small Rocks Glass — ice)

GREEN STINGER-
3 parts Brandy, 1 part Green Crème de Menthe
(Mix into Cocktail Glass — no ice)

GREEN TURTLE-
1 part Jägermeister®, 1 part Melon Liqueur
Orange Juice *(Mix into Highball Glass — ice)*

GREENBACK-
2 parts Gin, 1 part Green Crème de Menthe
Lime Juice *(Mix into Small Rocks Glass — ice)*

GREMLIN-
2 parts Vodka, 1 part Blue Curaçao, 1 part Light Rum
Orange Juice *(Mix into Highball Glass — ice)*

GRENADA-
2 parts Brandy, 1 part Dry Sherry, splash Triple Sec
fill Tonic Water *(Mix into Highball Glass—ice)*

GRENADE-
2 parts Vodka, 1 part Triple Sec
Grenadine *(Mix into Small Rocks Glass—ice)*

GRENADIER-
1 part Gin, 1 part Light Rum
Pineapple Juice, Lime Juice, splash Grenadine
(Mix into Cocktail Glass—no ice)

GREYHOUND-
Vodka
Grapefruit Juice *(Mix into Highball Glass—ice)*

GRINGO SWIZZLE-
4 parts Tequila, 1 part Crème de Cassis
Orange Juice, Pineapple Juice, Lime Juice, fill Ginger Ale
(Mix into Highball Glass—ice)

GRIZZLY BEAR (1)-
2 parts Dark Rum, 1 part Amaretto
Vanilla Ice Cream, Chocolate Syrup, splash Vanilla Extract
(Blend with ice in Daiquiri Glass)

GRIZZLY BEAR (2)-
1 part Amaretto, 1 part Brown Crème de Caçao, 1 part Dark Rum,
    1 part Vanilla Liqueur
Light Cream or Milk *(Mix into Highball Glass—ice)*

GROG-
Jamaican Rum
Hot Water, Sour Mix, Cloves, Cinnamon Stick
(Mix into Irish Coffee Cup—no ice)

GROUND ZERO-
1 part Bourbon Whiskey, 1 part Coffee Liqueur, 1 part Peppermint Schnapps,
    1 part Vodka *(Mix into Cocktail Glass—no ice)*

GUGGENHEIM-
1 part Brandy, 1 part Gin, 1 part Triple Sec *(Mix into Cocktail Glass—no ice)*

GULF STREAM-
1 part Blue Curaçao, 1 part Brandy, 1 part Light Rum, fill Champagne
Lemonade, Lime Juice, Strawberry Garnish *(Blend with ice in Daiquiri Glass)*

GULL'S WING-
4 parts Tequila, 1 part Banana Liqueur
Lime Juice *(Mix into Small Rocks Glass—ice)*

GUMBO FIZZ-
Gin, splash Triple Sec
Sour Mix, splash Light Cream or Milk, splash Club Soda
(Mix into Highball Glass—ice)

GUMDROP MARTINI-
4 parts Lemon Rum, 2 parts Vodka, 1 part Southern Comfort®,
   splash Dry Vermouth
Splash Lime Juice *(Mix into Cocktail Glass—no ice)*

GUMMY BEAR-
1 part Amaretto, 1 part Melon Liqueur, 1 part Southern Comfort®
Orange Juice, Pineapple Juice, splash Grenadine
(Mix into Highball Glass—ice)

GUNGA DIN-
3 parts Gin, 1 part Dry Vermouth
Orange Juice, Pineapple Slice *(Mix into Cocktail Glass—no ice)*

GYPSY (1)-
1 part Gin, 1 part Sweet Vermouth *(Mix into Cocktail Glass—no ice)*

GYPSY (2)-
4 parts Vodka, 1 part Bénédictine
splash Orange Juice, splash Lime Juice *(Mix into Small Rocks Glass—ice)*

– NOTES –

Gimlet - Muddled limes, Gin or Vodka, lime juice, shaken + poured over ice or in cocktail glass.

H & H-
2 parts Gin, 1 part Lillet, splash Triple Sec *(Mix into Cocktail Glass—no ice)*

H. P. W.-
Gin, splash Dry Vermouth, splash Sweet Vermouth
Orange Peel Garnish *(Mix into Cocktail Glass—no ice)*

HABANEROS-
Light Rum
Lime Juice, splash Grenadine *(Mix into Cocktail Glass—no ice)*

HABITANT-
Canadian Whiskey
Lime Juice, Maple Syrup *(Mix into Cocktail Glass—no ice)*

HAIDIN-HAIDIN-
4 parts Light Rum, 1 part Dry Vermouth
splash Bitters *(Mix into Cocktail Glass—no ice)*

HAIKU-
Sake, splash Dry Vermouth
Onion Garnish *(Mix into Cocktail Glass—no ice)*

HAIR OF THE DOG-
Scotch Whiskey
Light Cream or Milk, Honey *(Mix into Highball Glass—ice)*

HAIR RAISER-
3 parts 100-proof Vodka, 1 part Rock & Rye
Lime Juice *(Mix into Cocktail Glass—no ice)*

HAIRBALL-
6 oz. Hard Cider, 6 oz. Stout *(Layer in Order in Beer Mug)*,
    1 part Irish Whiskey
(drop Irish Whiskey in shot glass into Beer Mug)
(Beer Mug/Shot Glass)

HAIRY BITCH-
2 parts Light Rum, 1 part Triple Sec
Pineapple Juice
(Mix into Highball Glass with ice or blend with ice in Daiquiri Glass)

HAIRY NAVEL-
1 part Peach Schnapps, 1 part Vodka
Orange Juice *(Mix into Highball Glass—ice)*

HAIRY SLUT-
2 parts Light Rum, 1 part Triple Sec
Pineapple Juice
(Mix into Highball Glass with ice or blend with ice in Daiquiri Glass)

HAIRY SUNRISE-
1 part Tequila, 1 part Triple Sec, 1 part Vodka
Orange Juice, Grenadine (lace) (stir with straw for "sunrise")
(Mix into Highball Glass—ice)

HAIRY VIRGIN-
  2 parts Light Rum, 1 part Triple Sec
  Pineapple Juice, Cherry Garnish
  (Mix into Highball Glass with ice or blend with ice in Daiquiri Glass)

HALEAKALA MARTINI-
  3 parts Vodka, 1 part Raspberry Liqueur
  Pineapple Juice *(Mix into Cocktail Glass—no ice)*

HALF MOON STREET-
  Brandy, splash 151-proof Rum (float)
  Pineapple Juice, Sour Mix, fill Club Soda
  (Mix into Highball Glass—ice)

HALLEY'S COMFORT-
  1 part Southern Comfort®, 1 part Peach Schnapps
  Club Soda *(Mix into Highball Glass—ice)*

HAMMERHEAD-
  1 part Amaretto, 1 part Light Rum, 1 part Triple Sec, splash Southern Comfort®
  (Mix into Cocktail Glass—no ice)

HAMMERTOE-
  3 parts Light Rum, 1 part Blue Curaçao, splash Amaretto
  Lime Juice *(Mix into Highball Glass—ice)*

HAND GRENADE-
  Tequila
  Cranberry Juice *(Mix into Highball Glass—ice)*

HANDBALL COOLER-
  Vodka
  Club Soda, splash Orange Juice *(Mix into Highball Glass—ice)*

HANDICAPPER'S CHOICE-
  1 part Amaretto, 1 part Irish Whiskey
  Coffee, top Whipped Cream *(Mix in Irish Coffee Cup—no ice)*

HAPPY APPLE-
  Light Rum
  Apple Cider, splash Lime Juice *(Mix into Highball Glass—ice)*

HAPPY FELLER, THE-
  3 parts Vodka, 1 part Raspberry Liqueur, 1 part Triple Sec
  splash Lime Juice *(Mix into Cocktail Glass—no ice)*

HAPPY HAWAIIAN-
  1 part Coffee Liqueur, 1 part Irish Cream Liqueur
  Pineapple Juice *(Mix into Highball Glass—ice)*

HAPPY RANCHER-
  1 part Melon Liqueur, 1 part Peach Schnapps, 1 part Scotch Whiskey,
     1 part Vodka
  splash Lemon-Lime Soda
  (Mix into Cocktail Glass—no ice)

HAPPY YOUTH-
Cherry Brandy, fill Champagne
Orange Juice, Sugar *(Mix in Champagne Flute—no ice)*

HARBOR LIGHTS (1)-
1 part Cognac, 1 part Galliano® *(Mix into Cocktail Glass—no ice)*

HARBOR LIGHTS (2)-
1 part Light Rum, 1 part Raspberry Liqueur
Orange Juice *(Mix into Highball Glass—ice)*

HARBOR LIGHTS (3)-
1 part Galliano®, 1 part Metaxa *(Mix into Cocktail Glass—no ice)*

HARD CORE-
1 part Amaretto, 1 part 100-proof Vodka, 1 part Triple Sec,
1 part 151-proof Rum
fill Cola *(Mix into Highball Glass—ice)*

HARD DICK-
1 part Hazelnut Liqueur, 1 part Vodka
splash Club Soda *(Mix into Cocktail Glass—no ice)*

HARD ON-
1 part Coffee Liqueur, 1 part Amaretto, 1 part Irish Cream Liqueur
(Layer in Order in Cocktail Glass—no ice)

HARI KARI-
1 part Brandy, 1 part Triple Sec
Orange Juice *(Mix into Cocktail Glass—no ice)*

HARLEM-
Gin, splash Maraschino Liqueur
Pineapple Juice *(Mix into Cocktail Glass—no ice)*

HARPER'S FERRY-
Dry Vermouth, splash Light Rum, splash Southern Comfort®, splash Triple Sec
(Mix into Cocktail Glass—no ice)

HARPIC-
1 part Blue Curaçao, 1 part Coffee Liqueur, 1 part Vodka
Lemonade *(Mix into Highball Glass—ice)*

HARROVIAN-
Gin
Orange Juice, splash Lime Juice, splash Bitters
(Mix into Cocktail Glass—no ice)

HARRY'S-
2 parts Gin, 1 part Sweet Vermouth, splash Licorice Liqueur
Mint Leaves *(Mix into Cocktail Glass—no ice)*

HARVARD COCKTAIL (1)-
2 parts Brandy, 1 part Sweet Vermouth
Lime Juice, Grenadine, Bitters *(Mix into Cocktail Glass—no ice)*

HARVARD COCKTAIL (2)-
1 part Brandy, 1 part Sweet Vermouth
Sour Mix, splash Bitters *(Mix into Cocktail Glass—no ice)*

HARVARD COOLER-
Apple Brandy
Club Soda, Sugar, fill Ginger Ale *(Mix into Highball Glass—ice)*

HARVARD WINE-
1 part Brandy, 1 part Dry Vermouth
splash Orange Bitters, top Club Soda *(Mix into Cocktail Glass—no ice)*

HARVARD YARD-
2 parts Gin, 1 part Cranberry Brandy, 1 part Peppermint Schnapps,
   splash Triple Sec
Orange Slice Garnish *(Mix into Cocktail Glass—no ice)*

HARVEY WALLBANGER-
2 parts Vodka, 1 part Galliano® (lace)
Orange Juice *(Mix into Highball Glass—ice)*

HASTY-
2 parts Gin, 1 part Dry Vermouth, splash Anisette
splash Grenadine *(Mix into Cocktail Glass—no ice)*

HAT TRICK-
1 part Dark Rum, 1 part Light Rum, 1 part Sweet Vermouth
(Mix into Cocktail Glass—no ice)

HAVANA-
Light Rum
Pineapple Juice, splash Lime Juice *(Mix into Cocktail Glass—no ice)*

HAVANA BANANA FIZZ-
Light Rum
Pineapple Juice, Lime Juice, splash Bitters, Bananas, top Lemon-Lime Soda
(Blend with ice in Daiquiri Glass)

HAVANA BANDANA-
Light Rum, splash Banana Liqueur (float)
Lime Juice, Bananas *(Blend with ice in Daiquiri Glass)*

HAVANA BEACH-
Dark Rum
Pineapple Juice, splash Lime Juice *(Mix into Cocktail Glass—no ice)*

HAVANA CLUB-
Light Rum, splash Dry Vermouth *(Mix into Cocktail Glass—no ice)*

HAVE A HEART-
3 parts Gin, 1 part Citrus Rum
Lime Juice, splash Grenadine *(Mix into Cocktail Glass—no ice)*

HAWAII 5-0-
1 part Dark Rum, 1 part Gin, 1 part Red Wine
Orange Juice *(Mix into Highball Glass—ice)*

HAWAII 7-0-
2 parts Blended Whiskey, 1 part Amaretto, 1 part Coconut Liqueur
Orange Juice
(Mix into Highball Glass with ice or blend with ice in Daiquiri Glass)

HAWAII 8-0-
Vodka
Pineapple Juice *(Mix into Highball Glass—ice)*

HAWAIIAN BULL-
3 parts Scotch Whiskey, 1 part Amaretto (float)
Pineapple Garnish *(Mix into Small Rocks Glass—ice)*

HAWAIIAN COCKTAIL (1)-
Gin, splash Triple Sec
Pineapple Juice *(Mix into Cocktail Glass—no ice)*

HAWAIIAN COCKTAIL (2)-
1 part Amaretto, 1 part Vodka
Cranberry Juice *(Mix into Cocktail Glass—no ice)*

HAWAIIAN EYE-
2 parts Bourbon Whiskey, 1 part Banana Liqueur, 1 part Coffee Liqueur,
   1 part Vodka, splash Licorice Liqueur
Light Cream or Milk
(Blend with ice in Daiquiri Glass)

HAWAIIAN LEMONADE-
Vodka
Lemonade, Pineapple Juice *(Mix into Highball Glass—ice)*

HAWAIIAN ORANGE BLOSSOM-
1 part Gin, 1 part Triple Sec
Orange Juice, Pineapple Juice *(Mix into Highball Glass—ice)*

HAWAIIAN PUNCH (1)-
1 part Sloe Gin, 1 part Southern Comfort®, 1 part Triple Sec
Orange Juice *(Mix into Highball Glass—ice)*

HAWAIIAN PUNCH (2)-
1 part Amaretto, 1 part Southern Comfort®, 1 part 100-proof Vodka
Pineapple Juice *(Mix into Cocktail Glass—no ice)*

HAWAIIAN SEABREEZE-
Vodka
Cranberry Juice, Pineapple Juice *(Mix into Highball Glass—ice)*

HAZEL NUT COCKTAIL-
2 parts Hazelnut Liqueur, 1 part Brown Crème de Cacao
Light Cream or Milk
(Mix into Cocktail Glass—no ice)

HEAD BANGER-
1 part Licorice Liqueur, 1 part 151-proof Rum
splash Grenadine *(Mix into Cocktail Glass—no ice)*

HEAD FOR THE HILLS-
4 parts Dry Vermouth, 1 part Triple Sec
Club Soda *(Mix into Highball Glass—ice)*

HEAD ROOM-
1 part Banana Liqueur, 1 part Melon Liqueur, 2 parts Irish Cream Liqueur
(Layer in Order in Cocktail Glass—no ice)

HEADLESS HORSEMAN-
Vodka
Ginger Ale, splash Bitters *(Mix into Highball Glass—ice)*

HEADWALL-
1 part Gin, 1 part Light Rum
splash Lime Juice, splash Grenadine, fill Ginger Ale
(Mix into Highball Glass—ice)

HEARTS-
Cherry Brandy
Lemon-Lime Soda *(Mix into Highball Glass—ice)*

HEARTY SUSAN-
3 parts Blended Whiskey, 1 part Cherry Brandy
(Mix into Cocktail Glass—no ice)

HEAT WAVE-
3 parts Coconut Rum, 1 part Peach Schnapps
Pineapple Juice, Orange Juice, Grenadine
(Mix into Highball Glass—ice)

HEATHCLIFF-
2 parts Apple Brandy, 2 parts Scotch Whiskey, 1 part Gin
Sugar *(Mix into Cocktail Glass—no ice)*

HEATHER BLUSH-
3 parts Sparkling Wine, 1 part Scotch Whiskey, 1 part Strawberry Schnapps
(Mix in Champagne Flute—no ice)

HEAVENLY BODY-
1 part Pear Schnapps, 1 part Hazelnut Liqueur, 1 part Irish Cream Liqueur
(Layer in Order in Cocktail Glass—no ice)

HEAVYWEIGHT SAILOR-
2 parts Dark Rum, 2 parts 151-proof Rum, 1 part Light Rum,
    splash Coffee Liqueur
Lime Juice *(Mix into Highball Glass—ice)*

HELP WANTED-
1 part Apricot Brandy, 1 part Bourbon Whiskey
splash Lime Juice *(Mix into Small Rocks Glass—ice)*

HER NAME IN LIGHTS-
2 parts Vodka, 1 part Yellow Chartreuse, splash Blue Curaçao, splash Galliano®
splash Lime Juice
(Mix into Cocktail Glass—no ice)

HERE TODAY-
Gin
splash Lime Juice, Cherry Garnish *(Mix into Small Rocks Glass—ice)*

HESITATION-
1 part Citrus Vodka, 1 part Rye Whiskey
splash Lime Juice *(Mix into Cocktail Glass—no ice)*

HI RISE-
2 parts Vodka, 1 part Triple Sec
Orange Juice, Sour Mix, splash Grenadine
(Mix into Highball Glass with ice or blend with ice in Daiquiri Glass)

HIGH JAMAICAN WIND-
3 parts Dark Rum, 1 part Coffee Liqueur
Light Cream or Milk (float) *(Mix into Cocktail Glass—no ice)*

HIGH ROLLER-
2 parts Vodka, 1 part Grand Marnier®
Orange Juice, splash Grenadine *(Mix into Highball Glass—ice)*

HIGH VOLTAGE-
2 parts Scotch Whiskey, 1 part Triple Sec
Lime Juice *(Mix into Cocktail Glass—no ice)*

HIGHBALL (GENERIC)-
(Any Liqueur)
Ginger Ale or Club Soda *(Mix into Highball Glass—ice)*

HIGHLAND COOLER-
Scotch Whiskey
Sugar, Club Soda or Ginger Ale *(Mix into Highball Glass—ice)*

HIGHLAND FLING-
2 parts Scotch Whiskey, 1 part Sweet Vermouth
Orange Bitters, Olive Garnish *(Mix into Cocktail Glass—no ice)*

HILGERT-
2 parts Dry Vermouth, 1 part Gin, splash Maraschino Liqueur
splash Grapefruit Juice, splash Bitters *(Mix into Cocktail Glass—no ice)*

HILLARY WALLBANGER-
1 part White Wine, 1 part Galliano® (lace)
Orange Juice *(Mix in Wine Glass—ice)*

HIROSHIMA-
4 parts Blended Whiskey, 1 part Dry Vermouth, splash Anisette
(Mix into Cocktail Glass—no ice)

HO-HO-KUS POCUS-
1 part Apple Brandy, 1 part Brandy, splash Bourbon Whiskey
(Mix into Cocktail Glass—no ice)

HOFFMAN HOUSE-
2 parts Gin, 1 part Dry Vermouth
Orange Bitters *(Mix into Cocktail Glass—no ice)*

HOKKAIDO-
2 parts Gin, 2 parts Sake, 1 part Triple Sec *(Mix into Cocktail Glass—no ice)*

HOLE-IN-ONE (1)-
2 parts Scotch Whiskey, 1 part Dry Vermouth
Lime Juice, Orange Bitters *(Mix into Cocktail Glass—no ice)*

HOLE-IN-ONE (2)-
3 parts Melon Liqueur, 1 part Apple Brandy, splash Light Cream or Milk (lace)
(Layer in Order in Cocktail Glass—no ice)

HOLLAND HOUSE-
2 parts Gin, 1 part Dry Vermouth, splash Maraschino Liqueur
Lime Juice, Pineapple Slice Garnish *(Mix into Cocktail Glass—no ice)*

HOLLYWOOD-
1 part Raspberry Liqueur, 1 part Vodka
Pineapple Juice *(Mix into Highball Glass—ice)*

HOLLYWOOD MARTINI-
Gin, splash Dry Vermouth, splash Triple Sec *(Mix into Cocktail Glass—no ice)*

HOME RUN-
1 part Bourbon Whiskey, 1 part Brandy, 1 part Light Rum
Sour Mix *(Mix into Cocktail Glass—no ice)*

HOMECOMING-
1 part Amaretto, 1 part Irish Cream Liqueur *(Mix into Cocktail Glass—no ice)*

HOMESTEAD-
2 parts Gin, 1 part Sweet Vermouth *(Mix into Cocktail Glass—no ice)*

HONEYBEE-
Dark Rum
Lime Juice, Honey *(Mix into Cocktail Glass—no ice)*

HONEYMOON-
1 part Apple Brandy, 1 part Bénédictine, splash Triple Sec
Lime Juice *(Mix into Cocktail Glass—no ice)*

HONG KONG-
1 part Dry Vermouth, 1 part Gin
Sour Mix, splash Bitters *(Mix into Cocktail Glass—no ice)*

HONG KONG SUNDAE-
1 part Galliano®, 1 part Triple Sec
Orange Sherbet *(Blend with ice in Daiquiri Glass)*

HONOLULU-
Gin
Orange Juice, Pineapple Juice, Sour Mix, Bitters
(Mix into Cocktail Glass—no ice)

HONOLULU HAMMER-
3 parts Vodka, 1 part Amaretto
Pineapple Juice, splash Amaretto *(Mix into Cocktail Glass—no ice)*

HONOLULU LULU-
1 part Bénédictine, 1 part Gin, 1 part Maraschino Liqueur
(Mix into Cocktail Glass—no ice)

HONOLULU PUNCH-
1 part Amaretto, 1 part Southern Comfort®, 1 part 151-proof Rum
Pineapple Juice, Orange Juice, splash Grenadine
(Mix into Highball Glass—ice)

HOOP LA-
1 part Brandy, 1 part Lillet, 1 part Triple Sec
Lime Juice *(Mix into Cocktail Glass—no ice)*

HOOT MON-
2 parts Scotch Whiskey, 1 part Sweet Vermouth, splash Bénédictine
(Mix into Cocktail Glass—no ice)

HOOTER-
1 part Amaretto, 1 part Vodka
Orange Juice, Grenadine *(Mix into Highball Glass—ice)*

HOP SCOTCH (1)-
Scotch Whiskey, splash Triple Sec
splash Orange Bitters *(Mix into Cocktail Glass—no ice)*

HOP SCOTCH (2)-
1 part Irish Cream Liqueur, 1 part Butterscotch Schnapps
(Layer in Order in Cocktail Glass—no ice)

HOP SCOTCH (3)-
1 part Butterscotch Schnapps, 1 part Irish Cream Liqueur
Light Cream or Milk *(Mix into Highball Glass—ice)*

HOP, SKIP & GO NAKED-
1 part Gin, 1 part Vodka, fill Beer
Lime Juice *(Beer Mug)*

HOP TOAD-
1 part Apricot Brandy, 1 part Light Rum
Lime Juice *(Mix into Cocktail Glass—no ice)*

HORN PIPE-
Gin, splash Cherry Brandy *(Mix into Cocktail Glass—no ice)*

HORNY BULL (1)-
Tequila
Orange Juice *(Mix into Highball Glass—ice)*

HORNY BULL (2)-
1 part Vodka, 1 part Light Rum, 1 part Tequila
(Layer in Order in Cocktail Glass—no ice)

HORNY MOHICAN-
1 part Banana Liqueur, 1 part Irish Cream Liqueur, 1 part Coconut Rum
(Layer in Order in Cocktail Glass—no ice)

HORSE & JOCKEY-
2 parts Light Rum, 2 parts Southern Comfort®, 1 part Sweet Vermouth
splash Bitters *(Mix into Cocktail Glass—no ice)*

HORSE FEATHERS-
Blended Whiskey
Ginger Ale, splash Bitters *(Mix into Highball Glass—ice)*

HORSE'S NECK SPIKED-
Blended Whiskey
Ginger Ale, splash Lime Juice *(Mix into Highball Glass—ice)*

HORSE'S NECK WITH A KICK-
Blended Whiskey
Ginger Ale *(Mix into Highball Glass—ice)*

HOSS'S HOLDUP-
3 parts Vodka, 1 part Triple Sec
Orange Juice, splash Grenadine *(Mix into Highball Glass—ice)*

HOT APPLE PIE (1)-
Amaretto
Hot Apple Juice, top Whipped Cream *(Mix in Irish Coffee Cup—no ice)*

HOT APPLE PIE (2)-
4 parts Spiced Rum, 1 part Cinnamon Schnapps
Hot Apple Juice, top Whipped Cream *(Mix in Irish Coffee Cup—no ice)*

HOT BOMBER-
1 part Coffee Liqueur, 1 part Irish Cream Liqueur, 1 part Triple Sec
Coffee, top Whipped Cream *(Mix in Irish Coffee Cup—no ice)*

HOT BRANDY ALEXANDER-
1 part Brandy, 1 part Brown Crème de Caçao
Steamed Milk, top Whipped Cream, top Chocolate sprinkles
(Mix in Irish Coffee Cup—no ice)

HOT BRANDY FLIP-
Brandy
Hot Milk, Sugar *(Mix in Irish Coffee Cup—no ice)*

HOT BRICK TODDY-
Blended Whiskey
Hot Water, Butter, Sugar, sprinkle Cinnamon *(Mix in Irish Coffee Cup—no ice)*

HOT BROWN COW-
Dark Rum or Spiced Rum
Coffee, Hot Milk, sprinkle Nutmeg *(Mix in Irish Coffee Cup—no ice)*

HOT BUTTERED RUM (1)-
Dark Rum
Hot Water, Butter, Brown Sugar *(Mix in Irish Coffee Cup—no ice)*

HOT BUTTERED RUM (2)-***
3 parts Dark Rum, 1 part Butterscotch Schnapps
Hot Water, Melted Butter, Brown Sugar *(Mix in Irish Coffee Cup—no ice)*

HOT CINNAMON ROLL-
Cinnamon Schnapps
Hot Apple Cider, top Whipped Cream *(Mix in Irish Coffee Cup—no ice)*

HOT COCONUT COFFEE-
Coconut Rum
Coffee, top Whipped Cream *(Mix in Irish Coffee Cup—no ice)*

HOT DARLING DYLAN-
1 part Coffee Liqueur, 1 part Tequila
Mexican Hot Chocolate, top Whipped Cream
(Mix in Irish Coffee Cup—no ice)

HOT DECK-
2 parts Blended Whiskey, 1 part Green Ginger Wine, splash Sweet Vermouth
(Mix into Cocktail Glass—no ice)

HOT FLASH-
1 part Apricot Brandy, 1 part Sloe Gin
splash Lime Juice *(Mix into Cocktail Glass—no ice)*

HOT GOLD-
Amaretto
Warm Orange Juice *(Mix in Irish Coffee Cup—no ice)*

HOT IRISH NUT-
1 part Amaretto, 1 part Hazelnut Liqueur, 1 part Irish Cream Liqueur
Coffee, top Whipped Cream *(Mix in Irish Coffee Cup—no ice)*

HOT KISS-
2 parts Irish Whiskey, 1 part White Crème de Caçao, 1 part White
  Crème de Menthe
Coffee, top Whipped Cream *(Mix in Irish Coffee Cup—no ice)*

HOT MOLLIFIER-
3 parts Dark Rum, 1 part Tia Maria®
Coffee, top Whipped Cream *(Mix in Irish Coffee Cup—no ice)*

HOT NAIL-
2 parts Scotch Whiskey, 1 part Drambuie®
Hot Water, splash Lime Juice *(Mix in Irish Coffee Cup—no ice)*

HOT PANTS-
3 parts Tequila, 1 part Peppermint Schnapps
Grapefruit Juice, splash Grenadine, Salted Rim
(Mix into Small Rocks Glass—ice)

HOT PENNY RUM-
3 parts Light Rum, 1 part Bourbon Whiskey, splash Brown Crème de Caçao
Coffee, top Whipped Cream *(Mix in Irish Coffee Cup—no ice)*

HOT PEPPERMINT PATTY-
Peppermint Schnapps
Hot Chocolate, splash Light Cream or Milk, top Whipped Cream
(Mix in Irish Coffee Cup—no ice)

HOT PIPER-
4 parts Tequila, 1 part Brown Crème de Caçao
Coffee, top Whipped Cream *(Mix in Irish Coffee Cup—no ice)*

HOT RUM-
Light Rum
Hot Water, splash Sour Mix *(Mix in Irish Coffee Cup—no ice)*

HOT SCOTCH (1)-
Butterscotch Schnapps
Hot Chocolate, top Whipped Cream *(Mix in Irish Coffee Cup—no ice)*

HOT SCOTCH (2)-
2 parts Scotch Whiskey, 1 part Drambuie®
Hot Water, splash Sour Mix *(Mix in Irish Coffee Cup—no ice)*

HOT SHOTS-
1 part Peppermint Schnapps, 1 part Vodka
splash Hot Sauce *(Mix into Cocktail Glass—no ice)*

HOT SPRING-
White Wine, splash Maraschino Liqueur
Pineapple Juice, Orange Bitters *(Mix in Wine Glass—ice)*

HOT TODDY-
Brandy or Light Rum or Whiskey
Hot Water, Sugar, sprinkle Nutmeg *(Mix in Irish Coffee Cup—no ice)*

HOT TUB-
2 parts Vodka, 1 part Raspberry Liqueur
Ginger Ale, Pink Lemonade *(Mix into Highball Glass—ice)*

HOT TURTLE-
Butterscotch Schnapps
Hot Chocolate *(Mix in Irish Coffee Cup—no ice)*

HOT ZULTRY ZOE-
3 parts Tequila, 1 part Galliano®
Mexican Hot Chocolate, top Whipped Cream
(Mix in Irish Coffee Cup—no ice)

HOTEL CALIFORNIA-
Apricot Brandy
Orange Soda, Orange Sherbet *(Blend with ice in Daiquiri Glass)*

HOTEL PLAZA-
1 part Dry Vermouth, 1 part Gin, 1 part Sweet Vermouth
Pineapple Garnish *(Mix into Cocktail Glass—no ice)*

HOUSE FIRE-
Amaretto
Hot Apple Cider, top Whipped Cream *(Mix in Irish Coffee Cup—no ice)*

HOUSE STANDARD-
Tequila
Tomato Juice, splash Hot Sauce *(Mix into Highball Glass—ice)*

HOUSTON HURRICANE-
1 part Blended Whiskey, 1 part Gin, 1 part White Crème de Menthe
Lime Juice *(Mix into Cocktail Glass—no ice)*

HOWELL SAYS SO-
3 parts Dark Rum, 1 part Amaretto, 1 part Triple Sec
Lime Juice, splash Orange Bitters *(Mix into Small Rocks Glass—ice)*

HUDSON BAY-
2 parts Gin, 1 part Cherry Brandy, splash 151-proof Rum
Orange Juice, Lime Juice *(Mix into Cocktail Glass—no ice)*

HULA-HULA-
Gin, splash Triple Sec
Orange Juice, Sugar *(Mix into Cocktail Glass—no ice)*

HULA HOOP-
Gin
Orange Juice, Pineapple Juice *(Mix into Cocktail Glass—no ice)*

HUMMER (1)-
1 part Coffee Liqueur, 1 part Light Rum
Vanilla Ice Cream *(Blend with ice in Daiquiri Glass)*

HUMMER (2)-
1 part Coffee Liqueur, 1 part Light Rum
Light Cream or Milk *(Mix into Highball Glass—ice)*

HUNDRED PERCENT-
Citrus Rum
splash Orange Juice, splash Lime Juice, splash Grenadine
(Mix into Cocktail Glass—no ice)

HUNTER'S COCKTAIL-
3 parts Rye Whiskey, 1 part Cherry Brandy *(Mix into Cocktail Glass—no ice)*

HUNTINGTON SPECIAL-
Gin
Lime Juice, splash Grenadine *(Mix into Small Rocks Glass—ice)*

HUNTRESS-
1 part Bourbon Whiskey, 1 part Cherry Brandy, splash Triple Sec
Light Cream or Milk *(Mix into Cocktail Glass—no ice)*

HUNTSMAN-
3 parts Vodka, 1 part Jamaican Rum
Sour Mix *(Mix into Cocktail Glass—no ice)*

HURRICANE (1)-
Spiced Rum
Pineapple Juice, Orange Juice, Grenadine (float) *(Mix into Highball Glass—ice)*

HURRICANE (2)-
2 parts Dark Rum, 1 part Light Rum
Sour Mix, Passion Fruit Juice *(Mix into Highball Glass—ice)*

HURRICANE (3)-
2 parts Blended Whiskey, 1 part Apricot Brandy
Orange Juice, splash Bitters *(Mix into Highball Glass—ice)*

HURRICANE COCKTAIL-
1 part Blended Whiskey, 1 part White Crème de Menthe, splash Gin
Sour Mix *(Mix into Cocktail Glass—no ice)*

HURRICANE LEAH-
1 part Blue Curaçao, 1 part Cherry Brandy, 1 part Gin, 1 part Light Rum,
1 part Tequila, 1 part Vodka
Orange Juice, Sour Mix *(Mix into Highball Glass—ice)*

HYANNIS HIATUS-
Gin
Cranberry Juice, Orange Slice Garnish *(Mix into Highball Glass—ice)*

HYPNOTIC MARTINI-
2 parts Hpnotiq®, 1 part Coconut Liqueur
Pineapple Juice *(Mix into Cocktail Glass—no ice)*

– NOTES –

Hurricane – 1 oz Vodka, 1/4 oz. grenadine, 1 oz gin, 1 oz light
rum, 1/2 oz bacardi 151 rum, 1 oz amaretto almond
liquer, 1 oz. triple sec, grapefruit, pineapple
~ Pour all but juice in hurricane cup 3/4 full of ice,
fill equal part juice.

I. R. A. -
1 part Irish Cream Liqueur, 1 part Irish Whiskey
(Mix into Cocktail Glass—no ice)

I. V. (ITALIAN VALIUM)-
2 parts Amaretto, 1 part Gin
(Mix into Cocktail Glass—no ice)

ICE BALL-
2 parts Gin, 1 part Sambuca, 1 part White Crème de Menthe
Light Cream or Milk *(Blend with ice in Daiquiri Glass)*

ICE BEAR-
1 part Blue Curaçao, 1 part Vodka
Lemon-Lime Soda *(Mix into Highball Glass—ice)*

ICE BET-
1 part Tequila, 1 part Triple Sec
(Mix into Cocktail Glass—no ice)

ICE BOAT-
1 part Peppermint Schnapps, 1 part Vodka *(Mix into Cocktail Glass—no ice)*

ICE BREAKER (1)-
2 parts Dark Rum, 1 part Crème de Noyaux, 1 part Cognac, 1 part Gin
Lime Juice, Orange Juice *(Mix into Highball Glass—ice)*

ICE BREAKER (2)-
Tequila, splash Triple Sec
Grapefruit, splash Grenadine
(Mix into Highball Glass with ice or blend with ice in Daiquiri Glass)

ICE COFFEE-
Coffee Liqueur
Cold Coffee *(Mix into Highball Glass—ice)*

ICE CREAM FLIP-
1 part Maraschino Liqueur, 1 part Triple Sec
Vanilla Ice Cream *(Blend with ice in Daiquiri Glass)*

ICE PALACE-
2 parts Light Rum, 1 part Apricot Brandy, 1 part Galliano®
Pineapple Juice, splash Lime Juice *(Mix into Highball Glass—ice)*

ICE PICK, THE-
Vodka
Iced Tea, splash Lime Juice *(Mix into Highball Glass—ice)*

ICEBERG, THE-
Vodka, splash Licorice Liqueur *(Mix into Cocktail Glass—no ice)*

ICED COFFEE A L'ORANGE-
Triple Sec
Cold Coffee, Vanilla Ice Cream, top Whipped Cream
(Blend with ice in Daiquiri Glass)

ICED RUMMED CAÇAO-
1 part Brown Crème de Caçao, 1 part Dark Rum
Vanilla Ice Cream, top Chocolate sprinkles
(Blend with ice in Daiquiri Glass)

ICHBIEN (1)-
3 parts Brandy, 1 part Triple Sec
Light Cream or Milk *(Mix into Highball Glass—ice)*

ICHBIEN (2)-
2 parts Apple Brandy, 1 part Triple Sec
Light Cream or Milk *(Mix into Highball Glass—ice)*

IDEAL COCKTAIL-
1 part Dry Vermouth, 1 part Gin, splash Maraschino Liqueur
Grapefruit Juice or Lime Juice, Cherry Garnish
(Mix into Cocktail Glass—no ice)

IDONIS-
4 parts Vodka, 1 part Apricot Brandy
Pineapple Juice *(Mix into Cocktail Glass—no ice)*

IGUANA-
1 part Coffee Liqueur, 1 part Tequila, 1 part Vodka
Sour Mix *(Mix into Cocktail Glass—no ice)*

ILICIT AFFAIR-
1 part Irish Cream Liqueur, 1 part Peppermint Schnapps
top Whipped Cream *(Mix into Cocktail Glass—no ice)*

ILLUSION (1)-
1 part Light Rum, 1 part Melon Liqueur, 1 part Tequila, 1 part Triple Sec,
1 part Vodka
splash Lime Juice *(Mix into Cocktail Glass—no ice)*

ILLUSION (2)-
1 part Blue Curaçao, 1 part Light Rum, 1 part Melon Liqueur, 1 part Tequila,
1 part Vodka
splash Lime Juice *(Mix into Cocktail Glass—no ice)*

IMMACULATA-
3 parts Light Rum, 1 part Amaretto
Sour Mix *(Mix into Cocktail Glass—no ice)*

IMPERIAL COCKTAIL-
1 part Dry Vermouth, 1 part Gin, splash Maraschino Liqueur
Bitters, Cherry Garnish *(Mix into Cocktail Glass—no ice)*

IMPERIAL EGGNOG-
5 parts Brandy, 1 part Apricot Brandy
Eggnog, sprinkle Nutmeg *(Mix into Highball Glass—ice)*

IMPERIAL FIZZ-
3 parts Blended Whiskey, 1 part Light Rum
Sour Mix, splash Club Soda *(Mix into Highball Glass—ice)*

IMPERIAL HOTEL FIZZ-
2 parts Blended Whiskey, 1 part Light Rum
Lime Juice, fill Club Soda *(Mix into Highball Glass—ice)*

IMPERIAL MARTINI-
1 part Dry Vermouth, 1 part Gin, splash Maraschino Liqueur
splash Bitters *(Mix into Cocktail Glass—no ice)*

IN THE SACK-
1 part Apricot Brandy, 1 part Cream Sherry
Lime Juice, Orange Juice *(Mix into Highball Glass—ice)*

INCA-
1 part Dry Vermouth, 1 part Gin, 1 part Sherry, 1 part Sweet Vermouth
splash Orange Bitters *(Mix into Cocktail Glass—no ice)*

INCIDER-
Blended Whiskey
Apple Cider *(Mix into Highball Glass—ice)*

INCOME TAX-
Gin, splash Dry Vermouth, splash Sweet Vermouth
Orange Juice, Bitters *(Mix into Cocktail Glass—no ice)*

INCREDIBLE HULK-
Spiced Rum
Sugar, Mountain Dew® *(Mix into Highball Glass—ice)*

INDEPENDENCE SWIZZLE-
Dark Rum
Lime Juice, Honey, splash Bitters *(Mix into Highball Glass—ice)*

INDIAN RIVER-
3 parts Blended Whiskey, 1 part Raspberry Liqueur, 1 part Sweet Vermouth
Grapefruit Juice *(Mix into Highball Glass—ice)*

INDIAN SUMMER (1)-
Apple Schnapps
Hot Cider, Cinnamon Rim *(Mix into Irish Coffee Cup—no ice)*

INDIAN SUMMER (2)-
Coffee Liqueur, Vodka,
Pineapple Juice *(Mix into Highball Glass—ice)*

INDIFFERENT MISS-
Spiced Rum
Sugar, Club Soda *(Mix into Highball Glass—ice)*

INK SPOT-
1 part Blackberry Brandy, 1 part Peppermint Schnapps
(Layer in Order in Cocktail Glass—no ice)

INK STREET-
Blended Whiskey
splash Orange Juice, splash Lime Juice *(Mix into Cocktail Glass—no ice)*

INSTANT DEATH-
1 part 100-proof Vodka, 1 part Jägermeister®, 1 part 151-proof Rum
Salt, Water *(Mix into Highball Glass—ice)*

INTERNATIONAL, THE-
Cognac, splash Anisette, splash Triple Sec, splash Vodka
(Mix into Cocktail Glass—no ice)

INTERNATIONAL CREAM-
1 part Coffee Liqueur, 1 part Irish Cream Liqueur, splash Grand Marnier®
Vanilla Ice Cream, splash Light Cream or Milk
(Blend with ice in Daiquiri Glass)

INTERNATIONAL INCIDENT-
1 part Amaretto, 1 part Coffee Liqueur, 1 part Hazelnut Liqueur, 1 part Irish
     Cream Liqueur, 1 part Vodka
(Mix into Cocktail Glass—no ice)

INTERNATIONAL STINGER-
3 parts Metaxa, 1 part Galliano® *(Mix into Cocktail Glass—no ice)*

INVISIBLE MAN-
4 parts Gin, 1 part Brandy, 1 part Triple Sec
splash Orange Juice, fill Ginger Ale *(Mix into Highball Glass—ice)*

IRISH-
Irish Whiskey, splash Maraschino Liqueur, splash Licorice Liqueur,
     splash Triple Sec
splash Bitters *(Mix into Cocktail Glass—no ice)*

IRISH ANGEL-
3 parts Irish Whiskey, 1 part White Crème de Caçao, 1 part White
     Crème de Menthe
Light Cream or Milk *(Mix into Cocktail Glass—no ice)*

IRISH BERRY-
2 parts Irish Cream Liqueur, 1 part Vodka
Strawberry Daiquiri Mix, Coconut Milk, splash Grenadine
(Blend with ice in Daiquiri Glass)

IRISH CANADIAN-
3 parts Canadian Whiskey, 1 part Irish Mist®
(Mix into Cocktail Glass—no ice)

IRISH CHARLIE-
1 part Irish Cream Liqueur, 1 part White Crème de Menthe
(Mix into Cocktail Glass—no ice)

IRISH COFFEE-
Irish Whiskey, splash Green Crème de Menthe (lace on top of Whipped Cream)
Coffee, Sugar, top Whipped Cream *(Mix into Irish Coffee Cup—no ice)*

IRISH COOLER-
Irish Whiskey
Club Soda *(Mix into Highball Glass—ice)*

IRISH COW-
Irish Cream Liqueur
Light Cream or Milk *(Mix into Highball Glass—ice)*

IRISH CREAM FIZZ-
Irish Cream Liqueur
Club Soda *(Mix into Highball Glass—ice)*

IRISH DELIGHT-
Irish Whiskey
Light Cream or Milk *(Mix into Small Rocks Glass—ice)*

IRISH DREAM-
2 parts Brown Crème de Caçao, 1 part Hazelnut Liqueur,
    1 part Irish Cream Liqueur
Vanilla Ice Cream, top Whipped Cream, top Chocolate sprinkles
(Blend with ice in Daiquiri Glass)

IRISH ELEGANCE-
3 parts Jamaican Rum, 1 part Brandy, splash Crème de Yvette
Pineapple Juice, splash Lime Juice
(Mix into Highball Glass—ice)

IRISH EYES-
4 parts Irish Whiskey, 1 part Green Crème de Menthe
Light Cream or Milk *(Mix into Cocktail Glass—no ice)*

IRISH FIX-
4 parts Irish Whiskey, 1 part Irish Mist®
Pineapple Juice, splash Sour Mix *(Mix into Highball Glass—ice)*

IRISH FLAG (1)-
1 part Green Crème de Menthe, 1 part White Crème de Caçao, 1 part Triple
    Sec, 1 part Irish Whiskey *(Layer in Order in Cocktail Glass—no ice)*

IRISH FLAG (2)-
1 part Green Crème de Menthe, 1 part Irish Cream Liqueur, 1 part Grand
    Marnier® *(Layer in Order in Cocktail Glass—no ice)*

IRISH FROG-
1 part Melon Liqueur, 1 part Irish Cream Liqueur
(Layer in Order in Cocktail Glass—no ice)

IRISH HEADLOCK-
1 part Irish Cream Liqueur, 1 part Irish Whiskey, 1 part Amaretto, 1 part Brandy
(Layer in Order in Cocktail Glass—no ice)

IRISH HORSEMAN-
3 parts Irish Whiskey, 1 part Triple Sec, splash Raspberry Liqueur
Sour Mix *(Mix into Highball Glass—ice)*

IRISH KILT-
1 part Irish Whiskey, 1 part Scotch Whiskey
Sour Mix, splash Orange Bitters
(Mix into Cocktail Glass—no ice)

IRISH KISS-
2 parts Irish Whiskey, 1 part Peach Schnapps
Orange Juice, fill Ginger Ale *(Mix into Highball Glass—ice)*

IRISH KNIGHT-
Irish Whiskey, splash Bénédictine, splash Dry Vermouth
Orange Juice *(Mix into Small Rocks Glass—ice)*

IRISH MAGIC-
4 parts Irish Whiskey, 1 part White Crème de Caçao
Orange Juice *(Mix into Highball Glass—ice)*

IRISH MILK PUNCH-
Irish Whiskey
Light Cream or Milk, Sugar *(Mix into Highball Glass—ice)*

IRISH MONKEY-
1 part Irish Cream Liqueur, 1 part Banana Liqueur
(Layer in Order in Cocktail Glass—no ice)

IRISH MOUNTY-
1 part Canadian Whiskey, 1 part Irish Mist®
Light Cream or Milk, sprinkle Nutmeg *(Mix into Cocktail Glass—no ice)*

IRISH PRINCE-
Irish Whiskey
Tonic Water *(Mix into Highball Glass—ice)*

IRISH QUAALUDE-
1 part Hazelnut Liqueur, 1 part Irish Cream Liqueur, 1 part Vodka, 1 part White
Crème de Caçao *(Mix into Cocktail Glass—no ice)*

IRISH RAINBOW-
Irish Whiskey, splash Anisette, splash Maraschino Liqueur, splash Triple Sec
splash Bitters *(Mix into Small Rocks Glass—ice)*

IRISH RICKEY-
Irish Whiskey
Club Soda, splash Lime Juice *(Mix into Highball Glass—ice)*

IRISH SHILLELAGH-
Irish Whiskey, splash Light Rum, splash Sloe Gin
Sour Mix *(Mix into Highball Glass—ice)*

IRISH SPRING-
2 parts Irish Whiskey, 1 part Peach Brandy
Orange Juice, Sour Mix *(Mix into Highball Glass—ice)*

IRISH SUMMER COFFEE-
4 parts Irish Whiskey, 1 part Irish Cream Liqueur
Cold Coffee *(Mix into Highball Glass—ice)*

IRISH SUNRISE-
1 part Amaretto, 1 part Banana Liqueur, 1 part Irish Cream Liqueur
(Layer in Order in Cocktail Glass—no ice)

IRISH SUNSET-
    1 part Banana Liqueur, 1 part Amaretto, 1 part Irish Cream Liqueur
    (Layer in Order in Cocktail Glass—no ice)

IRISH TEA-
    Irish Whiskey
    Irish Tea, Sugar *(Mix into Irish Coffee Cup—no ice)*

IRISH WHISKEY COCKTAIL-
    Irish Whiskey, splash Anisette, splash Maraschino Liqueur, splash Triple Sec
    Bitters, Olive Garnish *(Mix into Cocktail Glass—no ice)*

IRISH WHISKEY HIGHBALL-
    Irish Whiskey
    Ginger Ale *(Mix into Highball Glass—ice)*

IRON BUTTERFLY-
    1 part Vodka, 1 part Coffee Liqueur, 1 part Light Cream or Milk
    (Layer in Order in Cocktail Glass—no ice)

IRON CROSS-
    1 part Apricot Brandy, 1 part Peppermint Schnapps
    (Mix into Small Rocks Glass—ice)

IRRESISTIBLE MANHATTAN, THE-
    1 part Amaretto, 1 part Canadian Whiskey, 1 part Sweet Vermouth
    splash Bitters *(Mix into Cocktail Glass—no ice)*

IS PARIS BURNING-
    2 parts Cognac, 1 part Raspberry Liqueur *(Mix into Cocktail Glass—no ice)*

ISLAND BREEZE-
    Coconut Rum
    Cranberry Juice *(Mix into Highball Glass—ice)*

ISLAND COCOA-
    Coconut Rum
    Hot Chocolate, top Whipped Cream *(Mix into Irish Coffee Cup—no ice)*

ISLAND JOY-
    4 parts Spiced Rum, 1 part Peach Schnapps
    Pineapple Juice, splash Lime Juice *(Mix into Highball Glass—ice)*

ISLAND MARTINI-
    Rum, splash Dry Vermouth, splash Sweet Vermouth
    (Mix into Cocktail Glass—no ice)

ISLAND MILK-
    4 parts Brandy, 1 part Dark Rum
    Light Cream or Milk, Sugar, sprinkle Nutmeg
    (Mix into Highball Glass—ice)

ISLAND REGGAE BEAT-
    1 part Cognac, 1 part Drambuie®, 1 part Scotch Whiskey
    Fruit Punch, splash Grenadine *(Blend with ice in Daiquiri Glass)*

ISLAND SEABREEZE-
1 part Dark Rum, 1 part Light Rum
Pineapple Juice *(Mix into Highball Glass—ice)*

ISLAND TOY-
4 parts Spiced Rum, 1 part Peach Schnapps
Pineapple Juice, Splash Lime Juice *(Mix into Highball Glass—ice)*

ISLE OF PINES-
Light Rum
Grapefruit Juice *(Mix into Highball Glass—ice)*

ISLE OF THE BLESSED COCONUT-
Light Rum, splash Amaretto
Orange Juice, Lime Juice, Coconut Milk
(Blend with ice in Daiquiri Glass)

ISRAELI COFFEE-
Sabra® Liqueur
Coffee, top Whipped Cream *(Mix into Irish Coffee Cup—no ice)*

ITALIAN BANANA-
1 part Banana Liqueur, 1 part Amaretto
Orange Juice, splash Lime Juice
(Mix into Highball Glass with ice or blend with ice in Daiquiri Glass)

ITALIAN COFFEE (1)-
Amaretto
Coffee, Coffee Ice Cream *(Mix into Irish Coffee Cup—no ice)*

ITALIAN COFFEE (2)-
Galliano®
Coffee, top Whipped Cream *(Mix into Irish Coffee Cup—no ice)*

ITALIAN COLADA-
3 parts Light Rum, 1 part Amaretto
Pineapple Juice, Coconut Milk, Light Cream or Milk
(Mix into Highball Glass with ice or blend with ice in Daiquiri Glass)

ITALIAN DELIGHT-
Amaretto
Light Cream or Milk, splash Orange Juice
(Mix into Highball Glass—ice)

ITALIAN DREAM-
3 parts Irish Cream Liqueur, 1 part Amaretto
Light Cream or Milk *(Blend with ice in Daiquiri Glass)*

ITALIAN HEATHER-
2 parts Scotch Whiskey, 1 part Galliano®
(Mix into Cocktail Glass—no ice)

ITALIAN PACIFIER-
White Crème de Menthe
splash Bitters *(Mix into Small Rocks Glass—ice)*

ITALIAN SCREWDRIVER-
Citrus Vodka
Orange Juice, Grapefruit Juice, splash Ginger Ale
(Mix into Highball Glass—ice)

ITALIAN SOMBRERO-
Amaretto
Light Cream or Milk
(Mix into Highball Glass with ice or blend with ice in Daiquiri Glass)

ITALIAN STALLION-
3 parts Bourbon Whiskey, 1 part Campari, 1 part Sweet Vermouth
splash Bitters *(Mix into Cocktail Glass—no ice)*

ITALIAN STINGER-
3 parts Brandy, 1 part Galliano® *(Mix into Cocktail Glass—no ice)*

ITALIAN SURFER-
1 part Amaretto, 1 part Brandy
Pineapple Juice *(Mix into Highball Glass—ice)*

ITALIAN SURFER WITH A RUSSIAN ATTITUDE-
1 part Amaretto, 1 part Coconut Rum, 1 part Vodka
Pineapple Juice, splash Cranberry Juice *(Mix into Highball Glass—ice)*

ITALIAN VALIUM (I. V.)-
2 parts Amaretto, 1 part Gin *(Mix into Cocktail Glass—no ice)*

IVY CLUB-
3 parts Gin, 1 part Amaretto
Lime Juice, splash Grenadine *(Mix into Cocktail Glass—no ice)*

IXTAPA-
2 parts Coffee Liqueur, 1 part Tequila *(Mix into Cocktail Glass—no ice)*

– NOTES –

_____

_____

_____

_____

_____

_____

_____

_____

_____

J. R. 'S GODCHILD-
4 parts Bourbon Whiskey, 1 part Amaretto
Light Cream or Milk *(Mix into Cocktail Glass—no ice)*

J. R. 'S GODFATHER-
4 parts Bourbon Whiskey, 1 part Amaretto *(Mix into Cocktail Glass—no ice)*

J. R. 'S REVENGE-
Bourbon Whiskey, splash Southern Comfort®
splash Bitters *(Mix into Cocktail Glass—no ice)*

JABBERWOCK-
1 part Dry Sherry, Gin, 1 part Red Dubonnet®
splash Orange Bitters *(Mix into Cocktail Glass—no ice)*

JACARANDA-
2 parts Dark Rum, 1 part Peppermint Schnapps, splash Peach Schnapps (float)
Orange Juice, Light Cream or Milk *(Mix into Cocktail Glass—no ice)*

JACK-IN-THE-BOX-
Apple Brandy
Pineapple Juice, Bitters *(Mix into Cocktail Glass—no ice)*

JACK FROST-
1 part Jack Daniel's® Tennessee Sour Mash Whiskey, 1 part Peppermint
Schnapps *(Mix into Small Rocks Glass—ice)*

JACK ME OFF-
3 parts Applejack® Apple Brandy, 1 part Melon Liqueur
Lemon-Lime Soda *(Mix into Highball Glass—ice)*

JACK RABBIT-
Apple Brandy
Orange Juice, Lime Juice, Maple Syrup *(Mix into Cocktail Glass—no ice)*

JACK ROBERT'S TREAT-
4 parts Brandy, 1 part Brown Crème de Caçao
Hot Chocolate, top Whipped Cream *(Mix in Irish Coffee Cup—no ice)*

JACK ROSE-
Apple Brandy
Lime Juice, Grenadine *(Mix into Cocktail Glass—no ice)*

JACK SLOAT-
Gin, splash Dry Vermouth, splash Sweet Vermouth
Pineapple Slice Garnish *(Mix into Cocktail Glass—no ice)*

JACK WITHERS-
1 part Dry Vermouth, 1 part Gin, 1 part Sweet Vermouth
Orange Juice *(Mix into Cocktail Glass—no ice)*

JACK'S JAM-
1 part Apple Schnapps, 1 part Banana Liqueur, 1 part Peach Schnapps,
1 part Strawberry Schnapps
Sour Mix, Orange Juice *(Mix into Highball Glass—ice)*

JACKALOPE-
　　1 part Amaretto, 1 part Coffee Liqueur, 1 part Jamaican Rum, splash Brown
　　　　Crème de Caçao (lace)
　　Pineapple Juice *(Mix into Highball Glass—ice)*

JACKATH-
　　Vodka, splash Brandy, splash Crème de Cassis, splash Triple Sec
　　splash Orange Bitters *(Mix into Cocktail Glass with no ice)*

JACKHAMMER (1)-
　　3 parts Root Beer Schnapps, 1 part Yukon Jack® Canadian Liqueur
　　(Mix into Cocktail Glass—no ice)

JACKHAMMER (2)-
　　1 part Jack Daniel's® Tennessee Sour Mash Whiskey, 1 part Root Beer Schnapps
　　(Mix into Small Rocks Glass—ice)

JACKHAMMER (3)-
　　1 part Yukon Jack® Canadian Liqueur, 1 part Yukon Jack® Perma Frost Schnapps
　　(Mix into Small Rocks Glass—ice)

JACKIE O'S ROSE-
　　Light Rum, splash Triple Sec
　　Sour Mix *(Mix into Cocktail Glass—no ice)*

JACKSON STANDARD-
　　1 part Gin, 1 part Red Dubonnet®
　　splash Orange Bitters *(Mix into Cocktail Glass—no ice)*

JACQUELINE-
　　2 parts Dark Rum, 1 part Triple Sec
　　Sour Mix *(Mix into Cocktail Glass—no ice)*

JADE-
　　Light Rum, splash Green Crème de Menthe, splash Triple Sec
　　Sour Mix *(Mix into Cocktail Glass—no ice)*

JAGER SHAKE-
　　1 part Amaretto, 1 part Irish Cream Liqueur, 1 part Jägermeister®,
　　　　1 part Root Beer Schnapps
　　Cola *(Mix into Highball Glass—ice)*

JAGUAR-
　　2 parts Galliano®, 1 part White Crème de Caçao
　　Light Cream or Milk
　　(Mix into Highball Glass with ice or blend with ice in Daiquiri Glass)

JAKE-
　　Jack Daniel's® Tennessee Sour Mash Whiskey
　　Cola *(Mix into Highball Glass—ice)*

JAMAICA BLUE-
　　2 parts Light Rum, 1 part Blueberry Schnapps, 1 part Blue Curaçao
　　Lime Juice, top Club Soda
　　(Mix into Highball Glass—ice)

JAMAICA COFFEE-
1 part Coffee Brandy, 1 part Light Rum
Coffee, top Whipped Cream *(Mix in Irish Coffee Cup—no ice)*

JAMAICA COOLER-
Dark Rum
splash Sour Mix, splash Orange Bitters, fill Lemon-Lime Soda
(Mix into Highball Glass—ice)

JAMAICA CREAM-
2 parts Dark Rum, 1 part Gin
Light Cream or Milk, Sour Mix, fill Club Soda *(Mix into Highball Glass—ice)*

JAMAICA GINGER-
Dark Rum, splash Maraschino Liqueur, splash Triple Sec
Grenadine, splash Bitters *(Mix into Cocktail Glass—no ice)*

JAMAICA GLOW-
Gin, splash Claret, splash Jamaican Rum
Orange Juice *(Mix into Cocktail Glass—no ice)*

JAMAICA GRANITO-
2 parts Brandy, 1 part Triple Sec
Club Soda, Lemon or Orange Sherbet, sprinkle Nutmeg
(Mix into Highball Glass—ice)

JAMAICA HOP-
1 part Coffee Brandy, 1 part White Crème de Caçao
Light Cream or Milk *(Mix into Cocktail Glass—no ice)*

JAMAICA ME CRAZY-
1 part Dark or Spiced Rum, 1 part Tia Maria®
Pineapple Juice *(Mix into Highball Glass—ice)*

JAMAICA MULE-
2 parts Light Rum, 1 part Dark Rum, splash Amaretto, fill Ginger Beer
Lime Juice *(Mix into Highball Glass—ice)*

JAMAICA SHAKE-
1 part Bourbon Whiskey, 1 part Dark Rum
Light Cream or Milk *(Mix into Cocktail Glass—no ice)*

JAMAICAN BANANA-
1 part Banana Liqueur, 1 part Light Rum, 1 part White Crème de Caçao
Light Cream or Milk, Vanilla Ice Cream, Banana
(Blend with ice in Daiquiri Glass)

JAMAICAN BEER-
1 part Blended Whiskey, 1 part Dry Vermouth, 1 part Gin, 1 part Sweet
    Vermouth, splash Blue Curaçao (lace), splash Red Vodka (lace), fill Beer
(Beer Mug)

JAMAICAN BLUES-
2 parts Coconut Rum, 2 parts Dark Rum, 1 part Blue Curaçao
Pineapple Juice
(Mix into Highball Glass with ice or blend with ice in Daiquiri Glass)

JAMAICAN CAB DRIVER-
Coconut Rum
Cranberry Juice, Orange Juice *(Mix into Highball Glass—ice)*

JAMAICAN COCKTAIL-
1 part Coffee Liqueur, 1 part Dark Rum
Lime Juice, splash Bitters, fill Lemon-Lime Soda *(Mix into Highball Glass—ice)*

JAMAICAN COFFEE (1)-
1 part Jamaican Rum, 1 part Tia Maria®
Coffee, top Whipped Cream *(Mix in Irish Coffee Cup—no ice)*

JAMAICAN COFFEE (2)-
1 part Coffee Liqueur, 1 part Jamaican Rum
Coffee, Sugared Rim, top Whipped Cream *(Mix in Irish Coffee Cup—no ice)*

JAMAICAN COFFEE (3)-
1 part Brandy, 1 part Light Rum
Coffee, top Whipped Cream *(Mix in Irish Coffee Cup—no ice)*

JAMAICAN CRAWLER-
1 part Light Rum, 1 part Melon Liqueur
Pineapple Juice, Grenadine (float) *(Mix into Highball Glass—ice)*

JAMAICAN CREAM-
1 part Dark Rum, 1 part Triple Sec
Light Cream or Milk *(Mix into Cocktail Glass—no ice)*

JAMAICAN DREAM-
Light Rum
Grapefruit Juice, Pineapple Juice, Orange Juice
(Blend with ice in Daiquiri Glass)

JAMAICAN DUST-
1 part Light Rum, 1 part Tia Maria®
Pineapple Juice *(Mix into Highball Glass—ice)*

JAMAICAN GLOW-
Dark Rum
Light Cream or Milk, Papaya Juice, Sour Mix *(Blend with ice in Daiquiri Glass)*

JAMAICAN KISS-
1 part Light Rum, 1 part Tia Maria®
Light Cream or Milk *(Mix into Cocktail Glass—no ice)*

JAMAICAN MARTINI-
Light Rum, splash Dry Sherry
Olive Garnish *(Mix into Cocktail Glass—no ice)*

JAMAICAN MILK SHAKE-
1 part Bourbon Whiskey, 1 part Jamaican Rum
Light Cream or Milk *(Blend with ice in Daiquiri Glass)*

JAMAICAN QUEEN-
2 parts Spiced Rum, 1 part Banana Liqueur
Vanilla Ice Cream, Strawberry Daiquiri Mix *(Blend with ice in Daiquiri Glass)*

JAMAICAN RUM COCKTAIL-
Jamaican Rum
Sour Mix *(Mix into Cocktail Glass—no ice)*

JAMAICAN SCREWDRIVER-
Coconut Rum
Orange Juice *(Mix into Highball Glass—ice)*

JAMAICAN SHAKIN'-
2 parts Bourbon Whiskey, 1 part Dark Rum
Light Cream or Milk *(Mix into Cocktail Glass—no ice)*

JAMAICAN SUNRISE-
1 part Peach Schnapps, 1 part Vodka
Cranberry Juice, Orange Juice *(Mix into Highball Glass—ice)*

JAMAICAN WIND-
2 parts Dark Rum, 1 part Coffee Liqueur
Light Cream or Milk *(Mix into Cocktail Glass—no ice)*

JAMAICAN YO YO-
1 part Dark Rum, 1 part Tia Maria®
(Mix into Small Rocks Glass—ice)

JAMBALAYA-
1 part Peach Schnapps, 1 part Southern Comfort®
Sour Mix, splash Grenadine *(Mix into Highball Glass—ice)*

JAMBO JACK-
4 parts Jamaican Rum, 1 part Apricot Brandy, 1 part Triple Sec, splash Amaretto
Lime Juice *(Mix into Highball Glass—ice)*

JAMBOREE-
1 part Raspberry Schnapps, 1 part Vodka
Cranberry Juice *(Mix into Highball Glass—ice)*

JAMES BOND MARTINI-
3 parts Gin, 1 part Vodka, splash Dry Vermouth
Lime Twist Garnish (shaken, not stirred) *(Mix into Cocktail Glass—no ice)*

JAMES THE SECOND COMES FIRST-
Scotch Whiskey, splash Dry Vermouth, splash Tawny Port
splash Bitters *(Mix into Cocktail Glass—no ice)*

JANET SPECIAL-
Brandy
splash Orgeat (Almond) Syrup, splash Bitters *(Mix into Cocktail Glass—no ice)*

JAP SLAP-
1 part Melon Liqueur, 1 part Vodka
Lime Juice or Sour Mix *(Mix into Highball Glass—ice)*

JAPAN TOWN-
Brandy, splash Amaretto
Lime Juice, splash Bitters *(Mix into Cocktail Glass—no ice)*

JAPANESE-
Brandy
Lime Juice, Orgeat (Almond) Syrup, Bitters *(Mix into Cocktail Glass—no ice)*

JAPANESE COFFEE-
Japanese Whiskey
Coffee, Sugar, top Whipped Cream *(Mix in Irish Coffee Cup—no ice)*

JAPANESE FIZZ-
2 parts Blended Whiskey, 1 part Port
Sour Mix, splash Club Soda *(Mix into Highball Glass—ice)*

JAPANESE FLIP-
Blended Whiskey or Japanese Whiskey, splash Port
Light Cream or Milk, Sugar, Pineapple Garnish
(Mix into Highball Glass—ice)

JAVA COOLER-
Gin
Lime Juice, splash Bitters, fill Tonic Water *(Mix into Highball Glass—ice)*

JAVA FLIP-
2 parts Brandy, 1 part Port
Coffee, Sugar *(Mix in Wine Glass—no ice)*

JEAN LAFITTE-
2 parts Gin, 1 part Anisette, 1 part Triple Sec
Sugar *(Mix into Cocktail Glass—no ice)*

JEFF TRACY-
1 part Cherry Brandy, 1 part Dry Vermouth, 1 part Gin, splash Sweet Vermouth
(Mix into Cocktail Glass—no ice)

JELLY BEANS (1)-
1 part Amaretto, 1 part Sambuca *(Mix into Cocktail Glass—no ice)*

JELLY BEANS (2)-
1 part Blackberry Brandy, 1 part Brandy, 1 part Sambuca
(Mix into Cocktail Glass—no ice)

JELLY BEANS (3)-
2 parts Blackberry Brandy, 2 parts Blended Whiskey, 1 part Anisette
(Mix into Cocktail Glass—no ice)

JELLY BEANS (4)-
1 part Anisette, 1 part Blackberry Brandy
(Mix into Cocktail Glass—no ice)

JELLY DOUGHNUT-
1 part Irish Cream Liqueur, 1 part Raspberry Liqueur
(Mix into Cocktail Glass—no ice)

JELLY FISH-
1 part Amaretto, 1 part Irish Cream Liqueur, 1 part White Crème de Caçao
Grenadine (lace) *(Mix into Cocktail Glass—no ice)*

JELLYBEAN-
   3 parts Brandy, 1 part Anisette
   splash Grenadine *(Mix into Small Rocks Glass—ice)*

JERICHO'S BREEZE-
   1 part Blue Curaçao, 1 part Vodka
   Sour Mix, splash Orange Juice, splash Lemon-Lime Soda
   (Mix into Highball Glass—ice)

JERSEY GENTLEMAN-
   3 parts Blended Whiskey, 1 part Licorice Liqueur
   Pineapple Juice *(Mix into Cocktail Glass—no ice)*

JERSEY LIGHTNING-
   3 parts Apple Brandy, 1 part Sweet Vermouth
   Lime Juice *(Mix into Cocktail Glass—no ice)*

JESSICA'S BLUE-
   2 parts Vodka, 1 part Blue Curaçao, splash Cherry Brandy
   (Mix into Cocktail Glass—no ice)

JET BLACK-
   2 parts Gin, 1 part Black Sambuca, splash Sweet Vermouth
   (Mix into Cocktail Glass—no ice)

JEWEL-
   1 part Gin, 1 part Green Chartreuse, 1 part Sweet Vermouth
   Orange Bitters, Cherry Garnish *(Mix into Cocktail Glass—no ice)*

JEWEL OF THE NILE-
   3 parts Gin, 1 part Green Chartreuse, 1 part Yellow Chartreuse
   (Mix into Cocktail Glass—no ice)

JEYPLAK-
   2 parts Gin, 1 part Sweet Vermouth, splash Anisette
   (Mix into Cocktail Glass—no ice)

JILLIONAIRE-
   4 parts Bourbon Whiskey, 1 part Triple Sec
   splash Grenadine *(Mix into Cocktail Glass—no ice)*

JOBURG-
   1 part Light Rum, 1 part Red Dubonnet®
   splash Orange Bitters *(Mix into Cocktail Glass—no ice)*

JOCK-IN-A-BOX-
   3 parts Scotch Whiskey, 1 part Sweet Vermouth
   Lime Juice *(Mix into Cocktail Glass—no ice)*

JOCK COLLINS-
   Scotch Whiskey
   splash Sour Mix, fill Club Soda *(Mix into Highball Glass—ice)*

JOCKEY CLUB COCKTAIL-
   Gin, splash White Crème de Caçao
   Lime Juice, Bitters *(Mix into Cocktail Glass—no ice)*

JOCOSE JULEP-
Bourbon Whiskey, splash Green Crème de Menthe
Sour Mix, Club Soda (top), Mint Leaves Garnish
(Blend with ice in Daiquiri Glass)

JOE COLLINS-
Scotch Whiskey
Sour Mix, splash Club Soda *(Mix into Highball Glass—ice)*

JOHN COLLINS-
Blended Whiskey or Bourbon Whiskey
Sour Mix, splash Club Soda
(Mix into Highball Glass—ice)

JOHNNIE-
2 parts Sloe Gin, 1 part Triple Sec, splash Anisette
(Mix into Cocktail Glass—no ice)

JOHNNY ON THE BEACH-
1 part Black Raspberry Liqueur, 1 part Melon Liqueur, 1 part Vodka
Pineapple Juice, Orange Juice, Grapefruit Juice, Cranberry Juice
(Mix into Highball Glass—ice)

JOLLY JULEP-
2 parts Bourbon Whiskey, 1 part Green Crème de Menthe
Sour Mix, fill Sparkling Water, Mint Leaves Garnish
(Mix into Highball Glass—ice)

JOLLY GREEN GIANT-
1 part Blue Curaçao, 1 part Gin, 1 part Light Rum, 1 part Tequila,
1 part Triple Sec *(Mix into Cocktail Glass—no ice)*

JOLLY RANCHER-
1 part Melon Liqueur, 1 part Peach Schnapps
Cranberry Juice *(Mix into Highball Glass—ice)*

JOLLY ROGER (1)-
1 part Banana Liqueur, 1 part Dark Rum
Lime Juice *(Mix into Cocktail Glass—no ice)*

JOLLY ROGER (2)-
2 parts Light Rum, 1 part Drambuie®, splash Scotch Whiskey
Lime Juice, fill Club Soda *(Mix into Highball Glass—ice)*

JONESEY-
4 parts Dark Rum, 1 part Brown Crème de Caçao
(Mix into Cocktail Glass—no ice)

JOSIAH'S BAY FLOAT-
2 parts Light Rum, 1 part Galliano®, fill Champagne
Pineapple Juice, Sour Mix *(Mix in Champagne Flute—no ice)*

JOULOUVILLE-
2 parts Gin, 1 part Apple Brandy, splash Sweet Vermouth
Lime Juice, Grenadine *(Mix into Cocktail Glass—no ice)*

JOUMBABA-
Tequila
Grapefruit Juice, fill Tonic Water *(Mix into Highball Glass—ice)*

JOURNALIST-
Gin, splash Dry Vermouth, splash Sweet Vermouth, splash Triple Sec
Lime Juice, Bitters *(Mix into Cocktail Glass—no ice)*

JOY JUMPER-
Vodka, splash Kümmel
Sour Mix *(Mix into Cocktail Glass—no ice)*

JOY TO THE WORLD-
3 parts Light Rum, 1 part Bourbon Whiskey, 1 part Brown Crème de Caçao
(Mix into Cocktail Glass—no ice)

JOYCE OF HILLHOUSE-
1 part Scotch Whiskey, 1 part Sweet Vermouth
splash Bitters *(Mix into Cocktail Glass—no ice)*

JU-JU-BE-
1 part Banana Liqueur, 1 part Strawberry Schnapps
Orange Juice, splash Lime Juice *(Mix into Small Rocks Glass—ice)*

JUAN BLUE-
Tequila, splash Blue Curaçao (float)
Orange Juice, Grapefruit Juice, splash Lime Juice, splash Bitters
(Mix into Highball Glass—ice)

JUBILEE-
2 parts Tequila, 1 part Blue Curaçao, 1 part Gin, 1 part Vodka
Sour Mix, fill Club Soda *(Mix into Highball Glass—ice)*

JUDGE JR.-
1 part Gin, 1 part Light Rum
Sour Mix, Grenadine *(Mix into Cocktail Glass—no ice)*

JUDGETTE-
1 part Dry Vermouth, 1 part Gin, 1 part Peach Brandy
Lime Juice *(Mix into Cocktail Glass—no ice)*

JUICY FRUIT-
1 part Melon Liqueur, 1 part Peach Schnapps, 1 part Vodka
Pineapple Juice *(Mix into Highball Glass—ice)*

JULIUS SPECIAL-
2 parts Jamaican Rum, 1 part Triple Sec
Sour Mix *(Mix into Cocktail Glass—no ice)*

JUMPING BEAN-
3 parts Tequila, 1 part Sambuca
Coffee Beans Garnish *(Mix into Cocktail Glass—no ice)*

JUNGLE JIM-
1 part Banana Liqueur, 1 part Vodka
Light Cream or Milk *(Mix into Highball Glass—ice)*

JUNGLE JOE-
1 part Banana Liqueur, 1 part Vodka
Light Cream or Milk *(Mix into Highball Glass—ice)*

JUNGLE JUICE-
2 parts Light Rum, 2 parts Vodka, 1 part Triple Sec
Cranberry Juice, Orange Juice, Pineapple Juice, splash Sour Mix
(Mix into Highball Glass—ice)

JUNIOR LEAGUE-
2 parts Blended Whiskey, 1 part Anisette *(Mix into Cocktail Glass—no ice)*

JUNIPER BLEND-
1 part Cherry Brandy, 1 part Gin, splash Dry Vermouth
(Mix into Cocktail Glass—no ice)

JUPITER-
2 parts Gin, 1 part Dry Vermouth, splash Crème de Yvette
Orange Juice *(Mix into Cocktail Glass—no ice)*

– NOTES –

K. C. B.-
Gin, splash Apricot Brandy, splash Cherry Brandy
splash Lime Juice *(Mix into Cocktail Glass—no ice)*

K. G. B.-
3 parts Gin, 1 part Kümmel, splash Apricot Brandy
Lime Juice *(Mix into Cocktail Glass—no ice)*

KABUKI-
Sake, splash Triple Sec
Lime Juice, Sour Mix, Salted Rim *(Mix into Highball Glass—ice)*

KAHLUA COCKTAIL-
1 part Crème de Noyaux, 1 part Kahlua® Coffee Liqueur
Light Cream or Milk
(Mix into Cocktail Glass—no ice)

KAHLUA FIZZ-
Kahlua® Coffee Liqueur
Light Cream or Milk, splash Cola *(Mix into Highball Glass—ice)*

KAHLUA HUMMER-
1 part Kahlua® Coffee Liqueur, 1 part Light Rum
Vanilla Ice Cream *(Blend with ice in Daiquiri Glass)*

KAHLUA SMITH & KEARNS-
Kahlua® Coffee Liqueur
splash Cream or Milk, fill Club Soda *(Mix into Highball Glass—ice)*

KAHLUA TOREADOR-
2 parts Brandy, 1 part Kahlua® Coffee Liqueur
(Mix into Small Rocks Glass—ice)

KAHLUACCINO-
2 parts Vodka, 1 part Kahlua® Coffee Liqueur
Cappuccino Mix, splash Light Cream or Milk
(Mix into Highball Glass—ice)

KAISER KOLA-
Cherry Brandy or Black Cherry Liqueur
Cola *(Mix into Highball Glass—ice)*

KAMIKAZE-
1 part Triple Sec, 1 part Vodka
Lime Juice or Sour Mix *(Mix into Highball Glass—ice)*

KANDY KANE-
1 part Crème de Noyaux, 1 part Peppermint Schnapps
(Mix into Cocktail Glass—no ice)

KANGAROO-
2 parts Vodka, 1 part Dry Vermouth *(Mix into Cocktail Glass—no ice)*

KANGAROO KICKER-
3 parts Vodka, 1 part French Vermouth *(Mix into Cocktail Glass—no ice)*

KAPPA COLADA-
Brandy
Pineapple Juice, Coconut Milk *(Blend with ice in Daiquiri Glass)*

KAROFF-
Vodka
Cranberry Juice, fill Club Soda *(Mix into Highball Glass—ice)*

KAYTEE-
1 part Dry Vermouth, 1 part Sherry, splash Licorice Liqueur
(Mix into Cocktail Glass—no ice)

KEMPINSKY FIZZ-
2 parts Vodka, 1 part Crème de Cassis
Lime Juice, splash Ginger Ale *(Mix into Highball Glass—ice)*

KENTUCKY-
Bourbon Whiskey
Pineapple Juice *(Mix into Cocktail Glass—no ice)*

KENTUCKY B & B-
4 parts Bourbon Whiskey, 1 part Bénédictine *(Snifter)*

KENTUCKY BLIZZARD-
Bourbon Whiskey
Cranberry Juice, Sour Mix, Grenadine *(Mix into Cocktail Glass—no ice)*

KENTUCKY CAPPUCCINO-
1 part Bourbon Whiskey, 1 part Coffee Liqueur
Light Cream or Milk, Instant Coffee Grinds, Club Soda, top Whipped Cream
(Blend with ice in Daiquiri Glass)

KENTUCKY COFFEE-
Bourbon Whiskey
Coffee, top Whipped Cream *(Mix in Irish Coffee Cup—no ice)*

KENTUCKY COLONEL-
3 parts Bourbon Whiskey, 1 part Bénédictine *(Mix into Cocktail Glass—no ice)*

KENTUCKY COOLER-
3 parts Bourbon Whiskey, 1 part Light Rum
Orange Juice, Lime Juice, splash Grenadine *(Mix into Cocktail Glass—no ice)*

KENTUCKY ORANGE BLOSSOM-
Bourbon Whiskey, splash Triple Sec
Orange Juice *(Mix into Highball Glass—ice)*

KENTUCKY SUNRISE-
Bourbon Whiskey
Orange Juice, Grenadine (lace) (stir with straw for "sunrise")
(Mix into Highball Glass—ice)

KEREMIKI-
1 part Goldschläger®, 1 part Peppermint Schnapps, 1 part 151-proof Rum
(Mix into Small Rocks Glass—ice)

KERRY COOLER-
2 parts Irish Whiskey, 1 part Sherry
Lime Juice, splash Orgeat (Almond) Syrup, fill Club Soda
(Mix into Highball Glass—ice)

KEY BISCAYNE-
3 parts Blended Whiskey, 1 part Sweet Vermouth, 1 part Triple Sec
Lime Juice *(Mix into Cocktail Glass—no ice)*

KEY CLUB-
4 parts Gin, 1 part Amaretto, 1 part Dark Rum
Lime Juice *(Mix into Cocktail Glass—no ice)*

KEY LARGO KOOLER-
2 parts Key Largo® Tropical Fruit Schnapps, 1 part Spiced Rum,
    1 part 151-proof Rum
Cranberry Juice, Orange Juice, Pineapple Juice
(Mix into Highball Glass with ice or blend with ice in Daiquiri Glass)

KEY LARGO MADRAS-
Key Largo® Tropical Fruit Schnapps
Orange Juice, Cranberry Juice *(Mix into Highball Glass—ice)*

KEY LARGO PARROT-
Key Largo® Tropical Fruit Schnapps
splash Orange Juice, Grenadine (lace) *(Mix into Small Rocks Glass—ice)*

KEY LIME QUENCHER-
1 part Coconut Rum, 1 part Dark Rum
Light Cream or Milk, Sour Mix
(Mix into Highball Glass with ice or blend with ice in Daiquiri Glass)

KEY WEST SONG-
1 part Spiced Rum
Coconut Milk, Orange Juice *(Mix into Highball Glass—ice)*

KIALOA-
2 parts Coffee Liqueur, 1 part Spiced Rum
Light Cream or Milk *(Mix into Small Rocks Glass—ice)*

KICKING COW-
Blended Whiskey
Light Cream or Milk, Maple Syrup *(Mix into Cocktail Glass—no ice)*

KILL DEVIL-
2 parts Light Rum, 1 part Brandy
Honey, splash Water *(Mix into Small Rocks Glass—ice)*

KILLER KOOL-AID-
3 parts Vodka, 1 part Peach Schnapps, 1 part Amaretto, Cranberry Juice
(Layer in Order in Highball Glass with no ice)

KINA-
2 parts Gin, 1 part Lillet, 1 part Sweet Vermouth
(Mix into Cocktail Glass—no ice)

KING ALFONSE-
Coffee Liqueur
Light Cream or Milk (float) *(Mix into Cocktail Glass—no ice)*

KING ALFONSO-
White Crème de Caçao
Light Cream or Milk *(Mix into Cocktail Glass—no ice)*

KING COLE-
Blended Whiskey
Orange Slice, Pineapple Slice, Sugar, muddle
(Mix into Small Rocks Glass with 2 ice cubes)

KING KENNETH-
3 parts Campari, 1 part Peach Schnapps
Orange Juice, splash Lime Juice, fill Tonic Water
(Mix into Highball Glass—ice)

KING OF KINGSTON-
2 parts Gin, 1 part Banana Liqueur
Pineapple Juice, Light Cream or Milk, splash Grapefruit Juice,
    splash Grenadine *(Mix into Cocktail Glass—no ice)*

KING'S PEG-
Brandy, fill Champagne *(Mix in Champagne Flute—no ice)*

KING'S RUIN-
Champagne, splash Cognac *(Mix in Champagne Flute—no ice)*

KINGDOM COME-
2 parts Dry Vermouth, 1 part Gin, splash White Crème de Menthe
splash Grapefruit Juice *(Mix into Small Rocks Glass—ice)*

KINGSTON-
2 parts Jamaican Rum, 1 part Gin
Sour Mix *(Mix into Cocktail Glass—no ice)*

KIOKI COFFEE-
3 parts Coffee Liqueur, 1 part Brandy
Coffee, top Whipped Cream *(Mix in Irish Coffee Cup—no ice)*

KIR-
White Wine, splash Crème de Cassis *(Mix into Wine Glass—ice)*

KIR GIN COCKTAIL-
4 parts Gin, 1 part Crème de Cassis
Club Soda *(Mix into Highball Glass—ice)*

KIR ROYALE-
Champagne, splash Crème de Cassis *(Mix in Champagne Flute—no ice)*

KISH WACKER-
1 part Brown Crème de Caçao, 1 part Coffee Liqueur, 1 part Irish Cream
    Liqueur, 1 part Vodka
(Mix into Cocktail Glass with no ice or blend with ice in Daiquiri Glass)

KISS, THE-
3 parts Vodka, 1 part Cherry Brandy, 1 part White Crème de Caçao
Light Cream or Milk *(Mix into Cocktail Glass—no ice)*

KISS & TELL-
1 part Apple Brandy, 1 part Sloe Gin
splash Lime Juice *(Mix into Cocktail Glass—no ice)*

KISS FROM HEAVEN-
2 parts Brandy, 1 part Drambuie®, 1 part Dry Vermouth
(Mix into Cocktail Glass—no ice)

KISS-IN-THE-DARK-
1 part Cherry Brandy, 1 part Dry Vermouth, 1 part Gin
(Mix into Cocktail Glass—no ice)

KISS ON THE LIPS (1)-
Bourbon Whiskey
Apricot Juice *(Mix into Highball Glass—ice)*

KISS ON THE LIPS (2)-
2 parts Bourbon Whiskey, 1 part Apricot Brandy
(Layer in Order in Cocktail Glass—no ice)

KISS ME AGAIN-
Scotch Whiskey, splash Licorice Liqueur *(Mix into Cocktail Glass—no ice)*

KISS ME QUICK-
2 parts Licorice Liqueur, splash Triple Sec
splash Bitters, Club Soda *(Mix into Highball Glass—ice)*

KISS ME SLOW-
2 parts Light Rum, 1 part Triple Sec
Lime Juice *(Mix into Small Rocks Glass—ice)*

KISS OFF-
1 part Cherry Marnier, 1 part Gin, splash Dry Vermouth
(Mix into Cocktail Glass—no ice)

KISS THE BOYS GOODBYE-
1 part Brandy, 1 part Sloe Gin
Lime Juice *(Mix into Cocktail Glass—no ice)*

KITCHEN SINK-
1 part Gin, 1 part Rye Whiskey, splash Apricot Brandy
Orange Juice, Sour Mix *(Mix into Cocktail Glass—no ice)*

KLINGON BLOOD WINE-
1 part Spiced Rum, 1 part Tequila
Cranberry Juice, splash Grenadine, splash Hot Sauce
(Mix into Highball Glass—ice)

KLONDIKE COOLER-
Blended Whiskey
splash Club Soda, Sugar, fill Ginger Ale *(Mix into Highball Glass—ice)*

KLONDIKE STRIKE-
Brandy
Orange Juice *(Mix into Highball Glass—ice)*

KNICKERBEIN-
1 part Brandy, 1 part Maraschino Liqueur
Grenadine *(Mix into Cocktail Glass—no ice)*

KNICKERBOCKER-
2 parts Gin, 1 part Dry Vermouth, splash Sweet Vermouth
(Mix into Cocktail Glass—no ice)

KNICKERBOCKER SPECIAL-
Light Rum, splash Raspberry Liqueur, splash Triple Sec
Orange Juice, Lime Juice *(Mix into Cocktail Glass—no ice)*

KNOCK OUT (1)-
1 part Anisette, 1 part Dry Vermouth, 1 part Gin, splash White Crème de
Menthe *(Mix into Cocktail Glass—no ice)*

KNOCK OUT (2)-
1 part Apricot Brandy, 1 part Sloe Gin, 1 part Southern Comfort®
Orange Juice *(Mix into Highball Glass—ice)*

KNUCKLEBUSTER-
2 parts Scotch Whiskey, 1 part Drambuie® *(Mix into Small Rocks Glass—ice)*

KOALA KOLADA-
2 parts Peach Schnapps, 1 part Melon Liqueur
Orange Juice, Pineapple Juice, Coconut Milk, Kiwi Fruit Garnish
(Blend with ice in Daiquiri Glass)

KOKOMO JOE-
1 part Banana Liqueur, 1 part Light Rum
Orange Juice, Coconut Milk, Banana *(Blend with ice in Daiquiri Glass)*

KON TIKI-
2 parts Scotch Whiskey, 1 part Dark Rum, 1 part Triple Sec
(Mix into Cocktail Glass—no ice)

KONA COOLER-
4 parts Blended Whiskey, 1 part Triple Sec, splash Sweet Vermouth
splash Lime Juice *(Mix into Cocktail Glass—no ice)*

KONA GOLD-
2 parts White Crème de Caçao, 1 part Peach Schnapps
Vanilla Ice Cream, Banana, sprinkle Nutmeg *(Blend with ice in Daiquiri Glass)*

KOOCH-
Peppermint Schnapps
Clam Juice, Onion Garnish *(Mix into Cocktail Glass—no ice)*

KOOL-ADE (1)-
1 part Amaretto, 1 part Melon Liqueur, 1 part Vodka
Cranberry Juice *(Mix into Highball Glass—ice)*

KOOL-ADE (2)-
1 part Melon Liqueur, 1 part Vodka
Cranberry Juice, Pineapple Juice *(Mix into Highball Glass—ice)*

KRAZEE KEITH-
Light Rum, splash Anisette, splash Cherry Brandy
splash Lime Juice, fill Cola *(Mix into Highball Glass—ice)*

KREMLIN-
1 part Vodka, 1 part White Crème de Caçao
Light Cream or Milk *(Mix into Highball Glass—ice)*

KREMLIN KERNEL-
Vodka
Sugar, Water *(Mix into Cocktail Glass—no ice)*

KRETCHMA-
1 part Vodka, 1 part White Crème de Caçao
Lime Juice, splash Grenadine *(Mix into Cocktail Glass—no ice)*

KRYPTONITE KOOLER-
2 parts Tropical Fruit Schnapps, 1 part Light Rum
Pineapple Juice *(Mix into Highball Glass—ice)*

KUP'S INDISPENSABLE-
2 parts Gin, 1 part Dry Vermouth
Bitters *(Mix into Cocktail Glass—no ice)*

KYOTO (1)-
3 parts Gin, 1 part Apricot Brandy, 1 part Dry Vermouth, 1 part Triple Sec
(Mix into Cocktail Glass—no ice)

KYOTO (2)-
3 parts Gin, 1 part Melon Liqueur, splash Dry Vermouth
splash Lime Juice *(Mix into Cocktail Glass—no ice)*

– NOTES –

_____

_____

_____

_____

_____

_____

_____

_____

_____

L'AIRD OF SUMMER ISLE-
3 parts Scotch Whiskey, 1 part Licorice Liqueur
Pineapple Juice *(Mix into Highball Glass—ice)*

L. A. COCKTAIL-
Blended Whiskey, splash Sweet Vermouth
Sour Mix *(Mix into Cocktail Glass—no ice)*

L. A. P. D. NIGHTSHIFT-
1 part Grenadine, 1 part Blue Curaçao, 1 part Tequila
(Layer in Order in Cocktail Glass—no ice)

L. A. SUNRISE-
2 parts Vodka, 1 part Banana Liqueur, 1 part Light Rum (float)
Orange Juice, Pineapple Juice, splash Grenadine
(Mix into Highball Glass—ice)

LA BANANE-
1 part Banana Liqueur, 1 part Vodka
Light Cream or Milk *(Mix into Cocktail Glass—no ice)*

LA BELLE QUEBEC-
3 parts Canadian Whiskey, 1 part Brandy, 1 part Cherry Brandy
Sour Mix *(Mix into Cocktail Glass—no ice)*

LA BOMBA (1)-
2 parts Gold Tequila, 1 part Triple Sec
Pineapple Juice, Orange Juice, splash Grenadine
(Mix into Cocktail Glass—no ice)

LA BOMBA (2)-
2 parts Light Rum, 1 part Anisette, 1 part Apricot Brandy, 1 part Triple Sec
Lime Juice *(Mix into Cocktail Glass—no ice)*

LA BOMBA (3)-
2 parts Light Rum, 1 part Anisette, 1 part Apricot Brandy, 1 part Blue Curaçao
Lime Juice *(Mix into Highball Glass—ice)*

LA CARRE-
Vodka, splash Dry Vermouth, splash Kümmel *(Mix into Cocktail Glass—no ice)*

LA JOLLA-
3 parts Brandy, 1 part Banana Liqueur
Orange Juice, Lime Juice *(Mix into Cocktail Glass—no ice)*

LA PUSSY-
1 part Brandy, 1 part Light Rum, 1 part Triple Sec, splash Apple Schnapps
(Mix into Cocktail Glass—no ice)

LA STEPHANIQUE-
3 parts Gin, 1 part Sweet Vermouth, 1 part Triple Sec
splash Bitters *(Mix into Cocktail Glass—no ice)*

LADIES' COCKTAIL-
Blended Whiskey, splash Anisette
Bitters, Pineapple Garnish *(Mix into Cocktail Glass—no ice)*

LADY BE GOOD-
3 parts Brandy, 1 part Sweet Vermouth, 1 part White Crème de Menthe
(Mix into Cocktail Glass—no ice)

LADY BUG-
2 parts Brandy, 1 part Dark Rum, splash Amaretto
Orange Juice, Lime Juice
(Mix into Highball Glass with ice or blend with ice in Daiquiri Glass)

LADY FINGER-
2 parts Cherry Brandy, 2 parts Gin, 1 part Black Cherry Liqueur
(Mix into Cocktail Glass—no ice)

LADY GODIVA-
Brandy, splash Triple Sec
Sour Mix *(Mix into Highball Glass—ice)*

LADY KILLER-
2 parts Gin, 1 part Dry Vermouth, 1 part Sweet Vermouth
splash Orange Bitters *(Mix into Cocktail Glass—no ice)*

LADY LOVE FIZZ-
Gin
Sour Mix, Light Cream or Milk, splash Club Soda
(Mix into Cocktail Glass—no ice)

LADY LUCK (1)-
4 parts Raspberry Liqueur, 1 part Banana Liqueur, 1 part Coconut Liqueur
(Mix into Cocktail Glass—no ice)

LADY LUCK (2)-
4 parts Raspberry Liqueur, 1 part Banana Liqueur
Coconut Milk *(Blend with ice in Daiquiri Glass)*

LADY LUV-
3 parts Blended Whiskey, 1 part Dark Rum, 1 part Light Rum,
splash White Crème de Caçao *(Mix into Cocktail Glass—no ice)*

LADY MADONNA-
2 parts Red Dubonnet®, 1 part Dry Vermouth *(Mix into Cocktail Glass—no ice)*

LADY'S PUNCH-
1 part Blue Curaçao, 1 part Red Wine
Boiling Water, Orange Slice Garnish *(Mix into Irish Coffee Cup—no ice)*

LAFAYETTE-
3 parts Bourbon Whiskey, 1 part Dry Vermouth, splash Lillet
Sugar *(Mix into Cocktail Glass—no ice)*

LAGER & LIME-
12 oz. Draft Beer
splash Lime Juice *(Beer Mug)*

LAGUNA (1)-
Blue Curaçao, fill Pineapple Wine *(Mix into Wine Glass—ice)*

LAGUNA (2)-
Brandy, splash Campari, splash Dry Vermouth, splash Vodka
splash Bitters *(Mix into Cocktail Glass—no ice)*

LALLAH ROOKH-
2 parts Light Rum, 1 part Brandy
Light Cream or Milk, Vanilla Extract, Sugar *(Blend with ice in Daiquiri Glass)*

LAMB BROTHERS-
3 parts Dark Rum, 1 part Crème de Cassis
Pineapple Juice *(Mix into Cocktail Glass—no ice)*

LAND SLIDE (1)-
1 part Irish Cream Liqueur, 1 part Grand Marnier®, 1 part Amaretto
(Layer in Order in Cocktail Glass—no ice)

LAND SLIDE (2)-
1 part Irish Cream Liqueur, 1 part Apricot Brandy, 1 part Banana Liqueur,
1 part Coffee Liqueur *(Layer in Order in Cocktail Glass—no ice)*

LANDED GENTRY-
3 parts Dark Rum, 1 part Tia Maria®
Light Cream or Milk *(Mix into Cocktail Glass—no ice)*

LARGO BREEZE-
Key Largo® Tropical Fruit Schnapps
Cranberry Juice, Grapefruit Juice *(Mix into Highball Glass—ice)*

LASER BEAM (1)-
1 part Amaretto, 1 part Galliano®, 1 part Jack Daniel's® Tennessee Sour Mash
Whiskey, 1 part Peppermint Schnapps
(Mix into Cocktail Glass with no ice or blend with ice in Daiquiri Glass)

LASER BEAM (2)-
1 part Bourbon Whiskey, 1 part Drambuie®, 1 part Peppermint Schnapps
(Mix into Cocktail Glass—no ice)

LASKY-
Gin, splash Citrus Rum
Grape Juice *(Mix into Cocktail Glass—no ice)*

LAST ROUND-
1 part Dry Vermouth, 1 part Gin, splash Anisette, splash Brandy
(Mix into Cocktail Glass—no ice)

LATHAM'S RULE-
3 parts Vodka, 1 part Grand Marnier®
Orange Juice, splash Bitters *(Mix into Highball Glass—ice)*

LATIN COOLER-
2 parts Light Rum, 1 part Peach Schnapps
Orange Juice *(Blend with ice in Daiquiri Glass)*

LATIN LOVER-
2 parts Tequila, 1 part Spiced Rum
Pineapple Juice, Lime Juice *(Mix into Highball Glass—ice)*

LATIN MANHATTAN-
Light Rum, splash Dry Vermouth, splash Sweet Vermouth
splash Bitters *(Mix into Cocktail Glass—no ice)*

LAUGHING AT THE WAVES-
3 parts Vodka, 1 part Campari, 1 part Dry Vermouth
(Mix into Cocktail Glass—no ice)

LAURA-
3 parts Bourbon Whiskey, 1 part Campari, 1 part Dry Vermouth,
1 part Galliano®, 1 part Sweet Vermouth
(Mix into Cocktail Glass—no ice)

LAURA'S LAKESIDE-***
1 part Banana Liqueur, 1 part Coconut Rum
Cranberry Juice, Pineapple Juice, Cherry Garnish
(Mix into Highball Glass—ice)

LAVA LAMP MARTINI-
4 parts Vodka, 1 part Raspberry Liqueur
Honey *(Mix into Cocktail Glass—no ice)*

LAVENDER SUNSET-
2 parts Peach Schnapps, 1 part White Crème de Caçao
Lime Sherbet, Grape Juice, Coconut Milk *(Blend with ice in Daiquiri Glass)*

LAWHILL-
2 parts Blended Whiskey, 1 part Dry Vermouth, splash Anisette,
splash Maraschino Liqueur
Bitters *(Mix into Cocktail Glass—no ice)*

LAYER CAKE-
1 part White Crème de Caçao, 1 part Apricot Brandy, 1 part Light Cream or
Milk *(Layer in Order in Cocktail Glass—no ice)*

LAZY AFTERNOON-
2 parts Dark Rum, 2 parts Light Rum, 1 part Cherry Brandy
Pineapple Juice
(Mix into Highball Glass—ice)

LEAF, THE-
2 parts Melon Liqueur, 1 part Light Rum
Light Cream or Milk *(Mix into Highball Glass—ice)*

LEANING TOWER-
Gin, splash Dry Vermouth
splash Orange Bitters *(Mix into Cocktail Glass—crushed ice)*

LEAP FROG-
3 parts Tequila, 1 part Sloe Gin, splash Sweet Vermouth
(Mix into Small Rocks Glass—ice)

LEAP FROG HIGHBALL-
Gin
Lime Juice, Ginger Ale *(Mix into Highball Glass—ice)*

LEAP YEAR (1)-
3 parts Gin, 1 part Orange Gin, 1 part Sweet Vermouth
Lime Juice *(Mix into Cocktail Glass—no ice)*

LEAP YEAR (2)-
3 parts Gin, 1 part Grand Marnier®, 1 part Sweet Vermouth
splash Lime Juice *(Mix into Cocktail Glass—no ice)*

LEATHER & LACE-
1 part Coffee Liqueur, 1 part Peppermint Schnapps, 1 part Irish Cream Liqueur
(Layer in Order in Cocktail Glass—no ice)

LEAVE-IT-TO-ME (1)-
2 parts Gin, 1 part Apricot Brandy, 1 part Dry Vermouth
Lime Juice, Grenadine *(Mix into Cocktail Glass—no ice)*

LEAVE-IT-TO-ME (2)-
Gin, splash Maraschino Liqueur, splash Raspberry Liqueur
Sour Mix *(Mix into Cocktail Glass—no ice)*

LEBANESE SNOW-
1 part Banana Liqueur, 1 part Strawberry Schnapps
Light Cream or Milk
(Blend with ice in Daiquiri Glass)

'LECTRIC LEMONAIDE-
1 part Gin, 1 part Light Rum, 1 part Tequila, 1 part Triple Sec, 1 part Vodka
Sour Mix, fill Lemon-Lime Soda *(Mix into Highball Glass—ice)*

LEG SPREADER-
3 parts Raspberry Liqueur, 1 part 100-proof Vodka
Cola *(Mix into Highball Glass—ice)*

LEI LANI-
Dark Rum
Orange Juice, Lime Juice, Papaya Juice, Pineapple Juice, splash Grenadine,
fill Club Soda
(Mix into Highball Glass—ice)

LEMON DROP (1)-
Vodka
Lemon Wedge Dipped in Sugar *(Mix into Small Rocks Glass—ice)*

LEMON DROP (2)-
Citrus Vodka
splash Lemon-Lime Soda, Lemon Wedge Dipped in Sugar
(Mix into Small Rocks Glass—ice)

LEMON DROP (3)-
1 part Tequila, 1 part Vodka
Lemon Wedge Dipped in Sugar *(Mix into Small Rocks Glass—ice)*

LEMONADE (1)-
Vodka
Lime Juice *(Mix into Highball Glass—ice)*

LEMONADE (2)-
1 part Sherry, 1 part Sloe Gin
Sour Mix, fill Club Soda *(Mix into Highball Glass—ice)*

LEMONAID-
Tequila
Lemon-Lime Soda, Lemonade *(Mix into Highball Glass—ice)*

LEMMINGS LEAP-
1 part Coconut Rum, 1 part Gin, 1 part Vodka
fill Orange Juice (float) *(Mix into Highball Glass—ice)*

LEO SPECIAL-
2 parts Gin, 1 part Triple Sec, splash Anisette
splash Lime Juice *(Mix into Cocktail Glass—no ice)*

LEO THE LION-
4 parts Dry Vermouth, 1 part Brandy, splash White Crème de Menthe
(Mix into Cocktail Glass—no ice)

LEPRECHAUN (1)-
Irish Whiskey
Tonic Water *(Mix into Highball Glass—ice)*

LEPRECHAUN (2)-
4 parts Irish Whiskey, 2 parts Light Rum, 1 part Sloe Gin
Sour Mix, Peaches, Raspberries *(Blend with ice in Daiquiri Glass)*

LETHAL INJECTION-
1 part Coconut Rum, 1 part Crème de Noyaux, 1 part Light Rum,
1 part Spiced Rum
Orange Juice, Pineapple Juice
(Mix into Highball Glass—ice)

LEXINGTON AVE. EXPRESS-
151-proof Rum
Lime Juice, splash Grenadine *(Mix into Highball Glass—ice)*

LIANO-
2 parts Cognac, 1 part Galliano®, 1 part Grand Marnier®
(Mix into Cocktail Glass—no ice)

LIBERTY-
2 parts Apple Brandy, 1 part Light Rum
Sugar *(Mix into Cocktail Glass—no ice)*

LICENSED VICTUALER'S CHAMPAGNE-
Champagne, splash Brandy
Sugar, splash Bitters
(Mix into Champagne Flute—no ice)

LICORICE MIST-
3 parts Sambuca, 1 part Coconut Liqueur
Light Cream or Milk, Licorice Stick Garnish
(Mix into Highball Glass with ice or blend with ice in Daiquiri Glass)

LICORICE SLUSH-
2 parts Anisette, 1 part Vodka
Lemon Sherbet *(Blend with ice in Daiquiri Glass)*

LICORICE STICK-
1 part Anisette, 1 part Triple Sec, 1 part Vodka
(Mix into Cocktail Glass—no ice)

LIEBFRAUMILCH-
White Crème de Caçao
Light Cream or Milk, splash Lime Juice *(Mix into Cocktail Glass—no ice)*

LIFE IS GOOD-***
1 part Banana Liqueur, 1 part Melon Liqueur, 1 part Raspberry Liqueur
Cranberry Juice, Orange Juice, Pineapple Juice
(Mix into Highball Glass—ice)

LIFESAVER (1)-
1 part Coconut Rum, 1 part Melon Liqueur, 1 part Vodka
Lemon-Lime Soda *(Mix into Highball Glass—ice)*

LIFESAVER (2)-
2 parts Brandy, 1 part Cherry Brandy, splash Triple Sec
Sour Mix, Grenadine *(Mix into Cocktail Glass—no ice)*

LIFETIMER-
3 parts Light Rum, 1 part Apricot Brandy, 1 part Brandy, splash Triple Sec
Sour Mix, fill Lemon-Lime Soda *(Mix into Highball Glass—ice)*

LIFT-
1 part Amaretto, 1 part Drambuie®, 1 part Tia Maria®
Coffee, top Whipped Cream *(Mix into Irish Coffee Cup—no ice)*

LIGHT HOUSE-
1 part Coffee Liqueur, 1 part Grand Marnier®, 1 part Tequila
(Layer in Order in Cocktail Glass—no ice)

LIGHTWEIGHT SAILOR-
1 part Dark Rum, 1 part Light Rum
Sour Mix *(Mix into Highball Glass—ice)*

LIL NAUE-
2 parts Brandy, 1 part Apricot Brandy, 1 part Port
Sugar, sprinkle Cinnamon *(Mix into Wine Glass—no ice)*

LILLET COCKTAIL-
4 parts Lillet, 1 part Gin *(Mix into Cocktail Glass—no ice)*

LIMBO-
2 parts Light Rum, 1 part Banana Liqueur
Orange Juice *(Mix into Cocktail Glass—no ice)*

LIME GIANT-
Lime Vodka
Lemon-Lime Soda *(Mix into Highball Glass—ice)*

LIME RICKEY-
Gin
Lime Juice, splash Club Soda *(Mix into Highball Glass—ice)*

LIMESTONE-
Bourbon Whiskey
Sour Mix *(Mix into Highball Glass—ice)*

LIMEY-
2 parts Light Rum, 2 parts Lime Liqueur, 1 part Triple Sec
Lime Juice *(Blend with ice in Daiquiri Glass)*

LIMP MOOSE-
1 part Canadian Whiskey, 1 part Irish Cream Liqueur
(Mix into Cocktail Glass—no ice)

LINSTEAD-
Blended Whiskey, splash Anisette
Sour Mix, Pineapple Juice *(Mix into Cocktail Glass—no ice)*

LINUX-
Vodka
splash Lime Juice, fill Cola *(Mix into Highball Glass—ice)*

LION TAMER-
Southern Comfort®
Lime Juice *(Mix into Cocktail Glass—no ice)*

LIQUID COCAINE 8-BALL-
1 part Amaretto, 1 part Light Rum, 1 part Southern Comfort®
Pineapple Juice, splash Grenadine *(Mix into Highball Glass—ice)*

LIQUID GOLD-
2 parts Vodka, 1 part Galliano®, 1 part White Crème de Caçao
Light Cream or Milk *(Mix into Cocktail Glass—no ice)*

LISBON-
1 part Port, 1 part Rye Whiskey
Sour Mix *(Mix into Small Rocks Glass—ice)*

LITTLE BASTARD-
Light Rum
Orange Juice, Pineapple Juice, Lemon-Lime Soda
(Mix into Highball Glass—ice)

LITTLE BISHOP-
Red Wine, splash Jamaican Rum (lace)
Orange Juice, Sour Mix *(Mix into Wine Glass—no ice)*

LITTLE COLONEL-
2 parts Bourbon Whiskey, 1 part Southern Comfort®
Lime Juice *(Mix into Cocktail Glass—no ice)*

LITTLE DEVIL-
1 part Gin, 1 part Light Rum, splash Triple Sec
Lime Juice *(Mix into Cocktail Glass—no ice)*

LITTLE DIX MIX-
4 parts Dark Rum, 1 part Banana Liqueur, splash Triple Sec
Lime Juice *(Mix into Highball Glass—ice)*

LITTLE EVA-
Burgundy Wine, splash Triple Sec
splash Lime Juice, Lemon-Lime Soda *(Mix into Wine Glass—no ice)*

LITTLE FLOWER-
1 part Light Rum, 1 part Triple Sec
Grapefruit Juice *(Mix into Cocktail Glass—no ice)*

LITTLE ITALY-
Amaretto
Orange Juice *(Mix into Highball Glass—ice)*

LITTLE PRINCESS-
1 part Light Rum, 1 part Sweet Vermouth
(Mix into Cocktail Glass—no ice)

LIZBUTH-
3 parts Coconut Rum, 1 part Amaretto
Light Cream or Milk, Pineapple Juice *(Mix into Highball Glass—ice)*

LOBOTOMY-
1 part Amaretto, 1 part Raspberry Liqueur
Pineapple Juice *(Mix into Highball Glass—ice)*

LOCH LOMOND (1)-
2 parts Blue Curaçao, 2 parts Scotch Whiskey, 1 part Peach Schnapps
Grapefruit Juice, Lime Juice *(Mix into Highball Glass—ice)*

LOCH LOMOND (2)-
Scotch Whiskey
Sugar, Bitters *(Mix into Cocktail Glass—no ice)*

LOCH LOMOND (3)-
4 parts Scotch Whiskey, 1 part Drambuie®, 1 part Dry Vermouth
(Mix into Cocktail Glass—no ice)

LOCH NESS-
2 parts Scotch Whiskey, 1 part Anisette, splash Sweet Vermouth
(Mix into Small Rocks Glass—ice)

LOCH NESS MONSTER-
Scotch Whiskey, splash Peppermint Schnapps
Club Soda *(Mix into Highball Glass—ice)*

LOCH NESS MYSTERY-
2 parts Scotch Whiskey, 1 part Apricot Brandy, splash Triple Sec
Grapefruit Juice, splash Lime Juice *(Mix into Highball Glass—ice)*

LOCO COCO-
2 parts Coconut Rum, 2 parts Light Rum, 1 part White Crème de Caçao
Lime Juice, fill Club Soda *(Mix into Highball Glass—ice)*

LOLITA-
 Tequila
 Lime Juice, Honey, splash Bitters *(Mix into Cocktail Glass—no ice)*

LOLLIPOP-
 1 part Cherry Brandy, 1 part Triple Sec, splash Green Chartreuse,
  splash Maraschino Liqueur *(Mix into Cocktail Glass—no ice)*

LOMA LOMA LULLABY-
 Light Rum, splash 151-proof Rum (lace)
 Passion Fruit Juice, Lime Juice *(Mix into Highball Glass—ice)*

LONDON BUCK-
 Gin
 Lime Juice, Ginger Ale *(Mix into Highball Glass—ice)*

LONDON COCKTAIL-
 Gin, splash Maraschino Liqueur
 Sugar, Orange Bitters *(Mix into Cocktail Glass—no ice)*

LONDON FOG-
 1 part Licorice Liqueur, 1 part White Crème de Menthe
 Vanilla Ice Cream *(Blend with ice in Daiquiri Glass)*

LONDON FRENCH "75"-
 Gin, fill Champagne
 Sour Mix *(Mix into Champagne Flute—no ice)*

LONDON SPECIAL-
 Champagne
 Bitters, Lump Sugar, Orange Peel Garnish *(Mix into Champagne Flute—no ice)*

LONDON TOWN-
 3 parts Gin, 1 part Maraschino Liqueur
 splash Orange Bitters *(Mix into Cocktail Glass—no ice)*

LONE TREE (1)-
 1 part Dry Vermouth, 1 part Gin, 1 part Sweet Vermouth
 splash Orange Bitters, Olive Garnish *(Mix into Cocktail Glass—no ice)*

LONE TREE (2)-
 2 parts Gin, 1 part Sweet Vermouth *(Mix into Cocktail Glass—no ice)*

LONE TREE COOLER-
 Gin, splash Dry Vermouth
 Sugar, Club Soda, fill Ginger Ale, Orange Spiral or Lemon Peel on Rim
 (Mix into Highball Glass—ice)

LONELY NIGHT-
 2 parts Hazelnut Liqueur, 2 parts Irish Cream Liqueur, 1 part Coffee Liqueur
 Vanilla Ice Cream, top Whipped Cream, top Chocolate sprinkles
 (Blend with ice in Daiquiri Glass)

LONG BEACH ICED TEA (1)-
 1 part Gin, 1 part Light Rum, 1 part Tequila, 1 part Triple Sec, 1 part Vodka
 Cranberry Juice, Sour Mix *(Mix into Highball Glass—ice)*

LONG BEACH ICED TEA (2)-
1 part Gin, 1 part Light Rum, 1 part Melon Liqueur, 1 part Triple Sec,
   1 part Vodka
Cranberry Juice *(Mix into Highball Glass—ice)*

LONG BEACH ICED TEA (3)-
2 parts Triple Sec, 1 part Dark Rum, 1 part Gin, 1 part Vodka
Cranberry Juice, Sour Mix *(Mix into Highball Glass—ice)*

LONG HOT NIGHT-
Bourbon Whiskey
Cranberry Juice, Pineapple Juice *(Mix into Highball Glass—ice)*

LONG ISLAND-
1 part Tequila, 1 part Triple Sec *(Mix into Cocktail Glass—no ice)*

LONG ISLAND ICED BERRY TEA-
1 part Amaretto, 1 part Blackberry Brandy, 1 part Sloe Gin,
   splash 151-proof Rum
Pineapple Juice *(Mix into Highball Glass—ice)*

LONG ISLAND ICED TEA (1)-
1 part Gin, 1 part Light Rum, 1 part Tequila, 1 part Triple Sec, 1 part Vodka
Sour Mix, Cola *(Mix into Highball Glass—ice)*

LONG ISLAND ICED TEA (2)-
1 part Gin, 1 part Light Rum, 1 part Tequila, 1 part Vodka
Sour Mix, Cola *(Mix into Highball Glass—ice)*

LONG ISLAND ICED TEA (3)-
1 part Gin, 1 part Light Rum, 1 part Tequila, 1 part Triple Sec
Sour Mix, Sugar, Cola *(Mix into Highball Glass—ice)*

LONG ISLAND SUNSET-
1 part Peach Schnapps, 1 part Spiced Rum
Cranberry Juice, Sour Mix *(Mix into Highball Glass—ice)*

LONG VODKA-
Vodka
Lime Juice, splash Bitters, fill Tonic Water *(Mix into Highball Glass—ice)*

LOOK OUT BELOW-
151-proof Rum
Lime Juice, Grenadine *(Mix into Small Rocks Glass—ice)*

LORD & LADY-
3 parts Dark Rum, 1 part Tia Maria® *(Mix into Small Rocks Glass—ice)*

LORD RODNEY-
2 parts Blended Whiskey, 1 part Coconut Rum, splash White Crème de Caçao
(Mix into Cocktail Glass—no ice)

LORD SUFFOLK-
Gin, splash Maraschino Liqueur, splash Sweet Vermouth, splash Triple Sec
(Mix into Cocktail Glass—no ice)

LORRAINE-
3 parts Black Cherry Liqueur, 1 part Bénédictine
Lime Juice *(Mix into Cocktail Glass—no ice)*

LOS ANGELES COCKTAIL-
Blended Whiskey, splash Sweet Vermouth
Sour Mix *(Mix into Highball Glass—ice)*

LOUD HAILER-
1 part Dry Vermouth, 1 part Gin, splash Triple Sec
Orange Juice, splash Grenadine
(Mix into Cocktail Glass—no ice)

LOUD SPEAKER-
Brandy, splash Gin, splash Triple Sec
Lime Juice *(Mix into Cocktail Glass—no ice)*

LOUISIANA LULLABY-
Dark Rum, splash Grand Marnier®, splash Red Dubonnet®
(Mix into Cocktail Glass—no ice)

LOUISIANA PLANTER'S PUNCH-
2 parts Gold Rum, 1 part Bourbon Whiskey, 1 part Cognac, splash Amaretto,
    splash Anisette
Sour Mix, splash Bitters, splash Club Soda
(Mix into Highball Glass—ice)

LOUISVILLE COOLER-
Bourbon Whiskey
Orange Juice, Sour Mix *(Mix into Small Rocks Glass—ice)*

LOUISVILLE LADY-
1 part Bourbon Whiskey, 1 part White Cream de Caçao
Light Cream or Milk *(Mix into Cocktail Glass—no ice)*

LOUISVILLE STINGER-
1 part Bourbon Whiskey, 1 part Light Rum, splash White Crème de Caçao,
    splash White Crème de Menthe *(Mix into Cocktail Glass—no ice)*

LOUNGE LIZARD (1)-
2 parts Dark Rum, 1 part Amaretto
Cola *(Mix into Highball Glass—ice)*

LOUNGE LIZARD (2)-
Dark Rum
Orange Juice, Cranberry Juice *(Mix into Highball Glass—ice)*

LOUNGE LIZARD (3)-
Dark Rum
Orange Juice, Pineapple Juice, Sour Mix, splash Grenadine
(Mix into Highball Glass—ice)

LOVE BIRD-
Amaretto
Light Cream or Milk
(Mix into Cocktail Glass with no ice or blend with ice in Daiquiri Glass)

LOVE COCKTAIL-
Sloe Gin, splash Raspberry Liqueur
Lime Juice *(Mix into Cocktail Glass—no ice)*

LOVE FOR TOBY-
3 parts Light Rum, 1 part Brandy, 1 part Cherry Brandy
Lime Juice *(Mix into Cocktail Glass—no ice)*

LOVE JUICE-
Light Rum
Apple Juice, Orange Juice, fill Lemon-Lime Soda
(Mix into Highball Glass—ice)

LOVE POTION-
Rum
Mango Juice, Piña Colada Mix, Strawberry Daiquiri Mix
(Blend with ice in Daiquiri Glass)

LOVER'S COCKTAIL-
Sloe Gin, splash Raspberry Liqueur
Lime Juice *(Mix into Cocktail Glass—no ice)*

LOVER'S DELIGHT-
1 part Brandy, 1 part Forbidden Fruit Liqueur, 1 part Triple Sec
(Mix into Cocktail Glass—no ice)

LOVER'S KISS-
1 part Amaretto, 1 part Brown Crème de Caçao, 1 part Cherry Brandy
Light Cream or Milk, top Chocolate sprinkles, Cherry Garnish
(Mix into Highball Glass—ice)

LOVER'S NOCTURNE-
3 parts Vodka, 1 part Drambuie®
splash Bitters *(Mix into Cocktail Glass—no ice)*

LOVING CUP-
Claret, splash Brandy, splash Triple Sec
Club Soda, Sugar *(Mix into Wine Glass—no ice)*

LUBE JOB-
1 part Irish Cream Liqueur, 1 part Vodka
(Mix into Small Rocks Glass—ice)

LUCKY DRIVER-
Coconut Rum
Grapefruit Juice, Orange Juice, Pineapple Juice, Sour Mix
(Mix into Highball Glass with ice or blend with ice in Daiquiri Glass)

LUCKY SHAMROCK-
2 parts Irish Whiskey, 1 part Dry Vermouth, splash Green Chartreuse,
    splash Green Crème de Menthe *(Mix into Cocktail Glass—no ice)*

LUDWIG & THE GANG-
2 parts Light Rum, 2 parts Vodka, 1 part Amaretto, 1 part Southern Comfort®
splash Bitters *(Mix into Cocktail Glass—no ice)*

LUGGER-
1 part Apple Brandy, 1 part Brandy, splash Apricot Brandy
(Mix into Cocktail Glass—no ice)

LULU-
1 part Amaretto, 1 part Light Rum, 1 part Peach Schnapps, 1 part Triple Sec,
1 part Vodka
Sour Mix, splash Pineapple Juice, splash Grenadine
(Mix into Highball Glass—ice)

LUMBERJACK-
2 parts Gin, 1 part Apple Brandy, 1 part Southern Comfort®
Maple Syrup *(Mix into Cocktail Glass—no ice)*

LUNCH PAIL-
12 oz. Beer, 1 part Amaretto
Orange Juice (drop Shot into Beer Mug) *(Beer Mug/Shot)*

LUSCIOUS LISA-
2 parts Brandy, 1 part Raspberry Liqueur (float), fill Champagne
(Mix into Champagne Flute—no ice)

LUTKIN'S SPECIAL-
1 part Dry Vermouth, 1 part Gin, splash Apricot Brandy
Orange Juice *(Mix into Cocktail Glass—no ice)*

LUXURY-
Brandy, fill Champagne
Orange Bitters *(Mix into Champagne Flute—no ice)*

LYING WITH THE TIGRESS-
1 part Dry Vermouth, 1 part Light Rum
splash Lime Juice, splash Orange Bitters *(Mix into Cocktail Glass—no ice)*

LYNCHBERG LEMONADE (1)-
Jack Daniel's® Tennessee Sour Mash Whiskey
Sour Mix, splash Club Soda *(Mix into Highball Glass—ice)*

LYNCHBERG LEMONADE (2)-
2 parts Jack Daniel's® Tennessee Sour Mash Whiskey, 1 part Triple Sec
Sour Mix *(Mix into Highball Glass—ice)*

LYNCHBERG LEMONADE (3)-
Jack Daniel's® Tennessee Sour Mash Whiskey, splash Triple Sec
Sour Mix, splash Lemon-Lime Soda *(Mix into Highball Glass—ice)*

– NOTES –

_____

_____

_____

_____

M'BATA-
1 part Blue Curaçao, 1 part Citrus Rum, 1 part Cognac
Light Cream or Milk *(Mix into Highball Glass—ice)*

M & M-
1 part Amaretto, 1 part Coffee Liqueur *(Mix into Cocktail Glass—no ice)*

MA BONNIE WEE HEN-
3 parts Scotch Whiskey, 1 part Cream Sherry
Orange Juice, Lime Juice, splash Grenadine *(Mix into Cocktail Glass—no ice)*

MA WEE HEN-
3 parts Scotch Whiskey, 1 part Dry Sherry
Orange Juice, Lime Juice, splash Grenadine
(Mix into Cocktail Glass—no ice)

MABEL SPECIAL-
1 part Citrus Rum, 1 part Sloe Gin
Lime Juice *(Mix into Cocktail Glass—no ice)*

MACARTHUR-
2 parts Light Rum, 1 part Triple Sec, splash Spiced Rum
(Mix into Cocktail Glass—no ice)

MACBETH'S DREAM-
Scotch Whiskey, splash Amaretto, splash Triple Sec
Sour Mix, splash Orange Bitters *(Mix into Cocktail Glass—no ice)*

MAD COW-
1 part Coffee Liqueur, 1 part 151-proof Rum
Light Cream or Milk *(Mix into Cocktail Glass—no ice)*

MAD HATTER-
Vodka
Cranberry Juice, Orange Juice, Sour Mix *(Mix into Highball Glass—ice)*

MAD MELON-ADE-
DeKuyper® Mad Melon Watermelon Schnapps
Lemonade *(Mix into Highball Glass—ice)*

MAD MELON SCREW-
1 part DeKuyper® Mad Melon Watermelon Schnapps, 1 part Vodka
Orange Juice *(Mix into Highball Glass—ice)*

MAD MONK-
1 part Hazelnut Liqueur, 1 part Irish Cream Liqueur
(Mix into Cocktail Glass—no ice)

MAD RUSSIAN-
1 part Coffee Liqueur, 1 part Irish Cream Liqueur, 1 part Vodka
(Mix into Small Rocks Glass—ice)

MADAME RENE-
4 parts Blended Whiskey, 1 part Light Rum
splash Bitters, splash Orange Bitters *(Mix into Cocktail Glass—no ice)*

MADEIRA COCKTAIL-
1 part Blended Whiskey, 1 part Madeira Wine
splash Lime Juice, splash Grenadine
(Mix into Cocktail Glass—no ice)

MADRAS-
Vodka
Cranberry Juice, Orange Juice *(Mix into Highball Glass—ice)*

MAEEK-
2 parts Blended Whiskey, 1 part Campari
Orange Juice *(Mix into Small Rocks Glass—ice)*

MAESTRO-
3 parts Light Rum, 1 part Cream Sherry
Lime Juice, fill Ginger Ale *(Mix into Highball Glass—ice)*

MAG PIE-
2 parts Melon Liqueur, 2 parts Vodka, 1 part White Crème de Caçao
Light Cream or Milk *(Mix into Highball Glass—ice)*

MAGENS BAY-
3 parts Light Rum, 1 part Apricot Brandy
Orange Juice, Sour Mix *(Mix into Cocktail Glass—no ice)*

MAGIQUE-
2 parts Dry Vermouth, 1 part Gin, splash Crème de Cassis
(Mix into Cocktail Glass—no ice)

MAGNOLIA BLOSSOM-
Gin
Light Cream or Milk, Lime Juice, splash Grenadine
(Mix into Cocktail Glass—no ice)

MAGNOLIA MAIDEN-
1 part Bourbon Whiskey, 1 part Grand Marnier®
Sugar, Club Soda *(Mix into Highball Glass—ice)*

MAH-JONNG-
2 parts Gin, 1 part Dark Rum, 1 part Triple Sec
(Mix into Cocktail Glass—no ice)

MAHUKONA-
3 parts Light Rum, 1 part Triple Sec, splash Amaretto
Lime Juice, splash Bitters *(Mix into Highball Glass—ice)*

MAI KAI NO-
2 parts Dark Jamaican Rum, 2 parts Light Rum, 1 part 151-proof Rum,
    splash Amaretto
Lime Juice, Passion Fruit Juice, fill Club Soda
(Mix into Highball Glass—ice)

MAI-TAI (1)-
2 parts Light Rum, 1 part Triple Sec, splash Amaretto
Sour Mix, splash Grenadine *(Mix into Highball Glass—ice)*

MAI-TAI (2)-
2 parts Light Rum, 1 part Triple Sec, 1 part 151-proof Rum (lace)
Sour Mix, splash Grenadine *(Mix into Highball Glass—ice)*

MAI-TAI (3)-
1 part Crème de Noyaux, 1 part Dark Rum, 1 part Light Rum, 1 part Triple Sec
Pineapple Juice, Orange Juice *(Mix into Highball Glass—ice)*

MAI-TAI (4)-
1 part Dark Rum, 1 part Light Rum, 1 part Triple Sec, splash Amaretto
splash Lime Juice, splash Grenadine *(Mix into Highball Glass—ice)*

MAI-TAI (5)-
3 parts Light Rum, 1 part Amaretto, 1 part Triple Sec
Lime Juice, Pineapple Juice *(Blend with ice in Daiquiri Glass)*

MAIDEN-NO-MORE-
3 parts Gin, 1 part Triple Sec, splash Brandy
Lime Juice *(Mix into Cocktail Glass—no ice)*

MAIDEN'S BLUSH-
Gin, splash Triple Sec
Lime Juice, splash Grenadine *(Mix into Cocktail Glass—no ice)*

MAIDEN'S DREAM-
1 part Anisette, 1 part Gin
Grenadine *(Mix into Small Rocks Glass—ice)*

MAIDEN'S PRAYER-
3 parts Gin, 1 part Triple Sec
Lime Juice *(Mix into Cocktail Glass—no ice)*

MAIER SPECIAL-
2 parts Vodka, 1 part Blackberry Brandy
Cranberry Juice *(Mix into Highball Glass—ice)*

MAINBRACE-
2 parts Gin, 1 part Triple Sec
Grape Juice *(Mix into Highball Glass—ice)*

MAJOR BAILEY-
Gin
Sour Mix, Sugar, Mint Leaves, muddle *(Mix into Small Rocks Glass—ice)*

MAJOR BRADBURY-
3 parts Canadian Whiskey, 1 part Grand Marnier®, splash Dry Vermouth,
splash Sweet Vermouth *(Mix into Cocktail Glass—no ice)*

MAJOR TOM-
3 parts Vodka, 1 part Cherry Brandy, 1 part Triple Sec
Grapefruit Juice *(Mix into Cocktail Glass—no ice)*

MALIBU BAY BREEZE-
Malibu® Coconut Rum
Cranberry Juice, Pineapple Juice *(Mix into Highball Glass—ice)*

M

MALIBU BUBY-
2 parts Malibu® Coconut Rum, 1 part Barbados Rum, splash Triple Sec
Orange Juice, Lime Juice *(Mix into Highball Glass—ice)*

MALIBU CAFE-
Malibu® Coconut Rum
Coffee, top Whipped Cream *(Mix in Irish Coffee Cup—no ice)*

MALIBU HOOTER-
1 part Malibu® Coconut Rum, 1 part Melon Liqueur
Cranberry Juice *(Mix into Highball Glass—ice)*

MALIBU WAVE-
3 parts Tequila, 1 part Blue Curaçao
Sour Mix *(Mix into Highball Glass—ice)*

MALLARD'S REEF-
3 parts Jamaican Rum, 1 part Galliano®
Orange Juice, splash Grenadine *(Mix into Highball Glass—ice)*

MALLELIEU-
3 parts Light Rum, 1 part Grand Marnier®
Orange Juice *(Mix into Highball Glass—ice)*

MALMAISON-
2 parts Light Rum, 1 part Cream Sherry, splash Anisette (lace)
Lime Juice *(Mix into Cocktail Glass—no ice)*

MAMBO'S DREAM-
2 parts Dark Rum, 1 part Banana Liqueur, 1 part Triple Sec
Pineapple Juice, splash Lime Juice *(Mix into Highball Glass—ice)*

MAMIE GILROY-
Scotch Whiskey
splash Lime Juice, fill Ginger Ale *(Mix into Highball Glass—ice)*

MAMIE TAYLOR-
Scotch Whiskey
Lime Juice, fill Ginger Ale *(Mix into Highball Glass—ice)*

MAMIE'S SISTER-
Gin
Lime Juice, Ginger Ale *(Mix into Highball Glass—ice)*

MAMMAMATTAWA-
3 parts Canadian Whiskey, 1 part Drambuie®, splash Cherry Brandy
(Mix into Cocktail Glass—no ice)

MAN EATER-
3 parts Brandy, 1 part Southern Comfort®
splash Orange Bitters *(Mix into Small Rocks Glass—ice)*

MAN IN THE MELON-
3 parts Melon Liqueur, 1 part Triple Sec, 1 part Vodka
Club Soda, Lemon-Lime Soda *(Mix into Highball Glass—ice)*

M

MAN O' WAR-
3 parts Bourbon Whiskey, 1 part Triple Sec, splash Sweet Vermouth
Lime Juice *(Mix into Cocktail Glass—no ice)*

MAN OF THE MOMENT-
1 part Grand Marnier®, 1 part Scotch Whiskey
Lime Juice, splash Grenadine *(Mix into Cocktail Glass—no ice)*

MAN OVERBOARD-
2 parts Vodka, 1 part Melon Liqueur, 1 part Raspberry Liqueur
Pineapple Juice *(Mix into Highball Glass—ice)*

MANDEVILLE-
1 part Dark Rum, 1 part Light Rum, splash Anisette
splash Lime Juice, splash Grenadine, fill Cola *(Mix into Highball Glass—ice)*

MANDINGO GRINGO-
3 parts Dark Jamaican Rum, 1 part Banana Liqueur
Pineapple Juice, Orange Juice, Lime Juice
(Mix into Highball Glass with ice or blend with ice in Daiquiri Glass)

MANGO DAIQUIRI-
4 parts Dark Rum, 1 part Triple Sec
Mango Juice, Sour Mix *(Blend with ice in Daiquiri Glass)*

MANHANDLER-
1 part Jack Daniel's® Tennessee Sour Mash Whiskey, 1 part Sloe Gin, 1 part
Southern Comfort®, 1 part Vodka *(Mix into Small Rocks Glass—ice)*

MANHASSET-
Blended Whiskey, splash Dry Vermouth, splash Sweet Vermouth
Lime Juice *(Mix into Cocktail Glass—no ice)*

MANHATTAN-
Blended Whiskey, splash Sweet Vermouth
Cherry Garnish *(Mix into Cocktail Glass—no ice)*

MANHATTAN (DRY)-
Blended Whiskey, splash Dry Vermouth *(Mix into Cocktail Glass—no ice)*

MANHATTAN (PERFECT)-
Blended Whiskey, splash Dry Vermouth, splash Sweet Vermouth
(Mix into Cocktail Glass—no ice)

MANHATTAN (SWEET)-
1 part Blended Whiskey, 1 part Sweet Vermouth
(Mix into Cocktail Glass—no ice)

MANHATTAN COCKTAIL-
Gin
splash Lime Juice, splash Orange Juice, Mint Leaves, muddle
(Mix into Cocktail Glass—no ice)

MANHATTAN COOLER-
Red Bordeaux Wine, splash Dark Rum
Sour Mix *(Mix into Cocktail Glass—no ice)*

MANHATTAN FOR ROME-
1 part Bourbon Whiskey, 1 part Hazelnut Liqueur
muddle cherry and ice *(Mix into Cocktail Glass)*

MANILA FIZZ-
Gin
Root Beer Soda, Sour Mix *(Mix into Highball Glass—ice)*

MANYANN-
1 part Gin, 1 part White Dubonnet®, splash Triple Sec
Lime Juice *(Mix into Cocktail Glass—no ice)*

MAPLE LEAF (1)-
4 parts Canadian Whiskey, 1 part Irish Mist®, splash Brown Crème de Caçao
Light Cream or Milk *(Mix into Cocktail Glass—no ice)*

MAPLE LEAF (2)-
Canadian Whiskey
Lime Juice, Maple Syrup *(Mix into Cocktail Glass—no ice)*

MARASCHINO CHERRY-
2 parts Light Rum, 1 part Amaretto, 1 part Peach Schnapps
Cranberry Juice, Pineapple Juice, Grenadine *(Blend with ice in Daiquiri Glass)*

MARBELLA CLUB-
Grand Marnier®, fill Champagne
Orange Juice, splash Orange Bitters *(Mix in Wine Glass—no ice)*

MARCO'S POLO-
2 parts Irish Whiskey, 1 part Triple Sec
Lime Juice *(Mix into Cocktail Glass—no ice)*

MARCONI WIRELESS-
3 parts Apple Brandy, 1 part Sweet Vermouth
splash Orange Bitters *(Mix into Cocktail Glass—no ice)*

MARDEE MINE-
3 parts Dark Rum, 1 part Sweet Vermouth *(Mix into Cocktail Glass—no ice)*

MARGARET IN THE MARKETPLACE-
Light Rum
splash Lime Juice, splash Light Cream or Milk, splash Grenadine
(Mix into Cocktail Glass—no ice)

MARGARITA-
4 parts Tequila, 1 part Triple Sec
Lime Juice or Sour Mix, Salted Rim (optional) *(Mix into Cocktail Glass—no ice)*

MARGUERITE'S STANDARD-
2 parts Gin, 1 part Dry Vermouth
splash Orange Bitters *(Mix into Cocktail Glass—no ice)*

MARIACHI-
Tequila
Pineapple Juice, splash Grenadine *(Mix into Highball Glass—ice)*

MARIACHI MELON MARGARITA-
4 parts Tequila, 1 part Melon Liqueur
Sour Mix
(Mix into Cocktail Glass with no ice or blend with ice in Daiquiri Glass)

MARIONETTE-
1 part Apricot Brandy, 1 part Cherry Brandy, 1 part Dry Sake, 1 part Light Rum
(Mix into Small Rocks Glass—ice)

MARIPOSA-
2 parts Light Rum, 1 part Brandy
Orange Juice, Lime Juice, Grenadine *(Mix into Cocktail Glass—no ice)*

MARLON BRANDO-
3 parts Scotch Whiskey, 1 part Amaretto
Light Cream or Milk *(Mix into Highball Glass—ice)*

MARMALADE-
Triple Sec
Tonic Water *(Mix into Highball Glass—ice)*

MARNIER CAFE-
Grand Marnier®
Coffee, top Whipped Cream *(Mix in Irish Coffee Cup—no ice)*

MARNY-
2 parts Gin, 1 part Grand Marnier® *(Mix into Cocktail Glass—no ice)*

MARTHA WASHINGTON-
2 parts Blended Whiskey, 1 part Cherry Brandy
splash Lime Juice, splash Grenadine *(Mix into Cocktail Glass—no ice)*

MARTHA'S VINEYARD-
Gin
Vanilla Ice Cream, Lime Juice, top Club Soda
(Blend with ice in Daiquiri Glass)

MARTINEZ COCKTAIL-
1 part Dry Vermouth, 1 part Gin, splash Triple Sec
Orange Bitters, Cherry Garnish *(Mix into Cocktail Glass—no ice)*

MARTINI-
Gin, splash Dry Vermouth (Drier=Less Dry Vermouth)
Olive or Lemon Twist Garnish *(Mix into Cocktail Glass—no ice)*

MARTINI (DRY)-
Gin, splash Dry Vermouth *(Mix into Cocktail Glass—no ice)*

MARTINI (MEDIUM)-
3 parts Gin, 1 part Dry Vermouth, 1 part Sweet Vermouth
(Mix into Cocktail Glass—no ice)

MARTINI (PERFECT)-
Gin, splash Dry Vermouth, splash Sweet Vermouth
(Mix into Cocktail Glass—no ice)

MARTINI (SWEET)-
Gin, splash Sweet Vermouth *(Mix into Cocktail Glass—no ice)*

MARVEL-
4 parts Jamaican Rum, 1 part Citrus Vodka
Grenadine *(Mix into Cocktail Glass—no ice)*

MARVELLAID-
1 part Orange Vodka, 1 part Cointreau
(Mix into Cocktail Glass—no ice)

MARY GARDEN-
2 parts Red Dubonnet®, 1 part Dry Vermouth
(Mix into Cocktail Glass—no ice)

MARY PICKFORD-
Light Rum, splash Maraschino Liqueur
Pineapple Juice, splash Grenadine *(Mix into Cocktail Glass—no ice)*

MARY'S DELIGHT-
2 parts Sweet Vermouth, 1 part Brandy
splash Orange Bitters *(Mix into Cocktail Glass—no ice)*

MARY'S DREAM-
4 parts Light Rum, 1 part Triple Sec
Orange Juice, splash Orange Bitters *(Mix into Highball Glass—ice)*

MASSACRE-
Tequila, splash Campari
Ginger Ale *(Mix into Highball Glass—ice)*

MASTER OF THE HOUNDS-
2 parts Blended Whiskey, 1 part Cherry Brandy
splash Bitters *(Mix into Cocktail Glass—no ice)*

MATADOR-
Tequila
Pineapple Juice, Splash Lime Juice *(Mix into Highball Glass—ice)*

MATINEE-
3 parts Gin, 1 part Green Chartreuse, 1 part Sweet Vermouth
Orange Juice, Splash Orange Bitters *(Mix into Cocktail Glass—no ice)*

MATTI NYKNEN-
Vodka
Sour Mix *(Mix into Highball Glass—ice)*

MAUI BREEZE-
1 part Amaretto, 1 part Brandy, 1 part Triple Sec
Orange Juice, Guava Juice, Sour Mix *(Blend with ice in Daiquiri Glass)*

MAURA'S COFFEE-
2 parts Irish Cream Liqueur, 1 part Irish Whiskey
Coffee, top Whipped Cream
(Mix in Irish Coffee Cup—no ice)

MAUREEN'S DREAM-
1 part Dry Vermouth, 1 part Sweet Vermouth, splash Anisette
(Mix into Small Rocks Glass—ice)

MAURICE-
2 parts Gin, 1 part Dry Vermouth, 1 part Sweet Vermouth
Orange Juice, Bitters *(Mix into Cocktail Glass—no ice)*

MAX THE SILENT-
2 parts Light Rum, 1 part Apple Brandy, 1 part Brandy, splash Anisette
(Mix into Cocktail Glass—no ice)

MAXIM-
2 parts Gin, 1 part Dry Vermouth, splash White Crème de Caçao
(Mix into Cocktail Glass—no ice)

MAY BLOSSOM FIZZ-
Citrus Rum
Lime Juice, Grenadine, splash Club Soda *(Mix into Highball Glass—ice)*

MAYAN WHORE-
1 part Tequila, 1 part Coffee Liqueur
Pineapple Juice, splash Club Soda, splash Grenadine
(Layer in Order in Cocktail Glass—no ice)

MAYFLOWER-
3 parts Sweet Vermouth, 1 part Brandy, 1 part Dry Vermouth, splash Anisette,
   splash Triple Sec
splash Orange Bitters *(Mix into Cocktail Glass—no ice)*

MAYOR BILLY-
2 parts Dry Vermouth, 2 parts Sweet Vermouth, 1 part Gin
splash Bitters, splash Orange Bitters *(Mix into Cocktail Glass—no ice)*

MAZATLAN-
1 part Coconut Rum, 1 part White Crème de Caçao
Light Cream or Milk *(Mix into Cocktail Glass—no ice)*

MAZRICK-
3 parts Vodka, 1 part Amaretto, 1 part Triple Sec, splash Galliano®
Orange Juice, Pineapple Juice, splash Bitters *(Mix into Highball Glass—ice)*

McCLELLAND-
2 parts Sloe Gin, 1 part Triple Sec
Orange Bitters *(Mix into Cocktail Glass—no ice)*

McDUFF-
3 parts Scotch Whiskey, 1 part Triple Sec
splash Bitters, Orange Slice Garnish *(Mix into Cocktail Glass—no ice)*

MEAD-
Irish Mist®, fill Beer *(Beer Mug)*

MEISTER MIND MELD-
Amaretto
Cola *(Mix into Highball Glass—one ice cube)*

MELBA-
  1 part Citrus Rum, 1 part Light Rum, splash Anisette
  Lime Juice, splash Grenadine *(Mix into Cocktail Glass—no ice)*

MELLOW YELLOW-
  1 part Galliano®, 1 part Southern Comfort® *(Mix into Small Rocks Glass—ice)*

MELON BALL (1)-
  1 part Melon Liqueur, 1 part Vodka
  Orange Juice *(Mix into Highball Glass—ice)*

MELON BALL (2)-
  1 part Melon Liqueur, 1 part Vodka
  Pineapple Juice *(Mix into Highball Glass—ice)*

MELON BALL SUNRISE-
  1 part Melon Liqueur, 1 part Vodka
  Orange Juice, splash Grenadine (lace) *(Mix into Highball Glass—ice)*

MELON COCKTAIL-
  Gin, splash Maraschino Liqueur
  Lime Juice *(Mix into Cocktail Glass—no ice)*

MELON COLADA-
  2 parts Light Rum, 1 part Melon Liqueur
  Pineapple Juice, Coconut Milk, splash Light Cream or Milk
  (Blend with ice in Daiquiri Glass)

MELON COOLER-
  2 parts Melon Liqueur, 1 part Peach Schnapps, 1 part Raspberry Liqueur
  Pineapple Juice *(Mix into Cocktail Glass—no ice)*

MELON DAIQUIRI-
  1 part Light Rum, 1 part Melon Liqueur
  Cantaloupe, Sugar *(Blend with ice in Daiquiri Glass)*

MELON FEVER-
  4 parts Melon Liqueur, 1 part Triple Sec
  Light Cream or Milk *(Mix into Highball Glass—ice)*

MELON PATCH-
  2 parts Melon Liqueur, 1 part Triple Sec, 1 part Vodka
  Club Soda *(Mix into Highball Glass—ice)*

MELON SPRITZ-
  4 parts Spiced Rum, 1 part Melon Liqueur
  Pineapple Juice, Club Soda *(Mix into Highball Glass—ice)*

MELON VODKA MARGARITA-
  4 parts Vodka, 1 part Melon Liqueur
  Sour Mix
  (Mix into Cocktail Glass with no ice or blend with ice in Daiquiri Glass)

MELTDOWN-
  2 parts Russian Vodka, 1 part Peach Schnapps
  (Layer in Order in Cocktail Glass—no ice)

MEMORY LOSS-
1 part Banana Liqueur, 1 part Raspberry Liqueur, 1 part Vodka
Cranberry Juice, Orange Juice *(Mix into Highball Glass—ice)*

MEMPHIS BELLE-
2 parts Brandy, 1 part Southern Comfort®
Lime Juice, splash Orange Bitters *(Mix into Cocktail Glass—no ice)*

MENAGE A TROIS-
1 part Dark Rum, 1 part Triple Sec
Light Cream or Milk *(Mix into Cocktail Glass—no ice)*

MENDAY'S PERIL-
3 parts Blended Whiskey, 1 part Cherry Brandy
Lime Juice, Orange Juice, splash Orange Bitters
(Mix into Small Rocks Glass—ice)

MERCENARY-
4 parts Dry Vermouth, 1 part Brandy, splash Green Crème de Menthe
(Mix into Cocktail Glass—no ice)

MERION'S CRICKET-
4 parts Apricot Brandy, 1 part Sloe Gin
Lime Juice *(Mix into Cocktail Glass—no ice)*

MERRY WIDOW (1)-
1 part Dry Vermouth, 1 part Gin, splash Anisette, splash Bénédictine
Orange Bitters *(Mix into Cocktail Glass—no ice)*

MERRY WIDOW (2)-
1 part Cherry Brandy, 1 part Maraschino Liqueur
(Mix into Cocktail Glass—no ice)

MERRY WIDOW FIZZ-
Sloe Gin
Sour Mix, Orange Juice, splash Club Soda *(Mix into Highball Glass—ice)*

MESA VERDE-
Light Rum, splash Green Crème de Menthe (lace)
Pineapple Juice, splash Lime Juice *(Mix into Highball Glass—ice)*

METRO-
2 parts Cognac, 1 part Dry Vermouth
Sugar, splash Orange Bitters *(Mix into Cocktail Glass—no ice)*

METROPOLITAN-
1 part Brandy, 1 part Sweet Vermouth
Sugar, Bitters *(Mix into Cocktail Glass—no ice)*

METROPOLITAN MARTINI-
Gin
Cranberry Juice, Splash Lime Juice *(Mix into Cocktail Glass—no ice)*

MEXICAN BERRY-
1 part Raspberry Liqueur, 1 part Tequila *(Mix into Cocktail Glass—no ice)*

MEXICAN BULL SHOT-
Tequila
Beef Bouillon, Lime Juice, splash Worcestershire Sauce, Celery Salt
(Mix into Highball Glass—ice)

MEXICAN COFFEE-
2 parts Coffee Liqueur, 1 part Tequila
Coffee, top Whipped Cream *(Mix in Irish Coffee Cup—no ice)*

MEXICAN FLAG (1)-
1 part Cherry Liqueur, 1 part Coffee Liqueur, 1 part Green Crème de Menthe,
    1 part 151-proof Rum
(Layer in Order in Cocktail Glass—no ice)

MEXICAN FLAG (2)-
1 part Sloe Gin, 1 part Vodka, 1 part Melon Liqueur
(Layer in Order in Cocktail Glass—no ice)

MEXICAN GRASSHOPPER-
1 part Coffee Liqueur, 1 part Green Crème de Menthe
Light Cream or Milk *(Mix into Cocktail Glass—no ice)*

MEXICAN MADRAS-
Gold Tequila
Cranberry Juice, splash Orange Juice, splash Lime Juice
(Mix into Highball Glass—ice)

MEXICAN MARTINI-
3 parts Tequila, 1 part Triple Sec *(Mix into Cocktail Glass—no ice)*

MEXICAN MARY-
Tequila
Tomato Juice, Worcestershire Sauce, Sour Mix, Horseradish, splash Lime Juice,
    dash Whole Black Pepper, dash Salt and Pepper, dash Celery Salt
(Mix into Highball Glass—ice)

MEXICAN MOTHER F**KER-
1 part Irish Cream Liqueur, 1 part Hazelnut Liqueur, 1 part Coffee Liqueur,
    1 part Tequila
(Layer in Order in Cocktail Glass—no ice)

MEXICAN PEPPER POT-
Tequila
Dr Pepper® Cola, Lime Garnish *(Mix into Highball Glass—ice)*

MEXICAN PUMPER-
1 part Grenadine, 1 part Coffee Liqueur, 1 part Tequila
(Layer in Order in Cocktail Glass—no ice)

MEXICAN RUIN-
3 parts Coffee Liqueur, 1 part Tequila *(Mix into Cocktail Glass—no ice)*

MEXICAN SCREWDRIVER-
Tequila
Orange Juice *(Mix into Highball Glass—ice)*

MEXICAN VIRGIN-
Tequila
Cherry Cider *(Mix into Highball Glass—ice)*

MEXICANA-
Tequila
Lime Juice, Pineapple Juice, Grenadine
(Mix into Cocktail Glass—no ice)

MEXICANO-
Light Rum, splash Kümmel
Orange Juice, splash Bitters *(Mix into Cocktail Glass—no ice)*

MEXICOLA-
Tequila
Cola, Lime Juice *(Mix into Highball Glass—ice)*

MEXICOLADA-
2 parts Tequila, 1 part Coffee Liqueur
Pineapple Juice, Coconut Milk, Light Cream or Milk
(Blend with ice in Daiquiri Glass)

MEXITALY COFFEE-
1 part Amaretto, 1 part Coffee Liqueur
Coffee, top Whipped Cream
(Mix in Irish Coffee Cup—no ice)

MIAMI-
3 parts Light Rum, 1 part White Crème de Menthe
Lime Juice *(Mix into Cocktail Glass—no ice)*

MIAMI BEACH-
1 part Dry Vermouth, 1 part Scotch Whiskey
Grapefruit Juice *(Mix into Cocktail Glass—no ice)*

MIAMI ICE-
1 part Banana Liqueur, 1 part Melon Liqueur, 1 part Strawberry Schnapps
Pineapple Juice, Coconut Milk, Grenadine, Orange Sherbet
(Blend with ice in Daiquiri Glass)

MIAMI MELONI-
1 part Light Rum, 1 part Melon Liqueur
Light Cream or Milk *(Mix into Cocktail Glass—no ice)*

MIAMI NICE-
1 part Bourbon Whiskey, 1 part Dark Rum, 1 part Gin, 1 part Triple Sec
Lime Juice *(Blend with ice in Daiquiri Glass)*

MIAMI VICE-
Rum
Piña Colada Mix, Strawberry Daiquiri Mix *(Blend with ice in Daiquiri Glass)*

MIAMI WHAMMY-
2 parts Dark Rum, 1 part Triple Sec
Orange Juice, Sour Mix, Grenadine *(Blend with ice in Daiquiri Glass)*

MICKEY WALKER-
2 parts Scotch Whiskey, 1 part Sweet Vermouth
splash Lime Juice, splash Grenadine *(Mix into Cocktail Glass—no ice)*

MICKEY'S FIN-
2 parts Coconut Rum, 2 parts Dark Rum, 1 part Banana Liqueur
Grapefruit Juice, Orange Juice, Pineapple Juice, splash Grenadine
(Mix into Highball Glass—ice)

MIDNIGHT-
2 parts Apricot Brandy, 1 part Triple Sec
Lime Juice *(Mix into Cocktail Glass—no ice)*

MIDNIGHT COWBOY-
2 parts Bourbon Whiskey, 1 part Dark Rum
Light Cream or Milk *(Mix into Cocktail Glass—no ice)*

MIDNIGHT EXPRESS-
3 parts Dark Rum, 1 part Triple Sec,
Sour Mix *(Mix into Small Rocks Glass—ice)*

MIDNIGHT MARTINI-
1 part Gin, 1 part Dry Vermouth
Black Olive Garnish *(Mix into Cocktail Glass—no ice)*

MIDNIGHT RENDEZVOUS-
1 part Apple Brandy, 1 part Campari, 1 part Gin
(Mix into Cocktail Glass—no ice)

MIDNIGHT SUN-
Vodka
splash Grenadine *(Mix into Cocktail Glass—no ice)*

MIDORI COCKTAIL-
Midori® Melon Liqueur, fill Champagne *(Mix in Champagne Flute—no ice)*

MIDORI COLADA-
2 parts Midori® Melon Liqueur, 1 part Light Rum
Pineapple Juice, Coconut Milk *(Blend with ice in Daiquiri Glass)*

MIDORI DREAM-
2 parts Vodka, 1 part Midori® Melon Liqueur
Lemon-Lime Soda *(Mix into Highball Glass—ice)*

MIDORI MARGARITA (1)-
4 parts Tequila, 1 part Midori® Melon Liqueur, 1 part Triple Sec
Lime Juice, Salted Rim (optional) *(Mix into Cocktail Glass—no ice)*

MIDORI MARGARITA (2)-
2 parts Midori® Melon Liqueur, 1 part Grand Marnier®
Lime Juice, Salted Rim (optional) *(Mix into Cocktail Glass—no ice)*

MIDORI SOUR-
Midori® Melon Liqueur
Sour Mix *(Mix into Sour Glass—ice)*

M

MIDORI SUNRISE-
Midori® Melon Liqueur
Orange Juice, Grenadine (lace) (stir with straw for "sunrise")
(Mix into Highball Glass—ice)

MIGUELITO-
Tequila
Lime Juice, Honey, splash Bitters *(Mix into Cocktail Glass—no ice)*

MIKADO-
Brandy, splash Crème de Noyaux, splash Triple Sec
Grenadine, Bitters *(Mix into Small Rocks Glass—ice)*

MIKE TYSON-
1 part Anisette, Jägermeister®, 1 part Tia Maria®
(Mix into Small Rocks Glass—ice)

MIKEY MIKE-
2 parts Coconut Rum, 1 part Peach Schnapps, 1 part Raspberry Liqueur
Orange Juice, Pineapple Juice
(Mix into Highball Glass—ice)

MILANO-
1 part Gin, 1 part Triple Sec
Lime Juice *(Mix into Cocktail Glass—no ice)*

MILES OF SMILE-
1 part Amaretto, 1 part Peppermint Schnapps, 1 part Rye Whiskey
(Layer in Order in Cocktail Glass—no ice)

MILK PUNCH-
Blended Whiskey
Sugar, Light Cream or Milk *(Mix into Highball Glass—ice)*

MILK SHAKE-
Irish Cream Liqueur
Light Cream or Milk, splash Sour Mix
(Mix into Cocktail Glass with no ice or blend with ice in Daiquiri Glass)

MILKY WAY-
1 part Swiss Chocolate Almond Liqueur, 1 part Irish Cream Liqueur,
    1 part Hazelnut Liqueur
(Layer in Order in Cocktail Glass—no ice)

MILLION-
Jamaican Rum
Sour Mix, splash Bitters *(Mix into Cocktail Glass—no ice)*

MILLION-DOLLAR COCKTAIL-
2 parts Gin, 1 part Sweet Vermouth
Pineapple Juice, Grenadine *(Mix into Cocktail Glass—no ice)*

MILLIONAIRE-
3 parts Blended Whiskey, 1 part Triple Sec
Grenadine *(Mix into Cocktail Glass—no ice)*

MILLIONAIRE, THE-
1 part Banana Liqueur, 1 part Spiced Rum
Orange Juice, Sour Mix, Grenadine *(Blend with ice in Daiquiri Glass)*

MILLIONAIRE'S COFFEE-
1 part Coffee Liqueur, 1 part Grand Marnier®, 1 part Hazelnut Liqueur,
    1 part Irish Cream Liqueur
Coffee, top Whipped Cream *(Mix in Irish Coffee Cup—no ice)*

MIMOSA-
Champagne
Orange Juice *(Mix in Champagne Flute—no ice)*

MIND ERASER-
1 part Coffee Liqueur, 1 part Vodka
fill Club Soda (Do Not Mix, Serve with Drinking Straw, Drink all at Once.)
(Mix into Highball Glass—ice)

MINT CHIP-
1 part Peppermint Schnapps, 1 part Coffee Liqueur
(Layer in Order in Cocktail Glass—no ice)

MINT CHOCOLATE CHILLER-
4 parts Green Crème de Menthe, 1 part White Crème de Caçao
Vanilla Ice Cream, Light Cream or Milk, Oreo® Cookies, top Whipped Cream
(Blend with ice in Daiquiri Glass)

MINT CHOCOLATE CHIP ICE CREAM (1)-
1 part Coffee Liqueur, 1 part Irish Cream Liqueur, 1 part Peppermint Schnapps,
    1 part Vodka, 1 part White Crème de Caçao, 1 part White Crème de
    Menthe
(Mix into Cocktail Glass with no ice or blend with ice in Daiquiri Glass)

MINT CHOCOLATE CHIP ICE CREAM (2)-
1 part Coffee Liqueur, 1 part Irish Cream Liqueur, 1 part Peppermint Schnapps,
    1 part Vodka, 1 part White Crème de Caçao, 1 part White Crème de
    Menthe
Light Cream or Milk *(Mix into Highball Glass—ice)*

MINT COLLINS-
1 part Gin, 1 part White Crème de Menthe
Sour Mix, splash Club Soda *(Mix into Highball Glass—ice)*

MINT CONDITION-
1 part Bourbon Whiskey, 1 part Coffee Liqueur, 1 part Peppermint Schnapps,
    1 part Vodka
(Mix into Cocktail Glass with no ice or blend with ice in Daiquiri Glass)

MINT COOLER-
Scotch Whiskey, splash White Crème de Menthe
fill Club Soda *(Mix into Highball Glass—ice)*

MINT GIN-
1 part Gin, 1 part White Crème de Menthe, 1 part White Port,
    splash Dry Vermouth *(Mix into Cocktail Glass—no ice)*

MINT HIGHBALL-
Green Crème de Menthe
Ginger Ale or Club Soda *(Mix into Highball Glass—ice)*

MINT JULEP-
Bourbon Whiskey
Water, Sugar, muddle, Mint Leaves *(Mix into Highball Glass—ice)*

MINT MARTINI-
1 part Chocolate Liqueur, 1 part Vodka, splash Crème de Menthe
(Mix into Cocktail Glass—no ice)

MINT ON THE ROCKS-
Green Crème de Menthe *(Mix into Small Rocks Glass—ice)*

MINT SMASH-
Blended Whiskey
Club Soda, Sugar, muddle, Mint Leaves *(Mix into Cocktail Glass—no ice)*

MINT SUNRISE-
3 parts Scotch Whiskey, 1 part Brandy, 1 part Triple Sec
Mint Leaf Garnish *(Mix into Small Rocks Glass—ice)*

MINT WHISPER-
2 parts White Crème de Menthe, 1 part Coffee Liqueur
Light Cream or Milk *(Mix into Highball Glass—ice)*

MINTY MARTINI-
2 parts Gin or Vodka, 1 part Peppermint Schnapps
(Mix into Cocktail Glass—no ice)

MIRACLE MILE-
2 parts Gin, 1 part Triple Sec
Orange Juice, splash Lime Juice *(Mix into Cocktail Glass—no ice)*

MIRAMAR-
4 parts Bourbon Whiskey, 1 part Bénédictine
(Mix into Cocktail Glass—no ice)

MISS BELLE-
3 parts Dark Rum, 1 part Brown Crème de Caçao, 1 part Grand Marnier®
(Mix into Cocktail Glass—no ice)

MISSION ACCOMPLISHED-
4 parts Vodka, 1 part Triple Sec
Lime Juice, splash Grenadine *(Mix into Cocktail Glass—no ice)*

MISSISSIPPI MIST-
1 part Bourbon Whiskey, 1 part Southern Comfort®
(Mix into Small Rocks Glass—ice)

MISSISSIPPI MUD-
1 part Coffee Liqueur, 1 part Southern Comfort®
Vanilla Ice Cream, top Chocolate sprinkles
(Blend with ice in Daiquiri Glass)

MISSISSIPPI MULE-
   4 parts Gin, 1 part Crème de Cassis
   Lime Juice *(Mix into Cocktail Glass—no ice)*

MISSISSIPPI PLANTERS PUNCH-
   2 parts Brandy, 1 part Bourbon Whiskey, 1 part Light Rum
   Sour Mix, Club Soda *(Mix into Highball Glass—ice)*

MISTER CHRISTIAN-
   3 parts Light Rum, 1 part Brandy
   Orange Juice, Lime Juice, splash Grenadine *(Mix into Cocktail Glass—no ice)*

MISTER (MR.) MANHATTAN-
   Gin
   Orange Juice, Lime Juice, muddle, Mint Leaves
   (Mix into Cocktail Glass—no ice)

MISTER (MR.) NEW YORKER-
   3 parts French Vermouth, 1 part Dry Sherry, 1 part Gin, splash Triple Sec
   (Mix into Cocktail Glass—no ice)

MISTER WU-
   2 parts Bourbon Whiskey, 1 part Vodka
   splash Orange Juice, fill Lemon-Lime Soda *(Mix into Highball Glass—ice)*

MISTRAL-
   2 parts White Wine, 1 part Raspberry Liqueur
   Strawberries, Raspberries *(Blend with ice in Daiquiri Glass)*

M

MITHERING BASTARD-
   3 parts Scotch Whiskey, 1 part Triple Sec
   Orange Juice *(Mix into Highball Glass—ice)*

MOCHA BRANDY-
   Brandy
   Chocolate Milk, Coffee, top Whipped Cream *(Mix in Irish Coffee Cup—no ice)*

MOCHA MINT-
   1 part Coffee Brandy, 1 part White Crème de Caçao, 1 part White Crème de
      Menthe *(Mix into Cocktail Glass—no ice)*

MOCKINGBIRD-
   Tequila, splash White Crème de Menthe
   Lime Juice *(Mix into Cocktail Glass—no ice)*

MODEL T-
   1 part Coffee Liqueur, 1 part Banana Liqueur, 1 part Swiss Chocolate Almond
      Liqueur *(Layer in Order in Cocktail Glass—no ice)*

MODERN COCKTAIL (1)-
   Scotch Whiskey, splash Anisette, splash Jamaican Rum
   Lime Juice, Orange Bitters *(Mix into Cocktail Glass—no ice)*

MODERN COCKTAIL (2)-
   2 parts Sloe Gin, 1 part Scotch Whiskey, splash Anisette
   splash Grenadine, splash Orange Bitters *(Mix into Cocktail Glass—no ice)*

MODERN COCKTAIL (3)-
Scotch Whiskey, splash Anisette, splash Dark Rum
splash Lime Juice, splash Orange Bitters *(Mix into Small Rocks Glass—ice)*

MODERN LEMONADE-
2 parts Dry Sherry, 1 part Sloe Gin
Sour Mix, Sugar, muddle, Club Soda *(Mix into Highball Glass—ice)*

MOFO-
1 part Cranberry Juice, 1 part Vodka, 1 part Peach Schnapps, 1 part Light
Cream or Milk *(Layer in Order in Cocktail Glass—no ice)*

MOI-
4 parts Dry Vermouth, 1 part Gin, splash Crème de Cassis
Lime Juice, fill Tonic Water *(Mix into Highball Glass—ice)*

MOJITO-
Dark Rum
Sour Mix, fill Club Soda, Mint Leaves Garnish *(Mix into Highball Glass—ice)*

MOLDAU-
2 parts Gin, 1 part Russian Vodka
Orange Juice, Lime Juice *(Mix into Cocktail Glass—no ice)*

MOLEHILL LOUNGER-
3 parts Blended Whiskey, 1 part Brown Crème De Caçao, splash White
Crème de Caçao *(Mix into Cocktail Glass—no ice)*

MOLL-
1 part Dry Vermouth, 1 part Gin, 1 part Sloe Gin
Sugar, splash Orange Bitters *(Mix into Cocktail Glass—no ice)*

MOLOTOV COCKTAIL-
2 parts Vodka, 1 part 151-proof Rum
Vanilla Ice Cream, top Whipped Cream
(Blend in Irish Coffee Cup, then add Coffee—no ice)

MON CHERIE-
1 part Cherry Brandy, 1 part White Crème de Caçao
Light Cream or Milk *(Mix into Cocktail Glass—no ice)*

MONASTERY COFFEE-
Bénédictine
Coffee, top Whipped Cream *(Mix in Irish Coffee Cup—no ice)*

MONJA LOCA-
1 part Anisette, 1 part Tequila *(Mix into Small Rocks Glass—ice)*

MONK'S ROPE COFFEE-
3 parts Hazelnut Liqueur, 1 part Brown Crème de Caçao
Coffee, top Whipped Cream *(Mix in Irish Coffee Cup—no ice)*

MONK'S SECRET-
Amaretto
splash Lime Juice, Lemon-Lime Soda *(Mix into Highball Glass—ice)*

MONKEY DEW-
Banana Liqueur
Mountain Dew® *(Mix into Highball Glass—ice)*

MONKEY GLAND-
1 part Bénédictine, 1 part Gin *(Mix into Highball Glass—ice)*

MONKEY SHINE-
1 part Banana Liqueur, 1 part Bourbon Whiskey, 1 part Irish Cream Liqueur
(Mix into Cocktail Glass—no ice)

MONKEY WRENCH-
Light Rum
Grapefruit Juice *(Mix into Highball Glass—ice)*

MONKEY'S MILK-
1 part Banana Liqueur, 1 part Coffee Liqueur
Light Cream or Milk *(Mix into Highball Glass—ice)*

MONKEY'S PUNCH-
1 part Coffee Liqueur, 1 part Green Crème de Menthe, 1 part Irish Cream
Liqueur *(Layer in Order in Cocktail Glass—no ice)*

MONT BLANC-
1 part Raspberry Liqueur, 1 part Vodka
Light Cream or Milk, Vanilla Ice Cream *(Blend with ice in Daiquiri Glass)*

MONTANA-
2 parts Brandy, 1 part Dry Vermouth, 1 part Port
splash Bitters *(Mix into Small Rocks Glass—ice)*

MONTANA STUMP PULLER-
2 parts Canadian Whiskey, 1 part White Crème de Caçao
(Mix into Small Rocks Glass—ice)

MONTE CARLO-
2 parts Bourbon Whiskey, 1 part Bénédictine
splash Bitters *(Mix into Cocktail Glass—no ice)*

MONTE CARLO IMPERIAL HIGHBALL-
Gin, splash White Crème de Menthe, fill Champagne
Lime Juice *(Mix in Champagne Flute—no ice)*

MONTEZUMA-
2 parts Tequila, 1 part Madeira Wine *(Blend in Champagne Flute— ice)*

MONTEZUMA'S REVENGE-
1 part Sherry, 1 part Tequila *(Mix into Cocktail Glass—no ice)*

MONTMARTRE-
2 parts Gin, 1 part Sweet Vermouth, 1 part Triple Sec
(Mix into Cocktail Glass—no ice)

MONTREAL CLUB BOUNCER-
3 parts Gin, 1 part Anisette *(Mix into Small Rocks Glass—ice)*

MONTREAL GIN SOUR-
Gin
Sour Mix *(Mix into Sour Glass—ice)*

MOOCH, THE-
Apricot Brandy
Lemon-Lime Soda *(Mix into Highball Glass—ice)*

MOON CHASER-
2 parts Dark Rum, 1 part Amaretto
Orange Juice, Coconut Milk, Orange Sherbet *(Blend with ice in Daiquiri Glass)*

MOON LIGHT-
Apple Brandy
Sour Mix *(Mix into Small Rocks Glass—ice)*

MOON QUAKE SHAKE-
1 part Coffee Brandy, 1 part Dark Rum
Lime Juice *(Mix into Cocktail Glass—no ice)*

MOON RAKER-
3 parts Tequila, 1 part Blue Curaçao
Pineapple Juice *(Mix into Highball Glass—ice)*

MOON RIVER-
3 parts Brandy, 1 part Peppermint Schnapps
Lemon-Lime Soda, splash Grenadine (lace) *(Mix into Highball Glass—ice)*

MOON SHINE COCKTAIL-
1 part Brandy, 1 part Peach Brandy, 1 part White Dubonnet®, splash Anisette
(Mix into Cocktail Glass—no ice)

MOON SHOT-
Gin
Clam Juice, splash Hot Sauce *(Mix into Highball Glass—ice)*

MOON STAR-
1 part Bénédictine, 1 part Vodka
Pineapple Juice *(Mix into Cocktail Glass—no ice)*

MOON STRUCK-
Gin
Clam Juice, splash Hot Sauce *(Mix into Cocktail Glass—no ice)*

MOONLIGHT-
Apple Brandy
Sour Mix *(Mix into Highball Glass—ice)*

MOOSE JAW-
1 part Apple Brandy, 1 part Canadian Whiskey, splash Peppermint Schnapps
Sour Mix, splash Grenadine *(Mix into Highball Glass—ice)*

MORE SUNRISE-
1 part Crème de Cassis, 1 part Gin
Orange Juice *(Mix into Highball Glass—ice)*

MORGAN MADRAS-
Captain Morgan® Original Spiced Rum
Cranberry Juice, Orange Juice *(Mix into Highball Glass—ice)*

MORGAN'S FAIR CHILD-
2 parts Melon Liqueur, 1 part Amaretto
Vanilla Ice Cream, top Whipped Cream *(Blend with ice in Daiquiri Glass)*

MORGAN'S JOLLY RANCHER-
1 part Captain Morgan® Original Spiced Rum, 1 part Cinnamon Schnapps
(Mix into Cocktail Glass—no ice)

MORGAN'S MOUNTAIN-
3 parts Light Rum, 1 part Brown Crème de Caçao, splash Coffee Liqueur (lace)
Light Cream or Milk *(Mix into Cocktail Glass—no ice)*

MORGAN'S WENCH-
1 part Amaretto, 1 part Brown Crème de Caçao, 1 part Captain Morgan®
Original Spiced Rum *(Mix into Cocktail Glass—no ice)*

MORLEY'S DRIVER-
3 parts Dark Rum, 1 part Cherry Brandy, splash Brown Crème de Caçao
Coffee, top Whipped Cream *(Mix in Irish Coffee Cup—no ice)*

MORNING-
1 part Brandy, 1 part Triple Sec, splash Anisette, splash Maraschino Liqueur,
splash Triple Sec
Orange Bitters *(Mix into Cocktail Glass—no ice)*

MORNING BECOMES ELECTRIC-
2 parts Dry Vermouth, 1 part Brandy, splash Port, splash Triple Sec
(Mix into Cocktail Glass—no ice)

MORNING DIP-
Gold Rum, splash Maraschino Liqueur
Orange Juice, Sugar *(Mix into Cocktail Glass—no ice)*

MORNING GLORY-
1 part Brandy, 1 part Scotch Whiskey, splash Anisette, splash Triple Sec
Sugar, splash Bitters, fill Club Soda *(Mix into Highball Glass—ice)*

MORNING GLORY FIZZ-
Scotch Whiskey, splash Anisette
Sour Mix, splash Club Soda *(Mix into Highball Glass—ice)*

MORNING JOY-
Gold Rum, splash Sloe Gin (lace)
Grapefruit Juice *(Mix into Highball Glass—ice)*

MORNING KISS-
1 part Apricot Brandy, 1 part Gin, fill Champagne
Orange Juice *(Mix in Champagne Flute—no ice)*

MORNING WITH THE LEPRECHAUNS-
1 part Irish Cream Liqueur, 1 part Irish Whiskey, splash Cherry Brandy
Cold Coffee *(Mix into Highball Glass—ice)*

M

MORRO-
2 parts Gin, 1 part Dark Rum
Pineapple Juice, Sour Mix, Sugared Rim
(Mix into Small Rocks Glass—ice)

MOSCOW MILK TODDY-
Vodka
Light Cream or Milk, splash Grenadine, sprinkle Cinnamon (top)
(Mix into Highball Glass—ice)

MOSCOW MIMOSA-
Vodka, fill Champagne
Orange Juice *(Mix in Champagne Flute—no ice)*

MOSCOW MULE (1)-
Vodka, fill Ginger Beer
Lime Juice *(Beer Mug)*

MOSCOW MULE (2)-
Vodka
Lime Juice, fill Ginger Ale *(Mix into Highball Glass—ice)*

MOSTLY MAL-
3 parts Light Rum, 1 part Dry Vermouth, 1 part Triple Sec
splash Grenadine *(Mix into Cocktail Glass—no ice)*

MOTHER SHERMAN-
Apricot Brandy
Orange Juice, splash Bitters *(Mix into Small Rocks Glass—ice)*

MOTHER'S WHISTLER-
Vodka, splash Amaretto, splash Apple Brandy
Pineapple Juice
(Mix into Highball Glass—ice)

MOULIN BLEU-
1 part Gin, 1 part Licorice Liqueur
Orange Slice Garnish *(Mix into Small Rocks Glass—ice)*

MOULIN ROUGE-
2 parts Sloe Gin, 1 part Sweet Vermouth
Bitters *(Mix into Cocktail Glass—no ice)*

MOUNT FUJI-
Gin, splash Cherry Brandy
Lime Juice, Light Cream or Milk, splash Pineapple Juice
(Mix into Highball Glass—ice)

MOUNT RED-
1 part Gin, 1 part Light Rum, 1 part Peach Schnapps, 1 part Vodka
Cranberry Juice *(Mix into Cocktail Glass—no ice)*

MOUNTAIN COCKTAIL-
Blended Whiskey, splash Dry Vermouth, splash Sweet Vermouth
Lime Juice *(Mix into Cocktail Glass—no ice)*

MOUNTAIN MELTER-
2 parts Tequila, 1 part Triple Sec, splash Cinnamon Schnapps
Hot Chocolate, top Whipped Cream *(Mix in Irish Coffee Cup—no ice)*

MOUNTAIN STRAWBERRY BREEZE-
DeKuyper® Mountain Strawberry Schnapps
Grapefruit Juice, Orange Juice *(Mix into Highball Glass—ice)*

MOUNTIE-
3 parts Canadian Whiskey, 1 part Campari *(Mix into Cocktail Glass—no ice)*

MOUSETRAP-
Southern Comfort®, fill White Wine
Orange Juice, splash Grenadine *(Mix in Wine Glass—ice)*

MOZART-
3 parts Light Rum, 1 part Sweet Vermouth, splash Triple Sec
splash Orange Bitters *(Mix into Cocktail Glass—no ice)*

MUCH FUSS FOR THE CONQUERING HERO-
1 part Apple Brandy, 1 part Sweet Vermouth, splash Apricot Brandy
Pineapple Juice, Lime Juice, splash Orange Bitters
(Mix into Cocktail Glass—no ice)

MUDDY RIVER-
Coffee Liqueur
Light Cream or Milk *(Mix into Small Rocks Glass—ice)*

MUDSLIDE (1)-
1 part Coffee Liqueur, 1 part Irish Cream Liqueur, 1 part Vodka
splash Light Cream or Milk *(Blend with ice in Daiquiri Glass)*

MUDSLIDE (2)-
1 part Coffee Liqueur, 1 part Irish Cream Liqueur, 1 part Tequila
splash Light Cream or Milk *(Blend with ice in Daiquiri Glass)*

MUDSLIDE (3)-
1 part Coffee Liqueur, 1 part Irish Cream Liqueur, 1 part Tia Maria®
splash Light Cream or Milk *(Blend with ice in Daiquiri Glass)*

MUFF DIVER-
White Crème de Caçao
Light Cream or Milk, splash Lime Juice *(Mix into Highball Glass—ice)*

MUFF RIDER-
2 parts Sake, 1 part Light Rum
Pineapple Juice, Lemon-Lime Soda (top) *(Mix into Highball Glass—ice)*

MULE'S HIND LEGS-
1 part Apple Brandy, 1 part Gin, splash Apricot Brandy, splash Bénédictine
Maple Sugar *(Mix into Small Rocks Glass—ice)*

MULTIPLE ORGASM-
2 parts Amaretto, 2 parts Tia Maria®, 1 part Vodka
Light Cream or Milk *(Mix into Highball Glass—ice)*

MUMBO JUMBO-
3 parts Dark Rum, 1 part Apple Brandy
Sour Mix, sprinkle Cinnamon, sprinkle Nutmeg
(Mix into Small Rocks Glass—ice)

MUMSICLE-
3 parts Dark Rum, 1 part Bourbon Whiskey
splash Bitters, Cherry Garnish *(Mix into Cocktail Glass—no ice)*

MUPPET-
Tequila
Lemon-Lime Soda *(Mix into Highball Glass—ice)*

MUSCLE BEACH-
2 parts Triple Sec, 1 part Vodka
Pink Lemonade *(Mix into Highball Glass—ice)*

MUSCOVY MARTINI-
2 parts Vodka, 1 part Cinnamon Schnapps, 1 part Triple Sec
Orange Juice *(Mix into Cocktail Glass—no ice)*

MUTINY-
3 parts Dark Rum, 1 part Red Dubonnet®
splash Bitters *(Mix into Cocktail Glass—no ice)*

MY FATHER'S MARTINI-
1 part Gin, 1 part Vodka
Olive, Lemon Twist Garnish *(Mix into Cocktail Glass—no ice)*

MYRTLE BANK PUNCH-
Dark Rum or Spiced Rum, splash Cherry Liqueur
Sour Mix, splash Grenadine *(Mix into Highball Glass—ice)*

– NOTES –

_____

_____

_____

_____

_____

_____

_____

_____

_____

_____

19 DUKE DRIVE-
   1 part Chocolate Mint Liqueur, 1 part Cherry Brandy, 1 part Banana Liqueur
   (Layer in Order in Cocktail Glass—no ice)

NADIR-
   4 parts Gin, 1 part Cherry Brandy, 1 part Strawberry Schnapps
   Lime Juice, Grenadine, Pineapple Juice, fill Club Soda
   (Mix into Highball Glass—ice)

NADIR BLUE-
   4 parts Gin, 1 part Cherry Brandy, 1 part Strawberry Schnapps,
      1 part Blue Curaçao (top)
   Lime Juice, Grenadine, Pineapple Juice, fill Club Soda
   (Mix into Highball Glass—ice)

NAKED LADY-
   1 part Light Rum, 1 part Sweet Vermouth, splash Apricot Brandy
   Lime Juice, splash Grenadine *(Mix into Cocktail Glass—no ice)*

NAKED PRETZEL-
   2 parts Melon Liqueur, 1 part Crème de Cassis, 1 part Vodka
   Pineapple Juice *(Mix into Small Rocks Glass—ice)*

NANTUCKET-
   Brandy
   Cranberry Juice, Grapefruit Juice *(Mix into Highball Glass—ice)*

NANTUCKET RED-
   2 parts Gin, 1 part Apricot Brandy
   Lime Juice, splash Bitters, splash Grenadine *(Mix into Cocktail Glass—no ice)*

NAPALM-
   1 part Cinnamon Schnapps, 1 part Peppermint Schnapps, splash 151-proof
      Rum (ignite, optional) {extinguish flame before drinking}
   (Layer in Order in Cocktail Glass—no ice)

NAPOLEON-
   Gin, splash Fernet Branca (optional), splash Red Dubonnet®, splash Triple Sec
   (Mix into Cocktail Glass—no ice)

NAPOLI-
   2 parts Campari, 2 parts Vodka, 1 part Dry Vermouth, 1 part Sweet Vermouth
   Club Soda *(Mix into Highball Glass—ice)*

NARRAGANSETT-
   2 parts Bourbon Whiskey, 1 part Sweet Vermouth, splash Anisette
   (Mix into Small Rocks Glass—ice)

NASSAU PAUL-
   2 parts Light Rum, 1 part Triple Sec
   Sour Mix *(Mix into Cocktail Glass—no ice)*

NATIONAL AQUARIUM-
   1 part Blue Curaçao, 1 part Gin, 1 part Light Rum, 1 part Vodka
   Sour Mix, splash Lemon-Lime Soda *(Mix into Highball Glass—ice)*

Z

NATIONAL COCKTAIL-
Light Rum, splash Apricot Brandy
Pineapple Juice, splash Lime Juice *(Mix into Cocktail Glass—no ice)*

NAUTICAL MARY-
Pepper Vodka
Clam Juice, Tomato Juice, splash Hot Sauce, splash Worcestershire Sauce,
Horseradish, Lime Juice *(Mix into Highball Glass—ice)*

NAVY GROG-
1 part Dark Rum, 1 part Light Rum, splash Amaretto
Orange Juice, Pineapple Juice, splash Sour Mix
(Mix into Highball Glass—ice)

NEGRIL STINGER-
2 parts Rum, 1 part Tia Maria® *(Mix into Small Rocks Glass—ice)*

NEGRONI-
1 part Campari, 1 part Gin, 1 part Sweet Vermouth
(Mix into Cocktail Glass—no ice)

NEGRONI COOLER-
1 part Campari, 1 part Gin, 1 part Sweet Vermouth
Club Soda *(Mix into Highball Glass—ice)*

NELSON'S BLOOD-
Tawny Port, fill Champagne *(Mix into Champagne Flute—no ice)*

NEON BIKINI-
1 part Melon Liqueur, 1 part Vodka
Pineapple Juice, Sour Mix *(Mix into Highball Glass—ice)*

NEON LIGHTS-
1 part Cranberry Schnapps, 1 part Peach Schnapps
Orange Juice *(Mix into Highball Glass—ice)*

NERVOUS BREAKDOWN (1)-
1 part Raspberry Liqueur, 1 part Vodka
splash Club Soda *(Mix into Cocktail Glass—no ice)*

NERVOUS BREAKDOWN (2)-
1 part Raspberry Liqueur, 1 part Vodka
Cranberry Juice *(Mix into Highball Glass—ice)*

NETHERLAND-
1 part Brandy, 1 part Triple Sec
splash Orange Bitters *(Mix into Small Rocks Glass—ice)*

NEUTRON BOMB (1)-
1 part Hazelnut Liqueur, 1 part Irish Cream Liqueur
Light Cream or Milk *(Mix into Highball Glass—ice)*

NEUTRON BOMB (2)-
1 part Butterscotch Schnapps, 1 part Irish Cream Liqueur
Light Cream or Milk *(Mix into Highball Glass—ice)*

NEUTRON BOMB (3)-
1 part Coffee Liqueur, 1 part Light Rum, 1 part Tequila, 1 part Swiss Chocolate Almond Liqueur *(Layer in Order in Cocktail Glass—no ice)*

NEVADA-
Light Rum
Grapefruit Juice, Sour Mix, splash Bitters *(Mix into Cocktail Glass—no ice)*

NEVINS-
Bourbon Whiskey, splash Apricot Brandy
splash Grapefruit Juice, splash Lime Juice, splash Bitters
(Mix into Cocktail Glass—no ice)

NEW AGE OLD-FASHIONED-
Bourbon Whiskey
splash Bitters, Lemon Garnish *(Mix into Small Rocks Glass—ice)*

NEW OLD-FASHIONED-
Whiskey
splash Bitters, fill Lemon-Lime Soda *(Mix into Highball Glass—ice)*

NEW ORLEANS COCKTAIL-
4 parts Bourbon Whiskey, 1 part Anisette
Sugar, splash Bitters, splash Orange Bitters *(Mix into Small Rocks Glass—ice)*

NEW ORLEANS BUCK-
Light Rum
Orange Juice, Lime Juice, Club Soda or Ginger Ale
(Mix into Highball Glass—ice)

NEW ORLEANS COFFEE-
Southern Comfort®
Coffee, top Whipped Cream *(Mix into Irish Coffee Cup—no ice)*

NEW ORLEANS FIZZ-
Gin
Light Cream or Milk, splash Orange Juice, Sugar
(Mix into Highball Glass—ice)

NEW ORLEANS GIN FIZZ-
Gin, splash Triple Sec
Sour Mix, splash Light Cream or Milk, splash Club Soda
(Mix into Highball Glass—ice)

NEW WAVE, THE-
Peach Schnapps
Orange Juice, splash Club Soda *(Mix into Highball Glass—ice)*

NEW WORLD-
Blended Whiskey
splash Lime Juice, splash Grenadine *(Mix into Small Rocks Glass—ice)*

NEW YORK-
Blended Whiskey
Sour Mix, splash Grenadine *(Mix into Cocktail Glass—no ice)*

Z

NEW YORK COOLER-
1 part Melon Liqueur, 1 part Vodka
Cranberry Juice, Club Soda *(Mix into Highball Glass—ice)*

NEW YORK LEMONADE-
2 parts Lemon Vodka, 1 part Grand Marnier®
Lime Juice, top Lemon-Lime Soda, Sugared Rim
(Mix into Cocktail Glass—no ice)

NEW YORK NUT-
1 part Amaretto, 1 part Hazelnut Liqueur, 1 part Tia Maria®, 1 part Vodka
splash Light Cream or Milk *(Mix into Cocktail Glass—no ice)*

NEW YORK SOUR-
1 part Blended Whiskey, 1 part Claret (float)
Sour Mix *(Mix into Sour Glass—ice)*

NEWBURY-
2 parts Gin, 1 part Sweet Vermouth, 1 part Triple Sec
(Mix into Cocktail Glass—no ice)

NEWPORT COOLER-
1 part Gin, splash Brandy, splash Peach Brandy
splash Lime Juice, fill Ginger Ale *(Mix into Highball Glass—ice)*

NEWTON'S GRAVITY APPLE-
3 parts Apple Brandy, 1 part Triple Sec
splash Bitters *(Mix into Cocktail Glass—no ice)*

NEWTON'S SPECIAL-
2 parts Brandy, 1 part Triple Sec
splash Bitters *(Mix into Cocktail Glass—no ice)*

NIAGARA FALLS-
1 part Tangerine Cognac, 1 part Vodka
Sour Mix, top splash Ginger Ale *(Mix into Highball Glass—ice)*

NICKEL COCKTAIL-
2 parts Currant Vodka, 1 part Melon Liqueur
Orange Juice, fill Lemon-Lime Soda *(Mix into Highball Glass—ice)*

NICKEL ALLOY-
2 parts Currant Vodka, 1 part Triple Sec
Orange Juice, fill Lemon-Lime Soda *(Mix into Highball Glass—ice)*

NICKY FINN-
1 part Brandy, 1 part Triple Sec, splash Anisette
Sour Mix *(Mix into Cocktail Glass—no ice)*

NIGHT CAP-
Light Rum
Warm Milk, Sugar, sprinkle Nutmeg *(Mix into Irish Coffee Cup—no ice)*

NIGHT FLIGHT-
1 part Banana Liqueur, 1 part Strawberry Schnapps
Hot Chocolate, top Whipped Cream *(Mix into Irish Coffee Cup—no ice)*

NIGHT IN OLD MANDALAY, A-
1 part Dark Rum, 1 part Light Rum
Orange Juice, splash Lime Juice, fill Ginger Ale *(Mix into Highball Glass—ice)*

NIGHT TRAIN-
2 parts Gin, 1 part Triple Sec, splash Apple Brandy
Lime Juice *(Mix into Cocktail Glass—no ice)*

NIGHTINGALE (1)-
2 parts Banana Liqueur, 1 part Triple Sec
Light Cream or Milk *(Mix into Cocktail Glass—no ice)*

NIGHTINGALE (2)-
2 parts Banana Liqueur, 1 part Blue Curaçao
Light Cream or Milk *(Mix into Cocktail Glass—no ice)*

NIGHTMARE-
3 parts Gin, 1 part Cherry Brandy, 1 part Madeira Wine
splash Orange Juice *(Mix into Cocktail Glass—no ice)*

NIJINSKI BLINI-
Vodka, splash Champagne, splash Peach Schnapps
Lime Juice, Pureed Peaches *(Blend with ice in Daiquiri Glass)*

NINE-PICK-
1 part Anisette, 1 part Brandy, 1 part Triple Sec
(Mix into Small Rocks Glass—ice)

NINETEEN-
4 parts Dry Vermouth, 1 part Cherry Brandy, 1 part Gin, splash Anisette
Sugar *(Mix into Cocktail Glass—no ice)*

NINETEEN PICK ME UP-
2 parts Anisette, 1 part Gin
Sugar, splash Bitters, splash Orange Bitters, fill Club Soda
(Mix into Highball Glass—ice)

NINETEEN TWENTY-
4 parts Gin, 1 part Cherry Brandy, 1 part Dry Vermouth
splash Orange Bitters *(Mix into Cocktail Glass—no ice)*

NINETEENTH HOLE-
2 parts Gin, 1 part Dry Vermouth, splash Sweet Vermouth
splash Bitters, Olive Garnish *(Mix into Cocktail Glass—no ice)*

NINJA-
1 part Brown Crème de Caçao, 1 part Melon Liqueur, 1 part Hazelnut Liqueur
(Layer in Order in Cocktail Glass—no ice)

NINJA TURTLE-
2 parts Gin, 1 part Blue Curaçao
Orange Juice *(Mix into Highball Glass—ice)*

NINOTCHKA-
3 parts Vodka, 1 part White Crème de Caçao
splash Lime Juice *(Mix into Cocktail Glass—no ice)*

NO PROBLEM-
1 part Banana Liqueur, 1 part Coconut Rum
Cranberry Juice, Grapefruit Juice, Orange Juice, Pineapple Juice, Lime Juice
(Mix into Highball Glass—ice)

NOB HILL CRICKET-
4 parts Apricot Brandy, 1 part Sloe Gin
Lime Juice *(Mix into Cocktail Glass—no ice)*

NOCTURNAL-
2 parts Bourbon Whiskey, 1 part Brown Crème de Caçao
splash Light Cream or Milk *(Mix into Small Rocks Glass—ice)*

NORMANDY-
3 parts Gin, 1 part Apple Brandy, 1 part Apricot Brandy
Lime Juice *(Mix into Cocktail Glass—no ice)*

NORMANDY COLLINS-
Apple Brandy
Sour Mix, splash Light Cream or Milk, splash Club Soda
(Mix into Highball Glass—ice)

NORMANDY GOLD-
1 part Apple Brandy, 1 part Apricot Brandy, 1 part Gin
Orange Juice, splash Grenadine
(Mix into Cocktail Glass—no ice)

NORMANDY JACK-
2 parts Blended Whiskey, 1 part Apple Brandy
Sour Mix *(Mix into Cocktail Glass—no ice)*

NORMANDY NIP-
2 parts Gin, 1 part Apple Brandy
Sour Mix *(Mix into Cocktail Glass—no ice)*

NORTH POLE-
2 parts Gin, 1 part Maraschino Liqueur
Lime Juice, top Whipped Cream *(Mix into Cocktail Glass—no ice)*

NORTH SIDE SPECIAL-
Dark Rum or Spiced Rum
Orange Juice, splash Lime Juice, fill Club Soda
(Mix into Highball Glass—ice)

NORTH STAR-
2 parts Blue Curaçao, 1 part Apricot Brandy, 1 part Spiced Rum, 1 part Vodka
Sour Mix, Orange Juice, Pineapple Juice *(Mix into Highball Glass—ice)*

NORTHERN EXPOSURE-
Aquavit
Grapefruit Juice, Sour Mix, splash Grenadine *(Mix into Cocktail Glass—no ice)*

NORTHERN LIGHTS-
Yukon Jack® Canadian Liqueur
Cranberry Juice, Orange Juice *(Mix into Highball Glass—ice)*

NUCLEAR ACCELERATOR-
1 part Vodka, 1 part Grand Marnier®, 1 part Peppermint Schnapps
(Layer in Order in Cocktail Glass—no ice)

NUCLEAR KAMIKAZE-
1 part Blue Curaçao, 1 part Vodka
Sour Mix *(Mix into Highball Glass—ice)*

NUCLEAR KOOL AID-
2 parts Southern Comfort®, 1 part Amaretto
Cranberry Juice, Lemon-Lime Soda *(Mix into Highball Glass—ice)*

NUCLEAR MELTDOWN-
1 part Brandy, 1 part Tequila *(Mix into Small Rocks Glass—ice)*

NUCLEAR WASTE (1)-
1 part Vodka, 1 part Melon Liqueur, 1 part Triple Sec, splash Lime Juice
(Layer in Order in Cocktail Glass—no ice)

NUCLEAR WASTE (2)-
2 parts Melon Liqueur, 1 part Vodka *(Mix into Small Rocks Glass—ice)*

NUCLEAR ZIMA-
Vodka, fill Zima®
splash Grenadine *(Mix into Highball Glass—ice)*

NUDE BOMB-
1 part Coffee Liqueur, Amaretto, 1 part Banana Liqueur
(Layer in Order in Cocktail Glass—no ice)

NUT & CREAM-
1 part Amaretto, 1 part Hazelnut Liqueur
splash Light Cream or Milk, Vanilla Ice Cream, sprinkle Nutmeg
(Blend with ice in Daiquiri Glass)

NUTCRACKER-
1 part DeKuyper® Coconut Amaretto, 1 part DeKuyper® Hazelnut Liqueur
Light Cream or Milk *(Mix into Highball Glass—ice)*

NUTS & BERRIES (1)-
1 part Hazelnut Liqueur, 1 part Raspberry Liqueur
Light Cream or Milk *(Mix into Highball Glass—ice)*

NUTS & BERRIES (2)-
1 part Crème de Noyaux, 1 part Strawberry Schnapps
Light Cream or Milk *(Mix into Highball Glass—ice)*

NUTTY BANANA-
4 parts Amaretto, 1 part Banana Liqueur
Orange Juice, Light Cream or Milk
(Mix into Highball Glass with ice or blend with ice in Daiquiri Glass)

NUTTY BUDDY (1)-
1 part Hazelnut Liqueur, 1 part Swiss Chocolate Almond Liqueur, 1 part
Peppermint Schnapps *(Layer in Order in Cocktail Glass—no ice)*

NUTTY BUDDY (2)-
1 part Coffee Liqueur, 1 part Irish Cream Liqueur
(Mix into Cocktail Glass—no ice)

NUTTY CAFE-
3 parts Amaretto, 1 part Hazelnut Liqueur
Coffee, top Whipped Cream *(Mix into Irish Coffee Cup—no ice)*

NUTTY COLADA-
Amaretto
Coconut Milk, Crushed Pineapple *(Blend with ice in Daiquiri Glass)*

NUTTY IRISHMAN (1)-
1 part Hazelnut Liqueur, 1 part Irish Cream Liqueur
(Mix into Cocktail Glass—no ice)

NUTTY IRISHMAN (2)-
1 part Hazelnut Liqueur, 1 part Irish Cream Liqueur
Light Cream or Milk *(Mix into Highball Glass—ice)*

NUTTY PROFESSOR-
1 part Grand Marnier®, 1 part Hazelnut Liqueur, 1 part Irish Cream Liqueur
(Mix into Cocktail Glass—no ice)

NUTTY RUSSIAN (1)-
1 part Coffee Liqueur, 1 part Hazelnut Liqueur, 1 part Vodka
(Mix into Cocktail Glass—no ice)

NUTTY RUSSIAN (2)-
1 part Coffee Liqueur, 1 part Hazelnut Liqueur, 1 part Vodka
Light Cream or Milk *(Mix into Highball Glass—ice)*

NUTTY STINGER-
2 parts Amaretto, 1 part White Crème de Menthe
(Mix into Cocktail Glass—no ice)

NUTTY TROPIC-
Amaretto
Light Cream or Milk, Coconut Milk *(Blend with ice in Daiquiri Glass)*

NYACK-
2 parts Gin, 1 part Cherry Brandy, splash Dry Vermouth
(Mix into Cocktail Glass—no ice)

NYMPHOMANIAC-
2 parts Spiced Rum, 1 part Coconut Rum, 1 part Melon Liqueur
(Mix into Cocktail Glass—no ice)

– NOTES –

_____

_____

_____

_____

100 MILES PER HOUR-
4 parts Blue Curaçao, 1 part 151-proof Rum, 1 part Bourbon Whiskey,
    1 part Peach Schnapps, 1 part Southern Comfort®
Grenadine *(Mix into Cocktail Glass—no ice)*

101 DEGREES IN THE SHADE-
Pepper Vodka, fill Beer
Tomato Juice, splash Hot Sauce *(Beer Mug)*

151 REASONS-
151-proof Rum
Orange Juice, Lemon-Lime Soda *(Mix into Highball Glass—ice)*

OAK ROOM SPECIAL-
1 part Brandy, 1 part Cherry Brandy, 1 part White Crème de Caçao
(Mix into Cocktail Glass—no ice)

OATMEAL COOKIE (1)-
1 part Goldschläger®, 1 part Hazelnut Liqueur, 1 part Irish Cream Liqueur
(Mix into Cocktail Glass—no ice)

OATMEAL COOKIE (2)-
1 part Goldschläger®, 1 part Hazelnut Liqueur, 1 part Irish Cream Liqueur
Light Cream or Milk *(Mix into Highball Glass—ice)*

OATMEAL COOKIE (3)-
1 part Coffee Liqueur, 1 part Irish Cream Liqueur, 1 part Jägermeister®
(Mix into Cocktail Glass—no ice)

OAXACA JIM-
Gin
Grapefruit Juice, Orange Juice, splash Bitters *(Mix into Highball Glass—ice)*

OCEAN CRUISER-
Melon Liqueur
Coconut Milk, Pineapple Juice *(Blend with ice in Daiquiri Glass)*

ODD McINTYRE-
1 part Brandy, 1 part Lillet, 1 part Triple Sec
Lime Juice *(Mix into Cocktail Glass—no ice)*

ODEON CASINO-
Champagne, splash Peach Schnapps
Peach Juice *(Mix into Champagne Flute—no ice)*

OH, HENRY-
3 parts Blended Whiskey, 1 part Bénédictine
Ginger Ale *(Mix into Highball Glass—ice)*

OH MY GOSH-
1 part Amaretto, 1 part Peach Schnapps *(Mix into Cocktail Glass—no ice)*

OIL SLICK-
1 part Bourbon Whiskey, 1 part Peppermint Schnapps
(Mix into Cocktail Glass—no ice)

OKANAGAN-
1 part Apricot Brandy, 1 part Strawberry Schnapps, 1 part Blueberry Schnapps
(Layer in Order in Cocktail Glass—no ice)

OLD ETONIAN-
1 part Gin, 1 part Lillet, splash Crème de Noyaux
splash Orange Bitters *(Mix into Cocktail Glass—no ice)*

OLD FASHION COOL ADE-
1 part Amaretto, 1 part Southern Comfort®
Cranberry Juice, Pineapple Juice *(Mix into Highball Glass—ice)*

OLD-FASHIONED-
Blended Whiskey
Sugar Cube, splash Bitters, Water, muddle *(Mix into Small Rocks Glass—ice)*

OLD-FASHIONED GIN-
Gin
Sugar Cube, splash Bitters, muddle *(Mix into Small Rocks Glass—ice)*

OLD GLORY-
1 part Grenadine, 1 part Light Cream or Milk, 1 part Crème de Yvette
(Layer in Order in Cocktail Glass—no ice)

OLD GROANER-
4 parts Canadian Whiskey, 1 part Amaretto *(Mix into Small Rocks Glass—ice)*

OLD GROANER'S WIFE-
4 parts Canadian Whiskey, 1 part Amaretto
Light Cream or Milk *(Mix into Small Rocks Glass—ice)*

OLD LAY-
2 parts Tequila, 1 part Triple Sec
Grenadine, splash Lime Juice *(Mix into Cocktail Glass—no ice)*

OLD NICK-
4 parts Canadian Whiskey, 1 part Drambuie®
Orange Juice, Lime Juice, splash Orange Bitters
(Mix into Small Rocks Glass—ice)

OLD ORCHARD SOUR-
Blended Whiskey, splash Strawberry Schnapps
Sour Mix, splash Club Soda *(Mix into Highball Glass—ice)*

OLD PAL-
2 parts Blended Whiskey, 1 part Sweet Vermouth
Grenadine *(Mix into Cocktail Glass—no ice)*

OLD PALE-
1 part Peppermint Schnapps, 1 part Vodka, splash Strawberry Schnapps
(Mix into Cocktail Glass—no ice)

OLD PEPPER-
Whiskey
splash Lime Juice, splash Tomato Juice, splash Worcestershire Sauce, splash
   Bitters, splash Hot Sauce *(Mix into Cocktail Glass—no ice)*

OLD TIME APPETIZER-
1 part Bourbon Whiskey, 1 part Red Dubonnet®, splash Anisette, splash Triple Sec
splash Bitters, Orange Garnish, Lemon Twist Garnish
(Mix into Cocktail Glass—no ice)

OLE-
2 parts Tequila, 1 part Coffee Liqueur
Sugar, Light Cream or Milk (float)
(Mix into Cocktail Glass—no ice)

OLYMPIA-
4 parts Dark Rum, 1 part Cherry Brandy
Lime Juice *(Mix into Cocktail Glass—no ice)*

OLYMPIC-
1 part Brandy, 1 part Triple Sec
Orange Juice *(Mix into Cocktail Glass—no ice)*

OLYMPIC CIRCLE-
1 part Triple Sec, 1 part Vodka
Orange Juice, Lime Juice *(Mix into Highball Glass—ice)*

OLYMPIC LADY-
3 parts Brandy, 2 parts Apricot Brandy, 1 part Amaretto
(Mix into Cocktail Glass—no ice)

ON THE TOWN-
2 parts Vodka, 1 part Campari
Orange Juice *(Mix into Small Rocks Glass—ice)*

ONCE UPON A TIME-
3 parts Gin, 1 part Apricot Brandy, 1 part Lillet
(Mix into Cocktail Glass—no ice)

ONE EXCITING NIGHT-
2 parts Gin, 1 part Dry Vermouth, 1 part Sweet Vermouth
splash Orange Juice
(Mix into Cocktail Glass—no ice)

ONE IRELAND-
4 parts Irish Whiskey, 1 part Green Crème de Menthe
Vanilla Ice Cream *(Blend with ice in Daiquiri Glass)*

OOM PAUL-
1 part Apple Brandy, 1 part Red Dubonnet®
splash Bitters *(Mix into Small Rocks Glass—ice)*

OPAL-
2 parts Gin, 1 part Triple Sec
Orange Juice, Sugar *(Mix into Cocktail Glass—no ice)*

OPALINE-
2 parts Gin, 1 part Triple Sec
Orange Juice, Sugar *(Mix into Highball Glass—ice)*

OPENING-
3 parts Blended Whiskey, 1 part Sweet Vermouth
Grenadine *(Mix into Cocktail Glass—no ice)*

OPENING NIGHT-
3 parts Blended Whiskey, 1 part Dry Vermouth, 1 part Strawberry Schnapps
(Mix into Cocktail Glass—no ice)

OPERA-
3 parts Gin, 1 part Red Dubonnet®, splash Maraschino Liqueur
(Mix into Cocktail Glass—no ice)

OPERETTA-
2 parts Brandy, 1 part Triple Sec
Hot Tea, Honey, Cinnamon Stick
(Mix into Irish Coffee Cup—no ice)

OPPENHEIM-
2 parts Bourbon Whiskey, 1 part Sweet Vermouth
Grenadine *(Mix into Cocktail Glass—no ice)*

ORANG-A-TANG-
2 parts Vodka, 1 part Triple Sec, 1 part 151-proof Rum (float)
Orange Juice, splash Grenadine, splash Sour Mix
(Mix into Highball Glass—ice)

ORANGE & WHITE-
1 part Triple Sec, 1 part Vodka
Orange Juice *(Mix into Highball Glass—ice)*

ORANGE BLOOM-
2 parts Gin, 1 part Sweet Vermouth, 1 part Triple Sec
(Mix into Cocktail Glass—no ice)

ORANGE BLOSSOM-
Gin
Orange Juice, Sugar *(Mix into Cocktail Glass—no ice)*

ORANGE BLOSSOM SPECIAL-
Peach Schnapps
Orange Sherbet, Vanilla Ice Cream, Light Cream or Milk, Lemon-Lime Soda
(Blend with ice in Daiquiri Glass)

ORANGE BUCK-
Gin
Orange Juice, splash Lime Juice, fill Ginger Ale
(Mix into Highball Glass—ice)

ORANGE COMFORT-
Southern Comfort®, splash Anisette
splash Orange Juice, splash Lime Juice *(Mix into Small Rocks Glass—ice)*

ORANGE CRUSH (1)-
1 part Triple Sec, 1 part Vodka
splash Club Soda *(Mix into Cocktail Glass—no ice)*

ORANGE CRUSH (2)-
1 part Triple Sec, 1 part Vodka
Orange Juice *(Mix into Cocktail Glass—no ice)*

ORANGE DELIGHT-
1 part Triple Sec, 1 part Vodka
Orange Juice, splash Lime Juice *(Mix into Highball Glass—ice)*

ORANGE FIZZ-
Gin, splash Triple Sec
Orange Juice, splash Sour Mix, splash Orange Bitters, splash Club Soda
(Mix into Highball Glass—ice)

ORANGE GIMLET-
2 parts Gin, 1 part Lillet
splash Orange Bitters *(Mix into Small Rocks Glass—ice)*

ORANGE MOCHA-
4 parts Spiced Rum, 1 part Triple Sec
Coffee, Hot Chocolate, top Whipped Cream
(Mix into Irish Coffee Cup—no ice)

ORANGE OASIS-
3 parts Gin, 1 part Cherry Brandy
Orange Juice, top Ginger Ale *(Mix into Highball Glass—ice)*

ORANGE THRILL-
1 part French Vanilla Liqueur, 1 part Vodka
Orange Juice *(Mix into Highball Glass—ice)*

ORANGE TREE-
2 parts Amaretto, 1 part Crème de Noyaux
Orange Juice, Vanilla Ice Cream, top Whipped Cream
(Blend with ice in Daiquiri Glass)

ORCHID-
Gin, splash Crème de Yvette
(Mix into Cocktail Glass—no ice)

OREO COOKIE-
1 part Coffee Liqueur, 1 part White Crème de Caçao, 1 part Irish Cream
Liqueur, splash Vodka
Light Cream or Milk *(Mix into Highball Glass—ice)*

ORGASM (1)-
1 part Amaretto, 1 part Coffee Liqueur, 1 part Irish Cream Liqueur
Light Cream or Milk *(Mix into Highball Glass—ice)*

ORGASM (2)-
1 part Coffee Liqueur, 1 part Grand Marnier®, 1 part Irish Cream Liqueur
Light Cream or Milk *(Mix into Highball Glass—ice)*

ORGASM (3)-
1 part Amaretto, 1 part Triple Sec, 1 part White Crème de Caçao
Light Cream or Milk *(Mix into Highball Glass—ice)*

ORIENTAL-
2 parts Rye Whiskey, 1 part Sweet Vermouth, 1 part Triple Sec
Lime Juice *(Mix into Cocktail Glass—no ice)*

ORIENTAL RUG-
1 part Coffee Liqueur, 1 part Hazelnut Liqueur, 1 part Irish Cream Liqueur,
   1 part Jägermeister®
Cola *(Mix into Highball Glass—ice)*

ORIGINAL SINGAPORE SLING, THE-
1 part Bénédictine, 1 part Cherry Brandy, 1 part Gin
Club Soda *(Mix into Highball Glass—ice)*

ORLY BIRD-
Blended Whiskey, splash Anisette, splash Cherry Brandy,
splash Sweet Vermouth *(Mix into Cocktail Glass—no ice)*

OSTEND FIZZ-
1 part Cherry Brandy, 1 part Crème de Cassis
Club Soda *(Mix into Highball Glass—ice)*

OTHER ORIGINAL SINGAPORE SLING, THE-
2 parts Gin, 1 part Cherry Brandy, splash Bénédictine (float),
   splash Brandy (float)
Lime Juice *(Mix into Highball Glass—ice)*

OUR HOME-
1 part Dry Vermouth, 1 part Gin, 1 part Sweet Vermouth, splash White
   Crème de Menthe
splash Orange Bitters *(Mix into Cocktail Glass—no ice)*

OUR STANLEY-
3 parts Vodka, 1 part Gin, 1 part Triple Sec
(Mix into Cocktail Glass—no ice)

OUT OF THE BLUE-
1 part Blueberry Schnapps, 1 part Blue Curaçao, 1 part Vodka
splash Sour Mix, top Club Soda *(Mix into Highball Glass—ice)*

OUTRIGGER (1)-
1 part Lime Vodka, 1 part Peach Schnapps
Pineapple Juice *(Mix into Small Rocks Glass—ice)*

OUTRIGGER (2)-
4 parts Gold Rum, 1 part Apricot Brandy, 1 part Triple Sec
Lime Juice *(Mix into Small Rocks Glass—ice)*

OVER THE RAINBOW-
2 parts Spiced Rum, 1 part Triple Sec
Rainbow Sherbet, Pureed Peaches, Strawberries
(Blend with ice in Daiquiri Glass)

OWDHAM EDGE-
2 parts Vodka, 1 part White Crème de Caçao, splash Sambuca
Light Cream or Milk *(Mix into Cocktail Glass—no ice)*

OWEN MOORE-

3 parts Light Rum, 1 part White Crème de Caçao, splash Blue Curaçao (float)
Light Cream or Milk *(Mix into Cocktail Glass—no ice)*

OXBEND-

2 parts Southern Comfort®, 1 part Tequila
Orange Juice, splash Grenadine *(Mix into Highball Glass—ice)*

OYSTER-

2 parts Irish Cream Liqueur, 1 part Vodka *(Mix into Cocktail Glass—no ice)*

– NOTES –

P. H.-
>1 part Southern Comfort®, 1 part Amaretto, 1 part Pineapple Juice, splash Lime Juice *(Layer in Order in Cocktail Glass—no ice)*

PMS-
>1 part Melon Liqueur, 1 part Peach Schnapps, 1 part Vodka *(Mix into Cocktail Glass—no ice)*

P. T. O.-
>3 parts Dark Rum, 1 part Triple Sec, 1 part Vodka
>Orange Juice *(Mix into Highball Glass—ice)*

P. V. DOYLE-
>2 parts Irish Whiskey, 1 part Green Crème de Menthe
>Light Cream or Milk *(Mix into Cocktail Glass—no ice)*

PACIFIC PACIFIER-
>2 parts Triple Sec, 1 part Banana Liqueur
>Light Cream or Milk *(Mix into Highball Glass—ice)*

PACIFIC PALISADES-
>Campari, fill Champagne
>Orange Juice *(Mix into Champagne Flute—no ice)*

PACIFIC SUNRISE-
>1 part Blue Curaçao, 1 part Tequila
>Sour Mix, splash Bitters *(Mix into Highball Glass—ice)*

PADDY-
>3 parts Irish Whiskey, 1 part Sweet Vermouth
>splash Bitters *(Mix into Cocktail Glass—no ice)*

PADUCAH PALOOKAH-
>3 parts Bourbon Whiskey, 1 part Apricot Brandy
>Sour Mix, splash Grenadine *(Mix into Highball Glass—ice)*

PAGO PAGO-
>Light Rum, splash Green Chartreuse, splash White Crème de Caçao
>Lime Juice, Pineapple Juice *(Mix into Small Rocks Glass—ice)*

PAIN KILLER-
>3 parts Dark Rum, 1 part Coconut Rum
>Orange Juice, Pineapple Juice, sprinkle Nutmeg *(Mix into Highball Glass—ice)*

PAINLESS-
>1 part Amaretto, 1 part Crown Royal®, 1 part Irish Cream Liqueur
>*(Mix into Cocktail Glass—no ice)*

PAINT BOX-
>1 part Banana Liqueur, 1 part Blue Curaçao, 1 part Cherry Liqueur
>*(Layer in Order in Cocktail Glass—no ice)*

PAISLEY MARTINI-
>4 parts Gin, 1 part Dry Vermouth, splash Scotch Whiskey
>*(Mix into Cocktail Glass—no ice)*

PALL MALL-
   3 parts Gin, 1 part Dry Vermouth, 1 part Sweet Vermouth, 1 part White
      Crème de Menthe *(Mix into Small Rocks Glass—ice)*

PALM BEACH-
   Gin, splash Sweet Vermouth
   Grapefruit Juice *(Mix into Cocktail Glass—no ice)*

PALM BEACH POLO SPECIAL-
   1 part Banana Liqueur, 1 part Peppermint Schnapps
   Light Cream or Milk *(Mix into Highball Glass—ice)*

PALM BEACHER-
   4 parts Dark Rum, 1 part Amaretto
   Orange Juice *(Mix into Highball Glass—ice)*

PALM BREEZE-
   2 parts Vodka, 1 part Peach Schnapps
   Blue Hawaiian Punch®, Orange Juice *(Mix into Highball Glass—ice)*

PALMER-
   Blended Whiskey
   Lime Juice, splash Bitters *(Mix into Cocktail Glass—no ice)*

PALMETTO-
   1 part Dry Vermouth, 1 part Light Rum
   splash Bitters *(Mix into Cocktail Glass—no ice)*

PAMMY KAY-
   2 parts Dry Vermouth, 1 part Apricot Brandy, 1 part Gin
   Lime Juice *(Mix into Cocktail Glass—no ice)*

PAN-GALACTIC GARGLE BLASTER (1)-
   1 part Blue Curaçao, 1 part Jack Daniel's® Tennessee Sour Mash Whiskey
   Orange Juice, Lime Juice *(Mix into Highball Glass—ice)*

PAN-GALACTIC GARGLE BLASTER (2)-
   1 part Apricot Brandy, 1 part Light Rum, 1 part Tequila
   Orange Juice, splash Grenadine *(Mix into Cocktail Glass—no ice)*

PAN-GALACTIC GARGLE BLASTER (3)-
   4 parts 151-proof Rum, 2 parts Blue Curaçao, 1 part Triple Sec, splash Gin
   splash Bitters, splash Grenadine, fill Ginger Ale *(Mix into Highball Glass—ice)*

PANAMA (1)-
   1 part Brandy, 1 part White Crème de Caçao
   Light Cream or Milk *(Mix into Cocktail Glass—no ice)*

PANAMA (2)-
   3 parts Dark Rum, 1 part White Crème de Caçao,
   Light Cream or Milk *(Mix into Highball Glass—ice)*

PANAMA RED-
   2 parts Tequila, 1 part Triple Sec
   Sour Mix, splash Grenadine *(Mix into Cocktail Glass—no ice)*

PANCHO VILLA-
1 part Gin, 1 part Light Rum, splash Apricot Brandy, splash Cherry Brandy
splash Pineapple Juice *(Mix into Small Rocks Glass—ice)*

PANDA, THE-
1 part Apple Brandy, 1 part Gin, 1 part Russian Vodka
Orange Juice, Sugar *(Mix into Cocktail Glass—no ice)*

PANDA BEAR-
2 parts Amaretto, 1 part Brown Crème de Caçao, 1 part White Crème de Caçao
Vanilla Ice Cream, Chocolate Syrup *(Blend with ice in Daiquiri Glass)*

PANTHER-
Tequila
Sour Mix *(Mix into Highball Glass—ice)*

PANTOMIME-
Dry Vermouth
splash Orgeat (Almond) Syrup, splash Grenadine
(Mix into Cocktail Glass—no ice)

PANTS ON FIRE-
1 part Banana Liqueur, 1 part Strawberry Schnapps, 1 part Vodka
Grapefruit Juice, Orange Juice *(Mix into Highball Glass—ice)*

PANTY DROPPER-
1 part Gin, 1 part Red Dubonnet®
(Layer in Order in Cocktail Glass—no ice)

PAP SMEAR-
12 oz. Beer, 1 part 100-proof Vodka
(drop Vodka in Shot Glass into Beer Mug) (drink all at once)

PAPAYA DAIQUIRI-
Light Rum
Papaya Juice, Sour Mix
(Mix into Cocktail Glass with no ice or blend with ice in Daiquiri Glass)

PAPAYA SLING-
Gin
Papaya Juice, Lime Juice, splash Bitters, Club Soda
(Mix into Highball Glass—ice)

PARADISE-
2 parts Apricot Brandy, 1 part Gin
Orange Juice *(Mix into Cocktail Glass—no ice)*

PARADISE QUENCHER-
4 parts Spiced Rum, 1 part Apricot Brandy
Cranberry Juice, Orange Juice, Passion Fruit Juice, Pineapple Juice
(Mix into Highball Glass—ice)

PARALYZER-
2 parts Tequila, 1 part Coffee Liqueur, 1 part White Crème de Caçao
Light Cream or Milk *(Mix into Highball Glass—ice)*

PARISIAN-
1 part Dry Vermouth, 1 part Gin, splash Crème de Cassis
(Mix into Cocktail Glass—no ice)

PARISIAN BLONDE-
1 part Jamaican Rum, 1 part Triple Sec
Light Cream or Milk *(Mix into Cocktail Glass—no ice)*

PARISIAN MANHATTAN-
3 parts Blended Whiskey, 1 part Sweet Vermouth, splash Amer Picon
(Mix into Cocktail Glass—no ice)

PARK AVENUE-
2 parts Gin, 1 part Sweet Vermouth
Pineapple Juice *(Mix into Cocktail Glass—no ice)*

PARK LANE-
3 parts Blended Whiskey, 1 part Sloe Gin
Sour Mix *(Mix into Cocktail Glass—no ice)*

PARK PARADISE-
3 parts Canadian Whiskey, 1 part Sweet Vermouth, splash Maraschino Liqueur
splash Bitters *(Mix into Cocktail Glass—no ice)*

PARKEROO-
2 parts Dry Sherry, 1 part Tequila *(Mix into Cocktail Glass—no ice)*

PARKNASILLA PALMS-
4 parts Irish Cream Liqueur, 1 part Triple Sec *(Mix into Cocktail Glass—no ice)*

PARKNASILLA PEG LEG-
Irish Whiskey
Pineapple Juice, Coconut Milk, Lime Juice, top Club Soda
(Mix into Highball Glass—ice)

PARTY AT THE BEACH, A-
2 parts Coconut Liqueur, 1 part Amaretto
Orange Juice, Grenadine *(Mix into Highball Glass—ice)*

PARTY GIRL-
3 parts Dry Vermouth, splash Gin, 1 part Crème de Cassis
(Layer in Order in Cocktail Glass—no ice)

PASSION-
1 part Brandy, 1 part Light Rum, 1 part Triple Sec
Orange Juice, Lime Juice, splash Grenadine *(Mix into Highball Glass—ice)*

PASSION COLADA-
Dark Rum
Passion Fruit Juice, Coconut Milk *(Blend with ice in Daiquiri Glass)*

PASSION DAIQUIRI-
Light Rum
Passion Fruit Juice, Sour Mix
(Mix into Cocktail Glass with no ice or blend with ice in Daiquiri Glass)

PASSION MIMOSA-
Champagne
Passion Fruit Juice *(Mix into Champagne Flute—no ice)*

PASSION PUNCH-
1 part Gin, 1 part Light Rum
Orange Juice, Passion Fruit Juice *(Blend with ice in Daiquiri Glass)*

PASSIONATE DAIQUIRI, A-
Light Rum
Passion Fruit Juice, Sour Mix *(Blend with ice in Daiquiri Glass)*

PATAGONIA-
2 parts Coffee Liqueur, 2 parts Peppermint Schnapps, 1 part Bourbon Whiskey,
1 part Vodka *(Mix into Cocktail Glass—no ice)*

PATTY'S PRIDE-
4 parts Irish Whiskey, 1 part Peppermint Schnapps
Club Soda *(Mix into Highball Glass—ice)*

PAULINE-
Light Rum, splash Anisette
Lime Juice *(Mix into Cocktail Glass—no ice)*

PAVAROTTI-
4 parts Amaretto, 1 part Brandy, 1 part White Crème de Caçao
(Mix into Cocktail Glass—no ice)

PAVLOVA-
2 parts Vodka, 1 part Light Rum, splash Strawberry Schnapps
(Mix into Cocktail Glass—no ice)

PAVLOVA SUPREME-
4 parts Vodka, 1 part Crème de Cassis *(Mix into Small Rocks Glass—ice)*

PEACEFUL TREASURE-
Dark Rum
Orange Juice, Sour Mix, splash Grenadine *(Mix into Highball Glass—ice)*

PEACH ALEXANDER-
2 parts Peach Schnapps, 1 part White Crème de Caçao
Light Cream or Milk *(Mix into Small Rocks Glass—ice)*

PEACH BLOSSOM-
Gin, splash Peach Schnapps
Sour Mix, Club Soda *(Mix into Highball Glass—ice)*

PEACH BLOW FIZZ-
Gin, splash Peach Schnapps
Sour Mix, Light Cream or Milk, splash Club Soda
(Mix into Highball Glass—ice)

PEACH BLUSH COOLER-
3 parts White Zinfandel, 1 part Peach Schnapps
fill Club Soda *(Mix into Wine Glass—ice)*

PEACH BUCK-
2 parts Vodka, 1 part Peach Schnapps
Lime Juice, fill Ginger Ale *(Mix into Highball Glass—ice)*

PEACH BUNNY-
1 part Peach Schnapps, 1 part White Crème de Caçao
Light Cream or Milk *(Mix into Cocktail Glass—no ice)*

PEACH COCONUT FLIP-
1 part Light Rum, 1 part Peach Schnapps
Light Cream or Milk, Sugar *(Mix into Highball Glass—ice)*

PEACH DAIQUIRI-
4 parts Dark Rum, 1 part Triple Sec
Sour Mix, Pitted Peach
(Mix into Cocktail Glass with no ice or blend with ice in Daiquiri Glass)

PEACH FUZZ-
Peach Schnapps
Sour Mix, Peach Slices, splash Grenadine *(Blend with ice in Daiquiri Glass)*

PEACH MARGARITA-
2 parts Tequila, 1 part Peach Schnapps, splash Triple Sec
Sour Mix, Salted Rim
(Mix into Cocktail Glass with no ice or blend with ice in Daiquiri Glass)

PEACH MELBA (1)-
2 parts Peach Schnapps, 1 part Black Raspberry Liqueur
Light Cream or Milk *(Mix into Highball Glass—ice)*

PEACH MELBA (2)-
1 part Raspberry Liqueur, 1 part Spiced Rum
Peach Juice, Light Cream or Milk, Pitted Peach
(Blend with ice in Daiquiri Glass)

PEACH MELBA FREEZE-
1 part Black Raspberry Liqueur, 1 part Hazelnut Liqueur,
1 part Peach Schnapps
Light Cream or Milk, Vanilla Ice Cream, Raspberry Jam
(Blend with ice in Daiquiri Glass)

PEACH PUNCH-
2 parts Coconut Rum, 1 part Peach Schnapps
Orange Juice *(Mix into Highball Glass—ice)*

PEACH REFRESHER-
3 parts White Wine, 1 part Peach Schnapps
fill Lemon-Lime Soda *(Mix into Wine Glass—ice)*

PEACH SANGAREE-
1 part Peach Brandy, 1 part Port (float)
Club Soda, sprinkle Nutmeg *(Mix into Highball Glass—ice)*

PEACH TART-
Peach Schnapps
Lime Juice *(Mix into Cocktail Glass—no ice)*

P

PEACH TREAT-
Peach Schnapps, fill Champagne
Orange Juice *(Mix into Champagne Flute—no ice)*

PEACH VELVET-
3 parts Peach Schnapps, 1 part White Crème de Caçao
Light Cream or Milk *(Mix into Highball Glass—ice)*

PEACH WEST INDIES-
Light Rum
Lime Juice, Grenadine, Peaches *(Blend with ice in Daiquiri Glass)*

PEACHES & CREAM-
1 part Peach Schnapps, 1 part Vodka
Light Cream or Milk *(Mix into Highball Glass—ice)*

PEACHIE KEEN-
2 parts Peach Schnapps, 1 part Triple Sec
Club Soda, splash Grenadine (optional)
(Mix into Highball Glass—ice)

PEACHIE KIR-
Peach Schnapps, fill Champagne *(Mix into Champagne Flute—no ice)*

PEACHY AMARETTO-
1 part Amaretto, 1 part Peach Schnapps
Vanilla Ice Cream *(Blend with ice in Daiquiri Glass)*

PEACHY COLADA-
4 parts Spiced Rum, 1 part Peach Schnapps
Pineapple Juice, Coconut Milk
(Blend with ice in Daiquiri Glass)

PEANUT BUTTER & JELLY-
1 part Hazelnut Liqueur, 1 part Raspberry Liqueur
(Mix into Small Rocks Glass—ice)

PEANUT BUTTER CHOCOLATE CHIP COOKIE (1)-
1 part Coffee Liqueur, 1 part Hazelnut Liqueur, 1 part Tia Maria®
(Mix into Cocktail Glass—no ice)

PEANUT BUTTER CHOCOLATE CHIP COOKIE (2)-
1 part Coffee Liqueur, 1 part Hazelnut Liqueur, 1 part Tia Maria®
Light Cream or Milk *(Mix into Highball Glass—ice)*

PEANUT BUTTER CUP-
1 part Brown Crème De Caçao, 1 part Chocolate Liqueur, 1 part Hazelnut
Liqueur *(Mix into Cocktail Glass—no ice)*

PEARL HARBOR-
1 part Melon Liqueur, 1 part Vodka
Pineapple Juice *(Mix into Highball Glass—ice)*

PEARL HARBOR MARTINI-
Vodka, splash Melon Liqueur *(Mix into Cocktail Glass—no ice)*

PEARL NECKLACE-
1 part Vodka, 1 part White Crème de Caçao
splash of Light Cream or Milk *(Mix into Cocktail Glass—no ice)*

PECKER HEAD-
1 part Amaretto, 1 part Southern Comfort®
Pineapple Juice *(Mix into Highball Glass—ice)*

PEEP SHOW-
1 part Anisette, 1 part Brandy, 1 part White Dubonnet®
Lime Juice *(Mix into Cocktail Glass—no ice)*

PEGGY-
2 parts Gin, 1 part Dry Vermouth, splash Anisette, splash Red Dubonnet®
(Mix into Cocktail Glass—no ice)

PEGU CLUB-
2 parts Gin, 1 part Triple Sec
splash Lime Juice, splash Bitters, splash Orange Bitters
(Mix into Cocktail Glass—no ice)

PELTIKATTO-
Vodka
Squeeze Juice from Lemon Garnish *(Mix into Small Rocks Glass—ice)*

PENALTY SHOT-
1 part White Crème de Menthe, 1 part Tia Maria®, 1 part Peppermint Schnapps
(Layer in Order in Cocktail Glass—no ice)

PENDENNIS-
Gin, splash Apricot Brandy
Lime Juice, splash Bitters *(Mix into Cocktail Glass—no ice)*

PENDENNIS TODDY-
Bourbon Whiskey
Sugar Cube, Water, muddle *(Mix into Small Rocks Glass—ice)*

PEP UP-
Peppermint Schnapps
Lemon-Lime Soda *(Mix into Highball Glass—ice)*

PEPPER BULL-
Pepper Vodka
Lime Juice, Beef Bouillon, splash Worcestershire Sauce
(Mix into Highball Glass—ice)

PEPPER MARTINI-
Pepper Vodka, splash Dry Vermouth *(Mix into Cocktail Glass—no ice)*

PEPPERCLEAR-
100-proof Everclear® Vodka
Dr Pepper® Cola *(Mix into Highball Glass—ice)*

PEPPERMINT BEACH-
1 part Coconut Rum, 1 part Peppermint Schnapps
(Mix into Small Rocks Glass—ice)

P

PEPPERMINT HOT CHOCOLATE-
Peppermint Schnapps
Hot Chocolate, top Whipped Cream *(Mix into Irish Coffee Cup—no ice)*

PEPPERMINT ICEBERG-
Peppermint Schnapps *(Mix into Small Rocks Glass—ice)*

PEPPERMINT PARK-
Gin, fill Champagne
Lime Juice *(Mix into Champagne Flute—no ice)*

PEPPERMINT PATTIE (1)-
1 part White Crème de Caçao, 1 part White Crème de Menthe
(Mix into Cocktail Glass—no ice)

PEPPERMINT PATTIE (2)-
1 part Brown Crème de Caçao, 1 part White Crème de Menthe
Light Cream or Milk *(Mix into Highball Glass—ice)*

PEPPERMINT PATTIE (3)-
1 part Brown Crème de Caçao, 1 part Coffee Liqueur,
    1 part Peppermint Schnapps
Light Cream or Milk *(Mix into Highball Glass—ice)*

PEPPERMINT PATTIE (4)-
1 part Brown Crème de Caçao, 1 part Peppermint Schnapps
Light Cream or Milk *(Mix into Highball Glass—ice)*

PEPPERMINT PENGUIN-
1 part Chocolate Mint Liqueur, 1 part Green Crème de Menthe
Light Cream or Milk *(Mix into Cocktail Glass—no ice)*

PEPPERMINT STICK-
1 part Peppermint Schnapps, 1 part White Crème de Caçao
Light Cream or Milk *(Mix into Champagne Flute—no ice)*

PEPPERMINT STINGER-
1 part Brandy, 1 part Peppermint Schnapps *(Mix into Small Rocks Glass—ice)*

PEPPERMINT TREAT-
1 part Green Crème de Menthe, 1 part Peppermint Schnapps
Light Cream or Milk *(Mix into Highball Glass—ice)*

PEPPERMINT TWIST-
2 parts Peppermint Schnapps, 1 part White Crème de Caçao
Vanilla Ice Cream, Peppermint Candy Stick Garnish
(Blend with ice in Daiquiri Glass)

PEREGRINE'S PERIL-
2 parts Dark Rum, 1 part Banana Liqueur, 1 part Southern Comfort®
Lime Juice *(Mix into Cocktail Glass—no ice)*

PERFECT COCKTAIL-
Gin, splash Dry Vermouth, splash Sweet Vermouth
splash Bitters *(Mix into Cocktail Glass—no ice)*

PERFECT COUPLE, THE-
(Two layers: Blend with ice & layer Part 2 on top of Part 1 in order in Daiquiri Glass)
Part 1: 1 part Dark Rum
          Sour Mix, Strawberries, blend
Part 2: 1 part Dark Rum
          Piña Colada Mix, Light Cream or Milk, blend, top Whipped Cream

PERFECT MANHATTAN-
Blended Whiskey, splash Dry Vermouth, splash Sweet Vermouth
(Mix into Cocktail Glass—no ice)

PERFECT MARTINI-
Gin, splash Dry Vermouth, splash Sweet Vermouth
(Mix into Cocktail Glass—no ice)

PERFECT ROB ROY-
Scotch Whiskey, splash Dry Vermouth, splash Sweet Vermouth
(Mix into Cocktail Glass—no ice)

PERFECT SCREW(DRIVER)-
4 parts Pear Schnapps, 1 part Vodka,
Orange Juice *(Mix into Highball Glass—ice)*

PERTH-
Scotch Whiskey, splash Amaretto, splash Triple Sec
Sour Mix *(Mix into Cocktail Glass—no ice)*

PETE'S PREFERENCE-***
2 parts Irish Cream Liqueur, 1 part Bärenjäger®
(Layer in Order in Cocktail Glass—no ice)

PETER PAN-
1 part Dry Vermouth, 1 part Gin
Orange Juice, splash Bitters *(Mix into Cocktail Glass—no ice)*

PETTICOAT LANE-
4 parts Gin, 1 part Campari, 1 part Sweet Vermouth
(Mix into Cocktail Glass—no ice)

PEYTON PLACE-
1 part Gin, 1 part Sloe Gin
Grapefruit Juice, Sugar, fill Club Soda *(Mix into Highball Glass—ice)*

PHILADELPHIA SCOTCHMAN-
1 part Apple Brandy, 1 part Port
Orange Juice, fill Club Soda *(Mix into Highball Glass—ice)*

PHOEBE SNOW-
1 part Brandy, 1 part Red Dubonnet®, splash Anisette
(Mix into Cocktail Glass—no ice)

PIANO PLAYER-
1 part Vodka, 1 part White Crème de Caçao
Light Cream or Milk *(Mix into Cocktail Glass—no ice)*

PICCADILLY-
2 parts Gin, 1 part Dry Vermouth, splash Anisette
splash Grenadine *(Mix into Cocktail Glass—no ice)*

PICK ME UP-
1 part Cherry Brandy, 1 part French Vermouth, splash Gin
(Mix into Cocktail Glass—no ice)

PICKLED BRAIN-
1 part Vodka, 1 part Irish Cream Liqueur, 1 part Green Crème de Menthe
(Layer in Order in Cocktail Glass—no ice)

PICON-
1 part Amer Picon, 1 part Sweet Vermouth
(Mix into Cocktail Glass—no ice)

PICON FIZZ-
4 parts Amer Picon, 1 part Brandy (float)
splash Grenadine, fill Club Soda *(Mix into Highball Glass—ice)*

PIECE OF MIND-
1 part Kümmel, 1 part Vodka *(Mix into Small Rocks Glass—ice)*

PIERCED NAVEL-
Peach Schnapps
Cranberry Juice, Orange Juice *(Mix into Highball Glass—ice)*

PIG SKIN-
1 part Melon Liqueur, 1 part Vodka
Sour Mix *(Mix into Highball Glass—ice)*

PIGGELIN-
1 part Melon Liqueur, 1 part Vodka
Orange Juice or Tang® *(Mix into Highball Glass—ice)*

PIGGOT'S PREFERENCE-
3 parts Dry Vermouth, 1 part Southern Comfort®, splash Light Rum,
    splash Triple Sec
splash Orange Bitters *(Mix into Cocktail Glass—no ice)*

PIKE'S PEAK-
1 part Coffee Liqueur, 1 part Peppermint Schnapps
Coffee, top Whipped Cream *(Mix into Irish Coffee Cup—no ice)*

PILE DRIVER-
Vodka
Prune Juice, splash Lime Juice *(Mix into Highball Glass—ice)*

PILOT BOAT-
1 part Banana Liqueur, 1 part Dark Rum
Lime Juice *(Mix into Cocktail Glass—no ice)*

PIÑA COCKTAIL-
Tequila
Pineapple Juice, Sour Mix *(Mix into Cocktail Glass—no ice)*

PIÑA COLADA-
Dark or Light Rum
Coconut Milk, Pineapple Juice *(Blend with ice in Daiquiri Glass)*

PIÑATA-
2 parts Tequila, 1 part Banana Liqueur
Lime Juice *(Mix into Cocktail Glass—no ice)*

PINEAPPLE BANANA REFRESHER-
1 part Banana Liqueur, 1 part Dark Rum
Pineapple Juice, Pineapple Sherbet *(Blend with ice in Daiquiri Glass)*

PINEAPPLE BASH-
1 part Melon Liqueur, 1 part Southern Comfort®
Pineapple Juice *(Mix into Highball Glass—ice)*

PINEAPPLE BOMB (1)-
1 part Coconut Rum, 1 part Dark Rum
Pineapple Juice *(Mix into Highball Glass—ice)*

PINEAPPLE BOMB (2)-
1 part Amaretto, 1 part Southern Comfort®
Pineapple Juice, splash Cranberry Juice *(Mix into Highball Glass—ice)*

PINEAPPLE BOMB (3)-
2 parts Southern Comfort®, 1 part Amaretto
Pineapple Juice, splash Grenadine *(Mix into Highball Glass—ice)*

PINEAPPLE BOMBER (1)-
1 part Southern Comfort®, 1 part Jack Daniel's® Tennessee Sour Mash Whiskey
Pineapple Juice *(Mix into Highball Glass—ice)*

PINEAPPLE BOMBER (2)-
2 parts Southern Comfort®, 2 parts Spiced Rum, 1 part Amaretto
Pineapple Juice *(Mix into Highball Glass—ice)*

PINEAPPLE COCKTAIL-
Light Rum
Pineapple Juice, Lime Juice *(Mix into Cocktail Glass—no ice)*

PINEAPPLE COOLER-
White Wine
Pineapple Juice, Sugar, top Club Soda *(Mix into Wine Glass—ice)*

PINEAPPLE DAIQUIRI-
Light Rum
Pineapple Juice, splash Sour Mix *(Blend with ice in Daiquiri Glass)*

PINEAPPLE FIZZ-
Light Rum
Pineapple Juice, Sugar, splash Club Soda *(Mix into Highball Glass—ice)*

PINEAPPLE FRANCINE-
1 part Apricot Brandy, 1 part Light Rum
Pineapple Juice, Light Cream or Milk, Pineapple Slices
(Mix into Highball Glass with ice or blend with ice in Daiquiri Glass)

PINEAPPLE GIMLET-
Gin
splash Lime Juice, splash Pineapple Juice *(Mix into Small Rocks Glass—ice)*

PINEAPPLE GRANDE-
3 parts Blended Whiskey, 1 part Amaretto
splash Pineapple Juice *(Mix into Small Rocks Glass—ice)*

PINEAPPLE MARGARITA-
Tequila
Sour Mix, Pineapple Juice
(Mix into Cocktail Glass with no ice or blend with ice in Daiquiri Glass)

PINEAPPLE SUNRISE-
Tequila
Pineapple Juice, Sour Mix, Grenadine (lace) (stir with straw for "sunrise")
(Mix into Highball Glass—ice)

PINEAPPLE UPSIDE DOWN CAKE-
1 part Butterscotch Schnapps, 1 part Irish Cream Liqueur, 1 part Vodka
Pineapple Juice *(Mix into Highball Glass—ice)*

PINE TREE-
Triple Sec
Lemonade, Mint Leaf Garnish *(Mix into Highball Glass—ice)*

PING-PONG-
Sloe Gin
Lime Juice *(Mix into Cocktail Glass—no ice)*

PINK ALMOND-
2 parts Blended Whiskey, 1 part Amaretto, 1 part Cherry Brandy,
1 part Crème de Noyaux
Lime Juice *(Mix into Cocktail Glass—no ice)*

PINK BABY-
2 parts Vodka, 1 part Cherry Brandy
Sour Mix *(Mix into Cocktail Glass—no ice)*

PINK BELLY-
1 part Amaretto, 1 part Bourbon Whiskey, 1 part Irish Cream Liqueur,
1 part Sloe Gin
Lemon-Lime Soda *(Mix into Highball Glass—ice)*

PINK CADILLAC MARGARITA-
2 parts Tequila, 1 part Triple Sec
Cranberry Juice, Sour Mix *(Mix into Cocktail Glass—no ice)*

PINK CREAM FIZZ-
Gin
Sour Mix, Light Cream or Milk, splash Grenadine, splash Club Soda
(Mix into Highball Glass—ice)

PINK CREOLE-
Light Rum
Lime Juice, Light Cream or Milk, Grenadine *(Mix into Cocktail Glass—no ice)*

PINK FLAMINGO (1)-
   Berry Schnapps
   Cranberry Juice, splash Sour Mix *(Mix into Highball Glass—ice)*

PINK FLAMINGO (2)-
   Sloe Gin
   Orange Juice, Pineapple Juice, splash Sour Mix
   (Mix into Highball Glass—ice)

PINK GIN-
   Gin
   splash Bitters *(Mix into Small Rocks Glass—ice)*

PINK GOODY-
   1 part Gin, 1 part Light Rum
   Lime Juice, splash Grenadine, splash Lemon-Lime Soda
   (Mix into Cocktail Glass—no ice)

PINK LADY (1)-
   Gin
   Lime Juice, Grenadine *(Mix into Cocktail Glass—no ice)*

PINK LADY (2)-
   Gin
   Light Cream or Milk, splash Grenadine *(Mix into Highball Glass—ice)*

PINK LEMONADE (1)-
   Citrus Vodka
   Cranberry Juice, splash Sour Mix *(Mix into Highball Glass—ice)*

PINK LEMONADE (2)-
   Citrus Vodka, splash Triple Sec
   Sour Mix, Cranberry Juice *(Mix into Highball Glass—ice)*

PINK LEMONADE (3)-
   Light Rum
   Cranberry Juice, splash Lime Juice, top Lemon-Lime Soda
   (Mix into Highball Glass—ice)

PINK LEMONADE (4)-
   2 parts Vodka, 1 part Maraschino Liqueur
   Lemonade *(Mix into Highball Glass—ice)*

PINK MARTINI-
   1 part Raspberry Liqueur, 1 part Vodka
   Lime Garnish *(Mix into Cocktail Glass—no ice)*

PINK MERMAID-
   Light Rum
   Lime Juice, splash Light Cream or Milk, splash Grenadine
   (Mix into Cocktail Glass—no ice)

PINK ORCHID-
   Spiced Rum
   Cranberry Juice, Pineapple Juice *(Mix into Highball Glass—ice)*

P

PINK PANTHER-
3 parts Vodka, 1 part Cherry Brandy, 1 part Dry Vermouth
Orange Juice *(Mix into Cocktail Glass—no ice)*

PINK PARADISE-
1 part Amaretto, 1 part Coconut Rum
Cranberry Juice, Pineapple Juice *(Mix into Highball Glass—ice)*

PINK PUSSY-
2 parts Campari, 1 part Peach Schnapps
splash Bitters, fill Lemon-Lime Soda *(Mix into Highball Glass—ice)*

PINK PUSSY CAT-
Gin or Vodka
Grapefruit or Pineapple Juice, splash Grenadine *(Mix into Highball Glass—ice)*

PINK ROSE FIZZ-
Gin
Light Cream or Milk, Sour Mix, splash Club Soda
(Mix into Highball Glass—ice)

PINK SQUIRREL-
1 part Crème de Noyaux, 1 part White Crème de Caçao
Light Cream or Milk *(Mix into Highball Glass—ice)*

PINK TOP-
2 parts Gin, 1 part Grand Marnier®
Lime Juice, splash Grenadine *(Mix into Cocktail Glass—no ice)*

PINK VERANDA-
2 parts Light Rum, 1 part Dark Rum
Cranberry Juice, splash Sour Mix *(Mix into Highball Glass—ice)*

PINK WHISKERS-
2 parts Apricot Brandy, 1 part Dry Vermouth, 1 part Port (float),
　　splash White Crème de Menthe
Orange Juice, splash Grenadine *(Mix into Small Rocks Glass—ice)*

PINO FRIO-
Spiced Rum
Pineapple Slices, Sugar *(Blend with ice in Daiquiri Glass)*

PIPELINE-
1 part Tequila, 1 part Vodka *(Layer in Order in Cocktail Glass—no ice)*

PIPER-
4 parts Tequila, 1 part Brown Crème de Caçao
Warm Coffee, splash Lime Juice *(Mix into Irish Coffee Cup—no ice)*

PIPER AT ARMS-
2 parts Scotch Whiskey, 1 part Dry Vermouth *(Mix into Cocktail Glass—no ice)*

PIPER AT THE GATES OF DAWN-
2 parts Scotch Whiskey, 1 part Coffee Liqueur, 1 part Maraschino Liqueur
Light Cream or Milk (float) *(Mix into Highball Glass—ice)*

PIRATE-
  3 parts Jamaican Rum, 1 part Sweet Vermouth
  splash Bitters *(Mix into Small Rocks Glass—ice)*

PIRATE'S FLOAT-
  1 part Root Beer Schnapps, 1 part Captain Morgan® Original Spiced Rum
  splash Cola *(Mix into Small Rocks Glass—ice)*

PIRATE'S SPICED RUM TEA-
  Captain Morgan® Original Spiced Rum
  Hot Tea, Honey, Cinnamon Stick *(Mix into Irish Coffee Cup—no ice)*

PISTACHIO CREAM-
  1 part Brandy, 1 part Pistachio Liqueur
  Vanilla Ice Cream, Light Cream or Milk
  (Mix into Highball Glass with ice or blend with ice in Daiquiri Glass)

PISTACHIO MINT ICE CREAM-
  2 parts Hazelnut Liqueur, 2 parts Vodka, 1 part Green Crème de Menthe
  Light Cream or Milk *(Blend with ice in Daiquiri Glass)*

PLANTATION PUNCH-
  2 parts Dark Jamaican Rum, 1 part Southern Comfort®, 1 part Port (float)
  Sour Mix, Brown Sugar, fill Club Soda
  (Mix into Highball Glass—ice)

PLANTER'S COCKTAIL-
  Jamaican Rum
  Sour Mix *(Mix into Cocktail Glass—no ice)*

PLANTER'S PUNCH (1)-
  Jamaican Rum
  Sour Mix, splash Bitters, Club Soda *(Mix into Highball Glass—ice)*

PLANTER'S PUNCH (2)-
  Dark or Light Rum
  Sour Mix, splash Grenadine, Club Soda *(Mix into Highball Glass—ice)*

PLANTER'S PUNCH (3)-
  2 parts Light Rum, 1 part Jamaican Rum, splash Triple Sec
  Orange Juice, Pineapple Juice, Sour Mix, splash Grenadine
  (Mix into Highball Glass—ice)

PLANTER'S PUNCH (4)-
  1 part Dark Rum, 1 part Jamaican Rum, 1 part Light Rum, 1 part Spiced Rum,
    1 part 151-proof Rum (float)
  Orange Juice, Pineapple Juice, Sour Mix, splash Grenadine
  (Mix into Highball Glass—ice)

PLANTER'S PUNCH (5)-
  1 part Dark Rum, 1 part Light Rum
  Orange Juice, Sour Mix, splash Grenadine *(Mix into Highball Glass—ice)*

PLATINUM BLONDE-
  1 part Light Rum, 1 part Triple Sec
  Light Cream or Milk *(Mix into Highball Glass—ice)*

P

PLAYBOY COOLER-
1 part Coffee Liqueur, 1 part Gold Rum
Pineapple Juice, Lime Juice, top Cola *(Mix into Highball Glass—ice)*

PLAZA-
1 part Dry Vermouth, 1 part Gin, 1 part Sweet Vermouth
Pineapple Garnish *(Mix into Cocktail Glass—no ice)*

PLENTY & GOOD-
1 part Coffee Liqueur, 1 part Licorice Liqueur
(Mix into Cocktail Glass—no ice)

POINSETTIA (1)-
Champagne
Cranberry Juice *(Mix into Champagne Flute—no ice)*

POINSETTIA (2)-
1 part Triple Sec (lace), Champagne (fill)
(Mix into Champagne Flute—no ice)

POKER-
1 part Light Rum, 1 part Sweet Vermouth *(Mix into Cocktail Glass—no ice)*

POKER FACE-
3 parts Tequila, 1 part Triple Sec
Pineapple Juice *(Mix into Highball Glass—ice)*

POLAR ATTRACTION-
Brandy
Tonic Water *(Mix into Highball Glass—ice)*

POLAR ICE CAP-
1 part Coffee Liqueur, 1 part Vodka
Light Cream or Milk, Coconut Milk *(Blend with ice in Daiquiri Glass)*

POLARBEAR-
Vodka
Lime Juice, splash Lemon-Lime Soda *(Mix into Cocktail Glass—no ice)*

POLISH SIDECAR-
1 part Blackberry Brandy, 1 part Gin
Sour Mix *(Mix into Highball Glass—ice)*

POLLY'S SPECIAL-
3 parts Scotch Whiskey, 1 part Triple Sec
Grapefruit Juice *(Mix into Highball Glass—ice)*

POLLYANNA-
4 parts Gin, 1 part Sweet Vermouth
Orange & Pineapple Slices, muddle, splash Grenadine
(Mix into Cocktail Glass—no ice)

POLO-
Gin
Orange Juice, Lime Juice *(Mix into Cocktail Glass—no ice)*

POLO DREAM-
3 parts Bourbon Whiskey, 1 part Amaretto
Orange Juice *(Mix into Cocktail Glass—no ice)*

POLONAISE-
3 parts Brandy, 1 part Dry Sherry, splash Blackberry Brandy
Lime Juice *(Mix into Small Rocks Glass—ice)*

POLYNESIAN-
2 parts Vodka, 1 part Cherry Brandy
Lime Juice, Sugared Rim *(Mix into Cocktail Glass—no ice)*

POMPANO-
2 parts Gin, 1 part Dry Vermouth
Grapefruit Juice *(Mix into Cocktail Glass—no ice)*

POND SCUM-
2 parts Vodka, 1 part Irish Cream Liqueur (float)
Club Soda *(Mix into Highball Glass—ice)*

POOLSIDE MARGARITA-
2 parts Triple Sec, 1 part Tequila, splash Blue Curaçao
Sour Mix *(Mix into Cocktail Glass—no ice)*

POOP DECK-
2 parts Blackberry Brandy, 1 part Brandy, 1 part Port
(Mix into Cocktail Glass—no ice)

POOR MAN'S MIMOSA-
Beer
Orange Juice *(Beer Mug)*

POOR TIM-
3 parts Blended Whiskey, 1 part Dry Vermouth, splash Raspberry Liqueur
(Mix into Cocktail Glass—no ice)

POP THE CHERRY-
Cherry Brandy
Orange Juice *(Mix into Highball Glass—ice)*

POPPED CHERRY-
1 part Cherry Brandy, 1 part Vodka
Cranberry Juice, Orange Juice, Popped Cherry Garnish
(Mix into Highball Glass—ice)

POPPER-
Tequila
Lemon-Lime Soda *(Mix into Highball Glass—ice)*

POPPY-
2 parts Gin, 1 part White Crème de Caçao *(Mix into Cocktail Glass—no ice)*

POPSICLE (1)-
Amaretto
Orange Juice, Light Cream or Milk *(Mix into Highball Glass—ice)*

P

POPSICLE (2)-
    1 part Apricot Brandy, 1 part Vodka, 1 part Irish Cream Liqueur
    (Layer in Order in Cocktail Glass—no ice)

PORT & STARBOARD-
    Green Crème de Menthe (float)
    Grenadine *(Mix into Cocktail Glass—no ice)*

PORT EGGNOG-
    Port
    Eggnog *(Mix into Highball Glass—no ice)*

PORT MILK PUNCH-
    Port Wine
    Light Cream or Milk, Sugar, sprinkle Nutmeg
    (Mix into Wine Glass—no ice)

PORT SANGAREE-
    Port Wine
    Water, Sugar, fill Club Soda *(Mix into Wine Glass—no ice)*

PORT WINE COBBLER-
    Port Wine
    Club Soda, Sugar *(Mix into Wine Glass—no ice)*

PORT WINE COCKTAIL-
    Port Wine, splash Brandy *(Mix into Wine Glass—no ice)*

PORT WINE FLIP-
    Port Wine
    Light Cream or Milk, Sugar, sprinkle Nutmeg *(Mix into Wine Glass—no ice)*

PORT WINE NEGUS-
    Port Wine
    Hot Water, Sugar, sprinkle Nutmeg *(Mix into Irish Coffee Cup—no ice)*

PORT WINE SANGAREE-
    1 part Brandy (float), Port Wine (fill)
    Club Soda, Sugar, sprinkle Nutmeg *(Mix into Wine Glass—no ice)*

PORTUGUESE DAISY-
    2 parts Ruby Port, 1 part Brandy
    Sour Mix, splash Grenadine *(Mix into Wine Glass—no ice)*

POST-MODERN LEMONADE-
    2 parts Dry Sherry, 2 parts Sloe Gin, 1 part Aquavit, splash Vodka
    Sour Mix, fill Club Soda *(Mix into Highball Glass—ice)*

POST-MODERN MARGARITA-
    1 part Blue Curaçao, 1 part Tequila
    Cranberry Juice, Lime Juice *(Mix into Cocktail Glass—no ice)*

POT 'O GOLD-
    1 part Goldschläger®, 1 part Irish Cream Liqueur
    (Mix into Small Rocks Glass—ice)

POTTED PARROT-
3 parts Gold Rum, 1 part Orange Curaçao, splash Amaretto,
    splash 151-proof Rum (float)
Orange Juice, Lime Juice *(Mix into Highball Glass—ice)*

POUSSE CAFE-
1 part Grenadine, 1 part Yellow Chartreuse, 1 part Crème de Cassis, 1 part
    White Crème de Menthe, 1 part Green Chartreuse, 1 part Brandy
(Layer in Order in Cocktail Glass with no ice)

POUSSE L'AMOUR-
splash Maraschino Liqueur, 1 part Bénédictine, 1 part Brandy
(Layer in Order in Cocktail Glass—no ice)

POWER SCREWDRIVER-
Vodka
Orange Juice, Cola *(Mix into Highball Glass—ice)*

PRADO-
Tequila, splash Maraschino Liqueur
Lime Juice, splash Grenadine *(Mix into Highball Glass—ice)*

PRAIRIE CHICKEN-
Gin
Salt, Pepper *(Mix into Cocktail Glass—no ice)*

PRAIRIE OYSTER-
Brandy
Worcestershire Sauce, Ketchup, Vinegar, Pepper
(Mix into Small Rocks Glass—no ice)

PREAKNESS-
2 parts Blended Whiskey, 1 part Sweet Vermouth, splash Bénédictine
Bitters *(Mix into Cocktail Glass—no ice)*

PRESBYTERIAN (CONSERVATIVE)-
Bourbon Whiskey (Less than that of the "Liberal")
Club Soda, splash Ginger Ale *(Mix into Highball Glass—ice)*

PRESBYTERIAN (LIBERAL)-
Bourbon Whiskey
Club Soda, splash Ginger Ale *(Mix into Highball Glass—ice)*

PRESIDENTE-
3 parts Light Rum, 1 part Dry Vermouth, splash Triple Sec
splash Grenadine *(Mix into Cocktail Glass—no ice)*

PRESTO-
2 parts Brandy, 1 part Sweet Vermouth, splash Anisette
Orange Juice *(Mix into Cocktail Glass—no ice)*

PRESTWICK-
3 parts Scotch Whiskey, 1 part Sweet Vermouth, splash Triple Sec,
    splash Drambuie® (float)
(Mix into Small Rocks Glass—ice)

P

PRETTY PAULA'S PLEASURE-***
3 parts Tequila, 1 part Triple Sec
Cranberry Juice, splash Sour Mix, Salted Rim (optional)
(Mix into Cocktail Glass—no ice)

PRETTY THING-
3 parts Vodka, 1 part Amaretto, 1 part Coconut Liqueur
Light Cream or Milk *(Mix into Highball Glass—ice)*

PRIMAL SCREAM-
1 part Coffee Liqueur, 1 part Tequila
Club Soda *(Mix into Highball Glass—ice)*

PRINCE-
Blended Whiskey, splash White Crème de Menthe
splash Orange Bitters *(Mix into Cocktail Glass—no ice)*

PRINCE CHARLES COFFEE-
Drambuie®
Coffee, top Whipped Cream *(Mix into Irish Coffee Cup—no ice)*

PRINCE CHARLIE-
1 part Brandy, 1 part Drambuie®
Lime Juice *(Mix into Cocktail Glass—no ice)*

PRINCE EDWARD-
3 parts Scotch Whiskey, 1 part Lillet, splash Drambuie®
(Mix into Cocktail Glass—no ice)

PRINCE OF WALES-
1 part Brandy, 1 part Madeira Wine, splash Triple Sec, Champagne (fill)
splash Bitters *(Mix into Champagne Flute—no ice)*

PRINCE RUPERT-
3 parts Blended Whiskey, 1 part Anisette *(Mix into Cocktail Glass—no ice)*

PRINCE'S SMILE-
2 parts Gin, 1 part Apple Brandy, 1 part Apricot Brandy
Lime Juice *(Mix into Cocktail Glass—no ice)*

PRINCES STREET-
Scotch Whiskey, splash Triple Sec
Sugar *(Mix into Cocktail Glass—no ice)*

PRINCESS MARY'S PRIDE-
Apple Brandy, splash Dry Vermouth, splash Red Dubonnet®
(Mix into Small Rocks Glass—ice)

PRINCESS MORGAN-
3 parts Captain Morgan® Original Spiced Rum, 1 part Banana Liqueur
Orange Juice, top Club Soda *(Mix into Highball Glass—ice)*

PRINCESS POUSSE CAFE-
1 part Apricot Brandy, 1 part Light Cream or Milk
(Layer in Order in Cocktail Glass—no ice)

PRINCETON-
   1 part Dry Vermouth, 1 part Gin
   Lime Juice *(Mix into Cocktail Glass—no ice)*

PROHIBITION-
   1 part Gin, 1 part Lillet, splash Apricot Brandy
   splash Orange Juice *(Mix into Cocktail Glass—no ice)*

PROVINCETOWN PLAYHOUSE-
   1 part Gold Rum, 1 part Vodka
   Cranberry Juice, Sour Mix *(Mix into Highball Glass—ice)*

PRUSSIAN SALUTE-
   3 parts Russian Vodka, 1 part Blackberry Brandy, 1 part Triple Sec
   (Mix into Cocktail Glass—no ice)

PUERTO APPLE-
   2 parts Apple Schnapps, 1 part Light Rum, splash Amaretto
   Lime Juice *(Mix into Small Rocks Glass—ice)*

PUERTO PLATA-
   3 parts Vodka, 1 part Banana Liqueur, splash Amaretto
   Pineapple Juice, splash Lime Juice
   (Mix into Highball Glass—ice)

PUERTO RICAN MONKEY F**K-
   1 part Banana Liqueur, 1 part Coffee Liqueur, 1 part 151-proof Rum (float)
   (Mix into Cocktail Glass—no ice)

PUFFER-
   Light Rum
   Grapefruit Juice, Orange Juice, splash Grenadine (lace)
   (Mix into Highball Glass—ice)

PUMPKIN EATER-
   1 part Light Rum, 1 part Triple Sec
   Light Cream or Milk, Orange Juice *(Mix into Highball Glass—ice)*

PUPPY'S NOSE-
   1 part Peppermint Schnapps, 1 part Tia Maria®, 1 part Irish Cream Liqueur
   (Layer in Order in Cocktail Glass—no ice)

PURGAVIE-
   3 parts Canadian Whiskey, 1 part Amer Picon
   Orange Juice, splash Orange Bitters, fill Club Soda
   (Mix into Highball Glass—ice)

PURPLE BUNNY-
   3 parts Cherry Brandy, 1 part White Crème de Caçao
   Light Cream or Milk *(Mix into Highball Glass—ice)*

PURPLE GECKO-
   3 parts Tequila, 1 part Blue Curaçao, 1 part Red Curaçao
   Cranberry Juice, Sour Mix
   (Mix into Cocktail Glass—no ice)

PURPLE HAZE (1)-
   3 parts Vodka, 1 part Raspberry Liqueur
   Cranberry Juice, Sour Mix
   (Mix into Highball Glass—ice)

PURPLE HAZE (2)-
   2 parts Raspberry Liqueur, 2 parts Vodka, 1 part Triple Sec
   splash Lime Juice, fill Club Soda (Do Not Mix, Serve with Drinking Straw,
      Drink all at once.)
   (Mix into Highball Glass—ice)

PURPLE HEATHER, THE-
   3 parts Scotch Whiskey, 1 part Crème de Cassis
   Club Soda *(Mix into Highball Glass—ice)*

PURPLE HOOTER (1)-
   3 parts Citrus Vodka, 1 part Black Raspberry Liqueur, 1 part Triple Sec
   (Mix into Cocktail Glass—no ice)

PURPLE HOOTER (2)-
   1 part Raspberry Liqueur, 1 part Vodka
   Cranberry Juice, Sour Mix *(Mix into Highball Glass—ice)*

PURPLE HOOTER (3)-
   1 part Raspberry Liqueur, 1 part Vodka
   Sour Mix, splash Cranberry Juice, fill Lemon-Lime Soda
   (Mix into Highball Glass—ice)

PURPLE HOOTER (4)-
   1 part Orange Juice, 1 part Raspberry Liqueur, 1 part Sour Mix, 1 part Vodka
   (Layer in Order in Cocktail Glass—no ice)

PURPLE HOOTER MARTINI-
   3 parts Vodka, 1 part Raspberry Liqueur, splash Dry Vermouth
   splash Sour Mix *(Mix into Cocktail Glass—no ice)*

PURPLE KISS-
   2 parts Gin, 1 part Crème de Noyaux, splash Cherry Brandy
   Lime Juice *(Mix into Cocktail Glass—no ice)*

PURPLE MASK-
   2 parts Vodka, 1 part White Crème de Caçao
   Grape Juice *(Mix into Cocktail Glass—no ice)*

PURPLE MOTHER FKER-**
   1 part Raspberry Liqueur, 1 part Vodka
   Orange Juice, Sour Mix *(Mix into Highball Glass—ice)*

PURPLE NIPPLE-
   1 part Jägermeister®, 1 part Melon Liqueur
   Cranberry Juice, Orange Juice *(Mix into Highball Glass—ice)*

PURPLE ORCHARD-
   1 part Blackberry Brandy, 1 part White Crème de Caçao
   Light Cream or Milk *(Mix into Highball Glass—ice)*

PURPLE PANCHO-
  2 parts Tequila, 1 part Blue Curaçao, 1 part Sloe Gin
  Sour Mix, Salted Rim *(Mix into Cocktail Glass—no ice)*

PURPLE PASSION-
  Vodka
  Grapefruit Juice, Grape Juice, Sour Mix *(Mix into Highball Glass—ice)*

PURPLE PASSION TEA-
  2 parts Black Raspberry Liqueur, 1 part Gin, 1 part Light Rum, 1 part Vodka
  Sour Mix, Lemon-Lime Soda *(Mix into Highball Glass—ice)*

PURPLE RAIN-
  2 parts Vodka, 1 part Blue Curaçao
  Cranberry Juice *(Mix into Highball Glass—ice)*

PUSHKIN'S PUNCH-
  1 part Grand Marnier®, 1 part Vodka, Champagne (fill)
  splash Lime Juice, splash Bitters *(Mix into Champagne Flute—no ice)*

PUSSY PAWS-
  Amaretto
  Cranberry Juice, Sour Mix, fill Club Soda *(Mix into Highball Glass—ice)*

PYEWACKET'S REVENGE-
  Scotch Whiskey
  Cola *(Mix into Highball Glass—ice)*

– NOTES –

_____

_____

_____

_____

_____

_____

_____

_____

_____

_____

_____

_____

_____

QUAALUDE-
1 part Coffee Liqueur, 1 part Hazelnut Liqueur, 1 part Vodka
splash Light Cream or Milk *(Mix into Small Rocks Glass—ice)*

QUAKER CITY COOLER-
Vodka, fill Chablis Wine (fill)
Sour Mix, Vanilla Extract, splash Grenadine (lace) *(Mix into Wine Glass—ice)*

QUAKER'S COCKTAIL-
1 part Brandy, 1 part Light Rum, splash Raspberry Liqueur
Sour Mix *(Mix into Cocktail Glass—no ice)*

QUARTER DECK-
2 parts Light Rum, 1 part Cream Sherry
Lime Juice *(Mix into Cocktail Glass—no ice)*

QUEBEC COCKTAIL-
3 parts Canadian Whiskey, 1 part Dry Vermouth, splash Amer Picon, splash
    Maraschino Liqueur
Sugared Rim *(Mix into Cocktail Glass—no ice)*

QUEEN-
2 parts Gin, 1 part Dry Vermouth, 1 part Sweet Vermouth
Pineapple Slices, muddle *(Mix into Cocktail Glass—no ice)*

QUEEN BEE-
2 parts Coffee Brandy, 2 parts Lime Vodka, 1 part Cream Sherry
(Mix into Cocktail Glass—no ice)

QUEEN CHARLOTTE-
Red Wine
Lemon-Lime Soda, Grenadine *(Mix into Wine Glass—no ice)*

QUEEN ELIZABETH (1)-
2 parts Gin, 1 part Triple Sec, splash Anisette *(Mix into Cocktail Glass—no ice)*

QUEEN ELIZABETH (2)-
1 part Brandy, 1 part Sweet Vermouth, splash Triple Sec
(Mix into Cocktail Glass—no ice)

QUEEN ELIZABETH (3)-
3 parts Gin, 1 part Dry Vermouth, splash Bénédictine
(Mix into Cocktail Glass—no ice)

QUEEN ELIZABETH WINE-
3 parts Bénédictine, 1 part Dry Vermouth
Lime Juice *(Mix into Cocktail Glass—no ice)*

QUEEN OF SCOTS-
Scotch Whiskey, splash Blue Curaçao, splash Green Chartreuse
splash Sour Mix, splash Water *(Mix into Cocktail Glass—no ice)*

QUEEN'S COUSIN-
2 parts Vodka, 1 part Grand Marnier®, splash Triple Sec, Champagne (fill)
splash Lime Juice, splash Bitters *(Mix into Champagne Flute—no ice)*

QUEEN'S TASTE-
2 parts Gin, 1 part French Vermouth
Crushed Mint *(Mix into Cocktail Glass—no ice)*

QUEENS PARK SWIZZLE-
Dark or Spiced Rum
Lime Juice, Sour Mix, Mint Leaves *(Mix into Highball Glass—ice)*

QUELLE VIE-
2 parts Brandy, 1 part Kümmel *(Mix into Cocktail Glass—no ice)*

QUENTIN-
3 parts Dark Rum, 1 part Coffee Liqueur
Light Cream or Milk, sprinkle Nutmeg *(Mix into Cocktail Glass—no ice)*

QUICK & EASY MINT JULEP-
Bourbon Whiskey
Water, Sugar, Mint Leaves, muddle *(Mix into Highball Glass—ice)*

QUICK F**K-
1 part Coffee Liqueur, 1 part Melon Liqueur, 1 part Irish Cream Liqueur
(Layer in Order in Cocktail Glass with no ice)

QUICK SILVER-
1 part Tequila, 1 part Banana Liqueur, 1 part Peppermint Schnapps
(Layer in Order in Cocktail Glass—no ice)

QUICKIE-
1 part Bourbon Whiskey, 1 part Light Rum, splash Triple Sec
(Mix into Cocktail Glass—no ice)

QUIET BUT QUICK-
3 parts Vodka, 1 part Cherry Brandy
Orange Juice, splash Orange Bitters *(Mix into Cocktail Glass—no ice)*

QUIET NUN-
2 parts Bénédictine, 1 part Triple Sec
Light Cream or Milk *(Mix into Cocktail Glass—no ice)*

– NOTES –

_____

_____

_____

_____

_____

_____

_____

_____

R & B-
Spiced Rum
Orange Juice, Pineapple Juice, splash Grenadine
(Mix into Highball Glass—ice)

R. A. F.-
2 parts Apple Brandy, 1 part Apricot Brandy
Lime Juice *(Mix into Cocktail Glass—no ice)*

RACE CUP-
1 part Sweet Vermouth, 1 part Tequila
Grapefruit Juice *(Mix into Highball Glass—ice)*

RACE WAR-
1 part Brown Crème de Cacao, 1 part Irish Cream Liqueur, 1 part Vodka
(Layer in Order in Cocktail Glass—no ice)

RACING DRIVER-
2 parts Vodka, 1 part Sloe Gin, splash Cherry Brandy (float)
Orange Juice *(Blend with ice in Daiquiri Glass)*

RACQUET CLUB-
2 parts Gin, 1 part Dry Vermouth,
splash Orange Bitters *(Mix into Cocktail Glass—no ice)*

RADNOR-
1 part Apricot Brandy, 1 part Gin
Sour Mix, splash Grenadine *(Mix into Cocktail Glass—no ice)*

RAGGED COMPANY-
4 parts Bourbon Whiskey, 1 part Sweet Vermouth, splash Bénédictine
splash Bitters *(Mix into Cocktail Glass—no ice)*

RAGING BULL-
2 parts Red Bull®, 1 part Vodka
Cranberry Juice *(Mix into Cocktail Glass—no ice)*

RAGNAR-
Currant Vodka
splash Lime Juice, fill Lemon-Lime Soda *(Mix into Highball Glass—ice)*

RAGTIME-
1 part Brandy, 1 part Coffee Liqueur
Light Cream or Milk, Coffee Bean Garnish *(Mix into Cocktail Glass—no ice)*

RAIDER-
1 part Irish Cream Liqueur, 1 part Grand Marnier®, 1 part Triple Sec
(Layer in Order in Cocktail Glass—no ice)

RAIL SPLITTER-
12 oz. Ginger Beer
Sour Mix *(Beer Mug)*

RAIN FOREST-
1 part Melon Liqueur, 1 part Vodka
Lemon-Lime Soda *(Mix into Highball Glass—ice)*

RAIN MAN-
2 parts 151-proof Rum, 1 part Melon Liqueur
Orange Juice *(Mix into Highball Glass—ice)*

RAINBOW-
4 parts Vodka, 1 part Blue Curaçao (lace)
Sour Mix, splash Grenadine *(Mix into Cocktail Glass—no ice)*

RAINBOW CRUSH-
1 part Melon Liqueur, 1 part Raspberry Liqueur, 1 part Vodka
Orange Juice, Coconut Milk, Orange Sherbet
(Blend with ice in Daiquiri Glass)

RAINBOW POUSSE CAFE-
1 part Brown Crème de Caçao, 1 part Crème de Yvette, 1 part Yellow
   Chartreuse, 1 part Maraschino Liqueur, 1 part Bénédictine, 1 part Green
   Chartreuse, 1 part Cognac
(Layer in Order in Cocktail Glass—no ice)

RAINBOW ROOM-
2 parts Brandy, 2 parts Triple Sec, 1 part Peach Schnapps
(Mix into Cocktail Glass—no ice)

RAMOS FIZZ-
Gin, splash Triple Sec
Sour Mix, splash Light Cream or Milk, splash Club Soda
(Mix into Highball Glass—ice)

RAMPART STREET PARADE-
2 parts Light Rum, 1 part Banana Liqueur, splash Southern Comfort®
Lime Juice *(Mix into Cocktail Glass—no ice)*

RANCHO MIRAGE-
1 part Banana Liqueur, 1 part Blackberry Brandy, 1 part Gin
Light Cream or Milk *(Mix into Cocktail Glass—no ice)*

RANGER-
1 part Gin, 1 part Light Rum
Sour Mix *(Mix into Cocktail Glass—no ice)*

RASPBERRY BERET-
1 part Raspberry Liqueur, 1 part Vodka
Light Cream or Milk, splash Club Soda (top) *(Mix into Highball Glass—ice)*

RASPBERRY CAPPUCCINO-
Black Raspberry Liqueur
Espresso, top Whipped Cream *(Mix into Irish Coffee Cup—no ice)*

RASPBERRY CHEESECAKE-
1 part Black Raspberry Liqueur, 1 part White Crème de Caçao
Vanilla Ice Cream, Cream Cheese *(Blend with ice in Daiquiri Glass)*

RASPBERRY CORDIAL-
Vodka
Raspberry Juice, Sugar *(Mix into Highball Glass—ice)*

RASPBERRY CREAM (1)-
1 part Vodka, 1 part White Crème de Caçao
Light Cream or Milk, Raspberry Yogurt, Raspberry Sherbet
(Blend with ice in Daiquiri Glass)

RASPBERRY CREAM (2)-
1 part Raspberry Liqueur, 1 part Vodka, 1 part White Crème de Caçao
Light Cream or Milk *(Mix into Highball Glass—ice)*

RASPBERRY GRENADE-
1 part Peach Schnapps, 1 part Raspberry Liqueur, 1 part Vodka
Lime Juice *(Mix into Cocktail Glass—no ice)*

RASPBERRY HOT CHOCOLATE-
1 part Raspberry Liqueur, 1 part White Crème de Caçao, splash Vodka
Hot Chocolate, top Whipped Cream *(Mix into Irish Coffee Cup—no ice)*

RASPBERRY KIR-
Champagne, splash Raspberry Liqueur *(Mix into Champagne Flute—no ice)*

RASPBERRY MARTINI-
4 parts Vodka, 1 part Raspberry Liqueur
splash Lemon-Lime Soda *(Mix into Cocktail Glass—no ice)*

RASPBERRY RELIEF-
2 parts Raspberry Liqueur, 1 part Coconut Liqueur
Pineapple Juice, splash Grenadine *(Mix into Highball Glass—ice)*

RASPBERRY RICKEY-
Raspberry Liqueur
Sour Mix, fill Club Soda *(Mix into Highball Glass—ice)*

RASPBERRY ROMANCE-
2 parts Irish Cream Liqueur, 1 part Black Raspberry Liqueur, 1 part Coffee
Liqueur
Club Soda *(Mix into Highball Glass—ice)*

RASPBERRY SMASH-
2 parts Vodka, 1 part Raspberry Liqueur
Pineapple Juice *(Mix into Highball Glass—ice)*

RASPBERRY THRILL-
2 parts Raspberry Liqueur, 1 part French Vanilla Liqueur
(Mix into Small Rocks Glass—ice)

RASPBERRY WARM-UP-
2 parts Raspberry Liqueur, 1 part Brandy
Hot Tea, Sugar *(Mix into Irish Coffee Cup—no ice)*

RASTA'S REVENGE-
2 parts Gin, 1 part Dark Rum, 1 part Ruby Port
Orange Juice, Sour Mix *(Mix into Cocktail Glass—no ice)*

RATTLER-
Tequila, splash Triple Sec
Grapefruit Juice, splash Lime Juice *(Mix into Cocktail Glass—no ice)*

RATTLESNAKE (1)-
1 part Coffee Liqueur, 1 part White Crème de Caçao,
   1 part Irish Cream Liqueur
(Layer in Order in Cocktail Glass—no ice)

RATTLESNAKE (2)-
Blended Whiskey, splash Anisette
Sour Mix *(Mix into Cocktail Glass—no ice)*

RAUHREIF-
2 parts Gin, 2 parts Triple Sec, 1 part Jamaican Rum
splash Grenadine, splash Lime Juice
(Mix into Cocktail Glass—no ice)

RAY LONG-
2 parts Brandy, 1 part Sweet Vermouth, splash Anisette
splash Bitters *(Mix into Cocktail Glass—no ice)*

RAZZARETTO-
1 part Amaretto, 1 part DeKuyper® Razzmatazz Raspberry Liqueur
Club Soda *(Mix into Highball Glass—ice)*

RAZZLE DAZZLE-
Coconut Liqueur
Pineapple Juice, Orange Juice, splash Grenadine, fill Lemon-Lime Soda
(Mix into Highball Glass—ice)

RAZZMATAZZ COCKTAIL-
2 parts DeKuyper® Razzmatazz Black Raspberry Liqueur, 1 part Coffee Liqueur,
   1 part Crème de Cassis
Hot Coffee, top Whipped Cream
(Mix into Irish Coffee Cup—no ice)

REAL GOLD-
1 part Goldschläger®, 1 part Vodka *(Mix into Cocktail Glass—no ice)*

REARBUSTER-
1 part Coffee Liqueur, 1 part Tequila
Cranberry Juice *(Mix into Highball Glass—ice)*

REBEL CHARGE-
2 parts Bourbon Whiskey, 1 part Triple Sec
Orange Juice, Lime Juice *(Mix into Small Rocks Glass—ice)*

REBEL PARTY SOUR-
1 part Bourbon Whiskey, 1 part Beer
Lime Juice *(Blend with ice in Daiquiri Glass)*

REBEL RINGER-
1 part Bourbon Whiskey, 1 part White Crème de Menthe
(Mix into Cocktail Glass—no ice)

REBEL YELL-
4 parts Bourbon Whiskey, 1 part Triple Sec
Lime Juice *(Mix into Small Rocks Glass—ice)*

RECEPTACLE-
Vodka
splash Cranberry Juice, splash Orange Juice, splash Pineapple Juice,
fill Lemon-Lime Soda *(Mix into Highball Glass—ice)*

RED APPLE-
100-proof Vodka
Apple Juice, splash Lime Juice, splash Grenadine
(Mix into Cocktail Glass—no ice)

RED APPLE MARTINI-
1 part Sour Apple Schnapps, 1 part Vodka
Cranberry Juice *(Mix into Cocktail Glass—no ice)*

RED BARON-
Gin
Sour Mix, Orange Juice, splash Grenadine *(Mix into Cocktail Glass—no ice)*

RED BIRD-
1 part Irish Cream Liqueur, 1 part Vodka
Light Cream or Milk, Pineapple Juice *(Mix into Highball Glass—ice)*

RED BIRD SPECIAL-
Vodka, Beer (fill)
Tomato Juice *(Beer Mug)*

RED BLUFF-
2 parts Cherry Brandy, 2 parts Gin, 1 part Dry Vermouth
Lime Juice, splash Orange Bitters *(Mix into Highball Glass—ice)*

RED CLOUD-
3 parts Gin, 1 part Apricot Brandy
splash Lime Juice, splash Grenadine *(Mix into Cocktail Glass—no ice)*

RED COAT-
3 parts Light Rum, 1 part Apricot Brandy, 1 part Vodka
Lime Juice, splash Grenadine *(Mix into Cocktail Glass—no ice)*

RED DEATH (1)-
1 part Amaretto, 1 part Sloe Gin, 1 part Southern Comfort®, 1 part Triple Sec,
1 part Vodka
splash Sour Mix, Orange Juice *(Mix into Highball Glass—ice)*

RED DEATH (2)-
1 part Amaretto, 1 part Southern Comfort®
Cranberry Juice, Sour Mix *(Mix into Highball Glass—ice)*

RED DEVIL-
1 part Banana Liqueur, 1 part Sloe Gin, 1 part Southern Comfort®,
1 part Triple Sec, 1 part Vodka
splash Lime Juice, Orange Juice
(Mix into Highball Glass—ice)

RED DRAGON-
1 part Campari, 1 part Tequila *(Mix into Small Rocks Glass—ice)*

RED EYE (1)-
   12 oz. Beer
   Tomato Juice *(Beer Mug)*

RED EYE (2)-
   12 oz. Beer
   Bloody Mary Mix *(Beer Mug)*

RED FACE-
   Tequila, splash Cranberry Brandy
   Cranberry Juice *(Mix into Highball Glass—ice)*

RED GIN-
   Gin, splash Cherry Brandy *(Mix into Cocktail Glass—no ice)*

RED HEADED SISTER-
   1 part Jägermeister®, 1 part Peach Schnapps
   Cranberry Juice *(Mix into Highball Glass—ice)*

RED HEADED SLUT-
   1 part Jägermeister®, 1 part Peach Schnapps
   Cranberry Juice *(Mix into Highball Glass—ice)*

RED HOT PASSION-
   2 parts Amaretto, 2 parts Bourbon Whiskey, 2 parts Southern Comfort®,
      1 part Sloe Gin, splash Triple Sec
   splash Orange Juice, splash Pineapple Juice *(Mix into Highball Glass—ice)*

RED LIGHT-
   1 part Cranberry Liqueur, 1 part Vodka
   splash Lime Juice *(Mix into Small Rocks Glass—ice)*

RED LION-
   1 part Gin, 1 part Grand Marnier®
   Lime Juice, Orange Juice *(Mix into Cocktail Glass—no ice)*

RED RAIDER-
   2 parts Bourbon Whiskey, 1 part Triple Sec
   Lime Juice, splash Grenadine *(Mix into Cocktail Glass—no ice)*

RED RAW ASS-
   3 parts Gin, 1 part Triple Sec
   Pineapple Juice, Strawberry Daiquiri Mix, splash Lime Juice
   (Mix into Highball Glass with ice or blend with ice in Daiquiri Glass)

RED ROOSTER-
   3 parts Red Dubonnet®, 1 part Blended Whiskey
   splash Lime Juice *(Mix into Small Rocks Glass—ice)*

RED ROVER-
   3 parts Bourbon Whiskey, 1 part Sloe Gin
   Sour Mix *(Mix into Cocktail Glass—no ice)*

RED RUBY (1)-
   3 parts Gin, 1 part Cherry Brandy, 1 part Dry Vermouth
   (Mix into Cocktail Glass—no ice)

R

RED RUBY (2)-
Amaretto
Cranberry Juice, Orange Juice, splash Grenadine, fill Ginger Ale
(Mix into Highball Glass—ice)

RED RUSSIAN (1)-
1 part Cranberry Schnapps, 1 part Vodka *(Mix into Cocktail Glass—no ice)*

RED RUSSIAN (2)-
1 part Strawberry Schnapps, 1 part Vodka
Light Cream or Milk *(Mix into Highball Glass—ice)*

RED SNAPPER (1)-
Gin
Bloody Mary Mix *(Mix into Highball Glass—ice)*

RED SNAPPER (2)-
1 part Crown Royal®, 1 part Peach Schnapps
Cranberry Juice *(Mix into Highball Glass—ice)*

RED SWIZZLE-
Brandy or Gin or Rum or Whiskey
Sour Mix, Grenadine, Water, splash Bitters
(Mix into Highball Glass—ice)

RED TONIC-
Vodka
Grenadine, Lime Juice, fill Tonic Water *(Mix into Highball Glass—ice)*

RED TOP-
3 parts Rye Whiskey, 1 part Claret (top)
Sour Mix *(Mix into Sour Glass—ice)*

REDCOAT-
3 parts Light Rum, 1 part Apricot Brandy, 1 part Vodka
Lime Juice, splash Grenadine *(Mix into Cocktail Glass—no ice)*

REDNECK BLITZKRIEG-
1 part Jägermeister®, 1 part Southern Comfort®
Club Soda *(Mix into Highball Glass—ice)*

REFORM-
2 parts Dry Sherry, 1 part Dry Vermouth
splash Orange Bitters *(Mix into Cocktail Glass—no ice)*

REGGAE-
2 parts Vodka, 1 part Banana Liqueur
Orange Juice, Grapefruit Juice, Pineapple Juice, splash Orange Bitters,
    splash Grenadine
(Mix into Highball Glass—ice)

REGGAE AMBASSADOR-
Citrus Vodka
Orange Juice, Pineapple Juice, Bananas, Strawberries, Sugar
(Blend with ice in Daiquiri Glass)

REINDEER'S TEAR-
1 part Finlandia® Vodka, 1 part Triple Sec
Lime Juice *(Mix into Highball Glass—ice)*

REMOTE CONTROL-
1 part Galliano®, 1 part Triple Sec
Orange Juice, Light Cream or Milk *(Mix into Highball Glass—ice)*

REMSEN COOLER-
Gin
Club Soda, Sugar, fill Club Soda or Ginger Ale
(Mix into Highball Glass—ice)

RENAISSANCE-
3 parts Gin, 1 part Dry Sherry
splash Light Cream or Milk, sprinkle Nutmeg
(Mix into Cocktail Glass—no ice)

RENDEZVOUS-
3 parts Gin, 1 part Campari, 1 part Cherry Brandy
(Mix into Cocktail Glass—no ice)

RESOLUTE-
2 parts Gin, 1 part Apricot Brandy
Lime Juice *(Mix into Cocktail Glass—no ice)*

RHETT BUTLER-
Southern Comfort®, splash Triple Sec
Sour Mix *(Mix into Small Rocks Glass—ice)*

RHODE ISLAND ICED COFFEE-
1 part Brandy, 1 part Coffee Liqueur, 1 part Vodka
Light Cream or Milk *(Mix into Highball Glass—ice)*

RICH BABE-
1 part Vodka, 1 part White Crème de Caçao
splash Lime Juice, splash Grenadine *(Mix into Cocktail Glass—no ice)*

RICKEY (GENERIC)-
(Any Liqueur)
splash Lime Juice, fill Club Soda *(Mix into Highball Glass—ice)*

RILEY'S SPARROW-
3 parts Dark Rum, 1 part Southern Comfort®
splash Bitters *(Mix into Cocktail Glass—no ice)*

RIPTIDE-
1 part Dark Rum, 1 part Light Rum, 1 part 151-proof Rum, splash Anisette,
    splash Triple Sec
Grapefruit Juice, Orange Juice
(Mix into Highball Glass—ice)

RISING SUN-
Sake
Orange Juice, Grenadine *(Mix into Highball Glass—ice)*

R

RISON SHINE-***
1 part Citrus Vodka, 1 part Melon Liqueur, 1 part Raspberry Liqueur
Cranberry Juice, Grapefruit Juice, Orange Juice, Pineapple Juice
(Mix into Highball Glass—ice)

RITCHIE RITCHIE-
Light Rum, splash Brown Crème de Caçao, splash White Crème de Caçao
Coffee, top Whipped Cream *(Mix into Irish Coffee Cup—no ice)*

RITZ FIZZ-
Champagne, splash Amaretto, splash Blue Curaçao
splash Lime Juice *(Mix into Champagne Flute—no ice)*

RIVIERA RASPBERRY-
2 parts Raspberry Liqueur, 1 part Coffee Liqueur
Coconut Milk, Chocolate Syrup, Vanilla Ice Cream
(Blend with ice in Daiquiri Glass)

ROAD KILL-
1 part Irish Whiskey, 1 part Wild Turkey® Bourbon Whiskey,
1 part 151-proof Rum *(Mix into Cocktail Glass—no ice)*

ROAD RUNNER (1)-
2 parts Vodka, 1 part Amaretto
Coconut Milk, sprinkle Nutmeg, Sugared and Nutmeged Rim, Orange Garnish
(Blend with ice in Daiquiri Glass)

ROAD RUNNER (2)-
4 parts Gin, 1 part Dry Vermouth, splash Anisette
splash Grenadine *(Mix into Cocktail Glass—no ice)*

ROARING TWENTIES MANHATTAN-
2 parts Dry or Sweet Vermouth, 1 part Rye Whiskey
splash Orange Bitters *(Mix into Cocktail Glass—no ice)*

ROASTED TOASTED ALMOND (1)-
2 parts Coffee Liqueur, 1 part Amaretto, 1 part Vodka
Light Cream or Milk
(Mix into Highball Glass—ice)

ROASTED TOASTED ALMOND (2)-
Coffee Liqueur, Irish Cream Liqueur, Grand Marnier®
(Mix into Cocktail Glass—no ice)

ROB ROY-
Scotch Whiskey, splash Sweet Vermouth
(Mix into Cocktail Glass—no ice)

ROBERT E. LEE COOLER-
Gin, splash Anisette
Sour Mix, Club Soda, fill Ginger Ale *(Mix into Highball Glass—ice)*

ROBIN HOOD-
Hazelnut Liqueur, splash Brandy
Lime Juice, splash Grenadine *(Mix into Cocktail Glass—no ice)*

ROBIN'S NEST-
　　2 parts Vodka, 1 part White Crème de Caçao
　　Cranberry Juice *(Mix into Cocktail Glass—no ice)*

ROBSON-
　　Jamaican Rum
　　Lime Juice, splash Orange Juice, splash Grenadine
　　(Mix into Cocktail Glass—no ice)

ROCHDALE COWBOY-
　　3 parts Blended Whiskey, 1 part Southern Comfort®
　　Orange Juice, splash Sour Mix, splash Bitters *(Mix into Highball Glass—ice)*

ROCK & RYE COCKTAIL-
　　1 part Rock & Rye, 1 part White Port, splash Dry Vermouth
　　(Mix into Cocktail Glass—no ice)

ROCK & RYE COOLER-
　　1 part Rock & Rye, 1 part Vodka
　　Lime Juice, Lemon-Lime Soda *(Mix into Highball Glass—ice)*

ROCK LOBSTER-
　　1 part Crown Royal®, 1 part Raspberry Liqueur
　　Cranberry Juice *(Mix into Highball Glass—ice)*

ROCKAWAY BEACH-
　　3 parts Light Rum, 1 part Dark Rum, 1 part Tequila, splash Crème de Noyaux
　　Orange Juice, Pineapple Juice, Cranberry Juice *(Mix into Highball Glass—ice)*

ROCKY GREEN DRAGON-
　　3 parts Gin, 1 part Brandy, 1 part Green Chartreuse
　　(Mix into Small Rocks Glass—ice)

ROCKY MOUNTAIN COCKTAIL-
　　1 part Amaretto, 1 part Southern Comfort®
　　Lime Juice *(Mix into Cocktail Glass—no ice)*

ROCKY MOUNTAIN COOLER-
　　Peach Schnapps
　　Pineapple Juice, Lemon-Lime Soda *(Mix into Highball Glass—ice)*

ROCKY MOUNTAIN MOTHER F**KER-
　　1 part Amaretto, 1 part Yukon Jack® Canadian Liqueur
　　Lime Juice *(Mix into Small Rocks Glass—ice)*

ROCKY POINT-
　　Tequila, splash Amaretto, splash Triple Sec
　　Grapefruit Juice, splash Lime Juice *(Mix into Highball Glass—ice)*

ROCKY'S DILEMMA-
　　3 parts Vodka, 1 part Grand Marnier® *(Mix into Cocktail Glass—no ice)*

ROCOCO-
　　2 parts Cherry Vodka, 1 part Triple Sec
　　Orange Juice *(Mix into Cocktail Glass—no ice)*

R

ROGER SWIMS A MILE-
3 parts Drambuie®, 1 part Blended Whiskey, 1 part Dry Vermouth
(Mix into Cocktail Glass—no ice)

ROLLING GREEN ELIXER-
3 parts Peach Schnapps, 2 parts Blue Curaçao, 1 part 100-proof Vodka
Cranberry Juice *(Mix into Highball Glass—ice)*

ROLLS-ROYCE-
3 parts Gin, 1 part Dry Vermouth, 1 part Sweet Vermouth, splash Bénédictine
(Mix into Cocktail Glass—no ice)

ROMAN CANDLE-
Campari
Cranberry Juice, splash Lime Juice *(Mix into Highball Glass—ice)*

ROMAN HOLIDAY-
1 part Amaretto, 1 part Blackberry Brandy, 1 part Sambuca
Light Cream or Milk *(Mix into Cocktail Glass—no ice)*

ROMAN PUNCH-
1 part Brandy, 1 part Dark Rum, splash Port (lace), splash Raspberry Liqueur
Lime Juice *(Mix into Cocktail Glass—no ice)*

ROMAN RIOT-
1 part Amaretto, 1 part Galliano®, 1 part Sambuca
(Mix into Cocktail Glass—no ice)

ROMAN SNOWBALL-
Sambuca
Coffee Beans *(Mix into Small Rocks Glass—ice)*

ROMAN STINGER-
3 parts Brandy, 1 part Sambuca, 1 part White Crème de Menthe
(Mix into Cocktail Glass—no ice)

ROMANCE-
1 part Amer Picon, 1 part Brandy, 1 part Dry Vermouth, 1 part French
Vermouth, 1 part Triple Sec *(Mix into Cocktail Glass—no ice)*

ROMANOFF APPLE, THE-
3 parts Vodka, 1 part Apple Brandy
Sour Mix, Apples *(Blend with ice in Daiquiri Glass)*

ROMULAN ALE (1)-
1 part Blue Curaçao, 1 part Light Rum
Lemon-Lime Soda, splash Hot Sauce (top), Salt (top)
(Mix into Highball Glass—ice)

ROMULAN ALE (2)-
1 part Blue Curaçao, 1 part Tequila, fill Zima®
splash Hot Sauce *(Mix into Highball Glass—ice)*

ROMULAN DREAM-
1 part Blue Curaçao, 1 part Grand Marnier®
Lime Juice *(Mix into Highball Glass—ice)*

ROOT BEER-
1 part Coffee Liqueur, 1 part Galliano®, 1 part Vodka
Cola *(Mix into Highball Glass—ice)*

ROOT BEER FIZZ-
Gin
splash Sour Mix, fill Root Beer *(Mix into Highball Glass—ice)*

ROOT BEER FLOAT (1)-
Root Beer Schnapps
Club Soda *(Mix into Highball Glass—ice)*

ROOT BEER FLOAT (2)-
1 part Galliano®, 1 part Vodka
Light Cream or Milk, fill Cola *(Mix into Highball Glass—ice)*

ROOT TOOTY-
Root Beer Schnapps
Orange Juice *(Mix into Small Rocks Glass—ice)*

ROOTARAMA BANANARAMA-
Root Beer Schnapps
Coconut Milk, Bananas, splash Club Soda *(Blend with ice in Daiquiri Glass)*

ROOTIE FROOTIE-
Root Beer Schnapps
Orange Juice, Pineapple Juice, Coconut Milk *(Blend with ice in Daiquiri Glass)*

RORY O'MORE-
2 parts Irish Whiskey, 1 part Sweet Vermouth
splash Orange Bitters *(Mix into Cocktail Glass—no ice)*

ROSE COCKTAIL (ENGLISH)-
2 parts Gin, 1 part Apricot Brandy, 1 part Dry Vermouth
Lime Juice, Grenadine *(Mix into Cocktail Glass—no ice)*

ROSE COCKTAIL (FRENCH)-
3 parts Gin, 1 part Cherry Brandy, 1 part Dry Vermouth
(Mix into Cocktail Glass—no ice)

ROSE HALL-
3 parts Jamaican Rum, 1 part Banana Liqueur
Orange Juice, splash Lime Juice *(Mix into Cocktail Glass—no ice)*

ROSELYN-
2 parts Gin, 1 part Dry Vermouth
Grenadine, Lemon Twist Garnish *(Mix into Cocktail Glass—no ice)*

ROSEY MANHATTAN-
3 parts Blended Whiskey, 1 part Dry Vermouth, 1 part Raspberry Liqueur
(Mix into Cocktail Glass—no ice)

ROSINGTON-
2 parts Gin, 1 part Sweet Vermouth
Orange Peel Garnish *(Mix into Cocktail Glass—no ice)*

R

ROSITA-
2 parts Campari, 2 parts Tequila, 1 part Dry Vermouth, 1 part Sweet Vermouth
Lemon Twist Garnish *(Mix into Small Rocks Glass—ice)*

ROSY DAWN-
(Gin, Light Rum, or Vodka)
Grapefruit Juice, Lime Juice, splash Grenadine
(Mix into Cocktail Glass—no ice)

ROTTEN PUSSY-
2 parts Melon Liqueur, 1 part Amaretto, 1 part Coconut Rum,
    1 part Southern Comfort®
Pineapple Juice, Sour Mix
(Mix into Highball Glass—ice)

ROUGE MARTINI-
Gin, splash Raspberry Liqueur *(Mix into Cocktail Glass—no ice)*

ROULETTE-
2 parts Apple Brandy, 1 part Citrus Rum, 1 part Light Rum
(Mix into Cocktail Glass—no ice)

ROUND ROBIN-
1 part Anisette, 1 part Brandy
Sugar *(Mix into Cocktail Glass—no ice)*

ROYAL CLOVER CLUB-
Gin
Lime Juice, splash Grenadine
(Mix into Highball Glass—ice)

ROYAL COCKTAIL-
Gin
Sour Mix *(Mix into Highball Glass—ice)*

ROYAL FIZZ-
Gin
Sour Mix, splash Club Soda *(Mix into Highball Glass—ice)*

ROYAL GIN FIZZ-
4 parts Gin, 1 part Grand Marnier®
Sour Mix, splash Club Soda *(Mix into Highball Glass—ice)*

ROYAL PEACH FREEZE-
1 part Champagne, 1 part Peach Schnapps
Orange Juice, Lime Juice *(Blend with ice in Daiquiri Glass)*

ROYAL ROOST-
2 parts Bourbon Whiskey, 1 part Red Dubonnet®, splash Anisette,
    splash Triple Sec
splash Bitters *(Mix into Small Rocks Glass—ice)*

ROYAL SCREW-
Cognac, fill Champagne
Orange Juice *(Mix into Champagne Flute—no ice)*

ROYAL SMILE-
2 parts Apple Brandy, 1 part Gin
Lime Juice, splash Grenadine *(Mix into Cocktail Glass—no ice)*

ROYALLY SCREWED-
1 part Grand Marnier®, 1 part Vodka
Orange Juice *(Mix into Highball Glass—ice)*

ROYALTY FIZZ-
Gin, splash Blue Curaçao
Sour Mix, splash Club Soda *(Mix into Highball Glass—ice)*

RUBY COCKTAIL-
2 parts Gin, 1 part Apple Brandy
splash Grenadine *(Mix into Cocktail Glass—no ice)*

RUBY FIZZ-
Sloe Gin
Sour Mix, splash Grenadine, splash Club Soda *(Mix into Highball Glass—ice)*

RUBY IN THE ROUGH-
3 parts Gin, 1 part Cherry Brandy, splash Sweet Vermouth
(Mix into Cocktail Glass—no ice)

RUBY TUESDAY (1)-
2 parts Raspberry Liqueur, 1 part Banana Liqueur
Pineapple Juice, Coconut Milk *(Blend with ice in Daiquiri Glass)*

RUBY TUESDAY (2)-
Raspberry Liqueur
Lemon-Lime Soda, splash Grenadine *(Mix into Highball Glass—ice)*

RUM ALEXANDER-
2 parts Light Rum, 1 part Brown Crème de Caçao
Light Cream or Milk, sprinkle Nutmeg *(Mix into Cocktail Glass—no ice)*

RUM APPLE-
2 parts Light Rum, 1 part Sweet Vermouth, splash Apple Brandy,
    splash Apricot Brandy
splash Lime Juice, splash Grenadine *(Mix into Cocktail Glass—no ice)*

RUM BANA-
Jamaican Rum
Sour Mix, Bananas *(Blend with ice in Daiquiri Glass)*

RUM BUCK-
Light Rum
Lime Juice, Ginger Ale *(Mix into Highball Glass—ice)*

RUM COBBLER-
Light Rum
Club Soda, Sugar *(Mix into Highball Glass—ice)*

RUM COLA-
Light Rum
Cola, Lime Wedge *(Mix into Highball Glass—ice)*

RUM COLLINS-
Light Rum
Sour Mix, splash Club Soda *(Mix into Highball Glass—ice)*

RUM COOLER-
Light Rum
Club Soda, Sugar, fill Club Soda or Ginger Ale *(Mix into Highball Glass—ice)*

RUM COW-
Dark Rum
Sugar, Bitters *(Mix into Small Rocks Glass—ice)*

RUM DAISY-
Light Rum
Sour Mix, splash Grenadine *(Mix into Sour Glass— ice)*

RUM DUBONNET
Light Rum, splash Red Dubonnet®
splash Lime Juice *(Mix into Cocktail Glass—no ice)*

RUM EGGNOG-
Light or Dark Rum
Light Cream or Milk, Sugar, sprinkle Nutmeg *(Mix into Highball Glass—ice)*

RUM FIX-
Light Rum
Sour Mix, splash Water *(Mix into Highball Glass—ice)*

RUM FIZZ-
Light Rum
Sour Mix, splash Club Soda *(Mix into Highball Glass—ice)*

RUM FLIP-
Light Rum
Light Cream or Milk, Sugar *(Mix into Highball Glass—ice)*

RUM GIMLET-
Light Rum
splash Lime Juice *(Mix into Small Rocks Glass—ice)*

RUM HIGHBALL-
Light or Dark Rum
Club Soda or Ginger Ale *(Mix into Highball Glass—ice)*

RUM HUMMER-
1 part Coffee Liqueur, 1 part Light Rum
Vanilla Ice Cream *(Blend with ice in Daiquiri Glass)*

RUM JULEP-
Dark Rum
Syrup, Mint Leaves, muddle *(Mix into Small Rocks Glass—ice)*

RUM MANHATTAN-
Light Rum, splash Sweet Vermouth
splash Bitters *(Mix into Cocktail Glass—no ice)*

RUM MARTINI-
Light Rum, splash Dry Vermouth *(Mix into Cocktail Glass—no ice)*

RUM MILK PUNCH-
Light Rum
Light Cream or Milk, Sugar, sprinkle Nutmeg *(Mix into Highball Glass—ice)*

RUM OLD-FASHIONED-
1 part Light Rum, 1 part 151-proof Rum (float)
Water, Sugar, Bitters *(Mix into Small Rocks Glass—ice)*

RUM PUNCH (1)-
Light Rum
Cranberry Juice, Orange Juice, Pineapple Juice
(Mix into Highball Glass—ice)

RUM PUNCH (2)-
Light Rum
Orange Juice, Pineapple Juice, Lime Juice, splash Grenadine, splash bitters
(Blend with ice in Daiquiri Glass)

RUM RELAXER-
Light Rum
Pineapple Juice, Grenadine, Lemon-Lime Soda
(Mix into Highball Glass—ice)

RUM RICKEY-
Light Rum
splash Lime Juice, Club Soda *(Mix into Highball Glass—ice)*

RUM RUNNER (1)-
1 part Banana Liqueur, 1 part Cherry Brandy, 1 part Dark Rum,
    1 part Light Rum
Orange Juice, Pineapple Juice *(Mix into Highball Glass—ice)*

RUM RUNNER (2)-
Gin
Pineapple Juice, Sour Mix, splash Bitters, Salted Rim
(Mix into Small Rocks Glass—ice)

RUM RUNNER (3)-
1 part Blackberry Brandy, 1 part Banana Liqueur, 1 part Dark Rum
Lime Juice, splash Grenadine *(Blend with ice in Daiquiri Glass)*

RUM SCOUNDREL-
Light Rum
Sour Mix, Sugared Rim *(Mix into Small Rocks Glass—ice)*

RUM SCREWDRIVER-
Light Rum
Orange Juice *(Mix into Highball Glass—ice)*

RUM SLING-
Jamaican Rum
splash Bitters, fill Club Soda *(Mix into Highball Glass—ice)*

R

RUM SOUR-
Light Rum
Sour Mix *(Mix into Sour Glass— ice)*

RUM STINGER-
1 part Jamaican Rum, 1 part White Crème de Menthe
(Mix into Cocktail Glass—no ice)

RUM SWEETIE-
2 parts Dark Rum, 1 part Amaretto
Apple Juice *(Blend with ice in Daiquiri Glass)*

RUM SWIZZLE-
Light or Dark Rum
Sour Mix, Water, Bitters *(Mix into Highball Glass—ice)*

RUM TODDY-
Light or Dark Rum
Sugar, Water *(Mix into Small Rocks Glass—ice)*

RUM TODDY (HOT)-
Light Rum or Dark Rum
Hot Water, Sugar, sprinkle Nutmeg *(Mix into Irish Coffee Cup—no ice)*

RUMMY SOUR-
Spiced Rum
Sour Mix *(Blend with ice in Daiquiri Glass)*

RUMPLESTILTSKIN-
1 part Cinnamon Schnapps, 1 part Peppermint Schnapps
(Mix into Small Rocks Glass—ice)

RUPTURED DUCK-
1 part Banana Liqueur, 1 part Crème de Noyaux
Light Cream or Milk *(Mix into Highball Glass—ice)*

RUSSIAN APPLE-
Vodka
Cranberry Juice, Pineapple Juice *(Mix into Highball Glass—ice)*

RUSSIAN BANANA-
1 part Banana Liqueur, 1 part Brown Crème de Caçao, 1 part Vodka
Light Cream or Milk *(Mix into Highball Glass—ice)*

RUSSIAN BEAR-
2 parts Vodka, 1 part Brown Crème de Caçao
Light Cream or Milk *(Mix into Cocktail Glass—no ice)*

RUSSIAN BRUNCH-
1 part Champagne, 1 part Vodka
Orange Juice *(Mix into Highball Glass—ice)*

RUSSIAN COCKTAIL-
1 part Gin, 1 part Vodka, 1 part White Crème de Caçao
(Mix into Cocktail Glass—no ice)

R

RUSSIAN COFFEE-
2 parts Coffee Liqueur, 2 parts Hazelnut Liqueur, 1 part Vodka
Coffee, top Whipped Cream *(Mix into Irish Coffee Cup—no ice)*

RUSSIAN ICE-
2 parts Vodka, 1 part Coffee Liqueur
splash Light Cream or Milk, Vanilla Ice Cream
(Blend with ice in Daiquiri Glass)

RUSSIAN KAMIKAZE-
Vodka, splash Raspberry Liqueur *(Mix into Cocktail Glass—no ice)*

RUSSIAN QUAALUDE (1)-
1 part Hazelnut Liqueur, 1 part Irish Cream Liqueur, 1 part Vodka
(Layer in Order in Cocktail Glass—no ice)

RUSSIAN QUAALUDE (2)-
1 part Amaretto, 1 part Hazelnut Liqueur, 1 part Irish Cream Liqueur,
1 part Vodka *(Mix into Cocktail Glass—no ice)*

RUSSIAN QUAALUDE (3)-
1 part Coffee Liqueur, 1 part Irish Cream Liqueur, 1 part Vodka, splash
Hazelnut Liqueur (lace) *(Mix into Cocktail Glass—no ice)*

RUSSIAN QUAALUDE (4)-
1 part Irish Cream Liqueur, 1 part Vodka
Grenadine *(Mix into Cocktail Glass—no ice)*

RUSSIAN ROB ROY-
3 parts Vodka, 1 part Dry Vermouth, 1 part Scotch Whiskey
(Mix into Cocktail Glass—no ice)

RUSSIAN ROSE-
Vodka
Grenadine, splash Bitters *(Mix into Cocktail Glass—no ice)*

RUSSIAN ROULETTE-
1 part Galliano®, 1 part Southern Comfort®, 1 part Vodka
(Layer in Order in Cocktail Glass—no ice)

RUSSIAN TURKEY-
Vodka
Cranberry Juice *(Mix into Highball Glass—ice)*

RUSSIAN WOLFHOUND-
Vodka
Grapefruit Juice, Lemon-Lime Soda, Salted Rim *(Mix into Highball Glass—ice)*

RUSSINA-
1 part Gin, 1 part Vodka, 1 part White Crème de Caçao
(Mix into Cocktail Glass—no ice)

RUSSJKOV-
3 parts Vodka, 2 parts Irish Cream Liqueur, 1 part Triple Sec
(Mix into Cocktail Glass—no ice)

RUSTY AGGRAVATION-
2 parts Coffee Liqueur, 2 parts Scotch Whiskey, 1 part Drambuie®
Light Cream or Milk *(Mix into Highball Glass—ice)*

RUSTY NAIL-
1 part Drambuie®, 1 part Scotch Whiskey *(Mix into Small Rocks Glass—ice)*

RUSTY NAVEL-
1 part Tequila, 1 part Amaretto *(Layer in Order in Cocktail Glass—no ice)*

RUSTY ZIPPER-
3 parts Peach Schnapps, 1 part Amaretto
(Layer in Order in Cocktail Glass with no ice)

RYE HIGHBALL-
Rye Whiskey
Club Soda or Ginger Ale *(Mix into Highball Glass—ice)*

RYE WHISKEY COCKTAIL-
Rye Whiskey
Sugar, splash Bitters *(Mix into Cocktail Glass—no ice)*

– NOTES –

R

69-
1 part Banana Liqueur, 1 part Anisette, 1 part Irish Cream Liqueur
(Layer in Order in Cocktail Glass—no ice)

69ER-
1 part Light Rum, 1 part Peach Schnapps
Cola *(Mix into Highball Glass—ice)*

747-
1 part Amaretto, 1 part Coffee Liqueur, 1 part Irish Cream Liqueur
(Mix into Cocktail Glass—no ice)

7 & 7-
Seagram's 7® Whiskey
Lemon-Lime Soda *(Mix into Highball Glass—ice)*

S. F. SOUR-
2 parts Blended Whiskey, 1 part Bénédictine
Lime Juice, splash Grenadine *(Mix into Sour Glass— ice)*

S. H. I. T.-
1 part Sambuca, 1 part Haagen Dazs® Cream Liqueur, 1 part Irish Mist®,
1 part Tequila *(Layer in Order in Cocktail Glass—no ice)*

S. O. B.-
1 part Brandy, 1 part Triple Sec, 1 part 151-proof Rum
(Mix into Cocktail Glass—no ice)

SACRIFICE-
2 parts Dark Rum, 2 parts Light Rum, 1 part White Crème de Caçao
Cranberry Juice, Orange Juice, Pineapple Juice, Coconut Milk,
splash Orange Bitters *(Blend with ice in Daiquiri Glass)*

SADIE SONG-
Bourbon Whiskey
Sugar, fill Club Soda, Mint Leaf Garnish *(Mix into Highball Glass—ice)*

SAINT (ST.) CHARLES PUNCH-
3 parts Port (layer on top), 1 part Brandy, splash Triple Sec
Sour Mix *(Mix into Highball Glass—ice)*

SAINT (ST.) CLOUD-
1 part Anisette, 1 part Blended Whiskey
Light Cream or Milk, sprinkle Nutmeg *(Mix into Cocktail Glass—no ice)*

SAINT (ST). LOUIS-
3 parts Blended Whiskey, 1 part Southern Comfort®, splash Amaretto
Lime Juice *(Mix into Cocktail Glass—no ice)*

SAINT (ST.) MORITZ-
Raspberry Liqueur
splash Light Cream or Milk *(Mix into Cocktail Glass—no ice)*

SAINT (ST). PATRICK'S DAY-
1 part Green Chartreuse, 1 part Green Crème de Menthe, 1 part Irish Whiskey
splash Bitters *(Mix into Cocktail Glass—no ice)*

S

SAINT (ST.) PETERSBURG-
Vodka
Orange Bitters *(Mix into Small Rocks Glass—ice)*

SAKINI (SAKE MARTINI)-
3 parts Gin, 1 part Sake *(Mix into Cocktail Glass—no ice)*

SALOM-
1 part Dry Vermouth, 1 part Gin, splash Sweet Vermouth
(Mix into Cocktail Glass—no ice)

SALT LICK-
Vodka
Grapefruit Juice, splash Bitters, top Lemon-Lime Soda
(Mix into Highball Glass—ice)

SALTY DOG-
Gin or Vodka
Grapefruit Juice, Salt *(Mix into Highball Glass—ice)*

SALTY DOG COLLINS-
Gin
Lime Juice, Salt *(Mix into Highball Glass—ice)*

SALTY JOHN-
Blended Whiskey
Grapefruit Juice, Salted Rim *(Mix into Highball Glass—ice)*

SAM-TINI-
Vodka, splash Blue Curaçao, splash Sambuca *(Mix into Cocktail Glass—no ice)*

SAMBUCA-GIN SHAKE-
4 parts Gin, 1 part Sambuca
Light Cream or Milk *(Mix into Highball Glass—ice)*

SAMBUCA SLIDE-
2 parts Sambuca, 1 part Vodka
Light Cream or Milk *(Mix into Cocktail Glass—no ice)*

SAME OLD SONG-
2 parts Gin, 2 parts Sweet Vermouth, 1 part Dry Vermouth
Orange Juice, splash Lime Juice, splash Bitters
(Mix into Cocktail Glass—no ice)

SAMOVAR SLING-
4 parts Vodka, 1 part Bénédictine, 1 part Cherry Brandy
Lime Juice, splash Bitters, splash Orange Bitters, fill Club Soda
(Mix into Highball Glass—ice)

SAMSON-
1 part Amaretto, 1 part Blackberry Brandy, 1 part Black Sambuca
Light Cream or Milk *(Mix into Highball Glass—ice)*

SAN FRANCISCO COCKTAIL-
1 part Dry Vermouth, 1 part Sloe Gin, 1 part Sweet Vermouth
splash Bitters, splash Orange Bitters *(Mix into Cocktail Glass—no ice)*

SAN JUAN-
Puerto Rican Rum, splash 151-proof Rum (lace)
Grapefruit Juice, Lime Juice, Coconut Milk
(Blend with ice in Daiquiri Glass)

SAN SEBASTIAN-
Gin, splash Light Rum, splash Triple Sec
splash Grapefruit Juice, splash Lime Juice *(Mix into Cocktail Glass—no ice)*

SANCTUARY-
2 parts Red Dubonnet®, 1 part Amer Picon, 1 part Triple Sec
(Mix into Small Rocks Glass—ice)

SAND BLASTER-
3 parts Jägermeister®, 1 part Light Rum
splash Lime Juice, Lime Wedge *(Mix into Small Rocks Glass—ice)*

SAND DANCE-
3 parts Blended Whiskey, 1 part Cherry Brandy
Cranberry Juice *(Mix into Highball Glass—ice)*

SAND MARTIN-
1 part Gin, 1 part Sweet Vermouth, splash Green Chartreuse
(Mix into Cocktail Glass—no ice)

SANDRA BUYS A DOG-
1 part Dark Rum, 1 part Light Rum
Cranberry Juice, splash Orange Juice, splash Bitters
(Mix into Highball Glass—ice)

SANGAREE (GENERIC)-
(Any Liqueur)
Water, Sugar, muddle, splash Club Soda *(Mix into Small Rocks Glass—ice)*

SANGRIA-
Red Wine, (Brandy, Gin, Light Rum, Triple Sec as optional additions)
Water, splash Club Soda, Sugar, Oranges, Limes, Bananas, Strawberries
(Mix into Wine Glass—no ice)

SANTA ANITA-
Scotch Whiskey
Lemon Twist Garnish *(Mix into Small Rocks Glass—ice)*

SANTA BARBARA SUNSET-
2 parts Gin, 1 part Apricot Brandy
Orange Juice, splash Lime Juice, splash Grenadine
(Mix into Cocktail Glass—no ice)

SANTA CLAUS IS COMING TO TOWN-
1 part Cinnamon Schnapps, 1 part Melon Liqueur, 1 part Peppermint Schnapps
top Whipped Cream *(Mix into Cocktail Glass—no ice)*

SANTA CRUZ DAISEY-
Dark Rum, splash Maraschino Liqueur
Sour Mix, splash Club Soda *(Mix into Highball Glass—ice)*

SANTA SHOT COCKTAIL-
1 part Grenadine, 1 part Green Crème de Menthe, 1 part Peppermint Schnapps
(Layer in Order in Cocktail Glass—no ice)

SANTIAGO-
Light Rum
Sour Mix, splash Grenadine *(Mix into Cocktail Glass—no ice)*

SANTINI'S POUSSE CAFE-
1 part Brandy, splash Maraschino Liqueur, 1 part Triple Sec, 1 part Light Rum
(Layer in Order in Cocktail Glass—no ice)

SARAH-
2 parts Vodka, 1 part Cherry Brandy, 1 part Dry Vermouth, splash Banana
Liqueur, splash Campari *(Mix into Cocktail Glass—no ice)*

SARATOGA-
Brandy, splash Maraschino Liqueur
splash Pineapple Juice, splash Lime Juice, splash Bitters
(Mix into Cocktail Glass—no ice)

SARONNO-
1 part Amaretto, 1 part Brandy
Light Cream or Milk *(Mix into Cocktail Glass—no ice)*

SASKATOON STINGER-
2 parts Canadian Whiskey, 1 part Peppermint Schnapps or White Crème de
Menthe *(Mix into Cocktail Glass—no ice)*

SATIN GLIDER-
2 parts Peppermint Schnapps, 2 parts White Crème de Caçao, 1 part Sambuca
Light Cream or Milk *(Mix into Cocktail Glass—no ice)*

SATIN'S WHISKERS-
3 parts Dry Vermouth, 3 parts Sweet Vermouth, 2 parts Gin,
1 part Grand Marnier®
Orange Juice, splash Orange Bitters
(Mix into Highball Glass—ice)

SAUCY SUE-
Apple Brandy, splash Apricot Brandy, splash Licorice Liqueur
(Mix into Cocktail Glass—no ice)

SAUZALIKY-
Tequila
Orange Juice, splash Lime Juice, Banana Garnish
(Mix into Highball Glass—ice)

SAVANNAH-
Gin, splash White Crème de Caçao
Orange Juice *(Mix into Cocktail Glass—no ice)*

SAVE THE PLANET-
1 part Melon Liqueur, 1 part Vodka, splash Blue Curaçao, splash Green
Chartreuse *(Mix into Cocktail Glass—no ice)*

SAVOY HOTEL-
1 part White Crème de Caçao, 1 part Bénédictine, 1 part Brandy
(Layer in Order in Cocktail Glass—no ice)

SAVOY SANGAREE-
Port or Sherry
Powdered Sugar *(Mix into Small Rocks Glass—ice)*

SAVOY TANGO-
2 parts Apple Brandy, 1 part Gin *(Mix into Cocktail Glass—no ice)*

SAXON-
Light Rum
Grenadine, splash Lime Juice *(Mix into Cocktail Glass—no ice)*

SAZERAC-
Bourbon Whiskey, splash Anisette
Sugar, splash Bitters *(Mix into Small Rocks Glass—ice)*

SCANDINAVIAN MARTINI-
2 parts Vodka, 1 part Aquavit
Sour Mix *(Mix into Cocktail Glass—no ice)*

SCARLET FEVER-
2 parts Light Rum, 2 parts Vodka, 1 part Gin
Cranberry Juice *(Mix into Highball Glass—ice)*

SCARLET LETTER-
2 parts Gin, 1 part Port (float)
Lime Juice, splash Grenadine *(Mix into Highball Glass—ice)*

SCARLETT O'HARA-
Southern Comfort®
Cranberry Juice *(Mix into Highball Glass—ice)*

SCEPTER-
Canadian Whiskey
Grapefruit Juice, splash Grenadine *(Mix into Highball Glass—ice)*

SEPTIC-
1 part Blue Curaçao, 1 part Coffee Liqueur, 1 part Vodka,
    1 part Stout Beer (float)
Lemonade *(Mix into Highball Glass—ice)*

SCHALALEY-
1 part Irish Cream Liqueur, 1 part Vodka *(Mix into Small Rocks Glass—ice)*

SCHNORKEL-
Light Rum, splash Anisette
Sour Mix *(Mix into Highball Glass—ice)*

SCOOBY SNACK-
1 part Coconut Rum, 1 part Melon Liqueur
Pineapple Juice, Light Cream or Milk
(Mix into Highball Glass—ice)

S

SCOOTER-
1 part Amaretto, 1 part Brandy
Light Cream or Milk *(Mix into Cocktail Glass—no ice)*

SCORPION (1)-
1 part Blackberry Brandy, 1 part Vodka
Grenadine *(Mix into Cocktail Glass—no ice)*

SCORPION (2)-
4 parts Light Rum, 1 part Brandy, 1 part Cherry Brandy
Orange Juice, Lime Juice
(Mix into Highball Glass with ice or blend with ice in Daiquiri Glass)

SCORPION (3)-
1 part Amaretto, 1 part Brandy, 1 part Dark Rum, 1 part Light Rum
Pineapple Juice, splash Sour Mix *(Mix into Highball Glass—ice)*

SCOTCH BIRD FLYER-
3 parts Scotch Whiskey, 1 part Triple Sec
Light Cream or Milk, Sugar *(Mix into Highball Glass—ice)*

SCOTCH BISHOP-
2 parts Scotch Whiskey, 1 part Dry Vermouth, splash Triple Sec
splash Orange Juice, Sugar *(Mix into Cocktail Glass—no ice)*

SCOTCH BOUNTY-
1 part Coconut Rum, 1 part Scotch Whiskey, 1 part White Crème de Caçao
Orange Juice, splash Grenadine *(Mix into Highball Glass—ice)*

SCOTCH BUCK-
Scotch Whiskey
splash Lime Juice, fill Ginger Ale *(Mix into Highball Glass—ice)*

SCOTCH COBBLER-
Scotch Whiskey, splash Brandy, splash Triple Sec
(Mix into Small Rocks Glass—ice)

SCOTCH COOLER-
Scotch Whiskey, splash White Crème de Menthe
Club Soda *(Mix into Highball Glass—ice)*

SCOTCH DAISY-
Scotch Whiskey
Sour Mix, splash Grenadine *(Mix into Highball Glass—ice)*

SCOTCH FIX-
Scotch Whiskey
Sour Mix, Water *(Mix into Highball Glass—ice)*

SCOTCH FIZZ (1)-
Scotch Whiskey
Sour Mix, fill Club Soda *(Mix into Highball Glass—ice)*

SCOTCH FIZZ (2)-
Scotch Whiskey, fill Strawberry Champagne
(Mix into Champagne Flute—no ice)

SCOTCH FIZZ (3)-
Scotch Whiskey, splash Strawberry Schnapps, fill Champagne
(Mix into Champagne Flute—no ice)

SCOTCH FLIP-
Scotch Whiskey
Light Cream or Milk, Sugar *(Mix into Highball Glass—ice)*

SCOTCH HIGHBALL-
Scotch Whiskey
Ginger Ale or Club Soda *(Mix into Highball Glass—ice)*

SCOTCH HOLIDAY SOUR-
3 parts Scotch Whiskey, 2 parts Cherry Brandy, 1 part Sweet Vermouth
Lime Juice *(Mix into Small Rocks Glass—ice)*

SCOTCH MILK PUNCH-
Scotch Whiskey
Light Cream or Milk, Sugar *(Mix into Highball Glass—ice)*

SCOTCH MIST-
Scotch Whiskey
Lemon Peel Garnish *(Mix into Small Rocks Glass—ice)*

SCOTCH OLD-FASHIONED-
Scotch Whiskey
Sugar Cube, splash Bitters, Water, muddle *(Mix into Small Rocks Glass—ice)*

SCOTCH ORANGE FIX-
Scotch Whiskey, splash Triple Sec
Water, Sour Mix *(Mix into Highball Glass—ice)*

SCOTCH RICKEY-
Scotch Whiskey
Lime Juice, Club Soda *(Mix into Highball Glass—ice)*

SCOTCH ROYALE-
Scotch Whiskey, fill Champagne
Sugar, Bitters *(Mix into Champagne Flute—no ice)*

SCOTCH SMASH-
Scotch Whiskey
Sugar, Mint Leaves, muddle, Club Soda *(Mix into Small Rocks Glass—ice)*

SCOTCH SOUR-
Scotch Whiskey
Sour Mix *(Mix into Sour Glass— ice)*

SCOTCH STINGER-
3 parts Scotch Whiskey, 1 part White Crème de Menthe
(Mix into Cocktail Glass—no ice)

SCOTCH STONE SOUR-
Scotch Whiskey
Sour Mix, Orange Juice *(Mix into Highball Glass—ice)*

SCOTCH TOM COLLINS-
Scotch Whiskey
splash Lime Juice, fill Club Soda *(Mix into Highball Glass—ice)*

SCOTTISH COBBLER-
3 parts Scotch Whiskey, 1 part Triple Sec
Honey, Mint Leaves Garnish *(Mix into Small Rocks Glass—ice)*

SCOTTISH COFFEE-
Drambuie®
Coffee, top Whipped Cream *(Mix into Irish Coffee Cup—no ice)*

SCOTTY WAS BEAMED UP-
4 parts Tequila, 1 part Galliano® *(Mix into Cocktail Glass—no ice)*

SCREAMING BANANA BANSHEE-
1 part Banana Liqueur, 1 part Vodka, 1 part White Crème de Caçao
Light Cream or Milk *(Mix into Highball Glass—ice)*

SCREAMING BLUE MESSIAH-
5 parts Goldschläger®, 1 part Blue Curaçao
(Layer in Order in Cocktail Glass with no ice)

SCREAMING HUDSON-
3 parts Canadian Whiskey, 1 part Drambuie®
splash Lime Juice *(Mix into Cocktail Glass—no ice)*

SCREAMING LIZARD-
1 part Tequila, 1 part Green Chartreuse
(Layer in Order in Cocktail Glass—no ice)

SCREAMING MULTIPLE ORGASM-
1 part Amaretto, 1 part Coffee Liqueur, 1 part Irish Cream Liqueur,
    1 part Light Rum
Orange Juice, Light Cream or Milk
(Mix into Highball Glass—ice)

SCREAMING MULTIPLE ORGASM ON THE BEACH-
1 part Amaretto, 1 part Coconut Rum, 1 part Melon Liqueur, 1 part Peach
    Schnapps, 1 part Triple Sec
Club Soda *(Mix into Highball Glass—ice)*

SCREAMING ORGASM (1)-
1 part Amaretto, 1 part Coffee Liqueur, 1 part Irish Cream Liqueur, 1 part Vodka
Light Cream or Milk *(Mix into Highball Glass—ice)*

SCREAMING ORGASM (2)-
1 part Coffee Liqueur, 1 part Grand Marnier®, 1 part Irish Cream Liqueur,
    1 part Vodka
Light Cream or Milk *(Mix into Highball Glass—ice)*

SCREAMING ORGASM (3)-
1 part Amaretto, 1 part Triple Sec, 1 part Vodka, 1 part White Crème de Caçao
Light Cream or Milk
(Mix into Highball Glass—ice)

S

SCREW 'EM UP-
Light Rum
Orange Juice, top Lemon-Lime Soda *(Mix into Highball Glass—ice)*

SCREW IN THE TROPICS-
Vodka
Orange Juice, Pineapple Juice *(Mix into Highball Glass—ice)*

SCREW UP AGAINST THE WALL-
Vodka, splash Galliano®
Orange Juice *(Mix into Highball Glass—ice)*

SCREWBALL-
(Any Whiskey)
Orange Juice *(Mix into Highball Glass—ice)*

SCREWDRIVER-
Vodka
Orange Juice *(Mix into Highball Glass—ice)*

SCREWLIMER-
Vodka
Lime Juice, Orange Juice *(Mix into Highball Glass—ice)*

SCRUMPY STRONG-
Blended Whiskey
Hard Cider *(Mix into Highball Glass—ice)*

SEA FIZZ-
Anisette
Sour Mix, fill Club Soda *(Mix into Highball Glass—ice)*

SEA MONKEY-
Goldschläger®, splash Blue Curaçao *(Mix into Small Rocks Glass—ice)*

SEA RAY-
2 parts Gin, 1 part Amaretto, 1 part Light Rum, splash Maraschino Liqueur
Orange Juice, splash Lime Juice
(Mix into Highball Glass—ice)

SEABOARD-
1 part Blended Whiskey, 1 part Gin
Sour Mix *(Mix into Small Rocks Glass—ice)*

SEABREEZE (1)-
Vodka
Cranberry Juice, Grapefruit Juice *(Mix into Highball Glass—ice)*

SEABREEZE (2)-
3 parts Vodka, 1 part Melon Liqueur, 1 part Raspberry Liqueur
Pineapple Juice *(Mix into Highball Glass—ice)*

SEAGIRT-
Bourbon Whiskey, splash Amaretto
Grapefruit Juice, Cranberry Juice *(Mix into Highball Glass—ice)*

S

SEAHAWKER-
1 part Blue Curaçao, 1 part Vodka, 1 part Melon Liqueur
(Layer in Order in Cocktail Glass—no ice)

SEAWEED-
1 part Melon Liqueur, 1 part Pineapple Vodka, splash Strawberry Schnapps
Pineapple Juice *(Mix into Highball Glass—ice)*

SECRET-
4 parts Scotch Whiskey, 1 part White Crème de Menthe
Club Soda *(Mix into Highball Glass—ice)*

SECRET PLACE-
3 parts Dark Rum, 1 part Cherry Brandy, splash Brown Crème de Caçao
Cold Coffee *(Mix into Highball Glass—ice)*

SEDUCTION-
1 part Hazelnut Liqueur, 1 part Banana Liqueur, 1 part Irish Cream Liqueur
(Layer in Order in Cocktail Glass—no ice)

SEETHING JEALOUSY-
2 parts Sweet Vermouth, 1 part Cherry Brandy, 1 part Scotch Whiskey
Orange Juice
(Mix into Cocktail Glass—no ice)

SELF-STARTER-
2 parts Gin, 1 part Lillet, splash Apricot Brandy, splash Licorice Liqueur
(Mix into Cocktail Glass—no ice)

SENSATION-
Gin, splash Maraschino Liqueur
Lime Juice *(Mix into Cocktail Glass—no ice)*

SEPARATOR-
2 parts Brandy, 1 part Coffee Liqueur
(Mix into Cocktail Glass—no ice)

SEPTEMBER MORNING-
Light Rum, splash Cherry Brandy
Lime Juice, splash Grenadine *(Mix into Cocktail Glass—no ice)*

SEPTEMBER SUNRISE-
Light Rum
Lime Juice, splash Grenadine (lace) *(Mix into Cocktail Glass—no ice)*

SERGEANT MAJOR-
2 parts Brandy, 1 part Galliano® *(Mix into Small Rocks Glass—ice)*

SERPENT'S TOOTH-
2 parts Sweet Vermouth, 1 part Irish Whiskey, splash Kümmel
Lime Juice, splash Bitters *(Mix into Small Rocks Glass—ice)*

SERPENTINE-
2 parts Light Rum, 1 part Brandy, 1 part Sweet Vermouth
Sour Mix *(Mix into Cocktail Glass—no ice)*

SEVENTH HEAVEN (1)-
3 parts Seagram's® 7 Whiskey, 1 part Amaretto
Orange Juice *(Mix into Highball Glass—ice)*

SEVENTH HEAVEN (2)-
Gin, splash Maraschino Liqueur
Grapefruit Juice *(Mix into Cocktail Glass—no ice)*

SEVILLA COCKTAIL (1)-
1 part Light Rum, 1 part Port
Sugar *(Mix into Wine Glass—no ice)*

SEVILLA COCKTAIL (2)-
1 part Dark Rum, 1 part Sweet Vermouth *(Mix into Cocktail Glass—no ice)*

SEVILLE-
3 parts Gin, 1 part Fino Sherry
Orange Juice, Sour Mix *(Mix into Highball Glass—ice)*

SEWER RAT-
1 part Coffee Liqueur, 1 part Peach Schnapps, 1 part Vodka
Orange Juice *(Mix into Highball Glass—ice)*

SEWER WATER-
2 parts 151-proof Rum, 1 part Gin, 1 part Melon Liqueur
Pineapple Juice, Grenadine, Lime Juice (float) *(Mix into Highball Glass—ice)*

SEX-
1 part Coffee Liqueur, 1 part Grand Marnier® *(Mix into Small Rocks Glass—ice)*

SEX IN A BUBBLEGUM FACTORY-
1 part Apricot Brandy, 1 part Banana Liqueur, 1 part Blue Curaçao,
1 part Light Rum
Lemon-Lime Soda *(Mix into Highball Glass—ice)*

SEX IN THE PARKING LOT-
1 part Apple Schnapps, 1 part Raspberry Liqueur, 1 part Vodka
Cranberry Juice, Orange Juice *(Mix into Highball Glass—ice)*

SEX, LIES & VIDEO POKER-
1 part Amaretto, 1 part Blended Whiskey, 1 part Spiced Rum
Cranberry Juice, Orange Juice, Pineapple Juice, Grenadine
(Mix into Highball Glass—ice)

SEX MACHINE-
1 part Coffee Liqueur, 1 part Irish Cream Liqueur
Light Cream or Milk *(Mix into Highball Glass—ice)*

SEX ME STRONG-
2 parts DeKuyper® Island Blue Pucker, 2 parts DeKuyper® Sour Apple
Schnapps, 1 part Tequila *(Mix into Cocktail Glass—no ice)*

SEX ON ACID-
1 part Blackberry Brandy, 1 part Jägermeister®, 1 part Melon Liqueur
Cranberry Juice, Pineapple Juice *(Mix into Highball Glass—ice)*

S

SEX ON THE BEACH (1)-
1 part Melon Liqueur, 1 part Raspberry Liqueur, 1 part Vodka
Pineapple Juice *(Mix into Highball Glass—ice)*

SEX ON THE BEACH (2)-
1 part Peach Schnapps, 1 part Vodka
Cranberry Juice, Orange Juice *(Mix into Highball Glass—ice)*

SEX ON THE BEACH (3)-
1 part Black Raspberry Liqueur, 1 part Melon Liqueur, 1 part Vodka
Cranberry Juice, Pineapple Juice *(Mix into Highball Glass—ice)*

SEX ON THE BEACH IN THE WINTER-
1 part Peach Schnapps, 1 part Vodka
Cranberry Juice, Pineapple Juice, Coconut Milk
(Blend with ice in Daiquiri Glass)

SEX ON THE BEACH (SOUTHERN STYLE)-
1 part Apple Schnapps, 1 part Peach Schnapps
Cranberry Juice, Pineapple Juice *(Mix into Highball Glass—ice)*

SEX ON THE BEACH WITH A FRIEND-
1 part Crème de Cassis, 1 part Melon Liqueur, 1 part Vodka
Pineapple Juice *(Mix into Highball Glass—ice)*

SEX ON THE BOAT-
4 parts Captain Morgan® Original Spiced Rum, 1 part Banana Liqueur
Orange Juice *(Mix into Highball Glass—ice)*

SEX ON THE LAKE-
1 part Banana Liqueur, 1 part Brown Crème de Caçao, splash Light Rum
Light Cream or Milk *(Mix into Highball Glass—ice)*

SEX ON THE SIDEWALK-
1 part Melon Liqueur, 1 part Raspberry Liqueur
Cranberry Juice *(Mix into Highball Glass—ice)*

SEX UNDER THE BOARDWALK-
1 part Melon Liqueur, 1 part Peach Schnapps, 1 part Raspberry Liqueur
Orange Juice *(Mix into Highball Glass—ice)*

SEX UNDER THE SUN-
2 parts Light Rum, 1 part Dark Rum
Orange Juice, Pineapple Juice, splash Grenadine
(Mix into Highball Glass—ice)

SEX UP AGAINST THE WALL-
Vodka, splash Galliano®
Cranberry Juice, Pineapple Juice, Sour Mix
(Mix into Highball Glass—ice)

SEX WITH AN ALLIGATOR-
1 part Melon Liqueur, 1 part Coconut Rum, 1 part Pineapple Juice,
     1 part Raspberry Liqueur, 1 part Jägermeister®
(Layer in Order in Cocktail Glass—no ice)

SEX WIH THE CAPTAIN-
1 part Amaretto, 1 part Captain Morgan® Original Spiced Rum,
    1 part Peach Schnapps
Cranberry Juice, Orange Juice *(Mix into Highball Glass—ice)*

SEXUAL CHOCOLATE-
1 part Brown Crème de Caçao, 1 part Coffee Liqueur, 1 part Irish Cream
    Liqueur, splash Raspberry Liqueur
Light Cream or Milk, splash Soda *(Mix into Highball Glass—ice)*

SEXUAL HARRASEMENT-
1 part Amaretto, 1 part Canadian Whiskey, 1 part Sloe Gin
Orange Juice, Pineapple Juice *(Mix into Highball Glass—ice)*

SEXUAL PEAK-
1 part Amaretto, 1 part Peach Schnapps, 1 part Vodka
Orange Juice, Pineapple Juice, Sour Mix *(Mix into Highball Glass—ice)*

SEXY ALLIGATOR-
1 part Jägermeister®, 1 part Melon Liqueur, 1 part Coconut Liqueur,
    splash Grenadine *(Layer in Order in Cocktail Glass—no ice)*

SHADY GROVE-
Gin, fill Ginger Beer
Sour Mix *(Beer Mug)*

SHADY LADY-
1 part Melon Liqueur, 1 part Tequila
Grapefruit Juice *(Mix into Highball Glass—ice)*

SHAKE THAT ASS-
1 part Banana Liqueur, 1 part Blue Curaçao
Orange Juice, Sour Mix *(Mix into Highball Glass—ice)*

SHAKER-
Tequila
Pineapple Juice, splash Lime Juice, splash Grenadine
(Mix into Cocktail Glass—no ice)

SHAKING BLUE MONDAY-
3 parts Canadian Whiskey, 1 part Blueberry Brandy, splash Brandy
Sour Mix *(Mix into Highball Glass—ice)*

SHALOM-
1 part Madeira Wine, 1 part 100-proof Vodka
splash Orange Juice *(Mix into Small Rocks Glass—ice)*

SHAMROCK (1)-
1 part Green Crème de Menthe, 1 part Brown Crème de Caçao, 1 part Irish
    Cream Liqueur
(Layer in Order in Cocktail Glass—no ice)

SHAMROCK (2)-
3 parts Irish Whiskey, 1 part Dry Vermouth, splash Green Crème de Menthe
(Mix into Cocktail Glass—no ice)

S

SHANAYNAY-
Light Rum
Lemonade, Water *(Mix into Highball Glass—ice)*

SHANDY-
12 oz. Beer
top Lemon-Lime Soda *(Beer Mug)*

SHANGHAI (1)-
Jamaican Rum, splash Anisette
Lime Juice, Grenadine *(Mix into Cocktail Glass—no ice)*

SHANGHAI (2)-
1 part Dark Rum, 1 part Sambuca
Lime Juice, splash Grenadine *(Mix into Cocktail Glass—no ice)*

SHARK-
1 part Tequila, 1 part Vodka
splash Hot Sauce *(Mix into Small Rocks Glass—ice)*

SHARK ATTACK-
Vodka
Lemonade, splash Grenadine *(Mix into Highball Glass—ice)*

SHARK BITE-
Dark Rum or Spiced Rum
Orange Juice, Grenadine *(Mix into Highball Glass—ice)*

SHARK'S TOOTH-
Dark Rum
Lime Juice, splash Grenadine, fill Club Soda *(Mix into Highball Glass—ice)*

SHARKY PUNCH-
3 parts Apple Brandy, 1 part Rye Whiskey
Sugar, fill Club Soda *(Mix into Highball Glass—ice)*

SHARPLES-
3 parts Dark Rum, 1 part Peppermint Schnapps
(Mix into Small Rocks Glass—ice)

SHAVETAIL-
Peppermint Schnapps
Light Cream or Milk, Pineapple Juice *(Mix into Cocktail Glass—no ice)*

SHEER ELEGANCE-
3 parts Amaretto, 3 parts Black Raspberry Liqueur, 1 part Vodka
(Mix into Cocktail Glass—no ice)

SHERBET-
1 part Raspberry Liqueur, 1 part Triple Sec
Orange Juice *(Mix into Highball Glass—ice)*

SHERMAN TANK-
4 parts Blended Whiskey, 1 part Bénédictine
Sour Mix, splash Bitters *(Mix into Cocktail Glass—no ice)*

SHERRY COBBLER-
Sweet Sherry
Club Soda, Sugar *(Mix into Highball Glass—ice)*

SHERRY COCKTAIL-
Cream Sherry
splash Bitters *(Mix into Cocktail Glass—no ice)*

SHERRY EGGNOG-
Cream Sherry
Light Cream or Milk, Sugar, sprinkle Nutmeg *(Mix into Highball Glass—ice)*

SHERRY FLIP-
Cream Sherry
Light Cream or Milk, Sugar *(Mix into Cocktail Glass—no ice)*

SHERRY MILK PUNCH-
Cream Sherry
Light Cream or Milk, Sugar *(Mix into Highball Glass—ice)*

SHERRY SANGAREE-
Cream Sherry, splash Port (float)
Water, Sugar, splash Club Soda *(Mix into Small Rocks Glass—ice)*

SHERRY TWIST-
2 parts Cream Sherry, 1 part Brandy, 1 part Dry Vermouth, 1 part Triple Sec
splash Lime Juice, Orange Peel Twist Garnish
(Mix into Cocktail Glass—no ice)

SHILLELAGH-
1 part Green Crème de Menthe, 1 part Spiced Rum
Sour Mix, Green Cherry Garnish
(Mix into Highball Glass—ice)

SHIP-
3 parts Sherry, 1 part Blended Whiskey, 1 part Light Rum
Sugar, splash Prune Juice, splash Orange Bitters
(Mix into Cocktail Glass—no ice)

SHOGUN-
1 part Citrus Vodka, 1 part Grand Marnier®
Lime Juice *(Mix into Small Rocks Glass with ice or into Snifter with no ice)*

SHOGUN FIZZ-
1 part Red Wine, 1 part Scotch Whiskey
Sour Mix, splash Club Soda *(Mix into Highball Glass—ice)*

SHOOT, THE-
1 part Dry Sherry, 1 part Scotch Whiskey
Orange Juice, Sour Mix *(Mix into Cocktail Glass—no ice)*

SHOW TUNE-
4 parts Spiced Rum, 1 part Amaretto
Grapefruit Juice, splash Grenadine, top Club Soda
(Mix into Highball Glass—ice)

SHRINER-
1 part Brandy, 1 part Sloe Gin
splash Bitters, Sugar *(Mix into Cocktail Glass—no ice)*

SIBERIAN SLEIGHRIDE-
2 parts Vodka, 1 part White Crème de Caçao, 1 part White Crème de Menthe
Light Cream or Milk *(Mix into Cocktail Glass—no ice)*

SIBERIAN SUNSET-
2 parts Vodka, 1 part Cherry Brandy or Raspberry Liqueur or
    Strawberry Schnapps
Lime Juice *(Mix into Cocktail Glass—no ice)*

SICILIAN KISS-
2 parts Southern Comfort®, 1 part Amaretto
(Mix into Cocktail Glass—no ice)

SICILIAN MARY-
Sambuca
Bloody Mary Mix *(Mix into Highball Glass—ice)*

SIDECAR-
2 parts Brandy, 1 part Triple Sec
splash Sour Mix *(Mix into Cocktail Glass—no ice)*

SIENNA-
2 parts Spiced Rum, 1 part Amaretto
Orange Juice, Ginger Ale *(Mix into Highball Glass—ice)*

SIGN OF THE CROSS-***
Red Wine
Orange Juice, splash Water, splash Club Soda, splash Grenadine (lace)
(Mix into Wine Glass—no ice)

SILENT BROADSIDER-
Light Rum, splash Brandy, splash Hazelnut Liqueur, splash Sweet Vermouth
splash Grenadine *(Mix into Cocktail Glass—no ice)*

SILENT GEORGE-
3 parts Vodka, 1 part Peppermint Schnapps
Pineapple Juice *(Mix into Highball Glass—ice)*

SILENT MONK-
2 parts Bénédictine, 1 part Triple Sec
Light Cream or Milk *(Mix into Cocktail Glass—no ice)*

SILENT THIRD-
2 parts Scotch Whiskey, 1 part Triple Sec
Lime Juice *(Mix into Cocktail Glass—no ice)*

SILK PANTIES (1)-
1 part Peach Schnapps, 1 part Sambuca *(Mix into Cocktail Glass—no ice)*

SILK PANTIES (2)-
1 part Peach Schnapps, 1 part Vodka *(Mix into Cocktail Glass—no ice)*

S

SILK STOCKINGS (1)-
3 parts Tequila, 1 part Brown Crème de Caçao, 1 part Raspberry Liqueur
Light Cream or Milk *(Mix into Highball Glass—ice)*

SILK STOCKINGS (2)-
2 parts Tequila, 1 part White Crème de Caçao
Light Cream or Milk, splash Grenadine
(Mix into Cocktail Glass—no ice)

SILVER BRONX-
4 parts Gin, 1 part Dry Vermouth, 1 part Sweet Vermouth
Orange Juice *(Mix into Highball Glass—ice)*

SILVER BULLET (1)-
1 part Dry Vermouth, 1 part Gin, splash Maraschino Liqueur
splash Orange Bitters, Sugar *(Mix into Cocktail Glass—no ice)*

SILVER BULLET (2)-
Gin, splash Scotch Whiskey *(Mix into Cocktail Glass—no ice)*

SILVER COCKTAIL-
2 parts Gin, 1 part Dry Vermouth, splash Maraschino Liqueur
splash Orange Bitters *(Mix into Cocktail Glass—no ice)*

SILVER DEVIL-
1 part Tequila, 1 part Peppermint Schnapps
(Layer in Order in Cocktail Glass—no ice)

SILVER FIZZ-
Gin
Sour Mix, splash Club Soda *(Mix into Highball Glass—ice)*

SILVER FOX-
2 parts Brown Crème de Caçao, 1 part Triple Sec
Cold Coffee, splash Light Cream or Milk
(Mix into Cocktail Glass—no ice)

SILVER JUBILEE-
1 part Gin, 1 part Light Rum
Sour Mix, splash Bitters *(Mix into Cocktail Glass—no ice)*

SILVER KING-
Gin
Sour Mix, splash Orange Bitters *(Mix into Cocktail Glass—no ice)*

SILVER MARGARITA-
3 parts Silver Tequila, 1 part Triple Sec
Lime Juice, Salted Rim (optional) *(Mix into Cocktail Glass—no ice)*

SILVER NIPPLE-
1 part Sambuca, 1 part Vodka *(Mix into Small Rocks Glass—ice)*

SILVER SHELL-
2 parts Gin, 1 part Jägermeister®
splash Lime Juice *(Mix into Cocktail Glass—no ice)*

S

SILVER SPIDER-
 1 part Light Rum, 1 part Triple Sec, 1 part Vodka, 1 part White Crème de
 Menthe *(Mix into Cocktail Glass—no ice)*

SILVER STALLION FIZZ-
 Gin
 Vanilla Ice Cream, Club Soda *(Mix into Highball Glass—ice)*

SILVER STREAK-
 2 parts Gin, 1 part Kümmel *(Mix into Cocktail Glass—no ice)*

SILVER SUNSET-
 3 parts Vodka, 1 part Apricot Brandy, 1 part Campari
 Orange Juice, Lime Juice *(Mix into Highball Glass—ice)*

SIMPLY BONKERS-
 1 part Light Rum, 1 part Raspberry Liqueur
 Light Cream or Milk *(Mix into Highball Glass—ice)*

SINGAPORE SLING (1)-
 4 parts Gin, 1 part Cherry Brandy
 Sour Mix, splash Grenadine, top Club Soda *(Mix into Highball Glass—ice)*

SINGAPORE SLING (2)-
 Gin, splash Cherry Brandy (float)
 Sour Mix, Club Soda *(Mix into Highball Glass—ice)*

SINGING ORCHARD-
 4 parts Dark Rum, 1 part Raspberry Liqueur
 Pineapple Juice, Coconut Milk, splash Grenadine (lace)
 (Blend with ice in Daiquiri Glass)

SINK OR SWIM-
 3 parts Brandy, 1 part Sweet Vermouth
 splash Bitters *(Mix into Small Rocks Glass—ice)*

SINO-SOVIET SPLIT-
 2 parts Vodka, 1 part Amaretto
 Light Cream or Milk *(Mix into Cocktail Glass—no ice)*

SIR WALTER-
 1 part Brandy, 1 part Light Rum, splash Triple Sec
 Lime Juice, Grenadine *(Mix into Cocktail Glass—no ice)*

SIR WALTER RALEIGH (1)-
 2 parts Brandy, 1 part Light Rum, splash Triple Sec
 splash Lime Juice, splash Grenadine *(Mix into Cocktail Glass—no ice)*

SIR WALTER RALEIGH (2)-
 2 parts Brandy, 1 part Light Rum, splash Blue Curaçao
 splash Lime Juice, splash Grenadine *(Mix into Cocktail Glass—no ice)*

SISTER STARSEEKER-
 Light Rum
 splash Lime Juice, splash Grenadine, fill Tonic Water
 (Mix into Highball Glass—ice)

SIT ON MY FACE-
1 part Irish Cream Liqueur, 1 part Hazelnut Liqueur, 1 part Coffee Liqueur
(Layer in Order in Cocktail Glass—no ice)

SITARSKI-
Dark Rum
Grapefruit Juice, Sour Mix *(Mix into Highball Glass—ice)*

SIZZLER-
1 part Beer, 1 part Jack Daniel's® Tennessee Sour Mash Whiskey, 1 part Vodka
Lemonade *(Mix into Highball Glass—ice)*

SKI LIFT-
2 parts Peach Schnapps, 1 part Coconut Rum
Hot Chocolate, top Whipped Cream *(Mix into Irish Coffee Cup—no ice)*

SKINNY TART-
Dark Rum
Grapefruit Juice, Pineapple Juice, Sugar
(Mix into Highball Glass with ice or blend with ice in Daiquiri Glass)

SKIP & GO NAKED-
Gin, fill Beer
Sour Mix *(Beer Mug)*

SKIP, RUN & GO NAKED-
Tequila, fill Beer
splash Bitters *(Beer Mug)*

SKITTLE-
2 parts Vodka, 1 part Banana Liqueur
Cranberry Juice, Sour Mix, splash Grenadine *(Mix into Highball Glass—ice)*

SKULL CRACKER-
4 parts Light Rum, 1 part White Crème de Caçao
Pineapple Juice, Lime Juice *(Mix into Highball Glass—ice)*

SKYSCRAPER-
Bourbon Whiskey *(Mix into Highball Glass—ice)*

SLACKER'S SLAMMER-
1 part Root Beer Schnapps, 1 part Vodka
Root Beer, Vanilla Ice Cream (optional) *(Mix into Highball Glass—ice)*

SLAM DANCER-
2 parts White Crème de Caçao, 1 part Brown Crème de Caçao, 1 part Coffee
Liqueur, splash Peppermint Schnapps
Light Cream or Milk *(Mix into Highball Glass—ice)*

SLAPSTICK-
2 parts Spiced Rum, 1 part Strawberry Schnapps
Pineapple Juice, Coconut Milk, Grenadine *(Blend with ice in Daiquiri Glass)*

SLEAZY SEX ON THE BEACH-
1 part Grand Marnier®, 1 part Vodka
Cranberry Juice, Orange Juice *(Mix into Highball Glass—ice)*

SLEDGEHAMMER-
1 part Apple Brandy, 1 part Brandy, 1 part Light Rum, splash Anisette
(Mix into Cocktail Glass—no ice)

SLEEPER-
1 part Coffee Liqueur, 1 part Galliano®, 1 part Tequila
(Mix into Small Rocks Glass—ice)

SLEEPY HEAD-
Brandy
Ginger Ale *(Mix into Highball Glass—ice)*

SLEEPY LEMON CLEGG-
3 parts Dark Rum, 1 part Banana Liqueur
Orange Juice, Pineapple Juice, Lime Juice *(Mix into Highball Glass—ice)*

SLING (GENERIC)-
(Any Liqueur)
Sour Mix, splash Water *(Mix into Small Rocks Glass—ice)*

SLIPPERY DICK-
1 part Banana Liqueur, 1 part Irish Cream Liqueur
(Mix into Cocktail Glass—no ice)

SLIPPERY KNOB-
Gin, splash Grand Marnier® *(Mix into Cocktail Glass—no ice)*

SLIPPERY NIPPLE (1)-
1 part Irish Cream Liqueur, 1 part Sambuca
(Mix into Cocktail Glass—no ice)

SLIPPERY NIPPLE (2)-
1 part Irish Cream Liqueur, 1 part Peppermint Schnapps
splash Grenadine (lace) *(Mix into Cocktail Glass—no ice)*

SLOE & BOUNCY-
3 parts Bourbon Whiskey, 1 part Sloe Gin
Sour Mix *(Mix into Cocktail Glass—no ice)*

SLOE BALL-
3 parts Sloe Gin, 1 part Gin, 1 part Vodka
Orange Juice, splash Lime Juice, splash Grenadine
(Mix into Highball Glass—ice)

SLOE BRANDY-
4 parts Brandy, 1 part Sloe Gin
splash Lime Juice *(Mix into Cocktail Glass—no ice)*

SLOE DRIVER-
Sloe Gin
Orange Juice *(Mix into Highball Glass—ice)*

SLOE GIN COCKTAIL-
Sloe Gin, splash Dry Vermouth
splash Orange Bitters *(Mix into Cocktail Glass—no ice)*

SLOE GIN COLLINS-
  Sloe Gin
  Sour Mix, splash Club Soda *(Mix into Highball Glass—ice)*

SLOE GIN FIZZ-
  Sloe Gin
  Sour Mix, Sugar, splash Club Soda *(Mix into Highball Glass—ice)*

SLOE GIN FLIP-
  Sloe Gin
  Light Cream or Milk, Sugar *(Mix into Highball Glass—ice)*

SLOE GIN RICKEY-
  Sloe Gin
  Lime Juice, Club Soda *(Mix into Highball Glass—ice)*

SLOE HAND JACKSON-
  3 parts Sloe Gin, 1 part Gin, 1 part Vodka
  Orange Juice, splash Lime Juice, splash Grenadine
  (Mix into Highball Glass—ice)

SLOE SCREW-
  3 parts Vodka, 1 part Sloe Gin
  Orange Juice *(Mix into Highball Glass—ice)*

SLOE TEQUILA-
  2 parts Tequila, 1 part Sloe Gin
  Lime Juice *(Mix into Highball Glass—ice)*

SLOE VERMOUTH-
  1 part Dry Vermouth, 1 part Sloe Gin
  Lime Juice *(Mix into Cocktail Glass—no ice)*

SLOEBERRY-
  Sloe Gin
  splash Bitters *(Mix into Cocktail Glass—no ice)*

SLOPPY JOE'S (1)-
  1 part Dry Vermouth, 1 part Light Rum, splash Triple Sec
  Lime Juice, Grenadine *(Mix into Cocktail Glass—no ice)*

SLOPPY JOE'S (2)-
  1 part Brandy, 1 part Port, splash Triple Sec
  Pineapple Juice, splash Grenadine
  (Mix into Cocktail Glass—no ice)

SLOW COMFORTABLE, FUZZY SCREW-
  1 part Peach Schnapps, 1 part Sloe Gin, 1 part Southern Comfort®,
    1 part Vodka
  Orange Juice *(Mix into Highball Glass—ice)*

SLOW COMFORTABLE, FUZZY SCREW AGAINST THE WALL-
  1 part Peach Schnapps, 1 part Sloe Gin, 1 part Southern Comfort®,
    1 part Vodka, splash Galliano®
  Orange Juice *(Mix into Highball Glass—ice)*

S

SLOW COMFORTABLE SCREW-
1 part Sloe Gin, 1 part Southern Comfort®, 1 part Vodka
Orange Juice *(Mix into Highball Glass—ice)*

SLOW COMFORTABLE SCREW AGAINST THE WALL-
1 part Sloe Gin, 1 part Southern Comfort®, 1 part Vodka,
    1 part Galliano® (float)
Orange Juice *(Mix into Highball Glass—ice)*

SLOW COMFORTABLE SCREW AGAINST THE WALL (MEXICAN STYLE)-
1 part Sloe Gin, 1 part Southern Comfort®, 1 part Tequila,
    1 part Galliano® (float)
Orange Juice *(Mix into Highball Glass—ice)*

SLOW SCREW-
Sloe Gin
Orange Juice *(Mix into Highball Glass—ice)*

SLUSH-
Gin
Cranberry Juice, Orange Juice, Sour Mix, Lemon-Lime Soda (float)
(Blend with ice in Daiquiri Glass)

SLY GOES TO HAVANA-
Light Rum, splash Green Chartreuse, splash White Crème de Caçao
Pineapple Juice, splash Lime Juice *(Mix into Highball Glass—ice)*

SMART CHRISTINE-
4 parts Gin, 1 part Bénédictine
Orange Juice *(Mix into Highball Glass—ice)*

SMARTIE-
1 part Grenadine, 1 part Swiss Chocolate Almond Liqueur, 1 part Tequila
(Layer in Order in Cocktail Glass—no ice)

SMILE-
Gin
Grenadine, splash Lime Juice *(Mix into Cocktail Glass—no ice)*

SMILER-
2 parts Gin, 1 part Dry Vermouth, 1 part Sweet Vermouth
Orange Juice, splash Bitters *(Mix into Cocktail Glass—no ice)*

SMITH & KEARNS COCKTAIL-
Coffee Liqueur
splash Light Cream or Milk, fill Club Soda *(Mix into Highball Glass—ice)*

SMITH & WESSON-
1 part Coffee Liqueur, 1 part Vodka
splash Light Cream or Milk, fill Cola *(Mix into Highball Glass—ice)*

SMOKY MARY-
Vodka
Tomato Juice, Barbecue Sauce, Lime Juice, splash Hot Sauce, splash
    Worcestershire Sauce *(Mix into Highball Glass—ice)*

SMOOTH MOVE-
Light Rum
Pineapple Juice, Prune Juice, Sour Mix *(Blend with ice in Daiquiri Glass)*

SMOOTH OPERATOR (1)-
2 parts Hazelnut Liqueur, 1 part Coffee Liqueur, 1 part Irish Cream Liqueur
Light Cream or Milk, Bananas
(Blend with ice in Daiquiri Glass)

SMOOTH OPERATOR (2)-
2 parts Hazelnut Liqueur, 1 part Banana Liqueur, 1 part Coffee Liqueur,
1 part Irish Cream Liqueur
Light Cream or Milk *(Mix into Highball Glass—ice)*

SMOOTH SAILING-
Bourbon Whiskey
Light Cream or Milk, fill Club Soda *(Mix into Highball Glass—ice)*

SMOOTH SCREW-
1 part Spiced Rum, 1 part Tia Maria®, 1 part Dark Rum (float)
Pineapple Juice *(Mix into Highball Glass—ice)*

SMURF JUICE-
1 part Blue Curaçao, 1 part White Wine
Ginger Ale *(Mix into Highball Glass—ice)*

SMURF PISS-
100-proof Vodka
Berry Blue Kool-Aid®, Mountain Dew® *(Mix into Highball Glass—ice)*

SMURF SNOT-
1 part Blue Curaçao, 1 part Blueberry Schnapps,
splash Irish Cream Liqueur (lace)
(Mix into Cocktail Glass—no ice)

SNAKE BITE (1)-
2 parts Yukon Jack® Canadian Liqueur, 1 part Peppermint Schnapps
(Mix into Cocktail Glass—no ice)

SNAKE BITE (2)-
Yukon Jack® Canadian Liqueur
splash Lime Juice *(Mix into Cocktail Glass—no ice)*

SNAP APPLE-
Apple Brandy, splash Sweet Vermouth
Orange Juice, splash Sour Mix *(Mix into Cocktail Glass—no ice)*

SNAP SHOT-
1 part Peppermint Schnapps, 1 part Irish Cream Liqueur
(Layer in Order in Cocktail Glass—no ice)

SNEAKY PEACH-
Peach Schnapps
Orange Juice, Coconut Milk, splash Grenadine, splash Sour Mix
(Blend with ice in Daiquiri Glass)

SNEAKY PETE (1)-
4 parts Tequila, 1 part White Crème de Menthe
Pineapple Juice, Lime Juice *(Mix into Cocktail Glass—no ice)*

SNEAKY PETE (2)-
Apple Brandy, fill Beer *(Beer Mug)*

SNOW BALL-
3 parts Gin, 1 part Anisette
Light Cream or Milk *(Mix into Cocktail Glass—no ice)*

SNOW BUNNY-
Triple Sec
Hot Chocolate, top Whipped Cream
(Mix into Irish Coffee Cup—no ice)

SNOW CAP-
1 part Tequila, 1 part Irish Cream Liqueur
(Layer in Order in Cocktail Glass—no ice)

SNOW JOB-
Pear Schnapps
Light Cream or Milk, sprinkle Nutmeg *(Mix into Highball Glass—ice)*

SNOW MELTER-
1 part Light Rum, 1 part Sambuca, 1 part White Crème de Caçao
Hot Chocolate, top Whipped Cream
(Mix into Irish Coffee Cup—no ice)

SNOW SHOE (1)-
1 part Bourbon Whiskey, 1 part Peppermint Schnapps
(Mix into Cocktail Glass—no ice)

SNOW SHOE (2)-
1 part Brandy, 1 part Peppermint Schnapps *(Mix into Cocktail Glass—no ice)*

SNOW WHITE-
3 parts Southern Comfort®, 1 part Vodka
Orange Juice, Pineapple Juice *(Mix into Highball Glass—ice)*

SNOWBALL-
1 part Cinnamon Schnapps, 1 part Coffee Liqueur
Coffee, top Whipped Cream *(Mix into Irish Coffee Cup—no ice)*

SNUGGLER-
Peppermint Schnapps
Hot Chocolate, top Whipped Cream *(Mix into Irish Coffee Cup—no ice)*

SNYDER-
3 parts Gin, 1 part Dry Vermouth, 1 part Triple Sec
(Mix into Cocktail Glass—no ice)

SO-SO-
2 parts Gin, 2 parts Sweet Vermouth, 1 part Apple Brandy
Grenadine *(Mix into Cocktail Glass—no ice)*

SOCIETY-
2 parts Gin, 1 part Dry Vermouth
splash Grenadine *(Mix into Cocktail Glass—no ice)*

SOCRATES-
3 parts Canadian Whiskey, 1 part Apricot Brandy, splash Triple Sec
splash Bitters *(Mix into Cocktail Glass—no ice)*

SOMBRERO-
Coffee Liqueur or Coffee Brandy
Light Cream or Milk *(Mix into Highball Glass—ice)*

SOMBRERO COOLER-
Dark Rum
Grapefruit Juice, Pineapple Juice *(Mix into Highball Glass—ice)*

SOMETHING DIFFERENT-
1 part Amaretto, 1 part Peach Schnapps
Cranberry Juice, Pineapple Juice *(Mix into Highball Glass—ice)*

SOMETHING PEACHIE-
1 part Light Rum or Vodka, 1 part Peach Schnapps, 1 part Triple Sec
Orange Juice, Pineapple Juice *(Mix into Highball Glass—ice)*

SON OF ADAM-
3 parts Light Rum, 1 part Apricot Brandy
Sour Mix *(Mix into Cocktail Glass—no ice)*

SONIC BLASTER-
1 part Banana Liqueur, 1 part Light Rum, 1 part Vodka
Cranberry Juice, Orange Juice, Pineapple Juice *(Mix into Highball Glass—ice)*

SONNY GETS KISSED-
3 parts Light Rum, 1 part Apricot Brandy
Sour Mix *(Mix into Cocktail Glass—no ice)*

SONOMA FIZZ-
Bourbon Whiskey
Sour Mix, splash Club Soda *(Mix into Highball Glass—ice)*

SONORA-
1 part Apple Brandy, 1 part Light Rum, splash Apricot Brandy
splash Lime Juice *(Mix into Cocktail Glass—no ice)*

SOOTHER-
1 part Apple Brandy, 1 part Brandy, 1 part Triple Sec
Sour Mix *(Mix into Cocktail Glass—no ice)*

SOUL KISS-
1 part Bourbon Whiskey, 1 part Dry Vermouth, splash Red Dubonnet®
Orange Juice *(Mix into Cocktail Glass—no ice)*

SOUR (GENERIC)-
(Any Liqueur)
Sour Mix, Cherry or Orange Garnish *(Mix into Sour Glass—ice)*

SOUR APPLE (1)-
1 part Amaretto, 1 part Melon Liqueur
Sour Mix *(Mix into Highball Glass—ice)*

SOUR APPLE (2)-
1 part Melon Liqueur, 1 part Tequila
Sour Mix *(Mix into Highball Glass—ice)*

SOUR APPLE (3)-
1 part Apple Schnapps, 1 part Melon Liqueur, 1 part Vodka
Lemon-Lime Soda *(Mix into Highball Glass—ice)*

SOUR APPLE MARTINI-
4 parts Vodka, 1 part Sour Apple Schnapps, 1 part Triple Sec
Lime Juice *(Mix into Cocktail Glass—no ice)*

SOUR GRAPES-
1 part Raspberry Liqueur, 1 part Vodka
splash Sour Mix *(Mix into Cocktail Glass—no ice)*

SOUTH BEND-
1 part Hazelnut Liqueur, 1 part Irish Cream Liqueur
Light Cream or Milk, Orange Juice *(Mix into Highball Glass—ice)*

SOUTH FORK COFFEE-
3 parts Bourbon Whiskey, 1 part Brown Crème de Caçao
Coffee, top Whipped Cream *(Mix into Irish Coffee Cup—no ice)*

SOUTH OF THE BORDER (1)-
1 part Coffee Liqueur or Coffee Brandy, 1 part Tequila
Lime Juice *(Mix into Highball Glass—ice)*

SOUTH OF THE BORDER (2)-
4 parts Blended Whiskey, 1 part Triple Sec
Sour Mix *(Mix into Highball Glass—ice)*

SOUTH PACIFIC-
2 parts Brandy, 1 part Vodka
Pineapple Juice, splash Lime Juice, splash Grenadine
(Mix into Cocktail Glass—no ice)

SOUTH PAW-
Brandy
Orange Juice, Lemon-Lime Soda *(Mix into Highball Glass—ice)*

SOUTH-SIDE COCKTAIL-
Gin
Sour Mix *(Mix into Cocktail Glass—no ice)*

SOUTH-SIDE FIZZ-
Gin
Sour Mix, splash Club Soda *(Mix into Highball Glass—ice)*

SOUTH STREET SEAPORT-
1 part Brandy, 1 part Madeira Wine, splash Dry Vermouth
(Mix into Small Rocks Glass—ice)

SOUTHAMPTON SLAM-
1 part Anisette, 1 part Green Crème de Menthe
(Mix into Cocktail Glass—no ice)

SOUTHERN BELLE (1)-
2 parts Jack Daniel's® Tennessee Sour Mash Whiskey, 1 part Triple Sec
Pineapple Juice, Orange Juice, splash Grenadine
(Mix into Highball Glass—ice)

SOUTHERN BELLE (2)-
1 part Apricot Brandy, 1 part Swiss Chocolate Almond Liqueur, 1 part Southern
    Comfort® *(Layer in Order in Cocktail Glass—no ice)*

SOUTHERN BRIDE-
Gin, splash Maraschino Liqueur
Grapefruit Juice *(Mix into Cocktail Glass—no ice)*

SOUTHERN COMFORT COCKTAIL-
2 parts Southern Comfort®, 1 part Triple Sec
Lime Juice *(Mix into Cocktail Glass—no ice)*

SOUTHERN COMFORT WATERMELON-
2 parts Southern Comfort®, 1 part Vodka
Pineapple Juice, splash Grenadine *(Mix into Highball Glass—ice)*

SOUTHERN FROST-
1 part Amaretto, 1 part Southern Comfort®, 1 part Triple Sec
Orange Juice, Pineapple Juice *(Blend with ice in Daiquiri Glass)*

SOUTHERN GIN-
Gin, splash Triple Sec
splash Orange Bitters *(Mix into Cocktail Glass—no ice)*

SOUTHERN GINGER-
4 parts Bourbon Whiskey, 1 part Ginger Brandy
splash Lime Juice, fill Ginger Ale *(Mix into Highball Glass—ice)*

SOUTHERN LADY-
2 parts Bourbon Whiskey, 1 part Crème de Noyaux, 1 part Southern Comfort®
Pineapple Juice, Lime Juice, Lemon-Lime Soda *(Mix into Highball Glass—ice)*

SOUTHERN MAIDEN-
2 parts Bourbon Whiskey, 1 part Triple Sec
Orange Juice, Pineapple Juice, splash Grenadine (float)
(Mix into Highball Glass—ice)

SOUTHERN PEACH-
1 part Bourbon Whiskey, 1 part Peach Schnapps
Orange Juice, Sour Mix, splash Grenadine
(Mix into Highball Glass with ice or blend with ice in Daiquiri Glass)

SOUTHERN PINK FLAMINGO-
1 part Coconut Rum, 1 part Southern Comfort®
Lime Juice, Pineapple Juice, splash Grenadine
(Mix into Cocktail Glass—no ice)

S

SOUTHERN SLAMMER-
3 parts Amaretto, 2 parts Southern Comfort®, 1 part Sloe Gin
Lime Juice *(Mix into Highball Glass—ice)*

SOUTHERN SODA-
Southern Comfort®
Ginger Ale *(Mix into Highball Glass—ice)*

SOUTHERN SPARKLER-
Southern Comfort®
Grapefruit Juice, Pineapple Juice, Soda *(Mix into Highball Glass—ice)*

SOUTHERN SUICIDE-
1 part Jack Daniel's® Tennessee Sour Mash Whiskey, 1 part Southern Comfort®
Orange Juice, Lemon-Lime Soda, splash Grenadine
(Mix into Highball Glass—ice)

SOUVENIR-
1 part Blended Whiskey, 1 part Dry Vermouth
splash Orange Juice *(Mix into Cocktail Glass—no ice)*

SOVIET-
3 parts Vodka, 1 part Dry Vermouth, 1 part Sherry
(Mix into Small Rocks Glass—ice)

SPANISH COFFEE-
1 part Brandy, 1 part Tia Maria®
Coffee, top Whipped Cream *(Mix into Irish Coffee Cup—no ice)*

SPANISH GOLD-
3 parts Gin, 1 part Red Wine, splash Dark Rum
Orange Juice *(Mix into Cocktail Glass—no ice)*

SPANISH MILKMAID-
Harvey's Bristol® Cream Sherry, splash Brandy
Orange Juice, splash Light Cream or Milk *(Mix into Cocktail Glass—no ice)*

SPANISH MOSS-
1 part Coffee Liqueur, 1 part Tequila, splash Green Crème de Menthe (lace)
(Mix into Cocktail Glass—no ice)

SPANISH TOWN-
Light Rum, splash Triple Sec *(Mix into Cocktail Glass—no ice)*

SPARK IN THE NIGHT-
3 parts Dark Rum, 1 part Coffee Liqueur
splash Lime Juice *(Mix into Cocktail Glass—no ice)*

SPARKLING STRAWBERRY MIMOSA-
Champagne
Orange Juice, Strawberry Margarita Mix
(Blend with ice in Champagne Flute)

SPARKLING WINE JULEP-
Brandy, fill Sparkling Wine
Sugar, Mint Leaves Garnish *(Mix into Champagne Flute—no ice)*

S

SPARKLING WINE POLONAISE-
splash Blackberry Brandy, splash Brandy, fill Sparkling Wine
(Mix into Champagne Flute—no ice)

SPEAKER OF THE HOUSE-
3 parts Canadian Whiskey, 1 part Ginger Schnapps, splash Cherry Brandy
splash Lime Juice *(Mix into Cocktail Glass—no ice)*

SPEARMINT LIFESAVER-
4 parts Jack Daniel's® Tennessee Sour Mash Whiskey,
1 part Peppermint Schnapps
Mountain Dew® *(Mix into Highball Glass—ice)*

SPECIAL (1)-
Rye Whiskey, splash Apricot Brandy
Club Soda *(Mix into Highball Glass—ice)*

SPECIAL (2)-
Rye Whiskey, splash Apricot Brandy
Sour Mix *(Mix into Highball Glass—ice)*

SPECIAL ROUGH-
1 part Apple Brandy, 1 part Brandy, splash Anisette
(Mix into Cocktail Glass—no ice)

SPEEDY GONZALEZ-
Tequila
Grapefruit Juice, Sugar, top Club Soda *(Mix into Highball Glass—ice)*

SPENCER-
2 parts Gin, 1 part Apricot Brandy
Orange Juice, splash Bitters *(Mix into Cocktail Glass—no ice)*

SPHINX-
Gin, splash Dry Vermouth, splash Sweet Vermouth
Lemon Garnish *(Mix into Cocktail Glass—no ice)*

SPICED BANANA DAIQUIRI-
2 parts Spiced Rum, 1 part Banana Liqueur
Sour Mix, Bananas *(Blend with ice in Daiquiri Glass)*

SPICED GINGER ALE-
Spiced Rum
Ginger Ale *(Mix into Highball Glass—ice)*

SPIKER-
2 parts Brandy, 1 part Green Crème de Menthe
(Mix into Small Rocks Glass—ice)

SPINNER-
Bourbon Whiskey
Orange Juice, splash Sour Mix *(Mix into Cocktail Glass—no ice)*

SPINSTER-
2 parts Cherry Brandy, 1 part Maraschino Liqueur
(Mix into Cocktail Glass—no ice)

S

SPINSTER'S DELIGHT-
1 part Brandy, 1 part Vodka, 1 part White Crème de Caçao
Light Cream or Milk *(Mix into Cocktail Glass—no ice)*

SPIRIT OF SCOTLAND-
2 parts Scotch Whiskey, 1 part Drambuie®
Lime Juice *(Mix into Cocktail Glass—no ice)*

SPIRITUAL ENLIGHTENMENT-
1 part Grand Marnier®, 1 part White Crème de Caçao, 1 part White Crème de
Menthe *(Mix into Small Rocks Glass—ice)*

SPLASH & CRASH-
1 part Amaretto, 1 part 151-proof Rum (float)
Cranberry Juice, Orange Juice *(Mix into Highball Glass—ice)*

SPRING FEELING-
2 parts Gin, 1 part Green Chartreuse
Lime Juice *(Mix into Cocktail Glass—no ice)*

SPRITZER-
White Wine
splash Club Soda or Ginger Ale *(Mix into Wine Glass—ice)*

SPUTNIK-
1 part Peach Schnapps, 1 part Vodka
Orange Juice, Light Cream or Milk *(Mix into Highball Glass—ice)*

SPY CATCHER-
2 parts Canadian Whiskey, 1 part Sambuca
(Mix into Cocktail Glass—no ice)

SPY MASTER-
2 parts Vodka, 1 part Banana Liqueur
Lime Juice *(Mix into Cocktail Glass—no ice)*

SQUID INK-***
1 part Blackberry Brandy, 1 part Black Sambuca
(Mix into Small Rocks Glass—ice)

SQUIRE RACINE-
3 parts Dark Rum, 1 part Southern Comfort®
Hot Milk, top Whipped Cream *(Mix into Irish Coffee Cup—no ice)*

SQUIRT (GENERIC)-
(Any Liqueur)
Grenadine, Sugar, Club Soda *(Mix into Highball Glass—ice)*

STAB IN THE BACK-
4 parts White Wine, 1 part Brandy
Orange Juice, Club Soda *(Mix into Highball Glass—ice)*

STALACTITE-
3 parts Sambuca, 1 part Irish Cream Liqueur, 1 part Black Raspberry Liqueur
(Layer in Order in Cocktail Glass—no ice)

STANLEY-
3 parts Gin, 1 part Light Rum
Lime Juice, splash Grenadine *(Mix into Cocktail Glass—no ice)*

STANLEY SENIOR-
Light Rum, splash Cranberry Schnapps
Grapefruit Juice *(Mix into Cocktail Glass—no ice)*

STAR-
1 part Apple Brandy, 1 part Sweet Vermouth
splash Bitters *(Mix into Cocktail Glass—no ice)*

STAR DAISY-
1 part Apple Brandy, 1 part Gin
Sour Mix, Grenadine *(Mix into Highball Glass—ice)*

STAR SEEKER-
Light Rum
Orange Juice, splash Grenadine, fill Tonic Water *(Mix into Highball Glass—ice)*

STAR WARS-
1 part Amaretto, 1 part Southern Comfort®, 1 part Triple Sec
splash Grenadine *(Mix into Cocktail Glass—no ice)*

STARBOARD-
1 part Dry Vermouth, 1 part Scotch Whiskey
Grapefruit Juice *(Mix into Highball Glass—ice)*

STARS & STRIPES-
1 part Grenadine, 1 part Light Cream or Milk, 1 part Blue Curaçao
(Layer in Order in Cocktail Glass—no ice)

STAY UP LATE-
4 parts Gin, 1 part Brandy
Sour Mix, Club Soda *(Mix into Highball Glass—ice)*

STEAMBOAT-
Gin, splash Crème de Cassis
Lime Juice *(Mix into Small Rocks Glass—ice)*

STEAMBOAT GIN-
2 parts Gin, 1 part Southern Comfort®
Grapefruit Juice, Lime Juice *(Mix into Cocktail Glass—no ice)*

STEAMING PEACH-
Peach Schnapps
Hot Water *(Mix into Irish Coffee Cup—no ice)*

STELLA'S STINGER-
Tequila, splash Anisette, splash White Crème de Menthe
(Mix into Cocktail Glass—no ice)

STEVIE RAY VAUGHAN-
1 part Jack Daniel's® Tennessee Sour Mash Whiskey, 1 part Southern Comfort®,
  1 part Triple Sec
Orange Juice, Sour Mix *(Mix into Highball Glass—ice)*

STEWART PLAID-
2 parts Coffee Liqueur, 2 parts Triple Sec, 1 part Irish Cream Liqueur
(Mix into Cocktail Glass—no ice)

STICKY NIPPLE-
1 part Amaretto, 1 part Irish Cream Liqueur *(Mix into Cocktail Glass—no ice)*

STILETTO-
4 parts Blended Whiskey, 1 part Amaretto
splash Lime Juice *(Mix into Cocktail Glass—no ice)*

STILETTO MANHATTAN-
2 parts Canadian Whiskey, 1 part Amaretto, splash Dry Vermouth
splash Orange Bitters, Cherry and Orange Garnish
(Mix into Cocktail Glass—no ice)

STINGER-
3 parts Brandy, 1 part White Crème de Menthe
(Mix into Cocktail Glass—no ice)

STINGER (AMARETTO STINGER)-
2 parts Amaretto, 1 part White Crème de Menthe
(Mix into Cocktail Glass—no ice)

STINGER (BEE STINGER)-
3 parts Blueberry Brandy, 1 part White Crème de Menthe
(Mix into Cocktail Glass—no ice)

STINGER (GIN STINGER)-
4 parts Gin, 1 part White Crème de Menthe *(Mix into Cocktail Glass—no ice)*

STINGER (GLADIATOR STINGER)-
1 part Brandy, 1 part Peppermint Schnapps, 1 part Sambuca
(Mix into Cocktail Glass—no ice)

STINGER (GREEN STINGER)-
3 parts Brandy, 1 part Green Crème de Menthe
(Mix into Cocktail Glass—no ice)

STINGER (INTERNATIONAL STINGER)-
3 parts Metaxa, 1 part Galliano® *(Mix into Cocktail Glass—no ice)*

STINGER (ITALIAN STINGER)-
3 parts Brandy, 1 part Galliano® *(Mix into Cocktail Glass—no ice)*

STINGER (LOUISVILLE STINGER)-
1 part Bourbon Whiskey, 1 part Light Rum, splash White Crème de Caçao,
splash White Crème de Menthe *(Mix into Cocktail Glass—no ice)*

STINGER (NEGRIL STINGER)-
2 parts Rum, 1 part Tia Maria® *(Mix into Small Rocks Glass—ice)*

STINGER (NUTTY STINGER)-
2 parts Amaretto, 1 part White Crème de Menthe
(Mix into Cocktail Glass—no ice)

STINGER (PEPPERMINT STINGER COCKTAIL)-
1 part Brandy, 1 part Peppermint Schnapps
(Mix into Small Rocks Glass—ice)

STINGER (ROMAN STINGER)-
3 parts Brandy, 1 part Sambuca, 1 part White Crème de Menthe
(Mix into Cocktail Glass—no ice)

STINGER (RUM STINGER)-
1 part Jamaican Rum, 1 part White Crème de Menthe
(Mix into Cocktail Glass—no ice)

STINGER (SASKATOON STINGER)-
2 parts Canadian Whiskey, 1 part Peppermint Schnapps or White Crème de
Menthe *(Mix into Cocktail Glass—no ice)*

STINGER (SCOTCH STINGER)-
3 parts Scotch Whiskey, 1 part White Crème de Menthe
(Mix into Cocktail Glass—no ice)

STINGER (STELLA'S STINGER)-
Tequila, splash Anisette, splash White Crème de Menthe
(Mix into Cocktail Glass—no ice)

STINGER (TEQUILA STINGER)-
2 parts Tequila, 1 part White Crème de Menthe
(Mix into Cocktail Glass—no ice)

STINGER (VODKA STINGER)-
1 part Vodka, 1 part White Crème de Menthe
(Mix into Cocktail Glass—no ice)

STIRRUP CUP-
1 part Brandy, 1 part Cherry Brandy
Sour Mix *(Mix into Small Rocks Glass—ice)*

STOCKHOLM 75-
Citrus Vodka, fill Champagne
Sour Mix *(Mix into Champagne Flute—no ice)*

STOLI BUTT-
2 parts Stolichnaya® Vodka, 1 part Butterscotch Schnapps
(Layer in Order in Cocktail Glass—no ice)

STONE-
2 parts Dry Sherry, 1 part Light Rum, 1 part Sweet Vermouth
(Mix into Cocktail Glass—no ice)

STONE FENCE-
Scotch Whiskey
splash Bitters, Club Soda or Cider *(Mix into Highball Glass—ice)*

STONE SOUR (1)-
Bourbon Whiskey, splash White Crème de Menthe
splash Sour Mix, Club Soda *(Mix into Highball Glass—ice)*

STONE SOUR (2)-
Apricot Brandy
Orange Juice, Sour Mix *(Mix into Sour Glass— ice)*

STONE SOUR (GENERIC)-
(Any Liqueur)
Orange Juice, Sour Mix *(Mix into Sour Glass— ice)*

STONEWALL-
Dark Rum
Apple Cider *(Mix into Highball Glass—ice)*

STONY BROOK-
3 parts Blended Whiskey, 1 part Triple Sec, splash Amaretto
(Mix into Cocktail Glass—no ice)

STOP LIGHT-
1 part Green Crème de Menthe, 1 part White Crème de Menthe, 1 part Sloe
Gin *(Layer in Order in Cocktail Glass—no ice)*

STORK CLUB-
Gin, splash Triple Sec
Orange Juice, splash Lime Juice, splash Bitters
(Mix into Cocktail Glass—no ice)

STRAIGHT LAW-
2 parts Dry Sherry, 1 part Gin *(Mix into Cocktail Glass—no ice)*

STRANGER IN TOWN-
3 parts Light Rum, 1 part Apple Brandy, 1 part Cherry Brandy, 1 part Sweet
Vermouth *(Mix into Cocktail Glass—no ice)*

STRATOSPHERE-
Crème de Yvette, fill Champagne *(Mix into Champagne Flute—no ice)*

STRAW HAT-
2 parts Coconut Rum, 1 part Vodka
Strawberry Garnish *(Mix into Cocktail Glass—no ice)*

STRAWBEERY COCKTAIL-
Strawberry Schnapps, fill Beer (Do Not Mix, Serve with Drinking Straw, Drink
all at once) *(Mix into Highball Glass—ice)*

STRAWBERRY ALEXANDER-
1 part Brandy, 1 part Brown Crème de Caçao, 1 part Strawberry Schnapps
Light Cream or Milk *(Mix into Cocktail Glass—no ice)*

STRAWBERRY ALEXANDRA-
1 part Brandy, 1 part White Crème de Caçao
Vanilla Ice Cream, Strawberry Daiquiri Mix *(Blend with ice in Daiquiri Glass)*

STRAWBERRIES & CREAM-
Strawberry Schnapps
Light Cream or Milk, Sugar, Strawberries
(Mix into Highball Glass with ice or blend with ice in Daiquiri Glass)

STRAWBERRY BANANA COLADA-
3 parts Dark Rum, 1 part Banana Liqueur, 1 part Strawberry Schnapps
Strawberry Daiquiri Mix, Bananas, Coconut Milk
(Blend with ice in Daiquiri Glass)

STRAWBERRY BANANA SPLIT-
1 part Banana Liqueur, 1 part Dark Rum, 1 part Strawberry Schnapps,
    splash Vanilla Liqueur
Light Cream or Milk
(Mix into Highball Glass with ice or blend with ice in Daiquiri Glass)

STRAWBERRY BANANA SPRITZ-
1 part Banana Liqueur, 1 part Strawberry Schnapps
Vanilla Ice Cream, Strawberry Daiquiri Mix, top Club Soda
(Blend with ice in Daiquiri Glass)

STRAWBERRY BOMB-
1 part 100-proof Vodka, 1 part Strawberry Schnapps
(Mix into Cocktail Glass—no ice)

STRAWBERRY COOLER-
White Wine, splash Strawberry Schnapps
Lemon-Lime Soda *(Mix into Wine Glass—ice)*

STRAWBERRY DAIQUIRI (1)-
2 parts Light Rum, 1 part Strawberry Schnapps
Sour Mix, Strawberry Daiquiri Mix
(Mix into Cocktail Glass with no ice or blend with ice in Daiquiri Glass)

STRAWBERRY DAIQUIRI (2)-
Light Rum
Sour Mix, Strawberry Daiquiri Mix
(Mix into Cocktail Glass with no ice or blend with ice in Daiquiri Glass)

STRAWBERRY DAWN-
Gin
Strawberry Daiquiri Mix, Coconut Milk *(Blend with ice in Daiquiri Glass)*

STRAWBERRY FIELDS FOREVER-
4 parts Strawberry Schnapps, 1 part Brandy
Club Soda *(Mix into Highball Glass—ice)*

STRAWBERRY KISS-
1 part Coffee Liqueur, 1 part Strawberry Schnapps, 1 part Irish Cream Liqueur
(Layer in Order in Cocktail Glass—no ice)

STRAWBERRY MARGARITA (1)-
2 parts Tequila, 1 part Strawberry Schnapps, 1 part Triple Sec
Lime Juice, Strawberry Daiquiri Mix, Salted Rim
(Mix into Cocktail Glass with no ice or blend with ice in Daiquiri Glass)

STRAWBERRY MARGARITA (2)-
Tequila, splash Triple Sec
Sour Mix, Strawberry Daiquiri Mix, Salted Rim
(Mix into Cocktail Glass with no ice or blend with ice in Daiquiri Glass)

S

STRAWBERRY QUICK (1)-
1 part Strawberry Schnapps, 1 part Vodka, splash Banana Liqueur
Light Cream or Milk, Orange Juice, splash Grenadine
(Mix into Highball Glass—ice)

STRAWBERRY QUICK (2)-
1 part Raspberry Liqueur, 1 part Vodka, splash Banana Liqueur
Light Cream or Milk, Orange Juice, splash Grenadine
(Mix into Highball Glass—ice)

STRAWBERRY ROYAL-
Champagne, splash Strawberry Schnapps *(Mix into Champagne Flute—no ice)*

STRAWBERRY SHORTCAKE (1)-
1 part Amaretto, 1 part Strawberry Schnapps
Light Cream or Milk *(Mix into Highball Glass—ice)*

STRAWBERRY SHORTCAKE (2)-
1 part Strawberry Schnapps, 1 part Vodka
Light Cream or Milk *(Mix into Highball Glass—ice)*

STRAWBERRY SHORTCAKE (3)-
3 parts Strawberry Schnapps, 1 part White Crème de Caçao
Strawberry Daiquiri Mix, Vanilla Ice Cream, top Whipped Cream
(Blend with ice in Daiquiri Glass)

STRAWBERRY SHORTCAKE SWIRL-
Amaretto
Strawberries, Light Cream or Milk *(Blend with ice in Daiquiri Glass)*

STRAWBERRY SUNRISE-
Strawberry Schnapps
Orange Juice, splash Grenadine, Sugar *(Mix into Highball Glass—ice)*

STREAMING PEACH-
Peach Schnapps
Hot Water *(Mix into Irish Coffee Cup—no ice)*

STRIP & GO NAKED-
1 part Beer, 1 part Vodka
Lemonade *(Beer Mug)*

STRONG ARM-
4 parts Blended Whiskey, 1 part Triple Sec
splash Lime Juice *(Mix into Cocktail Glass—no ice)*

STUFFY IN A SUIT-
2 parts Vodka, 1 part Lillet, 1 part Triple Sec
splash Orange Bitters *(Mix into Cocktail Glass—no ice)*

STUPID CUPID-
Citrus Vodka, splash Sloe Gin
splash Sour Mix, Cherry Garnish *(Mix into Cocktail Glass—no ice)*

SUBMARINO-
12 oz. Beer, Tequila (float) *(Beer Mug)*

S

SUE RIDING HIGH-
3 parts Dark Rum, 1 part Brown Crème de Caçao
Chocolate Milk, splash Light Cream or Milk (float)
(Mix into Highball Glass—ice)

SUFFERING BASTARD-
2 parts Gin, 1 part Brandy, fill Ginger Beer
Sour Mix, splash Bitters
(Mix into Highball Glass—ice)

SUFFRAGETTE CITY-
3 parts Light Rum, 1 part Grand Marnier®
Lime Juice, splash Grenadine *(Mix into Cocktail Glass—no ice)*

SUGAR DADDY-
Gin, splash Maraschino Liqueur
Pineapple Juice, splash Bitters *(Mix into Cocktail Glass—no ice)*

SUISSESSE-
Licorice Liqueur
Light Cream or Milk *(Mix into Cocktail Glass—no ice)*

SUMMER LEMONADE-
3 parts Vodka, 1 part Triple Sec
Sour Mix, fill Lemon-Lime Soda *(Mix into Highball Glass—ice)*

SUMMER SAILOR-
2 parts Vodka, 1 part Triple Sec
Grapefruit Juice *(Mix into Highball Glass—ice)*

SUMMER SCOTCH-
Scotch Whiskey, splash White Crème de Menthe
fill Club Soda *(Mix into Highball Glass—ice)*

SUMMER SHARE-
2 parts Light Rum, 2 parts Vodka, 1 part Tequila, splash Apricot Brandy
Cranberry Juice, top Lemon-Lime Soda
(Mix into Highball Glass—ice)

SUMMER SUNRISE-
2 parts Raspberry Liqueur, 1 part Apricot Brandy
Orange Juice, splash Cranberry Juice *(Mix into Highball Glass—ice)*

SUN KISS-
Amaretto
Orange Juice *(Mix into Highball Glass—ice)*

SUNBEAM-
3 parts Galliano®, 1 part Sweet Vermouth
(Mix into Small Rocks Glass—ice)

SUNBURN-
Tropical Fruit Liqueur
Grapefruit Juice, fill Club Soda, splash Grenadine
(Mix into Highball Glass—ice)

S

SUNDAY BRUNCH-
Bourbon Whiskey
Tomato Juice, Beef Bouillon, splash Lime Juice, splash Worcestershire Sauce
(Mix into Highball Glass—ice)

SUNDOWNER-
Light Rum
Lime Juice, splash Grenadine, fill Tonic Water *(Mix into Highball Glass—ice)*

SUNNIER SOUR-
Dark Rum
Grapefruit Juice, Sour Mix, fill Club Soda *(Mix into Sour Glass— ice)*

SUNNIEST SOUR-
Dark Rum
Orange Juice, Sour Mix, fill Club Soda *(Mix into Sour Glass— ice)*

SUNNY DAY-
Bénédictine
Grapefruit Juice *(Mix into Highball Glass—ice)*

SUNNY SOUR-
Dark Rum
Sour Mix *(Mix into Sour Glass—ice)*

SUNSET-
Cherry Brandy
Orange Juice *(Mix into Highball Glass—ice)*

SUNSHINE-
2 parts Gin, 1 part Sweet Vermouth
splash Bitters, Orange Garnish *(Mix into Cocktail Glass—no ice)*

SUNSPLASH-
3 parts Light Rum, 1 part Dry Vermouth, 1 part Sweet Vermouth
(Mix into Cocktail Glass—no ice)

SUNSTROKE-
Vodka, splash Triple Sec
Grapefruit Juice *(Mix into Highball Glass—ice)*

SUNTAN-
Tropical Fruit Liqueur
Orange Juice, fill Club Soda *(Mix into Highball Glass—ice)*

SUPER COFFEE-
1 part Brandy, 1 part Coffee Liqueur
Coffee, top Whipped Cream *(Mix into Irish Coffee Cup—no ice)*

SUPER SIDECAR-
2 parts Cognac, 1 part Triple Sec
Lime Juice *(Mix into Cocktail Glass—no ice)*

SUPER TART-
Berry Schnapps
Sour Mix, fill Lemon-Lime Soda *(Mix into Highball Glass—ice)*

SURF CITY LIFESAVER-
2 parts Gin, 1 part Grand Marnier®, 1 part Irish Cream Liqueur,
   1 part Licorice Liqueur
(Mix into Cocktail Glass with no ice or blend with ice in Daiquiri Glass)

SURF RIDER-
3 parts Vodka, 1 part Sweet Vermouth
Orange Juice, Lime Juice, splash Grenadine
(Mix into Cocktail Glass—no ice)

SURF'S UP-
1 part Banana Liqueur, 1 part White Crème de Caçao
Pineapple Juice, Light Cream or Milk
(Mix into Highball Glass with ice or blend with ice in Daiquiri Glass)

SURFER MARTINI-
2 parts Vodka, 1 part Banana Liqueur, 1 part Coconut Rum
(Mix into Cocktail Glass—no ice)

SURFER ON ACID-
1 part Coconut Rum, 1 part Jägermeister®
Orange Juice *(Mix into Highball Glass—ice)*

SURFER ON ACID IN HAWAII-
1 part Coconut Rum, 1 part Jägermeister®, 1 part Raspberry Liqueur
Cranberry Juice, Pineapple Juice
(Mix into Highball Glass—ice)

SURINAM SUNDOWNER-
3 parts Dark Jamaican Rum, 1 part Gin, 1 part Sweet Vermouth
splash Bitters *(Mix into Cocktail Glass—no ice)*

SURPUTTE-
1 part Triple Sec, 1 part Vodka
Lime Juice, Lemon-Lime Soda *(Mix into Highball Glass—ice)*

SURRY SLIDER-
3 parts Light Rum, 1 part Peach Schnapps
Orange Juice *(Mix into Highball Glass—ice)*

SUSAN LITTLER-
2 parts Dark Rum, 1 part Bourbon Whiskey, splash Galliano®
Orange Juice *(Mix into Highball Glass—ice)*

SUSIE TAYLOR-
Light Rum
Lime Juice, Ginger Ale *(Mix into Highball Glass—ice)*

SUZANNE'S SECRET (1)-***
Swiss Chocolate Liqueur, splash Peppermint Schnapps
Hot Chocolate, top Whipped Cream *(Mix into Irish Coffee Cup—no ice)*

SUZANNE'S SECRET (2)-***
Swiss Chocolate Liqueur, splash Peppermint Schnapps
Coffee, top Whipped Cream *(Mix into Irish Coffee Cup—no ice)*

SWAMP WATER-
2 parts Light Rum, 1 part Blue Curaçao
Orange Juice, splash Lime Juice *(Mix into Highball Glass—ice)*

SWEDISH LULLABY-
1 part Cherry Brandy, 1 part Citrus Rum
splash Lime Juice *(Mix into Cocktail Glass—no ice)*

SWEET & SILKY-
1 part Light Rum, 1 part Triple Sec
Light Cream or Milk *(Mix into Cocktail Glass—no ice)*

SWEET & SOUR BOURBON-
Bourbon Whiskey
Orange Juice, splash Sour Mix, Salt *(Mix into Highball Glass—ice)*

SWEET APPLE-
Apple Brandy, splash Ginger Brandy (float)
Lime Juice, splash Grenadine, fill Club Soda *(Mix into Highball Glass—ice)*

SWEET CREAM-
3 parts Coffee Liqueur, 1 part Irish Cream Liqueur (float)
(Mix into Cocktail Glass—no ice)

SWEET DREAMS-
Light Rum
Warm Milk, Sugar, top Whipped Cream, sprinkle Nutmeg
(Mix into Irish Coffee Cup—no ice)

SWEET GOLD-
1 part Light Rum, 1 part Triple Sec
Light Cream or Milk *(Mix into Cocktail Glass—no ice)*

SWEET HEART SIP-
Amaretto
Pineapple Juice *(Mix into Highball Glass—ice)*

SWEET MARIA-
2 parts Vodka, 1 part Amaretto
Light Cream or Milk *(Mix into Cocktail Glass—no ice)*

SWEET MARTINI-
4 parts Gin, 1 part Sweet Vermouth
splash Orange Bitters *(Mix into Cocktail Glass—no ice)*

SWEET NAN-
1 part Brandy, 1 part Sweet Vermouth, splash Bénédictine
(Mix into Small Rocks Glass—ice)

SWEET PATOOTIE-
2 parts Gin, 1 part Triple Sec
Orange Juice *(Mix into Cocktail Glass—no ice)*

SWEET PEACH-
1 part Amaretto, 1 part Peach Schnapps
splash Orange Juice *(Mix into Highball Glass—ice)*

SWEET SENSATION-
Southern Comfort®
Lemon-Lime Soda *(Mix into Highball Glass—ice)*

SWEET TART (1)-
1 part Melon Liqueur, 1 part Southern Comfort®
splash Sour Mix *(Mix into Cocktail Glass—no ice)*

SWEET TART (2)-
1 part Raspberry Liqueur, 1 part Vodka
Pineapple Juice, Lime Juice *(Mix into Highball Glass—ice)*

SWEET TART (3)-
1 part Melon Liqueur, 1 part Vodka
Sour Mix *(Mix into Highball Glass—ice)*

SWEET TART (4)-
Vodka
Cranberry Juice, Pineapple Juice, splash Lime Juice
(Mix into Highball Glass—ice)

SWEETIE BABY-
Amaretto
Vanilla Ice Cream, splash Light Cream or Milk
(Blend with ice in Daiquiri Glass)

SWIMMING POOL-
2 parts Coconut Rum, 1 part Vodka, splash Blue Curaçao (float)
Pineapple Juice, splash Light Cream or Milk
(Mix into Highball Glass—ice)

SWISS & WHOOSH-
1 part Tia Maria®, 1 part Hazelnut Liqueur, 1 part Irish Cream Liqueur
(Layer in Order in Cocktail Glass—no ice)

SWISS FAMILY-
2 parts Blended Whiskey, 1 part Dry Vermouth, splash Anisette
splash Bitters *(Mix into Cocktail Glass—no ice)*

SWISS HIKER-
1 part Swiss Chocolate Almond Liqueur, 1 part Banana Liqueur,
1 part Irish Cream Liqueur
(Layer in Order in Cocktail Glass—no ice)

SWISS MANHATTAN-
3 parts Blended Whiskey, 1 part Cherry Brandy, 1 part Dry Vermouth
(Mix into Cocktail Glass—no ice)

SWISS YODELER-
Light Rum
Sour Mix, splash Molasses *(Mix into Cocktail Glass—no ice)*

SWIZZLE (GENERIC)-
(Any Liqueur)
Sour Mix, Club Soda, Bitters *(Mix into Highball Glass—ice)*

S

– NOTES –

2BORG SPECIAL-
1 part Light Rum, 1 part Drambuie®, 1 part Cherry Brandy
(Layer in Order in Cocktail Glass—no ice)

357 MAGNUM-
2 parts Amaretto, 1 part 151 part-proof Rum, 1 part Vodka
Lemon-Lime Soda *(Mix into Highball Glass—ice)*

2000 FLUSHES-
1 part Blue Curaçao, 1 part Spiced Rum, 1 part Mango Rum
Lemon-Lime Soda *(Mix into Highball Glass—ice)*

T & T-
Tanqueray® Gin
Tonic Water *(Mix into Highball Glass—ice)*

T. K. O.-
1 part Coffee Liqueur, 1 part Licorice Liqueur, 1 part Tequila
(Mix into Cocktail Glass—no ice)

T. L. C. (TEQUILA, LIME, CAMPARI)-
2 parts Tequila, 1 part Campari
Lime Juice, top Club Soda *(Mix into Highball Glass—ice)*

T. L. C. (TEQUILA, LIME, COGNAC)-
2 parts Tequila, 1 part Cognac
Lime Juice *(Mix into Highball Glass—ice)*

T. L. C. (TEQUILA, LIME, COLA)-
Tequila
splash Lime Juice, fill Cola *(Mix into Highball Glass—ice)*

T. N. T. (1)-
1 part Anisette, 1 part Blended Whiskey *(Mix into Cocktail Glass—no ice)*

T. N. T. (2)-
Tequila
Tonic Water *(Mix into Highball Glass—ice)*

T. V. R.-
1 part Tequila, 1 part Vodka, 4 parts Red Bull®
(Layer in Order in Cocktail Glass—no ice)

T. T. T. (TEQUILA, TRIPLE SEC, TONIC)-
Tequila, splash Triple Sec,
Tonic Water *(Mix into Highball Glass—ice)*

T-BIRD-
2 parts Canadian Whiskey, 1 part Amaretto
Pineapple Juice, Orange Juice, splash Grenadine
(Mix into Highball Glass—ice)

T-SHOT-
1 part White Crème de Caçao, 1 part Tia Maria®, 1 part Irish Cream Liqueur,
1 part Light Cream or Milk *(Layer in Order in Cocktail Glass—no ice)*

TAHITI CLUB-
Light Rum, splash Maraschino Liqueur
Pineapple Juice, Lime Juice
(Mix into Small Rocks Glass—ice)

TAHITIAN TEA-
1 part Gin, 1 part Light Rum, 1 part Tropical Fruit Liqueur, 1 part Vodka
Cranberry Juice, Orange Juice, Lemon-Lime Soda
(Mix into Highball Glass—ice)

TAHOE JULIUS-
Vodka
Orange Juice, splash Light Cream or Milk, Sugar
(Blend with ice in Daiquiri Glass)

TAILSPIN-
1 part Gin, 1 part Green Chartreuse, 1 part Sweet Vermouth
splash Orange Bitters
(Mix into Cocktail Glass—no ice)

TAKE FIVE-
2 parts Vodka, 1 part Green Curaçao
Lime Juice *(Mix into Highball Glass—ice)*

TAKE ME HOME-
2 parts Blended Whiskey, 1 part Anisette, 1 part White Crème de Caçao
(Mix into Cocktail Glass—no ice)

TALL BLONDE-
2 parts Aquavit, 1 part Apricot Brandy
Lemon-Lime Soda *(Mix into Highball Glass—ice)*

TALL SHIP-
1 part Coffee Liqueur, 1 part Drambuie®, 1 part Irish Cream Liqueur
(Mix into Small Rocks Glass—ice)

TANGLE FOOT-
1 part Citrus Rum, 1 part Light Rum
Orange Juice, Lime Juice *(Mix into Cocktail Glass—no ice)*

TANGO-
2 parts Gin, 1 part Dry Vermouth, 1 part Sweet Vermouth, splash Triple Sec
Orange Juice *(Mix into Cocktail Glass—no ice)*

TANK-
1 part Jack Daniel's® Tennessee Sour Mash Whiskey, 1 part Gin
(Mix into Small Rocks Glass—ice)

TANNERSWORTH-
2 parts Red Dubonnet®, 1 part Dry Vermouth, 1 part Gin
(Mix into Cocktail Glass—no ice)

TANQUARITA-
Tanqueray® Gin, splash Triple Sec
Sour Mix *(Mix into Cocktail Glass—no ice)*

TANTALUS-
Brandy, splash Forbidden Fruit Liqueur
Lime Juice *(Mix into Small Rocks Glass—ice)*

TARANTULA-
1 part Amaretto, 1 part Canadian Whiskey, 1 part Irish Cream Liqueur
(Mix into Small Rocks Glass—ice)

TARTAN SWIZZLE-
Scotch Whiskey
Sour Mix, splash Bitters, fill Club Soda *(Mix into Highball Glass—ice)*

TARTANTULA-
3 parts Scotch Whiskey, 1 part Bénédictine, 1 part Sweet Vermouth
(Mix into Cocktail Glass—no ice)

TASTY ORGASM-
1 part Peppermint Schnapps, 1 part Irish Cream Liqueur
(Layer in Order in Cocktail Glass—no ice)

TAWNY RUSSIAN-
1 part Amaretto, 1 part Vodka *(Mix into Small Rocks Glass—ice)*

TCHOUPITOLAS STREET GUZZLE-
Light Rum, fill Ginger Beer *(Beer Mug)*

TEA GROG-
1 part Brandy, 1 part Dark Rum
Hot Tea, Honey *(Mix into Irish Coffee Cup—no ice)*

TEA-LISCIOUS-
Amaretto
Hot Tea, top Whipped Cream *(Mix into Irish Coffee Cup—no ice)*

TEACHER'S PET-
3 parts Blended Whiskey, 1 part Dry Vermouth, splash Sweet Vermouth
splash Bitters *(Mix into Small Rocks Glass—ice)*

TEDDY BEAR-
1 part Root Beer Schnapps, 1 part Vodka *(Mix into Cocktail Glass—no ice)*

TEED OFF-
2 parts Brandy, 1 part Peppermint Schnapps
Orange Juice, Pineapple Juice *(Mix into Cocktail Glass—no ice)*

TEMPTATION-
Blended Whiskey, splash Anisette, splash Red Dubonnet®, splash Triple Sec
(Mix into Cocktail Glass—no ice)

TEMPTER-
1 part Apricot Brandy, 1 part Port *(Mix into Cocktail Glass—no ice)*

TEN-GALLON-
1 part Coffee Liqueur, 1 part Gin, 1 part Sweet Vermouth
(Mix into Cocktail Glass—no ice)

TEN QUIDDER-
  2 parts Gin, 1 part Triple Sec, splash Blue Curaçao (lace)
  splash Bitters *(Mix into Small Rocks Glass—ice)*

TENNESSEE-
  Rye Whiskey, splash Maraschino Liqueur
  splash Lime Juice *(Mix into Small Rocks Glass—ice)*

TENNESSEE BOILER MAKER-
  12 oz. Beer, 1 part Jack Daniel's® Tennessee Sour Mash Whiskey
  (Drop Sour Mash Whiskey in Shot Glass into Mug of Beer)

TENNESSEE COFFEE-
  1 part Amaretto, 1 part Jack Daniel's® Tennessee Sour Mash Whiskey
  Coffee, top Whipped Cream *(Mix into Irish Coffee Cup—no ice)*

TENNESSEE MUD (1)-
  3 parts Coffee Liqueur, 3 parts Irish Cream Liqueur, 1 part Jack Daniel's®
    Tennessee Sour Mash Whiskey *(Mix into Small Rocks Glass—ice)*

TENNESSEE MUD (2)-
  1 part Amaretto, 1 part Blended Whiskey
  Coffee, top Whipped Cream *(Mix into Irish Coffee Cup—no ice)*

TENNESSEE TEA-
  1 part Jack Daniel's® Tennessee Sour Mash Whiskey, 1 part Gin, 1 part Light
    Rum, 1 part Triple Sec, 1 part Vodka
  Sour Mix, splash Orange Juice, splash Grenadine, splash Cola (top)
  (Mix into Highball Glass—ice)

TENNESSEE WALTZ-
  Peach Schnapps
  Pineapple Juice, Passion Fruit Juice, Vanilla Ice Cream
  (Blend with ice in Daiquiri Glass)

TEQUILA CANYON-
  Tequila, splash Triple Sec
  Cranberry Juice, splash Orange Juice, splash Pineapple Juice
  (Mix into Highball Glass—ice)

TEQUILA COCKTAIL-
  Tequila
  Lime Juice, splash Grenadine *(Mix into Cocktail Glass—no ice)*

TEQUILA COLADA-
  Tequila
  Sour Mix, Coconut Milk *(Blend with ice in Daiquiri Glass)*

TEQUILA COLLINS-
  Tequila
  Sour Mix, splash Club Soda *(Mix into Highball Glass—ice)*

TEQUILA COMFORT-
  1 part Southern Comfort®, 1 part Tequila
  Orange Juice *(Mix into Highball Glass—ice)*

TEQUILA DAISY-
Tequila, splash Grand Marnier®, splash Raspberry Liqueur
Sour Mix, splash Grenadine, splash Club Soda
(Mix into Sour Glass—ice)

TEQUILA FIZZ-
Tequila
Grenadine, Lime Juice, fill Ginger Ale *(Mix into Highball Glass—ice)*

TEQUILA FROST-
Tequila
Pineapple Juice, Grapefruit Juice, Honey, Grenadine, Vanilla Ice Cream
(Blend with ice in Daiquiri Glass)

TEQUILA GHOST-
2 parts Tequila, 1 part Anisette
splash Lime Juice *(Mix into Small Rocks Glass—ice)*

TEQUILA GIMLET-
Tequila
splash Lime Juice *(Mix into Small Rocks Glass—ice)*

TEQUILA MANHATTAN-
Tequila, splash Sweet Vermouth
splash Lime Juice *(Mix into Cocktail Glass—no ice)*

TEQUILA MARIA-
Tequila
Tomato Juice, Lime Juice, Horseradish, splash Hot Sauce,
    splash Worcestershire Sauce, Salt, Pepper
(Mix into Highball Glass—ice)

TEQUILA MARTINI-
Tequila, splash Sweet Vermouth *(Mix into Cocktail Glass—no ice)*

TEQUILA MATADOR-
Tequila
Pineapple Juice, Lime Juice *(Mix into Highball Glass—ice)*

TEQUILA MOCKINGBIRD (1)-
2 parts Tequila, 1 part Green Crème de Menthe
Lime Juice *(Mix into Cocktail Glass—no ice)*

TEQUILA MOCKINGBIRD (2)-
1 part Swiss Chocolate Almond Liqueur, 1 part Amaretto, 1 part Tequila
(Layer in Order in Cocktail Glass—no ice)

TEQUILA OLD-FASHIONED-
Tequila
Sugar, Bitters, Water, muddle, splash Club Soda
(Mix into Small Rocks Glass—ice)

TEQUILA PARALYZER-
1 part Coffee Liqueur, 1 part Tequila
splash Light Cream or Milk, fill Cola *(Mix into Highball Glass—ice)*

T

TEQUILA PINK-
2 parts Tequila, 1 part Dry Vermouth
Grenadine *(Mix into Cocktail Glass—no ice)*

TEQUILA RICKEY-
Tequila
splash Lime Juice, fill Club Soda *(Mix into Highball Glass—ice)*

TEQUILA ROSA-
2 parts Tequila, 1 part Dry Vermouth
splash Grenadine *(Mix into Cocktail Glass—no ice)*

TEQUILA SCREWDRIVER-
Tequila
Orange Juice *(Mix into Highball Glass—ice)*

TEQUILA SHRINKER-
Tequila
Sour Mix *(Mix into Highball Glass—ice)*

TEQUILA SOUR-
Tequila
Sour Mix *(Mix into Sour Glass— ice)*

TEQUILA STINGER-
2 parts Tequila, 1 part White Crème de Menthe
(Mix into Cocktail Glass—no ice)

TEQUILA SUNBURST-
2 parts Tequila, 1 part Cognac
Orange Juice, splash Grenadine
(Mix into Highball Glass—ice)

TEQUILA SUNRISE-
Tequila
Orange Juice, Grenadine (lace) (stir with straw for "sunrise")
(Mix into Highball Glass—ice)

TEQUILA SUNSET-
Tequila
Grapefruit Juice, Grenadine (lace) (stir with straw for "sunset")
(Mix into Highball Glass—ice)

TEQUILA SUNSET MARGARITA-
4 parts Tequila, 1 part Strawberry Schnapps, 1 part Triple Sec
Sour Mix, Orange Juice
(Mix into Cocktail Glass with no ice or blend with ice in Daiquiri Glass)

TEQUILA TANGO-
2 parts Tequila, 1 part Amaretto
Orange Juice, splash Lemon-Lime Soda *(Mix into Highball Glass—ice)*

TEQUILA TROPICAL-
Tequila
Orange Juice, Lime Juice, splash Grenadine *(Mix into Highball Glass—ice)*

TEQUINI-
Tequila, splash Dry Vermouth *(Mix into Cocktail Glass—no ice)*

TEQUONIC-
Tequila
Lime Juice, Tonic Water *(Mix into Highball Glass—ice)*

TERMINATOR (1)-
1 part Blackberry Brandy, 1 part 151-proof Rum
Cranberry Juice *(Mix into Highball Glass—ice)*

TERMINATOR (2)-
1 part Coffee Liqueur, 1 part Irish Cream Liqueur, 1 part Sambuca, 1 part
Grand Marnier®, 1 part Vodka *(Layer in Order in Cocktail Glass—no ice)*

TEXAS ROSE-
1 part Banana Liqueur, 1 part Light Rum
Orange Juice, Pineapple Juice *(Mix into Highball Glass—ice)*

TEXAS SWEAT-
1 part Grenadine, 1 part Green Crème de Menthe, 1 part Tequila, 1 part Light
Rum *(Layer in Order in Cocktail Glass—no ice)*

TEXAS TEA-
2 parts Tequila, 1 part Light Rum, 1 part Triple Sec, 1 part Vodka
Sour Mix, fill Cola *(Mix into Highball Glass—ice)*

THANKSGIVING COCKTAIL-
1 part Apricot Brandy, 1 part Dry Vermouth, 1 part Gin
splash Lime Juice, Cherry Garnish *(Mix into Cocktail Glass—no ice)*

THANKSGIVING SPECIAL-
1 part Apricot Brandy, 1 part Dry Vermouth, 1 part Gin
splash Lime Juice *(Mix into Cocktail Glass—no ice)*

THAT TIME OF THE MONTH-
1 part Coconut Rum, 1 part Peach Schnapps
Cranberry Juice, Pineapple Juice, splash Grenadine (lace)
(Mix into Highball Glass with ice or blend with ice in Daiquiri Glass)

THIRD DEGREE-
2 parts Gin, 1 part Dry Vermouth, splash Anisette
(Mix into Cocktail Glass—no ice)

THIRD EDITION-
1 part Dry Vermouth, 1 part Gin, 1 part Sweet Vermouth,
splash White Crème de Menthe
splash Orange Bitters *(Mix into Cocktail Glass—no ice)*

THIRD RAIL-
1 part Apple Brandy, 1 part Brandy, 1 part Light Rum, splash Anisette
(Mix into Cocktail Glass—no ice)

THISTLE-
1 part Scotch Whiskey, 1 part Sweet Vermouth
splash Bitters *(Mix into Cocktail Glass—no ice)*

T

THOROUGHBRED COOLER-
Bourbon Whiskey
Orange Juice, Sour Mix, splash Grenadine, fill Lemon-Lime Soda
(Mix into Highball Glass—ice)

THREE BASE HIT-
1 part Bourbon Whiskey, 1 part Brandy, 1 part Light Rum, splash Amaretto
splash Lime Juice *(Mix into Cocktail Glass—no ice)*

THREE MILES-
2 parts Brandy, 1 part Light Rum
splash Lime Juice, splash Grenadine *(Mix into Cocktail Glass—no ice)*

THREE MILLER-
2 parts Light Rum, 1 part Brandy
Lime Juice, Grenadine *(Mix into Cocktail Glass—no ice)*

THREE STRIPES-
2 parts Gin, 1 part Dry Vermouth
Orange Juice *(Mix into Cocktail Glass—no ice)*

THREE WISE MEN-
1 part Jack Daniel's® Tennessee Sour Mash Whiskey, 1 part Jim Beam® Whiskey,
1 part Johnnie Walker® Red Scotch Whiskey
(Mix into Cocktail Glass—no ice)

THRILLER-
Scotch Whiskey, fill Ginger Beer
Orange Juice *(Beer Mug)*

THUNDER-
Brandy
Sugar, Cayenne Pepper *(Mix into Cocktail Glass—no ice)*

THUNDER & LIGHTNING-
Brandy
Sugar *(Mix into Cocktail Glass—no ice)*

THUNDER CLAP-
2 parts Blended Whiskey, 1 part Brandy, 1 part Gin
(Mix into Cocktail Glass—no ice)

THUNDER CLOUD-
1 part Crème de Noyaux, 1 part Blue Curaçao, 1 part Amaretto, 1 part Vodka,
1 part Sour Mix, 1 part Lemon-Lime Soda
(Layer in Order in Highball Glass with no ice Use straw to "whirl" gently)

THURSTON HOWELL-
2 parts Spiced Rum, 1 part Banana Liqueur
Orange Juice, Sour Mix, splash Grenadine (lace after blend)
(Blend with ice in Daiquiri Glass)

TIDAL WAVE-
2 parts Melon Liqueur, 1 part Coconut Rum
Orange Juice, Pineapple Juice, Sour Mix
(Mix into Highball Glass with ice or blend with ice in Daiquiri Glass)

TIDBIT-
Gin, splash Dry Sherry
Vanilla Ice Cream *(Blend with ice in Daiquiri Glass)*

TIDY BOWL (1)-
1 part Blue Curaçao, 1 part Licorice Liqueur
(Mix into Small Rocks Glass—ice)

TIDY BOWL (2)-
1 part Blue Curaçao, 1 part Vodka *(Mix into Small Rocks Glass—ice)*

TIE ME TO THE BEDPOST-
1 part Citrus Vodka, 1 part Coconut Rum, 1 part Melon Liqueur
Sour Mix *(Mix into Cocktail Glass—no ice)*

TIGER JUICE-
Canadian Whiskey
Orange Juice, Lime Juice *(Mix into Cocktail Glass—no ice)*

TIGER TAIL-
Licorice Liqueur, splash Triple Sec
Orange Juice *(Mix into Highball Glass—ice)*

TIGER'S MILK-
1 part Brandy, 1 part Jamaican Rum
Sugar, Light Cream or Milk *(Mix into Small Rocks Glass—ice)*

TIGHT SNATCH-
2 parts Light Rum, 1 part Peach Schnapps
Pineapple Juice *(Mix into Highball Glass—ice)*

TIJUANA BLUES MARGARITA-
4 parts Tequila, 1 part Blue Curaçao
Sour Mix
(Mix into Cocktail Glass with no ice or blend with ice in Daiquiri Glass)

TIJUANA BULL DOG-
2 parts Tequila, 1 part Coffee Liqueur
Light Cream or Milk, splash Cola *(Mix into Highball Glass—ice)*

TIJUANA SUNRISE-
Tequila
Orange Juice, splash Bitters (lace) *(Mix into Highball Glass—ice)*

TIJUANA TAXI-
2 parts Tequila, 1 part Blue Curaçao, 1 part Tropical Fruit Schnapps
Lemon-Lime Soda *(Mix into Highball Glass—ice)*

TIKKI DREAM-
Melon Liqueur
Cranberry Juice *(Mix into Highball Glass—ice)*

TILT THE KILT-
Scotch Whiskey, splash Triple Sec (float)
Sour Mix, Water *(Mix into Cocktail Glass—no ice)*

TIME KILLER-
Tequila, fill Mexican Beer
Salt (optional) *(Beer Mug)*

TIN WEDDING-
1 part Brandy, 1 part Gin, 1 part Sweet Vermouth
splash Orange Bitters *(Mix into Cocktail Glass—no ice)*

TINTON-
1 part Apple Brandy, 1 part Port *(Mix into Cocktail Glass—no ice)*

TIPPERARY-
1 part Green Chartreuse, 1 part Irish Whiskey, 1 part Sweet Vermouth
(Mix into Cocktail Glass—no ice)

TIPSY TURTLE-
1 part Banana Liqueur, 1 part Coconut Rum, 1 part Dark Rum, 1 part Light
Rum, 1 part Vodka
Orange Juice, Pineapple Juice, splash Grenadine
(Mix into Highball Glass with ice or blend with ice in Daiquiri Glass)

TIVOLI-
3 parts Bourbon Whiskey, 1 part Aquavit, 1 part Sweet Vermouth,
splash Campari *(Mix into Cocktail Glass—no ice)*

TO HELL WITH SWORDS & GARTERS-
2 parts Scotch Whiskey, 1 part Dry Vermouth
Pineapple Juice *(Mix into Highball Glass—ice)*

TO THE MOON-
1 part Amaretto, 1 part Coffee Liqueur, 1 part Irish Cream Liqueur,
1 part 151-proof Rum *(Mix into Cocktail Glass—no ice)*

TOASTED ALMOND-
2 parts Coffee Liqueur, 1 part Amaretto
Light Cream or Milk *(Mix into Highball Glass—ice)*

TOBAGO CAYS-
Gold Rum, splash Maraschino Liqueur, splash Licorice Liqueur (float)
Sour Mix *(Blend with ice in Daiquiri Glass)*

TODDY (GENERIC)-
(Any Liqueur)
Water, Sugar *(Mix into Highball Glass—ice)*

TOE WARMER-
1 part Blended Whiskey, 1 part Coffee Liqueur, 1 part Hazelnut Liqueur,
1 part Irish Cream Liqueur, 1 part Tequila
Coffee, top Whipped Cream *(Mix into Irish Coffee Cup—no ice)*

TOKYO TEA-
1 part Gin, 1 part Light Rum, 1 part Melon Liqueur, 1 part Triple Sec,
1 part Vodka
Sour Mix, splash Orange Juice, splash Grenadine, splash Cola (top)
(Mix into Highball Glass—ice)

TOM & JERRY-
1 part Brandy, 1 part Dark Rum
Hot Milk or Hot Water, Sugar, sprinkle Nutmeg
(Mix into Irish Coffee Cup—no ice)

TOM COLLINS-
Gin
Sour Mix, splash Club Soda *(Mix into Highball Glass—ice)*

TOMAHAWK-
1 part Canadian Whiskey, 1 part Spiced Rum, splash Triple Sec
Sour Mix *(Mix into Highball Glass—ice)*

TOMAKAZI-
1 part Gin, 1 part Vodka
Sour Mix, splash Cola (optional) *(Mix into Highball Glass—ice)*

TOMBOY (1)-
Red Dubonnet®
Club Soda *(Mix into Highball Glass—ice)*

TOMBOY (2)-
Beer
Tomato Juice *(Mix into Highball Glass—ice)*

TOOTSIE ROLL (1)-
1 part Brown Crème de Cacao, 1 part Hazelnut Liqueur, 1 part Tia Maria®
(Mix into Small Rocks Glass—ice)

TOOTSIE ROLL (2)-
1 part Brown Crème de Cacao, 1 part Hazelnut Liqueur, 1 part Tia Maria®
Light Cream or Milk *(Mix into Highball Glass—ice)*

TOOTSIE ROLL (3)-
1 part Coffee Liqueur, 1 part Vodka
Orange Juice *(Mix into Highball Glass—ice)*

TOOTSIE ROLL (4)
Coffee Liqueur
Orange Juice *(Mix into Highball Glass—ice)*

TOP BANANA-
1 part Banana Liqueur, 1 part Vodka
Orange Juice *(Mix into Highball Glass—ice)*

TOP GUN-
Light Rum
Guava Juice, Orange Juice, Lime Juice *(Blend with ice in Daiquiri Glass)*

TOP TEN-
Spiced Rum
Light Cream or Milk, Coconut Milk, Cola *(Blend with ice in Daiquiri Glass)*

TOREADOR-
3 parts Tequila, 1 part Crème de Cacao
Light Cream or Milk, top Whipped Cream *(Mix into Cocktail Glass—no ice)*

TORONJA-
Gin
Grapefruit Juice, Lime Juice
(Mix into Cocktail Glass—no ice)

TORPEDO-
2 parts Apple Brandy, 1 part Brandy, splash Gin
(Mix into Cocktail Glass—no ice)

TORRIDORA-
3 parts Light Rum, 1 part Coffee Brandy, 1 part 151-proof Rum (float)
Light Cream or Milk *(Mix into Cocktail Glass—no ice)*

TOTAL MADNESS-
1 part DeKuyper® Mad Melon Watermelon Schnapps, 1 part Vodka
(Mix into Cocktail Glass—no ice)

TOVARICH-
2 parts Vodka, 1 part Kümmel
Lime Juice *(Mix into Cocktail Glass—no ice)*

TOWER TOPPER-
3 parts Canadian Whiskey, 1 part Grand Marnier®
Light Cream or Milk *(Mix into Cocktail Glass—no ice)*

TOXIC WASTE-
1 part Blue Curaçao, 1 part Melon Liqueur, 1 part Vodka
Orange Juice, Pineapple Juice, Sour Mix
(Mix into Highball Glass—ice)

TRADE WINDS-
4 parts Gold Rum, 1 part Plum Brandy
Sour Mix *(Mix into Highball Glass—ice)*

TRAFFIC LIGHT (1)-
1 part Green Crème de Menthe, 1 part Banana Liqueur, 1 part Sloe Gin
(Layer in Order in Cocktail Glass—no ice)

TRAFFIC LIGHT (2)-
1 part Crème de Noyaux, 1 part Galliano®, 1 part Melon Liqueur
(Layer in Order in Cocktail Glass—no ice)

TRAFFIC LIGHT COOLER-
2 parts Melon Liqueur, 2 parts Gold Tequila, splash Sour Mix, 1 part Orange
Juice, 1 part Sloe Gin
(Layer in Order in Cocktail Glass—no ice)

TRANSAMERICA-
Irish Whiskey
Pineapple Juice, Coconut Milk, splash Lime Juice, top Club Soda
(Blend with ice in Daiquiri Glass)

TRAVELER'S JOY-
1 part Cherry Brandy, 1 part Gin
Lime Juice *(Mix into Cocktail Glass—no ice)*

T

TREASURE CHEST-
2 parts Chocolate Almond Liqueur, 1 part Amaretto, 1 part Gold Rum
Light Cream or Milk
(Mix into Highball Glass with ice or blend with ice in Daiquiri Glass)

TRIAD-
1 part Amaretto, 1 part Light Rum, 1 part Sweet Vermouth
Ginger Ale *(Mix into Highball Glass—ice)*

TRICYCLE-
Triple Sec
Light Cream or Milk, Orange Juice *(Mix into Highball Glass—ice)*

TRIFECTA-
1 part 151-proof Rum, 1 part Banana Liqueur, 1 part Irish Cream Liqueur
Light Cream or Milk *(Mix into Highball Glass—ice)*

TRILBY-
2 parts Bourbon Whiskey, 1 part Sweet Vermouth
splash Orange Bitters *(Mix into Cocktail Glass—no ice)*

TRINIDAD-
Light Rum
Sour Mix, splash Bitters *(Mix into Cocktail Glass—no ice)*

TRINIDAD SWIZZLE-
1 part Dark Rum, 1 part Grand Marnier®, 1 part Light Rum
Lime Juice, Mango Juice, splash Grenadine *(Mix into Cocktail Glass—no ice)*

TRINITY-
1 part Dry Vermouth, 1 part Gin, 1 part Sweet Vermouth
(Mix into Cocktail Glass—no ice)

TRIPLE A-
1 part Cherry Brandy, 1 part Gin
Lime Juice *(Mix into Cocktail Glass—no ice)*

TRIPLE IRISH-
1 part Irish Whiskey, 1 part Irish Cream Liqueur, 1 part Irish Mist®
(Layer in Order in Cocktail Glass—no ice)

TRIPLE T-
1 part Tanqueray® Gin, 1 part Tequila, 1 part Wild Turkey® Bourbon Whiskey
(Mix into Cocktail Glass—no ice)

TRIPLET-
1 part Dry Vermouth, 1 part Gin, 1 part Peach Schnapps
splash Lime Juice *(Mix into Cocktail Glass—no ice)*

TROIS RIVIERES-
Canadian Whiskey, splash Red Dubonnet®, splash Triple Sec
(Mix into Small Rocks Glass—ice)

TROLLEY-
Bourbon Whiskey
Cranberry Juice, Pineapple Juice *(Mix into Highball Glass—ice)*

TROLLEY CAR (1)-
1 part Amaretto, 1 part Strawberry Schnapps
Vanilla Ice Cream, Strawberry Daiquiri Mix
(Blend with ice in Daiquiri Glass)

TROLLEY CAR (2)-
1 part Amaretto, 1 part Strawberry Schnapps
Light Cream or Milk *(Mix into Highball Glass—ice)*

TROPIC COLADA-
1 part Banana Liqueur, 1 part Strawberry Schnapps
Pineapple Juice, Coconut Milk *(Blend with ice in Daiquiri Glass)*

TROPIC FREEZE-
Spiced Rum
Orange Juice, Pineapple Juice, Coconut Milk, splash Grenadine
(Blend with ice in Daiquiri Glass)

TROPICA-
Light Rum
Pineapple Juice, Grapefruit Juice, splash Grenadine
(Mix into Highball Glass—ice)

TROPICAL-
1 part Dry Vermouth, 1 part Maraschino Liqueur, 1 part White Crème de Caçao
splash Bitters
(Mix into Cocktail Glass—no ice)

TROPICAL BIRD-
2 parts Gold Rum, 1 part Dark Jamaican Rum, 1 part Dry Vermouth,
splash Raspberry Liqueur
Lime Juice *(Mix into Cocktail Glass—no ice)*

TROPICAL BREEZE-
2 parts Light Rum, 1 part Banana Liqueur
Orange Juice, Coconut Milk, Pineapple Slice
(Blend with ice in Daiquiri Glass)

TROPICAL DELIGHT-
2 parts Spiced Rum, 1 part Banana Liqueur, 1 part Brown Crème de Caçao
Light Cream or Milk *(Blend with ice in Daiquiri Glass)*

TROPICAL HEART-
Tropical Fruit Schnapps
Hot Apple Cider *(Mix into Irish Coffee Cup—no ice)*

TROPICAL HEAT-
1 part Tropical Fruit Schnapps, 1 part Vodka
Pineapple Juice
(Mix into Highball Glass—ice)

TROPICAL ICED TEA-
1 part Gin, 1 part Light Rum, 1 part Triple Sec, 1 part Vodka
Cranberry Juice, Pineapple Juice, Sour Mix, Sugar, Grenadine
(Mix into Highball Glass—ice)

TROPICAL ITCH-
1 part Coconut Rum, 1 part Melon Liqueur
Pineapple Juice, Sour Mix *(Mix into Highball Glass—ice)*

TROPICAL PARADISE-
Spiced Rum
Orange Juice, Coconut Milk, splash Grenadine, Bananas
(Blend with ice in Daiquiri Glass)

TROPICAL PEACH-
Peach Schnapps
Orange Juice, Orange Sherbet, Sour Mix, Coconut Milk
(Blend with ice in Daiquiri Glass)

TROPICAL RAIN STORM-
3 parts Dark Rum, 1 part Cherry Brandy, splash Triple Sec
splash Lime Juice *(Mix into Cocktail Glass—no ice)*

TROPICAL SHOT (1)-
1 part Tropical Fruit Schnapps, 1 part Light Rum
Orange Juice, Pineapple Juice *(Mix into Highball Glass—ice)*

TROPICAL SHOT (2)-
2 parts Margarita Schnapps, 1 part Vodka
Pineapple Juice *(Mix into Highball Glass—ice)*

TROPICAL SPECIAL-
3 parts Gin, 1 part Triple Sec
Grapefruit Juice, Orange Juice, Lime Juice
(Mix into Highball Glass—ice)

TROPICAL SPICED TEA-
Spiced Rum
Iced Tea, splash Lime Juice *(Mix into Highball Glass—ice)*

TROPICAL STORM-
2 parts Dark Rum, 1 part Banana Liqueur
Orange Juice, splash Grenadine, Bananas
(Blend with ice in Daiquiri Glass)

TROPICAL STORM GIMLET-
1 part Amaretto, 1 part Vodka
Lime Juice, splash Grapefruit Juice *(Mix into Small Rocks Glass—ice)*

TROPICAL TREASURE-
2 parts Melon Liqueur, 1 part Banana Liqueur
Pineapple Juice, Coconut Milk *(Blend with ice in Daiquiri Glass)*

TROPICAL WAVE-
Coconut Rum
Orange Juice, splash Cranberry Juice *(Mix into Highball Glass—ice)*

TROPICANA-
1 part Gin, 1 part Grand Marnier®, splash Triple Sec
Orange Juice *(Mix into Cocktail Glass—no ice)*

TROUBLE FOR TINA-
  3 parts Light Rum, 1 part Dark Rum, 1 part Brown Crème de Cacao
  Warm Coffee, top Whipped Cream
  (Mix into Irish Coffee Cup—no ice)

TRUE TRIXIE-
  2 parts Campari, 1 part Dry Vermouth, 1 part Triple Sec
  (Mix into Small Rocks Glass—ice)

TU TU CHERRY-
  4 parts Dark Rum, 1 part Cherry Brandy
  Cranberry Juice, Orange Juice
  (Mix into Highball Glass—ice)

TULIP-
  1 part Apple Brandy, 1 part Sweet Vermouth, splash Apricot Brandy
  Lime Juice
  (Mix into Cocktail Glass—no ice)

TUMBLEWEED-
  1 part Amaretto, 1 part White Crème de Cacao
  Light Cream or Milk
  (Mix into Highball Glass—ice)

TURBO-
  1 part Apple Schnapps, 1 part Peach Schnapps, 1 part Vodka
  Cranberry Juice *(Mix into Highball Glass—ice)*

TURF-
  2 parts Gin, 1 part Dry Vermouth, splash Anisette, splash Maraschino Liqueur
  splash Bitters *(Mix into Small Rocks Glass—ice)*

TURKEY COCKTAIL-
  3 parts 101-proof Wild Turkey® Bourbon Whiskey, 1 part White Crème de
      Menthe (float) *(Mix into Cocktail Glass—no ice)*

TURKEY TROT-
  2 parts Wild Turkey® Bourbon Whiskey, 1 part 101-proof Wild Turkey®
      Bourbon Whiskey
  Lemon Peel Garnish
  (Mix into Small Rocks Glass—ice)

TURTLE-
  4 parts Canadian Whiskey, 1 part Bénédictine
  (Mix into Cocktail Glass—no ice)

TURTLE DOVE-
  4 parts Dark Rum, 1 part Amaretto
  Orange Juice
  (Mix into Highball Glass with ice or blend with ice in Daiquiri Glass)

TUTTI FRUITI-
  3 parts Gin, 1 part Amaretto, 1 part Maraschino Liqueur
  Apples, Peaches, Pears
  (Blend with ice in Daiquiri Glass)

TUTTI FRUITI CRUSH-
1 part Banana Liqueur, 1 part Melon Liqueur, 1 part Strawberry Schnapps
Pineapple Juice, Orange Sherbet, splash Grenadine
(Blend with ice in Daiquiri Glass)

TUXEDO (1)-
1 part Dry Vermouth, 1 part Gin, splash Anisette, splash Maraschino Liqueur
splash Bitters *(Mix into Cocktail Glass—no ice)*

TUXEDO (2)-
Fino Sherry, splash Anisette, splash Maraschino Liqueur
splash Bitters *(Mix into Cocktail Glass—no ice)*

TV TOWER-
1 part Grenadine, 1 part Blue Curaçao, 1 part Sherry
(Layer in Order in Cocktail Glass—no ice)

TWENTY THOUSAND LEAGUES-
2 parts Gin, 1 part Dry Vermouth, splash Anisette
splash Orange Bitters
(Mix into Cocktail Glass—no ice)

TWILIGHT ZONE-
1 part Light Rum, 1 part Spiced Rum
Grenadine *(Mix into Small Rocks Glass—ice)*

TWIN HILLS-
Blended Whiskey, splash Bénédictine
Sour Mix *(Mix into Sour Glass—ice)*

TWIN PEACH-
Peach Schnapps
Cranberry Juice
(Mix into Highball Glass—ice)

TWIN PEAKS-
3 parts Blended Whiskey, 1 part Red Dubonnet®, splash Triple Sec
(Mix into Cocktail Glass—no ice)

TWIN SIX-
2 parts Gin, 1 part Sweet Vermouth
Orange Juice, splash Grenadine
(Mix into Cocktail Glass—no ice)

TWISTER (1)-
Vodka
Lime Juice, Lemon-Lime Soda *(Mix into Highball Glass—ice)*

TWISTER (2)-
1 part Southern Comfort®, 1 part Tequila, 1 part Vodka
(Layer in Order in Cocktail Glass—no ice)

TWO TURTLES-
4 parts Canadian Whiskey, 1 part Bénédictine, 1 part Triple Sec
(Mix into Cocktail Glass—no ice)

TWO-WHEELER-
Triple Sec
Orange Juice, Light Cream or Milk *(Mix into Cocktail Glass—no ice)*

TYPHOON-
2 parts Gin, 1 part Anisette, fill Champagne
Lime Juice *(Mix into Champagne Flute—no ice)*

TYPHOON BETTY-
2 parts Cherry Marnier, 1 part Cherry Brandy, 1 part Ginger Brandy
(Mix into Cocktail Glass—no ice)

TYROL-
2 parts Galliano®, 1 part Brandy, 1 part Green Chartreuse
Light Cream or Milk, sprinkle Nutmeg *(Mix into Cocktail Glass—no ice)*

– NOTES –

_____

_____

_____

_____

_____

_____

_____

_____

_____

_____

_____

_____

_____

_____

_____

_____

_____

_____

UGLY-
2 parts Light Rum, 1 part Apricot Brandy, 1 part Blue Curaçao
Grenadine, Lime Juice, fill Ginger Ale *(Mix into Highball Glass—ice)*

ULANDA-
2 parts Gin, 1 part Triple Sec, splash Anisette *(Mix into Cocktail Glass—no ice)*

ULTIMATE ARCTIC MARTINI-
Finlandia® Vodka, splash Dry Vermouth
splash Lime Juice *(Mix into Cocktail Glass—no ice)*

ULTIMATE CHOCOLATE MARTINI-
2 parts Chocolate Liqueur, 2 parts Vodka, 1 part Irish Cream Liqueur,
1 part Raspberry Liqueur, 1 part White Crème de Caçao
(Mix into Cocktail Glass—no ice)

UNABOMBER-
1 part Gin, 1 part Vodka, 1 part Triple Sec
Lime Juice *(Mix into Highball Glass—ice)*

UNDER THE COVERS (1)-
1 part Irish Cream Liqueur, 1 part Peach Schnapps, 1 part Vodka
(Mix into Small Rocks Glass—ice)

UNDER THE COVERS (2)-
1 part Irish Cream Liqueur, 1 part Peach Schnapps, 1 part Sambuca
(Mix into Small Rocks Glass—ice)

UNIFIED TEAM (1)-
3 parts Vodka, 1 part Light Rum, 1 part Triple Sec
Sour Mix *(Mix into Cocktail Glass—no ice)*

UNIFIED TEAM COCKTAIL (2)-
3 parts Vodka, 1 part Blue Curaçao, 1 part Light Rum
Sour Mix *(Mix into Cocktail Glass—no ice)*

UNION JACK (1)-
2 parts Gin, 1 part Sloe Gin
splash Grenadine *(Mix into Cocktail Glass—no ice)*

UNION JACK (2)-
2 parts Dark Rum, 1 part Apple Brandy
Lime Juice, splash Grenadine (float) *(Mix into Cocktail Glass—no ice)*

UNION LEAGUE-
2 parts Gin, 1 part Port
splash Orange Bitters *(Mix into Small Rocks Glass—ice)*

UNIVERSITY-
Scotch Whiskey, splash Triple Sec
Chocolate Milk, top Chocolate sprinkles *(Mix into Highball Glass—ice)*

UNIVERSITY UNIVERSAL-
1 part Amaretto, 1 part Melon Liqueur, 1 part Vodka
Pineapple Juice, Sour Mix *(Mix into Highball Glass—ice)*

UP IN THE AIR-
  Gin, splash Maraschino Liqueur
  Lime Juice *(Mix into Cocktail Glass—no ice)*

UP TO DATE-
  1 part Blended Whiskey, 1 part Sherry, splash Triple Sec
  splash Bitters *(Mix into Cocktail Glass—no ice)*

UPGRADED LINUX-
  1 part Triple Sec, 1 part Vodka
  splash Lime Juice, fill Cola *(Mix into Highball Glass—ice)*

URBAN COWBOY-
  1 part Grand Marnier®, 1 part Jack Daniel's® Tennessee Sour Mash Whiskey,
    1 part Southern Comfort® *(Mix into Small Rocks Glass—ice)*

URBAN VIOLENCE-
  1 part Blue Curaçao, 1 part Coconut Rum, 1 part Vodka, splash Banana
    Liqueur, splash Strawberry Schnapps
  Orange Juice *(Mix into Highball Glass—ice)*

URINE SAMPLE (1)-
  1 part 100-proof Vodka, 1 part Yellow Gatorade®
  (Layer in Order in Cocktail Glass—no ice)

URINE SAMPLE (2)-
  1 part Amaretto, 1 part Coconut Rum
  Orange Juice, Pineapple Juice *(Mix into Highball Glass—ice)*

URQUHART CASTLE-
  Scotch Whiskey, splash Dry Vermouth, splash Triple Sec
  splash Orange Bitters *(Mix into Small Rocks Glass—ice)*

UVULA-
  Brandy, splash Maraschino Liqueur
  Pineapple Juice, splash Lime Juice *(Mix into Cocktail Glass—no ice)*

– NOTES –

_____

_____

_____

_____

_____

_____

_____

_____

_____

VALENCIA-
 Apricot Brandy
 splash Orange Juice, splash Orange Bitters *(Mix into Cocktail Glass—no ice)*

VAMPIRE-
 1 part Raspberry Liqueur, 1 part Vodka
 Cranberry Juice *(Mix into Highball Glass—ice)*

VAN-
 2 parts Gin, 1 part Dry Vermouth, splash Grand Marnier®
 (Mix into Cocktail Glass—no ice)

VAN DUSSEN-
 2 parts Gin, 1 part Dry Vermouth, splash Grand Marnier®
 (Mix into Cocktail Glass—no ice)

VAN VLEET-
 Light Rum
 Lime Juice, Maple Syrup *(Mix into Small Rocks Glass—ice)*

VANCOUVER COCKTAIL-
 2 parts Canadian Whiskey, 1 part Red Dubonnet®
 Sour Mix, splash Bitters *(Mix into Cocktail Glass—no ice)*

VANDERBILT-
 2 parts Brandy, 1 part Cherry Brandy
 Sugar, splash Bitters *(Mix into Cocktail Glass—no ice)*

VANESSA'S VICE-***
 1 part Amaretto, 1 part Bärenjäger®, 1 part Coffee Liqueur,
   1 part Goldschläger®, 1 part Irish Cream Liqueur
 Light Cream or Milk *(Mix into Highball Glass—ice)*

VANITY FAIR (1)-
 2 parts Apple Brandy, 1 part Cherry Brandy, splash Crème de Noyaux (float)
 (Mix into Cocktail Glass—no ice)

VANITY FAIR (2)-
 4 parts Apple Brandy, 2 parts Cherry Brandy, 1 part Maraschino Liqueur,
   splash Amaretto (float) *(Mix into Cocktail Glass—no ice)*

VELOCITY-
 2 parts Sweet Vermouth, 1 part Gin *(Mix into Cocktail Glass—no ice)*

VELVET DRESS-
 1 part Brandy, 1 part Coffee Liqueur, 1 part Triple Sec
 Light Cream or Milk *(Mix into Highball Glass—ice)*

VELVET HAMMER (1)-
 Vodka, splash Brown Crème de Cacao
 Light Cream or Milk *(Mix into Cocktail Glass—no ice)*

VELVET HAMMER (2)-
 1 part Triple Sec, 1 part White Crème de Cacao
 Light Cream or Milk *(Mix into Highball Glass—ice)*

VELVET KISS-
   3 parts Gin, 1 part Banana Liqueur
   Light Cream or Milk, splash Pineapple Juice
   (Mix into Cocktail Glass—no ice)

VELVET PEACH HAMMER-
   2 parts Vodka, 1 part Peach Schnapps
   splash Sour Mix *(Mix into Small Rocks Glass—ice)*

VENETIAN COFFEE-
   Brandy
   Coffee, Sugar, top Whipped Cream *(Mix into Irish Coffee Cup—no ice)*

VENOM-
   1 part Yukon Jack® Canadian Liqueur, 1 part Lime Juice
   (Layer in Order in Cocktail Glass—no ice)

VENUSIAN FLAME WATER-
   Pineapple Wine
   Grenadine *(Mix into Wine Glass—ice)*

VERACRUZ-
   3 parts Mexican Rum, 1 part Dry Vermouth
   Sour Mix, Pineapple Juice *(Mix into Highball Glass—ice)*

VERBOTEN-
   Gin, splash Forbidden Fruit Liqueur
   splash Orange Juice, splash Lime Juice *(Mix into Cocktail Glass—no ice)*

VERMOUTH CASSIS-
   2 parts Dry Vermouth, 1 part Crème de Cassis
   Club Soda *(Mix into Highball Glass—ice)*

VERMOUTH COCKTAIL-
   1 part Dry Vermouth, 1 part Sweet Vermouth
   splash Orange Bitters *(Mix into Cocktail Glass—no ice)*

VERONA-
   2 parts Amaretto, 2 parts Gin, 1 part Sweet Vermouth
   splash Lime Juice *(Mix into Small Rocks Glass—ice)*

VERY BERRY COLADA-
   2 parts Wild Berry Schnapps, 1 part Dark Rum
   Pineapple Juice, Coconut Milk *(Blend with ice in Daiquiri Glass)*

VESPER-
   2 parts Gin, 1 part Vodka, splash Lillet *(Mix into Cocktail Glass—no ice)*

VESUVIO (1)-
   2 parts Light Rum, 1 part Sweet Vermouth
   Sour Mix *(Mix into Small Rocks Glass—ice)*

VESUVIO (2)-
   White Wine, splash Amaretto, splash Apricot Brandy
   (Mix into Wine Glass—ice)

VETERAN-
4 parts Dark Rum, 1 part Cherry Brandy *(Mix into Small Rocks Glass—ice)*

VIA VENETO-
3 parts Brandy, 1 part Sambuca
Sour Mix *(Mix into Highball Glass—ice)*

VICIOUS SID-
3 parts Light Rum, 1 part Southern Comfort®, 1 part Triple Sec
splash Lime Juice, splash Bitters
(Mix into Small Rocks Glass—ice)

VICKER'S TREAT-
Vodka
Lemonade, splash Bitters *(Mix into Highball Glass—ice)*

VICTOR-
2 parts Gin, 1 part Brandy, 1 part Sweet Vermouth
(Mix into Cocktail Glass—no ice)

VICTORY-
Licorice Liqueur
splash Grenadine, fill Club Soda *(Mix into Highball Glass—ice)*

VICTORY COLLINS-
Vodka
Sour Mix, Grape Juice *(Mix into Highball Glass—ice)*

VIKING (1)-
1 part Aquavit, 1 part Galliano® *(Mix into Small Rocks Glass—ice)*

VIKING (2)-
1 part Aquavit, 1 part Citrus Rum
Lime Juice *(Mix into Small Rocks Glass—ice)*

VILE GREEN STUFF-
1 part Melon Liqueur, 1 part Peach Schnapps
Orange Juice, splash Club Soda (top)
(Mix into Highball Glass—ice)

VILLA BELLA FIZZ-
2 parts Cherry Brandy, 1 part Light Rum
Sour Mix, splash Club Soda *(Mix into Highball Glass—ice)*

VINCENNES-
2 parts Blended Whiskey, 2 parts Red Dubonnet®, 1 part Triple Sec,
splash Licorice Liqueur *(Mix into Cocktail Glass—no ice)*

VINCOW SOMBA-
1 part Triple Sec, 1 part Vodka
Pineapple Juice *(Mix into Highball Glass—ice)*

VIOLET CRUMBLE-
1 part Butterscotch Schnapps, 1 part Brown Crème de Caçao
(Layer in Order in Cocktail Glass—no ice)

VIOLET FIZZ-
3 parts Gin, 1 part Raspberry Liqueur
splash Light Cream or Milk, splash Sour Mix, fill Club Soda
(Mix into Highball Glass—ice)

VIRGIN-
2 parts Forbidden Fruit Liqueur, 2 parts Gin, 1 part White Crème de Menthe
(Mix into Cocktail Glass—no ice)

VIRGIN ISLANDS RUM PUNCH-
Light Rum
Grapefruit Juice, Orange Juice, Sour Mix, splash Grenadine, splash Bitters
(Mix into Highball Glass—ice)

VIRGIN'S KISS-
3 parts Dark Rum, 1 part Apricot Brandy, 1 part Galliano®
Pineapple Juice, Sour Mix
(Mix into Highball Glass—ice)

VIRTUAL REALITY-
2 parts Gin, 1 part Apple Brandy, splash Champagne (top)
Lime Juice, Grenadine
(Mix into Highball Glass—ice)

VIVA VILLA-
Tequila
Sour Mix, Salted Rim *(Mix into Small Rocks Glass—ice)*

VLADIMIR-
2 parts Vodka, 1 part Crème de Cassis
Grenadine *(Mix into Small Rocks Glass—ice)*

VODKA "7"-
Vodka
Lime Juice, Club Soda *(Mix into Highball Glass—ice)*

VODKA & TONIC-
Vodka
Tonic Water, Lime Garnish *(Mix into Highball Glass—ice)*

VODKA COLLINS-
Vodka
Sour Mix, splash Club Soda *(Mix into Highball Glass—ice)*

VODKA COOLER-
Vodka
Club Soda, Sugar, fill Ginger Ale *(Mix into Highball Glass—ice)*

VODKA DAISY-
Vodka
Sour Mix, splash Grenadine *(Beer Mug)*

VODKA GIBSON-
Vodka, splash Dry Vermouth
Onion Garnish *(Mix into Cocktail Glass—no ice)*

VODKA GIMLET-
Vodka
Lime Juice *(Mix into Small Rocks Glass—ice)*

VODKA GRAND MARNIER-
4 parts Vodka, 1 part Grand Marnier®
splash Lime Juice, Orange Garnish *(Mix into Cocktail Glass—no ice)*

VODKA GRASSHOPPER (1)-
1 part Green Crème de Menthe, 1 part Vodka, 1 part White Crème de Caçao
Light Cream or Milk *(Mix into Highball Glass—ice)*

VODKA GRASSHOPPER (2)-
1 part Green Crème de Menthe, 1 part Vodka, 1 part White Crème de Caçao
(Mix into Cocktail Glass—no ice)

VODKA MARTINI-
Vodka, splash Dry Vermouth
Lemon Twist or Olive Garnish *(Mix into Cocktail Glass—no ice)*

VODKA RICKEY-
Vodka
splash Lime Juice, fill Club Soda *(Mix into Highball Glass—ice)*

VODKA SAKETINI-
Vodka, splash Sake *(Mix into Cocktail Glass—no ice)*

VODKA SALTY DOG-
Vodka
Grapefruit Juice, Salt *(Mix into Highball Glass—ice)*

VODKA SLING-
Vodka
Sour Mix, splash Water *(Mix into Small Rocks Glass—ice)*

VODKA SOUR-
Vodka
Sour Mix *(Mix into Sour Glass— ice)*

VODKA STANDARD-
2 parts Vodka, 1 part Cherry Brandy
Lime Juice *(Mix into Cocktail Glass—no ice)*

VODKA STINGER-
1 part Vodka, 1 part White Crème de Menthe
(Mix into Cocktail Glass—no ice)

VODKA TWISTER-
Vodka
splash Lime Juice, fill Lemon-Lime Soda
(Mix into Highball Glass—ice)

VOLCANO (1)-
2 parts Vodka, 1 part Amaretto
Vanilla Ice Cream, Coconut Milk *(Blend with ice in Daiquiri Glass)*

VOLCANO (2)-
1 part Coffee Liqueur, 1 part Licorice Liqueur, 1 part Light Rum
(Layer in Order in Cocktail Glass—no ice)

VOLGA BOATMAN-
1 part Cherry Brandy, 1 part Vodka
Orange Juice *(Mix into Highball Glass—ice)*

VOLGA VOLGA-
2 parts Vodka, 1 part Blue Curaçao, splash Anisette
(Mix into Small Rocks Glass—ice)

VOODOO-
1 part Tia Maria®, 1 part Spiced Rum, 1 part 151-proof Rum
(Layer in Order in Cocktail Glass—no ice)

VOYAGER-
4 parts Spiced Rum, 1 part Banana Liqueur
Hot Apple Cider *(Mix into Irish Coffee Cup—no ice)*

VULCAN BLOOD-
1 part Blue Curaçao, 1 part Vodka
Orange Juice *(Mix into Highball Glass—ice)*

VULCAN MIND PROBE (1)-
1 part Irish Cream Liqueur, 1 part Peppermint Schnapps, 1 part 151-proof Rum
(Layer in Order in Cocktail Glass with no ice) (Serve with drinking straw, and drink all at once.)

VULCAN MIND PROBE (2)-
1 part Licorice Liqueur, 1 part 151-proof Rum, 1 part Bourbon Whiskey
(Layer in Order in Cocktail Glass—no ice)

– NOTES –

WAFFLE-
1 part Butterscotch Schnapps, 1 part Vodka
Orange Juice *(Mix into Highball Glass—ice)*

WAGON BURNER-
Yukon Jack® Canadian Liqueur
Cranberry Juice, Sour Mix *(Mix into Highball Glass—ice)*

WAGON WHEEL-
3 parts Southern Comfort®, 1 part Brandy
Lime Juice, Grenadine *(Mix into Cocktail Glass—no ice)*

WAHOO-
1 part Amaretto, 1 part 151-proof Rum
top Pineapple Juice *(Mix into Small Rocks Glass—ice)*

WAIKIKI BEACHCOMBER-
1 part Gin, 1 part Triple Sec
Pineapple Juice *(Mix into Cocktail Glass—no ice)*

WAIKIKI TEASE-
Dark Rum
Orange Juice, Pineapple Juice *(Mix into Highball Glass—ice)*

WAIKIKI TIKI-
Dark Rum
Orange Juice, Pineapple Juice *(Mix into Highball Glass—ice)*

WAIKOLOA FIZZ-
3 parts Spiced Rum, 1 part Coconut Rum, 1 part Jamaican Rum
Pineapple Juice, splash Passion Fruit Juice, splash Lemon-Lime Soda
(Mix into Highball Glass—ice)

WALDORF-
1 part Bourbon Whiskey, 1 part Licorice Liqueur, 1 part Sweet Vermouth
splash Bitters *(Mix into Cocktail Glass—no ice)*

WALLICK-
1 part Dry Vermouth, 1 part Gin, splash Triple Sec
(Mix into Cocktail Glass—no ice)

WALLIS BLUE-
1 part Gin, 1 part Triple Sec
Lime Juice, Sugared Rim *(Mix into Small Rocks Glass—ice)*

WALLY-
1 part Apple Brandy, 1 part Peach Brandy
Lime Juice *(Mix into Cocktail Glass—no ice)*

WALLY HARBANGER-
2 parts Bourbon Whiskey, 1 part Galliano®
Sour Mix *(Mix into Highball Glass—ice)*

WALTERS-
Scotch Whiskey
Orange Juice, Lime Juice *(Mix into Cocktail Glass—no ice)*

WALTZING MATILDA-
3 parts White Wine, 1 part Gin, splash Triple Sec
Passion Fruit Juice, top Club Soda or Ginger Ale *(Mix into Highball Glass—ice)*

WAM BAS-
1 part Southern Comfort®, 1 part Scotch Whiskey
(Layer in Order in Cocktail Glass—no ice)

WANDERING MINSTREL-
2 parts Brandy, 1 part Coffee Liqueur, 1 part Vodka, 1 part White
Crème de Menthe *(Mix into Cocktail Glass—no ice)*

WARD EIGHT-
Bourbon Whiskey
Sour Mix, Grenadine *(Mix into Highball Glass—ice)*

WARDAY'S COCKTAIL-
1 part Apple Brandy, 1 part Gin, 1 part Sweet Vermouth, splash Yellow
Chartreuse *(Mix into Cocktail Glass—no ice)*

WARM BLONDE-
1 part Southern Comfort®, 1 part Amaretto
(Layer in Order in Cocktail Glass—no ice)

WARM FUZZY-
1 part Peach Schnapps, 1 part Blue Curaçao
(Layer in Order in Cocktail Glass—no ice)

WARRIOR-
2 parts Dry Vermouth, 2 parts Sweet Vermouth, 1 part Brandy, 1 part Licorice
Liqueur, 1 part Triple Sec *(Mix into Cocktail Glass—no ice)*

WARSAW COCKTAIL-
2 parts Vodka, 1 part Blackberry Brandy, 1 part Dry Vermouth
Lime Juice *(Mix into Cocktail Glass—no ice)*

WASHINGTON COCKTAIL-
2 parts Dry Vermouth, 1 part Brandy
splash Bitters, Sugar *(Mix into Cocktail Glass—no ice)*

WASP-
1 part Banana Liqueur, 1 part Vodka
Ginger Ale *(Mix into Highball Glass—ice)*

WATERBURY-
Brandy
Sour Mix, Grenadine *(Mix into Cocktail Glass—no ice)*

WATERLOO-
2 parts Light Rum, 1 part Mandarin Liqueur (float)
Orange Juice *(Mix into Small Rocks Glass—ice)*

WATERMELON (1)-
1 part Strawberry Schnapps, 1 part Vodka
Orange Juice, Sour Mix *(Mix into Highball Glass—ice)*

WATERMELON (2)-
Melon Liqueur
Cranberry Juice *(Mix into Highball Glass—ice)*

WATERMELON CRAWL-
3 parts Amaretto, 1 part Melon Liqueur, 1 part Southern Comfort®
Orange Juice, Pineapple Juice *(Mix into Highball Glass—ice)*

WATERMELON RANCHER-
1 part Light Rum, 1 part Melon Liqueur
Cranberry Juice, Orange Juice *(Mix into Highball Glass—ice)*

WATERMELON SLUSHIE-
2 parts Watermelon Schnapps, 1 part Light Rum, splash Melon Liqueur
Strawberry Daiquiri Mix, splash Sour Mix, top Whipped Cream
(Blend with ice in Daiquiri Glass)

WATERMELON SMASH-
1 part Melon Liqueur, 1 part Vodka
Cranberry Juice *(Mix into Highball Glass—ice)*

WEBSTER-
2 parts Gin, 1 part Dry Vermouth, splash Apricot Brandy
Lime Juice *(Mix into Cocktail Glass—no ice)*

WEDDING BELLE-
1 part Gin, 1 part Red Dubonnet®, splash Cherry Brandy
Orange Juice *(Mix into Cocktail Glass—no ice)*

WEDDING CAKE-
2 parts Amaretto, 1 part White Crème de Caçao
Light Cream or Milk *(Mix into Highball Glass—ice)*

WEDDING DRESS-***
1 part Coconut Rum, 1 part Melon Liqueur
Pineapple Juice *(Mix into Highball Glass—ice)*

WEDDING MARCH-
Light Rum
splash Lime Juice, splash Bitters *(Mix into Cocktail Glass—no ice)*

WEDDING NIGHT-
Dark Rum
Lime Juice, Maple Syrup *(Mix into Cocktail Glass—no ice)*

WEEKENDER-
1 part Dry Vermouth, 1 part Gin, 1 part Sweet Vermouth, 1 part Triple Sec,
splash Licorice Liqueur *(Mix into Cocktail Glass—no ice)*

WEEP NO MORE-
1 part Brandy, 1 part Red Dubonnet®, splash Maraschino Liqueur
Lime Juice *(Mix into Cocktail Glass—no ice)*

WELCOME STRANGER-
1 part Brandy, 1 part Citrus Rum, 1 part Gin
Orange Juice, Lime Juice, Grenadine *(Mix into Highball Glass—ice)*

WELL HEELED-
    3 parts Dark Rum, 1 part Strawberry Schnapps
    Orange Juice *(Mix into Highball Glass—ice)*

WELLINGTON-
    Gin, splash Cherry Brandy, splash Citrus Rum
    splash Lime Juice *(Mix into Cocktail Glass—no ice)*

WEMBLY-
    2 parts Gin, 1 part Dry Vermouth, splash Apple Brandy, splash Apricot Brandy
    (Mix into Cocktail Glass—no ice)

WENCH-
    1 part Amaretto, 1 part Spiced Rum *(Mix into Small Rocks Glass—ice)*

WEREWOLF-
    1 part Drambuie®, 1 part Jack Daniel's® Tennessee Sour Mash Whiskey
    (Mix into Small Rocks Glass—ice)

WESTERN ROSE-
    2 parts Gin, 1 part Apricot Brandy, 1 part Dry Vermouth
    Lime Juice *(Mix into Cocktail Glass—no ice)*

WET DREAM (1)-
    4 parts Gin, 1 part Apricot Brandy
    Grenadine, splash Lime Juice *(Mix into Cocktail Glass—no ice)*

WET DREAM (2)-
    1 part Orange Juice, 1 part Galliano®, 1 part Triple Sec, 1 part Club Soda
    (Layer in Order in Cocktail Glass—no ice)

WET SPOT-
    1 part Irish Cream Liqueur, 1 part Tequila *(Mix into Small Rocks Glass—ice)*

WHAT THE HELL-
    1 part Apricot Brandy, 1 part Dry Vermouth, 1 part Gin
    splash Lime Juice *(Mix into Small Rocks Glass—ice)*

WHICH WAY-
    1 part Anisette, 1 part Brandy, 1 part Licorice Liqueur
    (Mix into Cocktail Glass—no ice)

WHIP-
    3 parts Brandy, 1 part Dry Vermouth, 1 part Sweet Vermouth, splash Anisette,
        splash Triple Sec
    (Mix into Cocktail Glass—no ice)

WHIPPET-
    2 parts Blended Whiskey, 1 part Peppermint Schnapps, 1 part White
        Crème de Cacao *(Mix into Small Rocks Glass—ice)*

WHIRLAWAY-
    2 parts Bourbon Whiskey, 1 part Blue Curaçao
    splash Bitters, Club Soda
    (Mix into Highball Glass—ice)

WHISKEY COBBLER-
Blended Whiskey
Club Soda, Sugar *(Mix into Highball Glass—ice)*

WHISKEY COCKTAIL-
Blended Whiskey
Sugar, splash Bitters *(Mix into Cocktail Glass—no ice)*

WHISKEY COLLINS-
Blended Whiskey
Sour Mix, splash Club Soda *(Mix into Highball Glass—ice)*

WHISKEY DAISY-
Blended Whiskey
Sour Mix, splash Grenadine *(Mix into Sour Glass—ice)*

WHISKEY FIX-
Blended Whiskey
Water, Sour Mix *(Mix into Highball Glass—ice)*

WHISKEY FLIP-
Blended Whiskey
Light Cream or Milk, Sugar *(Mix into Highball Glass—ice)*

WHISKEY HIGHBALL-
Blended Whiskey
Ginger Ale or Club Soda *(Mix into Highball Glass—ice)*

WHISKEY MAC-
Scotch Whiskey, fill Green Ginger Wine *(Mix into Wine Glass—ice)*

WHISKEY MILK PUNCH-
Blended Whiskey
Light Cream or Milk, Sugar *(Mix into Highball Glass—ice)*

WHISKEY ORANGE-
Blended Whiskey, splash Anisette
Orange Juice, Sugar *(Mix into Highball Glass—ice)*

WHISKEY RICKEY-
Blended Whiskey
splash Lime Juice, Club Soda *(Mix into Highball Glass—ice)*

WHISKEY SANGAREE-
1 part Blended Whiskey, 1 part Port (float)
Water, Sugar, muddle, splash Club Soda
(Mix into Small Rocks Glass—ice)

WHISKEY SKIN-
Blended Whiskey
Hot Water, Sugar *(Mix into Irish Coffee Cup—no ice)*

WHISKEY SLING-
Blended Whiskey
Water, Sour Mix *(Mix into Small Rocks Glass—ice)*

WHISKEY SMASH-
    Blended Whiskey
    Club Soda, Sugar, Mint Leaves *(Mix into Small Rocks Glass—ice)*

WHISKEY SOUR-
    Blended Whiskey
    Sour Mix *(Mix into Sour Glass—ice)*

WHISKEY SOUR ON THE SWEET SIDE-
    Rye Whiskey
    Sour Mix *(Mix into Sour Glass— ice)*

WHISKEY SQUIRT-
    Blended Whiskey
    Grenadine, Sugar, Club Soda *(Mix into Highball Glass—ice)*

WHISKEY SWIZZLE-
    Blended Whiskey
    Sour Mix, Club Soda, Bitters *(Mix into Highball Glass—ice)*

WHISKEY TODDY (COLD)-
    Blended Whiskey
    Water, Sugar *(Mix into Highball Glass—ice)*

WHISKEY TODDY (HOT)-
    Blended Whiskey
    Hot Water, Sugar *(Mix into Irish Coffee Cup—no ice)*

WHISPER-
    1 part French Vermouth, 1 part Italian Vermouth, 1 part Scotch Whiskey
    (Mix into Small Rocks Glass—ice)

WHISPER OF A KISS-
    2 parts Bourbon Whiskey, 1 part Apricot Brandy
    Lime Juice, splash Grenadine *(Mix into Cocktail Glass—no ice)*

WHISPERS OF THE FROST-
    1 part Blended Whiskey, 1 part Cream Sherry, 1 part Port
    Sugar *(Mix into Cocktail Glass—no ice)*

WHIST-
    2 parts Apple Brandy, 1 part Dark Rum, 1 part Sweet Vermouth
    (Mix into Cocktail Glass—no ice)

WHITE ALEXANDER-
    2 parts Gin, 1 part White Crème de Caçao
    Light Cream or Milk *(Mix into Cocktail Glass—no ice)*

WHITE BABY-
    1 part Gin, 1 part Triple Sec
    Light Cream or Milk *(Mix into Cocktail Glass—no ice)*

WHITE BULL-
    1 part Coffee Liqueur, 1 part Tequila
    Light Cream or Milk *(Mix into Small Rocks Glass—ice)*

WHITE CARGO-
　　Gin, splash Maraschino Liqueur
　　Vanilla Ice Cream *(Blend with ice in Daiquiri Glass)*

WHITE CARNATION-
　　Vodka
　　Lime Juice, Pineapple Juice, fill Club Soda *(Mix into Highball Glass—ice)*

WHITE CHOCOLATE MARTINI-
　　Vodka, splash White Crème de Caçao *(Mix into Cocktail Glass—no ice)*

WHITE CLOUDS-
　　Sambuca (Chilled)
　　splash Club Soda *(Mix into Cocktail Glass—no ice)*

WHITE ELEPHANT-
　　2 parts Gin, 1 part Sweet Vermouth
　　splash Light Cream or Milk (optional) *(Mix into Cocktail Glass—no ice)*

WHITE HEART-
　　1 part Sambuca, 1 part White Crème de Caçao
　　Light Cream or Milk *(Mix into Highball Glass—ice)*

WHITE HEAT-
　　2 parts Gin, 1 part Dry Vermouth, 1 part Triple Sec
　　Pineapple Juice *(Mix into Small Rocks Glass—ice)*

WHITE HOT CHOCOLATE-
　　White Crème de Caçao
　　Hot Chocolate, top Whipped Cream *(Mix into Irish Coffee Cup—no ice)*

WHITE LADY (1)-
　　Gin
　　Light Cream or Milk, Sugar *(Mix into Cocktail Glass—no ice)*

WHITE LADY (2)-
　　1 part Vodka, 1 part White Crème de Caçao
　　Light Cream or Milk *(Mix into Cocktail Glass—no ice)*

WHITE LADY (3)-
　　1 part Gin, 1 part Triple Sec
　　Lime Juice *(Mix into Cocktail Glass—no ice)*

WHITE LIE-
　　2 parts Gin, 1 part Maraschino Liqueur
　　Orange Juice, splash Sour Mix *(Mix into Cocktail Glass—no ice)*

WHITE LILY-
　　1 part Gin, 1 part Light Rum, 1 part Triple Sec, splash Anisette
　　(Mix into Cocktail Glass—no ice)

WHITE LION-
　　Light Rum
　　Sour Mix, splash Bitters, splash Grenadine
　　(Mix into Cocktail Glass—no ice)

WHITE MOUNTAIN-
　　Sake
　　Light Cream or Milk, Piña Colada Mix, top Whipped Cream
　　(Blend with ice in Daiquiri Glass)

WHITE OUT-
　　1 part Gin, 1 part White Crème de Caçao
　　Light Cream or Milk *(Mix into Cocktail Glass—no ice)*

WHITE PIGEON-
　　2 parts Light Rum, 1 part Anisette *(Mix into Cocktail Glass—no ice)*

WHITE PLUSH-
　　Blended Whiskey
　　Light Cream or Milk, Sugar *(Mix into Highball Glass—ice)*

WHITE ROSE-
　　2 parts Gin, 1 part Maraschino Liqueur
　　Lime Juice, splash Orange Juice *(Mix into Cocktail Glass—no ice)*

WHITE RUSSIAN-
　　2 parts Vodka, 1 part Coffee Liqueur
　　Light Cream or Milk *(Mix into Highball Glass—ice)*

WHITE SATIN-
　　1 part Galliano®, 1 part Tia Maria®
　　Light Cream or Milk *(Mix into Cocktail Glass—no ice)*

WHITE SPIDER (1)-
　　1 part Peppermint Schnapps, 1 part Vodka *(Mix into Small Rocks Glass—ice)*

WHITE SPIDER (2)-
　　1 part Vodka, 1 part White Crème de Menthe *(Mix into Cocktail Glass—no ice)*

WHITE WAY-
　　2 parts Gin, 1 part White Crème de Menthe *(Mix into Cocktail Glass—no ice)*

WHITE WIM-
　　Vodka
　　Pineapple Juice, Lime Juice, fill Club Soda *(Mix into Highball Glass—ice)*

WHITE WING-
　　2 parts Gin, 1 part White Crème de Menthe *(Mix into Cocktail Glass—no ice)*

WHITE WITCH-
　　1 part Vodka, 1 part White Crème de Caçao
　　Vanilla Ice Cream *(Blend with ice in Daiquiri Glass)*

WHIZZ-DOODLE-
　　1 part Gin, 1 part Scotch Whiskey, 1 part White Crème de Caçao
　　Light Cream or Milk *(Mix into Highball Glass—ice)*

WHORE-
　　1 part Triple Sec, 1 part Vodka
　　Sour Mix *(Mix into Cocktail Glass—no ice)*

WHY NOT?-
2 parts Apricot Brandy, 2 parts Gin, 1 part Dry Vermouth
Lime Juice *(Mix into Cocktail Glass—no ice)*

WIDGET-
Gin, splash Peach Schnapps *(Mix into Small Rocks Glass—ice)*

WIDOW WITH A SECRET-
1 part Gin, 1 part Sweet Vermouth, splash Bénédictine, splash Campari,
    splash Licorice Liqueur
splash Orange Bitters, Cherry Garnish *(Mix into Cocktail Glass—no ice)*

WIDOW WOOD'S NIGHTCAP-
4 parts Scotch Whiskey, 1 part Brown Crème de Caçao
Light Cream or Milk *(Mix into Highball Glass—ice)*

WIDOW'S DREAM-
Bénédictine
Light Cream or Milk (float) *(Mix into Cocktail Glass—no ice)*

WIDOW'S KISS-
2 parts Brandy, 1 part Bénédictine, 1 part Yellow Chartreuse
splash Bitters *(Mix into Cocktail Glass—no ice)*

WIKI WAKI WOO-
2 parts Amaretto, 1 part Light Rum, 1 part Tequila, 1 part Triple Sec,
    1 part Vodka, 1 part 151-proof Rum
Cranberry Juice, Orange Juice, Pineapple Juice *(Mix into Highball Glass—ice)*

WILD BANSHEE-
4 parts Spiced Rum, 1 part Amaretto
Light Cream or Milk, Bananas *(Blend with ice in Daiquiri Glass)*

WILD BLUE-
2 parts Hpnotiq®, 1 part Triple Sec
Cranberry Juice *(Mix into Highball Glass—ice)*

WILD BREW YONDER-
Vodka, splash Blue Curaçao, fill Beer *(Beer Mug)*

WILD FLING-
Wild Berry Schnapps
Pineapple Juice, Cranberry Juice (float) *(Mix into Highball Glass—ice)*

WILD IRISH ROSE-
Irish Whiskey
splash Lime Juice, splash Grenadine, fill Club Soda
(Mix into Highball Glass—ice)

WILD OATS-
3 parts Gin, 1 part Cherry Brandy, splash Apricot Brandy
splash Lime Juice *(Mix into Cocktail Glass—no ice)*

WILD THING-
Tequila
Cranberry Juice, Club Soda, splash Lime Juice *(Mix into Highball Glass—ice)*

WILDFLOWER-
Scotch Whiskey
Grapefruit Juice, splash Grenadine
(Mix into Highball Glass with ice or blend with ice in Daiquiri Glass)

WILL ROGERS-
3 parts Gin, 1 part Dry Vermouth, splash Triple Sec
splash Orange Juice *(Mix into Cocktail Glass—no ice)*

WILLAWA-
2 parts Brandy, 1 part Cherry Brandy, 1 part Galliano®
Light Cream or Milk, sprinkle Nutmeg *(Mix into Cocktail Glass—no ice)*

WILSON-
Gin, splash Dry Vermouth
splash Orange Juice *(Mix into Cocktail Glass—no ice)*

WIND SURF-
Chablis, splash Triple Sec
Pineapple Juice, Club Soda, Sugar *(Mix into Wine Glass—ice)*

WINDSURFER-
1 part Coffee Liqueur, 1 part Triple Sec, 1 part Yukon Jack® Canadian Liqueur
(Layer in Order in Cocktail Glass—no ice)

WINDWARD PASSAGE-
Light Rum, splash Cherry Brandy, splash Crème de Cassis
Pineapple Juice *(Mix into Cocktail Glass—no ice)*

WINDY CITY-
1 part Gold Rum, 1 part Port
Sour Mix, top Club Soda *(Mix into Highball Glass—ice)*

WINDY CORNER-
Blackberry Brandy
sprinkle Nutmeg *(Mix into Cocktail Glass—no ice)*

WINE COLLINS-
Red Wine
Sour Mix, splash Club Soda *(Mix into Wine Glass—no ice)*

WINE COOLER-
Wine
fill Lemon-Lime Soda *(Mix into Wine Glass—ice)*

WINE SPRITZER-
Wine
fill Club Soda *(Mix into Wine Glass—ice)*

WINTER WARMER-
2 parts Dark Rum, 1 part Cognac
Hot Milk, Maple Syrup *(Mix into Irish Coffee Cup—no ice)*

WITCH OF VENICE-
3 parts Vodka, 1 part Strega, splash Banana Liqueur
Orange Juice *(Mix into Cocktail Glass—no ice)*

WITCH'S BREW-
Coconut Rum
Orange Juice, Pineapple Juice *(Mix into Highball Glass—ice)*

WITCH'S TAIL-
4 parts Wild Berry Schnapps, 1 part Blue Curaçao
Sour Mix, fill Club Soda *(Mix into Highball Glass—ice)*

WITCH'S TIT-
Coffee Liqueur
splash Light Cream or Milk (float), Cherry Garnish
(Mix into Cocktail Glass—no ice)

WITCHING EVE-
White Crème de Caçao
Light Cream or Milk, splash Bitters
(Mix into Highball Glass—ice)

WOMAN OF THE MOMENT-
1 part Grand Marnier®, 1 part Rye Whiskey
Lime Juice, splash Grenadine *(Mix into Cocktail Glass—no ice)*

WOMAN WARRIOR-
3 parts Vodka, 1 part Blue Curaçao
Lime Juice *(Mix into Cocktail Glass—no ice)*

WOO WOO-
1 part Peach Schnapps, 1 part Vodka
Cranberry Juice *(Mix into Highball Glass—ice)*

WOO-WOO MARTINI-
3 parts Vodka, 1 part Peach Schnapps, splash Dry Vermouth
splash Sour Mix *(Mix into Cocktail Glass—no ice)*

WOODEN SHOE-
1 part Chocolate Mint Liqueur, 1 part Coffee Liqueur
Light Cream or Milk *(Mix into Highball Glass—ice)*

WOODSTOCK-
Gin
Lime Juice, Maple Syrup, splash Orange Bitters
(Mix into Cocktail Glass—no ice)

WOODWARD-
2 parts Scotch Whiskey, 1 part Dry Vermouth
Grapefruit Juice *(Mix into Cocktail Glass—no ice)*

WRATH OF GRAPES-
Dark Rum
Grape Juice, splash Sour Mix *(Mix into Highball Glass—ice)*

WRIGLEY'S DOUBLEMINT BLOWJOB-
2 parts Coffee Liqueur, 1 part Peppermint Schnapps, 1 part Light Cream or
   Milk, top Whipped Cream (optional)
(Layer in Order in Cocktail Glass—no ice)

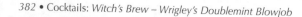

WRITE OFF-
1 part Banana Liqueur, 1 part Strawberry Schnapps, splash Dark Rum
Pineapple Juice *(Mix into Highball Glass—ice)*

WYOMING SWING-
1 part Dry Vermouth, 1 part Sweet Vermouth
Orange Juice, Sugar *(Mix into Cocktail Glass—no ice)*

WYSOOSLER-
1 part Green Chartreuse, 1 part Gin, 1 part Sweet Vermouth
splash Orange Bitters *(Mix into Cocktail Glass—no ice)*

– NOTES –

X.Y.Z.-
 2 parts Light Rum, 1 part Triple Sec
 Lime Juice *(Mix into Cocktail Glass—no ice)*

XANGO-
 3 parts Light Rum, 1 part Triple Sec
 Grapefruit Juice *(Mix into Cocktail Glass—no ice)*

XANTHIA-
 1 part Cherry Brandy, 1 part Gin, 1 part Yellow Chartreuse
 (Mix into Cocktail Glass—no ice)

XERES-
 Dry Sherry
 splash Orange Bitters *(Mix into Cocktail Glass—no ice)*

XYLOPHONE-
 2 parts Tequila, 1 part White Crème de Caçao
 Light Cream or Milk, Sugar
 (Mix into Highball Glass with ice or blend with ice in Daiquiri Glass)

– NOTES –

_____

_____

_____

_____

_____

_____

_____

_____

_____

_____

_____

_____

_____

_____

_____

_____

_____

YAKA-HULA-HICKY-DULA-
1 part Dark Rum, 1 part Dry Vermouth
Pineapple Juice *(Mix into Cocktail Glass—no ice)*

YALE COCKTAIL-
3 parts Gin, 1 part Dry Vermouth, splash Blue Curaçao
splash Bitters *(Mix into Cocktail Glass—no ice)*

YASHMAK-
2 parts Rye Whiskey, 1 part Dry Vermouth, splash Anisette
splash Bitters, Sugar *(Mix into Cocktail Glass—no ice)*

YELLOW BIRD (1)-
3 parts Banana Liqueur, 1 part Light Rum
Orange Juice, Pineapple Juice *(Mix into Highball Glass—ice)*

YELLOW BIRD (2)-
3 parts Spiced Rum, 1 part Banana Liqueur, 1 part Galliano®
Orange Juice, Pineapple Juice, splash Lime Juice
(Mix into Highball Glass—ice)

YELLOW BIRD (3)-
4 parts Light Rum, 1 part Apricot Brandy, 1 part Galliano®
Orange Juice, Lime Juice *(Mix into Highball Glass—ice)*

YELLOW BIRD (4)-
2 parts Vodka, 2 parts White Crème de Caçao, 1 part Galliano®
Light Cream or Milk, Orange Juice *(Mix into Highball Glass—ice)*

YELLOW BIRD (5)-
3 parts Light Rum, 1 part Galliano®, 1 part Triple Sec
Lime Juice *(Mix into Cocktail Glass—no ice)*

YELLOW BOXER-
4 parts Tequila, 1 part Galliano®
Orange Juice, Lime Juice *(Mix into Highball Glass—ice)*

YELLOW COCONUT-
1 part Citrus Vodka, 1 part Coconut Rum
Pineapple Juice *(Mix into Highball Glass—ice)*

YELLOW FEVER-
Vodka
Lemonade *(Mix into Highball Glass—ice)*

YELLOW FINGERS-
2 parts Gin, 1 part Banana Liqueur, 1 part Blackberry Brandy
Light Cream or Milk *(Mix into Cocktail Glass—no ice)*

YELLOW JERSEY-
Sweet Vermouth
Ginger Ale *(Mix into Highball Glass—ice)*

YELLOW PARROT-
1 part Anisette, 1 part Apricot Brandy, 1 part Yellow Chartreuse
(Mix into Cocktail Glass—no ice)

YELLOW RATTLER-
2 parts Gin, 1 part Dry Vermouth, 1 part Sweet Vermouth
Orange Juice *(Mix into Cocktail Glass—no ice)*

YELLOW RUSSIAN-
1 part Banana Liqueur, 1 part Vodka, splash Coconut Liqueur
Light Cream or Milk *(Mix into Highball Glass—ice)*

YELLOW STRAWBERRY (1)-
2 parts Light Rum, 1 part Banana Liqueur
Sour Mix, Strawberry Daiquiri Mix *(Blend with ice in Daiquiri Glass)*

YELLOW STRAWBERRY (2)-
2 parts Light Rum, 1 part Banana Liqueur, 1 part Strawberry Schnapps
Sour Mix *(Mix into Highball Glass—ice)*

YELLOW SUBMARINE-
1 part Light Rum, 1 part Orange Curaçao
Sour Mix *(Mix into Highball Glass—ice)*

YES & NO-
Brandy, splash Blue Curaçao
(Mix into Cocktail Glass—no ice)

YO HO-
1 part Apple Brandy, 1 part Citrus Rum, 1 part Light Rum
(Mix into Cocktail Glass—no ice)

YO MAMA (1)-
Citrus Vodka
Club Soda, splash Orange Juice (float) *(Mix into Highball Glass—ice)*

YO MAMA (2)-
1 part Triple Sec, 1 part Vodka
Club Soda, splash Orange Juice (float) *(Mix into Highball Glass—ice)*

YODEL-
Fernet Branca
Orange Juice, top Club Soda *(Mix into Highball Glass—ice)*

YOKOHAMA MAMA-
3 parts Brandy, 1 part Melon Liqueur, splash Amaretto
(Mix into Cocktail Glass—no ice)

YOLANDA-
2 parts Sweet Vermouth, 1 part Anisette, 1 part Brandy, 1 part Gin
splash Grenadine
(Mix into Cocktail Glass—no ice)

YORK SPECIAL-
Dry Vermouth, splash Maraschino Liqueur
splash Orange Bitters *(Mix into Cocktail Glass—no ice)*

YORSH-
12 oz. Beer, 1 part Vodka *(Beer Mug)*

YOUNG BLOOD-
3 parts Gin, 1 part Dry Vermouth, 1 part Sweet Vermouth,
 splash Strawberry Schnapps
Strawberries *(Blend with ice in Daiquiri Glass)*

YOUNG MAN-
3 parts Brandy, 1 part Sweet Vermouth, splash Triple Sec
splash Bitters *(Mix into Cocktail Glass—no ice)*

YUKON CORNELIUS-
Yukon Jack® Canadian Liqueur, splash Goldschläger® (top)
(Mix into Small Rocks Glass—ice)

– NOTES –

Gimlet – Vodka or Gin, muddled limes,
lemon juice, shaken & poured over rocks

Z-28-
1 part White Crème de Menthe, 1 part Banana Liqueur, 1 part Tequila
(Layer in Order in Cocktail Glass—no ice)

Z STREET-
2 parts Spiced Rum, 1 part Banana Liqueur
Pineapple Juice, Grenadine *(Mix into Highball Glass—ice)*

ZAGREB-
4 parts Blended Whiskey, 1 part Russian Vodka
Sour Mix, fill Club Soda *(Mix into Highball Glass—ice)*

ZAMBOANGA HUMMER-
1 part Brandy, 1 part Gin, 1 part Gold Rum, 1 part Triple Sec
Orange Juice, Pineapple Juice, splash Lime Juice, Brown Sugar (optional)
(Mix into Highball Glass—ice)

ZAMBODIAN-
1 part Blackberry Brandy, 1 part Vodka
Pineapple Juice *(Mix into Highball Glass—ice)*

ZANZIBAR-
2 parts Dry Vermouth, 1 part Gin
Sour Mix, splash Orange Bitters *(Mix into Cocktail Glass—no ice)*

ZARANES COCKTAIL-
1 part Apricot Brandy, 1 part Vodka
Bitters *(Mix into Cocktail Glass—no ice)*

ZAZA-
2 parts Gin, 1 part Red Dubonnet® *(Mix into Cocktail Glass—no ice)*

ZAZARAC-
2 parts Rye Whiskey, 1 part Anisette, 1 part Light Rum
Sugar, splash Bitters, splash Orange Bitters *(Mix into Cocktail Glass—no ice)*

ZERO MINT JULEP-
4 parts Blended Whiskey, 1 part Green Crème de Menthe
(Mix into Cocktail Glass—no ice)

ZERO MIST-
White Crème de Menthe
Water *(Mix into Cocktail Glass—no ice)*

ZHIVAGO STANDARD-
3 parts Vodka, 1 part Kümmel
Lime Juice *(Mix into Cocktail Glass—no ice)*

ZIPPER-
1 part Triple Sec, 1 part Tequila , 1 part Light Cream or Milk
(Layer in Order in Cocktail Glass—no ice)

ZIPPERHEAD-
1 part Raspberry Liqueur, 1 part Vodka
Club Soda *(Mix into Highball Glass—ice)*

ZOCOLO-
2 parts Dark Rum, 1 part Tequila
Grapefruit Juice, Pineapple Juice, top Club Soda *(Mix into Highball Glass—ice)*

ZOMBIE (1)-
2 parts Dark or Spiced Rum, 2 parts Light Rum, 1 part Apricot Brandy,
   splash 151-proof Rum (lace)
Orange Juice, Pineapple Juice *(Mix into Highball Glass—ice)*

ZOMBIE (2)-
1 part Apricot Brandy, 1 part Dark Rum, 1 part Jamaican Rum,
   1 part Light Rum
Orange Juice, Pineapple Juice, Sour Mix, splash Grenadine
(Mix into Highball Glass—ice)

ZOMBIE (3)-
2 parts Jamaican Rum, 2 parts Light Rum, 1 part Apricot Brandy,
   splash 151-proof Rum (lace)
Orange Juice, Pineapple Juice, Sour Mix
(Mix into Highball Glass with ice or blend with ice in Daiquiri Glass)

ZOMBIE (4)-
1 part Amaretto, 1 part Light Rum, 1 part Triple Sec,
   splash 151-proof Rum (lace)
Orange Juice, Sour Mix *(Mix into Highball Glass—ice)*

ZOOM-
Brandy
Light Cream or Milk, Honey *(Mix into Cocktail Glass—no ice)*

ZUC-
1 part Coffee Liqueur, 1 part Grand Marnier®, 1 part Green Crème de Menthe,
   1 part Irish Cream Liqueur
(Mix into Cocktail Glass—no ice)

ZULTRY ZOE-
Tequila, splash Galliano®
Hot Chocolate, top Whipped Cream *(Mix into Irish Coffee Cup—no ice)*

ZUZU'S PETALS-
2 parts Gin, 1 part Lillet, splash Crème de Yvette
splash Orange Bitters *(Mix into Cocktail Glass—no ice)*

– NOTES –

– NOTES –

Shooters

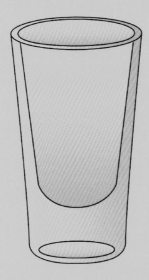

Shooters are meant to be fun. Pour the liquors and the mixers (if any) into a shaker with ice, shake or stir and strain into the shot glass with no ice.

Many shooters are layered for taste, show and meaning. Layering is exactly what it implies—pouring one ingredient on top of the other without allowing them to mix in the glass.

A. S. S.-
>1 part Absolut® Vodka, 1 part Sambuca, 1 part Spearmint Schnapps

A-BOMB-
>1 part Coffee Liqueur, 1 part Irish Cream Liqueur, 1 part Tia Maria®,
>1 part Vodka

ABORTION-
>1 part Sambuca, 1 part Irish Cream Liqueur (lace)
>splash Grenadine (lace second)

ABUSE MACHINE-
>2 parts Tequila, 1 part Sambuca, 1 part Blended Whiskey
>splash Hot Sauce, splash Worcestershire Sauce

ACID-
>1 part 151-proof Rum, 1 part Bourbon Whiskey

ACID COOKIE-
>1 part Butterscotch Schnapps, 1 part Cinnamon Schnapps, 1 part Irish Cream
>Liqueur, splash 151-proof Rum

ACID TRIP-
>3 parts Melon Liqueur, 1 part Gin, 1 part Light Rum, 1 part Tequila,
>1 part Vodka

ADIOS MOTHER-
>1 part Blue Curaçao, 1 part Gin, 1 part Spiced Rum, 1 part Vodka
>splash Sour Mix

ADIOS MOTHER F**KER-
>1 part Blue Curaçao, 1 part Gin, 1 part Light Rum, 1 part Tequila,
>1 part Triple Sec, 1 part Vodka
>splash Orange Juice, splash Pineapple Juice
>(Serve with Drinking Straw, Drink all at once)
>*(Mix into Highball Glass with ice)*

ADMIRAL X-RAY SHOOTER-***
>4 parts Spiced Rum, 1 part Amaretto, 1 part Melon Liqueur
>Cranberry Juice, Orange Juice, Pineapple Juice, splash Grenadine

AFTER EIGHT-
>1 part Coffee Liqueur, 1 part Irish Cream Liqueur, 1 part White
>Crème de Menthe (Layer in Order)

AFTER FIVE (1)-
>1 part Irish Cream Liqueur, 1 part Peppermint Schnapps

AFTER FIVE (2)-
>1 part Coffee Liqueur, 1 part Irish Cream Liqueur, 1 part Peppermint Schnapps
>(Layer in Order)

AFTER NINE-
>1 part Coffee Liqueur, 1 part Irish Cream Liqueur, 1 part Peach Schnapps
>(Layer in Order)

AFTERBURNER-
>1 part Peppermint Schnapps, 1 part Tia Maria®

AGENT 99-
>1 part Grand Marnier®, 1 part Blue Curaçao, 1 part Sambuca
>(Layer in Order)

AGENT ORANGE (1)-
>1 part Irish Cream Liqueur, 1 part Southern Comfort®

AGENT ORANGE (2)-
>1 part Apple Schnapps, 1 part Gin, 1 part Light Rum, 1 part Melon Liqueur,
>   1 part Southern Comfort®, 1 part Vodka, 1 part Yukon Jack® Canadian
>   Liqueur
>splash Grenadine, splash Orange Juice

AGENT ORANGE (3)-
>1 part Jack Daniel's® Tennessee Sour Mash Whiskey, 1 part Southern Comfort®
>splash Orange Juice

ALABAMA SLAMMER SHOOTER (1)-
>2 parts Amaretto, 2 parts Southern Comfort®, 1 part Sloe Gin
>splash Orange Juice

ALABAMA SLAMMER SHOOTER (2)-
>1 part Amaretto, 1 part Southern Comfort®, 1 part Sloe Gin
>splash Orange Juice, splash Pineapple Juice

ALABAMA SLAMMER SHOOTER (3)-
>1 part Galliano®, 1 part Southern Comfort®, 1 part Sloe Gin, 1 part Triple Sec
>splash Orange Juice

ALASKAN OIL SLICK-
>1 part Blue Curaçao, 1 part Peppermint Schnapps, splash Jägermeister®

ALGAE-
>1 part Blue Curaçao, 1 part Melon Liqueur, 1 part Raspberry Schnapps,
>   1 part Vodka
>Sour Mix

ALIEN-
>1 part Blue Curaçao, 1 part Irish Cream Liqueur (lace)

ALIEN NIPPLE-
>1 part Butterscotch Schnapps, splash Irish Cream Liqueur (top),
>   splash Melon Liqueur (lace)

ALIEN SECRETION-
>1 part Coconut Rum, 1 part Melon Liqueur
>splash Sour Mix

ALIEN URINE SAMPLE-
>1 part Banana Liqueur, 1 part Coconut Rum, 1 part Melon Liqueur,
>   1 part Peach Schnapps, splash Blue Curaçao
>splash Sour Mix, splash Club Soda

ALLIGATOR-
1 part Melon Liqueur, 1 part Triple Sec, 1 part Vodka
Orange Juice, Sour Mix, splash Lemon-lime Soda

ALMOND COOKIE-
1 part Amaretto, 1 part Butterscotch Schnapps

ALMOND DELIGHT-
2 parts Amaretto, 1 part Brown Crème de Caçao

ALMOND JOY-
1 part Amaretto, 1 part Brown Crème de Caçao, 1 part Coconut Liqueur

ALTERED STATE-
1 part Pear Schnapps, 1 part Irish Cream Liqueur, 1 part Coffee Liqueur
(Layer in Order)

AMERICAN DREAM-
1 part Amaretto, 1 part Brown Crème de Caçao, 1 part Coffee Liqueur,
1 part Hazelnut Liqueur

AMERICAN FLAG (1)-
1 part Grenadine, 1 part White Crème de Caçao, 1 part Blue Curaçao
(Layer in Order)

AMERICAN FLAG (2)-
1 part Blue Curaçao, 1 part Peppermint Schnapps, 1 part Crème de Noyaux
(Layer in Order)

ANABOLIC STEROIDS-
1 part Blue Curaçao, 1 part Melon Liqueur

ANAL PROBE-
2 parts Light Rum, 1 part Coffee Liqueur
splash Cola

ANEURYSM-
1 part Blackberry Brandy, 1 part Licorice Liqueur

ANGRY GERMAN, THE-
1 part Amaretto, 1 part Blackberry Brandy, 1 part Jägermeister®
splash Lime Juice

ANONYMOUS-
1 part Southern Comfort®, 1 part Raspberry Liqueur
Sour Mix

ANTIFREEZE-
1 part Green Crème de Menthe, 1 part Vodka

APACHE-
1 part Coffee Liqueur, 1 part Irish Cream Liqueur, 1 part Melon Liqueur
(Layer in Order)

APOCALYPSE-
2 parts Peppermint Schnapps, 1 part Bourbon Whiskey, 1 part Coffee Liqueur, 1 part Vodka

APPLE COBBLER-
1 part Apple Schnapps, 1 part Goldschläger®, 1 part Irish Cream Liqueur

APPLE CRISP-
1 part Butterscotch Schnapps, 1 part Sour Apple Schnapps, 1 part Vodka

APPLE PIE (1)-
1 part Apple Schnapps, 1 part Vodka
splash Pineapple Juice

APPLE PIE (2)-
Apple Schnapps, splash Cinnamon Schnapps

APPLE PIE A LA MODE-
2 parts Coconut Rum, 2 parts Spiced Rum, 1 part Apple Brandy
splash Light Cream or Milk

APPLE TART-
1 part Amaretto, 1 part Apple Brandy

ARCTIC JOY-
1 part Peppermint Schnapps, 1 part White Crème de Caçao

ARMY GREEN-
1 part Goldschläger®, 1 part Jägermeister®, 1 part Tequila

ASS-
1 part Green Crème de Menthe, 1 part Sambuca, 1 part Vodka

ASS KICKER-
1 part 100-proof Vodka, 1 part Goldschläger®, 1 part Peppermint Schnapps, 1 part Tequila, 1 part Triple Sec, 1 part Vodka
Orange Juice, Pineapple Juice

ASSASSIN-
1 part Jack Daniel's® Tennessee Sour Mash Whiskey, 1 part Peppermint Schnapps, 1 part Tequila
Cola

ASSISTED SUICIDE-
2 parts 100-proof Vodka, 1 part Jägermeister®
splash Jolt® Cola

ASTHMA ATTACK-
2 parts Amaretto, 1 part 151-proof Rum, 1 part 100-proof Vodka, 1 part Raspberry Liqueur

ASTROPOP-
1 part Goldschläger®, 1 part Melon Liqueur, 1 part Yukon Jack® Canadian Liqueur
splash Grenadine

ATOM BOMB-
1 part Apple Schnapps, 1 part Goldschläger®

ATOMIC BOMB-
1 part Rye Whiskey, 1 part Tequila
(Layer in Order)

ATTITUDE-
1 part Peach Schnapps, 1 part Vodka

AVALANCHE-
1 part Coffee Liqueur, 1 part White Crème de Caçao, 1 part Southern Comfort®
(Layer in Order)

B-1B-
1 part Amaretto, 1 part Coffee Liqueur, 1 part Irish Cream Liqueur, 1 part Vodka

B-51-
1 part Irish Cream Liqueur, 1 part Coffee Liqueur, 1 part Light Rum
(Layer in Order)

B-52-
1 part Coffee Liqueur, 1 part Irish Cream Liqueur, 1 part Grand Marnier®
(Layer in Order)

B-52 with a BOMBAY DOOR-
1 part Coffee Liqueur, 1 part Irish Cream Liqueur, 1 part Grand Marnier®,
    1 part Bombay® Gin
(Layer in Order)

B-53-
1 part Coffee Liqueur, 1 part Sambuca, 1 part Grand Marnier® (Layer in Order)

B-54-
1 part Coffee Liqueur, 1 part Irish Cream Liqueur, 1 part Grand Marnier®,
    1 part Tequila (Layer in Order)

B-57-
1 part Coffee Liqueur, 1 part Triple Sec, 1 part Sambuca (Layer in Order)

B. B. C.-
1 part Baileys® Irish Cream Liqueur, 1 part Banana Liqueur, 1 part Cointreau

B. P. RISER-
1 part Banana Liqueur, 1 part Melon Liqueur, 1 part Vodka

B. S.-
1 part Coffee Liqueur, 1 part Grand Marnier®, 1 part Irish Cream Liqueur

BABE RUTH-
1 part Hazelnut Liqueur, 1 part Vodka (Layer in Order)

BABY ASPIRIN-
3 parts Coconut Rum, 1 part Triple Sec
splash Orange Juice, splash Pineapple Juice, splash Grenadine

BABY'S BOTTOM-
> 3 parts Blended Whiskey, 1 part White Crème de Caçao, 1 part White
> Crème de Menthe

BACK DRAFT-
> 2 parts Tequila, 1 part Grand Marnier® (Layer in Order)
> splash Hot Sauce

BACK STREET BANGER-
> 1 part Jack Daniel's® Tennessee Sour Mash Whiskey, 1 part Irish Cream Liqueur

BACKBURNER-
> 2 parts Peppermint Schnapps, 1 part Coffee Liqueur, 1 part Light Rum

BACKFIRE-
> 1 part Coffee Liqueur, 1 part Irish Cream Liqueur, 1 part Vodka (Layer in Order)

BACON & TOMATO SANDWICH-
> 1 part Dark Rum, 1 part Gin, 1 part Light Rum
> splash Sour Mix

BAD STING-
> 1 part Grenadine, 1 part Sambuca, 1 part Grand Marnier®, 1 part Tequila
> (Layer in Order)

BALD EAGLE-
> 1 part Peppermint Schnapps, 1 part Tequila

BALD-HEADED WOMAN-
> 151-proof Rum
> splash Grapefruit Juice

BALL-PEEN HAMMER-
> 3 parts Vodka, 1 part Rye Whiskey
> splash Lime Juice

BALLISTIC MISSILE-
> 1 part Amaretto, 1 part Grand Marnier®
> Pineapple Juice

BANANA BANSHEE-
> 1 part Banana Liqueur, 1 part White Crème de Caçao

BANANA BERRY-
> 2 parts Raspberry Liqueur, 1 part Banana Liqueur

BANANA BIRD-
> Bourbon Whiskey, splash Banana Liqueur, splash Triple Sec

BANANA BOAT (1)-
> 1 part Banana Liqueur, 1 part Coffee Liqueur, 1 part Peppermint Schnapps

BANANA BOAT (2)-
> 1 part Banana Liqueur, 1 part Coconut Rum
> splash Pineapple Juice

BANANA BOAT (3)-
1 part Banana Liqueur, 1 part Tequila
splash Lime Juice

BANANA BOOMER-
1 part Banana Liqueur, 1 part Light Rum
splash Orange Juice, splash Pineapple Juice

BANANA COW-
1 part Banana Liqueur, 1 part Light Rum
splash Grenadine

BANANA CREAM PIE-
1 part Banana Liqueur, 1 part Vodka, 1 part White Crème de Caçao
Light Cream or Milk

BANANA NUT BREAD-
2 parts Banana Liqueur, 2 parts Hazelnut Liqueur, 1 part Vanilla Liqueur

BANANA PUDDING-
1 part Coffee Liqueur, 2 parts Banana Liqueur, 1 part Irish Cream Liqueur
(Layer in Order)

BANANA SLIP-
1 part Banana Liqueur, 1 part Irish Cream Liqueur
(Layer in Order)

BANANA SPLIT (1)-
4 parts Banana Liqueur, 1 part Crème de Noyaux, 1 part White
    Crème de Caçao
splash Light Cream or Milk, splash Grenadine

BANANA SPLIT (2)-
1 part Swiss Chocolate Almond Liqueur, 1 part Strawberry Schnapps,
    1 part Banana Liqueur
(Layer in Order)

BANANA SPLIT (3)-
1 part Brown Crème de Caçao, 1 part Amaretto, 1 part Strawberry Schnapps,
    1 part Banana Liqueur
(Layer in Order)

BARBED WIRE-
1 part Goldschläger®, 1 part Sambuca

BARNEY ON ACID-
1 part Blue Curaçao, 1 part Jägermeister®
splash Cranberry Juice

BARNSTORMER-
3 parts Canadian Whiskey, 1 part Peppermint Schnapps, splash Brown Crème
    de Caçao, splash White Crème de Caçao
splash Lime Juice

BARRACUDA-
1 part Southern Comfort®, 1 part Triple Sec, 1 part Vodka

BAT BITE-
     3 parts Light Rum, 1 part Raspberry Liqueur
     Cranberry Juice

BATTERED, BRUISED & BLEEDING-
     1 part Grenadine, 1 part Melon Liqueur, 1 part Blue Curaçao (Layer in Order)

BAY BOMBER-
     1 part Bombay® Gin, 1 part Light Rum, 1 part Tequila, 1 part Triple Sec,
          1 part Vodka, 1 part 151-proof Rum (lace)
     splash Cranberry Juice, splash Orange Juice, splash Pineapple Juice,
          splash Sour Mix

BAZOOKA-
     2 parts Southern Comfort®, 1 part Banana Liqueur
     splash Grenadine

BAZOOKA JOE-
     1 part Blue Curaçao, 1 part Banana Liqueur, 1 part Irish Cream Liqueur
     (Layer in Order)

BEAM ME UP SCOTTY-
     1 part Banana Liqueur, 1 part Coffee Liqueur, 1 part Irish Cream Liqueur

BEAUTY & THE BEAST-
     1 part Jägermeister®, 1 part Tequila

BEAUTY SPOT-
     Gin, splash White Crème de Cacao, splash Grenadine
     (Do Not Mix)

BEAVIS & BUTTHEAD-
     1 part Apple Schnapps, 1 part Cinnamon Schnapps

BEETLEJUICE-
     2 parts Brown Crème de Cacao, 2 parts White Crème de Cacao, 1 part Coffee
          Liqueur, 1 part Peppermint Schnapps

BEND ME OVER-
     1 part Amaretto, 1 part Vodka
     Orange Juice, Sour Mix

BERMUDA TRIANGLE-
     2 parts Peach Schnapps, 1 part Spiced Rum
     splash Orange Juice

BERRISSIMO-
     1 part Blackberry Brandy, 1 part Strawberry Schnapps
     splash Orange Juice, splash Pineapple Juice

BETTER THAN SEX-
     1 part Coffee Liqueur, 1 part Grand Marnier®, 1 part Haagen Dazs® Cream
          Liqueur, 1 part Hazelnut Liqueur
     splash Light Cream or Milk

BETWEEN THE SHEETS (1)-
 1 part Brandy, 1 part Light Rum, 1 part Triple Sec
 splash Sour Mix

BETWEEN THE SHEETS (2)-
 1 part Blue Curaçao, 1 part Brandy, 1 part Light Rum
 splash Sour Mix

BIG BLUE SKY-
 1 part Blue Curaçao, 1 part Coconut Liqueur, 1 part Light Rum
 splash Pineapple Juice

BIG CHILL-
 1 part Coffee Liqueur, 1 part Green Crème de Menthe

BIG DIPPER-
 1 part Apricot Brandy, 1 part White Crème de Caçao

BIG O-
 1 part Peppermint Schnapps, 1 part Irish Cream Liqueur (Layer in Order)

BIG RED HOOTER-
 1 part Amaretto, 1 part Tequila
 splash Pineapple Juice, splash Grenadine

BIG ROLLER-
 1 part Amaretto, 1 part Banana Liqueur, 1 part Coffee Liqueur

BIG UNIT-
 Tequila, splash Blue Curaçao

BIKINI LINE-
 1 part Raspberry Liqueur, 1 part Tia Maria®, 1 part Vodka

BIKINI WAX-
 2 parts Vodka, 1 part Light Rum
 Light Cream or Milk, splash Sour Mix

BIRD SH*T-
 Blackberry Brandy, splash Tequila
 splash Light Cream or Milk (lace)

BIRTH CONTROL-
 1 part Gin, 1 part Rye Whiskey

BIT O' HONEY (1)-
 3 parts Butterscotch Schnapps, 1 part Irish Cream Liqueur
 (Layer in Order)

BIT O' HONEY (2)-
 1 part Apple Schnapps, 1 part Hazelnut Liqueur

BITCH ON WHEELS-
 4 parts Gin, 1 part Dry Vermouth, 1 part White Crème de Menthe,
  splash Sambuca

BITE OF THE IGUANA-
2 parts Tequila, 1 part Triple Sec, 1 part Vodka
splash Orange Juice, splash Sour Mix, splash Lemon-Lime Soda

BLACK & BLUE-
1 part Black Raspberry Liqueur, 1 part Blue Curaçao, 1 part Tequila

BLACK & GOLD-
1 part Black Sambuca, 1 part Goldschläger®

BLACK ARMY-
1 part Galliano®, 1 part Jägermeister® (Layer in Order)

BLACK BANDITO-
1 part Blackberry Liqueur, 1 part Tequila

BLACK BITCH-
1 part Black Sambuca, 1 part Irish Cream Liqueur, 2 parts 151-proof Rum
(Layer in Order)

BLACK GOLD-
1 part Jägermeister®, 1 part Goldschläger®

BLACK DEATH-
1 part Jägermeister®, 1 part Peppermint Schnapps

BLACK DEVIL-
1 part Dark Rum, 1 part Green Crème de Menthe
(Layer in Order)

BLACK DRAGON-
1 part Mint Liqueur, 1 part Coffee Liqueur, 1 part Scotch Whiskey
(Layer in Order)

BLACK FOREST-
1 part Vodka, 1 part Raspberry Liqueur (lace)
splash Sour Mix

BLACK HOLE-
1 part Jägermeister®, 1 part Peppermint Schnapps

BLACK JACK-
1 part Coffee Liqueur, 1 part Anisette (Layer in Order)

BLACK KENTUCKY-
1 part Black Sambuca, 2 parts Bourbon Whiskey (Layer in Order)

BLACK LEATHER WHIP-
1 part Jägermeister®, 1 part Peppermint Schnapps

BLACK LICORICE-
1 part Coffee Liqueur, 1 part Sambuca

BLACK MAGIC (1)-
2 parts Vodka, 1 part Coffee Liqueur
splash Sour Mix

BLACK MAGIC (2)-
1 part Black Sambuca, 1 part Vodka

BLACK NUTS-
1 part Black Sambuca, 1 part Hazelnut Liqueur

BLACK ORGASM-
1 part Blue Curaçao, 1 part Peach Schnapps, 1 part Sloe Gin, 1 part Vodka

BLACK PEPPER-
1 part Blackberry Brandy, 1 part Pepper Vodka

BLACK SAND-
1 part Coffee Liqueur, 1 part Sambuca, 1 part Amaretto
(Layer in Order)

BLACK TIE-
1 part Drambuie®, 1 part Scotch Whiskey, 1 part Amaretto (Layer in Order)

BLACK WIDOW (1)-
1 part Dark Rum, 1 part Southern Comfort®
splash Sour Mix

BLACK WIDOW (2)-
1 part Jägermeister®, 1 part Orange Vodka

BLACKBERRY SLAMMER-
2 parts Brandy, 2 parts Coffee Liqueur, 1 part Amaretto, 1 part Blackberry
Brandy
splash Lime Juice

BLASTER-
1 part Triple Sec, 1 part Coffee Liqueur, 1 part Irish Cream Liqueur
(Layer in Order)

BLEACHER CREATURE-
1 part Butterscotch Schnapps, 1 part 151-proof Rum (Layer in Order)

BLOOD CLOT-
Southern Comfort®
fill Lemon-Lime Soda, splash Grenadine (lace)
(Do Not Mix, Serve with Drinking Straw, Drink all at once)
(Mix into Highball Glass with ice)

BLOODY BRAIN-
1 part Blended Whiskey, 1 part Irish Cream Liqueur
Grenadine (Float)

BLOODY STOOL-
1 part Campari, 1 part Irish Cream Liqueur, 1 part 151-proof Rum
splash Lime Juice

BLOW JOB (1)-
1 part Coffee Liqueur, 1 part Irish Cream Liqueur, 1 part Vodka
top Whipped Cream

BLOW JOB (2)-
1 part Banana Liqueur, 1 part Coffee Liqueur, 1 part Irish Cream Liqueur
top Whipped Cream

BLOW JOB (3)-
Irish Cream Liqueur
top Whipped Cream

BLOW JOB (4)-
Amaretto
top Whipped Cream

BLUE BALLS-
1 part Blue Curaçao, 1 part Coconut Rum, 1 part Peach Schnapps
Sour Mix, splash Lemon-Lime Soda

BLUE BANANA-
1 part Banana Liqueur, 1 part Blue Curaçao

BLUE BAYOU (1)-
2 parts Spiced Rum, 1 part Blue Curaçao

BLUE BAYOU (2)-
1 part Blue Curaçao, 1 part Vodka
splash Grapefruit Juice, splash Pineapple Juice

BLUE CABOOSE-
1 part Irish Cream Liqueur, 1 part Blended Whiskey, 1 part Amaretto
(Layer in Order)

BLUE CARNATION-
1 part Blue Curaçao, 1 part White Crème de Caçao

BLUE CHIMNEY SMOKE-
Tequila, splash Blue Curaçao (float)
Orange Juice

BLUE COOL-
2 parts Peppermint Schnapps, 1 part Blue Curaçao

BLUE DEVIL-
4 parts Gin, 1 part Blue Curaçao, 1 part Cherry Liqueur
splash Sour Mix

BLUE GLORY-
Peppermint Schnapps, splash Blue Curaçao

BLUE HAWAII-
1 part Blue Curaçao, 1 part Light Rum, 1 part White Crème de Caçao
splash Pineapple Juice, splash Light Cream or Milk

BLUE HAWAIIAN-
1 part Blue Curaçao, 1 part Coconut Rum
splash Pineapple Juice

BLUE ICE-
1 part Blue Curaçao, 1 part Citrus Vodka
(Layer in Order)

BLUE KAMIKAZE -
1 part Blue Curaçao, 1 part Vodka
splash Lime Juice

BLUE LEMON DROP-
Vodka, splash Blue Curaçao
splash Sour Mix

BLUE MARBLE-
1 part Black Sambuca, 1 part Light Rum, 1 part Light Cream or Milk,
1 part Gin
(Layer in Order)

BLUE MOON-
2 parts Gin, 1 part Blue Curaçao

BLUE NEON-
3 parts Goldschläger®, 1 part 151-proof Rum, splash Blue Curaçao
(Layer in Order)

BLUE NUT-
1 part Blueberry Schnapps, 1 part Hazelnut Liqueur

BLUE PASSION-
1 part Blue Curaçao, 1 part Spiced Rum
splash Sour Mix

BLUE PEACH-
2 parts Blue Curaçao, 1 part Peach Schnapps

BLUE POLAR BEAR-
1 part Peppermint Schnapps, 1 part Vodka

BLUE SHARK-
2 parts Tequila, 2 parts Vodka, 1 part Blue Curaçao

BLUE SMURF PISS-
1 part 151-proof Rum, 1 part Blue Curaçao, 1 part Goldschläger®,
1 part Jägermeister®, 1 part Peppermint Schnapps

BLUE TAIL FOX-
1 part Blue Curaçao, 1 part Brown Crème de Caçao

BLUE TRAIN-
1 part Blue Curaçao, 1 part Gin
splash Lime Juice

BLUE WAVE-
1 part Blue Curaçao, 1 part Light Rum
splash Lime Juice, splash Pineapple Juice

BLUE WHALE-
1 part Blue Curaçao, 1 part Vodka or Light Rum
splash Sour Mix

BLUEBEARD-
1 part Blueberry Brandy, 1 part Vodka

BLUEBERRY RHUMBA-
2 parts Light Rum, 1 part Blueberry Schnapps, 1 part Blue Curaçao,
    1 part Dark Rum, 1 part Triple Sec
splash Lime Juice, splash Pineapple Juice

BLUE-EYED BLONDE-
1 part Banana Liqueur, 1 part Blue Curaçao, 1 part Irish Cream Liqueur
(Layer in Order)

BLURRICANE-
1 part Blue Curaçao, 1 part Peppermint Schnapps, 1 part Goldschläger®,
    1 part Jägermeister®, 1 part Bourbon Whiskey, 1 part Licorice Liqueur
(Layer in Order)

BOB MARLEY-
1 part Melon Liqueur, 1 part Jägermeister®, 1 part Goldschläger®
(Layer in Order)

BOMB, THE-
1 part Banana Liqueur, 1 part Peach Schnapps, 1 part Sour Apple Schnapps
Pineapple Juice, Lemon-Lime Soda

BONFIRE-
3 parts Irish Cream Liqueur, 1 part Goldschläger®
sprinkle Cinnamon (Layer in Order)

BONG WATER-
1 part Jägermeister®, 1 part Melon Liqueur
Orange Juice

BONSAI PIPELINE (1)-
2 parts Tropical Fruit Schnapps, 1 part Vodka

BONSAI PIPELINE (2)-
3 parts Bourbon Whiskey, 3 parts Melon Liqueur,
    1 part 151-proof Rum (Layer in Order)

BOOGER-
1 part Banana Liqueur, 1 part Coconut Rum, 1 part Melon Liqueur,
    splash Irish Cream Liqueur (lace)

BOOGERS IN THE GRASS-
1 part Melon Liqueur, 1 part Peach Schnapps, splash Irish Cream Liqueur (lace)

BOOTLEGGER-
1 part Jack Daniel's® Tennessee Sour Mash Whiskey, 1 part Southern Comfort®,
    1 part Tequila

BOSTON GOLD-
2 parts Vodka, 1 part Banana Liqueur
splash Orange Juice

BOSTON STRANGLER-***
1 part Jägermeister®, 1 part Peppermint Schnapps, 1 part Tequila

BOTTOM BOUNCER-
1 part Irish Cream Liqueur, 1 part Butterscotch Schnapps (Layer in Order)

BOURBON STREET-
1 part Amaretto, 1 part Bourbon Whiskey

BRAIN (1)-
3 parts Irish Cream Liqueur, 1 part Peach Schnapps

BRAIN (2)-
1 part Coffee Liqueur, 1 part Peach Schnapps, 1 part Irish Cream Liqueur
(Layer in Order)

BRAIN (3)-
1 part Strawberry Schnapps, 1 part Peach Schnapps, 1 part Irish Cream Liqueur
(Layer in Order)

BRAIN BLENDER-
2 parts Southern Comfort®, 1 part Banana Liqueur, 1 part Light Rum,
1 part Peach Schnapps
splash Grenadine, splash Orange Juice

BRAIN DAMAGE-
1 part Amaretto, 1 part 151-proof Rum, splash Irish Cream Liqueur (lace)

BRAIN DEAD-
1 part Triple Sec, 1 part Vodka
Sour Mix

BRAIN DESTROYER-
1 part Amaretto, 1 part Coffee Liqueur, 1 part Irish Cream Liqueur,
splash 151-proof Rum (lace)

BRAIN ERASER-
2 parts Vodka, 1 part Amaretto, 1 part Coffee Liqueur
fill Club Soda (Do Not Mix, Serve with Drinking Straw, Drink all at once)
(Mix into Highball Glass with ice)

BRAIN HEMORRHAGE (1)-
3 parts Irish Cream Liqueur, 1 part Peach or Strawberry Schnapps
splash Grenadine (lace)

BRAIN HEMORRHAGE (2)-
1 part Coffee Liqueur, 1 part Vodka, splash Irish Cream Liqueur (top)
splash Grenadine (lace)

BRAIN TUMOR-
Irish Cream Liqueur, splash Peach or Strawberry Schnapps

BRAIN WAVE-
1 part Irish Cream Liqueur, 1 part Vodka (Layer in Order)
splash Grenadine (lace)

BRASS BALLS-
1 part Grand Marnier®, 1 part Peach Schnapps
Pineapple Juice

BRAVE BULL-
2 parts Tequila, 1 part Coffee Liqueur

BREATHALYZER-
1 part Light Rum, 1 part Peppermint Schnapps

BROADWAY SMILE-
1 part Triple Sec, 1 part Citrus Rum, 1 part Crème de Cassis
(Layer in Order)

BROKEN DOWN GOLF CART-
1 part Melon Liqueur, 1 part Amaretto, 1 part Cranberry Juice
(Layer in Order)

BROWN BOMBER-
1 part Peanut Liqueur, 1 part White Crème de Caçao

BROWN COW-
1 part Brown Crème de Caçao, 1 part Vodka

BROWN EYE OPENER-
1 part Amaretto, 1 part Butterscotch Schnapps, 1 part Coffee Liqueur,
1 part 100-proof Vodka, 1 part Irish Cream Liqueur

BRUISED HEART-
1 part Peach Schnapps, 1 part Raspberry Liqueur, 1 part Vodka
Cranberry Juice

BUBBLEGUM (1)-
1 part Banana Liqueur, 1 part Melon Liqueur, 1 part Vodka
splash Orange Juice, splash Grenadine

BUBBLEGUM (2)-
1 part Amaretto, 1 part Banana Liqueur, 1 part Yukon Jack® Canadian Liqueur
splash Orange Juice, splash Light Cream or Milk, splash Grenadine

BUBBLEGUM (3)-
1 part Banana Liqueur, 1 part Peach Schnapps, 1 part Vodka
splash Orange Juice

BUBBLEGUM (4)-
1 part Banana Liqueur, 1 part Peach Schnapps, 1 part Southern Comfort®,
1 part Vodka

BUBBLEGUM (5)-
1 part Banana Liqueur, 1 part Southern Comfort®
splash Light Cream or Milk, splash Grenadine

BUFFALO SWEAT (1)-
   1 part Tequila, 1 part 151-proof Rum
   splash Hot Sauce

BUFFALO SWEAT (2)-
   Bourbon Whiskey
   splash Hot Sauce

BULL SH*T-
   1 part Light Rum, 1 part Peach Schnapps or Pear Schnapps

BUM F**KER-
   1 part Jack Daniel's® Tennessee Sour Mash Whiskey, 1 part Tequila

BUMBLEBEE (1)-
   1 part Coffee Liqueur, 1 part Irish Cream Liqueur, 1 part Sambuca

BUMBLEBEE (2)-
   1 part Vanilla Liqueur, 1 part Vodka

BUMBLEBEE (3)-
   3 parts Blackberry Brandy, 1 part White Crème de Menthe

BUSHWHACKER-
   1 part Amaretto, 1 part Coffee Liqueur, 1 part Irish Cream Liqueur,
      1 part Light Rum

BUTTER PECAN SHOOTER-
   2 parts Hazelnut Liqueur, 1 part Butterscotch Schnapps,
      1 part Vanilla Liqueur

BUTTERBALL-
   1 part Irish Cream Liqueur, 1 part Butterscotch Schnapps
   (Layer in Order, optional)

BUTTERY FINGER-
   1 part Butterscotch Schnapps, 1 part Coffee Liqueur, 1 part Irish Cream
      Liqueur, 1 part Vodka

BUTTERY JAGER RIPPLE-
   1 part Butterscotch Schnapps, 1 part Jägermeister®, 1 part Irish Cream Liqueur

BUTTERY NIPPLE-
   1 part Butterscotch Schnapps, 1 part Irish Cream Liqueur, 1 part Vodka

BUTTERY NIPPLE WITH AN ATTITUDE-
   1 part Butterscotch Schnapps, 1 part Irish Cream Liqueur,
      splash Peppermint Schnapps

BUTTERY NIPPLE WITH A CHERRY KISS-
   1 part Butterscotch Schnapps, 1 part Irish Cream Liqueur,
      splash Cranberry Liqueur

BUTTMEISTER-
   3 parts Jägermeister®, 1 part Butterscotch Schnapps

BUTTOCK CLENCHER-
 1 part Gin, 1 part Tequila, splash Melon Liqueur
 splash Sour Mix, splash Pineapple Juice

BUZZARD'S BREATH-
 1 part Amaretto, 1 part Coffee Liqueur, 1 part Peppermint Schnapps

C-SPOT-
 Peach Schnapps
 Cranberry Juice

CACTUS SPIKE-
 1 part Margarita Schnapps, 1 part Sloe Gin
 splash Orange Juice, splash Sour Mix

CACTUS THORN-
 2 parts Tequila, 1 part Green Crème de Menthe
 Lime Juice

CALIFORNIA SURFER-
 1 part Coconut Rum, 1 part Jägermeister®
 Pineapple Juice

CAMEL DRIVER-
 1 part Sambuca, 1 part Irish Cream Liqueur (Layer in Order)

CAMSHAFT-
 1 part Jägermeister®, 1 part Irish Cream Liqueur, 1 part Root Beer Schnapps

CANADIAN MOOSE-
 1 part Coffee Liqueur, 1 part Irish Cream Liqueur, 1 part Crown Royal®
  Canadian Whiskey (Layer in Order)

CANADIAN SALAD-
 2 parts Canadian Whiskey, 1 part Brandy, 1 part Irish Mist®,
  1 part Scotch Whiskey
 splash Orange Juice, splash Sour Mix

CANDY-
 1 part Brandy, 1 part Galliano®, splash Maraschino Liqueur
 splash Orange Juice

CANDY APPLE (1)-
 1 part Apple Schnapps, 1 part Cinnamon Schnapps

CANDY APPLE (2)-
 1 part Apple Schnapps, 1 part Peach Schnapps
 splash Cranberry Juice

CANDY ASS-
 1 part Irish Cream Liqueur, 1 part Raspberry Liqueur,
  1 part White Crème de Caçao

CANDY BAR (1)-
 1 part Hazelnut Liqueur, 1 part Vodka

CANDY BAR (2)-
1 part Brown Crème de Caçao, 1 part Coffee Liqueur, 1 part Hazelnut Liqueur
Light Cream or Milk

CANDY CANE-
1 part Green Crème de Menthe, 1 part Peppermint Schnapps (Layer in Order)

CANDY PANTS-
3 parts Blended Whiskey, 1 part Cherry Brandy
splash Sour Mix, splash Grenadine

CANDY STORE-
1 part Amaretto, 1 part Crème de Noyaux, 1 part Irish Cream Liqueur,
1 part Raspberry Liqueur

CANYON QUAKE-
1 part Amaretto, 1 part Brandy, 1 part Irish Cream Liqueur

CAPITAL PUNISHMENT-
1 part Amaretto, 1 part Jack Daniel's® Tennessee Sour Mash Whiskey

CAR CRASH-
1 part Amaretto, 1 part Peach Schnapps, 1 part Southern Comfort®
Orange Juice, Sour Mix, splash Grenadine

CARAMEL APPLE-
1 part Butterscotch Schnapps, 1 part Sour Apple Schnapps

CARAMEL NUT-
2 parts Butterscotch Schnapps or Caramel Liqueur, 2 parts Hazelnut Liqueur,
1 part White Crème de Caçao

CARIBBEAN BERRY-
2 parts Spiced Rum, 1 part Coconut Rum, 1 part Melon Liqueur,
1 part Peach Schnapps
Cranberry Juice

CARIBBEAN BREEZE-
4 parts Dark Rum, 1 part Banana Liqueur
splash Pineapple Juice, splash Lime Juice, splash Grenadine,
splash Orange Bitters

CARIBBEAN GRASSHOPPER-
1 part Coconut Liqueur, 1 part Green Crème de Menthe, 1 part White
Crème de Caçao

CARIBBEAN ROMANCE-
1 part Amaretto, 1 part Light Rum
splash Orange Juice, splash Pineapple Juice, Grenadine (Float)

CARIBBEAN SMUGGLER-
2 parts Dark Rum, 1 part Triple Sec
splash Orange Juice, splash Sour Mix

CARROT CAKE-
1 part Butterscotch Schnapps, 1 part Goldschläger®, 1 part Irish Cream Liqueur

CEMENT MIXER-
Irish Cream Liqueur
layer Lime Juice (shoot, swish around in mouth before swallowing)

CEREBRAL HEMORRHAGE-
1 part Coffee Liqueur, 1 part Peach Schnapps, 1 part Irish Cream Liqueur,
1 part Grenadine (lace) (Layer in Order)

CHAIN GANG-
1 part Amaretto, 1 part Banana Liqueur, 1 part Coffee Liqueur

CHANNEL 64-
1 part Banana Liqueur, 1 part Irish Cream Liqueur, 1 part Eggnog Liqueur
(Layer in Order)

CHARTBUSTER-
1 part Coconut Liqueur, 1 part Strawberry Schnapps
splash Pineapple Juice

CHASTITY BELT-
2 parts Tia Maria®, 1 part Hazelnut Liqueur, 1 part Irish Cream Liqueur,
splash Light Cream or Milk (Layer in Order)

CHEAP SUNGLASSES-
2 parts Melon Liqueur, 1 part Peach Schnapps
splash Orange Juice, splash Pineapple Juice, splash Sour Mix

CHEESE SANDWICH-
3 parts Melon Liqueur, 1 part Triple Sec, splash Dark Rum
splash Sour Mix

CHERRY KISS-
1 part Irish Cream Liqueur, 1 part Raspberry Liqueur
(Layer in Order)

CHERRY REPAIR KIT-
1 part Amaretto, 1 part White Crème de Caçao, splash Maraschino Liqueur
splash Grenadine

CHERRY TREE CLIMBER-
2 parts Cherry Brandy, 2 parts White Crème de Caçao,
1 part Peppermint Schnapps

CHICKEN DROP-
1 part Jägermeister®, 1 part Peach Schnapps
Orange Juice

CHINESE TORTURE-
1 part Canton Liqueur, 1 part 151-proof Rum

CHOCOLATE ALMOND-
1 part Amaretto, 1 part White Crème de Caçao

CHOCOLATE BANANA-
1 part Banana Liqueur, 1 part Brown Crème de Caçao, 1 part Dark Rum

CHOCOLATE BANANA BANSHEE-
1 part Banana Liqueur, 1 part Coffee Liqueur, 1 part White Crème de Caçao

CHOCOLATE BLACK RUSSIAN SHOOTER-
2 parts Vodka, 1 part Brown Crème de Caçao, 1 part Coffee Liqueur

CHOCOLATE CHIMP-
1 part White Crème de Caçao, 1 part Coffee Liqueur, 1 part Banana Liqueur (Layer in Order)

CHOCOLATE CHIP-
1 part Amaretto, 1 part White Crème de Caçao, 1 part Irish Cream Liqueur (Layer in Order)

CHOCOLATE CORVETTE-
2 parts Dark Rum, 1 part Brown Crème de Caçao, 1 part Coffee Liqueur

CHOCOLATE COVERED BANANA-
1 part Banana Liqueur, 1 part Brown Crème de Caçao, 1 part Coconut Rum, 1 part Vanilla Liqueur

CHOCOLATE COVERED CHERRY-
1 part Amaretto, 1 part Coffee Liqueur, 1 part White Crème de Caçao splash Grenadine (lace)

CHOCOLATE COVERED STRAWBERRY-
1 part Strawberry Schnapps, 1 part White Crème de Caçao splash Light Cream or Milk

CHOCOLATE MINT-
1 part Coffee Liqueur, 1 part Gin, 1 part Green Crème de Menthe, 1 part Peppermint Schnapps

CHOCOLATE MINT KISS (1)-
2 parts Brown Crème de Caçao, 1 part White Crème de Menthe

CHOCOLATE MINT KISS (2)-
1 part Brown Crème de Caçao, 1 part Coffee Liqueur, 1 part White Crème de Menthe

CHOCOLATE MINT RUM-
2 parts Dark Rum, 1 part Brown Crème de Caçao, 1 part 151-proof Rum, splash White Crème de Menthe

CHOCOLATE MONKEY-
2 parts Banana Liqueur, 1 part White Crème de Caçao, 1 part Light Rum

CHOCOLATE RUM-
2 parts Light Rum, 1 part White Crème de Caçao, 1 part White Crème de Menthe, splash 1 part 151-proof Rum

CHOCOLATE SIN-
1 part White Crème de Caçao, 1 part Peppermint Schnapps

CHOCOLATE SNOW BEAR-
 1 part Amaretto, 1 part French Vanilla Liqueur, 1 part White Crème de Caçao

CHOCOLATE SUNDAE-
 1 part Irish Cream Liqueur, 1 part White Crème de Cação,
  1 part Coffee Liqueur, top Whipped Cream
 (Layer in Order)

CHOCOLATE TOASTED ALMOND-
 1 part Amaretto, 1 part Brown Crème de Cação,
  1 part Coffee Liqueur

CHOCOLATE VICE-
 2 parts Dark Rum, 1 part Bourbon Whiskey, 1 part Brown Crème de Cação,
  1 part Coffee Liqueur

CHOCOLATE XS-
 1 part Brown Crème de Cação, 1 part Dark Rum, 1 part Irish Cream Liqueur

CHOCOLATIER CAKE-
 1 part Brown Crème de Cação, 1 part Brandy, 1 part Light Cream or Milk
 (Layer in Order)

CHRISTMAS SHOT-
 1 part Melon Liqueur, 1 part Raspberry Liqueur (Layer in Order)

CHRISTMAS TREE-
 1 part Green Crème de Menthe, 1 part Grenadine, 1 part Irish Cream Liqueur
 (Layer in Order)

CHUCK RASPBERRY-
 3 parts Raspberry Liqueur, 1 part Amaretto
 splash Pineapple Juice, splash Grenadine

CINNAMON ROLL-
 Cinnamon Schnapps, splash Apple Schnapps

CINNAMON TOAST (1)-
 1 part Apple Schnapps, 1 part Cinnamon Schnapps, 1 part Spiced Rum

CINNAMON TOAST (2)-
 1 part Goldschläger®, 1 part Irish Cream Liqueur

CINNAMON TOAST CRUNCH-
 1 part Butterscotch Schnapps, 1 part Irish Cream Liqueur, 1 part Goldschläger®
 (Layer in Order)

CITRON BOMB-
 1 part Citrus Vodka, 1 part Grand Marnier®
 splash Orange Juice

CITRON NEON-
 3 parts Citrus Vodka, 2 parts Melon Liqueur, 1 part Blue Curaçao
 splash Sour Mix

CIVIL WAR-
1 part Jack Daniel's® Tennessee Sour Mash Whiskey, 1 part Yukon Jack®
    Canadian Liqueur
splash Cranberry Juice

CLIMAX (1)-
1 part Amaretto, 1 part Banana Liqueur, 1 part Triple Sec, 1 part Vodka,
    1 part White Crème de Caçao

CLIMAX (2)-
1 part Coffee Liqueur, 1 part Southern Comfort®
top Whipped Cream

CLOUD 9-
1 part Amaretto, 1 part Black Raspberry Liqueur, 1 part Irish Cream Liqueur

CLUB MED SHOOTER-
2 parts Vodka, 1 part Raspberry Liqueur
splash Pineapple Juice, splash Lime Juice

COBANA SHOOTER-
1 part Banana Liqueur, 1 part Coffee Liqueur, 1 part Strawberry Schnapps

COBRA-
1 part Irish Cream Liqueur, 1 part Jägermeister®, 1 part Peppermint Schnapps
(Layer in Order)

COBRA'S BITE-
1 part Pepper Vodka, 1 part Green Crème de Menthe

COCAINE (1)-
1 part Raspberry Liqueur, 1 part Southern Comfort®, 1 part Vodka
splash Cranberry Juice, splash Orange Juice

COCAINE (2)-
1 part Raspberry Liqueur, 1 part Vodka
Grapefruit Juice

COCAINE LADY-
1 part Coffee Liqueur, 1 part Irish Cream Liqueur, 1 part Light Rum,
    1 part Vodka
splash Light Cream or Milk, splash Cola (float)

COCKROACH-
1 part Drambuie®, 1 part Coffee Liqueur

COCONUT BROWNIE-
2 parts Spiced Rum, 1 part Brown Crème de Caçao, 1 part Coconut Rum

COCONUT CLIMBER-
2 parts Coconut Rum, 1 part Mango Liqueur, 1 part Spiced Rum
splash Light Cream or Milk, splash Orange Juice, splash Grenadine

COFFEE BERRY-
1 part Coffee Liqueur, 1 part Hazelnut Liqueur, 1 part Raspberry Liqueur

COFFEE GRASSHOPPER-
1 part Coffee Liqueur, 1 part White Crème de Menthe

COFFEE STICK-
3 parts Coffee Liqueur, 1 part Sambuca

COLD PORRIDGE-
Scotch Whiskey
splash Light Cream or Milk, Honey

COMA (1)-
1 part Triple Sec, 1 part Coffee Liqueur, 1 part Sambuca
(Layer in Order)

COMA (2)-
1 part Cinnamon Schnapps, 1 part Dark Rum

COMFORTABLE BROTHER-
1 part Hazelnut Liqueur, 1 part Southern Comfort®

COMFORTABLE PIRATE-
3 parts Spiced Rum, 1 part Southern Comfort®
splash Pineapple Juice

CONEY ISLAND BABY-
2 parts Peppermint Schnapps, 1 part Brown Crème de Caçao

COOKIE MONSTER-
1 part Coffee Liqueur, 1 part Irish Cream Liqueur, 1 part 151-proof Rum (lace)
(ignite, optional) {extinguish flame before drinking}

COOL-AID (1)-
1 part Amaretto, 1 part Melon Liqueur
splash Pineapple Juice

COOL-AID (2)-
1 part Amaretto, 1 part Melon Liqueur, 1 part Southern Comfort®
splash Cranberry Juice

COOL KISS-
Amaretto, splash Strawberry Schnapps

COOL OPERATOR-
2 parts Melon Liqueur, 1 part Light Rum, 1 part Vodka
splash Grapefruit Juice, splash Orange Juice, splash Lime Juice

COON DOG-
1 part Blackberry Liqueur, 1 part Jack Daniel's® Tennessee Sour Mash Whiskey

COPPER PENNY-
2 parts Amaretto, 1 part White Crème de Caçao

CORAL GOLD-
2 parts Gold Rum, 2 parts Triple Sec, 1 part Peppermint Schnapps

CORAL REEF-
2 parts Coconut Rum, 1 part Strawberry Schnapps, 1 part Vodka
splash Sour Mix

CORPSE REVIVER-
1 part Citrus Rum, 1 part Gin, 1 part Triple Sec, splash Licorice Liqueur
splash Lime Juice

CORRIDOR OF FIRE-
2 parts Coffee Liqueur, 1 part Cognac, 2 parts Irish Cream Liqueur
(Layer in Order)

CORTISONE-
1 part Coffee Liqueur, 1 part Dark Rum, splash Vanilla Liqueur

COUGH DROP-
1 part Blackberry Brandy, 1 part Peppermint Schnapps

COUGH SYRUP (1)-
1 part Amaretto, 1 part Southern Comfort®
splash Grenadine

COUGH SYRUP (2)-
1 part Blue Curaçao, 1 part Crème de Menthe, 1 part Vodka

COUGH SYRUP (3)-
1 part Cherry Vodka, 1 part Root Beer Schnapps

COUNTRY & WESTERN-
1 part Coconut Rum, 1 part Dark Rum
splash Orange Juice, splash Pineapple Juice

COWBOY COCKSUCKER-
1 part Butterscotch Schnapps, 1 part Irish Cream Liqueur,
    splash Goldschläger®

CRACK PIPE-
1 part 151-proof Rum, 1 part Bourbon Whiskey, 1 part Peppermint Schnapps

CRANIUM MELTDOWN-
1 part 151-proof Rum, 1 part Coconut Rum, 1 part Raspberry Liqueur
Pineapple Juice

CRAZY ITALIAN-
1 part Amaretto, 1 part Irish Cream Liqueur

CRAZY NUN-
1 part Anisette, 1 part Tequila

CREAMSICLE (1)-
Vanilla Liqueur
splash Orange Juice, splash Light Cream or Milk

CREAMSICLE (2)-
Amaretto
splash Orange Juice, splash Light Cream or Milk

CREAMSICLE (3)-
1 part Triple Sec, 1 part White Crème de Caçao
splash Light Cream or Milk

CREAMY BUSH-
1 part Bushmill's® Irish Whiskey, 1 part Irish Cream Liqueur

CREAMY NUTS-
1 part Banana Liqueur, 1 part Hazelnut Liqueur

CREATURE FROM THE BLACK LAGOON-
1 part Black Sambuca, 1 part Jägermeister®

CRÈMESICKLE (1)-
1 part Galliano®, 1 part White Crème de Caçao
splash Orange Juice, splash Light Cream or Milk

CRÈMESICKLE (2)-
1 part Galliano®, 1 part Triple Sec
splash Orange Juice, splash Light Cream or Milk

CRIMSON TIDE-
1 part 151-proof Rum, 1 part Coconut Rum, 1 part Raspberry Liqueur,
    1 part Southern Comfort®, 1 part Tropical Fruit Schnapps, 1 part Vodka
Cranberry Juice, Lemon-Lime Soda

CRISP APPLE-
2 parts Apple Brandy, 1 part Amaretto, 1 part Tequila, splash Triple Sec
splash Lime Juice

CRISPY CRUNCH-
1 part Hazelnut Liqueur, 1 part White Crème de Caçao

CROCODILE-
2 parts Citrus Vodka, 2 parts Melon Liqueur, 1 part Triple Sec
splash Sour Mix

CRUISE CONTROL-
1 part Apricot Brandy, 1 part Light Rum, 1 part Triple Sec
splash Lime Juice

CRYPTO NUGGET-
2 parts Apple Schnapps, 1 part Blue Curaçao, 1 part Vodka
splash Lime Juice

CUCARACHA-
1 part Coffee Liqueur, 1 part Tequila, 1 part Vodka

CUM DROP-
2 parts Coffee Liqueur, 2 parts Irish Cream Liqueur,
    1 part Banana Liqueur

CUM IN A HOT TUB-
Irish Cream Liqueur (lace)
Orange Juice

CUM IN A POND-
1 part Blue Curaçao, 1 part Vodka, splash Irish Cream Liqueur (lace)

CUM SCORCHER-
1 part Butterscotch Schnapps, 1 part Vodka, 1 part Coffee Liqueur,
  splash Irish Cream Liqueur (Layer in Order)

CUM SHOT
1 part Butterscotch Schnapps, 1 part Irish Cream Liqueur
top Whipped Cream

CUPID'S KISS-
2 parts Crème de Noyaux, 1 part White Crème de Caçao

CYCLONE ATTACK-
1 part Blue Curaçao, 1 part Lime Juice (Layer in Order)

CYRANO-
1 part Irish Cream Liqueur, 1 part Grand Marnier®, splash Raspberry Liqueur
(Layer in order)

DC-
1 part Irish Cream Liqueur, 1 part Tequila (Layer in Order)

DC-3-
1 part Brown Crème De Caçao, 1 part Sambuca, 1 part Irish Cream Liqueur
(Layer in Order)

DC-9-
1 part Coffee Liqueur, 1 part Sambuca, 1 part Light Rum (Layer in Order)

D-DAY-
1 part 151-proof Rum, 1 part Banana Liqueur, 1 part Citrus Vodka,
  1 part Raspberry Liqueur
Orange Juice

D. O. A. (1)-
1 part Bärenjäger®, 1 part Jägermeister®, 1 part Peppermint Schnapps

D. O. A. (2)-
1 part Hazelnut Liqueur, 1 part Peach Schnapps, 1 part White Crème de Caçao

DAGGER-
1 part Tequila, 1 part White Crème de Caçao, 1 part Peach Schnapps
(Layer in Order)

DAKOTA-
1 part Bourbon Whiskey, 1 part Tequila

DAILY MAIL-
Scotch Whiskey, splash Amaretto, splash Blue Curaçao
splash Sour Mix

DAMNED IF YOU DO-
3 parts Blended Whiskey, 1 part Cinnamon Schnapps

DANCIN' COWBOY-
1 part Banana Liqueur, 1 part Coffee Liqueur, 1 part Irish Cream Liqueur (Layer in Order)

DANGEROUOS GRANDMA-
2 parts Coffee Liqueur, 1 part Amaretto, 1 part Blended Whiskey

DANGEROUS LIASONS-
1 part Tia Maria®, 1 part Triple Sec
splash Sour Mix

DANGEROUS SHOT-
1 part Banana Liqueur, 1 part Coffee Liqueur, 1 part Dark Rum,
    1 part Light Rum

DARK & LOVELY-
1 part Coffee Liqueur, 1 part Hazelnut Liqueur, 1 part Irish Cream Liqueur

DARK EYES-
3 parts Vodka, 1 part Blackberry Brandy
splash Lime Juice

DARK NIGHTMARE-
4 parts Coffee Liqueur, 1 part Goldschläger®
splash Light Cream or Milk

DARTH VADER-
2 parts Jägermeister®, 1 part Gin, 1 part Light Rum, 1 part Tequila,
    1 part Triple Sec, 1 part Vodka
splash Sour Mix

DEAD BIRD-
1 part Jägermeister®, 1 part Wild Turkey® Bourbon Whiskey

DEAD FROG-
3 parts Melon Liqueur, 1 part Irish Cream Liqueur
splash Grenadine (lace)

DEAD NAZI-
1 part Jägermeister®, 1 part Peppermint Schnapps

DEAD HITLER-
1 part Goldschläger®, 1 part Jägermeister®, 1 part Peppermint Schnapps

DEATH BY CHOCOLATE-
2 parts Brown Crème de Caçao, 1 part Irish Cream Liqueur, 1 part Vodka

DEATH BY FIRE-
1 part Cinnamon Schnapps, 1 part Peppermint Schnapps
Hot Sauce

DEATH BY SEX-
1 part Amaretto, 1 part Peach Schnapps, 1 part Sloe Gin, 1 part Southern
    Comfort®, 1 part Triple Sec, 1 part Vodka
Cranberry Juice, Orange Juice

DEATH FROM WITHIN-
1 part Dark Rum, 1 part Light Rum, 1 part Vodka

DEATH ROW-
1 part 151-proof Rum, 1 part Blended Whiskey

DEATH WISH-
1 part Grenadine, 1 part Bourbon Whiskey, 1 part Peppermint Schnapps,
1 part 151-proof Rum (Layer in Order)

DECADENCE-
1 part Coffee Liqueur, 1 part Hazelnut Liqueur, 1 part Irish Cream Liqueur
(Layer in Order)

DECEIVER-
2 parts Tequila, 1 part Galliano®

DEEP DARK SECRET-
3 parts Dark Rum, 1 part Coffee Liqueur, 1 part Light Rum
splash Light Cream or Milk

DEEP SEA DIVER-
3 parts Dark Rum, 1 part Light Rum, 1 part Triple Sec, 1 part 151-proof Rum
splash Sour Mix

DEEP THROAT (1)-
1 part Coffee Liqueur, 1 part Vodka
top Whipped Cream

DEEP THROAT (2)-
1 part Coffee Liqueur, 1 part Grand Marnier®
top Whipped Cream

DEER SPERM-
1 part Jägermeister®, 1 part Irish Cream Liqueur (lace)

DESERT GLOW-
1 part Peach Schnapps, 1 part Tequila
splash Orange Juice

DESERT SUNRISE SHOOTER-
1 part Blue Curaçao, 1 part Margarita Schnapps
splash Orange Juice, splash Sour Mix

DEVIL YOU DON'T KNOW, THE-
1 part Brown Crème de Cacao, 1 part Jägermeister® (Layer in Order)

DEVIL'S MOUTHWASH-
1 part Black Sambuca, 1 part Southern Comfort®

DIESEL FUEL-
1 part Jägermeister®, 1 part Spiced Rum

DINGO-
1 part Amaretto, 1 part Light Rum, 1 part Southern Comfort®
splash Sour Mix, splash Orange Juice, splash Grenadine

Shooters

DINNER CLUB BABES-***
1 part Amaretto, 1 part Southern Comfort®
splash Cranberry Juice, splash Orange Juice

DIRTY BANANA-
2 parts Coffee Liqueur, 1 part Banana Liqueur, 1 part Light Rum

DIRTY DIAPER-
1 part Amaretto, 1 part Melon Liqueur, 1 part Raspberry Liqueur,
    1 part Southern Comfort®, 1 part Vodka
Orange Juice

DIRTY GIRL SCOUT-
1 part Coffee Liqueur, 1 part Irish Cream Liqueur, 1 part Vodka,
    splash Green Crème de Menthe

DIRTY GIRL SCOUT COOKIE-
2 parts Irish Cream Liqueur, 1 part Green Crème de Menthe

DIRTY HARRY-
1 part Grand Marnier®, 1 part Tia Maria®

DIRTY LEPRECHAUN-
1 part Jägermeister®, 1 part Irish Cream Liqueur, 1 part Melon Liqueur
(Layer in Order)

DIRTY MOTHER-
2 parts Brandy, 1 part Coffee Liqueur

DIRTY NIPPLE-
1 part Sambuca, 1 part Irish Cream Liqueur (Layer in Order)

DIRTY OATMEAL-
1 part Jägermeister®, 1 part Irish Cream Liqueur (Layer in Order)

DIRTY ORGASM-
1 part Triple Sec, 1 part Galliano®, 1 part Irish Cream Liqueur (Layer in Order)

DIRTY SEX ON THE BEACH-
2 parts Peach Schnapps, 1 part Melon Liqueur, 1 part Raspberry Liqueur
Pineapple Juice

DIRTY SOCK-
Scotch Whiskey
splash Pineapple Juice

DIRTY VIRGIN-
3 parts Gin, 1 part Brown Crème de Caçao

DIRTY WHITE MOTHER (1)-
3 parts Brandy, 1 part Coffee Liqueur
splash Light Cream or Milk (float)

DIRTY WHITE MOTHER (2)-
1 part Coffee Liqueur, 1 part Tequila
splash Light Cream or Milk (float)

DISAPPOINTED LADY-
1 part Brandy, 1 part Crème de Noyaux, 1 part Tia Maria®
splash Orange Juice, splash Grenadine

DIZZY BUDDHA SHOOTER-
1 part Amaretto, 1 part Banana Liqueur, 1 part Coconut Rum, 1 part Coffee
Liqueur, 1 part Melon Liqueur, 1 part Dark Rum, 1 part Southern
Comfort®, 1 part Vodka
splash Orange Juice, splash Pineapple Juice, splash Grenadine

DIZZY DAMAGE-
1 part Goldschläger®, 1 part Jägermeister®, 1 part Peppermint Schnapps

DOCTOR PEPPER-
1 part Amaretto, 1 part Spiced Rum
splash Cola

DOLLAR BILL-
1 part Light Rum, 1 part Melon Liqueur
splash Lime Juice

DOMINATOR-
1 part Coffee Liqueur, 1 part Peppermint Schnapps, 1 part Triple Sec

DOUBLE HOMICIDE-
1 part Goldschläger®, 1 part Jägermeister®
Orange Juice

DOUBLEMINT BLOW JOB-
1 part Coffee Liqueur, 1 part Peppermint Schnapps
splash Light Cream or Milk

DOUBLEMINT SHOOTER-
1 part Spearmint Schnapps, splash Coffee Liqueur,
splash Green Crème de Menthe

DRAGON FIRE-
1 part Green Crème de Menthe, 1 part Pepper Vodka

DRAGON'S BREATH-
2 parts Beer, 2 parts Gin, 2 parts 100-proof Vodka, 2 parts Vodka, 1 part Dark
Rum, 1 part Peppermint Schnapps
splash Cola

DREAMY MONKEY-
2 parts Vodka, 1 part Banana Liqueur, 1 part Brown Crème de Caçao

DRINK OF THE GODS-
2 parts Vodka, 1 part Blueberry Schnapps
splash Pineapple Juice

DRY HOLE-
2 parts Light Rum, 1 part Apricot Brandy, 1 part Triple Sec
splash Lime Juice, splash Club Soda

DUCK FART (1)-
1 part Coffee Liqueur, 1 part Irish Cream Liqueur,
1 part Canadian Rye Whiskey
(Layer in Order)

DUCK FART (2)-
1 part Coffee Liqueur, 1 part Brown Crème de Caçao,
1 part Irish Cream Liqueur (Layer in Order)

DUMB F**K-
1 part Canadian Whiskey, 1 part Cinnamon Schnapps

DUTCH VELVET-
1 part Banana Liqueur, 1 part Chocolate Mint Liqueur

DYNASTY-
1 part Amaretto, 1 part Southern Comfort®

E. T.-
1 part Irish Cream Liqueur, 1 part Melon Liqueur, 1 part Vodka

EAGER BEAVER-
2 parts Coffee Liqueur, 2 parts Light Rum, 1 part Triple Sec

EARTHQUAKE-
1 part Amaretto, 1 part Southern Comfort®, 1 part Sambuca
(Layer in Order)

EASTER EGG-
1 part Raspberry Liqueur, 1 part Tia Maria®, 1 part Light Cream or Milk
(Layer in Order)

EAT HOT DEATH-
151-proof Rum
splash Lime Juice

EH BOMB-
1 part Tequila, 1 part White Crème de Menthe, 1 part Licorice Liqueur,
1 part Irish Cream Liqueur (Layer in Order)

EIGHT SECONDS-
1 part Cinnamon Schnapps, 1 part Goldschläger®, 1 part Jägermeister®,
1 part Peppermint Schnapps

EL CID-
Tequila, splash Amaretto
splash Lime Juice, splash Grenadine

EL DIABLO-
Tequila, splash Crème de Cassis
splash Lime Juice

EL REVOLTO-
1 part Peppermint Schnapps, 1 part Irish Cream Liqueur, 1 part Triple Sec
(Layer in Order)

ELECTRIC BANANA-
 2 parts Banana Liqueur, 1 part Coconut Liqueur, 1 part Melon Liqueur

ELECTRIC JAM-
 3 parts Vodka, 1 part Blue Curaçao
 splash Sour Mix

ELECTRIC KAMIKAZE-
 1 part Blue Curaçao, 1 part Triple Sec, 1 part Vodka
 Lime Juice

ELECTRICAL STORM-
 1 part Irish Cream Liqueur, 1 part Peppermint Schnapps, 1 part Goldschläger®,
  1 part Jägermeister®
 (Layer in Order)

ELECTRIC SURFBOARD-
 Blue Curaçao
 Pineapple Juice, splash Grenadine, splash Lemon-Lime Soda (top)

ELECTRIC WATERMELON-
 1 part Light Rum, 1 part Melon Liqueur, 1 part Triple Sec, 1 part Vodka
 splash Orange Juice, splash Grenadine (lace)

ELEPHANT LIPS-
 3 parts Dark Rum, 1 part Banana Liqueur
 splash Lime Juice

EMBRYO-
 Peppermint Schnapps
 splash Light Cream or Milk (lace), splash Grenadine (lace)

END OF MY ROPE-
 Hazelnut Liqueur, splash Banana Liqueur
 splash Pineapple Juice, splash Bitters

END OF THE WORLD-
 1 part 151-proof Rum, 1 part Bourbon Whiskey, 1 part Vodka

ENEBRIATOR-
 1 part Amaretto, 1 part Gin, 1 part Triple Sec, 1 part Vodka
 Pineapple Juice

EPIDURAL-
 1 part Coconut Rum, 1 part 100-proof Vodka

ERECT NIPPLE-
 1 part Tequila, 1 part Sambuca

ERUPTION-
 Canadian Whiskey, splash Crème de Cassis

EVERYBODY'S IRISH-
 Irish Whiskey, splash Green Chartreuse, splash Green Crème de Menthe

EVERYTHING BUT-
1 part Blended Whiskey, 1 part Gin, splash Apricot Brandy
splash Orange Juice, splash Sour Mix

EXTACY-
2 parts Melon Liqueur, 1 part 151-proof Rum, 1 part Citrus Vodka,
    1 part Blue Curaçao (lace)
Pineapple Juice

EXTERMINATOR-
Vodka, splash Sherry

EYE BALL-
splash Grenadine, 2 parts Irish Cream Liqueur, 1 part Blue Curaçao
(Layer in Order)

EYE DROP-
1 part Licorice Liqueur, 1 part Peppermint Schnapps, 1 part Vodka

EYE OPENER (1)-
Light Rum, splash Anisette, splash Triple Sec, splash White Crème de Caçao

EYE OPENER (2)-
1 part Dark Rum, 1 part Jamaican Rum, splash Triple Sec
splash Orange Juice, splash Grapefruit Juice

44D-
1 part Coffee Liqueur, 1 part Peach Schnapps, 1 part Vodka
splash Grenadine

401-
1 part Coffee Liqueur, 1 part Banana Liqueur, 1 part Irish Cream Liqueur,
    1 part Yukon Jack® Canadian Liqueur (Layer in Order)

'57 CHEVY-
1 part Grand Marnier®, 1 part Southern Comfort®, 1 part Vodka
splash Pineapple Juice

'57 CHEVY (WITH A WHITE LICENSE PLATE)-
1 part White Crème de Caçao, 1 part Vodka

'57 T-BIRD-
1 part Amaretto, 1 part Grand Marnier®, 1 part Southern Comfort®
Pineapple Juice

501 BLUE-
1 part Blueberry Schnapps, 1 part Blue Curaçao, 1 part Vodka
splash Sour Mix

F-16-
1 part Coffee Liqueur, 1 part Hazelnut Liqueur, 1 part Irish Cream Liqueur
(Layer in Order)

F-52-
1 part Coffee Liqueur, 1 part Irish Cream Liqueur, 1 part Hazelnut Liqueur
(Layer in Order)

FACE OFF-
1 part Grenadine, 1 part Green Crème de Menthe, 1 part Blue Curaçao, 1 part Sambuca (Layer in Order)

FAT CAT-
2 parts Irish Cream Liqueur, 1 part Amaretto, 1 part Banana Liqueur

FENCE JUMPER-
1 part Light Rum, 1 part Tequila
Hot Sauce

FIRE & ICE (1)-
1 part Tequila, 1 part Green Crème de Menthe (Layer in Order)

FIRE & ICE (2)-
1 part Tequila, 1 part Peppermint Schnapps (Layer in Order)

FIRE BALL (1)-
Cinnamon Schnapps
splash Hot Sauce

FIRE BALL (2)-
Cinnamon Schnapps, splash Cherry Brandy

FIRE BALL (3)-
1 part Coffee Liqueur, 1 part Licorice Liqueur (Layer in Order)

FIRE BALL (4)-
1 part Brandy, 1 part Sambuca (Layer in Order)

FIRE BOMB-
1 part Sour Mash Whiskey, 1 part Tequila, 1 part Vodka
splash Hot Sauce

FIRE BREATHING DRAGON-
1 part Campari, 1 part Tequila, 1 part 151-proof Rum

FIRE IN HEAVEN-
151-proof Rum
splash Hot Sauce

FIRE IN THE HOLE-
Cinnamon Schnapps
splash Hot Sauce

FIRECRACKER (1)-
1 part Cherry Brandy, 1 part Cinnamon Schnapps
splash Hot Sauce

FIRECRACKER (2)-
1 part Raspberry Liqueur, 1 part Vodka
splash Sour Mix

FIRECRACKER (3)-
1 part Raspberry Liqueur, 1 part Tequila
splash Sour Mix

FIRECRACKER (4)-
1 part Blended Whiskey, 1 part Raspberry Liqueur
splash Sour Mix

FIRESTORM-
1 part Cinnamon Schnapps, 1 part Peppermint Schnapps, 1 part 151-proof Rum

FIVE STAR GENERAL-
1 part 151-proof Rum, 1 part Goldschläger®, 1 part Jägermeister®,
    1 part Peppermint Schnapps, 1 part Tequila

FLAMING ARMADILLO-
1 part Tequila, 1 part Amaretto, 1 part 151-proof Rum (Layer in Order)
(ignite, optional) {extinguish flame before drinking}

FLAMING ASSHOLE-
1 part Blueberry Brandy, 1 part 151-proof Rum, 1 part Tequila
(Layer in Order)

FLAMING BEE-
1 part Bärenjäger®, 1 part Sambuca
(Layer in Order)

FLAMING BLUE FK-**
1 part Sambuca, 1 part Blue Curaçao (Layer in Order) (ignite, optional)
(Drink through straw) {extinguish flame before drinking}

FLAMING COCAINE-
1 part Cinnamon Schnapps, 1 part Vodka
Cranberry Juice

FLAMING COURAGE-
1 part Cinnamon Schnapps, 1 part Melon Liqueur, 1 part Peppermint
    Schnapps, splash 151-proof rum (ignite, optional)
{extinguish flame before drinking}

FLAMING DIAMOND-
1 part Strawberry Schnapps, 1 part Peppermint Schnapps,
    1 part Grand Marnier® (Layer in Order)

FLAMING DOCTOR PEPPER-
1 part Amaretto, 1 part Light Rum *(Layer in Order in Shot Glass),* 12 oz. Beer
(ignite, optional) {extinguish flame before drinking}
(drop Shot Glass into Mug of Beer)

FLAMING GORILLA-
1 part Coffee Liqueur, 1 part Peppermint Schnapps, splash 1 part 151-proof
    rum (ignite, optional) {extinguish flame before drinking}

FLAMING ORGY-
1 part Grenadine, 1 part Green Crème de Menthe, 1 part Brandy, 1 part Tequila
(Layer in Order)

FLAT TIRE-
2 parts Tequila, 1 part Sambuca

FLINTSTONE SHOOTER-
3 parts Bourbon Whiskey, 1 part Apple Brandy, 1 part Peppermint Schnapps
splash Lime Juice, splash Grenadine

FLORIDA BANANA-
2 parts Vodka, 1 part Banana Liqueur, 1 part Coconut Liqueur
splash Orange Juice

FLORIDA GATOR-
3 parts Gold Rum, 1 part Maraschino Liqueur, 1 part Triple Sec
splash Orange Juice

FLYING F**K-
1 part Sambuca, 1 part Sour Mash Whiskey (Layer in Order)

FLYING GRASSHOPPER-
1 part Green Crème de Menthe, 1 part Vodka,
1 part White Crème de Menthe

FLYING KANGAROO-
1 part Coconut Rum, 1 part Vodka, splash Galliano®
Orange Juice, Pineapple Juice, splash Light Cream or Milk

FLYING MONKEY-
1 part Coffee Liqueur, 1 part Banana Liqueur, 1 part Irish Cream Liqueur
(Layer in Order)

FOG CITY BLUES-
3 parts Blue Curaçao, 1 part White Crème de Caçao

FOGGY AFTERNOON-
2 parts Vodka, 1 part Apricot Brandy, 1 part Triple Sec,
splash Banana Liqueur
splash Lime Juice

FOOL'S GOLD-
1 part Galliano®, 1 part Vodka

FORBIDDEN JUNGLE-
3 parts Coconut Rum, 1 part Peach Schnapps
Pineapple Juice, splash Lime Juice, splash Grenadine

FORNICATION-
1 part Irish Cream Liqueur, 1 part Tia Maria®
(Layer in Order)

FOUR LEAF CLOVER-
1 part Green Crème de Menthe, 1 part Irish Whiskey

FOURTH (4TH) OF JULY (1)-
1 part Grenadine, 2 parts Blue Curaçao, 2 parts Light Rum
(Layer in Order)

FOURTH (4TH) OF JULY (2)-
1 part Grenadine, 2 parts Vodka, 2 parts Blue Curaçao
(Layer in Order)

FOURTH (4TH) OF JULY TOOTER-
1 part Grenadine, 1 part Vodka, 1 part Blue Curaçao
(Layer in Order)

FOXY LADY-
2 parts Amaretto, 1 part Brown Crème de Caçao

FREDDY KRUGER-
1 part Jägermeister®, 1 part Sambuca, 1 part Vodka

FREEBASE-
1 part Coffee Liqueur, 1 part Light Rum, 1 part Dark Rum,
   1 part 151-proof Rum (float)

FREIGHT TRAIN-
1 part Jack Daniel's® Tennessee Sour Mash Whiskey, 1 part Tequila

FRENCH DREAM-
3 parts Irish Cream Liqueur, 1 part Raspberry Liqueur

FRENCH FANTASY-
1 part Black Raspberry Liqueur, 1 part Grand Marnier®
splash Orange Juice, splash Cranberry Juice

FRENCH TICKLER-
1 part Goldschläger®, 1 part Grand Marnier®

FRENCH TOAST-
1 part Butterscotch Schnapps, 1 part Cinnamon Schnapps,
   1 part Irish Cream Liqueur

FRIGID HAIRY VIRGIN-
2 parts Light Rum, 1 part Triple Sec
splash Pineapple Juice

FRISKY WITCH-
1 part Sambuca, 1 part Vodka

FROG LICK-
1 part Vodka, 1 part Yukon Jack® Canadian Liqueur
splash Lime Juice

FROOT LOOP-
2 parts Apple Brandy, 1 part Cherry Brandy, 1 part Vodka
splash Orange Juice

FROSTBITE-
4 parts Tequila, 1 part White Crème de Caçao, splash Blue Curaçao

FROST HEAVES-
1 part Jägermeister®, 1 part Yukon Jack® Perma Frost Schnapps

FRUIT OF THE LOOM-
1 part Apple Schnapps, 1 part Peach Schnapps
splash Cranberry Juice

FRUIT LOOP (1)-
1 part Amaretto, 1 part Blue Curaçao
Grenadine, Light Cream or Milk

FRUIT LOOP (2)-
Citrus Rum
splash Cranberry Juice, splash Pineapple Juice

FRU-FRU SHOOTER-
1 part Banana Liqueur, 1 part Peach Schnapps
splash Pineapple Juice, splash Lime Juice

F**K ME UP-
1 part Cinnamon Schnapps, 1 part Jägermeister®, 1 part Peppermint Schnapps,
1 part 151-proof Rum (Float)

F**KIN' HOT-
1 part Cinnamon Schnapps, 1 part Pepper Vodka
splash Hot Sauce

FUNKY MONKEY-
1 part Coffee Liqueur, 1 part Irish Cream Liqueur, 1 part Peach Schnapps

FUZZY BALLS-
1 part Melon Liqueur, 1 part Peach Schnapps, 1 part Vodka
splash Cranberry Juice, splash Grapefruit Juice

FUZZY CHARLIE (1)-
2 parts Coconut Rum, 2 parts Spiced Rum, 1 part Peach Schnapps
splash Orange Juice

FUZZY CHARLIE (2)-
3 parts Dark Rum, 1 part Banana Liqueur, 1 part Coconut Rum
splash Pineapple Juice

FUZZY FRUIT-
Peach Schnapps
splash Grapefruit Juice

FUZZY IRISHMAN-
1 part Raspberry Liqueur, 1 part Butterscotch Schnapps,
1 part Irish Cream Liqueur
(Layer in Order)

FUZZY MEXICAN-
1 part Peach Schnapps, 1 part Tequila

FUZZY MONKEY-
1 part Banana Liqueur, 1 part Peach Schnapps, 1 part Vodka
Orange Juice

FUZZY MOTHER-
1 part Tequila, 1 part 151-proof Rum (lace) (ignite, optional)
{extinguish flame before drinking}

FUZZY NAVEL-
Peach Schnapps
splash Orange Juice

FUZZY NUT-
4 parts Peach Schnapps, 1 part Amaretto, 1 part White Crème de Caçao

FUZZY RUSSIAN-
1 part Peach Schnapps, 1 part Vodka

FUZZY SMURF-
1 part Apricot Brandy, 1 part Blue Curaçao

FUZZY WUZZY-
1 part Peach Schnapps, 1 part Vodka
splash Orange Juice

G4-
1 part Amaretto, 1 part Irish Cream Liqueur
(Layer in Order)

G-BOMB-
1 part Goldschläger®, 1 part Vodka

G-BOY-
1 part Grand Marnier®, 1 part Hazelnut Liqueur, 1 part Irish Cream Liqueur

G-SPOT-
1 part Southern Comfort®, 1 part Peach Schnapps
splash Orange Juice

G-STRING-
Vodka, splash Brown Crème de Caçao
splash Light Cream or Milk

G. T. O.-
1 part Amaretto, 1 part Gin, 1 part Light Rum, 1 part Southern Comfort®,
1 part Vodka
Orange Juice, splash Grenadine

GALACTIC ALE SHOOTER-
3 parts Blue Curaçao, 3 parts Vodka, 1 part Black Raspberry Liqueur
splash Lime Juice

GANGREEN-
1 part Green Crème de Menthe, 1 part Jägermeister®,
1 part Irish Cream Liqueur

GASOLINE-
1 part Southern Comfort®, 1 part Tequila (Layer in Order)

GATES OF HELL-
Tequila, splash Cherry Brandy (lace)
splash Lime Juice

GENE SPLICE-
1 part Raspberry Liqueur, 1 part Tequila, 1 part Vodka
splash Lime Juice, splash Pineapple Juice

GENEVA CONVENTION-
4 parts Vodka, 1 part 100-proof Vodka, 1 part Goldschläger®

GENTLE BULL-
2 parts Tequila, 1 part Coffee Liqueur

GERMAN BURRITTO-
1 part Jägermeister®, 1 part Tequila

GET LAID-
2 parts Vodka, 1 part Raspberry Liqueur
splash Cranberry Juice, splash Pineapple Juice

GHETTO BLASTER-
1 part Coffee Liqueur, 1 part Metaxa, 1 part Tequila, 1 part Rye Whiskey
(Layer in Order)

GHOSTBUSTER-
1 part Coffee Liqueur, 1 part Irish Cream Liqueur, 1 part Vodka

GILA MONSTER-
1 part Orange Juice, 1 part Jägermeister®, 1 part Tequila (Layer in Order)

GILLIGAN'S ISLAND-
3 parts Light Rum, 1 part Maraschino Liqueur
splash Grapefruit Juice, splash Lime Juice

GINGERBREAD-
1 part Butterscotch Schnapps, 1 part Cinnamon Schnapps,
1 part Irish Cream Liqueur

GINGERBREAD MAN-
1 part Coffee Liqueur, 1 part Irish Cream Liqueur, 1 part Goldschläger®
(Layer in Order)

GIRL MOM WARNED YOU ABOUT, THE-
1 part Grenadine, 1 part Triple Sec, 1 part Light Rum, 1 part Melon Liqueur,
1 part Blue Curaçao
(Layer in Order)

GIRL SCOUT COOKIE (1)-
2 parts Coffee Liqueur, 1 part Green Crème de Menthe

GIRL SCOUT COOKIE (2)-
2 parts Coffee Liqueur, 1 part Peppermint Schnapps

GIRL SCOUT COOKIE (3)-
1 part Brown Crème de Caçao, 1 part Green Crème de Menthe

GIRL SCOUT COOKIE (4)-
1 part Coffee Liqueur, 1 part Irish Cream Liqueur, 1 part Peppermint Schnapps

GLACIER MINT-
3 parts Vodka, 1 part Citrus Vodka, 1 part Green Crème de Menthe

GLADIATOR-
1 part Amaretto, 1 part Southern Comfort®
splash Orange Juice, splash Lemon-Lime Soda

GLASS TOWER-
2 parts Light Rum, 2 parts Peach Schnapps, 2 parts Triple Sec, 2 parts Vodka,
1 part Sambuca

GLITTERBOX-
1 part Coffee Liqueur, 1 part Sambuca

GO GIRL!-
1 part Raspberry Liqueur, 1 part Vodka
splash Sour Mix, splash Club Soda

GODZILLA-
1 part Green Crème de Menthe, 1 part Pepper Vodka

GOLD BARON-
1 part Peppermint Schnapps, 1 part Goldschläger® (Layer in Order)

GOLD DIGGER-
1 part Goldschläger®, 1 part Jack Daniel's® Tennessee Sour Mash Whiskey

GOLD FURNACE-
Goldschläger®
splash Hot Sauce

GOLD RUSH-
1 part Goldschläger®, 1 part Tequila

GOLDEN COMFORT-
1 part Goldschläger®, 1part Jägermeister®, 1 part Southern Comfort®

GOLDEN DREAM (1)-
2 parts Galliano®, 1 part White Crème de Caçao, splash Triple Sec

GOLDEN DREAM (2)-
4 parts Galliano®, 1 part Triple Sec

GOLDEN FLASH-
1 part Sambuca, 1 part Triple Sec, 1 part Amaretto (Layer in Order)

GOLDEN GLOW-
1 part Blackberry Brandy, 1 part Galliano®, 1 part Green Crème de Menthe

GOLDEN NIGHT-
1 part Amaretto, 1 part Irish Cream Liqueur, 1 part Hazelnut Liqueur
(Layer in Order)

GOLDEN NIPPLE-
1 part Goldschläger®, 1 part Butterscotch Schnapps, splash Irish Cream Liqueur
(Layer in Order)

GOLDEN OLDIE-
2 parts Dark Rum, 1 part Banana Liqueur
splash Pineapple Juice

GOLDEN SHOWER-
2 parts Tequila, 1 part Yellow Chartreuse

GOLDEN SLIPPER-
2 parts Apricot Brandy, 1 part Yellow Chartreuse

GOOBER-
1 part Black Raspberry Liqueur, 1 part Melon Liqueur, 1 part Triple Sec,
1 part Vodka

GOOD & PLENTY (1)-
1 part Anisette, 1 part Blackberry Brandy

GOOD & PLENTY (2)-
1 part Anisette, 1 part Licorice Liqueur

GOOD & PLENTY (3)-
1 part Coffee Liqueur, 1 part Vanilla Liqueur, 1 part Vodka, splash Anisette

GORILLA-
1 part Jägermeister®, 1 part 151-proof Rum

GORILLA FART-
1 part Licorice Liqueur, 1 part Jack Daniel's® Tennessee Sour Mash Whiskey,
1 part 151-proof Rum

GORILLA MILK-
2 parts Light Rum, 1 part Banana Liqueur, 1 part Coffee Liqueur,
1 part Irish Cream Liqueur

GRAND FINALE-
2 parts Amaretto, 1 part Coconut Liqueur, 1 part Hazelnut Liqueur

GRAPE CRUSH-
1 part Raspberry Liqueur, 1 part Vodka
splash Cranberry Juice, splash Sour Mix

GRASSHOPPER-
1 part Green Crème de Menthe, 1 part White Crème de Caçao

GRATEFUL DEAD-
3 parts Blended Whiskey, 1 part Apple Schnapps (Layer in Order)

GRAVE DIGGER-
1 part Irish Cream Liqueur, 1 part Jägermeister®, 1 part Peppermint Schnapps

GREAT BALLS OF FIRE-
1 part Goldschläger®, 1 part Cinnamon Schnapps, 1 part Cherry Brandy
(Layer in Order)

GREAT HEAD-
3 parts Canadian Whiskey, 1 part Apple Brandy

GREEK REVOLUTION-
1 part Grenadine, 1 part Licorice Liqueur, 1 part Galliano® (Layer in Order)

GREEN APPLE-
Southern Comfort®, splash Melon Liqueur
splash Sour Mix

GREEN CHARTREUSE NECTAR-
2 parts Apricot Schnapps, 1 part Green Chartreuse

GREEN CHILI-
1 part Peach Schnapps, 1 part Melon Liqueur
splash Hot Sauce

GREEN DRAGON (1)-
2 parts Russian Vodka, 1 part Green Chartreuse

GREEN DRAGON (2)-
3 parts Gin, 1 part Green Crème de Menthe, 1 part Jägermeister®

GREEN EMERALD-
1 part Green Crème de Menthe, 1 part Amaretto (Layer in Order)

GREEN FLY-
3 parts Vodka, 1 part Green Crème de Menthe, 1 part White Crème de Menthe

GREEN GENIE-
1 part Green Chartreuse, 1 part Tequila

GREEN HORNET-
3 parts Brandy, 1 part Green Crème de Menthe

GREEN LIZARD-
2 parts Green Chartreuse, 1 part 151-proof Rum

GREEN PUSSY-
1 part Sour Mix, 1 part Melon Liqueur, 1 part Light Rum (Layer in Order)

GREEN SNEAKER-
2 parts Vodka, 1 part Melon Liqueur, 1 part Triple Sec
Orange Juice

GREEN TURTLE-
1 part Jägermeister®, 1 part Melon Liqueur

GREMLIN-
2 parts Vodka, 1 part Blue Curaçao, 1 part Light Rum
Orange Juice

GRIZZLY BEAR-
1 part Amaretto, 1 part Brown Crème de Caçao, 1 part Dark Rum,
1 part Vanilla Liqueur

GROUND ZERO-
1 part Bourbon Whiskey, 1 part Coffee Liqueur, 1 part Peppermint Schnapps,
1 part Vodka

GUILLOTINE-
1 part Butterscotch Schnapps, 1 part Irish Cream Liqueur,
1 part Cinnamon Schnapps (Layer in Order)

GUMBALL-
1 part Blue Curaçao, 1 part Sambuca

GUMMY BEAR-
1 part Amaretto, 1 part Melon Liqueur, 1 part Southern Comfort®
Orange Juice, Pineapple Juice, splash Grenadine

HAIRY NAVEL-
1 part Peach Schnapps, 1 part Vodka
splash Orange Juice

HAMMERHEAD-
1 part Amaretto, 1 part Light Rum, 1 part Triple Sec, splash Southern Comfort®

HAMMERTOE-
3 parts Light Rum, 1 part Blue Curaçao, splash Amaretto
splash Lime Juice

HAND GRENADE-
Tequila
splash Cranberry Juice

HAPPY HAWAIIAN-
1 part Coffee Liqueur, 1 part Irish Cream Liqueur
splash Pineapple Juice

HAPPY RANCHER-
1 part Melon Liqueur, 1 part Peach Schnapps, 1 part Scotch Whiskey,
1 part Vodka

HARBOR LIGHTS (1)-
1 part Light Rum, 1 part Raspberry Liqueur
splash Orange Juice

HARBOR LIGHTS (2)-
1 part Galliano®, 1 part Metaxa

HARD CORE-
1 part Amaretto, 1 part 100-proof Vodka, 1 part Triple Sec,
1 part 151-proof Rum
splash Cola

HARD DICK-
1 part Hazelnut Liqueur, 1 part Vodka
splash Club Soda

HARD ON-
1 part Coffee Liqueur, 1 part Amaretto, 1 part Irish Cream Liqueur
(Layer in Order)

HARSH-
1 part Jägermeister®, 1 part Tequila

HAWAIIAN PUNCH SHOOTER-
1 part Amaretto, 1 part Southern Comfort®, 1 part 100-proof Vodka
splash Pineapple Juice

HAWAIIAN SHOOTER-
1 part Amaretto, 1 part Vodka
Cranberry Juice

HAZEL NUT-
2 parts Hazelnut Liqueur, 1 part Brown Crème de Caçao

HEAD BANGER-
1 part Licorice Liqueur, 1 part 151-proof Rum
splash Grenadine

HEAD ROOM-
1 part Banana Liqueur, 1 part Melon Liqueur, 2 parts Irish Cream Liqueur
(Layer in Order)

HEAT WAVE-
3 parts Coconut Rum, 1 part Peach Schnapps
Pineapple Juice, Orange Juice, Grenadine

HEAVENLY BODY-
1 part Pear Schnapps, 1 part Hazelnut Liqueur, 1 part Irish Cream Liqueur
(Layer in Order)

HEAVYWEIGHT SAILOR-
2 parts Dark Rum, 2 parts 151-proof Rum, 1 part Light Rum,
    splash Coffee Liqueur
splash Lime Juice

HOLE-IN-ONE-
3 parts Melon Liqueur, 1 part Apple Brandy
splash Light Cream or Milk (lace)
(Layer in Order)

HOLLYWOOD SHOT-
1 part Raspberry Liqueur, 1 part Vodka
splash Pineapple Juice

HOME RUN-
1 part Bourbon Whiskey, 1 part Brandy, 1 part Light Rum
splash Sour Mix

HOMECOMING-
1 part Amaretto, 1 part Irish Cream Liqueur

HONOLULU PUNCH SHOOTER-
1 part Amaretto, 1 part Southern Comfort®, 1 part 151-proof Rum
splash Pineapple Juice, splash Orange Juice, splash Grenadine

HOOTER SHOOTER-
1 part Amaretto, 1 part Vodka
Orange Juice, Grenadine

HOP SCOTCH-
1 part Irish Cream Liqueur, 1 part Butterscotch Schnapps
(Layer in Order, optional)

HORNY BULL-
1 part Vodka, 1 part Light Rum, 1 part Tequila
(Layer in Order)

HORNY MOHICAN-
1 part Banana Liqueur, 1 part Irish Cream Liqueur, 1 part Coconut Rum
(Layer in Order)

HOT NUTS-
1 part Cinnamon Schnapps, 1 part Hazelnut Liqueur

HOT SHOT SHOOTER-
1 part Peppermint Schnapps, 1 part Vodka
splash Hot Sauce

HOT TO SHOT-
1 part Cinnamon Schnapps, 1 part Tequila
splash Lime Juice

HOWLING COYOTE-
3 parts Tequila, 1 part Raspberry Liqueur

HUMMER-
1 part Coffee Liqueur, 1 part Light Rum

HURRICANE SHOOTER-
1 part Jägermeister®, 1 part Yukon Jack® Canadian Liqueur,
    splash Irish Cream Liqueur

HYNOMEISTER-
1 part Hpnotiq®, 1 part Jägermeister®

I. R. A. SHOT-
1 part Irish Cream Liqueur, 1 part Irish Whiskey

I. V. (ITALIAN VALIUM)-
2 parts Amaretto, 1 part Gin

ICE BALL-
2 parts Gin, 1 part Sambuca, 1 part White Crème de Menthe

ICE BOAT-
1 part Peppermint Schnapps, 1 part Vodka

IGUANA-
1 part Coffee Liqueur, 1 part Tequila, 1 part Vodka
splash Sour Mix

ILICIT AFFAIR-
1 part Irish Cream Liqueur, 1 part Peppermint Schnapps
top Whipped Cream

ILLUSION (1)-
1 part Light Rum, 1 part Melon Liqueur, 1 part Tequila, 1 part Triple Sec,
1 part Vodka
splash Lime Juice

ILLUSION (2)-
1 part Blue Curaçao, 1 part Light Rum, 1 part Melon Liqueur, 1 part Tequila,
1 part Vodka
splash Lime Juice

IN THE SACK-
1 part Apricot Brandy, 1 part Cream Sherry
splash Lime Juice, splash Orange Juice

INK SPOT-
1 part Blackberry Brandy, 1 part Peppermint Schnapps (Layer in Order)

INSTANT DEATH-
1 part 100-proof Vodka, 1 part Jägermeister®, 1 part 151-proof Rum

INTERNATIONAL CREAM-
1 part Coffee Liqueur, 1 part Irish Cream Liqueur, splash Grand Marnier®
splash Light Cream or Milk

INTERNATIONAL INCIDENT-
1 part Amaretto, 1 part Coffee Liqueur, 1 part Hazelnut Liqueur, 1 part Irish
Cream Liqueur, 1 part Vodka

IRISH ANGEL-
3 parts Irish Whiskey, 1 part White Crème de Caçao, 1 part White
Crème de Menthe

IRISH CHARLIE-
1 part Irish Cream Liqueur, 1 part White Crème de Menthe

IRISH DREAM-
2 parts Brown Crème de Caçao, 1 part Hazelnut Liqueur,
1 part Irish Cream Liqueur

IRISH EYES-
4 parts Irish Whiskey, 1 part Green Crème de Menthe

IRISH FLAG (1)-
1 part Green Crème de Menthe, 1 part White Crème de Caçao,
1 part Triple Sec, 1 part Irish Whiskey (Layer in Order)

IRISH FLAG (2)-
1 part Green Crème de Menthe, 1 part Irish Cream Liqueur,
1 part Grand Marnier® (Layer in Order)

IRISH FROG-
1 part Melon Liqueur, 1 part Irish Cream Liqueur (Layer in Order)

IRISH HEADLOCK-
1 part Irish Cream Liqueur, 1 part Irish Whiskey, 1 part Amaretto, 1 part Brandy
(Layer in Order)

IRISH HORSEMAN-
   3 parts Irish Whiskey, 1 part Triple Sec, splash Raspberry Liqueur

IRISH KISS-
   2 parts Irish Whiskey, 1 part Peach Schnapps
   splash Orange Juice

IRISH MONKEY-
   1 part Irish Cream Liqueur, 1 part Banana Liqueur

IRISH QUAALUDE-
   1 part Hazelnut Liqueur, 1 part Irish Cream Liqueur, 1 part Vodka, 1 part White
      Crème de Caçao

IRISH SUNRISE-
   1 part Amaretto, 1 part Banana Liqueur, 1 part Irish Cream Liqueur
   (Layer in Order)

IRISH SUNSET-
   1 part Banana Liqueur, 1 part Amaretto, 1 part Irish Cream Liqueur
   (Layer in Order)

IRON BUTTERFLY-
   1 part Vodka, 1 part Coffee Liqueur, 1 part Light Cream or Milk (Layer in Order)

IRON CROSS-
   1 part Apricot Brandy, 1 part Peppermint Schnapps

ISLAND JOY-
   4 parts Spiced Rum, 1 part Peach Schnapps
   splash Lime Juice, splash Pineapple Juice

ITALIAN DREAM-
   3 parts Irish Cream Liqueur, 1 part Amaretto

ITALIAN STALLION-
   1 part Amaretto, 1 part Hazelnut Liqueur, 1 part Sambuca

ITALIAN SURFER-
   1 part Amaretto, 1 part Brandy
   splash Pineapple Juice

ITALIAN SURFER WITH A RUSSIAN ATTITUDE-
   1 part Amaretto, 1 part Coconut Rum, 1 part Vodka
   splash Cranberry Juice, splash Pineapple Juice

ITALIAN VALIUM (I.V.)-
   2 parts Amaretto, 1 part Gin

JACK & JILL-
   1 part Jack Daniel's® Tennessee Sour Mash Whiskey, 1 part Root Beer Schnapps

JACK FROST-
   1 part Jack Daniel's® Tennessee Sour Mash Whiskey,
      1 part Peppermint Schnapps

JACK'S JAM-
1 part Apple Schnapps, 1 part Banana Liqueur, 1 part Peach Schnapps,
    1 part Strawberry Schnapps
splash Sour Mix, splash Orange Juice

JACKHAMMER (1)-
3 parts Root Beer Schnapps, 1 part Yukon Jack® Canadian Liqueur

JACKHAMMER (2)-
1 part Jack Daniel's® Tennessee Sour Mash Whiskey, 1 part Root Beer Schnapps

JACKHAMMER (3)-
1 part Yukon Jack® Canadian Liqueur, 1 part Yukon Jack® Perma Frost Schnapps

JAMAICA BLUE-
2 parts Light Rum, 1 part Blueberry Schnapps, 1 part Blue Curaçao
splash Lime Juice

JAMAICAN BLUES-
2 parts Coconut Rum, 2 parts Dark Rum, 1 part Blue Curaçao
splash Pineapple Juice

JAMAICAN CRAWLER-
1 part Light Rum, 1 part Melon Liqueur
splash Pineapple Juice, Grenadine (Float)

JAMAICAN YO YO-
1 part Dark Rum, 1 part Tia Maria® (Layer in Order)

JAMBALAYA-
1 part Peach Schnapps, 1 part Southern Comfort®
splash Sour Mix, splash Grenadine Juice

JAP SLAP-
1 part Melon Liqueur, 1 part Vodka
splash Lime Juice, splash Sour Mix

JAWBREAKER-
Cinnamon Schnapps
splash Hot Sauce

JEDI MIND PROBE-
1 part Butterscotch Schnapps, 1 part Irish Cream Liqueur, 1 part Jägermeister®

JELLY BEANS (1)-
1 part Amaretto, 1 part Sambuca

JELLY BEANS (2)-
1 part Blackberry Brandy, 1 part Brandy, 1 part Sambuca

JELLY BEANS (3)-
2 parts Blackberry Brandy, 2 parts Blended Whiskey, 1 part Anisette

JELLY BEANS (4)-
1 part Anisette, 1 part Blackberry Brandy

JELLY DOUGHNUT-
1 part Irish Cream Liqueur, 1 part Raspberry Liqueur

JELLY FISH-
1 part Amaretto, 1 part Irish Cream Liqueur, 1 part White Crème de Caçao
Grenadine (lace)

JELLYBEAN-
3 parts Brandy, 1 part Anisette
splash Grenadine

JOHNNY ON THE BEACH-
1 part Black Raspberry Liqueur, 1 part Melon Liqueur, 1 part Vodka
Pineapple Juice, Orange Juice, Grapefruit Juice, Cranberry Juice

JOLLY GREEN GIANT-
1 part Blue Curaçao, 1 part Gin, 1 part Light Rum, 1 part Tequila,
   1 part Triple Sec

JOLLY RANCHER-
1 part Melon Liqueur, 1 part Peach Schnapps
splash Cranberry Juice

JU-JU-BE-
1 part Banana Liqueur, 1 part Strawberry Schnapps
splash Orange Juice, splash Lime Juice

JUICY FRUIT-
1 part Melon Liqueur, 1 part Peach Schnapps, 1 part Vodka
splash Pineapple Juice

JUMPING BEAN-
3 parts Tequila, 1 part Sambuca

JUNGLE JIM-
1 part Banana Liqueur, 1 part Vodka

JUNGLE JUICE-
2 parts Light Rum, 2 parts Vodka, 1 part Triple Sec
Cranberry Juice, Orange Juice, Pineapple Juice, splash Sour Mix

KAMIKAZE-
1 part Triple Sec, 1 part Vodka
splash Lime Juice

KANDY KANE-
1 part Crème de Noyaux, 1 part Peppermint Schnapps

KEREMIKI-
1 part Goldschläger®, 1 part Peppermint Schnapps, 1 part 151-proof Rum

KILL ME NOW-
1 part 151-proof Rum, 1 part Amaretto, 1 part Gin, 1 part Tequila, 1 part Vodka

KILLER BEE-
1 part Bärenjäger®, 1 part Jägermeister®

KILLER KOOL-AID-
  3 parts Vodka, 1 part Peach Schnapps, 1 part Amaretto, Cranberry Juice
  (Layer in Order)

KLINGON DISRUPTER-
  1 part Bourbon Whiskey, 1 part Cinnamon Schnapps, 1 part Tequila

KOOL-ADE (1)-
  1 part Amaretto, 1 part Melon Liqueur, 1 part Vodka
  splash Cranberry Juice

KOOL-ADE (2)-
  1 part Melon Liqueur, 1 part Vodka
  splash Cranberry Juice, splash Pineapple Juice

KRYPTONITE SHOT-
  Citrus Rum, 6 oz. Beer
  Orange Juice *(Drop Shot Glass of Citrus Rum into Mug of Beer & OJ)*

L. A. P. D. NIGHTSHIFT-
  1 part Grenadine, 1 part Blue Curaçao, 1 part Tequila (Layer in Order)

LA BOMBA (1)-
  2 parts Gold Tequila, 1 part Triple Sec
  Pineapple Juice, Orange Juice, splash Grenadine

LA BOMBA (2)-
  2 parts Light Rum, 1 part Anisette, 1 part Apricot Brandy, 1 part Blue Curaçao
  splash Lime Juice

LADY LUCK-
  4 parts Raspberry Liqueur, 1 part Banana Liqueur, 1 part Coconut Liqueur

LAND MINE-
  1 part Jägermeister®, 1 part 151-proof Rum

LAND SLIDE (1)-
  1 part Irish Cream Liqueur, 1 part Grand Marnier®, 1 part Amaretto
  (Layer in Order)

LAND SLIDE (2)-
  1 part Irish Cream Liqueur, 1 part Apricot Brandy, 1 part Banana Liqueur,
    1 part Coffee Liqueur (Layer in Order)

LASER BEAM (1)-
  1 part Amaretto, 1 part Galliano®, 1 part Jack Daniel's® Tennessee Sour Mash
    Whiskey, 1 part Peppermint Schnapps

LASER BEAM (2)-
  1 part Bourbon Whiskey, 1 part Drambuie®, 1 part Peppermint Schnapps

LATIN LOVER-
  2 parts Tequila, 1 part Spiced Rum
  splash Pineapple Juice, splash Lime Juice

LAURA'S LAKESIDE-***
1 part Banana Liqueur, 1 part Coconut Rum
Cranberry Juice, Pineapple Juice

LAYER CAKE-
1 part White Crème de Caçao, 1 part Apricot Brandy, 1 part Light Cream or
  Milk (Layer in Order)

LEATHER & LACE-
1 part Coffee Liqueur, 1 part Peppermint Schnapps, 1 part Irish Cream Liqueur
(Layer in Order)

LEBANESE SNOW-
1 part Banana Liqueur, 1 part Strawberry Schnapps

LEG SPREADER-
3 parts Raspberry Liqueur, 1 part 100-proof Vodka
splash Cola

LEMON DROP (1)-
Vodka
Lemon Wedge Dipped in Sugar

LEMON DROP (2)-
Citrus Vodka
splash Lemon-Lime Soda, Lemon Wedge Dipped in Sugar

LEMON DROP (3)-
1 part Tequila, 1 part Vodka
Lemon Wedge Dipped in Sugar

LETHAL INJECTION-
1 part Coconut Rum, 1 part Crème de Noyaux, 1 part Light Rum,
  1 part Spiced Rum
splash Orange Juice, splash Pineapple Juice

LICORICE MIST-
3 parts Sambuca, 1 part Coconut Liqueur

LICORICE STICK-
1 part Anisette, 1 part Triple Sec, 1 part Vodka

LIFE IS GOOD-***
1 part Banana Liqueur, 1 part Melon Liqueur, 1 part Raspberry Liqueur
Cranberry Juice, Orange Juice, Pineapple Juice

LIFESAVER (1)-
1 part Coconut Rum, 1 part Melon Liqueur, 1 part Vodka

LIFESAVER (2)-
2 parts Brandy, 1 part Cherry Brandy, splash Triple Sec
splash Sour Mix, splash Grenadine

LIQUID ASPHALT
1 part Sambuca, 1 part Jägermeister® (Layer in Order)

LIQUID COCAINE (1)-
2 parts Jägermeister®, 2 parts Peppermint Schnapps, 1 part 151-proof Rum

LIQUID COCAINE (2)-
1 part Amaretto, 1 part Grand Marnier®, 1 part Southern Comfort®,
    1 part Vodka
splash Pineapple Juice

LIQUID COCAINE 8-BALL-
1 part Amaretto, 1 part Light Rum, 1 part Southern Comfort®
splash Pineapple Juice, splash Grenadine

LIQUID CRACK-
1 part Goldschläger®, 1 part Jägermeister®, 1 part Peppermint Schnapps,
    1 part 151-proof Rum

LIQUID GOLD-
2 parts Vodka, 1 part Galliano®, 1 part White Crème de Caçao
Light Cream or Milk

LIQUID HEROIN-
1 part Peppermint Schnapps, 1 part Jägermeister®, 1 part 151-proof Rum
(Layer in Order)

LIQUID QUAALUDE-
1 part Jägermeister®, 1 part Irish Cream Liqueur

LIQUID VALIUM-
1 part Amaretto, 1 part Blended Whiskey, 1 part Tequila, 1 part Triple Sec

LOBOTOMY-
1 part Amaretto, 1 part Raspberry Liqueur
splash Pineapple Juice

LOLLIPOP-
1 part Cherry Brandy, 1 part Triple Sec, splash Green Chartreuse,
    splash Maraschino Liqueur

LUBE JOB-
1 part Irish Cream Liqueur, 1 part Vodka

LUCKY LINDA-***
1 part Coffee Liqueur, 1 part White Crème de Caçao, 1 part Irish Cream
(Layer in Order)

LULU-
1 part Amaretto, 1 part Light Rum, 1 part Peach Schnapps, 1 part Triple Sec,
    1 part Vodka
splash Pineapple Juice, splash Grenadine

M & M-
1 part Amaretto, 1 part Coffee Liqueur

MACHINE SHOT-
1 part Mountain Dew®, 1 part 151-proof Rum (Layer in Order)

MAD COW-
1 part Coffee Liqueur, 1 part 151-proof Rum
splash Light Cream or Milk

MAD MONK-
1 part Hazelnut Liqueur, 1 part Irish Cream Liqueur

MAD RUSSIAN-
1 part Coffee Liqueur, 1 part Irish Cream Liqueur, 1 part Vodka

MAG PIE-
2 parts Melon Liqueur, 2 parts Vodka, 1 part White Crème de Caçao

MALIBU HOOTER SHOOTER-
1 part Malibu® Coconut Rum, 1 part Melon Liqueur
splash Cranberry Juice

MALIBU WAVE-
3 parts Tequila, 1 part Blue Curaçao
splash Sour Mix

MAN OVERBOARD-
2 parts Vodka, 1 part Melon Liqueur, 1 part Raspberry Liqueur
Pineapple Juice

MANHANDLER-
1 part Jack Daniel's® Tennessee Sour Mash Whiskey, 1 part Sloe Gin,
1 part Southern Comfort®, 1 part Vodka

MARASCHINO CHERRY-
2 parts Light Rum, 1 part Amaretto, 1 part Peach Schnapps
Cranberry Juice, Pineapple Juice, Grenadine

MARGARITA SHOOTER-
Tequila
Sour Mix, splash Orange Juice

MAYAN WHORE-
1 part Tequila, 1 part Coffee Liqueur, 1 part Pineapple Juice, splash Club Soda,
splash Grenadine (Layer in Order)

MELLOW YELLOW-
1 part Galliano®, 1 part Southern Comfort®

MELON COOLER SHOOTER-
2 parts Melon Liqueur, 1 part Peach Schnapps, 1 part Raspberry Liqueur
splash Pineapple Juice

MELON FEVER-
4 parts Melon Liqueur, 1 part Triple Sec
splash Light Cream or Milk

MELTDOWN-
2 parts Russian Vodka, 1 part Peach Schnapps (Layer in Order)

MEMORY LOSS-
1 part Banana Liqueur, 1 part Raspberry Liqueur, 1 part Vodka
Cranberry Juice, Orange Juice

MEXICAN ASSHOLE-
Tequila
splash Hot Sauce, splash Worcestershire Sauce

MEXICAN BERRY-
1 part Raspberry Liqueur, 1 part Tequila

MEXICAN FLAG (1)-
1 part Cherry Liqueur, 1 part Coffee Liqueur, 1 part Green Crème de Menthe,
1 part 151-proof Rum (Layer in Order)

MEXICAN FLAG (2)-
1 part Sloe Gin, 1 part Vodka, 1 part Melon Liqueur (Layer in Order)

MEXICAN GRASSHOPPER-
1 part Coffee Liqueur, 1 part Green Crème de Menthe

MEXICAN LEPRECHAUN-
1 part Tequila, 1 part Green Crème de Menthe (Layer in Order)

MEXICAN MOTHER F**KER-
1 part Irish Cream Liqueur, 1 part Hazelnut Liqueur, 1 part Coffee Liqueur,
1 part Tequila (Layer in Order)

MEXICAN MOUTHWASH-
1 part Peppermint Schnapps, 1 part Tequila

MEXICAN PUMPER-
1 part Grenadine, 1 part Coffee Liqueur, 1 part Tequila (Layer in Order)

MEXICAN RUIN-
3 parts Coffee Liqueur, 1 part Tequila

MIAMI ICE SHOOTER-
1 part Banana Liqueur, 1 part Melon Liqueur, 1 part Strawberry Schnapps,
splash Coconut Rum, splash Triple Sec
splash Grenadine, splash Pineapple Juice

MIKE TYSON-
1 part Anisette, 1 part Jägermeister®, 1 part Tia Maria®

MIKEY MIKE-
2 parts Coconut Rum, 1 part Peach Schnapps, 1 part Raspberry Liqueur
splash Orange Juice, splash Pineapple Juice

MILES OF SMILES-
1 part Amaretto, 1 part Peppermint Schnapps, 1 part Rye Whiskey
(Layer in Order)

MILK SHAKE SHOOTER-
Irish Cream Liqueur
splash Light Cream or Milk, splash Sour Mix

MILKY WAY-
>1 part Swiss Chocolate Almond Liqueur, 1 part Irish Cream Liqueur,
>>1 part Hazelnut Liqueur (Layer in Order)

MIND ERASER-
>1 part Coffee Liqueur, 1 part Vodka
>fill Club Soda (Do Not Mix, Serve with Drinking Straw, Drink all at Once)
>*(Mix into Highball Glass with ice)*

MINT CHIP-
>1 part Peppermint Schnapps, 1 part Coffee Liqueur (Layer in Order)

MINT CHOCOLATE CHIP ICE CREAM-
>1 part Coffee Liqueur, 1 part Irish Cream Liqueur, 1 part Peppermint Schnapps,
>>1 part Vodka, 1 part White Crème de Caçao, 1 part White
>>Crème de Menthe

MINT CONDITION-
>1 part Bourbon Whiskey, 1 part Coffee Liqueur, 1 part Peppermint Schnapps,
>>1 part Vodka

MINT WHISPER-
>2 parts White Crème de Menthe, 1 part Coffee Liqueur

MISSION ACCOMPLISHED-
>4 parts Vodka, 1 part Triple Sec
>splash Lime Juice, splash Grenadine

MODEL T-
>1 part Coffee Liqueur, 1 part Banana Liqueur, 1 part Swiss Chocolate Almond
>>Liqueur (Layer in Order)

MONKEY SHINE-
>1 part Banana Liqueur, 1 part Bourbon Whiskey, 1 part Irish Cream Liqueur

MONKEY'S PUNCH-
>1 part Coffee Liqueur, 1 part Green Crème de Menthe, 1 part Irish Cream
>>Liqueur (Layer in Order)

MONTANA STUMP PULLER-
>2 parts Canadian Whiskey, 1 part White Crème de Caçao

MONTEZUMA'S REVENGE-
>1 part Sherry, 1 part Tequila

MORGAN'S JOLLY RANCHER-
>1 part Captain Morgan® Original Spiced Rum, 1 part Cinnamon Schnapps

MORGAN'S WENCH-
>1 part Amaretto, 1 part Brown Crème de Caçao, 1 part Captain Morgan®
>>Original Spiced Rum

MOTOR OIL-
>1 part Jägermeister®, 1 part Peppermint Schnapps, 1 part Goldschläger®,
>>1 part Coconut Rum (Layer in Order)

MOUTHWASH-
1 part Blue Curaçao, 1 part Peppermint Schnapps, 1 part Vodka

MUDSLIDE SHOOTER (1)-
1 part Coffee Liqueur, 1 part Irish Cream Liqueur, 1 part Vodka

MUDSLIDE SHOOTER (2)-
1 part Coffee Liqueur, 1 part Irish Cream Liqueur, 1 part Tequila

MUDSLIDE SHOOTER (3)-
1 part Coffee Liqueur, 1 part Irish Cream Liqueur, 1 part Tia Maria®

MUFF DIVER-
White Crème de Caçao
splash Lime Juice, splash Light Cream or Milk

MULTIPLE ORGASM-
2 parts Amaretto, 2 parts Tia Maria®, 1 part Vodka

MUSHROOM-
1 part Grenadine, 1 part Irish Cream Liqueur, 1 part Melon Liqueur
(Layer in Order)

19 DUKE DRIVE-
1 part Chocolate Mint Liqueur, 1 part Cherry Brandy, 1 part Banana Liqueur
(Layer in Order)

911-
1 part Cinnamon Schnapps, 1 part Peppermint Schnapps

NAKED PRETZEL-
2 parts Melon Liqueur, 1 part Crème de Cassis, 1 part Vodka
splash Pineapple Juice

NAPALM-
1 part Cinnamon Schnapps, 1 part Peppermint Schnapps,
    splash 151-proof Rum (Layer in Order) (ignite, optional)
{extinguish flame before drinking}

NAZI FROM HELL-
1 part Peppermint Schnapps, 1 part Jägermeister® (Layer in Order)

NEUTRON BOMB (1)-
1 part Hazelnut Liqueur, 1 part Irish Cream Liqueur

NEUTRON BOMB (2)-
1 part Butterscotch Schnapps, 1 part Irish Cream Liqueur

NEUTRON BOMB (3)-
1 part Coffee Liqueur, 1 part Light Rum, 1 part Tequila, 1 part Swiss Chocolate
    Almond Liqueur (Layer in Order)

NINJA-
1 part Brown Crème de Caçao, 1 part Melon Liqueur, 1 part Hazelnut Liqueur
(Layer in Order)

NINJA TURTLE-
2 parts Gin, 1 part Blue Curaçao
splash Orange Juice

NIPPLE ON FIRE-
1 part Cinnamon Schnapps, 1 part Butterscotch Schnapps, 1 part Irish Cream
   Liqueur (Layer in Order)

NIRVANA-
1 part Amaretto, 1 part Southern Comfort®, 1 part Vodka
Mango Juice

NUCLEAR ACCELERATOR-
1 part Vodka, 1 part Grand Marnier®, 1 part Peppermint Schnapps
(Layer in Order)

NUCLEAR KAMIKAZE-
1 part Blue Curaçao, 1 part Vodka
splash Lime Juice

NUCLEAR KOOL AID-
2 parts Southern Comfort®, 1 part Amaretto
splash Cranberry Juice

NUCLEAR MELTDOWN-
1 part Brandy, 1 part Tequila

NUCLEAR RAINBOW-
1 part Grenadine, 1 part Peppermint Schnapps, 1 part Jägermeister®,
   1 part Melon Liqueur, 1 part Canadian Whiskey, 1 part 151-proof Rum,
   1 part Amaretto
(Layer in Order)

NUCLEAR WASTE (1)-
1 part Vodka, 1 part Melon Liqueur, 1 part Triple Sec, splash Lime Juice
(Layer in Order)

NUCLEAR WASTE (2)-
2 parts Melon Liqueur, 1 part Vodka

NUDE BOMB-
1 part Coffee Liqueur, 1 part Amaretto, 1 part Banana Liqueur
(Layer in Order)

NUTCRACKER-
1 part DeKuyper® Coconut Amaretto, 1 part DeKuyper® Hazelnut Liqueur

NUTS & BERRIES (1)-
1 part Hazelnut Liqueur, 1 part Raspberry Liqueur

NUTS & BERRIES (2)-
1 part Crème de Noyaux, 1 part Strawberry Schnapps

NUTTY BANANA-
4 parts Amaretto, 1 part Banana Liqueur

NUTTY BUDDY (1)-
1 part Hazelnut Liqueur, 1 part Swiss Chocolate Almond Liqueur,
1 part Peppermint Schnapps (Layer in Order)

NUTTY BUDDY (2)-
1 part Coffee Liqueur, 1 part Irish Cream Liqueur

NUTTY IRISHMAN-
1 part Hazelnut Liqueur, 1 part Irish Cream Liqueur

NUTTY PROFESSOR-
1 part Grand Marnier®, 1 part Hazelnut Liqueur, 1 part Irish Cream Liqueur

NUTTY RUSSIAN-
1 part Coffee Liqueur, 1 part Hazelnut Liqueur, 1 part Vodka

NYMPHOMANIAC-
2 parts Spiced Rum, 1 part Coconut Rum, 1 part Melon Liqueur

NYQUIL-
2 parts Triple Sec, 1 part Sambuca
Grenadine

100 MILES PER HOUR-
4 parts Blue Curaçao, 1 part 151-proof Rum, 1 part Bourbon Whiskey,
1 part Peach Schnapps, 1 part Southern Comfort®
Grenadine

OATMEAL COOKIE (1)-
1 part Goldschläger®, 1 part Hazelnut Liqueur, 1 part Irish Cream Liqueur

OATMEAL COOKIE (2)-
1 part Coffee Liqueur, 1 part Irish Cream Liqueur, 1 part Jägermeister®

OH MY GOSH-
1 part Amaretto, 1 part Peach Schnapps

OIL SLICK-
1 part Bourbon Whiskey, 1 part Peppermint Schnapps

OKANAGAN-
1 part Apricot Brandy, 1 part Strawberry Schnapps, 1 part Blueberry Schnapps
(Layer in Order)

OLD FASHION COOL ADE SHOOTER-
1 part Amaretto, 1 part Southern Comfort®
splash Cranberry Juice, splash Pineapple Juice

OLD LAY-
2 parts Tequila, 1 part Triple Sec
Grenadine, splash Lime Juice

ORANGE CRUSH-
1 part Triple Sec, 1 part Vodka
Orange Juice

OREO COOKIE-
1 part Coffee Liqueur, 1 part White Crème de Caçao, 1 part Irish Cream Liqueur, splash Vodka (Layer in Order)

ORGASM (1)-
1 part Amaretto, 1 part Coffee Liqueur, 1 part Irish Cream Liqueur

ORGASM (2)-
1 part Coffee Liqueur, 1 part Grand Marnier®, 1 part Irish Cream Liqueur

ORGASM (3)-
1 part Amaretto, 1 part Triple Sec, 1 part White Crème de Caçao

ORIENTAL RUG-
1 part Coffee Liqueur, 1 part Hazelnut Liqueur, 1 part Irish Cream Liqueur, 1 part Jägermeister®

OUT OF THE BLUE-
1 part Blueberry Schnapps, 1 part Blue Curaçao, 1 part Vodka
splash Sour Mix

OVER THE RAINBOW-
2 parts Spiced Rum, 1 part Triple Sec, splash Peach Schnapps

OYSTER-
2 parts Irish Cream Liqueur, 1 part Vodka

P. H.-
1 part Southern Comfort®, 1 part Amaretto, 1 part Pineapple Juice, splash Lime Juice (Layer in Order)

PMS-
1 part Melon Liqueur, 1 part Peach Schnapps, 1 part Vodka

PAIN KILLER-
3 parts Dark Rum, 1 part Coconut Rum
Orange Juice, Pineapple Juice

PAINLESS-
1 part Amaretto, 1 part Canadian Whiskey, 1 part Irish Cream Liqueur

PAINT BOX-
1 part Banana Liqueur, 1 part Blue Curaçao, 1 part Cherry Liqueur
(Layer in Order)

PANTS ON FIRE-
1 part Banana Liqueur, 1 part Strawberry Schnapps, 1 part Vodka
Grapefruit Juice, Orange Juice

PANTY DROPPER-
1 part Gin, 1 part Red Dubonnet® (Layer in Order)

PANTY QUIVER-
1 part Blackberry Liqueur, 1 part Jägermeister®

Shooters

PAP SMEAR-
12 oz. Beer, 1 part 100-proof Vodka
(drop Vodka in Shot Glass into Beer Mug) (drink all at once)

PARALYZER-
2 parts Tequila, 1 part Coffee Liqueur, 1 part White Crème de Caçao

PARTY AT THE BEACH, A-
2 parts Coconut Liqueur, 1 part Amaretto
Orange Juice, Grenadine

PEACH BUNNY-
1 part Peach Schnapps, 1 part White Crème de Caçao

PEACH MELBA-
2 parts Peach Schnapps, 1 part Black Raspberry Liqueur

PEACH TART-
Peach Schnapps
splash Lime Juice

PEACH VELVET-
3 parts Peach Schnapps, 1 part White Crème de Caçao

PEANUT BUTTER & JELLY-
1 part Hazelnut Liqueur, 1 part Raspberry Liqueur

PEANUT BUTTER CHOCOLATE CHIP COOKIE-
1 part Coffee Liqueur, 1 part Hazelnut Liqueur, 1 part Tia Maria®

PEANUT BUTTER CUP-
1 part Brown Crème De Caçao, 1 part Chocolate Liqueur,
    1 part Hazelnut Liqueur

PEARL HARBOR SHOOTER-
1 part Melon Liqueur, 1 part Vodka
splash Pineapple Juice

PEARL NECKLACE-
1 part Vodka, 1 part White Crème de Caçao
splash of Light Cream or Milk

PECKER HEAD-
1 part Amaretto, 1 part Southern Comfort®
splash Pineapple Juice

PENALTY SHOT-
1 part White Crème de Menthe, 1 part Tia Maria®,
    1 part Peppermint Schnapps (Layer in Order)

PEPPERMINT BEACH-
1 part Coconut Rum, 1 part Peppermint Schnapps

PEPPERMINT PATTIE (1)-
1 part White Crème de Caçao, 1 part White Crème de Menthe

PEPPERMINT PATTIE (2)-
1 part Brown Crème de Caçao, 1 part White Crème de Menthe

PEPPERMINT PATTIE (3)-
1 part Brown Crème de Caçao, 1 part Coffee Liqueur,
1 part Peppermint Schnapps

PEPPERMINT PATTIE (4)-
1 part Brown Crème de Caçao, 1 part Peppermint Schnapps

PEPPERMINT PENGUIN-
1 part Chocolate Mint Liqueur, 1 part Green Crème de Menthe

PEPPERMINT STICK-
1 part Peppermint Schnapps, 1 part White Crème de Caçao

PEPPERMINT TREAT-
1 part Green Crème de Menthe, 1 part Peppermint Schnapps

PEPPERMINT TWIST-
2 parts Peppermint Schnapps, 1 part White Crème de Caçao

PETE'S PREFERENCE-
2 parts Irish Cream Liqueur, 1 part Bärenjäger®
(Layer in Order)

PETER RISON-***
3 parts Bourbon Whiskey, 1 part Drambuie®, splash Raspberry Liqueur

PETROLEUM-
Tequila
Mexican Seasoning, splash Hot Sauce

PHLEGM-
3 parts Dark Rum, 1 part Banana Liqueur
Lime Juice

PHOTON TORPEDO-
1 part Cinnamon Schnapps, 1 part Vodka

PICKLED BRAIN-
1 part Vodka, 1 part Irish Cream Liqueur,
1 part Green Crème de Menthe
(Layer in Order)

PIERCED NAVEL-
Peach Schnapps
Cranberry Juice, Orange Juice

PIGSKIN-
1 part Melon Liqueur, 1 part Vodka
Sour Mix

PINEAPPLE BASH-
1 part Melon Liqueur, 1 part Southern Comfort®
splash Pineapple Juice

PINEAPPLE BOMB (1)-
1 part Coconut Rum, 1 part Dark Rum
splash Pineapple Juice

PINEAPPLE BOMB (2)-
1 part Amaretto, 1 part Southern Comfort®
splash Pineapple Juice, splash Cranberry Juice

PINEAPPLE BOMB (3)-
2 parts Southern Comfort®, 1 part Amaretto
splash Pineapple Juice, splash Grenadine

PINEAPPLE BOMBER (1)-
1 part Southern Comfort®, 1 part Jack Daniel's® Tennessee Sour Mash Whiskey
splash Pineapple Juice

PINEAPPLE BOMBER (2)-
2 parts Southern Comfort®, 2 parts Spiced Rum, 1 part Amaretto
splash Pineapple Juice

PINEAPPLE UPSIDE DOWN CAKE-
1 part Butterscotch Schnapps, 1 part Irish Cream Liqueur, 1 part Vodka
splash Pineapple Juice

PINK BELLY-
1 part Amaretto, 1 part Bourbon Whiskey, 1 part Irish Cream Liqueur,
    1 part Sloe Gin
splash Lemon-Lime Soda

PINK FLAMINGO-
Berry Schnapps
Cranberry Juice, splash Sour Mix

PINK LEMONADE (1)-
Citrus Vodka
Cranberry Juice, splash Sour Mix

PINK LEMONADE (2)-
Citrus Vodka, splash Triple Sec
Sour Mix, Cranberry Juice

PINK LEMONADE (3)-
Light Rum
Cranberry Juice, splash Lime Juice

PINK PARADISE-
1 part Amaretto, 1 part Coconut Rum
splash Cranberry Juice, splash Pineapple Juice

PINK SQUIRREL -
1 part Crème de Noyaux, 1 part White Crème de Caçao

PISTACHIO MINT-
2 parts Hazelnut Liqueur, 2 parts Vodka, 1 part Green Crème de Menthe

PITBULL ON CRACK-
1 part 151-proof Rum, 1 part Licorice Liqueur

PLATINUM BLONDE-
1 part Light Rum, 1 part Triple Sec
splash Light Cream or Milk

PLENTY & GOOD-
1 part Coffee Liqueur, 1 part Licorice Liqueur

POND SCUM-
2 parts Vodka, 1 part Irish Cream Liqueur (Float)

POPSICLE (1)-
Amaretto
splash Orange Juice, splash Light Cream or Milk

POPSICLE (2)-
1 part Apricot Brandy, 1 part Vodka, 1 part Irish Cream Liqueur (Layer in Order)

PORT & STARBOARD-
Green Crème de Menthe (Float)
Grenadine

POT 'O GOLD-
1 part Goldschläger®, 1 part Irish Cream Liqueur

PRAIRIE FIRE-
Tequila
splash Hot Sauce

PRAIRIE WILDFIRE-
Tequila
splash Hot Sauce

PRETTY PAULA'S PLEASURE-***
3 parts Tequila, 1 part Triple Sec
Cranberry Juice, splash Sour Mix

PRETTY THING-
3 parts Vodka, 1 part Amaretto, 1 part Coconut Liqueur

PRIMAL SCREAM-
1 part Coffee Liqueur, 1 part Tequila
splash Club Soda (shoot it, scream, shout out loud)

PUERTO APPLE-
2 parts Apple Schnapps, 1 part Light Rum, splash Amaretto
splash Lime Juice

PUERTO RICAN MONKEY F**K-
1 part Banana Liqueur, 1 part Coffee Liqueur, splash 151-proof Rum (Float)

PUMPKIN EATER-
1 part Light Rum, 1 part Triple Sec
Light Cream or Milk, Orange Juice

PUPPY'S NOSE-
1 part Peppermint Schnapps, 1 part Tia Maria®, 1 part Irish Cream Liqueur
(Layer in Order)

PURPLE GECKO-
3 parts Tequila, 1 part Blue Curaçao, 1 part Red Curaçao
Cranberry Juice, Sour Mix

PURPLE HAZE (1)-
3 parts Vodka, 1 part Raspberry Liqueur
Cranberry Juice, Sour Mix

PURPLE HAZE (2)-
2 parts Raspberry Liqueur, 2 parts Vodka, 1 part Triple Sec
splash Lime Juice, fill Club Soda
(Do Not Mix, Serve with Drinking Straw, Drink all at once)
(Mix into Highball Glass with ice)

PURPLE HOOTER (1)-
3 parts Citrus Vodka, 1 part Black Raspberry Liqueur, 1 part Triple Sec

PURPLE HOOTER (2)-
1 part Raspberry Liqueur, 1 part Vodka
Cranberry Juice, Sour Mix

PURPLE HOOTER (3)-
1 part Orange Juice, 1 part Raspberry Liqueur, 1 part Sour Mix,
1 part Vodka
(Layer in Order)

PURPLE MOTHER F**KER-
1 part Raspberry Liqueur, 1 part Vodka
splash Orange Juice, splash Sour Mix

PURPLE NIPPLE-
1 part Jägermeister®, 1 part Melon Liqueur
splash Cranberry Juice, splash Orange Juice

PURPLE NURPLE-
2 parts Tequila, 1 part Blue Curaçao, 1 part Sloe Gin

PURPLE PANCHO-
2 parts Tequila, 1 part Blue Curaçao, 1 part Sloe Gin
splash Sour Mix

PURPLE RAIN (1)-
2 parts Vodka, 1 part Blue Curaçao
Cranberry Juice

PURPLE RAIN (2)-
2 parts Hpnotiq®, 1 part Peach Schnapps, 1 part Raspberry Schnapps,
1 part Vanilla Liqueur

PUSSY PAWS-
Amaretto
splash Cranberry Juice, splash Sour Mix

QUAALUDE-
1 part Coffee Liqueur, 1 part Hazelnut Liqueur, 1 part Vodka

QUICK F**K-
1 part Coffee Liqueur, 1 part Melon Liqueur, 1 part Irish Cream Liqueur
(Layer in Order)

QUICK SILVER-
1 part Tequila, 1 part Banana Liqueur, 1 part Peppermint Schnapps
(Layer in Order)

RACE WAR-
1 part Brown Crème de Caçao, 1 part Irish Cream Liqueur, 1 part Vodka
(Layer in Order)

RAIN MAN-
2 parts 151-proof Rum, 1 part Melon Liqueur
splash Orange Juice

RAINBOW-
4 parts Vodka, 1 part Blue Curaçao (lace)
Sour Mix, splash Grenadine

RAINBOW CRUSH-
1 part Melon Liqueur, 1 part Raspberry Liqueur, 1 part Vodka
splash Orange Juice

RASPBERRY BERET-
1 part Raspberry Liqueur, 1 part Vodka
Light Cream or Milk, splash Soda (top)

RASPBERRY CHEESECAKE-
1 part Black Raspberry Liqueur, 1 part White Crème de Caçao

RASPBERRY CREAM-
1 part Raspberry Liqueur, 1 part Vodka, 1 part White Crème de Caçao
splash Light Cream or Milk

RASPBERRY GRENADE-
1 part Peach Schnapps, 1 part Raspberry Liqueur, 1 part Vodka
splash Lime Juice

RASPBERRY ROMANCE-
2 parts Irish Cream Liqueur, 1 part Black Raspberry Liqueur,
1 part Coffee Liqueur

RASPBERRY THRILL-
2 parts Raspberry Liqueur, 1 part French Vanilla Liqueur

RATTLESNAKE-
1 part Coffee Liqueur, 1 part White Crème de Caçao, 1 part Irish Cream
(Layer in Order)

RAZZMATAZZ SHOOTER-
2 parts DeKuyper® Razzmatazz Black Raspberry Liqueur, 1 part Coffee Liqueur,
1 part Crème de Cassis

REAL GOLD-
  1 part Goldschläger®, 1 part Vodka

REARBUSTER-
  1 part Coffee Liqueur, 1 part Tequila
  splash Cranberry Juice

REBEL RINGER-
  1 part Bourbon Whiskey, 1 part White Crème de Menthe

REBEL YELL-
  4 parts Bourbon Whiskey, 1 part Triple Sec
  splash Lime Juice

RED DEATH (1)-
  1 part Amaretto, 1 part Sloe Gin, 1 part Southern Comfort®, 1 part Triple Sec,
    1 part Vodka
  splash Sour Mix, Orange Juice

RED DEATH (2)-
  1 part Amaretto, 1 part Southern Comfort®
  Cranberry Juice, Sour Mix

RED DEVIL-
  1 part Banana Liqueur, 1 part Sloe Gin, 1 part Southern Comfort®,
    1 part Triple Sec, 1 part Vodka
  splash Lime Juice, Orange Juice

RED DRAGON-
  1 part Campari, 1 part Tequila

RED FACE-
  Tequila, splash Cranberry Brandy
  splash Cranberry Juice

RED HEADED SISTER-
  1 part Jägermeister®, 1 part Peach Schnapps
  splash Cranberry Juice

RED HEADED SLUT-
  1 part Jägermeister®, 1 part Peach Schnapps
  splash Cranberry Juice

RED HOT-
  1 part Cinnamon Schnapps, 1 part Tequila, splash Hot Sauce (Layer in Order)

RED HOT PASSION-
  2 parts Amaretto, 2 parts Bourbon Whiskey, 2 parts Southern Comfort®,
    1 part Sloe Gin, splash Triple Sec
  splash Orange Juice, splash Pineapple Juice

RED RUSSIAN (1)-
  1 part Cranberry Schnapps, 1 part Vodka

RED RUSSIAN (2)-
  1 part Strawberry Schnapps, 1 part Vodka

RED SNAPPER-
1 part Canadian Whiskey, 1 part Peach Schnapps
Cranberry Juice

REDNECK BLITZKRIEG -
1 part Jägermeister®, 1 part Southern Comfort®
splash Soda

REGGAE SHOOTER-
2 parts Vodka, 1 part Banana Liqueur
Orange Juice, Grapefruit Juice, Pineapple Juice, splash Orange Bitters,
    splash Grenadine

REMOTE CONTROL-
1 part Galliano®, 1 part Triple Sec
splash Orange Juice, splash Light Cream or Milk

RISE & SHINE-***
1 part Citrus Vodka, 1 part Melon Liqueur, 1 part Raspberry Liqueur
Cranberry Juice, Grapefruit Juice, Orange Juice, Pineapple Juice

ROAD KILL-
1 part Irish Whiskey, 1 part Wild Turkey® Bourbon Whiskey,
    1 part 151-proof Rum

ROAD RUNNER-
2 parts Vodka, 1 part Amaretto, 1 part Coconut Liqueur

ROASTED TOASTED ALMOND (1)-
2 parts Coffee Liqueur, 1 part Amaretto, 1 part Vodka

ROASTED TOASTED ALMOND (2)-
1 part Coffee Liqueur, 1 part Grand Marnier®, 1 part Irish Cream Liqueur

ROCK LOBSTER-
1 part Canadian Whiskey, 1 part Raspberry Liqueur
Cranberry Juice

ROCKET FUEL-
1 part Peppermint Schnapps, 1 part 151-proof Rum (Layer in Order)

ROCKY MOUNTAIN-
1 part Amaretto, 1 part Southern Comfort®
splash Lime Juice

ROCKY MOUNTAIN MOTHER F**KER-
1 part Amaretto, 1 part Yukon Jack® Canadian Liqueur
splash Lime Juice

ROOSTER PISS-
1 part Cinnamon Schnapps, 1 part Jack Daniel's® Tennessee Sour
    Mash Whiskey

ROOSTER POOP-
1 part Bourbon Whiskey, 1 part Peppermint Schnapps

ROOT BEER SHOOTER-
1 part Coffee Liqueur, 1 part Galliano®, 1 part Vodka
splash Cola

ROTTEN PUSSY-
2 parts Melon Liqueur, 1 part Amaretto, 1 part Coconut Rum,
1 part Southern Comfort®
splash Pineapple Juice, splash Sour Mix

ROYAL BITCH-
1 part Crown Royal® Canadian Whiskey, 1 part Hazelnut Liqueur

RUM RUNNER SHOOTER-
1 part Banana Liqueur, 1 part Cherry Brandy, 1 part Dark Rum,
1 part Light Rum
splash Orange Juice, splash Pineapple Juice

RUMPLESTILTSKIN-
1 part Cinnamon Schnapps, 1 part Peppermint Schnapps

RUPTURED DUCK-
1 part Banana Liqueur, 1 part Crème de Noyaux

RUSSIAN BANANA
1 part Banana Liqueur, 1 part Brown Crème de Caçao, 1 part Vodka

RUSSIAN BEAR-
2 parts Vodka, 1 part Brown Crème de Caçao

RUSSIAN KAMIKAZE-
Vodka, splash Raspberry Liqueur

RUSSIAN QUAALUDE (1)-
1 part Hazelnut Liqueur, 1 part Irish Cream Liqueur, 1 part Vodka
(Layer in Order)

RUSSIAN QUAALUDE (2)-
1 part Amaretto, 1 part Hazelnut Liqueur, 1 part Irish Cream Liqueur,
1 part Vodka

RUSSIAN QUAALUDE (3)-
1 part Coffee Liqueur, 1 part Irish Cream Liqueur, 1 part Vodka,
splash Hazelnut Liqueur (lace)

RUSSIAN QUAALUDE (4)-
1 part Irish Cream Liqueur, 1 part Vodka
splash Grenadine

RUSSIAN ROULETTE (1)-
2 parts Gin, 1 part Coffee Liqueur (Layer in Order)

RUSSIAN ROULETTE (2)-
1 part Galliano®, 1 part Southern Comfort®, 1 part Vodka (Layer in Order)

RUSTY NAVEL-
1 part Tequila, 1 part Amaretto (Layer in Order)

RUSTY ZIPPER-
3 parts Peach Schnapps, 1 part Amaretto (Layer in Order)

69-
1 part Banana Liqueur, 1 part Anisette, 1 part Irish Cream Liqueur
(Layer in Order)

69ER IN A POOL-
1 part Vodka, 1 part 151-proof Rum, splash Lime Juice, splash Hot Sauce
(Layer in Order)

747-
1 part Amaretto, 1 part Coffee Liqueur, 1 part Irish Cream Liqueur

S. H. I. T.-
1 part Sambuca, 1 part Haagen Dazs® Cream Liqueur, 1 part Irish Mist®,
1 part Tequila (Layer in Order)

S. O. B.-
1 part Brandy, 1 part Triple Sec, 1 part 151-proof Rum

SAINT (ST.) PATRICK'S DAY SHOOTER-
1 part Green Chartreuse, 1 part Green Crème de Menthe, 1 part Irish Whiskey

SAMBUCA SLIDE-
2 parts Sambuca, 1 part Vodka

SAMPLE (URINE SAMPLE)-
1 part 100-proof Vodka, 1 part Yellow Gatorade® (Layer in Order)

SAND BLASTER-
3 parts Jägermeister®, 1 part Light Rum
splash Lime Juice

SANTA CLAUS IS COMING TO TOWN-
1 part Cinnamon Schnapps, 1 part Melon Liqueur, 1 part Peppermint Schnapps
top Whipped Cream

SANTA SHOT-
1 part Grenadine, 1 part Green Crème de Menthe, 1 part Peppermint Schnapps
(Layer in Order)

SATIN GLIDER-
2 parts Peppermint Schnapps, 2 parts White Crème de Caçao, 1 part Sambuca

SAVE THE PLANET-
1 part Melon Liqueur, 1 part Vodka, splash Blue Curaçao,
splash Green Chartreuse

SCOOBY SNACK-
1 part Coconut Rum, 1 part Melon Liqueur
Pineapple Juice, splash Light Cream or Milk

SCOTTY WAS BEAMED UP-
4 parts Tequila, 1 part Galliano®

Shooters

SCREAMING BLUE MESSIAH-
　　5 parts Goldschläger®, 1 part Blue Curaçao (Layer in Order)

SCREAMING DEAD NAZI DIGGING FOR GOLD-
　　1 part Yellow Chartreuse, 1 part Jägermeister®, 1 part Peppermint Schnapps,
　　　　1 part Vodka

SCREAMING LIZARD-
　　1 part Tequila, 1 part Green Chartreuse (Layer in Order)

SCREAMING MULTIPLE ORGASM-
　　1 part Amaretto, 1 part Coffee Liqueur, 1 part Irish Cream Liqueur,
　　　　1 part Light Rum
　　Orange Juice, Light Cream or Milk

SCREAMING MULTIPLE ORGASM ON THE BEACH-
　　1 part Amaretto, 1 part Coconut Rum, 1 part Melon Liqueur, 1 part Peach
　　　　Schnapps, 1 part Triple Sec
　　splash Soda

SCREAMING NAZI-
　　1 part Jägermeister®, 1 part Peppermint Schnapps

SCREAMING ORGASM (1)-
　　1 part Amaretto, 1 part Coffee Liqueur, 1 part Irish Cream Liqueur, 1 part Vodka

SCREAMING ORGASM (2)-
　　1 part Coffee Liqueur, 1 part Grand Marnier®, 1 part Irish Cream Liqueur,
　　　　1 part Vodka

SCREAMING ORGASM (3)-
　　1 part Amaretto, 1 part Triple Sec, 1 part Vodka, 1 part White Crème de Cacao

SEA MONKEY-
　　Goldschläger®, splash Blue Curaçao

SEDUCTION-
　　1 part Hazelnut Liqueur, 1 part Banana Liqueur, 1 part Irish Cream Liqueur
　　(Layer in Order)

SEWER RAT-
　　1 part Coffee Liqueur, 1 part Peach Schnapps, 1 part Vodka
　　splash Orange Juice

SEWER WATER-
　　2 parts 151-proof Rum, 1 part Gin, 1 part Melon Liqueur
　　splash Pineapple Juice, splash Grenadine, splash Lime Juice (float)

SEX IN A BUBBLEGUM FACTORY-
　　1 part Apricot Brandy, 1 part Banana Liqueur, 1 part Blue Curaçao,
　　　　1 part Light Rum

SEX IN THE PARKING LOT-
　　1 part Apple Schnapps, 1 part Raspberry Liqueur, 1 part Vodka

SEX, LIES & VIDEO POKER-
1 part Amaretto, 1 part Blended Whiskey, 1 part Spiced Rum
Cranberry Juice, Orange Juice, Pineapple Juice, Grenadine

SEX MACHINE-
1 part Coffee Liqueur, 1 part Irish Cream Liqueur
splash Light Cream or Milk

SEX ME STRONG-
2 parts DeKuyper® Island Blue Pucker, 2 parts DeKuyper® Sour Apple
    Schnapps, 1 part Tequila

SEX ON ACID-
1 part Blackberry Brandy, 1 part Jägermeister®, 1 part Melon Liqueur
Cranberry Juice, Pineapple Juice

SEX ON THE BEACH (1)-
1 part Melon Liqueur, 1 part Raspberry Liqueur, 1 part Vodka
splash Pineapple Juice

SEX ON THE BEACH (2)-
1 part Peach Schnapps, 1 part Vodka
splash Cranberry Juice, splash Orange Juice

SEX ON THE BEACH (3)-
1 part Black Raspberry Liqueur, 1 part Melon Liqueur, 1 part Vodka
splash Cranberry Juice, splash Pineapple Juice

SEX ON THE BEACH (SOUTHERN STYLE)-
1 part Apple Schnapps, 1 part Peach Schnapps
splash Cranberry Juice, splash Pineapple Juice

SEX ON THE BEACH WITH A FRIEND-
1 part Crème de Cassis, 1 part Melon Liqueur, 1 part Vodka
splash Pineapple Juice

SEX ON THE LAKE-
1 part Banana Liqueur, 1 part Brown Crème de Caçao, splash Light Rum
Light Cream or Milk

SEX SHOOTER-
1 part Coffee Liqueur, 1 part Grand Marnier®

SEX UNDER THE BOARDWALK-
1 part Melon Liqueur, 1 part Peach Schnapps, 1 part Raspberry Liqueur
Orange Juice

SEX UNDER THE SUN-
2 parts Light Rum, 1 part Dark Rum
Orange Juice, Pineapple Juice, splash Grenadine

SEX UP AGAINST THE WALL-
Vodka, splash Galliano®
Cranberry Juice, Pineapple Juice, Sour Mix

SEX WITH AN ALLIGATOR-
 1 part Melon Liqueur, 1 part Coconut Rum, 1 part Pineapple Juice,
  splash Raspberry Liqueur (lace), 1 part Jägermeister® (float) (Layer in Order)

SEX WITH THE CAPTAIN-
 1 part Amaretto, 1 part Captain Morgan® Original Spiced Rum,
  1 part Peach Schnapps
 splash Cranberry Juice, splash Orange Juice

SEXUAL CHOCOLATE-
 1 part Brown Crème de Caçao, 1 part Coffee Liqueur, 1 part Irish Cream
  Liqueur, splash Raspberry Liqueur
 Light Cream or Milk

SEXUAL HARRASEMENT-
 1 part Amaretto, 1 part Canadian Whiskey, 1 part Sloe Gin
 Orange Juice, Pineapple Juice

SEXUAL PEAK-
 1 part Amaretto, 1 part Peach Schnapps, 1 part Vodka
 Orange Juice, Pineapple Juice, Sour Mix

SHADY LADY-
 1 part Melon Liqueur, 1 part Tequila
 splash Grapefruit Juice

SHAKE THAT ASS-
 1 part Banana Liqueur, 1 part Blue Curaçao
 Orange Juice, Sour Mix

SHAMROCK-
 1 part Green Crème de Menthe, 1 part Brown Crème de Caçao, 1 part Irish
  Cream Liqueur (Layer in Order)

SHARK-
 1 part Tequila, 1 part Vodka
 splash Hot Sauce

SHARK BITE-
 Dark Rum or Spiced Rum
 splash Orange Juice, splash Grenadine

SHAVETAIL-
 Peppermint Schnapps
 splash Light Cream or Milk, splash Pineapple Juice

SHEER ELEGANCE-
 3 parts Amaretto, 3 parts Black Raspberry Liqueur, 1 part Vodka

SHERBET-
 1 part Raspberry Liqueur, 1 part Triple Sec
 splash Orange Juice

SHILLELAGH-
 1 part Irish Cream Liqueur, 1 part Vodka

SHOT FROM HELL-
1 part Jägermeister®, 1 part Peppermint Schnapps (Layer in Order)

SIBERIAN SLEIGHRIDE-
2 parts Vodka, 1 part White Crème de Caçao, 1 part White Crème de Menthe
splash Light Cream or Milk

SICILIAN KISS-
2 parts Southern Comfort®, 1 part Amaretto

SILK PANTIES (1)-
1 part Peach Schnapps, 1 part Sambuca

SILK PANTIES (2)-
1 part Peach Schnapps, 1 part Vodka

SILK STOCKINGS (1)-
3 parts Tequila, 1 part Brown Crème de Caçao, 1 part Raspberry Liqueur

SILK STOCKINGS (2)-
2 parts Tequila, 1 part White Crème de Caçao
splash Grenadine

SILVER DEVIL-
1 part Tequila, 1 part Peppermint Schnapps (Layer in Order)

SILVER NIPPLE-
1 part Sambuca, 1 part Vodka

SILVER SHELL-
2 parts Gin, 1 part Jägermeister®
splash Lime Juice

SILVER SPIDER-
1 part Light Rum, 1 part Triple Sec, 1 part Vodka, 1 part White
Crème de Menthe

SIT ON MY FACE-
1 part Irish Cream Liqueur, 1 part Hazelnut Liqueur, 1 part Coffee Liqueur
(Layer in Order)

SKITTLE-
2 parts Vodka, 1 part Banana Liqueur
Cranberry Juice, Sour Mix, splash Grenadine

SLAM DANCER-
2 parts White Crème de Caçao, 1 part Brown Crème de Caçao, 1 part Coffee
Liqueur, splash Peppermint Schnapps

SLEAZY SEX ON THE BEACH-
1 part Grand Marnier®, 1 part Vodka
splash Cranberry Juice, splash Orange Juice

SLIPPERY DICK-
1 part Banana Liqueur, 1 part Irish Cream Liqueur

SLIPPERY NIPPLE (1)-
1 part Irish Cream Liqueur, 1 part Sambuca

SLIPPERY NIPPLE (2)-
1 part Irish Cream Liqueur, 1 part Peppermint Schnapps
splash Grenadine (lace)

SMARTIE-
1 part Grenadine, 1 part Swiss Chocolate Almond Liqueur, 1 part Tequila
(Layer in Order)

SMOOTH OPERATOR-
2 parts Hazelnut Liqueur, 1 part Banana Liqueur, 1 part Coffee Liqueur
splash Light Cream or Milk

SMURF JUICE-
1 part Blue Curaçao, 1 part White Wine

SMURF PISS-
1 part 100-proof Vodka, 1 part Blueberry Schnapps, splash Blue Curaçao

SMURF SNOT-
1 part Blue Curaçao, 1 part Blueberry Schnapps,
    splash Irish Cream Liqueur (lace)

SNAKE BITE-
2 parts Yukon Jack® Canadian Liqueur, 1 part Peppermint Schnapps

SNAP SHOT-
1 part Peppermint Schnapps, 1 part Irish Cream Liqueur (Layer in Order)

SNOW CAP-
1 part Tequila, 1 part Irish Cream Liqueur (Layer in Order)

SNOW SHOE-
1 part Bourbon Whiskey, 1 part Peppermint Schnapps

SNOW WHITE-
3 parts Southern Comfort®, 1 part Vodka
splash Orange Juice, splash Pineapple Juice

SOMETHING DIFFERENT-
1 part Amaretto, 1 part Peach Schnapps
splash Cranberry Juice, splash Pineapple Juice

SOUR APPLE (1)-
1 part Amaretto, 1 part Melon Liqueur
splash Sour Mix

SOUR APPLE (2)-
1 part Melon Liqueur, 1 part Tequila
splash Sour Mix

SOUR APPLE (3)-
1 part Apple Schnapps, 1 part Melon Liqueur, 1 part Vodka

SOUR GRAPES-
1 part Raspberry Liqueur, 1 part Vodka
splash Sour Mix

SOUTHERN BELLE-
1 part Apricot Brandy, 1 part Swiss Chocolate Almond Liqueur,
    1 part Southern Comfort® (Layer in Order)

SOUTHERN COMFORT WATERMELON-
2 parts Southern Comfort®, 1 part Vodka
Pineapple Juice, splash Grenadine

SOUTHERN PEACH-
1 part Bourbon Whiskey, 1 part Peach Schnapps
splash Orange Juice, splash Sour Mix, splash Grenadine

SOUTHERN PINK FLAMINGO-
1 part Coconut Rum, 1 part Southern Comfort®
splash Lime Juice, splash Pineapple Juice, splash Grenadine

SOUTHERN SLAMMER-
3 parts Amaretto, 2 parts Southern Comfort®, 1 part Sloe Gin
splash Lime Juice

SPANISH MOSS-
1 part Coffee Liqueur, 1 part Tequila, splash Green Crème de Menthe (lace)

SPARK IN THE NIGHT-
3 parts Dark Rum, 1 part Coffee Liqueur
splash Lime Juice

SPARK PLUG-
1 part Peppermint Schnapps, 1 part 151-proof Rum

SPEARMINT LIFESAVER-
4 parts Jack Daniel's® Tennessee Sour Mash Whiskey,
    1 part Peppermint Schnapps

SPERM-
1 part Tequila, 1 part Vodka
splash of Light Cream or Milk (lace)

SPIRITUAL ENLIGHTENMENT-
1 part Grand Marnier®, 1 part White Crème de Caçao, 1 part White
    Crème de Menthe

SPLASH & CRASH-
1 part Amaretto, 1 part 151-proof Rum (Float)
splash Cranberry Juice, splash Orange Juice

SPUTNIK-
1 part Peach Schnapps, 1 part Vodka
splash Orange Juice, splash Light Cream or Milk

SPY CATCHER-
2 parts Canadian Whiskey, 1 part Sambuca

SPY MASTER-
2 parts Vodka, 1 part Banana Liqueur
splash Lime Juice

SQUID INK-***
1 part Blueberry Brandy, 1 part Black Sambuca

STALACTITE-
3 parts Sambuca, 1 part Irish Cream Liqueur, 1 part Black Raspberry Liqueur
(Layer in Order)

STAR WARS-
1 part Amaretto, 1 part Southern Comfort®, 1 part Triple Sec
splash Grenadine

STARS & STRIPES-
1 part Grenadine, 1 part Light Cream or Milk, 1 part Blue Curaçao
(Layer in Order)

STEVIE RAY VAUGHAN-
1 part Jack Daniel's® Tennessee Sour Mash Whiskey, 1 part Southern Comfort®,
   1 part Triple Sec
splash Orange Juice, splash Sour Mix

STICKY NIPPLE-
1 part Amaretto, 1 part Irish Cream Liqueur

STIFF DICK-
1 part Butterscotch Schnapps, 1 part Irish Cream Liqueur
(Layer in Order)

STOLI BUTT-
2 parts Stolichnaya® Vodka, 1 part Butterscotch Schnapps (Layer in Order)

STOP LIGHT-
1 part Green Crème de Menthe, 1 part White Crème de Menthe,
   1 part Sloe Gin (Layer in Order)

STORM TROOPER-
1 part Jägermeister®, 1 part Peppermint Schnapps

STRAWBERRY BANANA SPLIT-
1 part Banana Liqueur, 1 part Dark Rum, 1 part Strawberry Schnapps,
   splash Vanilla Liqueur

STRAWBERRY BOMB-
1 part 100-proof Vodka, 1 part Strawberry Schnapps

STRAWBERRY KISS-
1 part Coffee Liqueur, 1 part Strawberry Schnapps, 1 part Irish Cream Liqueur
(Layer in Order)

STRAWBERRY QUICK (1)-
1 part Strawberry Schnapps, 1 part Vodka, splash Banana Liqueur
Light Cream or Milk, Orange Juice, splash Grenadine

STRAWBERRY QUICK (2)-
1 part Raspberry Liqueur, 1 part Vodka, splash Banana Liqueur
Light Cream or Milk, Orange Juice, splash Grenadine

STRAWBERRY SHORTCAKE (1)-
1 part Amaretto, 1 part Strawberry Schnapps

STRAWBERRY SHORTCAKE (2)-
1 part Strawberry Schnapps, 1 part Vodka

STRAWBERRY SHORTCAKE (3)-
3 parts Strawberry Schnapps, 1 part White Crème de Caçao

STUMBLE F**K-
1 part Cinnamon Schnapps, 1 part Jägermeister®, 1 part Peppermint Schnapps

SUMMER SUNRISE-
2 parts Raspberry Liqueur, 1 part Apricot Brandy
splash Orange Juice, splash Cranberry Juice

SUNOCO 251-
1 part 151-proof Rum, 1 part 100-proof Vodka, splash Yellow Chartreuse

SUPER TART-
Berry Schnapps
splash Sour Mix

SURFER ON ACID-
1 part Coconut Rum, 1 part Jägermeister®
splash Orange Juice

SURFER ON ACID IN HAWAII-
1 part Coconut Rum, 1 part Jägermeister®, 1 part Raspberry Liqueur
Cranberry Juice, Pineapple Juice

SURF'S UP-
1 part Banana Liqueur, 1 part White Crème de Caçao

SWAMP WATER-
2 parts Light Rum, 1 part Blue Curaçao
splash Orange Juice, splash Lime Juice

SWEDISH QUAALUDE-
1 part Hazelnut Liqueur, 1 part Vodka

SWEET CREAM-
3 parts Coffee Liqueur, 1 part Irish Cream Liqueur (float)

SWEET PEACH-
1 part Amaretto, 1 part Peach Schnapps
splash Orange Juice

SWEET TART (1)-
1 part Melon Liqueur, 1 part Southern Comfort®
splash Sour Mix

SWEET TART (2)-
1 part Raspberry Liqueur, 1 part Vodka
splash Pineapple Juice, splash Lime Juice

SWEET TART (3)-
1 part Melon Liqueur, 1 part Vodka
splash Sour Mix

SWISS & WHOOSH-
1 part Tia Maria®, 1 part Hazelnut Liqueur, 1 part Irish Cream Liqueur
(Layer in Order)

SWISS HIKER-
1 part Swiss Chocolate Almond Liqueur, 1 part Banana Liqueur, 1 part Irish
Cream Liqueur (Layer in Order)

2 BORG SPECIAL-
1 part Light Rum, 1 part Drambuie®, 1 part Cherry Brandy (Layer in Order)

24 KARAT NIGHTMARE-
1 part Goldschläger®, 1 part Peppermint Schnapps

252-
1 part 101-proof Wild Turkey® Bourbon Whiskey, 1 part 151-proof Rum

2000 FLUSHES-
1 part Blue Curaçao, 1 part Spiced Rum, 1 part Mango Rum
Lemon-Lime Soda

T .K. O.-
1 part Coffee Liqueur, 1 part Licorice Liqueur, 1 part Tequila

T-SHOT-
1 part White Crème de Caçao, 1 part Tia Maria®, 1 part Irish Cream Liqueur,
1 part Light Cream or Milk (Layer in Order)

TANK-
1 part Gin, 1 part Jack Daniel's® Tennessee Sour Mash Whiskey

TARANTULA-
1 part Amaretto, 1 part Canadian Whiskey, 1 part Irish Cream Liqueur

TASTY ORGASM-
1 part Peppermint Schnapps, 1 part Irish Cream Liqueur (Layer in Order)

TEDDY BEAR-
1 part Root Beer Schnapps, 1 part Vodka

TENNESSEE MUD-
3 parts Coffee Liqueur, 3 parts Irish Cream Liqueur, 1 part Jack Daniel's®
Tennessee Sour Mash Whiskey

TENEMENT FIRE-
Vodka
splash Hot Sauce

TEQUILA FIRE-
Tequila
splash Hot Sauce

TEQUILA MOCKINGBIRD (1)-
2 parts Tequila, 1 part Green Crème de Menthe
splash Lime Juice

TEQUILA MOCKINGBIRD (2)-
1 part Swiss Chocolate Almond Liqueur, 1 part Amaretto, 1 part Tequila
(Layer in Order)

TEQUILA PARALYZER-
1 part Coffee Liqueur, 1 part Tequila
splash Light Cream or Milk

TERMINATOR (1)-
1 part Blackberry Brandy, 1 part 151-proof Rum
splash Cranberry Juice

TERMINATOR (2)-
1 part Coffee Liqueur, 1 part Irish Cream Liqueur, 1 part Sambuca,
1 part Grand Marnier®, 1 part Vodka (Layer in Order)

TEST TUBE BABY-
1 part Grand Marnier®, 1 part Anisette, splash Irish Cream Liqueur
(Layer in Order)

TETANUS SHOT-
1 part Drambuie®, 1 part Rye Whiskey (Layer in Order)

TEXAS CHAINSAW MASSACRE-
1 part Strawberry Schnapps, 1 part Vodka
(Layer in Order)

TEXAS SWEAT-
1 part Grenadine, 1 part Green Crème de Menthe, 1 part Tequila,
1 part Light Rum (Layer in Order)

THAT TIME OF THE MONTH-
1 part Coconut Rum, 1 part Peach Schnapps
Cranberry Juice, Pineapple Juice, splash Grenadine (lace)

THREE WISE MEN-
1 part Jack Daniel's® Tennessee Sour Mash Whiskey, 1 part Jim Beam® Whiskey,
1 part Johnnie Walker® Red Scotch Whiskey

THUNDER & LIGHTNING-
1 part Peppermint Schnapps, 1 part 151-proof Rum

TIDAL WAVE-
2 parts Melon Liqueur, 1 part Coconut Rum
splash Orange Juice, splash Pineapple Juice

TIDY BOWL (1)-
1 part Blue Curaçao, 1 part Licorice Liqueur

TIDY BOWL (2)-
1 part Blue Curaçao, 1 part Vodka

TIE ME TO THE BEDPOST-
1 part Citrus Vodka, 1 part Coconut Rum, 1 part Melon Liqueur
splash Sour Mix

TIGHT SNATCH-
2 parts Light Rum, 1 part Peach Schnapps
splash Pineapple Juice

TIJUANA TAXI-
2 parts Tequila, 1 part Blue Curaçao, 1 part Tropical Fruit Schnapps

TO THE MOON-
1 part Amaretto, 1 part Coffee Liqueur, 1 part Irish Cream Liqueur,
    1 part 151-proof Rum

TOASTED ALMOND-
2 parts Coffee Liqueur, 1 part Amaretto

TOMAKAZI-
1 part Gin, 1 part Vodka
Sour Mix, splash Cola (optional)

TOOTSIE ROLL (1)-
1 part Brown Crème de Caçao, 1 part Hazelnut Liqueur, 1 part Tia Maria®

TOOTSIE ROLL (2)-
1 part Coffee Liqueur, 1 part Vodka
splash Orange Juice

TOOTSIE ROLL (3)-
Coffee Liqueur
splash Orange Juice

TOTAL MADNESS-
1 part DeKuyper® Mad Melon Watermelon Schnapps, 1 part Vodka

TOXIC WASTE-
1 part Blue Curaçao, 1 part Melon Liqueur, 1 part Vodka
splash Orange Juice, splash Pineapple Juice, splash Sour Mix

TRAFFIC LIGHT (1)-
1 part Green Crème de Menthe, 1 part Banana Liqueur, 1 part Sloe Gin
(Layer in Order)

TRAFFIC LIGHT (2)-
1 part Crème de Noyaux, 1 part Galliano®, 1 part Melon Liqueur
(Layer in Order)

TREASURE CHEST-
2 parts Chocolate Almond Liqueur, 1 part Amaretto, 1 part Gold Rum

TRIAL OF THE CENTURY-
1 part Jägermeister®, 1 part Goldschläger®, 1 part Grenadine (Layer in Order)

TRIFECTA-
1 part 151-proof Rum, 1 part Banana Liqueur, 1 part Irish Cream Liqueur
splash Light Cream or Milk

TROLLEY CAR-
1 part Amaretto, 1 part Strawberry Schnapps

TROPICAL SHOT (1)-
1 part Tropical Fruit Schnapps, 1 part Light Rum
splash Orange Juice, splash Pineapple Juice

TROPICAL SHOT (2)-
2 parts Margarita Schnapps, 1 part Vodka
splash Pineapple Juice

TROPICAL TREASURE-
2 parts Melon Liqueur, 1 part Banana Liqueur
splash Pineapple Juice

TUMBLEWEED-
1 part Amaretto, 1 part White Crème de Caçao

TURBO SHOT-
1 part Apple Schnapps, 1 part Peach Schnapps, 1 part Vodka
splash Cranberry Juice

TURKEY SHOOTER-
3 parts 101-proof Wild Turkey® Bourbon Whiskey, 1 part White
Crème de Menthe (float)

TUTTI FRUITI-
1 part Banana Liqueur, 1 part Melon Liqueur, 1 part Strawberry Schnapps

UNDER THE COVERS (1)-
1 part Irish Cream Liqueur, 1 part Peach Schnapps, 1 part Vodka

UNDER THE COVERS (2)-
1 part Irish Cream Liqueur, 1 part Peach Schnapps, 1 part Sambuca

URBAN COWBOY-
1 part Grand Marnier®, 1 part Jack Daniel's® Tennessee Sour Mash Whiskey,
1 part Southern Comfort®

URBAN VIOLENCE-
1 part Blue Curaçao, 1 part Coconut Rum, 1 part Vodka, splash Banana
Liqueur, splash Strawberry Schnapps
splash Orange Juice

URINE SAMPLE (1)-
1 part 100-proof Vodka, 1 part Yellow Gatorade® (Layer in Order)

URINE SAMPLE (2)-
1 part Amaretto, 1 part Coconut Rum
Orange Juice, Pineapple Juice

VANESSA'S VICE SHOOTER-*
　1 part Amaretto, 1 part Bärenjäger®, 1 part Coffee Liqueur,
　　1 part Goldschläger®, 1 part Irish Cream Liqueur

VARICOSE VEINS-
　1 part Green Crème de Menthe, 1 part Irish Cream Liqueur

VENOM-
　1 part Yukon Jack® Canadian Liqueur, 1 part Lime Juice (Layer in Order)

VIBRATOR-
　1 part Southern Comfort®, 1 part Irish Cream Liqueur (Layer in Order)

VIKING FUNERAL-
　1 part Goldschläger®, 1 part Jägermeister®, 1 part Peppermint Schnapps

VILE GREEN STUFF-
　1 part Melon Liqueur, 1 part Peach Schnapps
　splash Orange Juice

VIOLET CRUMBLE-
　1 part Butterscotch Schnapps, 1 part Brown Crème de Caçao (Layer in Order)

VIRGIN'S KISS-
　3 parts Dark Rum, 1 part Apricot Brandy, 1 part Galliano®
　splash Pineapple Juice, splash Sour Mix

VODKA GRASSHOPPER-
　1 part Green Crème de Menthe, 1 part Vodka, 1 part White Crème de Caçao

VULCAN BLOOD-
　1 part Blue Curaçao, 1 part Vodka
　Orange Juice

VULCAN DEATH GRIP-
　1 part Licorice Liqueur, 1 part 151-proof Rum (Layer in Order)

VULCAN MIND MELD-
　1 part Licorice Liqueur, 1 part 151-proof Rum

VULCAN MIND PROBE (1)-
　1 part Irish Cream Liqueur, 1 part Peppermint Schnapps, 1 part 151 part-proof
　　Rum *(Layer in Order in Cocktail Glass with no ice)* (Serve with drinking
　　straw, and drink all at once)

VULCAN MIND PROBE (2)-
　1 part Licorice Liqueur, 1 part 151-proof Rum, 1 part Bourbon Whiskey
　(Layer in Order)

WAFFLE-
　1 part Butterscotch Schnapps, 1 part Vodka
　splash Orange Juice

WAHOO-
　1 part Amaretto, 1 part 151-proof Rum
　splash Pineapple Juice (top)

WARM BLONDE-
1 part Southern Comfort®, 1 part Amaretto (Layer in Order)

WARM FUZZY-
1 part Peach Schnapps, 1 part Blue Curaçao
(Layer in Order)

WARM PUKE-
1 part Banana Liqueur, 1 part Irish Cream Liqueur, 1 part Coconut Liqueur
(Layer in Order)

WARP CORE BREACH-
1 part Blended Whiskey, 1 part Goldschläger®, 1 part Tequila

WATERMELON (1)-
1 part Strawberry Schnapps, 1 part Vodka
splash Orange Juice, splash Sour Mix

WATERMELON (2)-
Melon Liqueur
Cranberry Juice

WATERMELON CRAWL-
3 parts Amaretto, 1 part Melon Liqueur, 1 part Southern Comfort®
splash Orange Juice, splash Pineapple Juice

WATERMELON RANCHER-
1 part Light Rum, 1 part Melon Liqueur
splash Cranberry Juice, splash Orange Juice

WATERMELON SMASH-
1 part Melon Liqueur, 1 part Vodka
splash Cranberry Juice

WEDDING CAKE-
2 parts Amaretto, 1 part White Crème de Caçao

WEDDING DRESS-***
1 part Coconut Rum, 1 part Melon Liqueur
splash Pineapple Juice

WELL HEELED-
3 parts Dark Rum, 1 part Strawberry Schnapps
splash Orange Juice

WENCH-
1 part Amaretto, 1 part Spiced Rum

WET DREAM (1)-
4 parts Gin, 1 part Apricot Brandy
Grenadine, splash Lime Juice

WET DREAM (2)-
1 part Orange Juice, 1 part Galliano®, 1 part Triple Sec, 1 part Club Soda
(Layer in Order)

WET SPOT-
  1 part Irish Cream Liqueur, 1 part Tequila

WHITE HEART-
  1 part Sambuca, 1 part White Crème de Caçao

WHITE SATIN-
  1 part Galliano®, 1 part Tia Maria®
  splash Light Cream or Milk

WHITE SPIDER (1)-
  1 part Peppermint Schnapps, 1 part Vodka

WHITE SPIDER (2)-
  1 part Vodka, 1 part White Crème de Menthe

WHORE-
  1 part Triple Sec, 1 part Vodka
  splash Sour Mix

WIDGET-
  Gin, splash Peach Schnapps

WIKI WAKI WOO-
  2 parts Amaretto, 1 part Light Rum, 1 part Tequila, 1 part Triple Sec,
      1 part Vodka, 1 part 151-proof Rum
  splash Cranberry Juice, splash Orange Juice, splash Pineapple Juice

WILD BLUE-
  2 parts Hpnotiq®, 1 part Triple Sec
  Cranberry Juice

WILD FLING-
  Berry Schnapps
  splash Pineapple Juice, splash Cranberry Juice (float)

WINDEX (1)-
  1 part Blue Curaçao, 1 part Vodka

WINDEX (2)-
  1 part Blue Curaçao, 1 part Triple Sec, 1 part Vodka
  splash Lime Juice

WINDSURFER-
  1 part Coffee Liqueur, 1 part Triple Sec, 1 part Yukon Jack® Canadian Liqueur
  (Layer in Order)

WITCH'S TAIL-
  4 parts Berry Schnapps, 1 part Blue Curaçao
  splash Sour Mix

WOMAN WARRIOR-
  3 parts Vodka, 1 part Blue Curaçao
  splash Lime Juice

WOO WOO-
1 part Peach Schnapps, 1 part Vodka
splash Cranberry Juice

WOODEN SHOE-
1 part Chocolate Mint Liqueur, 1 part Coffee Liqueur

WRIGLEY'S DOUBLEMINT BLOWJOB-
2 parts Coffee Liqueur, 1 part Peppermint Schnapps, 1 part Light Cream or Milk
(Layer in Order)

WRITE OFF-
1 part Banana Liqueur, 1 part Strawberry Schnapps, splash Dark Rum
splash Pineapple Juice

XYLOPHONE-
2 parts Tequila, 1 part White Crème de Caçao

YELLOW BIRD (1)-
3 parts Banana Liqueur, 1 part Light Rum
splash Orange Juice, splash Pineapple Juice

YELLOW BIRD (2)-
3 parts Spiced Rum, 1 part Banana Liqueur, 1 part Galliano®

YELLOW BIRD (3)-
4 parts Light Rum, 1 part Apricot Brandy, 1 part Galliano®
splash Orange Juice, splash Lime Juice

YELLOW BIRD (4)-
2 parts Vodka, 2 parts White Crème de Caçao, 1 part Galliano®

YELLOW BIRD (5)-
3 parts Light Rum, 1 part Galliano®, 1 part Triple Sec
splash Lime Juice

YELLOW RUSSIAN-
1 part Banana Liqueur, 1 part Vodka, splash Coconut Liqueur

YELLOW SNOW-
3 parts Irish Cream Liqueur, 1 part Yellow Chartreuse (Layer in Order)

YELLOW STRAWBERRY-
2 parts Light Rum, 1 part Banana Liqueur, 1 part Strawberry Schnapps

YOKOHAMA MAMA-
3 parts Brandy, 1 part Melon Liqueur, splash Amaretto

YUKON CORNELIUS-
Yukon Jack® Canadian Liqueur, splash Goldschläger® (top)

Z-28-
1 part White Crème de Menthe, 1 part Banana Liqueur, 1 part Tequila
(Layer in Order)

Z STREET-

2 parts Spiced Rum, 1 part Banana Liqueur
Pineapple Juice, Grenadine

ZIPPERHEAD-

1 part Raspberry Liqueur, 1 part Vodka

ZUC-

1 part Coffee Liqueur, 1 part Grand Marnier®, 1 part Green Crème de Menthe,
1 part Irish Cream Liqueur

– NOTES –

Shooters (sidebar)

Manhattans

Manhattans will be requested in two ways—up (or neat) or on the rocks. Up drinks should be prepared in a cocktail glass and in a rocks glass when on the rocks. Pour the liquors and the mixers into a shaker with ice, shake or stir and strain into the glass.

APPLE MANHATTAN-
2 parts Bourbon Whiskey, 1 part Apple Brandy

BLACK MANHATTAN-
Irish Whiskey, splash Sweet Vermouth

CUBAN MANHATTAN-
1 part Dry Vermouth, 1 part Light Rum, 1 part Sweet Vermouth
splash Bitters

DUBONNET MANHATTAN-
1 part Blended Whiskey, 1 part Red Dubonnet®
Cherry Garnish

EASTERN MANHATTAN-
Japanese Whiskey, splash Anisette, splash Sweet Vermouth

IRRESISTIBLE MANHATTAN, THE-
1 part Amaretto, 1 part Canadian Whiskey, 1 part Sweet Vermouth
splash Bitters

LATIN MANHATTAN-
Light Rum, splash Dry Vermouth, splash Sweet Vermouth
splash Bitters

MANHATTAN-
Blended Whiskey, splash Sweet Vermouth
Cherry Garnish

MANHATTAN (DRY)-
Blended Whiskey, splash Dry Vermouth

MANHATTAN (PERFECT)-
Blended Whiskey, splash Dry Vermouth, splash Sweet Vermouth

MANHATTAN (SWEET)-
1 part Blended Whiskey, 1 part Sweet Vermouth

MANHATTAN FOR ROME-
1 part Bourbon Whiskey, 1 part Hazelnut Liqueur
muddle cherry and ice

MANHATTAN SOUTH-
2 parts Gin, 1 part Dry Vermouth, 1 part Southern Comfort®
splash Bitters

PARISIAN MANHATTAN-
3 parts Blended Whiskey, 1 part Sweet Vermouth, splash Amer Picon

ROARING TWENTIES MANHATTAN-
2 parts Dry or Sweet Vermouth, 1 part Rye Whiskey
splash Orange Bitters

ROB ROY-
Scotch Whiskey, splash Sweet Vermouth

ROSY MANHATTAN-
3 parts Blended Whiskey, 1 part Dry Vermouth, 1 part Raspberry Liqueur

RUM MANHATTAN-
Light Rum, splash Sweet Vermouth

RUSTY NAIL-
1 part Drambuie®, 1 part Scotch Whiskey

STILETTO MANHATTAN-
2 parts Canadian Whiskey, 1 part Amaretto, splash Dry Vermouth
splash Orange Bitters, Cherry and Orange Garnish

SWISS MANHATTAN-
3 parts Blended Whiskey, 1 part Cherry Brandy, 1 part Dry Vermouth

TEQUILA MANHATTAN-
Tequila, splash Sweet Vermouth
splash Lime Juice

– NOTES –

_____

_____

_____

_____

_____

_____

_____

_____

_____

_____

_____

_____

_____

_____

_____

_____

– NOTES –

Margaritas

Frozen, up, or on the rocks? Salt or no salt?
Margaritas can be enjoyed in any combination
and will vary by person. To make a margarita
with salt (either frozen or on the rocks) you should
take a lime wedge and use it to moisten the rim of
the glass. Then dip the glass into cocktail
salt and proceed to mix the recipe. Either blend
into a daiquiri glass or serve it up or on the
rocks in a cocktail glass.

Margaritas

BAJA BANANA-BOAT MARGARITA-
2 parts Tequila, 1 part Banana Liqueur
Sour Mix, Bananas (optional), blend (optional)

BLACK CHERRY MARGARITA-
2 parts Black Cherry Liqueur, 1 part Tequila
Orange Juice, Sour Mix, blend (optional)

BLUE MARGARITA-
3 parts Tequila, 1 part Blue Curaçao
Sour Mix, blend (optional)

CACTUS MARGARITA-
Tequila
Pineapple Juice, Sour Mix, blend (optional)

CARIBBEAN MARGARITA-
1 part Banana Liqueur, 1 part Tequila
Coconut Milk, Sour Mix, Pineapple Juice, Grenadine, blend

CATALINA MARGARITA-
3 parts Tequila, 1 part Blue Curaçao, 1 part Peach Schnapps
Sour Mix

CHERRY MARGARITA-
2 parts Cherry Brandy, 2 part Tequila, 1 part Triple Sec
Sour Mix, blend (optional)

CHITA RIVER MARGARITA-
1 part Beer, 1 part Tequila
Lime Juice

DESERT THRILLER MARGARITA-
Margarita Schnapps
Lime Juice, Salted Rim, blend (optional)

FROZEN MARGARITA-
3 parts Tequila, 1 part Triple Sec
Sour Mix, blend, Salted Rim (optional)

FROZEN FRUIT MARGARITA-
2 parts Tequila, 1 part Triple Sec, 1 part (Fruit Liqueurs)
Sour Mix, Fruits, blend

FRUIT MARGARITA-
2 parts Tequila, 1 part Triple Sec, 1 part (Fruit Liqueurs)
Sour Mix

GOLD MARGARITA (1)-
3 parts Tequila, 1 part Grand Marnier®
Sour Mix

GOLD MARGARITA (2)-
3 parts Gold Tequila, 1 part Triple Sec
Lime Juice

MARGARITA-
4 parts Tequila, 1 part Triple Sec
Lime Juice or Sour Mix, Salt Rim (optional)

MARIACHI MELON MARGARITA-
4 parts Tequila, 1 part Melon Liqueur
Sour Mix, blend (optional)

MELON VODKA MARGARITA-
4 parts Vodka, 1 part Melon Liqueur
Sour Mix

MY HONEY MARGARITA-
3 parts Gold Tequila, 1 part Triple Sec
Sour Mix, Honey, splash Orange Juice, blend (optional)

PEACH MARGARITA-
2 parts Tequila, 1 part Peach Schnapps, splash Triple Sec
Sour Mix, Salted Rim, blend (optional)

PINEAPPLE MARGARITA-
Tequila
Sour Mix, Pineapple Juice, blend (optional)

PINK CADILLAC MARGARITA-
2 parts Tequila, 1 part Triple Sec
Cranberry Juice, Sour Mix

POOLSIDE MARGARITA-
2 parts Triple Sec, 1 part Tequila, splash Blue Curaçao
Sour Mix

POST-MODERN MARGARITA-
1 part Blue Curaçao, 1 part Tequila
Cranberry Juice, Lime Juice

PRETTY PAULA'S PLEASURE-***
3 parts Tequila, 1 part Triple Sec
Cranberry Juice, splash Sour Mix, Salted Rim (optional)

SILVER MARGARITA-
3 parts Silver Tequila, 1 part Triple Sec
Lime Juice, Salted Rim (optional)

STRAWBERRY MARGARITA (1)-
2 parts Tequila, 1 part Strawberry Schnapps, 1 part Triple Sec
Lime Juice, Strawberry Daiquiri Mix, blend (optional), Salted Rim

STRAWBERRY MARGARITA (2)-
Tequila, splash Triple Sec
Sour Mix, Strawberry Daiquiri Mix, blend (optional), Salted Rim

TEQUILA SUNSET MARGARITA-
4 parts Tequila, 1 part Strawberry Schnapps, 1 part Triple Sec
Sour Mix, Orange Juice, blend (optional)

TIJUANA BLUE MARGARITA-
4 parts Tequila, 1 part Blue Curaçao
Sour Mix, blend (optional)

– NOTES –

– NOTES –

– NOTES –

SAKETINI-
3 parts Gin, 1 part Sake

SCANDINAVIAN MARTINI-
2 parts Vodka, 1 part Aquavit
Sour Mix

SILVER BRONX-
4 parts Gin, 1 part Dry Vermouth, 1 part Sweet Vermouth
Orange Juice

SILVER BULLET (1)-
1 part Dry Vermouth, 1 part Gin, splash Maraschino Liqueur
splash Orange Bitters, Sugar

SILVER BULLET (2)-
Gin, splash Scotch Whiskey

SILVER MARTINI-
2 parts Gin, 1 part Dry Vermouth, splash Maraschino Liqueur
splash Orange Bitters

SOUR APPLE MARTINI-
4 parts Vodka, 1 part Sour Apple Schnapps, 1 part Triple Sec
Lime Juice

SURFER MARTINI-
2 parts Vodka, 1 part Banana Liqueur, 1 part Coconut Rum

SWEET MARTINI-
4 parts Gin, 1 part Sweet Vermouth
splash Orange Bitters

TEQUILA MARTINI-
Tequila, splash Sweet Vermouth

TRADITIONAL MARTINI-
2 parts Gin, 1 part Dry Vermouth
Olive or Lemon Twist Garnish

ULANDA-
2 parts Gin, 1 part Triple Sec, splash Anisette

ULTIMATE ARCTIC MARTINI-
Finlandia® Vodka, splash Dry Vermouth
splash Lime Juice

ULTIMATE CHOCOLATE MARTINI-
2 parts Chocolate Liqueur, 2 parts Vodka, 1 part Irish Cream Liqueur,
1 part Raspberry Liqueur, 1 part White Crème de Cacao

VESPER-
2 parts Gin, 1 part Vodka, splash Lillet

WHITE CHOCOLATE MARTINI-
Vodka, splash White Crème de Cacao

Martinis

MIDNIGHT MARTINI-
1 part Gin, 1 part Dry Vermouth
Black Olive Garnish

MINT MARTINI-
1 part Chocolate Liqueur, 1 part Vodka, splash Crème de Menthe

MINTY MARTINI-
2 parts Gin or Vodka, 1 part Peppermint Schnapps

MIRACLE MILE-
2 parts Gin, 1 part Triple Sec
Orange Juice, splash Lime

MUSCOVY MARTINI-
2 parts Vodka, 1 part Cinnamon Schnapps, 1 part Triple Sec
Orange Juice

MY FATHER'S MARTINI-
1 part Gin, 1 part Vodka
Olive, Lemon Twist Garnish

NEGRONI-
1 part Campari, 1 part Gin, 1 part Sweet Vermouth

PAISLEY MARTINI-
4 parts Gin, 1 part Dry Vermouth, splash Scotch Whiskey

PEARL HARBOR MARTINI-
Vodka, splash Melon Liqueur

PEPPER MARTINI-
Pepper Vodka, splash Dry Vermouth

PINK MARTINI-
1 part Raspberry Liqueur, 1 part Vodka
Lime Garnish

PURPLE HOOTER MARTINI-
3 parts Vodka, 1 part Raspberry Liqueur, splash Dry Vermouth
splash Sour Mix

RASPBERRY MARTINI-
4 parts Vodka, 1 part Raspberry Liqueur
splash Lemon-Lime Soda

RED APPLE MARTINI-
1 part Sour Apple Schnapps, 1 part Vodka
Cranberry Juice

ROUGE MARTINI-
Gin, splash Raspberry Liqueur

RUM MARTINI-
Light Rum, splash Dry Vermouth

Martinis

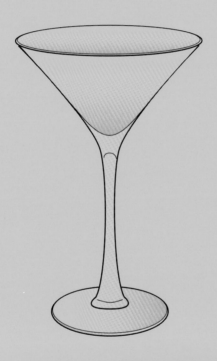

Martinis are trendy and range broadly from area to area. Most will be requested in two ways—up (or neat) or on the rocks. Usually martinis are prepared in cocktail glasses in varying sizes. Both up and rocks requests are usually poured into cocktail glasses.

ABBEY (1)-
Gin
Orange Juice, splash Orange Bitters

ABBEY (2)-
Gin, splash Sweet Vermouth
Orange Juice, splash Bitters

AFTER EIGHT-
2 parts Irish Cream Liqueur, 2 parts Vodka, 1 part Green Crème de Menthe

ALABAMA MARTINI-
4 parts Vodka, 1 part Blended Whiskey, 1 part Galliano®
Orange Juice

ALBERTO-
Citrus Vodka
Cranberry Juice

ALGONQUIN-
2 parts Blended Whiskey, 1 part Dry Vermouth
Pineapple Juice

ALMOND JOY MARTINI-
1 part Hazelnut Liqueur, 1 part Vodka, 1 part White Crème de Caçao
splash Coconut Milk

ALOHA-
2 parts Vodka, 1 part Apricot Brandy
Pineapple Juice

ANGEL-
3 parts Vodka, 1 part Hazelnut Liqueur

APPLETINI-
1 part Apple Brandy, 1 part Vodka, 1 part Triple Sec

ASIAN MARTINI-
Vodka, splash Ginger Schnapps
Orange Twist Garnish

ATOMIC ORANGE MARTINI-
1 part Melon Liqueur, 1 part Vodka
Orange Juice

AVIATION-
Gin, splash Apricot Brandy, splash Cherry Brandy
Lime Juice

BABY BLUE MARTINI-
1 part Blue Curaçao, 1 part Vodka
Sour Mix

BALD HEAD-
Gin, splash Anisette, splash Dry Vermouth

BEADLESTONE-
1 part Dry Vermouth, 1 part Scotch Whiskey

BERLIN MARTINI-
Vodka, splash Black Sambuca, splash Peach Schnapps

BLACK MARTINI-
Vodka, splash Raspberry Liqueur
Lemon Twist Garnish

BLONDE MARTINI-
Vodka, splash Lillet
Orange Twist Garnish

BLUE MOON MARTINI-
2 parts Gin, 1 part Blue Curaçao

BLUEBERRY MARTINI-
Gin, splash Blue Curaçao, splash Raspberry Liqueur

BRANTINI-
2 parts Brandy, 1 part Gin, splash Dry Vermouth

BROADWAY MARTINI-
Gin, splash White Crème de Menthe

BRONX COCKTAIL-
1 part Dry Vermouth, 1 part Gin, 1 part Sweet Vermouth
splash Orange Juice

BRONX MARTINI-
Vodka
splash Bitters, Orange Twist Garnish

BURNT MARTINI-
2 parts Gin, 1 part Blended Whiskey

CAJUN MARTINI (1)-
Vodka, splash Dry Vermouth
Jalapeno Pepper Garnish

CAJUN MARTINI (2)-
Pepper Vodka, splash Dry Vermouth

CARAMEL APPLE MARTINI-
2 parts Vodka, 1 part Butterscotch Schnapps,
1 part Sour Apple Schnapps

CARIBBEAN MARTINI-
2 parts Vodka, 1 part Coconut Rum
Splash Pineapple Juice

CHOCOLATE MARTINI-
Vodka, splash White Crème de Caçao

COOL BLUE MARTINI-
Gin or Vodka, splash Blue Curaçao, splash Dry Vermouth
splash Lime Juice

COSMOPOLITAN-
2 parts Vodka, 1 part Triple Sec
Cranberry Juice, Lime Juice

DIRTY MARTINI-
Gin, Splash Dry Vermouth
splash Olive Juice, Olive garnish

FINO MARTINI-
Gin, splash Fino Sherry

FLYING DUTCHMAN MARTINI-
Gin, splash Triple Sec

FRENCH MARTINI-
1 part Black Raspberry Liqueur, 1 part Vodka

FUSION COSMO-
3 parts Vodka, 1 part Triple Sec
Cranberry Juice, splash Lime Juice

GIBSON-
Gin or Vodka, splash Vermouth
Onion Garnish

GILROY-
Cherry Brandy, splash Dry Vermouth
Lime Juice, splash Orange Bitters

GIMLET-
Gin or Vodka
splash Lime Juice

GIMLEY-
Gin or Vodka
splash Sour Mix

GUMDROP MARTINI-
4 parts Lemon Rum, 2 parts Vodka, 1 part Southern Comfort®,
splash Dry Vermouth
splash Lime Juice

GYPSY (1)-
1 part Gin, 1 part Sweet Vermouth

GYPSY (2)-
4 parts Vodka, 1 part Bénédictine
splash Orange Juice, splash Lime Juice

HALEAKALA MARTINI-
3 parts Vodka, 1 part Raspberry Liqueur
Pineapple Juice

HOLLYWOOD MARTINI-
Gin, splash Dry Vermouth, splash Triple Sec

HYPNOTIC MARTINI-
2 parts Hpnotiq®, 1 part Coconut Liqueur
Pineapple Juice

IDEAL-
1 part Dry Vermouth, 1 part Gin, splash Maraschino Liqueur
Grapefruit Juice or Lime Juice, Cherry Garnish

IMPERIAL MARTINI-
1 part Dry Vermouth, 1 part Gin, splash Maraschino Liqueur
splash Bitters

ISLAND MARTINI-
Rum, splash Dry Vermouth, splash Sweet Vermouth

JAMAICAN MARTINI-
Light Rum, splash Dry Sherry
Olive Garnish

JAMES BOND MARTINI-
3 parts Gin, 1 part Vodka, splash Dry Vermouth
Lime Twist Garnish (Shaken, not stirred)

KNOCK OUT-
1 part Anisette, 1 part Dry Vermouth, 1 part Gin, splash White
Crème de Menthe

LAVA LAMP MARTINI-
4 parts Vodka, 1 part Raspberry Liqueur
Honey

MARTINI-
Gin, splash Dry Vermouth (Drier=Less Dry Vermouth)
Olive or Lemon Twist Garnish

MARTINI (DRY)-
Gin, splash Dry Vermouth

MARTINI (MEDIUM)-
3 parts Gin, 1 part Dry Vermouth, 1 part Sweet Vermouth

MARTINI (PERFECT)-
Gin, splash Dry Vermouth, splash Sweet Vermouth

MARTINI (SWEET)-
Gin, splash Sweet Vermouth

METROPOLITAN MARTINI-
Gin
Cranberry Juice, splash Lime Juice

MEXICAN MARTINI-
3 parts Tequila, 1 part Triple Sec

WOO-WOO MARTINI-
   3 parts Vodka, 1 part Peach Schnapps, splash Dry Vermouth
   splash Sour Mix

– NOTES –

_____

_____

_____

_____

_____

_____

_____

_____

_____

_____

_____

_____

_____

_____

_____

_____

_____

_____

_____

_____

_____

_____

_____

Martinis

Frozen Drinks

Making frozen drinks can be an art. Add your ice and all of the ingredients into the blender and blend. For recipes that require ice cream you may want to use less ice than for those that just contain juices. Remember to add any carbonated mixers like sodas, beer or champagne after you blend the other ingredients to avoid carbonation overflow.

A LA MODE-
1 part Amaretto, 1 part Apple Schnapps
Cider, Vanilla Ice Cream, Cinnamon, blend

ACAPULCO JOY-
1 part Coffee Liqueur, 1 part Peach Schnapps
Vanilla Ice Cream, Banana, blend, top Whipped Cream

ADULT ROOT BEER FLOAT-
1 part Coffee Liqueur, 1 part Galliano®
Vanilla Ice Cream, blend, fill Cola

ALL-AMERICAN DAIQUIRI, THE-
(Three layers: Blue, Red, White: Blended with ice & layered in order in Daiquiri Glass)
1. 1 part Light Rum or Vodka
   Sour Mix, Blueberry Daiquiri Mix, blend
2. 1 part Light Rum or Vodka
   Sour Mix, Strawberry Daiquiri Mix, blend
3. Whipped Cream

ALMOND FROST-
2 parts Amaretto, 1 part Cognac, 1 part Coconut Liqueur
Orange Juice, Light Cream or Milk, blend

AMBER DAIQUIRI-
4 parts Dark Rum, 1 part Triple Sec
Lime Juice, blend

AMBROSIA-
2 parts Coconut Rum, 1 part Dark Rum, 1 part Triple Sec
Orange Juice, Light Cream or Milk, blend

AMORE-
2 parts Amaretto, 1 part Coffee Liqueur
Light Cream or Milk, Vanilla Ice Cream, blend

AMOROUS DUO-
4 parts Raspberry Liqueur, 1 part Amaretto
Vanilla Ice Cream, blend

ANATOLE COFFEE-
1 part Coffee Liqueur, 1 part Cognac, 1 part Hazelnut Liqueur
Cold Coffee, blend, top Whipped Cream

ANEJO BANGER-
4 parts Tequila, 1 part Galliano® (Float)
Orange Juice, blend

ANNA'S BANANA-
Vodka
Lime Juice, Bananas, Honey, blend

APPLE BLOSSOM-
Apple Brandy
Apple Juice, splash Sour Mix, blend

Frozen Drinks

APPLE CALABASH-
1 part Apple Brandy, 1 part Coconut Rum, 1 part Cranberry Brandy,
    1 part Spiced Rum
Pineapple Juice, Light Cream or Milk, blend

APPLE COLADA-
Apple Schnapps
Coconut Milk, splash Light Cream or Milk, blend

APPLE GRANNY CRISP-
2 parts Apple Schnapps, 1 part Brandy, 1 part Irish Cream Liqueur
Vanilla Ice Cream, Graham Cracker Crumbs, blend, top Whipped Cream

APPLE RIVER INNER TUBE-
1 part Brandy, 1 part Brown Crème de Caçao
Vanilla Ice Cream, blend, Spiced Apple Ring Garnish

APRICOT JERK-
2 parts Apricot Brandy, 1 part Coconut Rum, 1 part Dark Rum
Light Cream or Milk, blend

APRICOT SWEETIE-
1 part Apricot Brandy, 1 part Dark Rum, 1 part Gin
Lime Juice, Grenadine, blend

APRIL FOOL-
Apple Schnapps
Cranberry Juice, Vanilla Ice Cream, blend

AZULUNA-
2 parts Light Rum, 1 part Blue Curacao
Pineapple Juice, Coconut Milk, blend

BAHAMA BREEZE-
1 part Banana Liqueur, 1 part Melon Liqueur
Coconut Milk, Pineapple Juice, Orange Juice, blend

BAJA BANANA-BOAT MARGARITA-
2 parts Tequila, 1 part Banana Liqueur
Sour Mix, Bananas (optional), blend

BANANA B. JONES-
Banana Liqueur
Coconut Milk, Vanilla Ice Cream, Bananas, blend, top Whipped Cream

BANANA BERRY BLENDER-
2 parts Raspberry Liqueur, 1 part Banana Liqueur
Vanilla Ice Cream, blend

BANANA CHI CHI-
1 part Banana Liqueur, 1 part Vodka
Coconut Milk, Pineapple Juice, Banana, blend

BANANA COLADA-
1 part Light Rum, 1 part Dark Rum
Pineapple Juice, Coconut Milk, Bananas, blend

BANANA DAIQUIRI-
3 parts Light Rum, 1 part Triple Sec
Sour Mix, Bananas, Honey, blend

BANANA DI AMORE-
1 part Amaretto, 1 part Banana Liqueur
Orange Juice, Sour Mix, blend

BANANA FOSTER-
3 parts Dark Rum, 1 part Banana Liqueur
Vanilla Ice Cream, Banana, blend

BANANA ITALIANO-
1 part Banana Liqueur, 1 part Galliano®
Light Cream or Milk, blend

BANANA MAMA-
1 part Banana Liqueur, 1 part Coconut Rum, 1 part Dark Rum,
1 part Light Rum
Pineapple Juice, Strawberry Daiquiri Mix, blend

BANANA MILK SHAKE-
2 parts Light Rum, 1 part Banana Liqueur
Light Cream or Milk, splash Grenadine, blend

BANANA NUT BREAD-
2 parts Banana Liqueur, 2 parts Hazelnut Liqueur, 1 part Dry Sherry
Vanilla Ice Cream, blend

BANANA POPSICLE-
Banana Liqueur
Coconut Milk, Orange Sherbet, blend

BANANA SLUSHEE-
1 part Banana Liqueur, 1 part Dark Rum
Orange Juice, Sugar, blend

BANANA SPLIT-
4 parts Banana Liqueur, 1 part Crème de Noyaux, 1 part White
Crème de Caçao
splash Light Cream or Milk, splash Grenadine, blend

BANANA TREE-
2 parts Banana Liqueur, 1 part Galliano®, 1 part White Crème de Caçao
Vanilla Ice Cream, Bananas, blend

BARRIER REEF-
2 parts Gin, 1 part Triple Sec, splash Blue Curaçao, splash Grand Marnier®
Vanilla Ice Cream, blend

BAY BOMBER-
1 part Gin, 1 part Light Rum, 1 part Tequila, 1 part Triple Sec, 1 part Vodka,
1 part 151-proof Rum (lace)
Cranberry Juice, Orange Juice, Pineapple Juice, Sour Mix, blend

Frozen Drinks

BAY CITY BOMBER-
1 part Gin, 1 part Rum, 1 part Tequila, 1 part Vodka,
   splash 1 part 151-proof Rum (top)
Orange Juice, Pineapple Juice, Cranberry Juice, Sour Mix, blend

BEACH BUM'S COOLER-
4 parts Irish Cream Liqueur, 1 part Banana Liqueur, 1 part Light Rum
Coconut Milk, Vanilla Ice Cream, Milk, Banana, blend

BIG CHILL, THE-
1 part Coconut Rum, 1 part Dark Rum
Cranberry Juice, Orange Juice, Pineapple Juice, blend

BLACK CHERRY MARGARITA-
2 parts Black Cherry Liqueur, 1 part Tequila
Orange Juice, Sour Mix, blend

BLACK DAIQUIRI-
3 parts Dark Rum, 1 part Triple Sec
Sour Mix, Honey, blend

BLACKBERRIES & CREAM-
1 part Banana Liqueur, 1 part Blackberry Brandy,
   1 part Coconut Liqueur
Pineapple Juice, splash Light Cream or Milk, blend

BLIZZARD-
Blended Whiskey
Cranberry Juice, splash Sour Mix, blend

BLIZZARD, THE-
1 part Brandy, 1 part Coffee Liqueur, 1 part Irish Cream Liqueur,
   1 part Light Rum
Light Cream or Milk, Vanilla Ice Cream, blend

BLUE BAYOU-
2 parts Spiced Rum, 1 part Blue Curaçao
Light Cream or Milk, Vanilla Ice Cream, blend

BLUE CLOUD-
2 parts Amaretto, 1 part Blue Curaçao
Vanilla Ice Cream, top Whipped Cream

BLUE DAIQUIRI-
3 parts Light Rum, 1 part Blue Curaçao
Sour Mix, Honey, blend

BLUE MARGARITA-
3 parts Tequila, 1 part Blue Curaçao
Sour Mix, blend

BLUE VELVET-
1 part Melon Liqueur, 1 part Raspberry Liqueur
Vanilla Ice Cream, blend, top Whipped Cream
(Drizzle Whipped Cream with splash Blue Curaçao)

BLUEBERRY FREEZE-
1 part Blueberry Schnapps, 1 part Vodka
Coconut Milk, Pineapple Juice, Vanilla Ice Cream, blend

BLUSHIN' RUSSIAN-
1 part Coffee Liqueur, 1 part Vodka
Vanilla Ice Cream, Strawberries, blend

BRANDIED PEACHES & CREAM-
1 part Peach Brandy, 1 part Peach Schnapps
Coconut Milk, Vanilla Ice Cream, blend

BRANDY HUMMER-
1 part Brandy, 1 part Coffee Liqueur
Vanilla Ice Cream, blend

BRASS FIDDLE, THE-
2 parts Peach Schnapps, 1 part Sour Mash Whiskey
Pineapple Juice, Orange Juice, splash Grenadine, blend

BRAZILIAN MONK-
1 part Brown Crème de Caçao, 1 part Coffee Liqueur, 1 part Hazelnut Liqueur,
    splash Dry Sherry
Vanilla Ice Cream, blend

BRUTE-
1 part Amaretto, 1 part Brown Crème de Caçao
Vanilla Ice Cream, blend

BUCCANEER-
1 part Coffee Liqueur, 1 part Dark Rum, 1 part Light Rum
Pineapple Juice, Light Cream or Milk, blend

BUNKY PUNCH-
1 part Melon Liqueur, 1 part Peach Schnapps, 1 part Vodka
Grape Juice, Orange Juice, Cranberry Juice, blend

BUTTER COLADA-***
3 parts Butterscotch Schnapps, 1 part Light Rum
Coconut Milk, splash Light Cream or Milk, blend

BUTTER PECAN-***
Hazelnut Liqueur
Vanilla Ice Cream, Butter Pecan Ice Cream, blend

CACTUS COLADA-
2 parts Tequila, 1 part Melon Liqueur
Coconut Milk, Pineapple Juice, blend

CANDY-
1 part Brandy, 1 part Galliano®, splash Maraschino Liqueur
Orange Sherbet, blend

CANDY STORE-
1 part Amaretto, 1 part Crème de Noyaux, 1 part Raspberry Liqueur
Cookies n' Cream Ice Cream, blend, top Whipped Cream

CANYON QUAKE-
1 part Amaretto, 1 part Brandy, 1 part Irish Cream Liqueur
Light Cream or Milk, blend

CAPE COLADA-
1 part Peach Schnapps, 1 part Vodka
Coconut Milk, Cranberry Juice, Sour Mix, blend

CARAMEL NUT-
1 part Butterscotch Schnapps or Caramel Liqueur, 1 part White
    Crème de Caçao
Vanilla Ice Cream, Chopped Nuts Garnish

CARIB BREEZER-
1 part Banana Liqueur, 1 part Melon Liqueur, 1 part Vodka
Pineapple Juice, blend

CARIBBEAN BEACH PARTY-
1 part Banana Liqueur, 1 part Dark Rum
Coconut Milk, Pineapple Juice, Cranberry Juice, Grenadine, blend

CARIBBEAN BREEZE-
1 part Banana Liqueur, 1 part Dark Rum
Coconut Milk, Pineapple Juice, Sour Mix, Grenadine, blend

CAVANAUGH'S SPECIAL-
1 part Amaretto, 1 part Coffee Liqueur (layer on top), 1 part White
    Crème de Caçao
Vanilla Ice Cream, blend, top Whipped Cream

CHAMPAGNE CHARISMA-
2 parts Champagne, 1 part Vodka, splash Peach Schnapps
Cranberry Juice, Raspberry Sherbet, blend

CHAMPAGNE CORNUCOPIA SWIRL-
1 part Champagne, 1 part Peach Schnapps, 1 part Vodka
Rainbow Sherbet, blend, Pour over Cranberry Juice

CHEAP MAN'S PINA COLADA-
Coconut Rum
Pineapple Juice, splash Light Cream or Milk, blend

CHERRY CHOCOLATE FREEZE-
1 part Brown Crème de Caçao, 1 part Cherry Brandy
Chocolate Ice Cream, blend

CHERRY DAIQUIRI-
3 parts Light Rum, 1 part Cherry Brandy
Sour Mix, blend

CHERRY MARGARITA (FROZEN)-
2 parts Cherry Brandy, 2 parts Tequila, 1 part Triple Sec
Sour Mix, blend

CHERRY REPAIR KIT COCKTAIL (FROZEN)-
1 part Amaretto, 1 part White Crème de Caçao, splash Maraschino Liqueur
Light Cream or Milk, splash Grenadine, blend

CHERRY TREE CLIMBER COCKTAIL-
2 parts Cherry Brandy, 2 parts White Crème de Caçao,
    1 part Peppermint Schnapps
Vanilla Ice Cream, blend

CHERRY VANILLA-
2 parts Maraschino Liqueur, 1 part Cherry Liqueur, 1 part White
    Crème de Caçao
Light Cream or Milk, Vanilla Ice Cream, Maraschino Cherries, blend

CHI-CHI (FROZEN)-
Vodka
Coconut Milk, Pineapple Juice, blend

CHILLY CHOCOLATE MINT-
1 part Coconut Rum, 1 part Dark Rum, 1 part Peppermint Schnapps
Light Cream or Milk, Chocolate Syrup, blend

CHILLY IRISHMAN-
2 parts Irish Whiskey, 1 part Coffee Liqueur, 1 part Irish Cream Liqueur
Cold Espresso, Vanilla Ice Cream, Sugar, blend

CHOCO-BANANA SMASH-
Irish Cream Liqueur
Light Cream or Milk, Vanilla Extract, Vanilla Ice Cream,
    top Chocolate Sprinkles

CHOCOLADA-
3 parts Light Rum, 1 part Coffee Liqueur, 1 part Dark Rum
Chocolate Syrup, Coconut Milk, blend

CHOCOLATE ALMOND CREAM-
1 part Amaretto, 1 part White Crème de Caçao
Vanilla Ice Cream, blend

CHOCOLATE BLACK RUSSIAN-
2 parts Vodka, 1 part Coffee Liqueur
Chocolate Ice Cream, blend

CHOCOLATE BRANDY HUMMER-
1 part Brandy, 1 part Coffee Liqueur
Chocolate Ice Cream, blend

CHOCOLATE COVERED BANANA-
Coconut Rum
Chocolate Syrup, Bananas, Vanilla Ice Cream, blend,
    top Whipped Cream

CHOCOLATE MONKEY-
2 parts Banana Liqueur, 1 part Light Rum
Chocolate Ice Cream, Bananas, blend

Frozen Drinks

CHOCOLATE SNOW BEAR-
1 part Amaretto, 1 part Brown Crème de Caçao
Chocolate Syrup, French Vanilla Ice Cream, Vanilla Extract, blend,
    top Whipped Cream

CHOCOLATE XS-
1 part Brown Crème de Caçao, 1 part Dark Rum, 1 part Irish Cream Liqueur
Chocolate Milk, Chocolate Ice Cream, blend, top Chocolate Sprinkles

CHOCOLATIER-
1 part Light Rum, 1 part White Crème de Caçao
Chocolate Ice Cream, blend, top Whipped Cream

CIAO BABY-
Dark Rum
Strawberry Daiquiri Mix, Sour Mix, splash Grenadine, blend

CITRUS BANANA FLIP-
Dark Rum
Club Soda, Orange Juice, Light Cream or Milk, Lime Juice, Brown Sugar,
    Bananas, blend

CLOUD 9-
1 part Amaretto, 1 part Black Raspberry Liqueur, 1 part Irish Cream Liqueur
Vanilla Ice Cream, blend, Half Peanut Butter Cup Garnish

COCO LOCO-
1 part Coconut Rum, 1 part Dark Rum
Coconut Milk, Papaya Juice, Pineapple Juice, Orange Juice, Grenadine, blend

COCOBANANA-
2 parts Banana Liqueur, 2 parts Light Rum, 1 part Amaretto,
    1 part Coconut Rum
Pineapple Juice, Coconut Milk, Bananas, Vanilla Ice Cream, blend

COCONUT DAIQUIRI-
1 part Coconut Rum, 1 part Dark Rum
Sour Mix, Coconut Milk, blend

COFFEE BRANDY HUMMER-
1 part Brandy, 1 part Coffee Liqueur
Coffee, Ice Cream, blend

COFFEE COOLER-
1 part Coffee Liqueur, 1 part Vodka
Cold Coffee, splash Light Cream or Milk, Sugar,
    Coffee Ice Cream, blend

COFFEE EGGNOG-
2 parts Blended Whiskey, 1 part Coffee Liqueur
Light Cream or Milk, Instant Coffee, Sugar, blend

COFFEE HUMMER-
1 part Coffee Liqueur, 1 part Light Rum
Vanilla Ice Cream, blend

COFFEE NUT SUNDAE-
1 part Amaretto, 1 part Hazelnut Liqueur
Coffee Ice Cream, blend, top Whipped Cream

COLADA (APPLE COLADA)-
Apple Schnapps
Coconut Milk, splash Light Cream or Milk, blend

COLADA (BANANA COLADA)-
1 part Light Rum, 1 part Dark Rum
Pineapple Juice, Coconut Milk, Bananas, blend

COLADA (BUTTER COLADA)-***
3 parts Butterscotch Schnapps, 1 part Light Rum
Coconut Milk, splash Light Cream or Milk, blend

COLADA (CACTUS COLADA)-
2 parts Tequila, 1 part Melon Liqueur
Coconut Milk, Pineapple Juice, blend

COLADA (CAPE COLADA)-
1 part Peach Schnapps, 1 part Vodka
Coconut Milk, Cranberry Juice, Sour Mix, blend

COLADA (CHEAP MAN'S PINA COLADA)-
Coconut Rum
Pineapple Juice, splash Light Cream or Milk, blend

COLADA (CHOCOLADA)-
3 parts Light Rum, 1 part Coffee Liqueur, 1 part Dark Rum
Chocolate Syrup, Coconut Milk, blend

COLADA (COLADASCOPE)-
2 parts Light Rum, 1 part Triple Sec
Pineapple Juice, Lime Juice, Coconut Milk, blend

COLADA (FRENCH COLADA)-
2 parts Light Rum, 1 part Cognac, splash Crème de Cassis
Pineapple Juice, Coconut Milk, blend

COLADA (GINGER COLADA)-
2 parts Dark Rum, 1 part Coconut Rum, 1 part Ginger Brandy
Pineapple Juice, blend

COLADA (ITALIAN COLADA)-
3 parts Light Rum, 1 part Amaretto
Pineapple Juice, Coconut Milk, Light Cream or Milk, blend

COLADA (KAPPA COLADA)-
Brandy
Pineapple Juice, Coconut Milk, blend

COLADA (MELON COLADA)-
2 parts Light Rum, 1 part Melon Liqueur
Pineapple Juice, Coconut Milk, splash Light Cream or Milk, blend

COLADA (MEXICOLADA)-
2 parts Tequila, 1 part Coffee Liqueur
Pineapple Juice, Coconut Milk, Light Cream or Milk, blend

COLADA (MIDORI COLADA)-
2 parts Midori® Melon Liqueur, 1 part Light Rum
Pineapple Juice, Coconut Milk, blend

COLADA (NUTTY COLADA)-
Amaretto
Coconut Milk, Crushed Pineapple, blend

COLADA (PASSION COLADA)-
Dark Rum
Passion Fruit Juice, Coconut Milk, blend

COLADA (PEACHY COLADA)-
4 parts Spiced Rum, 1 part Peach Schnapps
Pineapple Juice, Coconut Milk, blend

COLADA (PIÑA COLADA)-
Dark or Light Rum
Coconut Milk, Pineapple Juice, blend

COLADA (STRAWBERRY BANANA COLADA)-
3 parts Dark Rum, 1 part Banana Liqueur, 1 part Strawberry Schnapps
Strawberry Daiquiri Mix, Bananas, Coconut Milk, blend

COLADA (TEQUILA COLADA)-
Tequila
Sour Mix, Coconut Milk, blend

COLADA (TROPIC COLADA)-
1 part Banana Liqueur, 1 part Strawberry Schnapps
Pineapple Juice, Coconut Milk, blend

COLADA (VERY BERRY COLADA)-
2 parts Wild Berry Schnapps, 1 part Dark Rum
Pineapple Juice, Coconut Milk, blend

COLADASCOPE-
2 parts Light Rum, 1 part Triple Sec
Pineapple Juice, Lime Juice, Coconut Milk, blend

COLDCOCKED-
Southern Comfort®
Piña Colada Mix, Cola, blend, top Whipped Cream

COOL KISS-
Amaretto
Vanilla Ice Cream, Strawberry Margarita Mix, blend

COOL OPERATOR-
2 parts Melon Liqueur, 1 part Light Rum, 1 part Vodka
Grapefruit Juice, Orange Juice, splash Lime Juice, blend

Frozen Drinks

CORAL REEF-
2 parts Coconut Rum, 1 part Vodka
Strawberry Margarita Mix, blend

COUNTRY CREAM-
2 parts Coffee Liqueur, 2 parts Pear Brandy, 1 part Campari,
    1 part Raspberry Liqueur
Vanilla Ice Cream, blend

CREAMY SCREWDRIVER-
Vodka
Orange Juice, Sugar, blend

CRIME OF PASSION-
Dark Rum, splash Raspberry Liqueur
Passion Fruit Juice, Vanilla Ice Cream, blend, fill Cream Soda

DAIQUIRI-
Light Rum, splash Triple Sec (optional)
Sour Mix, blend

DAIQUIRI (ALL-AMERICAN DAIQUIRI, THE)-
(Three layers: Blue, Red, White. Blended and layered in order)
1. Light Rum or Vodka
   Sour Mix, Blueberry Daiquiri Mix, blend
2. Light Rum or Vodka
   Sour Mix, Strawberry Daiquiri Mix, blend
3. Whipped Cream

DAIQUIRI (AMBER DAIQUIRI)-
4 parts Dark Rum, 1 part Triple Sec
Lime Juice, blend

DAIQUIRI (BANANA DAIQUIRI)-
3 parts Light Rum, 1 part Triple Sec
Sour Mix, Bananas, Honey, blend

DAIQUIRI (BLACK DAIQUIRI)-
3 parts Dark Rum, 1 part Triple Sec
Sour Mix, Honey, blend

DAIQUIRI (BLUE DAIQUIRI)-
3 parts Light Rum, 1 part Blue Curaçao
Sour Mix, Honey, blend

DAIQUIRI (CHERRY DAIQUIRI)-
3 parts Light Rum, 1 part Cherry Brandy
Sour Mix, blend

DAIQUIRI (COCONUT DAIQUIRI)-
1 part Coconut Rum, 1 part Dark Rum
Sour Mix, Coconut Milk, blend

DAIQUIRI (DERBY DAIQUIRI)-
Light Rum
Orange Juice, splash Sour Mix, blend

Frozen Drinks

DAIQUIRI (EVE'S APPLE DAIQUIRI)-
Spiced Rum, splash Apple Brandy
Orange Juice, Sour Mix, blend

DAIQUIRI (FLORIDA DAIQUIRI)-
4 parts Dark Rum, 1 part Cherry Brandy
Grapefruit Juice, Sour Mix, blend

DAIQUIRI (FRENCH DAIQUIRI)-
Light Rum, splash Crème de Cassis
Sour Mix, blend

DAIQUIRI (FROZEN DAIQUIRI)-
Light Rum, splash Triple Sec (optional)
Sour Mix, blend

DAIQUIRI (FROZEN MINT DAIQUIRI)-
Light Rum
Sour Mix, Mint Leaves, blend

DAIQUIRI (FROZEN PINEAPPLE DAIQUIRI)-
Light Rum
Pineapple Slices, Sour Mix, blend

DAIQUIRI (FRUIT DAIQUIRI)-
2 parts Light Rum, 1 part White Crème de Caçao, 1 part (Fruit Liqueurs)
Fruit, splash Sour Mix, blend

DAIQUIRI (GIN DAIQUIRI)-
3 parts Gin, 1 part Light Rum
Sour Mix, blend

DAIQUIRI (MANGO DAIQUIRI)-
4 parts Dark Rum, 1 part Triple Sec
Mango Juice, Sour Mix, blend

DAIQUIRI (MELON DAIQUIRI)-
1 part Light Rum, 1 part Melon Liqueur
Cantaloupe, Sugar, blend

DAIQUIRI (PAPAYA DAIQUIRI)-
Light Rum
Papaya Juice, Sour Mix, blend

DAIQUIRI (PASSION DAIQUIRI)-
Light Rum
Passion Fruit Juice, Sour Mix, blend

DAIQUIRI (PASSIONATE DAIQUIRI, A)-
Light Rum
Passion Fruit Juice, Sour Mix, blend

DAIQUIRI (PEACH DAIQUIRI)-
4 parts Dark Rum, 1 part Triple Sec
Sour Mix, Pitted Peach, blend

DAIQUIRI (PINEAPPLE DAIQUIRI)-
Light Rum
Pineapple Juice, splash Sour Mix, blend

DAIQUIRI (SPICED BANANA DAIQUIRI)-
2 parts Spiced Rum, 1 part Banana Liqueur
Sour Mix, Bananas, blend

DAIQUIRI (STRAWBERRY DAIQUIRI 1)-
2 parts Light Rum, 1 part Strawberry Schnapps
Sour Mix, Strawberry Daiquiri Mix, blend

DAIQUIRI (STRAWBERRY DAIQUIRI 2)-
Light Rum
Sour Mix, Strawberry Daiquiri Mix, blend

DEATH BY CHOCOLATE-
2 parts Irish Cream Liqueur, 1 part Brown Crème de Caçao, 1 part Vodka
Chocolate Ice Cream, blend

DERBY DAIQUIRI-
Light Rum
Orange Juice, splash Sour Mix, blend

DERBY SPECIAL-
3 parts Light Rum, 1 part Triple Sec
Orange Juice, Sour Mix, blend

DESERT THRILLER MARGARITA-
Margarita Schnapps
Lime, Salted Rim, blend

DEVIL'S TAIL-
2 parts Light Rum, 1 part Vodka, splash Apricot Brandy
Lime Juice, Grenadine, blend

DI AMORE DREAM-
2 parts Amaretto, 1 part White Crème de Caçao
Orange Juice, Vanilla Ice Cream, blend

DIRTY BANANA-
2 parts Coffee Liqueur, 1 part Light Rum
Light Cream or Milk, Bananas, Sugar, blend

DREAMSICLE-
Amaretto
Vanilla Ice Cream, splash Orange Juice, splash Light Cream or Milk, blend

DREAMY MONKEY-
2 parts Vodka, 1 part Banana Liqueur, 1 part Brown Crème de Caçao
Light Cream or Milk, Banana, Vanilla Ice Cream, blend, Garnish Half Banana

ECLIPSE-
Amaretto, splash Brown Crème de Caçao
Orange Juice, Chocolate Ice Cream, blend

ELECTRIC ICED TEA-
1 part Blue Curaçao, 1 part Gin, 1 part Light Rum, 1 part Tequila, 1 part Vodka
Sour Mix, fill Lemon-Lime Soda, blend

EMERALD ISLE-
1 part Green Crème de Menthe, 1 part Irish Whiskey
Vanilla Ice Cream, blend, top Club Soda

EVE'S APPLE DAIQUIRI-
Spiced Rum, splash Apple Brandy
Orange Juice, Sour Mix, blend

FELONY FRAPPE-***
2 parts Blueberry Schnapps, 1 part Light Rum
Strawberry Daiquiri Mix, splash Sour Mix, blend, top Whipped Cream

FLORIDA BANANA-
2 parts Vodka, 1 part Banana Liqueur, 1 part Coconut Liqueur
Orange Juice, Banana Garnish, blend

FLORIDA DAIQUIRI-
4 parts Dark Rum, 1 part Cherry Brandy
Grapefruit Juice, Sour Mix, blend

FLORIDA FREEZE-
1 part Coconut Rum, 1 part Dark Rum
Pineapple Juice, Orange Juice, blend

FOUR WHEELER-
Dark Rum
Orange Juice, Pineapple Juice, Coconut Milk, blend

FRAPPE-
(Any Liqueur)
Crushed Ice

FRENCH COLADA-
2 parts Light Rum, 1 part Cognac, splash Crème de Cassis
Pineapple Juice, Coconut Milk, blend

FRENCH DAIQUIRI-
Light Rum, splash Crème de Cassis
Sour Mix, blend

FRIDAY-
Light Rum
Orange Juice or Mango Juice, splash Lime Juice, blend

FRIGID HAIRY VIRGIN-
2 parts Light Rum, 1 part Triple Sec
Pineapple Juice, blend

FROSTBITE-
4 parts Tequila, 1 part White Crème de Caçao, splash Blue Curaçao
Light Cream or Milk, blend

FROSTY NOGGIN-
3 parts Light Rum, 1 part White Crème de Menthe
Eggnog, Vanilla Ice Cream, blend, top Whipped Cream

FROZEN APPLE-
Apple Schnapps
Sour Mix, blend

FROZEN BERKELEY-
3 parts Light Rum, 1 part Brandy
Passion Fruit Juice, Lime Juice, blend

FROZEN BIKINI-
2 parts Vodka, 1 part Peach Schnapps, fill Champagne
Orange Juice, Peach Juice, splash Sour Mix, blend

FROZEN BRANDY & RUM-
1 part Brandy, 1 part Light Rum
Sour Mix, blend

FROZEN CITRON NEON-
3 parts Citrus Vodka, 2 parts Melon Liqueur, 1 part Blue Curaçao
Sour Mix, blend

FROZEN CRAN RAZZ-
2 parts Tequila, 1 part DeKuyper® Razzmatazz Black Raspberry Liqueur
Cranberry Juice, splash Sour Mix, blend

FROZEN DAIQUIRI-
Light Rum, splash Triple Sec (Optional)
Sour Mix, blend

FROZEN FUZZY-
2 parts Peach Schnapps, 1 part Triple Sec
Lime Juice, Grenadine, splash Lemon-Lime Soda, blend

FROZEN MARGARITA-
3 parts Tequila, 1 part Triple Sec
Sour Mix, blend

FROZEN MATADOR-
Tequila
Pineapple Juice, splash Lime Juice, blend

FROZEN MINT DAIQUIRI-
Light Rum
Sour Mix, Mint Leaves, blend

FROZEN PINEAPPLE DAIQUIRI-
Light Rum
Pineapple Slices, Sour Mix, blend

FROZEN SNOWBALL-
2 parts Gin, 1 part Sambuca, 1 part White Crème de Menthe
Light Cream or Milk, blend

FRUIT DAIQUIRI-
2 parts Light Rum, 1 part White Crème de Caçao, 1 part (Fruit Liqueurs)
Fruit, splash Sour Mix, blend

FRUIT MARGARITA (FROZEN)-
2 parts Tequila, 1 part Triple Sec, 1 part (Fruit Liqueurs)
Fruit, splash Sour Mix, blend

FRUIT RUM FRAPPE-
2 parts Light Rum, 1 part Banana Liqueur, 1 part Crème de Cassis
Orange Juice, blend

FRUITY SMASH-
1 part Banana Liqueur, 1 part Cherry Brandy
Vanilla Ice Cream, blend

GALWAY BAY-
1 part Coffee Liqueur, 1 part Irish Cream Liqueur, 1 part Peppermint Schnapps
Light Cream or Milk, blend

GIN & BERRIES-
4 parts Gin, 1 part Strawberry Liqueur
splash Sour Mix, Strawberry Daiquiri Mix, blend, top Club Soda

GIN DAIQUIRI-
3 parts Gin, 1 part Light Rum
Sour Mix, blend

GINGER COLADA-
2 parts Dark Rum, 1 part Coconut Rum, 1 part Ginger Brandy
Pineapple Juice, blend

GINGER SNAP-
3 parts Spiced Rum, 1 part Ginger Brandy
Eggnog, Ginger Snap Cookie, blend

GOOD & PLENTY-
1 part Coffee Liqueur, 1 part Vodka, splash Anisette
Vanilla Ice Cream, blend

GOOMBAY SMASH-
1 part Coconut Rum, 1 part Dark Rum, splash Triple Sec
Pineapple Juice, Sour Mix, Orange Juice, Grenadine, blend

GRAPEFRUIT NOG-
Brandy
Grapefruit Juice, Lime Juice, Honey, blend

GREEN FROG, THE-
4 parts Dark Rum, 1 part Blue Curaçao, splash White Crème de Menthe
Orange Juice, blend

GRIZZLY BEAR-
2 parts Dark Rum, 1 part Amaretto
Vanilla Ice Cream, Chocolate Syrup, splash Vanilla Extract, blend

GULF STREAM-
1 part Blue Curaçao, 1 part Brandy, 1 part Light Rum, fill Champagne
Lemonade, Lime Juice, blend, Strawberry Garnish

HAIRY BITCH-
2 parts Light Rum, 1 part Triple Sec
Pineapple Juice, blend

HAIRY SLUT-
2 parts Light Rum, 1 part Triple Sec
Pineapple Juice, blend

HAIRY VIRGIN-
2 parts Light Rum, 1 part Triple Sec
Pineapple Juice, blend, Cherry Garnish

HAVANA BANANA FIZZ-
Light Rum
Pineapple Juice, Lime Juice, splash Bitters, Bananas, blend,
    top Lemon-Lime Soda

HAVANA BANDANA-
Light Rum, splash Banana Liqueur (Float)
Lime Juice, Bananas, blend

HAWAII 7-0-
2 parts Blended Whiskey, 1 part Amaretto, 1 part Coconut Liqueur
Orange Juice, blend

HAWAIIAN EYE-
2 parts Bourbon Whiskey, 1 part Banana Liqueur, 1 part Coffee Liqueur,
    1 part Vodka, splash Licorice Liqueur
Light Cream or Milk, blend

HI RISE-
2 parts Vodka, 1 part Triple Sec
Orange Juice, Sour Mix, splash Grenadine, blend

HONG KONG SUNDAE-
1 part Galliano®, 1 part Triple Sec
Orange Sherbet, blend

HOTEL CALIFORNIA-
Apricot Brandy
Orange Soda, Orange Sherbet, blend

HUMMER-
1 part Coffee Liqueur, 1 part Light Rum
Vanilla Ice Cream, blend

ICE BALL-
2 parts Gin, 1 part Sambuca, 1 part White Crème de Menthe
Light Cream or Milk, blend

ICE BREAKER-
Tequila, splash Triple Sec
Grapefruit, splash Grenadine, blend

ICE CREAM FLIP-
1 part Maraschino Liqueur, 1 part Triple Sec
Vanilla Ice Cream, blend

ICED COFFEE A L'ORANGE-
Triple Sec
Cold Coffee, Vanilla Ice Cream, blend, top Whipped Cream

ICED RUMMED CACAO-
1 part Brown Crème de Caçao, 1 part Dark Rum
Vanilla Ice Cream, blend, top Chocolate Sprinkles

INTERNATIONAL CREAM-
1 part Coffee Liqueur, 1 part Irish Cream Liqueur, splash Grand Marnier®
Vanilla Ice Cream, splash Light Cream or Milk, blend

IRISH BERRY-
2 parts Irish Cream Liqueur, 1 part Vodka
Strawberry Daiquiri Mix, Coconut Milk, splash Grenadine, blend

IRISH DREAM-
2 parts Brown Crème de Caçao, 1 part Hazelnut Liqueur,
    1 part Irish Cream Liqueur
Vanilla Ice Cream, blend, top Whipped Cream, top Chocolate Sprinkles

ISLAND REGGAE BEAT-
1 part Cognac, 1 part Drambuie®, 1 part Scotch Whiskey
Fruit Punch, splash Grenadine, blend

ISLE OF THE BLESSED COCONUT-
Light Rum, splash Amaretto
Orange Juice, Lime Juice, Coconut Milk, blend

ITALIAN BANANA-
1 part Banana Liqueur, 1 part Amaretto
Orange Juice, splash Lime Juice, blend

ITALIAN COLADA-
3 parts Light Rum, 1 part Amaretto
Pineapple Juice, Coconut Milk, Light Cream or Milk, blend

ITALIAN DREAM-
3 parts Irish Cream Liqueur, 1 part Amaretto
Light Cream or Milk, blend

ITALIAN SOMBRERO-
Amaretto
Light Cream or Milk, blend

JAGUAR-
2 parts Galliano®, 1 part White Crème de Caçao
Light Cream or Milk, blend

Frozen Drinks

JAMAICAN BANANA-
1 part Banana Liqueur, 1 part Light Rum, 1 part White Crème de Cacao
Light Cream or Milk, Vanilla Ice Cream, Banana, blend

JAMAICAN BLUES-
2 parts Coconut Rum, 2 parts Dark Rum, 1 part Blue Curaçao
Pineapple Juice, blend

JAMAICAN DREAM-
Light Rum
Grapefruit Juice, Pineapple Juice, Orange Juice, blend

JAMAICAN GLOW-
Dark Rum
Light Cream or Milk, Papaya Juice, Sour Mix, blend

JAMAICAN MILK SHAKE-
1 part Bourbon Whiskey, 1 part Jamaican Rum
Light Cream or Milk, blend

JAMAICAN QUEEN-
2 parts Captain Morgan® Original Spiced Rum, 1 part Banana Liqueur
Vanilla Ice Cream, Strawberry Daiquiri Mix, blend

JOCOSE JULEP-
Bourbon Whiskey, splash Green Crème de Menthe
Sour Mix, blend, Club Soda (top), Mint Leaves Garnish

KAPPA COLADA-
Brandy
Pineapple Juice, Coconut Milk, blend

KENTUCKY CAPPUCCINO-
1 part Bourbon Whiskey, 1 part Coffee Liqueur
Light Cream or Milk, Instant Coffee Grinds, Club Soda, blend,
    top Whipped Cream

KEY LIME QUENCHER-
1 part Coconut Rum, 1 part Dark Rum
Light Cream or Milk, Sour Mix, blend

KISH WACKER-
1 part Brown Crème de Cacao, 1 part Coffee Liqueur, 1 part Irish Cream
    Liqueur, 1 part Vodka, blend

KOALA KOLADA-
2 parts Peach Schnapps, 1 part Melon Liqueur
Orange Juice, Pineapple Juice, Coconut Milk, blend, Kiwi Fruit Garnish

KOKOMO JOE-
1 part Banana Liqueur, 1 part Light Rum
Orange Juice, Coconut Milk, Banana, blend

KONA GOLD-
2 parts White Crème de Cacao, 1 part Peach Schnapps
Vanilla Ice Cream, Banana, blend, sprinkle Nutmeg

LADY BUG-
2 parts Brandy, 1 part Dark Rum, splash Amaretto
Orange Juice, Lime Juice, blend

LADY LUCK-
4 parts Raspberry Liqueur, 1 part Banana Liqueur
Coconut Milk, blend

LALLAH ROOKH-
2 parts Light Rum, 1 part Brandy
Light Cream or Milk, Vanilla Extract, Sugar, blend

LASER BEAM-
1 part Amaretto, 1 part Galliano®, 1 part Jack Daniel's® Tennessee Sour Mash
Whiskey, 1 part Peppermint Schnapps, blend

LATIN COOLER-
2 parts Light Rum, 1 part Peach Schnapps
Orange Juice, blend

LAVENDER SUNSET-
2 parts Peach Schnapps, 1 part White Crème de Caçao
Lime Sherbet, Grape Juice, Coconut Milk, blend

LEBANESE SNOW-
1 part Banana Liqueur, 1 part Strawberry Schnapps
Light Cream or Milk, blend

LEPRECHAUN-
4 parts Irish Whiskey, 2 parts Light Rum, 1 part Sloe Gin
Sour Mix, Peaches, Raspberries, blend

LICORICE MIST-
3 parts Sambuca, 1 part Coconut Liqueur
Light Cream or Milk, blend, Licorice Stick Garnish

LICORICE SLUSH-
2 parts Anisette, 1 part Vodka
Lemon Sherbet, blend

LIMEY-
2 parts Light Rum, 2 parts Lime Liqueur, 1 part Triple Sec
Lime Juice, blend

LONDON FOG-
1 part Licorice Liqueur, 1 part White Crème de Menthe
Vanilla Ice Cream, blend

LONELY NIGHT-
2 parts Hazelnut Liqueur, 2 parts Irish Cream Liqueur, 1 part Coffee Liqueur
Vanilla Ice Cream, blend, top Whipped Cream, top Chocolate Sprinkles

LOVE POTION-
Rum
Mango Juice, Piña Colada Mix, Strawberry Daiquiri Mix, blend

LUCKY DRIVER-
Coconut Rum
Grapefruit Juice, Orange Juice, Pineapple Juice, Sour Mix, blend

MAI-TAI (FROZEN)-
3 parts Light Rum, 1 part Amaretto, 1 part Triple Sec
Lime Juice, Pineapple Juice, blend

MANDINGO GRINGO-
3 parts Dark Jamaican Rum, 1 part Banana Liqueur
Pineapple Juice, Orange Juice, Lime Juice, blend

MANGO DAIQUIRI-
4 parts Dark Rum, 1 part Triple Sec
Mango Juice, Sour Mix, blend

MARASCHINO CHERRY-
2 parts Light Rum, 1 part Amaretto, 1 part Peach Schnapps
Cranberry Juice, Pineapple Juice, Grenadine, blend

MARGARITA (FROZEN MARGARITA)-
3 parts Tequila, 1 part Triple Sec
Sour Mix, blend, Salted Rim (optional)

MARIACHI MELON MARGARITA-
4 parts Tequila, 1 part Melon Liqueur
Sour Mix, blend

MARTHA'S VINEYARD-
Gin
Vanilla Ice Cream, Lime Juice, blend, top Club Soda

MELON COLADA-
2 parts Light Rum, 1 part Melon Liqueur
Pineapple Juice, Coconut Milk, splash Light Cream or Milk, blend

MELON DAIQUIRI-
1 part Light Rum, 1 part Melon Liqueur
Cantaloupe, Sugar, blend

MELON VODKA MARGARITA-
4 parts Vodka, 1 part Melon Liqueur
Sour Mix, blend

MEXICOLADA-
2 parts Tequila, 1 part Coffee Liqueur
Pineapple Juice, Coconut Milk, Light Cream or Milk, blend

MIAMI ICE-
1 part Banana Liqueur, 1 part Melon Liqueur, 1 part Strawberry Schnapps
Pineapple Juice, Coconut Milk, Grenadine, Orange Sherbet, blend

MIAMI NICE-
1 part Bourbon Whiskey, 1 part Dark Rum, 1 part Gin, 1 part Triple Sec
Lime Juice, blend

Frozen Drinks

MIAMI VICE-
Rum
Piña Colada Mix, Strawberry Daiquiri Mix, blend

MIAMI WHAMMY-
2 parts Dark Rum, 1 part Triple Sec
Orange Juice, Sour Mix, Grenadine, blend

MIDORI COLADA-
2 parts Midori® Melon Liqueur, 1 part Light Rum
Pineapple Juice, Coconut Milk, blend

MILK SHAKE-
Irish Cream Liqueur
Light Cream or Milk, splash Sour Mix, blend

MILLIONAIRE, THE-
1 part Banana Liqueur, 1 part Spiced Rum
Orange Juice, Sour Mix, Grenadine, blend

MINSTRAL-
2 parts White Wine, 1 part Raspberry Liqueur
Strawberries, Raspberries, blend

MINT CHOCOLATE CHILLER-
4 parts Green Crème de Menthe, 1 part White Crème de Caçao
Vanilla Ice Cream, Light Cream or Milk, Oreo® Cookies, blend,
    top Whipped Cream

MINT CHOCOLATE CHIP ICE CREAM-
1 part Coffee Liqueur, 1 part Irish Cream Liqueur, 1 part Peppermint Schnapps,
    1 part Vodka, 1 part White Crème de Caçao, 1 part White Crème de
    Menthe, blend

MINT CONDITION-
1 part Bourbon Whiskey, 1 part Coffee Liqueur, 1 part Peppermint Schnapps,
    1 part Vodka, blend

MISSISSIPPI MUD-
1 part Coffee Liqueur, 1 part Southern Comfort®
Vanilla Ice Cream, blend, top Chocolate Sprinkles

MONT BLANC-
1 part Raspberry Liqueur, 1 part Vodka
Light Cream or Milk, Vanilla Ice Cream, blend

MOON CHASER-
2 parts Dark Rum, 1 part Amaretto
Orange Juice, Coconut Milk, Orange Sherbet, blend

MORGAN'S FAIR CHILD-
2 parts Melon Liqueur, 1 part Amaretto
Vanilla Ice Cream, blend, top Whipped Cream

MUDSLIDE (FROZEN 1)-
1 part Coffee Liqueur, 1 part Irish Cream Liqueur, 1 part Vodka
splash Light Cream or Milk, blend

MUDSLIDE (FROZEN 2)-
1 part Coffee Liqueur, 1 part Irish Cream Liqueur, 1 part Tequila
splash Light Cream or Milk, blend

MUDSLIDE (FROZEN 3)-
1 part Coffee Liqueur, 1 part Irish Cream Liqueur, 1 part Tia Maria®
splash Light Cream or Milk, blend

NIJINSKI BLINI-
Vodka, splash Champagne, splash Peach Schnapps
Lime Juice, Pureed Peaches, blend

NUT & CREAM-
1 part Amaretto, 1 part Hazelnut Liqueur
splash Light Cream or Milk, Vanilla Ice Cream, blend, sprinkle Nutmeg

NUTTY BANANA-
4 parts Amaretto, 1 part Banana Liqueur
Orange Juice, Light Cream or Milk, blend

NUTTY COLADA-
Amaretto
Coconut Milk, Crushed Pineapple, blend

NUTTY TROPIC-
Amaretto
Light Cream or Milk, Coconut Milk, blend

OCEAN CRUISER-
Melon Liqueur
Coconut Milk, Pineapple Juice, blend

ONE IRELAND-
4 parts Irish Whiskey, 1 part Green Crème de Menthe
Vanilla Ice Cream, blend

ORANGE BLOSSOM SPECIAL-
Peach Schnapps
Orange Sherbet, Vanilla Ice Cream, Light Cream or Milk,
    Lemon-Lime Soda, blend

ORANGE TREE-
2 parts Amaretto, 1 part Crème de Noyaux
Orange Juice, Vanilla Ice Cream, blend, top Whipped Cream

OVER THE RAINBOW-
2 parts Spiced Rum, 1 part Triple Sec
Rainbow Sherbet, Pureed Peaches, Strawberries, blend

PANDA BEAR-
2 parts Amaretto, 1 part Brown Crème de Caçao, 1 part White Crème de Caçao
Vanilla Ice Cream, Chocolate Syrup, blend

PAPAYA DAIQUIRI-
Light Rum
Papaya Juice, Sour Mix, blend

PASSION COLADA-
Dark Rum
Passion Fruit Juice, Coconut Milk, blend

PASSION DAIQUIRI-
Light Rum
Passion Fruit Juice, Sour Mix, blend

PASSION PUNCH-
1 part Gin, 1 part Light Rum
Orange Juice, Passion Fruit Juice, blend

PASSIONATE DAIQUIRI, A-
Light Rum
Passion Fruit Juice, Sour Mix, blend

PEACH DAIQUIRI-
4 parts Dark Rum, 1 part Triple Sec
Sour Mix, Pitted Peach, blend

PEACH FUZZ-
Peach Schnapps
Sour Mix, Peach Slices, splash Grenadine, blend

PEACH MARGARITA-
2 parts Tequila, 1 part Peach Schnapps, splash Triple Sec
Sour Mix, Salted Rim, blend

PEACH MELBA-
1 part Raspberry Liqueur, 1 part Spiced Rum
Peach Juice, Light Cream or Milk, Pitted Peach, blend

PEACH MELBA FREEZE-
1 part Black Raspberry Liqueur, 1 part Hazelnut Liqueur,
    1 part Peach Schnapps
Light Cream or Milk, Vanilla Ice Cream, Raspberry Jam, blend

PEACH WEST INDIES-
Light Rum
Lime Juice, Grenadine, Peaches, blend

PEACHY AMARETTO-
1 part Amaretto, 1 part Peach Schnapps
Vanilla Ice Cream, blend

PEACHY COLADA-
4 parts Spiced Rum, 1 part Peach Schnapps
Pineapple Juice, Coconut Milk, blend

PEPPERMINT TWIST-
2 parts Peppermint Schnapps, 1 part White Crème de Caçao
Vanilla Ice Cream, blend, Peppermint Candy Stick Garnish

PERFECT COUPLE, THE-
(Two layers: Blend with ice & layer Part 2 on top of Part 1 in order in Daiquiri Glass)
Part 1: 1 part Dark Rum
Sour Mix, Strawberries, blend
Part 2: 1 part Dark Rum
Piña Colada Mix, Light Cream or Milk, blend, top Whipped Cream

PIÑA COLADA-
Dark or Light Rum
Coconut Milk, Pineapple Juice, blend

PINEAPPLE BANANA REFRESHER-
1 part Banana Liqueur, 1 part Dark Rum
Pineapple Juice, Pineapple Sherbet, blend

PINEAPPLE FRANCINE-
1 part Apricot Brandy, 1 part Light Rum
Pineapple Juice, Light Cream or Milk, Pineapple Slices, blend

PINEAPPLE MARGARITA-
Tequila
Sour Mix, Pineapple Juice, blend

PINO FRIO-
Spiced Rum
Pineapple Slices, Sugar, blend

PISTACHIO CREAM-
1 part Brandy, 1 part Pistachio Liqueur
Vanilla Ice Cream, Light Cream or Milk, blend

PISTACHIO MINT ICE CREAM-
2 parts Hazelnut Liqueur, 2 parts Vodka, 1 part Green Crème de Menthe
Light Cream or Milk, blend

POLAR ICE CAP-
1 part Coffee Liqueur, 1 part Vodka
Light Cream or Milk, Coconut Milk, blend

RACING DRIVER-
2 parts Vodka, 1 part Sloe Gin, splash Cherry Brandy (Float)
Orange Juice, blend

RAINBOW CRUSH-
1 part Melon Liqueur, 1 part Raspberry Liqueur, 1 part Vodka
Orange Juice, Coconut Milk, Orange Sherbet, blend

RASPBERRY CHEESECAKE-
1 part Black Raspberry Liqueur, 1 part White Crème de Caçao
Vanilla Ice Cream, Cream Cheese, blend

RASPBERRY CREAM-
1 part Vodka, 1 part White Crème de Caçao
Light Cream or Milk, Raspberry Yogurt, Raspberry Sherbet, blend

REBEL PARTY SOUR-
1 part Bourbon Whiskey, 1 part Beer
Lime Juice, blend (slowly)

REGGAE AMBASSADOR-
Citrus Vodka
Orange Juice, Pineapple Juice, Bananas, Strawberries, Sugar, blend

RIVIERA RASPBERRY-
2 parts Raspberry Liqueur, 1 part Coffee Liqueur
Coconut Milk, Chocolate Syrup, Vanilla Ice Cream, blend

ROAD RUNNER-
2 parts Vodka, 1 part Amaretto
Coconut Milk, blend, sprinkle Nutmeg, Sugared and Nutmeged Rim,
    Orange Garnish

ROMANOFF APPLE, THE-
3 parts Vodka, 1 part Apple Brandy
Sour Mix, Apples, blend

ROOTARAMA BANANARAMA-
Root Beer Schnapps
Coconut Milk, Bananas, splash Club Soda, blend

ROOTIE FROOTIE-
Root Beer Schnapps
Orange Juice, Pineapple Juice, Coconut Milk, blend

ROYAL PEACH FREEZE-
1 part Champagne, 1 part Peach Schnapps
Orange Juice, Lime Juice, blend

RUBY TUESDAY-
2 parts Raspberry Liqueur, 1 part Banana Liqueur
Pineapple Juice, Coconut Milk, blend

RUM BANA-
Jamaican Rum
Sour Mix, Bananas, blend

RUM HUMMER-
1 part Coffee Liqueur, 1 part Light Rum
Vanilla Ice Cream, blend

RUM PUNCH-
Light Rum
Orange Juice, Pineapple Juice, Lime Juice, splash Grenadine,
    splash bitters, blend

RUM RUNNER-
1 part Blackberry Brandy, 1 part Banana Liqueur, 1 part Dark Rum
Lime Juice, splash Grenadine, blend

Frozen Drinks

RUM SWEETIE-
2 parts Dark Rum, 1 part Amaretto
Apple Juice, blend

RUMMY SOUR-
Spiced Rum
Sour Mix, blend

RUSSIAN ICE-
2 parts Vodka, 1 part Coffee Liqueur
splash Light Cream or Milk, Vanilla Ice Cream, blend

SACRIFICE-
2 parts Dark Rum, 2 parts Light Rum, 1 part White Crème de Caçao
Cranberry Juice, Orange Juice, Pineapple Juice, Coconut Milk,
    splash Orange Bitters, blend

SAN JUAN-
1 part Puerto Rican Rum, splash 1 part 151-proof Rum (lace)
Grapefruit Juice, Lime Juice, Coconut Milk, blend

SCORPION-
4 parts Light Rum, 1 part Brandy, 1 part Cherry Brandy
Orange Juice, Lime Juice, blend

SEX ON THE BEACH IN THE WINTER-
1 part Peach Schnapps, 1 part Vodka
Cranberry Juice, Pineapple Juice, Coconut Milk, blend

SINGING ORCHARD-
4 parts Dark Rum, 1 part Raspberry Liqueur
Pineapple Juice, Coconut Milk, blend, splash Grenadine (lace)

SKINNY TART-
Dark Rum
Grapefruit Juice, Pineapple Juice, Sugar, blend

SLAPSTICK-
2 parts Spiced Rum, 1 part Strawberry Schnapps
Pineapple Juice, Coconut Milk, Grenadine, blend

SLUSH-
Gin
Cranberry Juice, Orange Juice, Sour Mix, blend, Lemon-Lime Soda (Float)

SMOOTH MOVE-
Light Rum
Pineapple Juice, Prune Juice, Sour Mix, blend

SMOOTH OPERATOR-
2 parts Hazelnut Liqueur, 1 part Coffee Liqueur, 1 part Irish Cream Liqueur
Light Cream or Milk, Bananas, blend

SNEAKY PEACH-
Peach Schnapps
Orange Juice, Coconut Milk, splash Grenadine, splash Sour Mix, blend

SOUTHERN FROST-
1 part Amaretto, 1 part Southern Comfort®, 1 part Triple Sec
Orange Juice, Pineapple Juice, blend

SOUTHERN PEACH-
1 part Bourbon Whiskey, 1 part Peach Schnapps
Orange Juice, Sour Mix, splash Grenadine, blend

SPICED BANANA DAIQUIRI-
2 parts Spiced Rum, 1 part Banana Liqueur
Sour Mix, Bananas, blend

STRAWBERRIES & CREAM-
Strawberry Schnapps
Light Cream or Milk, Sugar, Strawberries, blend

STRAWBERRY ALEXANDRA-
1 part Brandy, 1 part White Crème de Caçao
Vanilla Ice Cream, Strawberry Daiquiri Mix, blend

STRAWBERRY BANANA COLADA-
3 parts Dark Rum, 1 part Banana Liqueur, 1 part Strawberry Schnapps
Strawberry Daiquiri Mix, Bananas, Coconut Milk, blend

STRAWBERRY BANANA SPLIT-
1 part Banana Liqueur, 1 part Dark Rum, 1 part Strawberry Schnapps,
   splash Vanilla Liqueur
Light Cream or Milk, blend

STRAWBERRY BANANA SPRITZ-
1 part Banana Liqueur, 1 part Strawberry Schnapps
Vanilla Ice Cream, Strawberry Daiquiri Mix, blend, top Club Soda

STRAWBERRY DAIQUIRI (1)-
2 parts Light Rum, 1 part Strawberry Schnapps
Sour Mix, Strawberry Daiquiri Mix, blend

STRAWBERRY DAIQUIRI (2)-
Light Rum
Sour Mix, Strawberry Daiquiri Mix, blend

STRAWBERRY DAWN-
Gin
Strawberry Daiquiri Mix, Coconut Milk, blend

STRAWBERRY MARGARITA (1)-
2 parts Tequila, 1 part Strawberry Schnapps, 1 part Triple Sec
Lime Juice, Strawberry Daiquiri Mix, blend, Salted Rim

STRAWBERRY MARGARITA (2)-
Tequila, splash Triple Sec
Sour Mix, Strawberry Daiquiri Mix, blend, Salted Rim

STRAWBERRY SHORTCAKE-
3 parts Strawberry Schnapps, 1 part White Crème de Caçao
Strawberry Daiquiri Mix, Vanilla Ice Cream, blend, top Whipped Cream

STRAWBERRY SHORTCAKE SWIRL-
Amaretto
Strawberries, Light Cream or Milk, blend

SURF CITY LIFESAVER-
2 parts Gin, 1 part Grand Marnier®, 1 part Irish Cream Liqueur, 1 part Licorice
    Liqueur, blend

SURF'S UP-
1 part Banana Liqueur, 1 part White Crème de Caçao
Pineapple Juice, Light Cream or Milk, blend

SWEETIE BABY-
Amaretto
Vanilla Ice Cream, splash Light Cream or Milk, blend

TAHOE JULIUS-
Vodka
Orange Juice, splash Light Cream or Milk, Sugar, blend

TENNESSEE WALTZ-
Peach Schnapps
Pineapple Juice, Passion Fruit Juice, Vanilla Ice Cream, blend

TEQUILA COLADA-
Tequila
Sour Mix, Coconut Milk, blend

TEQUILA FROST-
Tequila
Pineapple Juice, Grapefruit Juice, Honey, Grenadine, Vanilla Ice Cream, blend

TEQUILA SUNSET MARGARITA-
4 parts Tequila, 1 part Strawberry Schnapps, 1 part Triple Sec
Sour Mix, Orange Juice, blend

THAT TIME OF THE MONTH-
1 part Coconut Rum, 1 part Peach Schnapps
Cranberry Juice, Pineapple Juice, blend, splash Grenadine (lace)

THURSTON HOWELL-
2 parts Spiced Rum, 1 part Banana Liqueur
Orange Juice, Sour Mix, blend, splash Grenadine (lace after blend)

TIDAL WAVE-
2 parts Melon Liqueur, 1 part Coconut Rum
Orange Juice, Pineapple Juice, Sour Mix, blend

TIDBIT-
Gin, splash Dry Sherry
Vanilla Ice Cream, blend

TIJUANA BLUES MARGARITA-
4 parts Tequila, 1 part Blue Curaçao
Sour Mix, blend

Frozen Drinks

TIPSY TURTLE-
1 part Banana Liqueur, 1 part Coconut Rum, 1 part Dark Rum,
   1 part Light Rum, 1 part Vodka
Orange Juice, Pineapple Juice, splash Grenadine, blend

TOBAGO CAYS-
Gold Rum, splash Maraschino Liqueur, splash Licorice Liqueur (float)
Sour Mix, blend

TOP GUN-
Light Rum
Guava Juice, Orange Juice, Lime Juice, blend

TOP TEN-
Spiced Rum
Light Cream or Milk, Coconut Milk, Cola, blend

TRANSAMERICA-
Irish Whiskey
Pineapple Juice, Coconut Milk, splash Lime Juice, blend, top Club Soda

TREASURE CHEST-
2 parts Chocolate Almond Liqueur, 1 part Amaretto, 1 part Gold Rum
Light Cream or Milk, blend

TROLLEY CAR-
1 part Amaretto, 1 part Strawberry Schnapps
Vanilla Ice Cream, Strawberry Daiquiri Mix, blend

TROPIC COLADA-
1 part Banana Liqueur, 1 part Strawberry Schnapps
Pineapple Juice, Coconut Milk, blend

TROPIC FREEZE-
Spiced Rum
Orange Juice, Pineapple Juice, Coconut Milk, splash Grenadine, blend

TROPICAL BREEZE-
2 parts Light Rum, 1 part Banana Liqueur
Orange Juice, Coconut Milk, Pineapple Slice, blend

TROPICAL DELIGHT-
2 parts Spiced Rum, 1 part Banana Liqueur, 1 part Brown Crème de Caçao
Light Cream or Milk, blend

TROPICAL PARADISE-
Spiced Rum
Orange Juice, Coconut Milk, splash Grenadine, Bananas, blend

TROPICAL PEACH-
Peach Schnapps
Orange Juice, Orange Sherbet, Sour Mix, Coconut Milk, blend

TROPICAL STORM-
2 parts Dark Rum, 1 part Banana Liqueur
Orange Juice, splash Grenadine, Bananas, blend

TROPICAL TREASURE-
2 parts Melon Liqueur, 1 part Banana Liqueur
Pineapple Juice, Coconut Milk, blend

TURTLE DOVE-
4 parts Dark Rum, 1 part Amaretto
Orange Juice, blend

TUTTI FRUITI-
3 parts Gin, 1 part Amaretto, 1 part Maraschino Liqueur
Apples, Peaches, Pears, blend

TUTTI FRUITI CRUSH-
1 part Banana Liqueur, 1 part Melon Liqueur, 1 part Strawberry Schnapps
Pineapple Juice, Orange Sherbet, splash Grenadine, blend

VERY BERRY COLADA-
2 parts Wild Berry Schnapps, 1 part Dark Rum
Pineapple Juice, Coconut Milk, blend

VOLCANO-
2 parts Vodka, 1 part Amaretto
Vanilla Ice Cream, Coconut Milk, blend

WATERMELON SLUSHIE-
2 parts Watermelon Schnapps, 1 part Light Rum, splash Melon Liqueur
Strawberry Daiquiri Mix, splash Sour Mix, blend, top Whipped Cream

WHITE CARGO-
Gin, splash Maraschino Liqueur
Vanilla Ice Cream, blend

WHITE MOUNTAIN-
Sake
Light Cream or Milk, Piña Colada Mix, blend, top Whipped Cream

WHITE WITCH-
1 part Vodka, 1 part White Crème de Caçao
Vanilla Ice Cream, blend

WILD BANSHEE-
4 parts Spiced Rum, 1 part Amaretto
Light Cream or Milk, Bananas, blend

WILDFLOWER-
Scotch Whiskey
Grapefruit Juice, splash Grenadine, blend

XYLOPHONE-
2 parts Tequila, 1 part White Crème de Caçao
Light Cream or Milk, Sugar, blend

YELLOW STRAWBERRY-
2 parts Light Rum, 1 part Banana Liqueur
Sour Mix, Strawberry Daiquiri Mix, blend

Frozen Drinks

YOUNG BLOOD-
3 parts Gin, 1 part Dry Vermouth, 1 part Sweet Vermouth,
  splash Strawberry Schnapps
Strawberries, blend

ZOMBIE COCKTAIL-
2 parts Jamaican Rum, 2 parts Light Rum, 1 part Apricot Brandy,
  splash 1 part 151-proof Rum (lace)
Orange Juice, Pineapple Juice, Sour Mix, blend

– NOTES –

_____

_____

_____

_____

_____

_____

_____

_____

_____

_____

_____

_____

_____

_____

_____

_____

_____

_____

_____

Frozen Drinks

Hot Drinks

ADULT HOT CHOCOLATE-
Peppermint Schnapps
Hot Chocolate, top Whipped Cream

ALHAMBRA ROYALE-
Brandy
Hot Chocolate, top Whipped Cream

ALMOND CHOCOLATA-
Amaretto
Hot Chocolate, top Whipped Cream

ALMOND COFFEE-
Amaretto
Coffee, top Whipped Cream

AMARETTO CAFE-
Amaretto
Coffee, top Whipped Cream

ANISETTE COFFEE-
1 part Anisette, 1 part Gin
Coffee, top Whipped Cream

B. M. A.-
1 part Amaretto, 1 part Brandy
Hot Chocolate, Coffee

BANANAS BARBADOS-
2 parts Spiced Rum, 1 part Banana Liqueur
Hot Chocolate, top Whipped Cream

BARRIER BREAKER-
3 parts Dark Rum, 1 part Triple Sec, splash Blue Curaçao
Coffee, top Whipped Cream

BAVARIAN COFFEE-
1 part Coffee Liqueur, 1 part Peppermint Schnapps
Coffee, sprinkle Chocolate

BEDROOM FARCE-
2 parts Dark Rum, 1 part Bourbon Whiskey, splash Galliano®
Hot Chocolate, top Whipped Cream

BLACK FOREST-
1 part Chocolate Liqueur, 1 part Raspberry Liqueur
Cappuccino

BLACK HONEY-
2 parts Coffee Liqueur, 1 part Drambuie®
Coffee, top Whipped Cream

BLACK JACK-
2 parts Cherry Brandy, 1 part Brandy
Coffee, top Whipped Cream

Hot Drinks

BLACK MARIA-
1 part Coffee Brandy, 1 part Light Rum
Coffee, Sugar, top Whipped Cream

BLACK ROSE-
Light Rum
Coffee, Sugar, top Whipped Cream

BRAZILIAN COFFEE-
Bahai® Coffee Liqueur
Coffee, top Whipped Cream

BUTTERNUT COFFEE-
1 part Amaretto, 1 part Butterscotch Schnapps
Coffee, top Whipped Cream

CAFE AMARETTO-
Amaretto
Coffee, top Whipped Cream

CAFE AMOUR-
2 parts Cognac, 1 part Amaretto
Coffee, top Whipped Cream

CAFE AUX COGNAC-
Cognac
Coffee, Sugar, top Whipped Cream

CAFE BARBADOS-
2 parts Dark Rum, 1 part Tia Maria®
Coffee, top Whipped Cream

CAFE BONAPARTE-
Brandy
Cappuccino, top Whipped Cream

CAFE CARIBBEAN-
1 part Amaretto, 1 part Light Rum
Coffee, Sugar, top Whipped Cream

CAFE DI AMARETTO-
Amaretto
Coffee, top Whipped Cream

CAFE DIABLO-
2 parts Cognac, 1 part Triple Sec (ignite optional)
{extinguish flame before drinking}
Coffee, top Whipped Cream

CAFE DON JUAN-
1 part Coffee Liqueur, 1 part Dark Rum
Coffee, Sugared Rim

CAFE FOSTER-
2 parts Dark Rum, 1 part Banana Liqueur
Coffee, top Whipped Cream

Hot Drinks

CAFE FRENCH-
> 2 parts Amaretto, 2 parts Triple Sec, 1 part Irish Cream Liqueur
> Coffee, top Whipped Cream

CAFE GRANDE-
> 1 part Brown Crème de Caçao, 1 part Grand Marnier®, 1 part Tia Maria®
> Coffee, Cherry Garnish

CAFE HENRY THE THIRD-
> 1 part Brandy, 1 part Coffee Liqueur, 1 part Galliano®,
>   1 part Grand Marnier®
> Coffee, Cinnamon Rim, top Whipped Cream

CAFE L'ORANGE
> 2 parts Grand Marnier®, 1 part Cognac, 1 part Triple Sec
> Coffee, top Whipped Cream

CAFE MARNIER-
> Grand Marnier®
> Coffee, top Whipped Cream

CAFE MICHELLE-
> 2 parts Amaretto, 2 parts Coffee Liqueur, 1 part Irish Cream Liqueur
> Coffee, top Whipped Cream

CAFE NELSON-
> 1 part Hazelnut Liqueur, 1 part Irish Cream Liqueur
> Coffee, top Whipped Cream, sprinkle Nuts

CAFE PREGO-
> 3 parts Amaretto, 1 part Brandy
> Coffee, top Whipped Cream

CAFE ROYALE-
> Brandy or Cognac
> Coffee, Sugar Cube
> (Soak Sugar Cube in Brandy, Ignite, Drop in Coffee, optional)
>   {extinguish flame before drinking}

CAFE SEIYOKEN-
> 1 part Light Rum, 1 part Melon Liqueur, 1 part Sake
> Coffee, splash Lime Juice, top Whipped Cream

CAFE THEATRE-
> 1 part Irish Cream Liqueur, 1 part White Crème de Caçao,
>   splash Brown Crème de Caçao, splash Hazelnut Liqueur
> Coffee, top Whipped Cream

CAFE TOLEDO-
> 1 part Coffee Liqueur, 1 part Irish Cream Liqueur
> Coffee, Chocolate Syrup, top Whipped Cream

CAFE ZURICH-
> 1 part Amaretto, 1 part Anisette, 1 part Cognac
> Coffee, Honey, top Whipped Cream

Hot Drinks

CALIFORNIA COFFEE-
1 part California Brandy, 1 part California Sherry
Coffee, splash Orange Juice, splash Lime Juice, top Whipped Cream

CALYPSO COFFEE-
1 part Jamaican Rum, 1 part Tia Maria®
Coffee, top Whipped Cream

CALYPSO COFFEE (USA)-
1 part Brown Crème de Caçao, 1 part Light Rum,
    splash Amaretto (top)
Coffee

CANADIAN COFFEE-
Canadian Whiskey
Coffee, top Whipped Cream

CANDLE IN THE WINDOW-
Light Rum, splash Bourbon Whiskey, splash Brown Crème de Caçao,
    splash Cherry Brandy
Coffee, splash Light Cream or Milk, top Whipped Cream

CAPPUCCINO MOCHA-
1 part Brown Crème de Caçao, 1 part Coffee Liqueur
Cappuccino, top Whipped Cream

CAPPUCCINO SAUSALITO-
1 part Amaretto, 1 part Coffee Liqueur
Coffee, Hot Chocolate, top Whipped Cream

CAPRICCIO-
2 parts Amaretto, 1 part Brandy, 1 part Coffee Liqueur
Coffee, top Whipped Cream

CARIBBEAN COFFEE-
Dark Rum
Coffee, splash Light Cream or Milk, Sugar, top Whipped Cream

CASINO COFFEE-
1 part Amaretto, 1 part Brandy, 1 part Brown Crème de Caçao
Coffee, top Whipped Cream, Chocolate Sprinkles

CHARRO-
Tequila
Coffee, splash Light Cream or Milk, top Whipped Cream

CHOCOLATE BANANA-
1 part Banana Liqueur, 1 part Brown Crème de Caçao,
    1 part Dark Rum
Hot Chocolate, top Whipped Cream

CHOCOLATE COFFEE-
2 parts Cognac, 1 part Brown Crème de Caçao
Coffee, splash Light Cream or Milk, top Whipped Cream

CHOCOLATE COFFEE KISS-
1 part Coffee Liqueur, 1 part Irish Cream Liqueur, splash Brown Crème de Caçao, splash Grand Marnier®
Coffee, Chocolate Syrup, top Whipped Cream

CHOCOLATE CORVETTE-
3 parts Dark Rum, 1 part Brown Crème de Caçao
Hot Chocolate, splash Light Cream or Milk, top Whipped Cream

CHOCOLATE KISS-
2 parts Cognac, 1 part Raspberry Liqueur
Hot Chocolate, top Whipped Cream

CHOCOLATE MINT-
2 parts Gin, 1 part Green Crème de Menthe, 1 part Peppermint Schnapps
Hot Chocolate, top Whipped Cream

CHOCOLATE SIN-
Peppermint Schnapps
Hot Chocolate, top Whipped Cream

CHOCOLATE VICE-
3 parts Dark Rum, 1 part Bourbon Whiskey, 1 part Brown Crème de Caçao
Hot Chocolate, top Whipped Cream

CINNACCINO-
2 parts Spiced Rum, 1 part Cinnamon Schnapps
Cappuccino

CLAM DIGGER'S BLANKET-***
Irish Cream Liqueur
Hot Chocolate, top Whipped Cream

COBANA COFFEE-
1 part Banana Liqueur, 1 part Strawberry Schnapps
Coffee, Sugar, top Whipped Cream

COCO JAVA-
1 part Coconut Liqueur, 1 part Coffee Liqueur
Hot Chocolate, top Whipped Cream

COCONUT BROWNIE-
2 parts Spiced Rum, 1 part Coconut Rum
Hot Chocolate, top Whipped Cream

COFFEE BERRY-
1 part Hazelnut Liqueur, 1 part Raspberry Liqueur
Coffee, top Whipped Cream

COFFEE BREAK-
1 part Brandy, 1 part Coffee Liqueur
Coffee, top Whipped Cream, Cherry Garnish

COFFEE CHASER-
1 part Coffee Liqueur, 1 part Grand Marnier®
Coffee, top Whipped Cream

COFFEE FLING-
Drambuie®
Coffee, Sugar, top Whipped Cream

COFFEE KEOKEE-
1 part Brandy, 1 part Coffee Liqueur
Coffee, top Whipped Cream

COFFEE NUT-
1 part Amaretto, 1 part Hazelnut Liqueur
Coffee, top Whipped Cream

COFFEE ROYALE-
Brandy
Coffee, splash Light Cream or Milk, Sugar, top Whipped Cream

COMFORTABLE MOCHA-
Southern Comfort®
Hot Chocolate, Coffee, top Whipped Cream

COMFORTING COFFEE-
1 part Bourbon Whiskey, 1 part Southern Comfort®, splash Brown
     Crème de Caçao
Coffee, splash Light Cream or Milk, top Whipped Cream

CUPID'S COCOA-
1 part Amaretto, 1 part Coffee Liqueur
Coffee, top Whipped Cream

DANISH COFFEE-
Haagen-Dazs® Cream Liqueur
Coffee, top Whipped Cream

DOUBLEMINT-
Spearmint Schnapps, splash Green Crème de Menthe
Hot Coffee, top Whipped Cream

DUTCH COFFEE-
Chocolate Liqueur
Coffee, top Whipped Cream

ENGLISH COFFEE-
1 part Coffee Liqueur, 1 part Gin, splash Triple Sec
Coffee, top Whipped Cream

FIVE BEFORE FLYING-
1 part Banana Liqueur, 1 part Bourbon Whiskey,
     1 part Southern Comfort®, splash Brandy,
     splash White Crème de Caçao
Coffee, splash Light Cream or Milk, top Whipped Cream

FRENCH COFFEE-
Grand Marnier®
Coffee, top Whipped Cream

Hot Drinks

FRIAR'S COFFEE-
Bénédictine
Coffee, Sugar, top Whipped Cream

FUZZY DICK-
1 part Coffee Liqueur, 1 part Grand Marnier®
Coffee, top Whipped Cream

FUZZY NUT-
4 parts Peach Schnapps, 1 part Amaretto
Hot Chocolate, top Whipped Cream

GAELIC COFFEE-
2 parts Brown Crème de Caçao, 1 part Irish Cream Liqueur,
1 part Irish Whiskey
Coffee, splash Light Cream or Milk, top Whipped Cream

GALLIANO HOT SHOT-
Galliano®
Coffee, top Whipped Cream

GOOD COFFEE-
100-proof Vodka
Double Espresso

GOOD GOLLY-
3 parts Dark Rum, 1 part Galliano®, splash Brown Crème de Caçao
Coffee, Light Cream or Milk (float)

GREEK COFFEE-
Metaxa
Coffee, top Whipped Cream

HANDICAPPER'S CHOICE-
1 part Amaretto, 1 part Irish Whiskey
Coffee, top Whipped Cream

HOT BOMBER-
1 part Coffee Liqueur, 1 part Irish Cream Liqueur, 1 part Triple Sec
Coffee, top Whipped Cream

HOT BROWN COW-
Dark Rum or Spiced Rum
Coffee, Hot Milk, sprinkle Nutmeg

HOT COCONUT COFFEE-
Coconut Rum
Coffee, top Whipped Cream

HOT DARLING DYLAN-
1 part Coffee Liqueur, 1 part Tequila
Mexican Hot Chocolate, top Whipped Cream

HOT IRISH NUT-
1 part Amaretto, 1 part Hazelnut Liqueur, 1 part Irish Cream Liqueur
Coffee, top Whipped Cream

Hot Drinks

HOT KISS-
2 parts Irish Whiskey, 1 part White Crème de Caçao, 1 part White
    Crème de Menthe
Coffee, top Whipped Cream

HOT MOLLIFIER-
3 parts Dark Rum, 1 part Tia Maria®
Coffee, top Whipped Cream

HOT PENNY RUM-
3 parts Light Rum, 1 part Bourbon Whiskey, splash Brown Crème de Caçao
Coffee, top Whipped Cream

HOT PEPPERMINT PATTY-
Peppermint Schnapps
Hot Chocolate, splash Light Cream or Milk, top Whipped Cream

HOT PIPER-
4 parts Tequila, 1 part Brown Crème de Caçao
Coffee, top Whipped Cream

HOT SCOTCH-
Butterscotch Schnapps
Hot Chocolate, top Whipped Cream

HOT TURTLE-
Butterscotch Schnapps
Hot Chocolate

HOT ZULTRY ZOE-
3 parts Tequila, 1 part Galliano®
Mexican Hot Chocolate, top Whipped Cream

IRISH COFFEE-
Irish Whiskey, splash Green Crème de Menthe (lace on top of Whipped Cream)
Coffee, Sugar, top Whipped Cream

ISLAND COCOA-
Coconut Rum
Hot Chocolate, top Whipped Cream

ISRAELI COFFEE-
Sabra® Liqueur
Coffee, top Whipped Cream

ITALIAN COFFEE (1)-
Amaretto
Coffee, Coffee Ice Cream

ITALIAN COFFEE (2)-
Galliano®
Coffee, top Whipped Cream

JACK ROBERT'S TREAT-
4 parts Brandy, 1 part Brown Crème de Caçao
Hot Chocolate, top Whipped Cream

JAMAICA COFFEE-
1 part Coffee Brandy, 1 part Light Rum
Coffee, top Whipped Cream

JAMAICAN COFFEE (1)-
1 part Jamaican Rum, 1 part Tia Maria®
Coffee, top Whipped Cream

JAMAICAN COFFEE (2)-
1 part Coffee Liqueur, 1 part Jamaican Rum
Coffee, Sugared Rim

JAMAICAN COFFEE (3)-
1 part Brandy, 1 part Light Rum
Coffee

JAPANESE COFFEE-
Japanese Whiskey
Coffee, Sugar, top Whipped Cream

KENTUCKY COFFEE-
Bourbon Whiskey
Coffee, top Whipped Cream

KIOKI COFFEE-
3 parts Coffee Liqueur, 1 part Brandy
Coffee, top Whipped Cream

LIFT-
1 part Amaretto, 1 part Drambuie®, 1 part Tia Maria®
Coffee, top Whipped Cream

MARNIER CAFE-
Grand Marnier®
Coffee, top Whipped Cream

MAURA'S COFFEE-
2 parts Irish Cream Liqueur, 1 part Irish Whiskey
Coffee, top Whipped Cream

MEXICAN COFFEE-
2 parts Coffee Liqueur, 1 part Tequila
Coffee, top Whipped Cream

MEXITALY COFFEE-
1 part Amaretto, 1 part Coffee Liqueur
Coffee, top Whipped Cream

MILLIONAIRE'S COFFEE-
1 part Coffee Liqueur, 1 part Grand Marnier®, 1 part Hazelnut Liqueur,
    1 part Irish Cream Liqueur
Coffee, top Whipped Cream

MOCHA BRANDY-
Brandy
Chocolate Milk, Coffee, top Whipped Cream

MOLOTOV COCKTAIL-
2 parts Vodka, 1 part 151-proof Rum
Vanilla Ice Cream, blend, then add Coffee, top Whipped Cream

MONASTERY COFFEE-
Bénédictine
Coffee, top Whipped Cream

MONK'S ROPE COFFEE-
3 parts Hazelnut Liqueur, 1 part Brown Crème de Caçao
Coffee, top Whipped Cream

MORLEY'S DRIVER-
3 parts Dark Rum, 1 part Cherry Brandy, splash Brown Crème de Caçao
Coffee, top Whipped Cream

MOUNTAIN MELTER-
2 parts Tequila, 1 part Triple Sec, splash Cinnamon Schnapps
Hot Chocolate, top Whipped Cream

NEW ORLEANS COFFEE-
Southern Comfort®
Coffee, top Whipped Cream

NIGHT FLIGHT-
1 part Banana Liqueur, 1 part Strawberry Schnapps
Hot Chocolate, top Whipped Cream

NUTTY CAFE-
3 parts Amaretto, 1 part Hazelnut Liqueur
Coffee, top Whipped Cream

ORANGE MOCHA-
4 parts Spiced Rum, 1 part Triple Sec
Coffee, Hot Chocolate, top Whipped Cream

PEPPERMINT HOT CHOCOLATE-
Peppermint Schnapps
Hot Chocolate, top Whipped Cream

PIKE'S PEAK-
1 part Coffee Liqueur, 1 part Peppermint Schnapps
Coffee, top Whipped Cream

PIPER-
4 parts Tequila, 1 part Brown Crème de Caçao
Warm Coffee, splash Lime Juice

PRINCE CHARLES COFFEE-
Drambuie®
Coffee, top Whipped Cream

RASPBERRY CAPPUCCINO-
Black Raspberry Liqueur
Espresso, top Whipped Cream

RASPBERRY HOT CHOCOLATE-
1 part Raspberry Liqueur, 1 part White Crème de Caçao, splash Vodka
Hot Chocolate, top Whipped Cream

RAZZMATAZZ COCKTAIL-
2 parts DeKuyper® Razzmatazz Black Raspberry Liqueur, 1 part Coffee Liqueur,
1 part Crème de Cassis
Hot Coffee, top Whipped Cream

RITCHIE RITCHIE-
Light Rum, splash Brown Crème de Caçao, splash White Crème de Caçao
Coffee, top Whipped Cream

RUSSIAN COFFEE-
2 parts Coffee Liqueur, 2 parts Hazelnut Liqueur, 1 part Vodka
Coffee, top Whipped Cream

SCOTTISH COFFEE-
Drambuie®
Coffee, top Whipped Cream

SKI LIFT-
2 parts Peach Schnapps, 1 part Coconut Rum
Hot Chocolate, top Whipped Cream

SNOW BUNNY-
Triple Sec
Hot Chocolate, top Whipped Cream

SNOWBALL-
1 part Cinnamon Schnapps, 1 part Coffee Liqueur
Coffee, top Whipped Cream

SNUGGLER-
Peppermint Schnapps
Hot Chocolate, top Whipped Cream

SOUTH FORK COFFEE-
3 parts Bourbon Whiskey, 1 part Brown Crème de Caçao
Coffee, top Whipped Cream

SPANISH COFFEE-
1 part Brandy, 1 part Tia Maria®
Coffee, top Whipped Cream

SUPER COFFEE-
1 part Brandy, 1 part Coffee Liqueur
Coffee, top Whipped Cream

SUZANNE'S SECRET (1)-***
Swiss Chocolate Liqueur, splash Peppermint Schnapps
Hot Chocolate, top Whipped Cream

SUZANNE'S SECRET (2)-***
Swiss Chocolate Liqueur, splash Peppermint Schnapps
Coffee, top Whipped Cream

Hot Drinks

TENNESSEE COFFEE-
1 part Amaretto, 1 part Jack Daniel's® Tennessee Sour Mash Whiskey
Coffee, top Whipped Cream

TENNESSEE MUD-
1 part Amaretto, 1 part Blended Whiskey
Coffee, top Whipped Cream

TOE WARMER-
1 part Blended Whiskey, 1 part Coffee Liqueur, 1 part Hazelnut Liqueur,
    1 part Irish Cream Liqueur, 1 part Tequila
Coffee, top Whipped Cream

TROUBLE FOR TINA-
3 parts Light Rum, 1 part Dark Rum, 1 part Brown Crème de Caçao
Warm Coffee, top Whipped Cream

VENETIAN COFFEE-
Brandy
Coffee, Sugar, top Whipped Cream

WHITE HOT CHOCOLATE-
White Crème de Caçao
Hot Chocolate, top Whipped Cream

ZULTRY ZOE-
Tequila, splash Galliano®
Hot Chocolate, top Whipped Cream

– NOTES –

_____

_____

_____

_____

_____

_____

_____

_____

_____

_____

_____

_____

Hot Drinks